The Culture of Sensibility

THE CULTURE OF SENSIBILITY

Sex and Society in Eighteenth-Century Britain

G. J. BARKER-BENFIELD

The University of Chicago Press
Chicago and London

The University of Chicago Press, Chicago 60637
The University of Chicago Press, Ltd., London

Paperback edition 1996
Printed in the United States of America

01 00 99 98 97 96 5 4 3 2

ISBN 0-226-03713-4 (cloth)
ISBN 0-226-03714-2 (paper)

Library of Congress Cataloging-in-Publication Data
Barker-Benfield, G. J.
The culture of sensibility : sex and society in eighteenth-century Britain / G. J. Barker-Benfield.
p. cm.
Includes bibliographical references and index.
1. Women—Great Britain—History—18th century. 2. Women—Psychology—History—18th century. 3. Men—Great Britain—History—18th century. 4. Men—Psychology—History—18th century. 5. Emotions. 6. Sex role—Great Britain—History—18th century. 7. Great Britain—Social conditions—18th century. I. Title.
HQ1593.B37 1992
305.3'0941'09033—dc20 91-47945
CIP

♾ The paper used in this publication meets the minimum requirements of the American National Standard for Information Sciences—Permanence of Paper for Printed Library Materials, ANSI Z39.48-1984.

To

Patricia

To draw characters from nature, though not from life, and to mark the manners of the times, is the attempted plan of the following letters. For this purpose, a young female, educated in the most secluded retirement, makes, at the age of seventeen, her first appearance upon the great and busy stage of life; with a virtuous mind, a cultivated understanding, and a feeling heart, her ignorance of the forms, and inexperience in the manners, of the world, occasion all the little incidents which these volumes record, and which form the natural progression of the life of a young woman of obscure birth, but conspicuous beauty, for the first six months after her entrance into the world.

—Frances Burney, Preface, *Evelina* (1778)

The world cannot be seen by an unmoved spectator; we must mix with the throng and feel as men feel, before we can judge of their feelings. If we mean . . . to live in the world, to grow wiser and better, and not merely enjoy the good things of life, we must attain a knowledge of others at the same time that we become acquainted with ourselves. Knowledge acquired any other way only hardens the heart, and perplexes the understanding.

I may be told that the knowledge thus acquired is sometimes purchased at too dear a rate. I can only answer that I very much doubt whether any knowledge can be attained without labour and sorrow.

—Mary Wollstonecraft, "Animadversions on Some Writers Who Have Rendered Women Objects of Pity, Bordering on Contempt," *Vindication of the Rights of Woman* (1792)

Contents

Illustrations

Acknowledgments

The State University of New York at Albany has supported the writing of this book with special grants of time and money, sympathetically distributed by Robert Wesser and John Webb, their efforts augmented by the Center for the Humanities. The assistance of Sally Stevenson and her staff at the University Library's Interlibrary Loan Office has been invaluable. I thank Kevin Gilbert for bibliographical help. James Bissett, H. T. Dickinson, Paul Dove, Danny Friedman, M. M. Goldsmith, Don Locke, William McCarthy, Barbara Brandon Schnorrenberg, Keith Thomas, and Jean Fagan Yellin kindly answered my inquiries. Robert Glen, Deborah Kennedy, and Beth Kowaleski-Wallace sent me valuable unpublished papers.

It was a stroke of great good fortune that David Alexander, a friend from undergraduate days at Trinity College, Cambridge, happens to be a leading authority on eighteenth-century British prints. He placed his expertise at my service and provided me with one of his own pictures. The assistance of Joan Sussler, curator of the fabulous collection of prints at the Lewis Walpole Library, was invaluable. Evelyn Newby of the Photo Archive of the Paul Mellon Center for Studies in British Art, London, also deserves a special note of thanks. I am very grateful to Myles Hildyard for permitting me to reproduce his "Bible Lesson" and, for the rest of the pictures, to the Guildhall Library, the Corporation of London; the Photograph and Slide Library of the Metropolitan Museum of Art; the National Gallery of Victoria, Melbourne, Australia; the Tate Gallery; the Picture Library of the Victoria and Albert Museum; and the Yale Center for British Art, a great resource because its photographic collection guides the scholar to all the other picture libraries.

Friends who gave me important feedback and moral support include Don and Sarah Birn, Catherine Clinton (who suggested the subtitle), Daniel Colbert, Miriam Dixson, Lawrence and Sharon

Friedman, Vasant Kaiwar, Melinda Lawson, Karyn Loscocco, Sucheta Mazumdar, Charles and Ann McLaughlin, Linda and Sheldon Mehr, Bruce Miroff, Lawrence Schell, Dorothy Tristman, and Frank and Pat West. I have gained a great deal from the tough-minded perspective of my co-teacher and friend, Judith Fetterley. Phyllis Palmer and Mary Sykes Wylie gave insightful readings to early forays into the subject. The friendship of my colleague, Dan White, has meant a great deal in keeping me going.

Debbie Neuls, my highly skilled coworker, has borne all of the plagues of manuscript, typing and retyping them with the patience of Job, but with far more grace, inventiveness, and good humor.

My relationship with the University of Chicago Press has been a joy. My editor, Douglas Mitchell, has nourished this project since it was a mere seed, seeing it unflinchingly through several metamorphoses, encouraging me always with his faith and imagination. He made a superb choice of readers; the first, Mary Poovey, went far beyond her responsibility to suggest very specifically how the statue might emerge from the slab; the second, Carolyn Lougee, prodded me to clarify the scaffolding. My copyeditor, Lila Weinberg, exemplifies the extraordinarily high standards of the whole team at the press.

Randy McGowen provided valuable criticism of the whole manuscript. Jim Walvin assessed it with his usual miraculous powers of mind and made very clear what was necessary. Terry Murphy, backed up by Martha Murphy, brought his formidable knowledge of British history and his mastery of theory to bear on the book, reassuring a fellow iconoclast from way back.

My dear friend and colleague, Larry Wittner, always put aside his own, pressing history to listen to mine. John Callahan's mastery of American literature and politics, and his fearless playfulness in expressing himself, heartened me throughout, as they have since the 60s. Michael Hollington, who read an early draft and answered innumerable questions, was my first and most influential teacher of reading literature; he has continued to exemplify the life of the mind, urging me on as he has done since we were schoolboys together. As ever, the Axons, the Katzes, and the Shapiros have sustained me through thick and through thin: Linda's English account speeded the pictures across the Atlantic. Michael and Marianne Shapiro have brought their superb scholarship to our many discussions over the years, always suggesting fresh perspectives on every subject. Warren Roberts read more drafts and asked more questions than anyone, and his marathonic support and advice are beyond estimate. Donald Meyer introduced me and a fortunate band of students to women's history at UCLA nearly thirty years ago, when I was fresh off the boat, and has given me his friendship, as well as his inspiration, ever since. In this he has been beautifully abetted by Jean Meyer. Finally, fortune has smiled on me most in that I have been able to try out all of the book's ideas and their expression on Patricia West. She lavished her extraordinary talents on the work and on its author, too.

Introduction

"Sensibility" signified revolution, promised freedom, threatened subversion, and became convention. The word denoted the receptivity of the senses and referred to the psychoperceptual scheme explained and systematized by Newton and Locke. It connoted the operation of the nervous system, the material basis for consciousness. During the eighteenth century, this psychoperceptual scheme became a paradigm, meaning not only consciousness in general but a particular kind of consciousness, one that could be further sensitized in order to be more acutely responsive to signals from the outside environment and from inside the body. While sensibility rested on essentially materialist assumptions, proponents of the cultivation of sensibility came to invest it with spiritual and moral values. The flexibility of a word synonymous with consciousness, with feeling, and eventually identifiable with sexual characteristics, permitted a continuous struggle over its meanings and values.[1]

Scholars have long identified a literature of sensibility or "sentimentalism," a cognate word.[2] They have argued, too, that women dominated the writing and reading of this literature. The identification of a gendered constituency for sentimental fiction accorded with the gendering of sensibility. The promise that the new psychoperceptual paradigm held for women's equal mental development was recognized immediately. In fact, environmental psychology's invention followed women's earlier seventeenth-century demands for better education. Environmental psychology argued that human selves were made, not born. Therefore, women could capitalize on the "potentialities for mankind" stemming from this aspect of the scientific revolution.[3] But the promise soon began to be short-circuited by the restoration of a model of innate sexual difference. This was a gendered view of the nerves: not only were women's nerves interpreted as more delicate and more susceptible than men's, but women's ability to operate their nerves by acts of will (part of Newton's account) was seriously questioned. The short circuiting threatened to perpetuate past views of women, whereby they merely suffered the experience of the world, in contrast to the willful engagement and self-fashioning that Lockean psychology promised all men. Still, women would resist and even turn the gendering of nerves to their own purposes. The invention, popularization, and gendering of the new psychoperceptual paradigm is the subject of Chapter 1, which also suggests some of its relationships with a spreading material culture of consumerism.

One of the best-known representations of the literature of sensibility is the figure of "virtue in distress," the virtue a woman's, and her distress caused by a man. Men cultivated sensibility, too, but unlike women their doing so was not to be at the expense of the cultivation of other qualities and their participation in larger and more various goals, including the elaboration of a public culture of their own. Nor did they have to overcome sexual subordination. When women first gained the opportunity to publicize their awakening to self-consciousness as a group, they made their suffering at the hands of men a central focus. If feminism was in part born in women's "awareness of their mistreatment by men," of "felt oppression" and victimization, then it was born in the culture of sensibility.[4] However, there were many other possibilities advanced and contained by the culture as it changed over time.

This culture was brought into existence in decisive part by the public "awakening" of a critical mass of Englishwomen.[5] This can be seen as another aspect of the transition to modernity marked by the Protestant Revolution. Among the culture's roots were the sharp increase in women's literacy during the seventeenth century and the associated challenges by Puritan women to the patriarchal order during the Civil War. They brought to "fruition a tradition of independent action by laywomen" dating back to the Henrician Reformation.[6] Keith Thomas has charted the activities of women of the civil war sects, describing their

> lively discussion of polygamy and marriage . . . , the unusual part played by women in war, litigation, pamphleteering, and politics [including the petitioning of Parliament]; the appearance in English of continental feminist writings; and the attacks, sometimes by women themselves, on their limited educational activities, their confinement to domestic activity, their subjection to their husbands, and the injustices of the commercial marriage market.

Women also founded churches and preached. Thomas associates these challenges with the emergence of the individual instead of the family as the primary political unit. There was a direct relationship here with the dramatic acceleration of women's publishing. Patricia Crawford has tabulated the high points of women's publication during the Civil War and Interregnum, although women continued to publish at a comparable rate from then through the end of the century.[7] By 1700 women's publications would enter a rapidly expanding domestic market. Women's increasing literacy and their writing novels would be fundamental to the creation of the culture of sensibility.

The novel was first in establishing "sentimental fashion" because of the market and because "the disconnection of its form from precedent . . . allowed it to explore most extravagantly the powers of a language of feeling."[8] The power of sentimental fiction was compounded because it was "semireligious." "Sensibility" and the "sentimental" were "mystic."[9] Literary critics and historians, from the earliest to the most recent, have characterized the relationship between writers and readers of sentimental literature (it included poetry and plays as well as fiction) as "the cult of sensibility."[10] This cult, they assume, was coterminous with others; a cult of feeling, a cult of melancholy, a cult of distress, a cult of refined emotionalism, a cult of benevolence, and cults of individual writers (Rousseau's the most famous), and of some of their characters, a "Werther cult," for example.[11] All may be grouped with the cult of sensibility. But contemplating the magnitude and pervasiveness of the phenomenon, embedded in a much wider range of evidence than literature, it must be concluded that the cult was an epiphenomenon of a "culture" of sensibility. The tendency toward the aggrandizement of feeling and its investment with moral value was furthered by preachers and congregants, parents and children, and manufacturers and customers as well as writers and readers, all making or coming to terms with the rise of a consumer society. Moreover, the constellation of ideas, feelings, and events which comprised the culture was a central feature of eighteenth-century Britain.

The rise of women to the point where they could publicize their wishes was contingent on a series of developments of English social and economic history which are well-known. The "long, slow, cumulative process" culminating in the industrial revolution dated back to the sixteenth century. Then began the "one-way road" on which Britons set out, leading from "the undeveloped society's comparative poverty, insecurity, and dependence on the bounty of nature to the comparative wealth, security and freedom of choice of the developed society."[12] This would have profound meanings for each sex, although men saw themselves preceding women along this road because they continued to identify women with nature.[13]

Transcendence of long-standing forms of the suffering brought about by natural and human causes preceded the widespread expression of the refined kind of suffering that preoccupied cultivators of sensibility. In *Robinson Crusoe* (1719), Defoe characterized the English middle class by its consciousness of distance from suffering—"calamities," "miseries," "hardships," "disasters," "vicissitudes," "hard labour," "want of necessaries and mean or insufficient diet." Instead, the middle class enjoyed "peace and plenty," "agreeable diversions," and "desirable pleasures." These were not the "vicious" or "extravagant" luxuries of the upper class but the virtuous and moderate "happiness" associated with "temperance, moderation, quietness, health [and] society." In "easy circumstances" the middle class could slide "gently through the world . . . sensibly tasting the sweets of living." In short, it could have its material cake and eat it morally, too. One of its pleasures was its belief in its superiority to the other classes.[14]

Recent historians of England describe and explain the same distancing from suffering Defoe was able to assume. Peter Laslett suggests that it was in the decade prior to Robinson Crusoe's birth in 1632 that English peasants last endured an "elongated crisis of subsistence."[15] Demographic pressure was reduced by the combination of a slowdown in the rate of population growth (5.2 million in 1650 to 5.8 million in 1750), and the increasing and more elastic production of food, created by such "agricultural breakthroughs as the spread of convertible husbandry, new rotations, fodder crops, and fen drainage."[16] Enclosure had been underway since the sixteenth century; much of it was completed by 1700, as individuals destroyed communal rights, notably common grazing, in order to commercialize farming more thoroughly.[17] In addition to the destructive effects of enclosure, however, the consequent "spread of specialization and diversification" in agriculture improved prospects for employment in the countryside. Relative "price stability and rising real wages" sponsored "new consumer industries," so job opportunities also sharply improved in towns.[18] A new "communications infrastructure" was pegged to provincial towns, "the engines of the commercial system, pumping goods to and fro along the arteries of trade."[19] London, whose population rose from 200,000 in 1600 to 900,000 in 1800, was a massive growth center for the English economy, a center of manufacturing, commerce, and display; through it passed continuously a very significant proportion of the provincial population, transmitting news of its promise and fashions. Towns benefited from foreign trade, too, which together with all other indices showed an "upturn" around 1745, marking "the initial acceleration of the run-up for take-off," that is, the industrial revolution. Richardson's novels were all published over the next ten years, marking an upturn in the literature of sensibility.[20]

Defoe's middle class could feel still more insulated from disaster and calamity after 1660 because towns were not so subject to fire, since many houses were now built of brick, and firefighting was made more effective by better equipment, water supplies, and civic regulations. The plague disappeared from England after the last terrible visitation in the 1660s.[21]

Finally, by the time Defoe was writing, the scourge of civil war was past, although so, too, were its possibilities for more radical revolution.[22] The "Glorious Revolution" established a stable political regime in England, thoroughly devoted to commercial expansion. It was followed by the "Financial Revolution." Public institutions—the Bank of England, the stock market, the public debt—necessary "to transform a fledgling capitalist trading economy into a commercial capitalist economy" were introduced in the 1690s. If England remained "a land of elites and oligarchies," its aristocracy was as hip-deep in agrarian capitalism as it would be in the industrial capitalism growing from these earlier developments. Of course, by 1688, England was also well embarked on empire. The accession of William and Mary made the Dutch Empire "a virtual English protectorate," and the 1707 union with Scotland expanded "what was already the largest free trade area in the world," to the advantage of those Scots able to capitalize on it. During the 1690s, and despite a downturn in the middle of the decade, English wealth increased by an estimated 20 percent.[23]

Historians have also described the plenty and the pleasures Defoe's middle class could enjoy. Joan Thirsk locates the roots of a consumer society in the sixteenth century; by its end, luxuries were "in the reach of every man." Keith Thomas concludes that by "1700 Englishmen enjoyed a higher level of material welfare than the inhabitants of any other country in the world, save Holland." And, recently, Peter Borsay suggests that the prosperity of towns between 1660 and 1770 paid for an "urban renaissance," manifest in the houses, streets, promenades, squares, and public buildings built by and for those who had crossed a higher "consumer threshold." From the 1690s, towns specialized in "the undiluted pursuit of pleasure" in meeting a massive upsurge in demand.[24] No longer was consumerism the preserve of the aristocracy, nor even of the burgeoning middle class. (Lorna Weatherill estimates that half the population was of the middling ranks in the late seventeenth century and a million households out of the total million and a half by the mid-eighteenth century.)[25]

By the 1730s, at least, the decline in the price of food and a rise in wages allowed "many working people to choose public pleasures and to introduce a greater volume and variety of goods into their homes."[26]

At the same time there were great class, regional, and chronological differences in the new consumption patterns. And while the general trend between 1650 and 1750 was one of economic growth and a rise in living standards, there were periods of fluctuation and crisis, particularly between 1705 and 1715.[27] This gives specific meaning to Defoe's reference to the "vicissitudes" affecting the poor. His increasingly self-conscious middle portion of mankind defined itself against a lower portion that remained vulnerable to much of the suffering the middle class had escaped. That "poverty was an inescapable part of life" for others was a feature of English society throughout the century, one on which the cultivators of sensibility depended.[28] The "edge" may have been taken off urban poverty by "administrative improvements for poor relief," and overall statistics suggest that the proportion of laboring poor in the population declined from over half in 1688 to a third in 1803. (This shrinkage may be correlated with the absorption of cheap consumer goods.) But that was still a very wide base to the social pyramid.[29] By the 1790s the real income of agricultural workers, in general, was "stagnating."[30] In the north and midlands, however, living standards generally had risen over the same period because of the first phase of the industrial revolution. The extent to which that enormous series of events were "grievously disruptive" in their early years is open to debate, and then they were mingled with the related effects of a growing population, war, and poor harvests, conditions resembling those prior to 1650.[31] Eventually the industrial revolution would consolidate the "escape from the tyranny and niggardliness of nature."[32]

It is important to recognize that Britain became a mass consumer society in the preindustrial period, 1650–1750, or even earlier. The industrial revolution would answer to and vastly stimulate needs and appetites (for "white bread, tea, china cups, cotton prints, and muslins"), but they had long been expressed by the majority of English women and men.[33] One central theme of Carole Shammas's important and scrupulous study of the preindustrial consumer is the change in the most literal form of consumption, that is, in diet, a subject to which Defoe was sensitive. Enclosure had a more dramatic effect on the livestock holding of "the less wealthy segment of the rural population" than it did on the cultivation of field crops, because the latter had been far less "ubiquitous" than the ownership of livestock. The long-range dietary effects of the loss of livestock, that is, the reduction in the intake of meat, milk, and cheese, was accompanied by Britain's imperial ingestion of tobacco, sugar, and caffeine drinks (all termed "groceries" by contemporaries).[34]

Enclosure also resulted in an increase in rural artisanry (including commercial baking and butchering) and, consequently, in the number of shops; this increase was augmented by more shops selling goods made or processed by others.[35] The extraordinary proliferation of shops in towns (100,000 in London in 1686 and a proportionately high number in provincial capitals by 1700) coincided with "the rise of the country shop." There are rich meanings to be culled from the fact that England was "a nation of shopkeepers"—and, therefore, of customers, so early and so long. "Groceries" in shops were followed by stocks of salt, soap, candles, butter, cheese, flour, and bacon, much of this now purchased instead of being produced at home. "By the end of the early modern period, many English labouring families bought nearly their entire diet" from the local village shops. Furthermore, there was a clear link between dietary change and the increasing demand for the vessels and equipment whereby groceries were literally consumed.[36] In 1711 *The Spectator* attached itself to the new appetite for tea, its authors asking that their journal be "served up" every morning, "looked upon as a part of the tea equipage." While types of tea and its ceremonial serving have remained indices of class, the flow of tea could not be confined to middle-class palates. From 1730 or so, "plebeian versions" of glassware, tea sets, knives, and forks became a familiar part of "nearly everyone's daily life."[37]

Clothing was the second most vital consumption need, along with food. Here, too, much of the productive process moved from the household to that increased artisanry. "The biggest development in the English textile trade at the turn of the century [1700] was the appearance of ready made garments in the stock-in-trade of retailers." Finished garments included coats, suits, breeches, shirts, petticoats, and gowns.[38]

If groceries—and the imported china with which they were at first associated—were the fruits of empire, so, too, were the new textiles from which many of these garments were made. Cheap muslins and calicoes from India were augmented at the end of the seventeenth century by fine Holland linens (together with delftware, the symbols of the new relations with the prosperous Netherlands), their prices soon declining sharply. These fabrics joined regionally produced, light woolen cloth. The domestic production of textiles was the most important large-scale industry of this early phase of Britain's commercialization. Similarly, the importation of china was followed by its English manufacture, which also became "a staple of domestic industry."[39]

In Defoe's view the relationship between these goods and the consumer was a cultic one. During the 1690s, he said in his *Tour through Great Britain* (1724–6), Queen Mary had brought in the love of "fine East-India calicoes . . . which after descended into the humours of the common people," and she also "brought in the custom or humour of furnishing houses with China-ware, which increased to a strange degree afterwards, [the common people] piling their China upon the tops of cabinets, scrutores, and every chimney piece, to the tops of the ceilings, and even setting up shelves for their china-ware." These two customs "by the people's imitating them, became the two idols of the town and indeed of the whole kingdom." Defoe also noted that William had introduced two consumer appetites, "the love of painting and the love of gardening." He said that such tastes were men's: "all the gentlemen in England began to fall in" with William's lead. In "a few years fine gardens and fine houses began to grow up in every corner."[40]

In assessing the economic dynamism of preindustrial society, Harold Perkin notes the particular openness of the ranks of English landowners to *novi homines*; the "upflow" of new men "became spectacular between the Reformation and the Civil War." Their mobility was greater even than in the "nascent capitalisms" of Venice, Florence, and Holland. After the Restoration, "the road to the gentry was now a beaten one, with any number of new gates of access." Perkin suggests that, after the Restoration, "the emphasis at the highest level . . . switched from the rise to the consolidation of the great families."[41] But at lesser levels, men continued to emerge: Robinson Crusoe rejected his father's "commands" and his mother's "entreaties" that he merely capitalize on the immigrant, self-made success of his father's merchandising, which could have permitted the son to combine "application and industry, with a life of ease and pleasure." Instead, Crusoe insisted on risking himself as his father had done, in "desperate" and "ambitious" "adventure" and "enterprise," on which Defoe thus tells his readers, middle-class complacency depended. In doing so, Robinson Crusoe became the very model of *homo economicus*.[42]

The prospects of creating and furthering commerce led men to change themselves as males, changes nourished by and nourishing the elaboration of a public, popular, male culture in a process dating back to the English Reformation. Chapter 2 describes this process, synthesizing the brilliant advances made recently by scholars on the bridgehead established by Weber and Tawney, their subject the connections between religion, individualism, and the rise of capitalism. Here and elsewhere I have incorporated sociologist Colin Campbell's recent assimilation of consumerism to Weber's account of "the Protestant ethic." It was in the interests of commerce that men cultivated politeness and sensibility, this tendency coinciding with the goals of "the reformation of manners." Men wanted this reformation, and they associated it with greater heterosociality abroad and at home. At the same time, they marked their apprehensions over relinquishing the older male ideals associated with classical warriors and farmers at a boundary they named "effeminacy," the subject of Chapter 3. Political discourse was fraught with the issue throughout the century. My summary of the transformation of men moves from the subject of the public manners displayed in the street, in alehouse, tavern, and coffee house, to their new circumstances at home, where material abundance could enhance egotism, the capacity for "self-fashioning."[43] Cultural change was generated privately as well as in the public institutions monopolized by men. Here, mothers were seen to be crucial.

Chapter 4 takes up the meanings of eighteenth-century consumerism to women; it was basic to their cultivation of sensibility. Women's subordination in medieval England had been "rooted . . . in the household," its economy subject to the crises of subsistence, to the human and natural disasters mentioned earlier.[44] The transformation of the economy and the elaboration of a public male sphere was accompanied by the transformation of women's lives in the household, their elaboration within a sphere already becoming what it would be for women in the nineteenth century, a "precinct of culture all their own."[45] Home demand was of central importance to eighteenth-century commercial capitalism, a "bellows for workshop-based manufacturing," as later it would be "the ultimate economic key to the Industrial Revolution."[46] And because women were "a major force in promoting . . . enhancements to the domestic environment," home demand was "dominated by female consumer choice."[47] The home became the primary site for consumption on a broad social scale and women gained significant authority over the relations of new objects to human activities therein, creating what we think of as domesticity. No longer did they tend the livestock as ubiquitously as they had before and the consequent dietary shift, expressed in the new cooking and eating equipment and the rituals they mediated, further transformed the configuration of women's work. Over time and varying in accordance with class, that work shifted in fundamental ways, from household production and ancillary fieldwork to new and increased foci on cleanliness, mealtimes, and childrearing. The growing concern over the damaging effects of maternal "indulgence" on children of both sexes in fact signified women's new power in childrearing, a power that also served men's needs and purposes. Self-indulgence, the "luxury" of feeling, was at the heart of the culture of sensibility, and it was basic to the consumer psychology the polite and commercial economy required.

By the same token, "bourgeois" women were not confined to the home. On the contrary, they now were enabled to enter a new public world, comprised of those walks, streets, shopping parades, and amusement centers of the "urban renaissance," spaces intended for the enjoyment and cultivation of new heterosocial manners, albeit construable as valuable new counters in the marriage market, a dimension of the market economy as a whole. Those entrances, minglings, and possibilities for self-expression were tantamount to a public leisure culture women had not enjoyed before. Previously their appearance in public had been sharply circumscribed by a web of male rules, enforced by violence at times. Women's publication of their wishes and feelings on an unprecedented scale was a parallel development; they articulated their sense of real and potential victimization by men, as well as their rising expectations on this and other fronts.

As each gender changed, so it wished to control the direction of change. The culture of sensibility became a culture of reform, aiming to discipline women's consumer appetites in tasteful domesticity, but thence reforming male behavior. This, the subject of Chapter 5, can be seen as the most ambitious reform movement of the eighteenth century, fundamental to the well-known expressions of humanitarianism. Better educated wives and more comfortable houses would draw men home from the extravagant and cruel pleasures of tavern culture. The campaign for the reformation of manners targeted the male behavior women now had the resources more effectively to oppose. A dramatic vehicle for this reform and for the wishes of women was Methodism, its rise coinciding with the rise of the cult and culture of sensibility. Religious efforts may well have helped modify male manners; however, they cannot be disentangled from a far more powerful source of change—the requirements and attractions of commercial capitalism—on which such efforts and the transformative effects of domesticity were dependent. In short, women's wishes converged with men's to a significant degree.

At the same time, their intertwined histories were fraught with conflicts between and among each group as well as within individual minds. The culture of sensibility provides dramatic evidence of women's wishes for the individual pursuit of self-expression and heterosocial pleasure in a wider world, the unambiguous expression of which was epitomized by the figure of the rake. The expressive consciousness connoted by "sensibility" extended even so far as women's own sexual wishes, perhaps most disturbing of all. Conflict over the possibilities for women's selfhood in the culture of sensibility and over the directions their wishes should take is the subject of Chapter 6. There was a dialectic between the solidification of sensibility's potentials into a female culture and its ongoing sponsorship of romantic individualism among women. A focus on gender places the classicism/romanticism debate in a new light. Women continued to find their expressions of mind associated with the exclusively reproductive and marital identity on which their economic survival still was held to depend, despite new potentials in the middle-class transcendence of a subsistence economy. The dominant terms of eighteenth-century history led women to capitalize on their "naturalized"[48] gender characteristics, above all, the moral authority of their putatively finer sensibility. Here they had to attempt to purge it of subversive sexual potentials. Many women had long been ambivalent over sensibility because of its materialist underpinnings in the nerve paradigm. On one hand, they claimed an improved education on the basis of this sensational, environmental psychology; on the other, they held that women should maintain a Christian unworldliness as creatures above the mere expression of sense. They warned that godless men—rakes—treated women as yet more consumer objects of sense, capitalizing on women's own new pursuit of pleasure. This position was expressed in the eighteenth century's "feminization of religion."

The gendering of sensibility and its claim to moral superiority promised obvious advantages, including the reform of men on women's terms, but it also carried some dangerous, self-destructive consequences (mindlessness and solipsism, for example), of which many cultivators of sensibility were well aware. Women's temptation to identify themselves as "virtue in distress" also posed another danger against which Mary Wollstonecraft warned. Paradoxically, perhaps, the gendering of sensibility sexualized it, associating desire with the rake/victim dyad. Men, too, gendered and sexualized sensibility, as they tried to make sense of a manhood now expressing itself more immediately in commerce rather than war. Their wish to avoid effeminacy became more clearly marked the more mannerly they became and the more women pressed outward with their own wishes, including the wish that men have more in common with women. Conversely, women's boundary was marked by the figure of the Amazon. In publicly expressing their minds and their wishes, women faced the continued resistance of men.

Women's entering public space for pleasure (making it heterosocial) and men's being attracted into more comfortable homes (promising pleasurable heterosociality there, too) began to transform previous alignments of gender. This permeability contributed to the attempted clarification and hardening of new definitions of being female and male, and the spheres with which women and men were most usually identified.[49] The transcendence of nature and of traditional categories in religion, politics, and philosophy was accompanied by a rethinking of sexual categories. From now on, increasing numbers of women would publicize the fact that they were conscious human beings, equal in that respect to men. "The eighteenth century invented the modern terminology of class" without "the notion of class conflict . . . in its modern sense." The eighteenth century invented the modern terminology of sex (or in its very recent updating, gender) but with acute awareness of conflict.[50]

Fluctuating struggles over the shaping of women's emergent, self-assertive consciousness were most explicitly politicized during the 1790s, when they came to a head under the threat of revolution. Facing the bogey of a Wollstonecraft depicted as both an Amazon and a woman of sexually unbridled sensibility, literate women consolidated their claim to mind and domesticity at the expense of politics and the sexual promise in sensibility. This story, presented in my final chapter, set the stage for Victorian separate spheres and further fruitful conflict.

I have attempted to allow the cultivators of sensibility to disclose themselves in their own terms. I have been helped by the doubters, critics, and opponents of the culture of sensibility. One figure who was deeply ambivalent in her views of sensibility was Wollstonecraft. It was her *Vindication of the Rights of Woman* (1792) that first suggested to me that sensibility was a culture, and a culture of women. Her most famous book has much in common with the large-scale, psycho-sociological-historical studies of societies that founded modern approaches to understanding human culture, most notably in Britain those produced by the Scottish Enlightenment. Because Wollstonecraft made sex the conscious and central subject of her study, I have woven her analysis through my text. Wollstonecraft's book is passionate and confessional, one in which she said, "I myself . . . shall certainly appear, head and heart," so it combined the analytical with the romantic, the sociological with the individual voice.[51]

She presented herself in the *Rights of Woman* as a "philosopher" and a "moralist." Her vision of the past was a story of the "whole species" raising itself "in the scale of animal being," of men gaining preeminence over the brute creation" by way of "Reason" and their "acquirement" of "Virtue." In the "infancy of society" men emerged from chief- and priest-ridden "barbarism" into unstable "aristocracy," in turn giving way to the "monarchy and hierarchy" founded on "feudal tenures." Ensuing foreign and civil wars allowed "the people" to gain some power, obliging "their rulers to gloss over their oppression with a show of right."[52] In Wollstonecraft's own age, liberty challenged despotism by way of the unfolding of the faculties of men "in the middle rank of life." They had seized the opportunities supplied by "wars, agriculture, commerce, and literature," to "expand the mind." All this Wollstonecraft regarded as "the progress of civilization." One of her larger objections to Rousseau was that he preferred "a state of nature" to "civilization."[53]

According to this same vision, one she expressed throughout her other books, Wollstonecraft believed there should be an equivalent progress in individual lives. Absorbing Lockean and Smithean psychology, Wollstonecraft described the development of the personality from "infancy" to "maturity," under the aegis of "parental affection." In the "ductile" mind of "childhood," "an habitual association of ideas . . . 'grows with our growth,'" giving "a turn to the mind that commonly remains throughout life." From a parent's point of view, "the affection which we inspire always resembles that we cultivate." In connection with the familiarity to us of these and others of Wollstonecraft's psychological observations, we can note that she referred to "instinct" being "sublimated."[54]

In some sense, therefore, Wollstonecraft suggested that ontogeny recapitulated phylogeny. But Wollstonecraft's view was historical as well as anthropological, sociological, and psychological. Habits of mind differed in accordance with social circumstances which changed over time.

> Men and women must be educated in a great degree by the opinions and manners of the society they live in. In every age there has been a stream of popular opinion that has carried all before it, and given a family character, as it were, to the century.

That popular, familial "character" stemmed from the family, also, therefore, changing over time; the way in which individual minds are "turned" by the habitual association of ideas as well as by the yearning for individual freedom, "has a great effect on the moral character of mankind." Like her predecessors in Enlightenment sociology, Wollstonecraft aligned her view of progress with her wish for a reformation of manners.[55]

The full growth of character depended on the "cultivation" of both the "understanding" and of the "heart." The self-made, middle-class men Wollstonecraft admired combined strong minds with generous feelings, that is, with sensibility. And here we reach Wollstonecraft's chief point. So far in history, only men had been able to "ennoble" themselves above brute nature and to "perfect" themselves by the full exercise of reason. It was men's progress that provided Wollstonecraft the standard whereby she judged "one half of the human species"—women—to have remained "degraded" and "oppressed," kept in "a state of childhood."[56] Woman was "scarcely raised by her employments above the animal kingdom." Instead of being "strengthened" by the challenges men's minds faced—of "business, extensive plans, or . . . the discursive flights of ambition"—women's mental development was stunted, and women were directed into the consequently exaggerated cultivation of sensibility. "With respect to the culture of the heart it is unanimously allowed that sex is out of the question; but the line of subordination in the mental powers is never to be passed over." Hence Wollstonecraft presented sensibility as a sexual culture.[57]

While Wollstonecraft placed high value on sensibility, in this book especially she concentrated on the damage its cultivation did women because it was not accompanied by the cultivation of reason. Consequently women's capacity to develop, to individuate themselves, and to rise was forestalled, and they were kept in "the night of sensual ignorance." In unmistakable invocation of the model of progress represented by *Robinson Crusoe* at the beginning of the century, Wollstonecraft asked: "When do we hear of women who, starting out of obscurity, boldly claim respect on account of their great abilities or daring virtues?" Implicitly she believed that English women, particularly "those in the middle class" to whom she addressed her book, had that capacity. Somehow, women's acculturation, including their acculturation into properly modified sensibility, could not prevent their emergence; indeed, it must have contained the potentials to advance it.[58]

This was implicit in Wollstonecraft's writing the *Rights of Woman* and her appearance in it "head and heart." She recognized that she had been educated into an exaggerated sensibility, synonymous as we shall see with "delicacy." She wrote once to her friend and publisher, Joseph Johnson, "I am a mere animal and instinctive emotions too often silence the suggestions of reason." She treated herself as her parents treated her, her ambivalent terms in this same letter redolent with the values of the culture of sensibility.

> I have nourished a sickly kind of delicacy . . . I am a strange compound of weakness and resolution! However, if I must

> suffer, I will endeavor to suffer in silence. There is certainly a great defect in my mind—my wayward heart creates its own misery . . . I must be content to weep and dance like a child—[59]

Yet believing that "genius will educate itself," and choosing "intellectual pursuits" over the thus blighted "domestic comforts," she became, in Emily Sunstein's phrase, "a self-made woman."[60] Wollstonecraft declared, "I never yet resolved to do anything of consequence, that I did not adhere resolutely to it, till I had accomplished my purpose." Her purpose was "to be the first of a new genus," and the *Rights of Woman* was a summons to the development of the whole human species: "as sound politics diffuse liberty, mankind, including woman, will become more wise and virtuous."[61]

Wollstonecraft referred to mankind generally, and she dedicated her book to Talleyrand because the revolutionary system of state education he had just proposed to the Constituent Assembly in France was confined to boys. She hoped that, in its stead, her alternative "national" system of education (the subject of Chapter 12 of the *Rights of Woman*) would be diffused throughout "the European world," to which she assumed her diagnosis of sensibility was germane.[62] She saw herself as a member of the international republic of letters, but at the same time she kept eighteenth-century British culture and society to the forefront of her book. We may think of "the cult of sensibility" in the same way. It was an international phenomenon, appearing in Europe and its colonies, but it was strongly flavored and delineated by the characteristics of each nation in which it came into existence. Throughout much of the century, there were continuous feedback loops between England and Continental Europe in the matter of sensibility as, of course, there had been in the courtly culture with which it was connected.

The most recent description of "the cult of sensibility" in France, one which looks back to its English origins and ahead to its role in the Revolution, is Simon Schama's. He links the blooming of the phenomenon there to the growth of a consumer culture in Paris and to the cognate high literacy rate. But there was a sharp reaction to the emergence of women in the Revolution and powerful cultural and political checks to the spread of consumption in France until much later. The development of the cult was also retarded by its association with the court, above all, with Marie-Antoinette.[63] In addition, as Paul Langford points out, "the sentimental tradition" in France was associated with secularism, in contrast to evangelized England, where sentiment "became a tool of piety."[64] As we shall see, this English development was united with the uniquely widespread extent of consumer demand and supply. It would be in 1857, in *Madame Bovary*, that Flaubert would make sentimentalism a central target of his assault on the French bourgeoisie then reaching full flower.

Norman Fiering writes that "England, France, and Holland composed a remarkably well-integrated republic of letters." It may be inferred from Schama's superb portrait of Dutch culture that there was a relationship there, too, between commercial prosperity and consumption, the consequent aggrandizement of women's position in domestic interiors, and with what he calls the "cult of sensibility." Dutch prosperity and culture underwrote "the first sustained image of parental love that European art has to show us." It also underwrote "one of the oldest, richest traditions in feminism in Europe."[65] Schama's theme is that unprecedented wealth, distinguishing the Netherlands from "the miserable conditions that Europe had experienced since the fourteenth century," converged with ancient and recently refreshed religious standards, which were profoundly suspicious of such worldliness. The result was a profound cultural "embarrassment," where "riches seemed to provoke their own discomfort." The morality dispensed by women from their plush but obsessively cleaned homes was one powerful expression of this "syndrome." Schama suggests it was "a self-inflicted dilemma encountered in all nascent capitalisms." In this regard, sixteenth-century Venice, seventeenth-century Amsterdam, and eighteenth-century London anticipated Tocqueville's America. America's sentimental culture already has had its historian.[66] Schama's own later work makes it clear eighteenth-century Paris should be added to this list.

As we have seen, Defoe had attempted to reconcile plenty with morality, claiming that despite its pursuit of material pleasures, the English middle class was not "embarrassed with the pride, luxury, ambition, and envy of the upper part of mankind." There was a tension subsumed by this view, comparable to the one Schama describes. The Dutch immigrant Mandeville called it a "contradiction" and made it the premise of his analysis of the commercial and puritanical society he described. This tension was to be a running theme in eighteenth-century Britain. According to a Manchester "Cobbler" in 1756,

> Townsmen are constantly purchasing; and thereby laying the Foundations of a new Race of Gentry! Not adorn'd with Coats of Arms and a long Parchment Pedigree of useless Members of Society, but deck'd with Virtue and Frugality; and who, knowing both how, and when to be content, retire, decently to enjoy their well-got Wealth, leaving the Coast open for new Adventurers, to follow their worthy Example.

Among its other purposes, the British culture of sensibility expressed the attempt to solve the same "dilemma" Schama describes, by way of women's moralization and mastery of decent enjoyment, that is, of "taste." This may be seen as another aspect of the attempted spiritualization of sensibility and of the culture's reform impulse.[67]

While informed by other disciplines, my approach to evidence, including literature, has been the self-conscious discipline of the historian. I would repeat my grateful sense of indebtedness to literary scholars, from Edith Birkhead, writing in the 1920s, to Jane Spencer, writing today.[68] In my view, the most brilliant book devoted entirely to the literature of sensibility remains R. F. Brissenden's *Virtue in Distress* (1974), but valuable monographs published in 1986 and 1988 illustrate the continuing liveliness of a subject on which feminist scholarship is now pouring new light.[69]

As an historian, I am less sympathetic to the poststructuralist notions being applied to the literature of sensibility, among them Foucault's contention that "discourses about sex," produced by "institutions," are "mechanisms" of power, successfully penetrating and controlling individuals' "everyday pleasure."[70] There were efforts by individual people and organizations of people to effect such control, but the history of sensibility is one of increasingly self-conscious conflict, culminating in the work and reputation of Wollstonecraft. What follows is in agreement with Donald Meyer in his judgment of Foucault.

> In its liberation from the demographic anxieties of the old order, modern industrial society would take up the challenge of sex and sensuality as a realm for more autonomous and individualistic explorations, and the key to its success here would be in language, the ability to free experience from sociological norms. The arguments of Michael Foucault on modern sexuality as "discourse" have made the point, only backward. There was no natural sexuality wanting to be released from thrall by philosophical criticism, only a new sexuality created by new discourse, new poetry.[71]

My subject is the history of Britain preceding its industrialization, already showing signs, in its threshold-crossing, commercial-capitalist phase, of the "explorations" Meyer describes.

Like Meyer, I locate sources of change in human consciousness. I sometimes use general terms like "capitalism" and "consumerism" but I always mean capitalists and consumers. E. P. Thompson refreshed Marxism with the reminder that all such relationships "must always be embodied in real people." It is true that human beings often feel they are up against vast, impersonal "forces," but, as G. R. Elton reminds the historian, forces are "generalized inferences from observation, used as a kind of shorthand in historical explanation, which at best can become active agents only when reconverted into the agglomerate of detail from which they were first derived."[72]

Historians as well as literary critics are placing increased significance on eighteenth-century "sensibility." Lawrence Stone's *The Family, Sex and Marriage in England 1500–1800* (1977) described the "growth of affective individualism" in eighteenth-century, English, middle-class families as the expression of "a new sensibility," its ideal type, "The Man of Feeling" representing a "genuinely moral" movement, an "upsurge of new attitudes and emotions." My subject is the same "movement" but viewed from a different perspective. In *Man and the Natural World* (1983), Thomas pointed to the eighteenth-century bourgeoisie's "vast" reorientation, its "new sensibilities" manifesting a watershed in the evolution of modern consciousness, and he subtitled his book *A History of Modern Sensibility*. Thomas Haskell took up the history of "Capitalism and the Origins of Humanitarian Sensibility" in the two-part article published in the 1985 volume of the flagship journal, the *American Historical Review*, although he confined the subject to men. Peter Earle's *The Making of the English Middle Class: Business, Society, and Family Life in London 1660–1730* (1989) concludes that, essential to the emergent mentality of its subject, was "a sensibility that sees the beginning of 'Victorian' attitudes toward the 'home' and the place of middle-class women within it." Langford's volume in the New Oxford History of England, *A Polite and Commercial People: England 1727–1783* (1989), devotes a lengthy chapter to "The Birth of Sensibility" and declares that the "triumph of sentiment was overwhelming." This triumph was the outcome of the "revolution in manners" invoked by Langford's title. His terms are in agreement with Norbert Elias's *The Civilizing Process*, an old book now coming into its own and one on which I have frequently drawn.[73]

Gratefully acknowledging my debt to these and other students of British literature and history, I must add that I owe much of my approach to the dramatic achievements of the students of American women's history over the past twenty-five years. It is in the light of their success that I have dramatized the centrality of sex to eighteenth-century British society.

ONE

Sensibility and the Nervous System

Wollstonecraft's Perspective: The Gendering of Sensibility

In the *Rights of Woman* Wollstonecraft made a systematic analysis of "the conduct and manners" of middle-class women. She attributed their "weak and wretched" minds and bodies to "a false system of education." By education she meant childrearing as well as schooling.[1] Women, she argued, were acculturated to an exaggerated identification with "sensibility." Parents were fundamental to this process, but other key players were writers of both sexes. They argued on behalf of "the superiority of man." They argued it not simply in degree but in "essence."[2] Wollstonecraft said that the reason they placed a high value on "feeling," that is, she makes clear, on "sensibility" in women, was "to soften" this argument for essential male superiority. Hence they labored to prove that

> the sexes ought not to be compared; man was made to reason, woman to feel: and that together, flesh and spirit, they make the most perfect whole, by blending happily reason and sensibility into one character.
>
> And what is sensibility? "Quickness of sensation; quickness of perception; delicacy." Thus is it defined by Dr. Johnson; and the definition gives me no other idea than of the most exquisitely polished instinct. I discern not a trace of the image of God in either sensation or matter. Refined seventy times seven, they are still material; intellect dwells not there; nor will fire ever make gold.[3]

The terms "sensation," "matter," and "instinct," along with Dr. Johnson's "quickness," "perceptions," and "delicacy" all referred to the late eighteenth-century's common understanding of the nervous system. Wollstonecraft was by no means alone in condemning sensibility for its materialism. Vicesimus Knox wrote: "Feelings! a fashionable word substituted for mental operations, and savouring much of materialism." But Wollstonecraft pressed the implications for women; when identified entirely with "sensibility," women were reduced to an entirely physiological system, albeit one that was "refined" and "exquisitely polished" into "delicacy." In her next sentence Wollstonecraft declared that "if woman be allowed to have an immortal soul, she must have, as the employment of life, an understanding to improve." "Improvement" was another great watchword of the eighteenth century, and, as we have seen, Wollstonecraft wished to include women in its vision of progress. Women's conduct and manners would be improved if they were educated "to reason." She connected this recommendation with the parable of "the talents," and with other virtues, "the exercise of which ennobles the human character." It was improper to call them "manly" or "masculine," Wollstonecraft wrote at the very beginning of her book, which aimed at a national system of coeducation; such talents and virtues "more properly" pertain to both sexes, "comprehensively termed mankind." Wollstonecraft's critique of the feminization of sensibility was at the heart of her feminism.[4]

Recent historians have explained the origins of the sentimentalization of women and the family as a reaction to the feminism[5] born in the seventeenth century along with the Puritan Revolution.[6] By 1700, the challenge to political, patriarchal authority had been formally and publicly extended to its exercise in the family, where popular culture suggests the challenge had always existed in some form. Arguments on behalf of equal education and of women's pursuing individual improvement now had been heard over several generations, and the revolutions that promised resting men's political and legal equality on their "freedom, individuality, and rationality" could be seen to promise the same for women.[7] The corollary of Locke's assumption that human minds were born as if they were blank sheets of paper was the unleashing of the power to shape their own lives. Whatever Locke's ambiguities on the score, others expressed directly the possible meanings to women of the power to construct selves and environment. From the seventeenth century they argued that "custom and prejudice, not Nature, exclude women from public life."[8] Following seventeenth- and early eighteenth-century generations of feminists, a series of writers insisted that if, in the words of one of them, "women had the benefits of liberal instruction, if they were inured to study, and accustomed to learned conversation . . . if they had the same opportunity of improvement as the men, there can be no doubt that they would be equally capable of reaching any intellectual attainment." Sensational psychology continued to provide scientific authority for the view that women's "natures" were not natural at all but the result of custom, of "climate and manners," as Gibbon said of Zenobia. This was true of those not generally thought of as feminists—Hume, for example, who, like Gibbon, was a believer in the application of sensational psychology to history. As Wollstonecraft had it in 1792, women were *made* weak, "artificial beings," reared "in a premature, unnatural manner," hence her emphasis on the effect of the "Early Association of Ideas" on the female "Character."[9]

Novelists testified to the dramatic changes in the ideals and practices of being female and being male. Since "one of the foundations of the eighteenth-century novel" was the Lockean "notion of the self constantly being remade as it became conscious of new sensations,"[10] it is not surprising that the fundamental issue for gender would be that of consciousness, of "mind" inevitably associated with feeling, in short, of "sensibility," as the eighteenth century understood the term. The revolutionary possibilities for women's consciousness were countered in the same terms, women's subordination naturalized on the basis of their finer sensibility. The potential for women in sensational psychology seemed to be short-circuited.

A New Psychoperceptual System

Modern anatomy expressed the "hankering after the bare Mechanical causes of things" which characterized post-Restoration philosophy and science generally.[11] Outstanding among anatomists was Thomas Willis, working with his disciples in the 1660s. Willis identified the soul with the brain and argued that it depended "on the nerves for all of its functions." The "nerves alone" were to be "held responsible for sensory impressions, and consequently for knowledge." After Willis's breakthrough, "it was just one step to an integrated physiology of man, and another to a theory of sensory perception, learning, and the further association of ideas." These steps were taken by Willis's best student at Oxford, John Locke, in his *Essay Concerning Human Understanding* (1690), which pivoted on "the concept and definition of sensation." The invention of sensational psychology preceded Locke, but he extended and systematized it into a philosophical theory, incorporating it into his "paradigmatic book," one of the two or three most influential books of the century.[12]

Locke dismissed the notion that human beings are born with innate ideas and replaced it with the famous image of the *tabula rasa*.[13] Just as these became the truisms of the next century so, too, did the nerve physiology Locke assumed from Willis. Locke wrote of the reception of "sensation," in this case, tastes and smells,

> by the Nose and Palate. And if these Organs, or the Nerves which are the Conduits, to convey them from without to their Audience in the Brain . . . are any of them so disordered, as not to perform their Functions, they have no Postern to be admitted by.

Locke added "the Association of Ideas" to the 1700 edition of his *Essay*. "REFLECTION" connected ideas by reason, but there was

> another connexion of ideas wholly owing to *chance* or *custom*; ideas, that come to be so united in some men's minds, that it is very hard to separate them; they always keep in company, and the one no sooner at any time comes into the understanding, but its associate appears with it . . . and the whole gang, always inseparable, show themselves together.

For Locke, association was "a source of error." It could seriously modify an individual's sense of personal control and freedom.[14] The proponents of sensibility, however, placed value on it because it helped dissolve "the barrier between thought and feeling" by considering the latter as "intricately interrelated" to "a series of feelings and responses to an external stimulus." Yet this evaluation held the danger of encouraging passivity.[15]

Locke's psychology rested on Newtonian physics. (Newton himself is recorded to have described how the "great Mr. Locke was the first who became a Newtonian philosopher.") Newton's enormous intellectual authority provided sensational psychology with its understanding of the specific operation of the nerves, which Locke expressly had left aside.[16] Newton's *Opticks* depended on his account of the physiology of perception. While he may have derived his notion of the "Sensorium" (the termination of all the nerves in the brain) from Willis, Newton differed from Willis's idea of the hollow nerve through which animal spirits flowed from brain to organs. Instead, Newton had argued from 1675 that the nerve was solid and transmitted sense impressions by vibrations.[17]

While Newton's *Principia* (1687) had referred in its "General Scholium" to ether as "a certain most subtle spirit which pervades and is hid in all gross bodies" and hypothesized that "all sensation is excited . . . by the vibrations of this spirit, mutually propagated along the solid filaments of the nerves," it was published in Latin and not made more widely available for over forty years, when the General Scholium would reinforce what *Opticks* had already wrought. By contrast, *Opticks* was first published in English, the sections explaining the relation of ethereal vibrations to vision and hearing amplified in the second

English edition of 1717–8. Its language and conceptions would reverberate through eighteenth-century literature. "Do not the Rays of Light in falling upon the bottom of the Eye excite Vibrations . . . Which, being propagated along the solid Fibres of the optick Nerves into the Brain, cause the sense of seeing?" Such vibrations "convey into the Brain the impressions made upon all the Organs of Sense." So the hearing, too, is "perform'd by the Vibrations . . . excited in the auditory Nerves by the Tremors of the Air, and propagated through the solid . . . Nerves into the place of Sensation[,]" that is, the "Sensorium." The "elastic force" of the ether is demonstrated by the "swiftness of its Vibrations." The ether was made up of "Particles" of "exceeding Smallness," smaller than particles of air and light. At the same time, that quality could be affected by the elasticity of the solids through which they pass. Motion could be lost when bodies are "either so absolutely hard or so soft as to be void of Elasticity."[18]

Newton emphasized that the vibrations of the ether could be "excited in the Brain by the power of the Will and propagated from thence" through "the Nerves into the Muscles." Newton did not gender this scheme in the least. After it was popularized, however, the question of will in the operation of weaker, feminized nerves was brought into serious question, compounding the potential for the passivity implicit in the association of ideas.[19]

Newton's view of the body's constitution corresponded to his presentation of the nature of space, wherein "every particle is *always*, and every indivisible moment of duration is everywhere," that is, manifesting God's omnipresence. Our "little sensoriums" were merely parts, vibrations, within God's "boundless uniform Sensorium." In arguing for the existence of God, Newton's science seemed to reconcile the seventeenth-century's rigorous induction to religious orthodoxy. Newton posed his view of "natural Philosophy" as a way of knowing this Godly Sensorium, against the "false Gods" which "blinded the Heathen," scorning their simple beliefs in "the four Cardinal Virtues; . . . The Transmigration of Souls, . . . worship [of] the Sun and Moon, and dead Heroes," and reconciling nature with the Bible by declaring in the last sentence of *Opticks* that the heathen's ancestors had worshipped the true "Author" of natural Philosophy "under the Government of *Noah* and his Sons before they corrupted themselves." Newton's authority was behind the incessant references to nature as the source of religious inspiration on which the culture of sensibility insisted. Yet one upshot of the passionate religious debates at the turn of the century was also the "ebbing away of theology into natural religion," that is, the resting of a belief in God on reason and "the book of nature" rather than simply on revelation. The Newtonian amalgam coexisted from the 1690s with deism and pantheism. They would be among the provocations to religious revival.[20]

The publication of Locke's *Essay Concerning Human Understanding* and Newton's *Opticks* in English was the key to their reaching a popular audience. Not only were they accessible to a literate audience unschooled in Latin, but Newton's work was also accessible to those unschooled in mathematics. *Opticks* was "a rich intellectual feast . . . for all amateurs of the human imagination at the highest degree of refinement." Another powerful source for the propagation of Newtonian and Lockean thought was the pulpit. An annual series of lectures beginning in 1692 was established by the will of scientist Robert Boyle to defend Christianity against atheists and libertines. These lectures were published, inspiring lesser ministers' sermons. Furthermore, sensational psychology was preached very widely by the Latitudinarian heirs of the Cambridge Platonists to whose thought Newton's was related. Another vehicle disseminating the ideas of Locke and Newton was *The Spectator* (1711–3), frequently reprinted over the whole century, and again a mode inspiring imitations.[21]

Still another route to the popularization of sensational psychology in its earlier phase was poetry. Following Newton's *Opticks*, poets were deeply intrigued with light and color and, therefore, with the psychology of perception. Queen Anne's doctor, Sir Richard Blackmore, in *The Creation* (1712) referred to the discovery of "animal spirits" and the structure of the brain revealed by those who "with anatomic art/ Dissect the mind, and thinking substance part." James Thomson's *The Seasons* (1726–30), "one of the most popular and frequently reprinted of English poems," transmitted the Newtonian worldview and referred frequently to the nervous system.[22] The same can be said of the earliest sentimental fiction. The 1740s "were the great heyday for literature of all types concerning the nerves."[23] The stage had been set for Richardson's novels, *Pamela* (1740), *Clarissa* (1747–8), and *Sir Charles Grandison* (1753–4). Sentimental fiction, next to the religion with which it overlapped, was to become the most powerful medium for the spread of popular knowledge of sensational psychology. The nerve was to provide popular, literate culture with a Kuhnian paradigm.[24]

The Application of the New System: George Cheyne, 1671–1743

Blackmore was one of a line of researchers and doctors who specialized in diseases of the nerves. Included among them was the Dutch immigrant, Bernard Mandeville (1670–1733), who published *A Treatise of Hypochondriack and Hysterick Passions* in 1711. The inventor of the term "physiology" was another Dutchman, Hermann Boerhaave

(1668–1738), of Leyden.[25] Boerhaave's shaping of the Leyden medical school provided the model for Edinburgh's, founded in 1726. In 1747, when he became professor of medicine at Edinburgh, Robert Whytt introduced his version of a "sentient principle" sealed in the nervous system, and Whytt, his fellow teacher, William Cullen, and two other Edinburgh doctors, Alexander Monro II and John Gregory, have been credited with imparting the new neurophysiological system to the school of moral philosophy headed by David Hume and Adam Smith.[26] One of Boerhaave's students was LaMettrie, the author of the notorious *L'homme machine* (1748), the French parallel to David Hartley's *summa* of Lockean associationist nerve theory, his *Observations on Man,* the latter published by Richardson in 1749. Hartley may well have come to his understanding of the nerves by way of his patient and friend, Dr. George Cheyne.[27]

Cheyne was Richardson's doctor and confidante, and Richardson printed Cheyne's books. Their correspondence shows Cheyne transmitting the physiological aspect of sensibility to Richardson by way of his detailed response to Richardson's most intimate physiological needs. While evidently there were other sources for Richardson's assumption and propagation of sensational psychology (his notion of rays and beams of light reflect his reading of *Opticks* and in the second part of *Pamela* Richardson quotes Locke's *Some Thoughts Concerning Education* of 1693), Cheyne seems to have been Richardson's primary source for the version of the nerve paradigm injected into his novels, and thereby into the mainstream of sentimental fiction.[28]

Born in Scotland in 1671, Cheyne received his medical degree from Aberdeen in 1701, where he was first brought into contact with mechanistic views of physiology.[29] He saw himself in the forefront of Protestant rationalism. Echoing Newton in his introduction to *The English Malady* (1733), Cheyne said that he hoped he had "explain'd the Nature and Causes of Nervous Distempers (which have hitherto been reckon'd Witchcraft, Enchantment, Sorcery, and Possession)." He wished to alter the way in which people traditionally referred to such illnesses, to replace vague terms with the precise language of the physiology of the nerves. Cheyne's way of seeing, he said, represented "the Laws of Nature and Mechanisms . . . the latest Discoveries in Natural History." Cheyne made it clear that such a view was compatible with orthodox Christianity. In 1705 he had published *The Philosophical Principles of Religion: Natural and Revealed*, hoping to "install" the "principle of natural religion" into students. Ten years later, following his conversion, he appended a section on revealed religion.[30]

According to Cheyne's popularized version of the nerve paradigm, "the Intelligent Principle, or *Soul,* resides somewhere in the Brain, where all the Nerves, or instruments of sensation terminate, like a *Musician* in a finely fram'd and well tim'd Organ—Case; these Nerves are like *Keys* which, being struck on or touch'd, convey the Sound and Harmony to this Sentient Principle, or *Musician*."[31] This was an extension of Newton's idea that hearing was "perform'd." The musician occupied "the Temple or Sensorium." Cheyne divided the "sensible or compound *Fibres*" into those of the muscles, the bones, and, third, grouped together, of the "Membranes, Tendons and Nerves." These fibers were smaller and were compressed into a smaller space. Thus, "their *elastick* Force is greater, they contract with greater Strength and Quickness . . ." The compactness and closer union of parts "seems to be the Reason for the greater Degree of Sensibility" with which they are "endued." Cheyne here deferred to "the late *sagacious and learned* Sir Isaac Newton" on the probable existence of "an infinitely subtil, elastick Fluid, or Spirit . . . distended through this whole *System*, penetrating all Bodies . . . this *Aether*, *Spirit*, or most subtil Fluid [drives] the Parts of Bodies forcibly together and their mutual attractive Virtue Arises."[32] Cheyne defined "Feeling" in a way even more specifically material than the Johnsonian definition later cited by Wollstonecraft.

> *Feeling* is nothing but the Impulse, Motion, or Action of Bodies, gently or violently impressing the Extremities or Sides of the Nerves, of the Skin, or other Parts of the Body, which by their Structure and *Mechanism*, convey this Motion to the *sentient* Principle in the Brain, or the *Musician*.[33]

Distemper or disease was represented by the weakening or breaking of this "machine" or "instrument." The "more delicate" parts, "being more delicate than others, are sooner disorder's or broken." Again following Newton, Cheyne summarized the pathological status of the nerves as their "too lax, feeble, and *unelastik* State." The "Degrees" of elasticity and, therefore, of "sensibility," the ability to transmit "sense" via vibrations to the brain, were susceptible to the Lockean environment. While sensibility could be cultivated, it also was seen to be inborn. Variations between people in degrees of sensibility expressed a combination of environmental and innate differences between them. Variations of elasticity could be joined with Newton's suggestions as to the speed of vibrations and even the size of the particles making them up, and then aligned with a vision of society. Given the eighteenth-century connotations of "degree," the quality of sensibility could be seen as a badge of rank. Applied socially, Newtonian science could rationalize hierarchy, as Darwinian science would in the next century. In Cheyne's words,

> There are as many and as different Degrees of *Sensibility* or of *Feeling* as there are Degrees of *Intelligence* and Perception in *human* Creatures; and the *Principle* of both may be perhaps one and the same. One shall suffer more from the Prick of a *Pin*, or *Needle*, from their extreme Sensibility, than others from being run thro' the Body; and the *first* sort, seem to be of the *Class* of these *Quick-Thinkers* I have formerly mentioned; and as none have it in their *Option* to choose for themselves their own particular *Frame* of Mind nor *Constitution* of Body; so none can choose *his* own Degree of *Sensibility*. That is given him by the *Author* of his *Nature*, and is already determined.[34]

This hierarchalization was of central importance to cultists of sensibility's definition of themselves. Richardson's paraphrase of this passage can illustrate his absorption and promulgation of Cheyne's representative work. Lovelace declared: "Some people are as sensible of a scratch from a pin's point as others from the push of a sword; and who can say anything for the sensibility of such fellows?"[35]

Degrees of sensibility, then, betokened both social and moral status. Paradoxically, however, an innate refinement of nerves was also identifiable with greater suffering, with weakness, and a susceptibility to disorder. If other versions of sensational psychology promised self-creation, the variant represented by Cheyne betokened vulnerability. Cheyne explained how people were "too sensibly and violently affected," and who felt "too much Pain and Uneasiness from cold or frosty Weather": their showing "too great a Degree of Sensibility or Easiness of being acted upon by external Objects" argued "a Weakness or Slenderness" in the nervous "fibres," "either natural or acquired."[36]

Cheyne had felt this ambiguity himself. He was born with a "great Sensibility" in which was rooted his wit and his intellectual accomplishments, but he characterized his inheritance, too, as "an original State of weak nerves." He said he was "naturally one of those quick-Thinkers who have a great Sensibility either of Pleasure or Pain." This quickness of thought and degree of responsiveness was "natural" because it inhered in the particular and inherited quality of his nerves their smallness of size, elasticity, compactness, and, therefore, closer union thus able to transmit subtle impressions uninterruptedly, with the "swiftness" Newton said they should be transmitted.[37]

The Reformation of Manners Combined with Consumerism

Cheyne's books on sensibility anticipated Rousseau's in their confessional mode. He was his own first patient and, he claimed, his first successful cure. Cheyne devoted thirty-three pages of *The English Malady* to his own case.[38] One reason for describing his sickness and cure was, he said, his "own Vindication" against "sneers," on his "*Regimen, Case* and *Sentiments*." In this connection, Cheyne said he decided to write his book "in a plain *narrative* Stile, . . . without supposing my *Reader* . . . to have look'd into a *physical* Book before." Cheyne claimed that readers will be able to identify with his case as a "*low, desponding, valetudinary, overgrown Person*," because he made it so accessible.[39] And overgrown he had been. Those "sneers" were literally personal. This is how a contemporary described Cheyne.

> Dr. Cheyne, a Scotchman, with an immense broad back, taking snuff incessantly out of a ponderous gold box, and thus ever and anon displaying his fat knuckles—a perfect Falstaff, a good portly man and corpulent. Almost as witty as the knight himself, his humor heightened by his northern brogue, his humor mirthful. The most excellent banterer of his time, a faculty he was often called on to exercise, to repel the lampoons made by others upon his extraordinary personal appearance.[40]

The bitterness one detects in Cheyne's reference to himself as a sneered-at, "overgrown Person" may have been intensified by the characterization of his Scots "brogue" as humorous. (Later in the century, a further "influx of Scottish doctors focused resentment on peculiarly sensitive relationships.") Indeed, when one thinks of the contributions of Hume, Smith, MacKenzie, and even Smollett, to the culture of sensibility, their responsiveness to such friction—"sensitivity" in our terms—however internalized, may have played some considerable part in it. Hume purged "Scotticisms" from his prose; MacKenzie modeled his Edinburgh literary magazines, *The Lounger* and *The Mirror*, on the London *Spectator*. And the Scot Cheyne identified himself with a malady he characterized as particularly "English."[41]

Cheyne believed his family had a hereditary disposition to corpulence. As a youth in Scotland, he said, his "almost constant Application to abstracted Science," that is, a "sedentary life," compounded this disposition, and he came to London as a result of the "Disorder" which previously he had kept a secret. It was a hernia, that had resulted from the drastic but successful measure—"repeated Vomits"—he had taken to reduce his size. "I had been so exceedingly fat, unwidely and overgrown beyond any one I believe in Europe, that weighed 34 stone," that is, 476 pounds.[42] This youthful condition was accompanied by a smorgasbord of symptoms, including a trembling of the hands and being "easily ruffled on a surprise." In London, where he became fat again, his symptoms included melancholy and remorse. "I went about like a Malefactor condemned."[43]

Even after he was successfully dieting to the extent that his body was melting away "like a Snow-ball in Summer," Cheyne remained guilt ridden because in London he had become "a frequenter of coffee houses and taverns," prime, public nodal points for the communication of irreligious habits of thought and deed, as well as sites encouraging a young outsider to gluttony.

> Upon my coming to London, I all of a sudden changed my whole Manner of Living. I found the Bottle-Companions, the younger Gentry, and Free-livers, to be the most easy of Access, and most susceptible of Friendship . . . nothing being necessary . . . but to be able to Eat lustily and swallow down much Liquor . . . I grew daily in Bulk.

Like Richardson and their fellow reformers, Cheyne sought ways to keep people "from the Playhouse and the Tavern and perhaps for worse Places." Eventually Cheyne combined his dietary conversion with a religious one, although this still did not melt him all away, as that Falstaffian picture attests. He was essentially torn between reform and consumerism.[44]

Cheyne warned Richardson "you must go through your State of Purification, in Body as well as Soul, before you can enter on the Land of Promise." His letters insisted on this correspondence between earthly and otherworldly processes. Cheyne arrogated to himself the priestly function long associated with doctoring.[45] He told Richardson; "your Purification must be lighter than mine has been because you have never been so luxurious nor hurt your Constitution so deeply. But I must not flatter you that you will not have your Purgatory and Purification. They pass through Death who do at Heaven arrive, says the Poet; but I think I can lead you through the State having passed it, I hope."[46] Cheyne interpreted Richardson's nervous illness and his own as divinely willed afflictions, transcending the comforts and sensuality that caused them, sufferings analogous to Christ's. The

> Kind of Disorder you Labour under . . . is . . . one of the most effectual Means infinite Goodness could contrive . . . to shew the Nothingness of Creature Comforts and sensual enjoyments . . . and happy are they who by them or any such Means . . . proceeding from a merciful Father in Conjunction

> with and Imitation of his own Son's, who was made perfect by Suffering became dead to every Thing but Infant Love and Beauty.[47]

Cheyne's diagnosis of the effects of his own luxurious and corrupting life also corresponded to his representation of Britain in 1733: it was suffering from "Luxury," too. His vision was shaped by a pseudo-historical contrast between the putative health of a pastoral age and the sickness engendered by subsequent economic success. "When Mankind was simple, plain, honest, and frugal; there were few or no Diseases. Temperance, Exercise, Hunting and Labour, and Industry kept the Juices sweet and the Solids brac'd."[48] (Doctors and moralists had made precisely the same argument in Holland, England's predecessor as a mass consuming nation. Schama entitles the chapter describing this argument, "Feasting, Fasting and Timely Atonement.") According to Cheyne, it was recently in British history that significant sections of the populace had been removed from the healthy circumstances of economic necessity.

> Since our Wealth has increas'd, and our Navigation has been extended, we have ransack'd all the Parts of the *Globe* to bring together its whole Stock of Materials for *Riot*, *Luxury*, and to provoke *Excess*. The Tables of the Rich and Great (and indeed all Ranks who can afford it) are furnish'd with Provisions of Delicacy, Number and Plenty, sufficient to provoke, and even gorge the most large and voluptuous Appetite.

Cheyne seems to have been inspired here by his own remarkable appetite, but we have seen that England's consumption pattern was in fact being transformed. He extended this vision of Augustan Britain's self-destructive consumerism to a widely held frame of historical reference. Earlier empires had found their histories following the same process from simplicity to luxury and decline, from "Politeness and Refinement" to "nervous diseases." The Greeks had "sunk to Effeminacy, Luxury, and Disease," and the Romans fell from "Bravery, Courage, *heroick Virtue*" according to the same pattern. His concern here was the degradation of males.[49]

Cheyne remarked that the only limitation to the pursuit of appetitive pleasure under Britain's prosperous circumstances was wealth ("all Ranks who can afford it"). Later Cheyne suggested that "the middling Sort" remained closest to "the Simplicity of Nature" as they followed "the Dictates of Reason and Experience and [did] not lust after *foreign Delicacies*." Cheyne proposed as long as the middle classes stayed simple they would stay healthy, "not yet [having] grown luxurious rich and wanton, or [having] frequent Commerce with other Nations." This was a warning; Cheyne's medical sociology was intended to establish a check on the material pursuit of pleasure, although it was a check whose authority was itself rooted in materialism, that is, in the nerve paradigm.[50]

Cheyne counted himself in those jostling ranks "among us" Britons, striving to out-do "one another in Kinds of Profusion." "Profusion" signified the potentials for material pleasures in a successfully commercializing country. One particular feature of "rioting in sensual Pleasure" which Cheyne felt called for lengthy exposition, indeed his first example of "voluptuous 'appetite,'" was gourmet eating. "*Invention* is rack'd to furnish the Materials of our Food the most delicate and Savoury possible." Cheyne detailed the "culinary Torments" to which animals were subjected in order to satisfy the sensualist's palate, and he thus contributed his note to the campaign against cruelty to animals. His warning echoed, too, the advice then being disseminated to English housewives in the face of increasing temptations to luxurious consumption. For example, *The Compleat Housewife or, Accomplished Gentlewoman's Companion*, published the following year, gave directions, for "dressing" food in the "natural manner," agreeable "to English Palates," as opposed to the fondness the English were in fact showing for "French *modes*, and French messes." In Cheyne's view, the "Manner of Dressing or Cooking Items . . . the ingenious mixing and compounding of *Sauces* with foreign *Spices* and Provocatives, are contriv'd not only to rouze a fickle Appetite to receive the unnatural Load, but to render a good one incapable of knowing when it has enough." Consumer psychology was deliberately stimulated. Part of the guilty burden of those who consumed these luxuries could be shifted to the unfair provocation or, rather, to those farmers, international merchants, and chefs who benefited from this, "one of the most profitable Trades." An element of self-righteousness is apparent—even a sense of victimization: if Cheyne offered diet and self-discipline as a ritual of purgation leading to eternal life, he also said that "we" were dying as "martyrs to our luxury."[51]

"Necessarily," Cheyne's diagnosis continued, this literal consumerism begot an "Inaptitude for Exercise" and led to an inevitable chain of less material consumer dissipation. Consumers of luxurious dishes were limited by physical bulk and weakness, to "*Assemblies, Musick, Meetings, Plays, Cards,* and *Dice,*" where participants were conveyed, "with the Least Pain and Uneasiness possible from Motion" by "*Coaches* improv'd with Springs" and specially trained horses and chairmen.[52] A third category of pathogens that Cheyne argued was afflicting Britons' nervous systems and, again, one of which Cheyne had personal experience was the increase of the "contemplative and sedentary *Professions*." He suggested that talented human beings were born with "Organs finer, quicker, more agile, and sensible, and perhaps more numerous than others." That selfsame, naturally refined group in "our own Nation, our own Times, and of the better Sort" was striving "to go beyond" previous generations "in all the *Arts* of *Ingenuity*, *Invention*, *Study*, [and] *Learning*," with profoundly weakening effects on their nerves of precisely the kind the studious young Cheyne had suffered. Nurture compounding nature, their originally finer endowment was turned into a liability. Thereafter, an inheritance of naturally "delicate and fine" nerves, "wasted and thinned even more by disease," were passed on to posterity. The next generation of children, their nerves normally more tender because of youth, were then "even longer preserved in their Sensibility and Refinement."[53]

Cheyne completed this weaving together of his own history with that of the growth and prospects of British commercial capitalism by adding the effects of living in "over-grown Cities." His own unhealthy corpulence corresponded to London's. It is "the greatest, most capacious, close and, populous City of the *Globe*." In contrast to the "sweet, balmy, and clear Air of the Country," London's atmosphere and streets were full of the discharges of human activities: the fumes of workshop and domestic fires; the lavishly burned lamp oil and candles, the exhalations of breaths and crowded bodies (both alive and dead); the "Ordure" of human beings and animals as well as other piles of dirt and waste in cesspools, slaughterhouses, and stables. Cheyne found particularly pathogenic the "mixture of such Variety of all Kinds of Atoms" as he had done in the case of food, a notion we can link with "profusion," marking the most striking material distinction of the urban commercial world. It was the opposite of the simple, pastoral, and unstimulated world of the wished-for past and one which Cheyne termed "natural."[54]

Cheyne specified the effects of all this luxury on the nerves, the body's organs and juices, laden with corrosive salts, building up and stagnating around the nerve fibers, constricting, relaxing, or hardening them, causing them to break, in accordance with Newton's view of elasticity. The nervous system of the luxuriating consumer became as clogged and polluted as the air and streets of modern London. His therapeutic intentions were to "thin, dilute," and "sweeten" the "whole mass of fluids," to "dissolve" the "saline" accretions in the vessels, "restore the tone and elastic force, crisp, wind up, and contract the fibres of the whole system."[55]

While Cheyne saw himself as a moral reformer, his reformism was dependent upon consumerism, not the least because of his assumption that his readers had the freedom to choose a more or less frugal diet, a circumstance reflecting his internal conflict. Moreover, the site for Cheyne's religious conversion, following his falling into London's iniquitous tavern life, had been that eighteenth-century pleasure center, Bath, made fashionable by Queen Anne's visit earlier in the century. It was there that Cheyne himself became fashionable, becoming "an annual summertime resident." In 1720 Cheyne wrote a book recommending the beneficial effects of the Bath waters on gout. One of his patients may have been Richard "Beau" Nash, "the arbiter of fashion" at Bath. Whether or not this was literally the case, it was symbolically so. Here was another route for the transmission of nerve expertise in relationship with degrees of sensibility; following and propagating his regimen, Cheyne made his fortune. "I will secure you," he assured Richardson, "you shall have Time to turn all your expense in this Paroxism into a double or triple annual Income to your Family. I have tripled my Fortune since I first suffered in your Way."[56]

In sum, Richardson's doctor embodied the campaign for the reformation of manners *and* consumerism. At one symbolic nerve center, where the culture's language was being generated, one finds a compressed combination of luxury and guilt, fashion and self-denial, sensuality and purgation; within such spirals, in fact, produced by them, was the elevation of ambiguously susceptible nerves, whose state could be a sign of social superiority and Christian grace, or of weakness and nervous disorder.

Nerve Theory in Novels

The flow of nerve ideas from scientists and diagnosticians into literature, illustrated by Cheyne's influence on Richardson's best-selling works, also could be demonstrated with reference to Sterne's and Smollett's reading of "the physiological debates of the forties and fifties in England, especially those centering around Albrecht von Haller's theory of 'sensibility' and 'irritability.'"[57] Smith's aborption of the ideas of Cullen and Whytt in *The Theory of Moral Sentiments* (1759) was in turn propagated by the best-selling novels of Henry MacKenzie. In addition, the neurology of Boerhaave, von Haller, and others entered the writings of Diderot and the *Encyclopedie*'s other authors and readers, including Rousseau's, and thence reinforced the prominence given neurology by later eighteenth-century English novelists.[58] Professor G. Rousseau suggests that the "myth" and "truth" of the nerves became "national, even European or universal, common knowledge" over the course of the eighteenth century.[59]

So while Wollstonecraft criticized the entire identification of women with their supposedly finer nervous system, she made her analysis in the paradigm's own terms. Her chapter which explained how everything that women "see or hear [these are Newton's illustrative senses] serves to fix impressions and call forth emotions, and associate ideas, that give a sexual character to the mind[,]" refers throughout to Locke and Newton, each now modified in the directions noted. She emphasized that over the "instantaneous associations we have little power," and this was because they are effected by "this subtle electric fluid" over which, she also exclaimed, "how little power do we possess, and over it how little power can reason possess." Her "we" means we human beings, women and men, and it is on that basis that she went on to describe the further weakening of that little power by females' upbringing. Thus the "habitual slavery to first impressions, has a more baneful effect on women." If she had criticized the materialism of the nervous "fire" in her earlier quotation of Johnson's definition of sensibility on the grounds of its materialism, here she acknowledged that her acceptance of the Newtonian paradigm put her in the same bind as others of his descendants. Adherence to the nerve paradigm betokened by sensibility forced her to recognize she could not fully distinguish herself from "materialists." With other believers, other writers especially, Wollstonecraft held that this "subtle electric fluid," that is, Newton's ether, is "the essence of genius" operating Locke's sensational psychology (as it had been updated by Hartley), in genius producing "in the most eminent degree that happy energy of associating thoughts that surprise, delight, and instruct." This was a typical version of Cheyne's hierarchy of "degrees" of sensibility. Their degree of sensibility distinguished geniuses from the generality of people who could not see or feel poetically, wanting "fancy." In a revealing joke Wollstonecraft asked whether "the passions might not be fine volatile fluids that embraced humanity, keeping the more refractory parts together—or whether they were simply a liquid fire that pervaded the mere sluggish materials, giving them life and heat?" The paradigm suggested a social vision based on a sense of "little power" but pointing to humanitarian reform.[60]

That the nerve paradigm was so widely popularized, and popularized in the directions Wollstonecraft here exemplifies, must be seen in large part as the result of literacy and the novel, above all, the novel of "sensibility." The appearance of that term will be illustrated throughout, but here we can note the pervasiveness of related expressions of the paradigm.

One of the first appearances of the word "nerve" in *Clarissa* is in volume 2, when Lovelace, deliberately poisoning himself to win Clarissa's sympathy, declared "every nerve and fibre of me is already to contribute its aid, whether by health or by ailment, or carry a resolved-on roguery into execution." Burke in his 1757 treatise on *The Philosophical Origins of the Sublime and the Beautiful*, declared that "pain and fear consist in an unnatural tension of the nerves." Or in Smollett's *Humphrey Clinker*, Matthew Bramble said "it was the nature of fear to brace up the nerves." We read of the heroine's father in Anne Radcliffe's *The Mysteries of Udolpho* that "sorrow had seized upon his nerves, weakened as they had been by the preceding illness." Amusing his mind would "restore them to their proper tone." Mary Hays's heroine of sensibility, Emma Courtney, found her "nerves firmly braced by [her] exertions."[61]

"Fibres," too, occur in Richardson's work. Lovelace's metaphor for Clarissa's "native" principle, her "LOVE OF VIRTUE," ("its fibres struck into her heart, and, as she grew up, blended and twisted with the strings of life"), closely resembles Addison's playful dissection of a coquette's heart in *The Spectator* of January 22, 1711–2, a connection many of Richardson's readers would have made.[62] Both Richardson and Burke used "fibres" and "nerves" interchangeably. Smollett's Matthew Bramble proposed to "brace up" his "fibres by sea-bathing." Elizabeth Inchbald referred to the torment caused "every fibre of the frame," the effects of jealousy mixed with love.[63]

Other terms, "sensation" and "impression," referred to the nervous system of sensational psychology. Fielding's Tom Jones asked a friend if he did not share "the warm rapturous sensations" which one feels "from the consciousness" of a "benevolent action," a view preached by Fielding's contemporary Latitudinarians. According to a sentimental protagonist of MacKenzie's *The Man of the World* (1773), the libertine's "degree" of pleasure produced by the gratification of "gross sense" was "obdurated by the repetition of debauch" and therefore "unsusceptible" of "the delight which the finer sensations produce, which thrill through the bosom of delicacy and virtue."[64] The moral value attached to the capacity for the "finer sensations" is apparent. Frances Burney's villain in *The Wanderer* had a "constitutional hardness of nerve that cannot feel," an essential characteristic of all the villains in the literature of sensibility. Versions of the Burney quotation include the typical phrase used by Mercy Otis Warren, appealing to "every mind of the least sensibility" and Radcliffe's own similar appeal, referring to the Burkean effects of a landscape: "the heart must be insensible that does not soften to its influence." Hays's 1793 *Essays* illustrate how readers were flattered or elevated by the assumption of this common body of values and knowledge. Saying she would "draw a veil" over her subject's grief, Hays wrote that "to sensible hearts, such descriptions are unnecessary, to the cold and dissipated, they would be inconceivable." She then described the grief.[65]

"Impression" was one of the most frequently used nerve referents. Locke's usage had been preceded by the word's denoting the mark made by a signet ring on warmed wax. This former connection was sustained, for example in *Clarissa, Sir Charles Grandison,* Inchbald's *A Simple Story,* and Hays's *Essays.* A later adaptation was to the marks made by a printing press. Locke's *Essay on Understanding* had said, "Perception is only when the mind receives the impression," transmitted, that is, by the "conduits" of the nerves until it reached the famous blank sheet.[66] "Impressions" indicated sensationalist psychology in a wide-ranging way.[67] Sentimental writers and their critics also referred to "the association of ideas," references that may have become more frequent after the publication of Hartley's 1749 book and then of a popularized version by Joseph Priestley in 1775. Burke referred to the powerful effects of the association of ideas laid down in early childhood, a fact of central importance to his opponent, Wollstonecraft, from whom Hays probably derived her use of it in *Emma Courtney*. Radcliffe approvingly quoted Mark Akenside's version (Akenside studied in both Edinburgh and Leyden):

> Lull'd in the countless chambers of the brain,
> Our thoughts are linked by many a hidden chain:
> Awake but one, and lo! what myriads arise!
> Each stamps its image as the other flies![68]

"Spirits" was a more specific psychological and physiological referent, always indicating mood or body state. Cheyne presented "lowness of spirits" as a nervous symptom throughout. The new "mechanistic" nerve theories were grafted onto the ancient and, therefore, familiar vitalist meaning of the term. The state of one's spirits were a sensitive register of one's disposition and response to the world. Lovelace had "lively spirits," for example.[69] Very often, though, the exemplars of sensibility suffered from "lowness of spirits," "dejection of spirits," "weak spirits," "want of spirits," in what was always a vulnerable situation in relation to "the world" that was being mediated.[70] That world could be "too much for her spirits."[71] Heroines and heroes were "low-spirited."[72] Their spirits were "overcome," "overpowered," or "sunk," or "broken."[73] "Spirits" were "depressed" and "oppressed" in various combinations of these verbs.[74] One's spirits could "fail" or else be "sunk." Physical and mental states usually depended on each other.[75] Facing Lovelace, Clarissa wrote to her close friend, Anna Howe, "I had . . . less inclination to interrupt him, being excessively fatigued, and my spirits sunk to nothing, with even of the best prospects with such a man."[76]

The sense of spirits' vulnerability, above all in registering the wounds given women by men in the sexual warfare that the culture of sensibility embodied, is suggested by the phrase "harassed spirits."[77] That Clarissa could say, "I have been grievously harassed," with moral effects on her nervous system, dramatizes the connotations, which include those of warfare and hunting.[78] A related phrase (which Cheyne used in his account of nervous symptoms) was "Hurry of Spirits" and its variations which one finds scattered through the literature from Fielding and Richardson through Burke, Radcliffe (who was particularly influenced by Burke), the anonymous author of *Robert and Adela: or, The Rights of Woman Best Maintained by the Sentiments of Nature* (1795), and Maria Edgeworth's *Belinda* (1801).[79] Wollstonecraft shared this usages with the anti-Wollstonecraftian *Robert and Adela*. In her letters, her most frequent expression of anxiety is by way of the cognates "hurry," "harry," and "harassed."[80] "Spirits" were described as "better," "kept up," "amended," and "recruited." Following a Cheyne-like regimen brought Smollett's Matthew Bramble "a constant tide of spirits." And having plunged into the fashionable cure of sea bathing (one of the eighteenth-century therapies expressing this preoccupation), another of Smollett's characters exclaimed, "You cannot conceive what a flow of spirits it gives, and how it braces every sinew of the human frame."[81]

A word closely linked to "spirits" was "vapours." "My spirits sink again. . . Excuse this depth of vapourish dejection." Like "spirits," "vapours" was a traditional term, associated with the spleen and embodied in ancient humoral pathology. Cheyne referred to "Humors" and "the Choler" even while he attempted to update the meaning of "vapours." In this Cheyne had long been preceded by Mandeville in his 1711 *Treatise*.[82] This is another unsurprising overlap of traditional and new. Swift had given a satirical account of madness as "the redundancy of vapours" in *A Tale of a Tub* (1704), and Smollett was to refer to the same idea in *Humphrey Clinker* (1771).[83] Addison associated "the vapours" with women in two 1711 issues of *The Spectator*. Defoe's heroine, Moll Flanders (1722), occasionally suffers from "the vapours."[84] In *Sir Charles Grandison* (1753–4), Richardson puts the "loose" notion of "vapours" in the mouth of an unreconstructed male, Sir Charles's libertine father, Sir Thomas, by way of a folk saying: "A young wife makes a vapourish mother." But Clarissa's use of it in her metaphor for love is Cheyne's modern one.[85] Lovelace's use of the term refers to Mandeville's observation that the doctors' diagnose "vapours" as "a common Subterfuge for mere Ignorance of the Nature of Distempers." "The vapourish or splenetic patient is a fiddle for the doctors; and they are eternally playing upon it." Lovelace applies "vapourish" to himself to mean only slightly ill, but Clarissa uses it a number of times as a synonym for serious depression.[86]

"Vibration" was yet another sign of the nerve paradigm of the culture of sensibility; Burke insisted that the "vibrations must be sensitive" and Radcliffe echoed Burke in *Udolpho*. In her *Essays*, Hays wrote: "I have sometimes doubted, whether the acute sensibility arising from an organization peculiarly delicate, may not bring the happiness of the possessor, upon an average to nearly the same medium with that of others, whose nerves being of less flexible texture, feel no vibration from the thousand tremulous touches that convulse the tender and impassioned heart."[87]

Vibrations' more common synonym, one we have seen illustrated by MacKenzie's *Man of the World* but found, too, in Phillis Wheatley's "To Maecenas" (1773), or Hannah More's 1787 poem on sensibility as well as Wollstonecraft's *Letters Written in Sweden*, was "thrill." Radcliffe's heroine found thinking about a "terrible subject . . . thrilled her every nerve with horror." "Thrill" was an old verb (a variant of "drill") meaning to flow, trickle, or percolate. The Rev. Joseph Glanville, who had been a defender of natural philosophy in the last third of the seventeenth century and who was to incorporate the new nerve theory into his sermons, is recorded by the *Oxford English Dictionary* as the first to use the evolved meaning of thrill as a "subtle nervous tremor caused by intense emotion or excitement . . . producing a slight shudder or tingling through the body." In a 1672 sermon Glanville told his audience that joy "warms the . . . blood and sends it about with a pleasant thrill through all the channels of its motion." Akenside's later and thorough digestion of Newtonian neurology in *The Pleasures of the Imagination* allowed him to list an array of sensations, each one of which "Thrills through Imagination's tender frame, From nerve to nerve." Or Hays's Emma Courtney said of the voice of the man she loved, it "struck upon my ear—it thrilled through my nerves."[88]

The registering of sounds was an appealing illustration of Newton's vibrations along the nerves. A passage from his *Opticks* was the source for Cheyne's insistent comparison of the "Sensorium" to a "*Musician*" and of the nerves to "*Keys*." Richardson also paraphrased this aspect of Cheyne's thought in *Clarissa*. In a series of pictures illustrating the operation of the senses that he painted in 1744–7, Phillipe Mercier represented *The Sense of Hearing* by women playing musical instruments. Hence one of the most common nerve referents is "strings,"

Philippe Mercier (1689[?]-1760). *The Sense of Hearing*, 1744–7. Oil on canvas. 52 × 60 1/2 in. Yale Center for British Art, Paul Mellon Collection.

neatly assimilable to "vibration" or "thrill." And again (as in the cases of sense, spirits, and impressions) one may say that the new psycho-perceptual system capitalized on a traditional term. "String" had for centuries had meant muscle, acquiring the meaning of nerve only during the previous century (with the rise of dissection). Such capitalization surely was one factor in the eventually general acceptance of the new system.[89]

Hume emphasized the harmonic possibilities of the nervous system in his *Treatise of Human Nature* (1739–40), comparing the affections generated among human creatures to the sounds transmitted by musical instruments. Their "strings [were] equally wound up," a metaphor that would appear half a century later in *Udolpho*.[90] Recommending the sentimental poetry of Edward More, Henry Brooke said he aimed

> To touch the Strings that humanize our Kind,
> Man's sweetest Strain, the Music of the Mind.

"String" also denoted nerves in a nonmusical way. In one of his messages intended to impart the Protestant ethic, Wesley warned in 1786 that "the nerves are quite unstrung by lying too long abed in the morning." This was a version of Burke's 1757 remark about rest's effect on the tone of the fibers.[91]

The harmonious connotations were also embodied in the traditional old term "heart-strings." "Admirable mechanism! All the other strings of the heart vibrate when that of humanity has just been sounded."[92] Thus Radcliffe could describe sounds vibrating on her heroine's heart: the expansion of the old metaphor to the body's whole system is illustrated by the same heroine's capacity to hear familiar music "vibrate on the chords of unhappy memory."[93] We may bear in mind that the audience for which such sentimental literature was written also enjoyed a proliferating number of harpsichords, harps, and violins. Cheyne's "organ case" can be aligned with Clarissa's possession of a chamber organ and a harpsichord. Later in the century, the piano penetrated interiors further down the social scale. Heroines' and heroes' listening to and playing of affecting melodies, absorbing them into their own nervous instrumentality, was fostered by the new mass production of musical scores and instruments as well as of novels.[94] MacKenzie's Harley was thus moved in his absent lover's room. "My Emily's spinet stood . . . open with a book of music folded down at some of my favourite lessons. I touched the keys; there was a vibration in the sound that froze my blood: . . . methought the family-pictures on the walls gazed on me with compassion in their faces." This newly accessible mode for female self-expression was a significant new material circumstance of a consumer society in which to consider the proliferation of these metaphors. If Hartley in his 1749 *Observations* challenged the idea that "nerves themselves should vibrate like musical strings" (even though he adhered to Newton's doctrine of transmission by vibration), his challenge went unheeded in popular literature.[95]

Female Nerves and Sensibility's Ambiguity

In *The Book of the Courtier*, which, following its translation in 1561, had a "pervasive effect" on Elizabethan England, Castiglione declared that "the timidity of women, though it betrays a degree of imperfection, has a noble origin in the subtlety and readiness of their senses which conveys images very speedily to the mind, because they are easily moved by external things." One may see this as laying the courtly groundwork for bourgeois and scientized evaluation of delicate nerves. Castiglione went on to say that men were characterized by "a certain obtuse insensitivity." In 1674 Malebranche had "propounded the idea that women were intellectually inferior to men because of the greater sensibility of the nerve fibers in their brain." When asked in 1708 by a reader "whether women were as capable of learning as men," *The British Apollo* replied that women "are cast in too soft a mould, are made of too fine, too delicate composure to endure the severity of study, the drudgery of contemplation, the fatigue of profound speculation."[96] The question had been prompted by the growing number of publications by women, some of them making explicit the promise to women of sensational psychology.

Thomas Laqueur has suggested that, during the eighteenth century, a "new model of gender difference," an "anatomy and physiology of incommensurability replaced a metaphysics of hierarchy in the representation of women in relation to men." Crucial to feminist and antifeminist arguments was the Hobbesian view that there was "no basis in nature" for man's authority over woman. To a philosophy embodying the possibility that the definition of being human should exclude "half of humanity" was added revolution's argument that the social and cultural relations of mankind "could be remade." The potential engendered both "a new feminism and a new fear of women." Laqueur's subject is the late Enlightenment, the French Revolution, and its aftermath; the dialectic he describes focused on women's orgasmic and reproductive capabilities. But the dialectic between revolutionary possibilities had already occurred nearly a hundred years earlier. Although certainly opened by the materialism of Hobbesian thought, its focus was the nerves. Moreover, its context included the reconceptualization of men, about which women themselves had had a great deal to say in the intervening period. The nerves were gendered in accordance with the still older values expressed by Castiglione. As we have seen, Newton himself had not directed his science to such an end.[97]

Cheyne linked sedentary male intellectuals and women together as persons who, while scorned "among the multitude, for a lower Degree of lunacy," in fact suffered on account of their talented nerves. "I myself was thought a Fool, a weak and ignorant Coxcomb, and perhaps dismiss'd in Scorn." At the same time, his nervous disease could have happened only "to those of the liveliest and quickest natural Parts, whose Faculties are the brightest and most Spiritual, and whose Genius is most keen and penetrating, and particularly where there is the most delicate Sensation and Taste, both of Pleasure and Pain."[98] Yet, however delicate a man's system, it was firmer than a woman's. Cheyne's gendering of the nerves, although usually implicit, was fundamental to his thought. We have seen that he characterized the decline of the heroic virtues of the ancients as "effeminacy" and, therefore, nervous disease. Similarly, Cheyne wished to reconcile the prehistorical origins of the body to the account in Genesis of Eve's creation out of Adam's rib: he suggested that the human body's firmness and strength, its "original Stamina, the whole System of the Solids, the Firmness, Force, and strength of the Muscles, of the Viscera, and great Organs" were "owing to the Male." Combining this biblical explanation with Aristotle, he then asked: "does the Female *contribute* any more but a convenient Habitation, proper Nourishment, and an *Incubation* for the seminal Animalcule for a Time?" The male supplies the solids, the female the "fluids." "But it is on these Fluids that Medicines and Medical Operations have [effect] chiefly." In some sense, therefore, a human being's weakness and illness represented the overbalance of the originally female side. (The natural constituency for the specialist concentrating on the state of nervous liquids could be seen as a female one.) One may read Cheyne's characterization of those "born with weak nerves" in this light; they could never "expect the same Force, Strength, Vigour and Activity" as those born with "strong Fibres or robust Constitution." Women's finer, weaker nerves were "determined" by God and science. Lacking these literally male qualities, those born with innately fine or delicate nerves were not "made capable of running into the same Indiscretions or Excess of Sensual Pleasures" as were those born with "strong Fibres or Robust Constitutions."[99] According to this scheme, it could be claimed that women were naturally the moral superiors of most men, a superiority shared by men who were becoming more like women in this regard.

While Cheyne's general argument did not appear to gender nervous disorders, for example, the "hypochondriacal and Hysterical Distempers" of his book's subtitle, when it came to case studies, it did. Cheyne described eighteen cases of nervous diseases in *The English Malady*, seven women and eleven men. Of the latter, one was "a worthy merchant," another a "dignified Clergyman," the rest "gentlemen." All of the women were "ladies," one of them "of great Fortune" in London, another "of the first Quality," and a third of an "honourable and Opulent Family." Cheyne emphasizes these ladies' moral virtues of piety and charity, not mentioning such qualities in the cases of men. Part of his purpose was to claim the sheer respectability, indeed the fashionability (and profitability) of nervous disorders and of his treatment of them.[100] Although Cheyne's male patients shared some symptoms with the women ("lowness," for example), not one was described as having "Hysterical" disorders, while five of the seven women were. All were also subsumed under the rubric of "Nervous." "Hysterical" signified another profoundly traditional set of beliefs on which nerve diagnosticians capitalized. Mandeville's 1711 *Treatise* reflected his belief that women's normal condition "dispose them to be Hysterick." Later doctors who argued that women had a naturally more tender nervous system also linked it to the ancient female-associated disorder of "hysteria." As far as Cheyne's cases were concerned, three of the men had "Epileptick," "Nervous," and "Hypochondriacal Fits," while two of the women had "Hysterical Paroxysms" and "Hysterical Fits and Cholicks." Cheyne recommended regular exercise to five of the men but to only one of the women and to a second "on occasion."[101]

Cheyne may well have taken some of this from Mandeville's *Treatise of Hypochondriack and Hysterick Passions*, which was reprinted just three years before Cheyne's book. "Hypochondriasis" was the eighteenth-century's version of the ancient "melancholy" and the ancestor of modern "neurosis." Mandeville suggested that hypochondriasis was caused in large part by wealth. The qualities of wealth, leisure, and concentrated focus linked the man of business to the scholar as a potential sufferer from hypochondriasis. It was called "the Disease of the Learned," recorded Mandeville, because such men "continually fatigue their Heads with intense Thought and Study, whilst they neglect to give the other parts of their Bodies the Exercise they require." The same diagnosis had shown itself in the seventeenth century, keeping pace with the rise of the Protestant ethic and of the literate groups associated with it. That ethic's commercial successes potentiated the refinement of more and more men's bodies as well as their behavior. Nonetheless, according to Mandeville, women suffered from nervous disorders in greater numbers than men. Their susceptibility could be worsened by bad diet, idleness, and lack of exercise, all of which seem to have increased with prosperity.[102]

Shammas's book, demonstrating the permeation of "groceries" in the English diet, poses intriguing possibilities in this regard, that is, a connection between nervous susceptibility and nervous disorders and the new, mass consumption of tea and coffee, their caffeine compounded with lashings of sugar, as well as tobacco in its various forms. Boswell said of Dr. Johnson's "relish" for "the infusion of that fragrant leaf[,]" tea:

> The quantities that he drank of it at all hours were so great, that his nerves must have been uncommonly strong, not to have been extremely relaxed by such an intemperate use of it, he assured me, that he never felt the least inconvenience from it; which is a proof that the fault of his constitution was rather a too great tension of fibres than the contrary.

In his younger years, Dr. Johnson "drank freely," especially enjoying a port punch flavored with sugar and an orange. Feeling guilty, he converted to tea and is recorded to have drunk it in huge quantities, seventeen cups on one occasion, when he then asked for more.[103] Boswell assumes that men's nervous systems could be adversely affected by overindulgence in tea. Did women's particular pleasure in and identification with sugar-laden tea and its ceremonies, along with a less calorific diet, contribute to the apparent rise of nervous disorders among them? (The pourer of Johnson's seventeen plus cups was a vicar's wife.) Were the effects of a new pattern of consuming behavior judged differently in the case of each sex? Of course, any such material factors are always part of a denser history; in this case, the possible effects of tea drinking were coupled with the idealization/denigration of women's supposedly more susceptible nervous bodies and manners.[104]

Medical experts declared that women, unlike men, were born deficient, thereafter facing a debilitating reproductive history men did not experience. In Mandeville's view, women's "spirits" were inherently less than men's and their nerves were thinner, more delicate and softer. The effects permeated women's constitutions; women's vaunted "delicacy" reflected the weakness of their nervous systems, also termed "delicate." Such weakness explained why women were "unfit . . . for abstruse and elaborate thoughts, all Studies of Depth, Coherence and Solidity, that fatigue the Spirits and require a Steadiness and Assiduity of Thinking."[105] And even if women were educated and could exceed men "in Sprightliness of Fancy," they found that their nervous systems meant that "Grief, Joy, Anger, Fear, and the rest of the Passions, made greater Impression upon them, and sooner discompose their Bodies." Throughout the century doctors lent their expertise to the notion that all women had more delicate nerves and, therefore, greater sensibility than men: "their quickness of the pulse, in a healthy state is owing to the sensibility of the nerves in general." Conversely, women's liability to certain disorders was the price of "a finer texture of their Nerves."[106]

By 1734 Hume had absorbed the view that men and women had different nervous systems. Like Cheyne, Hume took his own case to illustrate his susceptibility to nervous disease. In accordance with Mandeville, he said he had "The Disease of the Learned," "the Vapours," and "a Weakness of Spirits." Following the experts, Hume took long rides daily as well as "Anti-hysteric Pills." At the same time Hume advocated the development of sensibility in men, in the interest of fostering "Delicacy of Taste and Passion," the title of one of his 1741 *Essays*. In considering the extent to which such delicacy reflected nervous physiology, Hume made it clear that he believed women had finer nerves than men.

> How far delicacy of taste, and that of passion, are connected together in the original frame of mind, it is hard to determine. To me there always appears very considerable connexion between them. For we may observe that women, who have more delicate passions than men, have also a more delicate taste of the ornaments of life . . . and the ordinary decencies of behaviour.

A further illustration of the "connexion" between a woman's behavior and her nervous system was that any "excelling" in such ornaments and decencies "hits" women's "taste much sooner than ours," that is, than men's. This assumed the "quickness" of the most refined nerves.[107]

The view that women's nerves were normatively distinct from men's, normatively making them creatures of greater sensibility, became a central convention of eighteenth-century literature. Richardson's Lovelace held that women's spirits were "naturally soft." The subject of sexuality "always makes women simper. A man that is gross in a woman's company ought to be knocked down with a club, for, like so many musical instruments, touch but a single wire, and the dear souls are sensible all over." Fielding (who, whatever his famous differences with Richardson, shared views of gender with him) referred to the "common opinion" that a women's "susceptibility" to the impression of a man's bravery proceeded from "the natural timidity of the sex." Horace Walpole expressed the same popular "opinion" in

1770, saying of the marquis of Granby that his "nerves trembled like a woman's." In the last third of the century, "tenderness" became synonymous with sensibility as a characteristic of women, above all, properly acculturated ones. "What is more suited to the tenderness which is allowed to be natural to our sex?" In "offering up to Heaven the thanksgiving of her artless rapture," Burney's Camilla found herself "dissolving in the soft tears of the tenderest sensibility, according to the quick changing impulses of her natural and lively, yet feeling and susceptible character." To be "Delicate-tender" was, in Jane Austen's Willoughby's words, to be "truly feminine." "Tender" can be added to the other popularized referents to the nervous system.[108]

A high value was placed on this greater sensibility. Like Mandeville, Clarissa attributed "liveliness and quickness," in fact, "all the powers that related to imagination" to women of all classes, in contrast to the generality of men. Moreover, men said they found women's greater sensibility a source of attraction. John Gregory told his female readers in 1774 that "extreme sensibility which blushing indicates, may be a weakness and encumbrance in our sex . . . but in yours it is peculiarly engaging." Conversely, novelist Frances Brooke declared in *Emily Montague* (1769) that sensibility was the "magnet which attracts all to itself, . . . virtue may command esteem, understanding and talents admiration, beauty a transient desire, but 'tis sensibility alone which inspires love." As Gregory and even Burney implied, however, those with the most refined nerves were naturally most susceptible to nervous disorders.[109]

The association between a gendered sensibility and nervous disorders was manifested in various ways. One of them was in women's consumerism, a proclivity linked to "Easiness of being acted upon by external objects." In February 1742, Cheyne wrote to Richardson:

> I hope Mrs. Richardson is not like the rest of her Sex or Kindred known to me who I fear would rather renounce Life than Luxury. My Female Family have been almost all forced into that Method to cure nervous and hysteric Disorders.

Cheyne linked women's nervous disorders to their appetite for consumer goods—elsewhere he recorded their appetite for coffee, tea, chocolate, and snuff—as he had done in his own case. He also illustrated how men could stand in the way of such appetite. In *Humphry Clinker* Smollett described how Mrs. Bayard used tears and fits to suck her husband "deeper and deeper into the vortex of extravagance and dissipation." Her being "seized with a violent fit . . . completed her triumph over the spirit of her consort . . . The family plate was sold for old silver, and a new service procured; fashionable furniture was provided." Mr. Bayard's old friend Matthew Bramble offered to persuade Mrs. Bayard of "the necessity of reforming her economy" (in keeping with the kind of advice offered by *The Compleat Housewife*) but Bayard declined "on the supposition that his wife's nerves were too delicate to bear expostulation."[110]

Fielding, who referred to "the learned Dr. Cheney" [sic] in *Tom Jones*, remarked in the same novel that "every physician hath his favourite disease, to which he ascribes all the victories over human nature. The gout, the rheumatism . . . the consumption . . . and none more than the nervous fever, or the fever of the spirits." Consumption, denoting both the "wasting" disease and the acquisition of new goods (Cheyne's work illustrating the integral relation of those meanings) took on fresh value in this century. We have seen that his logic led to the expectation that doctors could specialize in women's nervous disorders. A later Bath doctor, James Adair, a specialist in "women's nerves," recognized that fashion "has long influenced the great and the opulent in their choice of physicians. But it is not so obvious how it has influenced them also in their choice of diseases."[111] Poet George Crabbe, himself a doctor, suggested one answer in *The Village*:

> Ye, oppressed by some fantastic woes,
> Some jarring nerve that baffles your repose,
> Who press the downy couch . . .
> Who with sad prayers the weary doctor lease,
> To name the nameless ever-new disease;
> Who with mock patience dire complaints endure,
> Which real pain, and that alone can cure;
> How would ye bear in real pain to be . . . ?

Crabbe's point here was the contrast between "a class of glutted and neurotic consumers" and the pain of the lower-class laborers whose work sustained Crabbe's and Cheyne's voluptuaries. Other eighteenth-century writers made the same point, and it must be granted. Nonetheless, the distinction between the real and the feigned in nervous illness is far less easily dismissed in the case of the whole class of women suffering nervous "oppression," even as they pursued "fashion."[112]

And here, the gendered meaning implicit in "home demand" must be extended to embrace the importance of women's wishes in the related, external achievements of "a polite and commercial people." The connection between refined pleasure and women's susceptibility to nervous disorders played a fundamental part, for example, in the renaissance of spa towns during the eighteenth century. At the other kind of urban pleasure resorts—the urban centers on which hunts and race meets were based—men's pursuit of pleasure was the occasion. At spas, this was not so, and women's wishes, women's complaints, could be the purpose. At Bath, at least, where over the century the population increased from under three thousand to thirty-five thousand, at times women seem to have outnumbered men. And if thousands were already coming for the waters in the 1690s, it was after Queen Anne's visits in 1702 and 1703 that Bath became "the most fashionable of all provincial towns[,]" fashionable leadership we can compare to Queen Mary's in the case of china and calicoes. Borsay describes the magnificent rebuilding of spa towns' pleasure facilities, assembly rooms, shopping parades, public walks and gardens.[113] Of course, Bath and Tunbridge would be powerhouses for male as well as female manners, under the tutelage of Richard "Beau" Nash for one, but, very strikingly, those manners were formed in the public heterosociality of the joint pursuit of pleasure. But that "the line between recuperation and recreation was a thin one" took on a particular meaning in the case of women.[114]

Significantly, this meaning was rendered in the terms of a "well-established joke," that ladies (or women aspiring to be ladies) "sought social diversion and sexual dalliance" under cover of needing a visit to take the waters. Mandeville's 1711 treatise provided an early illustration of the form on which the spa-town joke was to capitalize (Mandeville in turn, drawing on ancient stereotype), and here he also could have been providing the material Richardson would fictionalize as the different values that Lovelace and Clarissa each attributed to "vapours," about which, of course, Lovelace joked.

> I never dare speak of Vapours, the very Name is become a Joke; and the general notion the Men have of them is, that they are nothing but a malicious Mood, and contriv'd Sullenness of willful, extravagant, and imperious Women, when they are denied, or thwarted in their unreasonable Desires; nay, even Physicians because they cannot cure them, are forced to ridicule them in their own Defence, and a Woman, that is really troubled with Vapours is pitied by none, but her unhappy Fellow-sufferers.

Women had "desires." They were typed as "extravagant" perhaps because legally anything a married woman spent was a man's. In an age in which the possibilities for spending were being transformed by an economic sea change, women daily faced an obstacle men did not. Somehow (and Mandeville later explained how) women would break through it, their "home demand" becoming central to that sea change. Doctors, too, like Dr. Adair, scratching his head in Bath, would learn how profitably to replace ridicule for specialization. Both of these changes were suffused by the reality of women's frustration of will, their unhappiness and their suffering, which Mandeville insists was gender specific.[115]

Mrs. Barbauld has left us a later, spa-town version of the joke. This was a 1786 fiction entitled "Letter on Watering Places," written under the pseudonym "Henry Homelove." The reluctant Homelove writes: "once . . . to recruit my wife's spirits after a tedious confinement from a laying-in, we passed a season at Bath." But his "Female Family," taking advantage of this single act of sympathy, then demanded that he authorize and, presumably, pay for

> spending [a] good part of every summer at a Watering place. I held out as long as I could. One may be allowed to resist the plans of dissipation, but the plea of health cannot decently be withstood.
>
> It was soon discovered that my eldest daughter wanted bracing, and my wife had a bilious complaint . . . Therefore, although it was my own private opinion that my daughter's nerves might have been braced by morning rides upon the Northamptonshore hills as by evening dances in the public rooms, and that my wife's bile would have been greatly lessened by compliance with her husband, I acquiesced.[116]

It may be unnecessary to appeal to Freud's reminder (in *Wit and Its Relation to the Unconscious*) of the potentially explosive meanings condensed in the form of jokes, to recognize the historical value of this one. The standpoint here—Barbauld endorsing Mandeville in suggesting it was characteristic of the joke—was a man's, its butt women's willfulness, its purpose to complain that the former had been victimized by the latter. Women's complaint was downgraded in favor of men's. The central feature, women's masking their pleasure-seeking wishes under questionable illness, may have caused men to complain, but the need for women to do so betrayed still deeper grounds for their "complaints." Nonetheless, the spa towns became as well-established as the joke and as home demand. The next chapter suggests that women's demand for consumer pleasures played a vital role in the rebuilding of hunt and racing towns, too. Here women were, at some level, operating their nervous systems by way of Newtonian "will."

Women's appetite for the "dissipation" of consumer pleasures was no joke to Thomas Clarkson, although his standpoint was identical to Mandeville's and Henry Homelove's. He observed in 1806 that having devoted years to the acquisition of music, young women threw them aside on marriage, under the necessity of subordinating themselves to domestic "employment amidst the cares of a family." Therefore, "great proficiency in music" was "a criminal waste of time." This was the underlying approach to his diagnosis: such proficiency was pathogenic as well as criminal because all "occupations of a sedentary nature are injurious to the human constitution, and weaken and disorder it in time." Music accelerated the degradation: "in proportion as the body is thus weakened by the sedentary nature of the employment, it is weakened again by the enervating powers of the art." Disease was appropriate because music was "a sensual gratification," and Clarkson applauded Quakerism's ban on instrumental music. He concluded that "the nervous system is acted upon by two enemies at once," sedentariness and music, and "the different disorders of hysteria are produced." Hence "the females of the present age, amongst whom this art has been cultivated to excess, are generally found to have a weak and languid constitution, and to be disqualified more than others from becoming healthy wives, or healthy mothers, or the parents of a health progeny." Clarkson, testifying to women's desire for "sensual gratification," for the self-expression and pleasure in the new consumer culture Mercier depicted in *The Sense of Hearing*, came close to saying they should suffer for it.[117]

Throughout the century novels of sensibility suggested that women's nervous illness could be a means of self-preservation, providing another dimension to the joke's suggestion of the value of illness to women. While sentimental heroines and heroes showed "signs or Symptoms" of nervous disorder on all kinds of occasions, the most powerful and most central was the stress ("distress") predatory males brought to bear on virtuous females.[118] Archetypal were the near-rape of Pamela and the actual rape of Clarissa. Surprised in bed and at Mr. B's mercy, Pamela called on God to "deliver me from this distress!" She screamed and screamed, then with "struggling, fright, terror, I fainted away quite . . . so from the cold sweats that I was in, thought me dying." She feared she had been raped while unconscious. Mr. B vowed he had not sexually assaulted her and "was frightened at the terrible manner I was taken with the fit." The result of her "fit," then, was that Mr. B desisted from his assault. Mrs. Jewkes was appalled: "And will you, sir, said the wicked wretch, for a fit or two, give up such an opportunity as this? I thought you had known the sex better. She is now, you see, quite well again!" According to Mrs. Jewkes, women used their faintings, their fits, and near-distractions as ways to escape the sexual demands of men. At these words, Pamela "fainted away once more," until the maid held a smell-

Joseph Highmore (1692–1780), *Pamela Fainting,* 1741–5. Oil on canvas. 63.5 × 76.2 cm. Felton Bequest 1921. National Gallery of Victoria, Melbourne.

ing bottle to her nose and Mrs. Jewkes left. Pamela experienced her illness as real. It was also a divine gift of personal power to preserve her from Mr. B's "indecency." She wrote her parents, "I . . . have reason to bless God, who, by disabling me in my faculties, empowered me to preserve my innocence; and, when all my strength would have signified nothing, magnified himself in my weakness." [119] Here the operation of will lay in God's hands; worked together, genuine weakness and moral superiority could succeed in defending a woman against a man, and in other circumstances, too.

By the same token, however, Mrs. Jewkes's suspicions could be borne out. Pamela herself had apprehended shortly before her successful resistance that "health" was "a blessing hardly to be coveted in my circumstances since that but exposes me to the calamity [rape] I am in continual apprehension of; whereas a weak and sickly state might possibly move compassion for me." What in *Tom Jones* Fielding called "the arts of counterfeiting illness" were characteristic of the culture of sensibility. Overpowered in a fight with her husband, Mrs. Partridge had recourse "to the softness of her sex . . . she presently dissolved in tears, which soon after concluded in a fit." The result was her victory over Mr. Partridge. Sophy Western used the excuse of "a violent headache" to escape the musical demands of her father. Embarrassed by the withdrawal of an offer of marriage by a man who afterward discovered the smallness of her fortune, Smollett's Tabitha Bramble withdrew from the assembly rooms at Bath, "imputing" her imprudence "to the flutter of her spirits." Or one of Godwin's many stereotypical sentimental female characters, unsuccessful in certain expedients, "had recourse to expedients of a different sort. She wept . . . she was seized with strong fits of sobbing and hysterical affections." [120]

In *Clarissa,* Richardson seemed to expose this kind of "empowerment" as a dangerous illusion. Under the exorbitant pressure of her father and his minions to marry Solmes, Clarissa was suspected by them of feigning sickness as a form of resistance. Lovelace joined them in expressing the view that women's illness was to be dismissed as a counter in sexual warfare. Clarissa, "like the rest of her sex, can be ill or well when she pleases." Lovelace warned her with horrible prescience, "fainting will not save you." Clarissa was up against the real horror: not a man who read her signs of weakness as power and desisted and, moreover, was then converted by them to the fantasy of deferential, sentimental husbandhood. Instead, Lovelace enjoyed Clarissa's tears and her distraction, her symptoms of virtuous distress, before he drugged and raped her. The power of a woman's weakness was revealed as fantasy, in contrast, to the reality of a man's power.[121]

Developing Cheyne's account of the mediatorship of the nerves, Richardson demonstrated the power of male hostility to affect women's health, particularly that of women who were most "sensible," most conscious. At the beginning of her story, while nursing her mother's nervous disorder which had been brought on by the "contentions of these fierce, these masculine spirits," Clarissa was tempted to believe that "we" women "may make the world allow for and respect us as we please, if we can but be sturdy in our wills." This, too, was prescient irony, since her most powerful will was its posthumous expression in the distribution of her letters—her story—and her property. In any case, persecuted by three of the forces of patriarchy with which the culture of sensibility was preoccupied, the arbitrary father, the potentially brutal husband, and the predatory rake, Clarissa became really disordered in body as well as mind. "Indeed," she said, "I am quite heartsick." Her sufferings and protracted dying provided a catalog of sensibility's symptoms. Clarissa's self-possessed suffering was "in humble imitation of the sublimest Exemplar, I often say: Lord, it is thy Will, and it shall be mine . . . I know Thou will not afflict me beyond what I can bear." This aligned her with Pamela and must be linked with the religious status claimed by sensibility as well as with Cheyne's association of nervous sufferers with Christ. Clarissa's detailed death is interpretable in contradictory ways, but certainly it should be thought of as a nervous disorder in extremis. And although it was too late, it was the power of Clarissa's illness that did finally get her family to reconcile themselves to her worldview.[122] It is not surprising, given the operation of the nerve paradigm, that, in the view of sentimental writers, feigned illness could shade into real: facing an interview with Montoni, Radcliffe's Emily found "her agitation increased so much that she almost resolved to excuse herself under what could scarcely be called a pretence of illness." Her psychological "suffering, . . . the pressure of her anxiety," sank Emily's physical health. "She was attacked by a slow fever, and the physicians prescribed air, gentle exercise and amusement." Wollstonecraft said in the *Rights of Woman* that woman was reared to be physically weak, *and* she "feign[ed] a sickly delicacy, in order to secure her husband's affection." Her letters suggest that sense of her own real symptoms competed in her mind with her sense of other people's affected ones, indeed with the feeling magnified by her own cultivation of her sensibility, and she found it painfully difficult to gauge whether or not her disorders were all in the mind.[123]

In sum, according to the evidence of sentimental fiction, the ambiguous values of a fine "sensibility" took on a particular meaning in the relations between women and men. The aggrandizement of a certain kind of consciousness on the one hand was associated with the powers of intellect, imagination, the pursuit of pleasure, the exercise of moral superiority, and wished-for resistance to men. On the other, it betokened physical and mental inferiority, sickness, and inevitable victimization, circumstances throwing severe doubt on the effectiveness of the female will.

TWO

The Reformation of Male Manners

The Public Manners of Men

The history of popular culture indicates that men had always separated their leisure activities from their comfortless homes. The distinction between public and private was also the distinction between leisure and work. Women left their households, but to work, trading clothing or selling foodstuffs at the market where, when single, they may have met their mates. Clearly women could glean some pleasure round the edges, but men claimed regular, even daily, leisure culture. Aside from trips to market, married women's "only public appearance," writes Peter Laslett, "their only expedition outside the circle of the family . . . was at service in church." Judith Bennett argues in her local study of Englishwomen that "a separation of the sexes—into private wives and public husbands—was . . . firmly established in the households of the medieval countryside." This was by and large the rule for all ranks. It was in the eighteenth century that middle-class women publicized their consciousness of segregation and identified it with specific psychological qualities. Within the "narrow sphere" of "domestic life," wrote a reviewer of Maria Susanna Cooper's *The Exemplary Mother* (1769), "the tender emotions of the heart are exerted in their utmost sensibility." This separation was the setting for the special claim of women writers to moral "authority in the private sphere." Sentimental ideology expressed a long and deep trend in social history, altering relations between men and the home and women and leisure outside it. It would tend to bring men closer to women in certain respects, although it also led to the articulation of their differences in new, more elaborate ways, and it was accompanied by very significant ambivalence among men. This trend included incremental, long-range changes outside the home as well as inside it. This chapter concentrates on these changes in the lives of men.[1]

In 1663 Lord Sackville and Sir Charles Sedley preached naked to a crowd from a Covent Garden tavern. They were among the "circle of influential rakes in the public eye" associated with Charles II's court and called "the merry gang." Charles II had been restored in May 1660, his restoration ostentatiously associated with the public revels the Puritans had banished. The maypole was set up for May games and morris dancing. With popular pleasures were restored more sophisticated ones: when "Charles landed at Dover . . . civilization, in the sense of the arts, poetry, painting, drama, and dissimulation, returned to England." The King's "dissimulation" was symbolized by his public kissing of the Bible, but the restoration was intended to display its repudiation of the brief puritan triumph rather than the return to a simply traditional past.[2] "Libertines" and "rakes" became targets of the ensuing campaign for the reformation of manners because they posed "the most serious threat of all to the clerical cause[,]" mocking it as Sackville and Sedley did. Used as invidious labels for amoral males who pursued their own appetites, these puritan terms originated, respectively, in the late sixteenth and mid-seventeenth centuries. Such men were the most flamboyant of a "whole movement of fashion." The Royal Society, the College of Physicians, the universities, clubs, coffeehouses, fashionable taverns, and playhouses—a new "cultural infrastructure"—seemed to be fostering infidelity and the pursuit of pleasure.[3]

Best known of Charles II's merry gang was John Wilmot, second earl of Rochester (1647–80). Rochester symbolizes a new kind of man. In his wit and dandyism, young Rochester was "the pattern of the modern fine gentleman," the leader of a new, postwar generation.[4] To the older Clarendon, this generation "affected" a manly style of "apparent hardness." Fortified by the new philosophy, "every man is unshaken at those Tales, at which his Ancestors trembled."[5]

Rochester's rationale for his "experiment of living the complete life of pleasure" was derived from Hobbes's disconnecting "*the pleasure of sense*" from religion's indivious label, "sensuality." Rochester said that his two "*Maxims* of *Morality* were that he should do nothing to the hurt of any other, or that might prejudice his own health: And he thought that all pleasure, when it did not interfere with these, was to be indulged as the gratification of our Natural Appetites."[6] His poetry, breaking "every kind of taboo," suggests that Rochester found in lovemaking "the ecstasy that annihilates space and time." Bishop Gilbert Burnet believed that Rochester and others who shared his views wished to "Reform the World" by bringing it under their "new System of Intellectual and Moral Principles"; Rochester wished to teach both sexes to face material reality, not only its great pleasures but the inevitably painful circumstances of life in its own terms.[7]

Rochester's realism extended to his expression of the view that women were reared to subordination by men, reflecting his inheritance of courtly culture and awareness of the public emergence of feminism. This is evident in a speech written by Rochester in 1672 for a sympathetic character named "Amaçoa," that is, Amazon. Its "passionate indignation against injustice" and unreason is characteristic of his "best satire."

> . . . Women is born
> With equall thirst of Humour and of Fame,
> But treacherous man misguides her in her aime;
> Makes her believe that all her Glories lye
> In dull Obedience, Truth, and Modesty
> That to bee Beautifull is to Bee Brave,
> And calls her Conqueror when she's most his Slave,
> Forbidding her those noble Paths to tread
> Which through bold daring deeds to Glory lead,
> With ye poor Hypocriticall pretence
> That Woman's merit is her Innocence
> Who treacherously advis'd, Retaining thus
> The sole Ambition to be Vertuous
> Thinks 'tis enough if she's not Infamous
> On these false grounds is mans stol'n Triumph laid
> Through Craft alone ye Nobler Creature made.[8]

Following the logic of this speech, Rochester assisted Aphra Behn with her writings, and both she and Anne Wharton eulogized him in fine poems. Like others among his contemporaries, they praised Rochester for the excoriating lessons of his satire and the instruction of his art, "his useful, kind instructing tongue."[9] Rochester recognized women's pleasure in sex ("What 'ere you gave, I paid you back in Blisse!") and he urged women to "love you[r] pleasures."[10] Rochester's letters and poetry at times demonstrate respect for the humanity and intelligence of women, including his wife; unusual for his age, he "designated her estate for her own use."[11]

His feminism was the expression of Rochester's negative capability, one he also demonstrated in the acting he taught his mistress, Elizabeth Barry. Rochester wrote elsewhere in the *personae* of women, declaring them "born, like Monarchs free." One poem, a "Satire on Men," begins, "What vaine unnecessary things are men." On occasion, he dressed up as a woman for playful purposes. His pleasure in "counterfeiting" character expressed his "imaginative recklessness," his fundamental sense of freedom. He has been described as "a champion of individualism and realism."[12]

The pleasure-seeking Rochester's "disposition to extravagant mirth led him to many odd Adventures and Frollicks." A "frollick" was a public prank, played for mirthful and diverting purpose, usually by a bibulous male group, although Rochester also enjoyed elaborate frolics on his own. He led different groups of "young blades" drawn from Charles II's "merry gang," one of them called the "Ballers."[13] Their actions were literally a display of a certain style of masculinity. Rochester and his companion "used . . . to run naked and particularly they did so once in Woodstock Park, upon a Sunday in the afternoon, expecting that several of the female sex would have been spectators but not one appear'd." They would dance naked with women who may have been volunteers but who, more likely, were paid, perhaps as prostitutes from a favorite bawdy house. Displaying their genitals to women was a characteristic that could be extended to direct physical assaults on them. Notable too in the Woodstock-Park episode was the deliberate violation of the Sabbath, perpetuating the triumph of the restoration of the maypole.[14] By the same token there was a powerful, younger-generation assertiveness in such frolics, ridiculing "the strange decay of manly parts since the days of dear Harry the Second." Once the Ballers were caught importing a dozen dildos, "means for the Support / of aged Letchers of the Court."[15] In addition to its post-Restoration display of anti-Puritanism, the "frollick" looked back to the traditionally unruly, public behavior of males at Carnival, for example, in their assaults on any representatives of status, law, and order. A frolic at Epsom in 1676 illustrates that period's form, including drunkenness, breaking into a house in search of a "whore," a violent assault on a constable, and a struggle with the watch.[16]

So Rochester treated women in shockingly contradictory ways. Another type of "rake-hell" frolic was the public exposure of a (usually lower-class) woman's genitals. Meeting a young woman taking butter to market, Rochester and his companions bought all of her butter and then smeared in on a tree. Waiting until they had gone, the women "took it off, thinking it a pity that it should be . . . spoiled. They observed her, and . . . as a punishment, set her upon her head, and clapt the butter upon her breach."[17] There is other evidence that rakes were accustomed to attack women going to market in the same way. When Rochester's life was publicized, his famous "raping away" of the heiress Elizabeth Malet (for which he was briefly imprisoned in the Tower) was grouped with his "frollicks" and other assaults on women. "At Charing Cross the horses were stopped by armed men under the direction of Rochester, and she was transferred by force to another coach with six horses, which was driven out of London."[18] This would provide a scene for several sentimental novels, including Harriet Byron's abduction in *Sir Charles Grandison.* Elizabeth Malet's later choosing Rochester for a husband as a way of escaping the clutches of her mercenary, marriage-minded family was also echoed in sentimental novels.[19]

Because his first "Principle," was his "violent love of Pleasure," which frequently "involved him in great sensuality[,]" Rochester left his wife in the country with their children and his mother.[20] He was "ever engaged in some amour or another," and his appetite extended from the ladies of the Court to "women of the lowest order, and the vilest prostitutes of the town."[21] Rochester believed in "the free use of Wine and Women." "The restraining a man from the Use of Women, Except one of the way of Marriage, and denying the remedy of Divorce, he thought unreasonable impositions on the freedom of Mankind."[22] Mary Hobart, a Maid of Honour, is reported to have issued the following warning: "there is no woman who listens to [Rochester] three times that does not lose her reputation . . . a woman cannot escape him since he can enjoy her in his writings if he cannot have her in any other way." The same writer recorded the technique women found so appealing; it gave the appearance of the sympathy Behn illustrates could be sincere. There was, Hobart wrote, "nothing more dangerous than the insinuating ways by which he gets possession of your confidence. He enters into all your tastes and your feelings, and makes you believe everything he says, though not a single word is sincere."[23] His elaborate and ruthless ingenuity in seducing women could end in tragic consequences, and it seems likely that the syphilis that killed him he brought to his wife. Both she and their oldest child died about a year after Rochester.[24]

On his deathbed, suffering an acute syphilitic decline, Rochester repented. One of his fellow rakes saw this change simply as going mad, but it was as "a Divine" that in *Some Passages of the Life and Death of Rochester* Burnet recorded Rochester's conversion. In key respects it was cognate with Bunyan's *Life and Death of Mr. Badman,* published the same year, and one of "scores of Puritan lives" sharing their form and message.[25] The purpose of Burnet's "Sermon" was to bring about the "Reformation of other rakes," and Burnet claimed that Rochester himself held up his dying as a lesson for others.[26]

Burnet's biography presents a clear contrast between opposing gender systems. Rochester's belief in "the use of Women" and "the remedy of Divorce" had been a sticking point during Burnet's earlier efforts to reason him to reformation. Burnet recognized the attraction in the "Variety" which "engage[d] men to a freer range of pleasure," but he reminded Rochester of "the far greater measure of mischiefs that must follow," in contrast to Christian monogamy. Those mischiefs included women's being "barbarously used." Monogamy meant giving up "some Pleasure," but it was exchanged for the marital "Harmony, which is one of the greatest joys of life." This was in keeping with Burnet's general argument in favor of the hierarchalizing of pleasures. He said that the governing of passions by reason "Ministers to a higher and more lasting Pleasure to a Man, than to give them their full scope and range."[27] As a matter of fact, Rochester had previously enjoyed both "domestic pleasures" and a life of sexual freedom. The pleasures of marriage, Burnet continued, were due to the fact that "man" was "of a sociable nature." The emphasis was in contrast to the individualism Rochester had embodied and clearly well on its way to suffusing English culture.

> In my dear self I center ev'ry thing,
> My *Servants, Friends,* My *Mrs.* and my *King.*[28]

Indissoluble marriage enforced the harmonizing of what Burnet saw as the essentially different natures of male and female. The man "may excel the wife in greatness of Mind and height of Knowledge, the Wife some way makes that up with her Affection and Tender Care." The "Laws of Marriage" reflected the concerns of women which protected them against rakes' barbarous usage. The reformation of manners posed "the quiet of our own Family at home, and others abroad" against "the mischiefs of being given up to pleasure, of running unordinately into it" and thereby "break through the restraints" governing "Appetites." Burnet's vision included a parallel spatial dimension, posing a quiet orderly home, secure in its lineage and property, against the violent running of men "abroad" in the streets, men who could burst through windows, doors, or even walls. The mischief was the damage done to patriarchy by way of the barbarous usage of the women it owned: Burnet's "Laws of Marriage" were to ensure "that Man have a property in their Wives and Daughters, so that to defile the one, or corrupt the other, is an unjust and injurious thing." In countering Rochester's maxim that he could not hurt another, Burnet made a familiar argument: the primary injury done by adultery and seduction did not involve body directly at all. It was the injury done to the male owner's feelings about his property. "If the difference is urged from the Injury that another Person [i.e. body] receives, the Injury is as great, if a Man's Wife is defiled or his Daughter corrupted."[29]

In sum, the contrast between Rochester's argument and Burnet's was between, on one hand, a sexual freedom that, while recognizing women's intellectual equality and her equal capacity for sexual pleasure, in effect also rationalized their exploitation in ways that led to syphilis, bearing illegitimate children, degradation, and early death;

and, on the other hand, a degree of patriarchal legal and moral protection against that exploitation but one that denied women equality of mind and repressed their sexuality.

Rochester seemed to be the reformers' greatest triumph, in spite of his change of heart being satirized later in the 1680s in a poem called "The Reformation of Manners." It was a triumph because of Rochester's virtually Satanic talents (in Behn's view, they were godlike), a meaning Burnet's Miltonic account suggests.[30] The dying but reformed Rochester had enough time left to exemplify the manners advocated by critics of the style of manhood he represented. He repudiated swearing and oaths and, Burnet implied, the drunkenness that previously had increased his proclivities for sexual "sensuality" and to "frollick." Burnet argued that the same reformation could save his rakish audience from several pangs Rochester suffered: "loathsome Diseases" as well as the "waste of Fortune and irregular Expence" in the pursuit of "wild Mirth and corporal Pleasure."[31]

A very significant dimension to Rochester's reformation was the domestic corollary to his repudiation of outdoor pleasures. The reformed Rochester, when he thought he might survive, "laid down . . . how retired, how strict, and how studious he intended to be." His orientation toward domesticity was also signified by the fact that he now "called often for his Children . . . and spoke to them with a sense and feeling that cannot be expressed in Writing." Similarly, Rochester was led to undo the damage he had done his wife when, in his perverse and anti-Puritan phase, he had induced her to become a Catholic. "During his whole Sickness, he expressed so much tenderness and true kindness to his Lady, that it easily defaced the remembrance of everything wherein he had been in fault formerly, so it drew from her the most passionate care and concern for him that was possible." Burnet implied that the conversion of her husband's rakish manners to those of religious convention and domesticity were very much in her interest. She was converted back to Protestantism by Rochester's death.[32]

Burnet's *Life of Rochester* was the model for subsequent rake confession-and-repentance biographies and narratives.[33] For example, it shaped *The Rake: or, The Libertine's Religion,* published in London in 1693. This hypothetical rake made "Pleasure his Heaven." His religion, wrote the sermonizing author of the preface, was another form of "Enthusiasm," although the rake himself argued that men's and women's pleasure-seeking appetite was "natural." To repress pleasure seeking out of fear of hell was to defer to a "Bugbear made by Priests . . . To keep the Headstrong Multitudes in aw[e]." The rake opposed his own natural life to the man driven by "Conscience" and defined by a "Priest-craft" of "pious knaves," duping the "multitudes with their "crabb'd Lectures." In keeping with his libertinism (its connotation literally liberty as well as the discreditable enthusiasm of the radical Reformation which had licensed the pursuit of pleasure on earth), he declared "I am free / And will enjoy my much-lov'd liberty[,]" a liberty to see the world as one of earthly delights, "his Garden and Confectionary." He was free to consume, to dress up in the latest clothes and go to the playhouse, "the Envy of the Dressing Sparks[,]" and see "the Ladies at my Rigging gaze." He indulged himself and his friends, inviting the latter to his "Treat": "Water, Earth and Air, ransackt I have / To purchase what the Nicest Stomachs eat": such delicacies were augmented by the "richest Wines, e're yet by Money bought / Or to Judicious Taste were brought." His freedom lay in his gratification of his "Taste," its possibilities decisively amplified by the commerce and empire betokened by the word "ransakt" and "money" (invoked in the same terms by Cheyne) but dependent, too, on the elevation of the pursuit of pleasure for its own sake. Essential to his ecumenical definition of pleasure—"all the Joys of Sense"—was "great Variety." He invoked such a value in explaining "the Joys of Women," those "Luscious Creatures, whom the Heavnly Pow'rs / Made to delight us." He wishes to taste their "Variety," too. Hence his opposition to the religious notion of marriage. Husbands missed out on the possibilities of freedom. Instead, the"poor slaves" were "Doom'd to the Drudgery of a Wife / Who, when they might be free, by pious Knaves / Are sentenc'd to Confinement during Life." The "[p]lodding sot" has internalized the "Rules" laid down by "Priest Craft," including "Be Temperate, be Chast, be Just, and Wise" and, hence, "all day on measures think / (if they to thinking can pretend) / To save the Trash they have no heart to spend." This was in stark contrast with the lavish and careless spending by the rake of his money and his body.[34]

Such salutary pamphlets (as well as the depiction of Rochester and other rakes on the Restoration stage) were followed by Hogarth's famous series of paintings, "The Rake's Progress," 1733–4, contrasting with *The Pilgrim's Progress.* Richardson's vignettes of the deaths of Lovelace's merry gang stemmed from the same reform impulse and provided another pipeline to later sentimental fiction. The correspondences between Lovelace and Rochester are ample and demonstrate Richardson's indebtedness to Burnet. We can note the example of Lovelace's consumer motives in sex, "a vehement aspiration after novelty," advertised by "those confounded poets, with their serenely-celestial descriptions, did as much, with me, as the lady: they fired my imagination, and set me upon a desire to become a goddess-maker."

Like Rochester, he expressed his appetite for novelty, his sexual enjoyment of women, in a variety of poetic forms. "I must needs try my new-fledged pinions in sonnet, elegy, and madrigal. I must have a Cynthia, a Stella, a Sacharissa, as well as the best of them." Richardson and his followers shared Burnet's views in opposing this infusion of sexuality with the variety and novelty permitted by consumption. Instead, they emphasized marriage, "with binding obligations," in opposition to the explicitly antimaritalism sentimental fiction put into the mouths of its rakes.[35] Rochester's reputation as a poet peaked in the 1720s and 1730s, thereafter being overwhelmed by an increasingly evangelized morality to the point in 1806 when his "licentious productions" were deemed to "forcibly warrant the sentence of outlawry that decorum and taste have passed upon them."[36]

Rochester's symbolic power was derived in part from his ambiguity. He combined elements of modernity with links to ancient Carnival, elements reiterated in his literary successors. In his "frollicks," his drinking, his participation in gang attacks on the watch and on accessible women, together with his expressions of misogyny, the rake symbolized the public manners of an older male leisure culture.[37] That Rochester was an aristocrat symbolized, too, that in Carnival, nobles had mingled with men of other ranks in such expressions of male culture, including, perhaps, the "peacetime" activities of privately raised armies of retainers. On the other hand, in his individualism, his secularism, his mastery of roles, his extravagant spending, his pursuit of pleasure, and his capacity for feminism, Rochester was modern.

Because rakes were symbolic of pervasive male behavior, one that was evolving into a new style on the basis of the old, their historical definition has been spongy. Two of the few historical works on the subject, old but still very useful, tend to conflate the stories of such notorious eighteenth-century aristocratic rakes as the duke of Wharton and Sir Francis Dashwood with the histories of societies and "impious clubs" devoted to various forms of all-male entertainment, traditional and novel, and with gangs of thieves or con men, or simply groups of drunken apprentices and other youths in the streets.[38] Many forms of their entertainment provided the opportunity for the wagering and gambling seen as characteristic of this male behavior.[39] Rakes were unrestrained consumers. Rochesterian prodigality, "Spending beyond their Pensions," living "as most Gentlemen of estate" were seen as characteristics of all classes of undisciplined rakes. Defoe illustrated (in 1727) that "rakish" was synonymous with extravagance and waste.[40]

It has been suggested that eighteenth-century "rakery" was only "a way of life for a colorful minority" and that for most it expressed "a passage stage of late adolescence." Eighteenth-century public schoolboys lived in a kind of "primitive subculture," engaged in immorality, indiscipline, riot, and rebellion. One newspaper referred to them as "brutes in human shapes" who terrorized the neighborhood in which they resided. As headmaster in one of the new pleasure centers, Tonbridge Wells, Vicesimus Knox attempted to replace the "indiscipline and degeneracy" of his charges with preparation for "commercial and professional" lives. Apprentices' being "prone to playgoing and rioting" suggests they enjoyed "an early form of youth culture." In 1712, *The Spectator* suggested that a gang of rakes called The Mohocks were "some thoughtless youngsters [who], out of a false sense of bravery and an immoderate fondness for fellows of fire, are insensibly hurried into his senseless, scandalous project." "Insensibly hurried" is a nice phrase for adolescent peer pressure. Youth has always seemed to moralists "a state of nature, a slippery age, full of passions, rashness, willfulness," and Keith Thomas asks if the campaigns for the reformation of manners "were not attempts to suppress all the great obstacles to the suppression of youth."[41]

The ranks of rakes and rioters also included university students. There had been serious attempts to control undergraduate disorders at Oxford and Cambridge during the sixteenth and seventeenth centuries. Rochester first "grew debauch'd" at Oxford, where the materialism he learned at Wadham could be implemented in the town's taverns and brothels. His exposure to temptation was compounded there by "the carnival of Restoration."[42] The Wesley brothers and their Holy Club at Oxford in the 1720s were mocked for its holiness, its fasting, and "endeavour to reform notorious whores." Gibbon describes the "manly Oxonian" going to London to "enjoy the taverns and bagnios of Covent Garden." Coleridge recorded the death of a student in a duel in 1791, the dead student and his opponent showing themselves "men of the World," a phrase synonymous with rakish behavior.[43]

Throughout the eighteenth century, novelists—reformers themselves—presented the university as a site for a young man's "entrance into the world," to appropriate Frances Burney's *Evelina*'s subtitle. There innocent young lads were corrupted, introduced to drinking, gambling, and prodigal spending as well as sex. The university was where young men, sexually maturing beings away from home and subject to peer pressure, could become "men of the world."[44] The 1814 edition of William Enfield's anthology, *The Speaker,* intended to "Facilitate the Improvement of Youth[,]" included a poem entitled "The Modern Rake's Progress," by James Hurdis. The decisive stage of its protagonist's decline was at the university (Hurdis was a professor of poetry at Oxford in 1793). The rake went from "sceptic" to "libertine" and then chose a "lewd" life of sensuality and extravagance, before being killed in a duel.[45]

Another characteristic of the socially varied, publicly riotous, extravagant, and youthful groups associated with rakes and libertines was that they assaulted people in public. Sedley "had an actor cudgelled in the park for imitating his dress." *The Spectator* recorded more extreme and permanent maiming by the Mohocks, flattening noses in order to gouge out eyes, something also done during wrestling matches outside taverns in British Virginia at the same time.[46] It seems that bystanders could be beaten on the buttocks, have their limbs broken, be stabbed, or have their teeth knocked out. At best, people were chased through the streets. Victims ranged from promenading gentlemen to beggars. A blind man might have his dog stolen. Violence extended to swordplay, from duels to the mock insult and challenge that resulted in the gang member's being paid off, the kind of setup that nearly hanged Magistrate Fielding's Tom Jones.[47] The public activities of immoral youth shaded into street crime of many kinds.[48] Prominent in the record was skirmishing with the watch. In 1680, a riotous nobleman, the seventh earl of Pembroke (lampooned as "boarish") killed one man in a duel and another "in a drunken scuffle in a Haymarket tavern." On another occasion Pembroke "killed an officer of the watch as he was coming out from a drinking bout at Turnham Green." Aubrey recorded that this street-fighting aristocrat kept "52 mastives, 30 greyhounds, some beares and a lyon and 60 fellows more bestiall than they[,]" all ready for popular sports of different kinds. It may have been one of Pembroke's gang who cudgeled Dryden in Rose Alley in 1679.[49]

Accounts of rakes and libertines, their minions, poor gentlemen, and riotous young undergraduates, pickup groups as it were, as well as the more continuous bands like Rochester's "Ballers" and the Mohocks, shade into stories of other named groups. Most notable were the "Hectors." In the aftermath of the Civil War the Hectors were recruited from the ranks of ex-soldiers flooding into London, soon joined by other "loose fellows." (Similarly, following the War of the Austrian Succession, "demobilization released into civilian society men of an age, disposition, and brutality . . . to commit crime on an unprecedented scale.")[50] That so many of the names of these male groups are synonymous with words connoting public male behavior of a riotous, bullying, "macho" sort points to their common historical denominator: Roysters, Hectors, Bucks, Bravadoes, Blades, Bloods. Rochester was called "ye Court Hector." In a poem Rochester, "Master of Ancient and Modern Wit," personified his penis as "a rude roaring hector in the streets."[51]

This brilliant image points to the best-known definition of "rake" and the common characteristic of this great variety of publicly violent men—nobles, "frollickers," veterans, apprentices, students, the unemployed—their public assault on women. On Shrove Tuesday 1630 (a vestige of Carnival in England), youths "arm'd with cudgels, stones, hammers, rules, trowels and handsaws put playhouses to the sack and bawdy houses to the spoil." Frequent targets of riotous males, playhouses and brothels, were linked together by their association with available women in the carnivalizing males' search for "food, sex, and violence." Brothels were "stormed" by drunken customers. Rochester told of,

> . . . Whores attacqu'd, their Lords at home,
> Bawds Quarters beaten up, and Fortress won.

His Epsom adventure included breaking into the constable's house in search of a "whore." According to *The Spectator's* 1712 description of the Mohocks, brothels also could be establishments of which such a male group declared itself "protector and guarantee."[52] In addition, at Carnival time "young men could openly express their desire for ladies of higher social status, and respectable ladies walk the streets." The notion carries an ambiguous meaning for women. It endorses the view that they were forbidden the streets for most of the year. It seems evident that this defining characteristic of public male culture was an extension and attempted perpetuation of "rough music processions," setting off from tippling houses "to ridicule local offenders against communal norms." The norms were those of sexual behavior, and they dictated that women only emerged into public on the sufferance of men.[53]

The dramatist and poet laureate Thomas Shadwell (1642[?]–1692) transformed Tirso de Molina's *El Burlador de Sevilla* (prototype for Don Juan) into English terms as *The Libertine,* and he satirized the "Scowrers" in his play of that name ("scowring" was cognate with "raking"): "I beat twenty Higling-women! spread their Butter about the Kennel, broke all their Eggs, let their sucking Pigs loose." Milton had suggested that, confronted by men in public, women could be forced to "expose" themselves "to avoid worse rape." The Mohocks of the 1720s were subdivided into specialists for street activity, one group called "tumblers" because they specialized in setting "women on their heads, [to] commit certain indecencies, or rather barbarities on the limbs which they expose."[54] The Mohocks are also recorded to have cut women's arms and rolled old women down hills in barrels.

That they slit noses may have reflected their identification with American Indians, albeit a confused one, although women's noses had long been the sensitive, highly visible targets for male disciplinary action, liable to be cut off for adultery in ancient English law.[55] "Modest" women were raped, it is probably unnecessary to say. Male pranksters used the newspapers to exploit the economic hardship of other women, too, according to a 1755 issue of *The Connoisseur.* It records false advertisements which, in one case, gathered unemployed wet-nurses for a nonexistent job and, in a second, brought together a number of old women by offering a big price for a male tabby cat. In sum, rakes treated rudely, "All that in Petticoats they meet." We can see "rakes" as the most egregious representatives of a male culture now being defined by its incompatibility with a new sense of public "decency," that is, order in the streets and the nonbrutalization of women. Conversely, it may be said that reformers defined themselves in opposition to this culture.[56]

It seemed to those who wished to reform it that the men they saw in the street were not anchored to a serious purposefulness abroad, let alone to a routine, to the inside of a workplace, or to a family. Reformers described such men as morally "loose," although the historian can link "looseness" to the mobility of labor characteristic of the modernizing economy. A contemporary of the Hectors said that they included men merely "unhappy in employment." A very significant proportion of seventeenth- and eighteenth-century migrants to these more distant parts of Britain fit the rake profile insofar as they were young, male, and footloose. Their migration was the "spillover" from the same kinds of people looking for work and a destiny in England. They were also unmarried.[57] In 1623 George Ferrars described Virginia's first, would-be gentlemen colonizers as "unruly Sparks . . . , poor Gentlemen, broken Tradesmen, Rakes and Libertines, Footmen." A missionary sent to Carolina by the Society for the Propagation of the Gospel in 1708 described the population as

> the Vilest race of Men upon the Earth they have neither honour, nor honesty nor Religion enough to entitle them to any tolerable Character, being a perfect Medley or Hotch potch made up of Bank[r]upts, pirates, decayed Libertines, Sectaries and Enthusiasts of all sorts who have transported themselves hither from [many other British colonies] . . . and as they are of large and loose principles so they live and Act accordingly.[58]

The Virginia Company added to the definition of these migrants by sending a boatload of women because "the plantation can never flourish till families be planted and the respect of wives and children fix the people on the soil."[59] New World geography favored the dramatic expression of the contrast between unruly, sexually untrameled males on one hand, and religious, familial orthodoxy on the other. In Plymouth Plantation in 1628, Thomas Morton, an ex-lawyer of Furnival's Inn, persuaded a group of young males bound to Virginia to break their indentures and gain his "dissolute" enclave at "Merrymount" where they set up "the idol maypole." William Bradford, the Puritan governor, interpreted it as an extended Carnival, a rival to Plymouth's permanent Lent, although the historian may see it as modern, too.[60]

The notion that rakes and libertines were more noisy or more troublesome representatives of male popular culture is reinforced by their association with taverns. In 1659 Evelyn had described a group of tavern drinkers who styled themselves "Hectors . . . a professed Atheistical order of Bravos." The tavern was the preferred scene whence, in the words of Milton, "flown with insolence and wine," the "sons of Belial" would sally forth into the street. There they would swagger and roar, swear and blaspheme.[61] One report described them as men wishing "to be merrye, and dryncke wyne, and take Tobaccoe, and call each other Brothers, without either Articles or other Agreement[s]," which met for supper at a tavern.[62] They were an informal group, identifying themselves by gender and meeting in a public place for pleasure. Turning to face the reformers in 1708, a defender of this culture said:

> we have been loaded with the pretended statutes of Reformation; Laws which if they were to be strictly executed, a Man must not be allow'd to drink a Pot of Ale, or take a Walk in the Fields, or play at Cudgels, or go to the Morrice Dancers, or any such things on the Sabbath Day. But, Thanks be to God, the Awe of those things, which by the Policy of our Puritanical Invaders, was Impressed on the Minds of Our People, begins to wear off again.[63]

Writing of the sixteenth and seventeenth centuries, Thomas points out that drinking "played a part in nearly every public and private ceremony, every commercial bargain, every craft ritual . . . and was the major focus of the "male-oriented, drink and betting-based" culture, including a great deal of cruelty to animals[,]" as well as violence among men. "There were badger-baiting, cock-fighting, bull-running, dog-fighting, bear-baiting and barefisted boxing."[64]

Of course, alehouses, inns, and taverns had been the sites for some drinking for centuries. (Their definitions overlapped and the terms came to be used interchangeably.)[65] They provided physical gathering places for a male culture. As Thomas's observation suggests, this culture was not one of simply riotous freedom but, to the contrary, one of knitting together for several purposes, long- and short-term. In towns the tavern was the base for the "craftsman culture" of male societies, each with its nickname, ceremonies, oaths, and insignia. Those rioting 1630 Shrove-Tuesday youths issuing into the street had made weapons of their craft implements, "hammers, rules, trowels, and handsaws." In the village, the alehouse long had been a key site in the public life of officeholding and peacekeeping, where men bound themselves "together in a political community" and developed a sense of "autonomy" independent of family life. Except as workers, women were excluded. Bennett records a medieval song berating wives who went to the alehouse "to spend their husbands money." Contemporary preachers enforced the same sexual order: "Dwell at home, daughter, and love thy work much."[66]

But as that 1708 defender suggested, the traditional male leisure culture had been given new meanings as a result of the English Reformation. Inns and alehouses replaced monasteries as "the natural resort of travellers and wayfarers," who connected locals to wider horizons. Second, "in the aftermath of the attack on church-oriented games, rituals and the like, the alehouse developed as a rival centre for communal and neighbourhood activities." Or it could be said that the church withdrew from "popular recreations."[67] At the same time, men's social drinking shifted from the household (to the extent the subsistence household economy had permitted it) to the alehouse, which became "an alternative to, rather than an extension of established family life." The 1639 author of *Sinne Stigmatized* noted that someone in search of a man could be told that "there is his house but his dwelling is at the alehouse."[68]

Until the late seventeenth century, "the comforts of home were by subsequent standards almost nonexistent." Home lacked the physical comforts of the furnished, lit, and heated alehouse, inn, and tavern. By relaxing at an alehouse, men "saved the expense of firewood and candles."[69] For "many lower-class men, even the rather basic facilities of the alehouse must have seemed august and attractive, compared with the sordid, cramped conditions of a poorly furnished cottage."[70] There were other attractions; at the alehouse, one could hobnob with other men, travelers, for example, familiar with different kinds of manners, and capable of extending the sense of possibilities associated with manhood, by way of pleasure, admiration, resentment, emulation, competition, and solidarity. "There all classes of the community—squire and parson, farmer and labourer, petty tradesman and artisan—could associate with some degree of freedom," to drink together, to transact local business, to exchange gossip about local politics and to play. Following the purge of the churchyards, landlords began to keep sports equipment on hand, footballs, bowls, and cudgels for outdoors, and cards, dice, game boards, and special tables for a host of indoor games, all of which were subject to wager. If later reformers would characterize alehouse-centered recreations as archaic, the historian should stress that much of it was relatively new.[71]

Business provided another significant amplification of traditional alehouse activities. By the early seventeenth century, benefiting from "the resurgence of internal trade," the alehouse was becoming a new kind of economic center, outside the regulated medieval market, more modern in its range and improvisatoriness. Not only did it supply small but critical amounts of credit to quite poor men for food, drink, and lodging, and by accepting goods in pawn; it became "an important venue for financial dealings of all kinds." Alehouses, inns, and taverns took on greater importance as employment exchanges, contributing to the massive mobilization of the labor market. There, too, men forged passports to get around Elizabethan officials' travel regulations. Alehouse keepers and their customers continually struggled against officialdom's efforts to regulate by licensing, and they joined shopkeepers in their resistance to official and semiofficial sabbatarianism. The alehouse—"the poor man's parliament"—developed a "new communal voice" and the "respectable" apprehended it as "a centre for popular irreligion." Such conflicts left ample testimony of a kind of populist appetite for freer trade as well as more pleasure, indeed, self-assertion in general. In sum, there was a relationship between the increasing elaboration of the sphere of public life enjoyed by men and the gradual transcendence of dearth in the early modern era. Reformers' preoccupation with the apparent wastefulness of men's consumer spending outside their household needs was a mark of this new dimension.[72]

Opposing visions of this masculine sphere were captured by a 1727 *Dissertation upon Drunkenness,* written from the same point of view as *The Rake: or, The Libertine's Religion.*

> The vile obscene talk, noise, nonsense and ribaldry discourses together with the fumes of tobacco, belchings and other foul breaking of wind . . . are enough to make any rational creature among them almost ashamed of his being. But all this the rude rabble esteem the highest degree of happiness and run themselves into the greatest straits imaginable to attain it.[73]

Instead of wasting money in the extravagant consumption of drink and tobacco, men should save it or spend it on other goods. Being rational in this way was connected to feeling "shame" over belching and farting (as out of control as consuming) and of playing with words connoting sex. We have to imagine how the obscene talk and ribaldry referred to women, but surely appetite and probably denigration were elements. It seems possible that among themselves men spoke to each other about sex in ways they did not talk to women.

The attainment of this masculine "happiness" was in large part dependent on a sense of "liberation" from the presence of "womenfolk" in the place where "most men spent the bulk of their time" when not working. Women were present at alehouses, taverns, and inns but, it must be emphasized, as workers—drudges, cooks, waitresses, and prostitutes (who worked in the backroom)—not as equal consumers of leisure.[74] In general, women marked their respectability by staying away from these institutions. Their presence was limited to special occasions: beginning or interrupting a journey, say, or christenings and churchings. Weddings "very often took place in taverns and inns" until the mid-eighteenth century.[75] Women never came alone but always in the company of a male relative, a mixed-sex group, or sometimes as one of a group of married women. These conditions articulated the existence of well-understood "rules" governing women's intrusion into a "masculine" sphere. To enter alone was to be considered a trespasser and/or a prostitute: if such a female entrant "was not assaulted or pushed outside by the victualler or other customers, she stood a good chance of a beating from her spouse." Of course, if she stayed home she risked a beating if he returned drunk. Women who worked in alehouses also risked assault: an Oxford landlady's nose was broken in 1633, and in 1635 a Lancashire woman was raped by two customers.[76]

Implicitly, then, women generally stayed at home in those cold, dark, cramped, poorly furnished cottages. The record of women's enjoying leisure is sparse. Women participated in those special occasions of weddings, christenings, churchings, and other feasts (for which they also did a disproportionate amount of the preparation and cleaning up). It was then, too, that they danced with men. Where possible, they sometimes attended the theater.[77] (At Carnival in some parts of Europe they may have had "some kind of special license" but there is no sign of festive organizations for young women as there was for men.)[78] A 1632 visitor to Barnsley, Gloucester, left an unusual account of two women's eking out a little leisure, significantly outdoors and linked to their permissible trip to church. It was recorded by way of the sabbatarian campaign, and the women improved on the punishment meted out to them:

> two Women who had bene at Church both before and after Noone, did but walke into the fields for their recreation, and they were put to their choice, either to pay six pence apiece for prophane walking or to be laid one houre in the stocks; and the pievish willfull women (though they were able enough to pay) to save their money and jest out the matter, lay both by the heels merrily one houre.[79]

But the usual target of reformers seems to have been male sabbath breaking. Women's leisure activities were occasional and heterosocial; they had no equivalent to the daily, public, institutional, homosociality of men.

The "popular culture" described recently as "the civilization of the crowd" was that of men. Its emblem was "the English Punch," captured at a particular moment: "in the act of beating his wife."[80] It is in light of this that one must read the characterization of the "recurring theme in working-class life and art" of "the war between the sexes" as "half-jocular, half-serious."[81] This is not to say that there is no record of the women's side: the good wife replied to her scornful husband in the "Ballad of the Tyrannical Husband" (such a man also is the subject of later, sentimental literature),

> Soo I loke to our good without and withyn,
> That there be none awey noder mor nor myn,
> Glade to pleas you to pay, lest any bate begyn,
> And for to chid thus with me, i-feught you be in synne.

The chief message that men's "popular culture" gave women was that they "had to know their place." The "types" of women recorded by popular culture were the saintly heroine, whose heroism inhered in her passively suffering; and the villainous shrew, causing trouble to the male's household economy. "At best, the medieval peasant wife was an object of pity, not esteem," and Bennett quotes the *fabliaux*'s lesson: "No man marries without regretting it." This attitude persisted; the 1639 reformer suggested that a chief cause of male drunkenness was "curst and shrewish wives at home," and his 1693 successor hinted that the "rake" called his wife a drudge. Anecdotes frequently warned of "the danger of [men's] trusting women."[82] (Conversely, men built trust with each other.) To such anecdotes may be added Mandeville's 1711 record of men's denigratory stereotyping of women and the invidiousness of male attitudes toward menstruation, part of the disorderliness associated with female physiology.[83] When women ventured into the public male sphere, they risked being targets of male violence. Because prostitutes depended on leisured male culture for work they were the most susceptible to assault. Their economic need to enter public space linked them to the other group of most susceptible women, those going to market, to whom can be added the notable presence of women peddlers going door to door. For most of the year respectable ladies could not walk the streets. In the countryside, Bennett suggests, women were unable to move "about the houses, lanes, and fields" with the "familiarity" that contributed to men's sense of autonomy.[84] The record suggests that every woman was vulnerable when she entered public spaces men saw as theirs. The medieval goodwife's advice to her daughter was succeeded by Mary Hobart's warning women about Rochester, and of all the warnings carried in eighteenth-century novel's targeting "rakes."

> Acquaint thee not with each man that goeth by the street,
> Though any man speak to thee, swiftly thou greet him;
> By him do not stand, but let his way depart,
> Lest he by his villainy should tempt thy heart.

While the verse intimates women's wish for pleasure, even for joining men abroad, it dictated repression. Physical and verbal assaults and cultural stereotypes demonstrate that the "popular" tradition, popular, that is, among men, was "misogyny" and, according to tradition, women did not enter the street for pleasure.[85]

The Campaign for the Reformation of Manners

During the late years of the seventeenth century a national campaign was implemented in Britain for "the reformation of manners." *The Libertine's Religion*, the *Dissertation upon Drunkenness*, and *Sinne Stigmatized* illustrate its values and its target. From one perspective it may be seen as part of a European pattern, where Reformation and counter-Reformation elites attempted "to reform the culture of ordinary people." Peter Burke argues that reformers wished to establish a permanent "Lenten" culture. Traditionally, Lent had been a time-limited, annual period of self-denial, preceded by Carnival, "the greatest popular festival of the year." It must be reiterated that Carnival was the outburst of appetites for "food, sex and violence." Facing daily denial because their economies were barely at a subsistence level, peasants traditionally had liberated their appetites spasmodically from their repression.[86] "Rather than sociability being mixed in with everyday life in the home, people of this [earlier] period seemed to go more for orgies on special occasions," feast days, for example. The inroads made by reformers on carnivalesque spasms would await the times and places where some of the fruits of commercial capitalism, signified by the growth of communications, penetrated subsistence culture, first sponsoring public male leisure in the tavern (when men nourished such growth) but then increasing "the furniture and utensils in peasant houses" from beds to forks, these items of material culture symbolizing a life of greater ease and the potential or regular, even daily, pleasures at home, too.[87] Psychologically speaking, no longer were pleasures to be confined to the sharp contrast of feast and famine. After the seventeenth-century Netherlands, which saw the same Protestant inroads on Carnival, it was in commercializing and then industrializing Britain that the widespread transcendence of subsistence was especially possible.[88]

There, the campaign for the reformation of manners took up the cause that Puritans had begun to institutionalize from early in the seventeenth century and by Acts of Parliament during the Interregnum, against adultery, fornication, and profane swearing and cursing, linking them with "atheistical opinions derogatory to the honour of God and destructive of human society[,]" above all, those of libertine sectarianism, which declared that the expressions of carnal, worldly appetite were "without sin."[89] While there had been some attempt to regulate alehouses in the medieval period, the beginnings of effective legislation were during the 1620s and 1630s. Religious societies, aiming to counteract Restoration manners, had existed from the 1670s. From the 1690s, societies for the reformation of manners, while still attacking the old targets, "fairs, gambling, masquerades, taverns, whores, obscene ballads," as well as bearbaiting, bullbaiting, and cockfighting, became more "essentially concerned with morals" and with "respectability." It was at this time that "the whole apparatus of regulation" of the alehouse was "put on a comprehensive, organized footing."[90]

Campaigners' views were strongly tinged with the reputability they associated with courtly manners, signified by their use of the words "gentleman" and "lady."[91] If there remained an antiaristocratic edge to the campaign through the century, it was very largely directed at the manners of the lower classes, whose public expression could be more easily checked than those of dissolute aristocrats. Undisciplined, disrespectful artisans and apprentices were to be restrained from "cursing, rioting, drinking, whoreing [and] blaspheming." A 1705 apprentice indenture wrote of its subject: "Taverns and alehouses he shall not haunt; dice, cards or any other unlawful games he shall not use; fornication with any woman he shall not commit," the latter adjuration referring to the prostitution in the backrooms of alehouses. Perhaps this part of the campaign drew some of its fuel from fears of riots and social disorder, reactions to the trauma of comparatively recent social revolution and civil war. But clearly it was responding most immediately and continuously to the proliferating, modernizing, "irreligious," masculine culture in post-Reformation Britain, centered on alehouse and tavern and invigorated in significant part by its assumption of activities driven out of the churchyard. This is a second perspective from which the historian should view the campaign for the reformation of manners. It was an attempt "to suppress individual deviance and sin, to exert tight control over the unruly forces of the market," the attempt no less intense because it was Protestantism that had contributed so evidently to the creation of those "forces."[92] The manners campaigners wished to reform were those of religious thought and observance, speech and other forms of expression, sexual behavior, work habits, trading on Sundays, and various forms of leisure—drinking, gambling, and sports. Reformers attacked the new, public, pleasure centers, playhouses and coffeehouses as well as taverns and alehouses, and the freer expressions of behavior associated with them, from masquerades to drunken brawls, from cursing to the expression of libertine opinions.

In 1689 the newly installed king requested the archbishops and the bishop of London to read in churches the statutes against "blasphemy, swearing, perjury, drunkenness, and profaning the sabbath." Mary's 1691 letter to Middlesex justices, urging them to prosecute immorality, has been credited with "providing a stimulus for a national movement for the reformation of manners" because 1692 saw the foundation of the Society for the Reformation of Manners.[93] There were something like twenty reform societies in London by the end of the century. Historians have described the modus operandi of the societies—paying informers, printing blank warrants, initiating prosecutions, and publishing their proceedings to encourage the establishment of other societies. They published "dissuasives" and "cautions" in a host of sermons and pamphlets, and they pressured the church, local magistrates, and the central government.[94] In 1699, following a petition by Parliament, William enacted a statute for the "more effectual suppressing of Blasphemy and Prophaneness," and that same year the Society for the Propagation of Christian Knowledge was formed. It became "the central directorate for the reforming societies." In 1702 Anne issued a "Proclamation for the Encouragement of Piety and Virtue and for the Preventing and Punishment of Vice, Profaneness and Immorality," to be read in churches four times a year. Sovereigns published edicts in 1712 and 1721, the first against "Great and Unusual Riots and Barbarities . . . committed in the Night-time in the open Streets," the second against certain "scandalous Clubs or Societies of Young Persons who . . . insult the most sacred Principles of our Holy Religion." Similar proclamations were issued by George II in 1755 and George III in 1787.[95]

Societies for the Reformation of Manners had been reestablished in 1738 and 1757. Their reestablishment signified both previous disappointment and the renewal of hope: the idea resurfaced in the 1760s, but it was not until after the 1770s that the "Evangelical ethic diffused itself through all sections of society." The 1770s and 1780s saw the fierce renewal of the campaign to regulate alehouses, even before the intense counterrevolutionaryism of the 1790s. William Wilberforce "secured . . . a royal proclamation against drunkenness" in 1787. The continually renewed campaign would culminate in the successful reform and charitable organizations of the early nineteenth century.[96]

The campaign was fostered at the highest level of politics. William and Mary had been expressing the moral ideology of those who had been in the forefront of the revolution which had enthroned them. The ideology was that of the "True Whig," "Country," or "Commonwealthman" tradition of political thought. Looking back to classical ideas revived by Machiavelli and anglicized by James Harrington in the context of the revolutionary and religious possibilities of the seventeenth century, this tradition of "civic humanism" emphasized public virtue ("the virtue of citizens or political leaders which established or maintained public spirit, liberty and happiness as opposed to vice, self-seeking, and corruption"), as well as the need to stamp out "private vice." The famous Commonwealthman, Algernon Sydney, wrote that "liberty cannot be preserved if manners are corrupt, nor absolute monarchy introduced where they are sincere." This was published in 1698. The ideology, evidently of great value to any oppositional politics, was absorbed by the Tories, too. Bolingbroke conflated the English government he opposed with that of the Emperor Augustus: "we must not wonder that the people, who bore the *tyrants,* bore the *libertines.*"[97] Indeed, writes Professor Goldsmith, wherever "we look in Augustan England (and Britain)—during the reigns of William and Mary, William, Anne, George I and ever afterwards—we discover a denunciation of vice, a fear of luxury, and corruption." The same moral ideology would be absorbed and propounded by sentimental fiction; Richardson was a Commonwealthman, excoriating "King Lovelace." The connection between public virtue and the "manners" generated in private coincided with Lockean psychology's elevation of the importance of childrearing to the creation of character. This could promise much to women as mothers and, if Locke was an unusual man in recognizing that "God had given powers to parents, not just fathers," his contemporaries included a significant number of women writers who drew upon the promise. Peter Earle suggests that among London's rising middle class, in the period 1660–1730, "it seems to have been the mother who provided most of the instruction and correction."[98]

To the reformers of manners the Restoration theater, as well as the alehouse, was a vortex of immorality. It flaunted behavior and values directly opposite to those the Puritans, following their earlier campaign against strolling players, had been able to institutionalize at a national level, closing down the playhouses in 1642. They had targeted brothels, too. These places were linked in several ways, not the least that black-vizored prostitutes found customers in the theater pit; they probably shared the reformers' view that the representation of libertinism on stage inspired the members of the audience. Moreover, after the Restoration, women's roles were played by women for the first time. Some actresses became famous mistresses of powerful aristocrats in addition to Rochester, including the king himself, and were celebrated by painters and poets.[99] Then there were the mere titles of the burgeoning numbers of plays: *The Costly Whore; Cupid's Whirligig; Amorous Old Woman; Love in the Dark; Marriage Night; The Husband His Own Cuckold; The Wild Gallant; The Merry Cuckold; The Politick Whore or the Conceited Cuckold;* and the "bawdy burlesque" entitled *Love lost in the dark, or the Drunken Couple.*[100] The campaigners poured out their horror, holding that "the stage has gone further [than anything else] in running us down to this low and almost brutal conduct."[101] Well-known among the spate of maxims, considerations, and dissuasives was the Rev. Jeremy Collier's *Short View of the Immorality and Profaneness of the English Stage* (1698). Going to the playhouse wasted time and money. It exposed audiences to what it judged as lewd women and to the libertine views exemplified by Rochester. In spite of such criticism the theater took off after 1689; there were statistical increases in audiences, theaters (both in London and everywhere in the provinces), theater capacity, numbers of performances. Entrepreneurs found that performing after hours at cheaper rates brought in lower-paid workers, all part of the "commercialization of leisure," which only added to the anxieties stirred up in moralists. At the turn of the century reformers began to consider using the theater itself as "a forum for mass moral elevation and discussion," to use its popularity rather than to oppose it.[102]

Reformers of manners also encouraged literacy in order to control it. The importance of the English Reformation to the origins of mass literacy must be emphasized, reformers' replacing the experience of Mass by reading the word of God for themselves.[103] The early eighteenth century was a significant stage in "the general transition from restricted to mass literacy," a transition tantamount to a "revolution."[104] The "steepest acceleration in literacy" occurred early in the previous century; by the 1750s, about 60 percent of men could read and 40 percent of women; by 1800 it was most men and at least a majority of women. Hunter argues that this increase was "broadly based" among "artisans, shopkeepers, yeomen, husbandmen, and servants." It seems likely, he writes, that those most likely to read were urban and young, with "an increased taste for commerce with a larger world." (It seems that alehouse keepers became more literate after the Restoration.) Parliament's 1695 refusal to renew the Licensing Act had been followed by an "unparallelled" growth in the publishing industry, with print of all kinds "flowing from the presses" and broadening the "horizons" of an increasing readership.[105] Reformers' schools, libraries, and the circulation of thousand upon thousand of tracts, prayer books, and Bibles fed the tiger they attempted to ride. Wesley's extension of this campaign "produced many simplified versions of textbooks on grammar, logic and mathematics . . . works of biography, poetry, travel, conduct books," his book on self-doctoring, and editions of Locke and Shakespeare, in addition, of course, to collections of prayers and hymns. Methodists claimed to be instrumental in diffusing "that general desire for reading now so prevalent among the inferior order of society."[106] The *Gentleman's Magazine* was shocked that "so many Persons in the lowest Stations of Life, are most intent upon cultivating their Minds than upon feeding and cloathing their Bodies." Elites saw this as a threat to "traditional standards."[107]

The Society for the Propagation of Christian Knowledge (SPCK) had been founded in 1698 to address the "profligacy" attributable to "ignorance." It shared Newton's and Cheyne's wish to leave behind "paganism and superstition" or, rather, to elevate the orthodox kind at the expense of "magic," and the "rational" above vulgar alehouse "nonsense." The attempt to flood the market with pamphlets and sermons, many of them distributed free, was one phase of the attempted management of literacy. Another was the "early and pious education of youth" in its charity schools. Third, the SPCK "attacked the printers and publishers of evil doctrines." Atheistic and pornographic books were censored, booksellers convicted, and books burnt by the common hangman. Mandeville said that if reformers had their way they would "break down the Printing-Presses, melt the Founts and burn all the Books on the Island, except those at Universities . . . and suffer no volume in private Hands but the Bible."[108] The early eighteenth-century debate over the liberty of the press expressed in part "the fear of the revolt of the literate."[109] Eventually the SPCK was able to advertise its success by parading hundreds of its schoolchildren at a time in the streets, surrounded by elaborate expressions of adult approval, all demonstrating moralized literacy in contrast with the usual activities of street youth.[110] In town after town, charity school buildings were more permanent public expressions of the movement's success.[111]

Like its predecessor, *The Tatler, The Spectator* shared the reformation goals of the SPCK. It provided statistical evidence of its success and said its own general intention was to "recover" the "age" out of its desperate state of vice and folly. The contrast between the lives of people enjoying leisure and consumerism on the one hand, and those of the poor on the other, was the setting for *The Spectator*'s advocacy of charity schools. It reported that in "the same street" as people rolling in "luxury" and in "power and wealth" lived "creatures" so miserable, hungry, and naked that one would have thought them a "different species."[112] *The Spectator* concluded its celebration of the charity school movement with a paragraph from "Dr. Snape's sermon on these charities," which argued that the "edifying education" the poor could now obtain exalted them in goodness and made poverty "in reality their preferment."[113] *The Spectator* gave several reasons for the rich to "edify" the poor in charity schools, but the most developed was the one historians currently interpret as the attempt to create "hegemony." Charity was an investment to produce a "servant" reared to "consider his master as his father, his friend, and his benefactor, upon easy terms, and in expectation of no other return, but moderate wages, and gentle usage." Lockean psychology could be turned to counterrevolutionary purpose, mediating luxurious privilege and stamping out the grumbling of the lower orders. Evidently the authors of *The Spectator* feared if not a revolt by the newly literate, certainly their wish to enjoy the fashionable vices the poor observed in their own streets.[114]

Addison, Steele, and their fellow reformers saw themselves facing the dissolution of any standard of morality and taste. In *The Guardian,* its title itself speaking its wish for Platonic authority (1713), Steele witnessed the

> unsettled way of reading . . . which naturally seduces us into an undetermined manner of thinking . . . That assemblage of words which is called a style becomes utterly annihilated . . . The common defence of these people is, that they have no design in reading but for *pleasure,* which I think should rather arise from reflection and remembrance of what one had read, than from the transient satisfaction of what one does, and we should be pleased proportionately as we are profited.

The Spectator wished to "lay down rules" of taste in the minds of the new consumers of literature and art, "that we may know whether we are possessed of [taste]," "how we may acquire . . . fine taste," and how to cultivate and improve it. In the series of papers "On the Pleasures of the Imagination," the reader was flattered to learn that a man of polite imagination would be "let into a great many pleasures that the vulgar are not capable of receiving."[115] The conscious target of *The Spectator* was the uncontrolled experience of pleasure. The authors confronted what they saw as a new historical situation in which many people (above all, readers) were pursuing pleasure for its own sake and doing so "transiently," skipping from one source of pleasure to the next.[116] They and their fellow moralists recognized what a twentieth-century historian terms the old "hierarchically structured" system for distributing consumption (whereby "the family, the master, the employer, and [sometimes] government authorities made a lot of consumer choices for those under their control") was breaking down, to be replaced by "consumer sovereignty." A multitude of new persons could now make the world "administer to [their] pleasures." An unprecedented number of people were extending their recognition of the potential for pleasure in the mere "play" of their individual minds.[117]

In order to shape such consumer appetite, *The Spectator* claimed that it controlled special keys to unlock still higher degrees of pleasure, including the mastery of ancient languages as well as those of Christian morality and self-discipline. They also included taking delight in descriptions that aroused "terror and grief"; or in descriptions of "dangers that are past or in looking at a precipice at a distance," "the apprehension of what is great or unlimited," the pleasure of "melancholy scenes and apprehensions of deaths and funerals or pleasing dreams of groves and elysiums."[118] The same distancing from "the world" was the optimal circumstance for one's relationship to God in which feeling played a vital part. "The devout man does not only believe, but feels there is a Deity." This experience of "giving life to a man's faith" was best obtained in "frequent retirement from the world," away from that world where the mind was liable to be "stunned and dazzled amidst the variety of objects in a great city . . . the cares or pleasures of the world."[119]

"We" readers, said *The Spectator,* could take pleasure in being distanced from life's calamities, a relation wherein Defoe defined the middle class a few years later:

> when we read of torments, wounds, deaths and the like dismal accidents, our pleasure does not flow so properly from

> the grief which such melancholy description gives us, as from the secret comparison which we make between ourselves and the person who suffers. Such representations teach us to set a just value upon our own condition, and make us prize our good fortune, which exempts us from the like calamities.[120]

The writer insisted on this distancing of reading as a necessary condition for deriving pleasure from pain. The significance of *The Spectator*'s title is redoubled in this context. The direct observation of pain and misery did not permit such pleasure: the assumed community of writers and readers needed "time and leisure" to pursue self-reflection. They depended for it on the pain of others, not only of their unleisured servants, perhaps reared to deference by charity schools, but also those "creatures" so miserable that they seemed to be of a different species. The pleasures of the imagination required clear social hierarchy. *The Spectator* aggrandized "pity," "love softened by a degree of sorrow . . . a kind of pleasing anguish, as well as generous sympathy, that knits mankind together," but implicit in that aggrandizement was the need for social distance. The pleasures *The Spectator* advocated were largely those of relief, complacency, and a sense of safety adequately remote from a pain on which they depended for "secret comparison." Shammas suggests that the "mass" preference for sugar and tea, even when more nutritious food was available, expressed the wish for distance from the "severe want" associated with the old, household-produced diet, which had been more subject to the vicissitudes of nature. In the eighteenth century, eating brown bread or drinking simply water "still carried the stigma of social deprivation."[121]

This feature of *The Spectator*'s recommended taste was implicit in reading itself. "Words, when well chosen have so great a force in them, that a description often gives us more lovely ideas than the sight of the things themselves." Second, the historical circumstances invoked by *The Spectator* were the spread of consumption and the elevation of a significantly greater number of people above the daily struggle for survival in the teeth of unmanageable social and natural disasters. They were able to transcend the feast and famine psychology of Lent and Carnival. We have noted *The Spectator's* keen awareness of the juxtaposition of luxury and poverty in "the same street." Langford remarks that it "often suited contemporaries to dwell on the extremes of social life." The cultivation of "secret comparison" by the constant juxtaposition of pleasure and pain allowed the constant reenactment of this recent elevation and the kinds of pleasures it brought. Third, the moralized order of this taste obviously represented the reassertion of a degree of control over the unleashing of pleasure, which corresponded to the social hierarchy symbolized by "polite" and "vulgar." A fourth explanation given by *The Spectator* itself was a characteristic of consumer pleasures generally, although *The Spectator* wished to attribute it to God rather than to the commerce on which *The Spectator* and its readers depended. God "has annexed a secret pleasure to the idea of anything that is new or uncommon."[122]

One consumer pleasure took "new" for its name, and the novel was "intellectually more accessible than any previous literary genre," the "most democratic of literary forms."[123] Like other displays of new consumer items, the novel offered "a degree of unsupervised choice, a limited freedom to exercise personal taste, and the chance to indulge in imaginative fantasies free from oppressive social duties." This, of course, is precisely what bothered the authors of *The Spectator* and other reformers of manners. Thus vulnerable to criticism, novelists themselves took up "the cause of religion and virtue," riding on the "wave already set in motion by early and organized attempts to propagate Christian belief and social orthodoxy through the teaching of reading skills."[124] Engendered in prenovelistic narratives, Christian storytelling, pious biographies, and Puritan conduct books; intertwined with the sermons they often resembled; accompanying an outpouring of religious publications; being accorded to "the official creed of authors, critics and public, that the function of the novel was explicitly educational and that its main business was to inculcate morality by example," the novel could be a weapon in the campaign for the reformation of manners.[125]

During the 1720s, Penelope Aubin (one of Richardson's several female predecessors), wrote expressly pious novels like *The Life and Amorous Adventures of Lucinda* (1722) and *The Life of Charlotte Du Pont* (1723), allegorizing "her familiar heroines into figures larger than life, very much in the manner of the writers of pious biography." Aubin became literally a popular preacher, "speaking in the York Buildings near Charing Cross." This was "a logical extension of the preaching she had already done in her novels." The famous anecdote of Dr. Benjamin Slocock's reading *Pamela: or, Virtue Rewarded* from his pulpit symbolizes the relationship between the sentimental novel and more traditional sermons.[126] In the "Postscript" to *Clarissa,* Richardson said he had advanced the novel as a more effective pulpit than the one from which clerical reformers preached the same message. Amidst a "general depravity, when even the pulpit has lost a great part of its weight, and the clergy are considered as a body of interested men, the author thought he should be able to answer it to his own heart

. . . if he threw in his mite towards introducing a general reformation so much wanted." He had investigated "the great doctrines of Christianity under the fashionable guise of an amusement" because he faced "an age given up to diversion and entertainment." His vision of the atheist problem, in which "scepticism and infidelity" were combined with consumerism—"a taste even to wantonness for out-door pleasure and luxury"—was identical to that of clerical reformers. Dr. Johnson's contemporaneous concern over "the young, the ignorant, and the idle," "easily following the current of fancy" in their reading, placed him in the camp of the reformers targeting young artisans and apprentices for their lack of discipline and morality. The novel's seventeenth-century precedents, aimed at a popular audience, had incorporated the same goal: Foxe's *Acts and Monuments* told the tale of "an idle and licentious apprentice who gambles away his masters money at dice," before being converted by reading the Bible and therefore turning to "industrious enterprise." Wesley attempted to reach a popular audience with cheap editions of several novels, for example, Henry Brooke's *The Fool of Quality* (1765–70), a typically pious work advocating the reformation of manners. Precisely how novelists contributed their efforts to the reformation of manners is the subject of later chapters.[127]

Heart Religion

E. P. Thompson has argued that the campaign for the reformation of manners was intended to inculcate "the Protestant ethic," that is, the formation of new work habits, aligning the campaign with the origins of industrial capitalism. In keeping with Weber's *The Protestant Ethic and the Spirit of Capitalism* and its modification by Tawney, Thompson writes that Puritanism provided "the necessary part of the work ethos which enabled the industrial world to break out of the poverty-stricken economies of the past."[128] Challenging Thompson, others suggest that, rather than repressing the "natural" work rhythm of the premodern economy in the interests of capitalists, evangelical nonconformity in general "echoed the aspirations rather than the despair of the working classes." Far down the social scale, eighteenth-century "men" were already according their behavior to an individual work pattern linked to their appetite for consumer goods. In fact, their new work pattern dated back to the sixteenth century and instead of requiring to be disciplined in the interests of capitalism, "popular culture" in eighteenth-century England was itself an early part of "the womb of an industrial and urban society."[129] The history of the elaboration of alehouse culture, including its sponsorship of consumerism and play, as well as of free market transactions, endorses such a view.

Whether men were converted to the Protestant ethic or not, however, there was one traditional dimension of their lives that still required reformation. That was their treatment of women. Even the recent proponents of the idea that the Protestant ethic had long penetrated popular male culture assert that culture remained "robust" and still appropriately emblemized by Punch. Sporting "squires and sturdy labourers rubbed shoulders in common appreciation of physical prowess, whether of man or animal." Updated pastimes maintained "the manliness of the race."[130] Reformers held that the alehouse threatened to unravel respectable society because it opposed the interests of "the family," notably those of women, by separating husbands from wives, for example, and by encouraging prostitution. Here reformers expressed the same view as Burnet. This is not to say that class was not vitally important as a consideration in definitions of self and other and as a counter in mobility, fashion, and other indications of power.[131] But, following and accompanying the development of male culture, gender emerged as just as fundamental an issue during the eighteenth century, one that could cut still deeper than class. Aristocratic libertines, wasteful drinkers and smokers, and rioting artisans were linked not only by their "atheism" but by their style of manhood.

Clarendon had said that the modern fine gentleman affected "hardness" and Burnet challenged those libertines given up to "hardness," their "Minds nummed" by their "dissolute Practices" as "to be wholly unfit for business."[132] Reformers not only wished to purge men of their wasteful libertine habits and to replace them with the Protestant ethic; they wished to persuade men to find and elevate their softer feelings of piety. These wishes were expressed theologically and ultimately were crystallized institutionally. Early expressions of this aspect of the campaign were the sermons of "numerous Anglican divines of the Latitudinarian tradition," preached "from hundreds of pulpits in London and the provinces." Their combined influence gained momentum from the 1660s and extended through the mid-eighteenth century. Among the divines listed by R. S. Crane in his pioneering effort to uncover the origins of the literary "cult of sensibility"[133] were Edward Calamy, William Colnett, and Jeremy Collier, the latter the author of a tract against dueling as well as the Restoration theater. All of them preached to the Society for the Reformation of Manners. Wishing to restore "all natural feelings and bodily passions" to a "Nature" they called "humane," the divines attacked "stoical insensibility," the gentlemanly hardness they saw making inroads among scholars and aristocrats. For example, the Rev. James Lowde told his congregants in 1694 that the "*Stoicks* would make Man so wholly rational, that they will scarce allow him to be sensible, and would wholly exclude all natural affections and bodily sensations out of human nature." This was one source for the rewriting of Stoicism so apparent in English letters from Shaftesbury's *Characteristics* of 1711 and Addison's *Cato* of 1713 to Hume's "The Stoic," of 1742.[134]

In turn, the Latitudinarians' intellectual origins lay with the Cambridge Platonists, who aimed to combat the grim view of human nature taken by the harsher forms of Calvinism. They also wished to counter the related doctrine of Hobbes, that people were at bottom utterly selfish and antisocial, motivated entirely by self-interest. By contrast, the Cambridge Platonists and their Latitudinarian successors argued that human nature was instinctively sympathetic and that their passions naturally inclined them to virtuous actions. Such actions were reinforced because of the pleasurable feelings they automatically brought.[135] People were naturally inclined to goodness, but it was still essential that they reinforce and cultivate such an inclination. The social setting was that increasingly widespread distancing from suffering which Defoe and *The Spectator* had emphasized. The Rev. Isaac Barrow, whose sermons provided models for "many other ministers," urged that since nature "hath made our neighbour's misery our pain and his content our pleasure . . . since by the discipline of our sense she instructs us . . . to the observance of our duty, let us follow her wise directions . . . let us not stifle or weaken by disuse, or contrary practice, but by comfortable action cherish and confirm the good inclinations of nature." Nature was to be reinforced by self-discipline. The intention was "make Men good."[136]

The material signs of virtuous responsiveness were as crucial as the more spiritual signs of grace had always been. In 1662 Robert South had contrasted Christ with the Stoics by pointing out that he "had been seen to weep." In the telling vision of the Cambridge Platonist Henry More, "Nature" had "bestowed on so many of the Creatures when they are oppressed, for the drawing of Compassion toward them," signals such as a "lamenting tone of Voice, the dejection of the Eyes and Countenances, Groaning, Howling, Sighs, and Tears, and the like." These expressions have the "Power to incline the mind to Compassion . . . to quicken [and] to Help or to retard the Mischiefs we Intended." Certain signs of distress or of oppression could become themselves a source of power. The signs given by both sides of this implicit human exchange served "as natural revelations of God's moral expectations of us."[137]

In explaining their new view of human nature, these divines were able to draw upon the most recent "results of psychological investigations," precisely as Dr. Cheyne had. Arguing that "nature" elevated feeling, Latitudinarians promoted Newtonian science. Several among the seventy divines described by Crane—Richard Bentley, Richard Kidder, and Samuel Clarke—gave the Boyle lectures.[138] Latitudinarians in general preached that God had "implanted in our very Frame and Make a compassionate sense of the Suffering . . . of our Fellow Creatures in Distress, and we are naturally, I had almost said, mechanically inclined to be helpful to them." It was their particular frame, their mechanism, that is, its finer nerve structure, which made those of "the finest Temper soonest affected by the Distresses of other Men" (1700). Barrow told his congregants that "mechanical Sympathy" to the groans of the afflicted forced "tears and sighs" from the generality of men because "their hearts are so tender." "Tenderness" was the quality essential for the receipt of "impressions." According to a sermon of 1685, "when our tempers are soft and sensible and easily receive impressions, we are pain'd within, and to ease ourselves, we are ready to succor them, and then Nature discharging Her Burthen and Oppression, creates both her own pleasure and satisfaction." Both pleasure and pain were seen as signs registered by one's interoceptive system. More categorized "feeling" as the first of the body's "internal powers of perception." One's exteroceptors were the outward receivers and transmitters of sensibility and were intrinsically capable of a greater range of signs.[139]

A Barrow sermon also illustrates the crucial part that "stories" and "fabulous reports" were already playing in the transmission of this new "state of mind," its morality, and in the amplification of the listener's imagination, precisely as *The Spectator* would soon recommend:

> the stories of calamities, that in ages long since past have happened to persons nowise related to us, yea, the fabulous reports of tragical events, do . . . melt our hearts with compassion, and draw tears from our eyes; and thereby signify that general sympathy which naturally intercedes between all men, since we can neither see nor hear of, nor imagine another's grief, without being afflicted ourselves.[140]

If, as Margaret Jacob has argued, the Latitudinarians rationalized the operation of a market economy as "natural," Colin Campbell has suggested that they also developed the potentials of consumer psychology inherent in Protestantism. In Campbell's view, Protestantism had disconnected the Christian from communal and "natural" controls, to agonize over his or her feelings but, under the aegis of Latitudinarian preaching, ultimately he or she was able to enjoy them. Sanctified at first as signs of grace, they came to be enjoyed for their own sake, as "dream-play," perpetually regenerated by their materialization in consumer goods promising ever more satisfaction. Such an evolution from Latitudinarianism through sentimental "Piety" and "pious sentimentalism," culminating in a consumer psychology of "autonomous hedonism," was marked by the frequency in sentimental literature of the notion of enjoying the "luxury of grief" or "indulging" one's feelings, luxury and indulgence essential members of sentimentalism's "family of words" which connected sensibility with consumerism.[141] "Pity," wrote J. Thistlethwaite in his 1770 *The Man of Experience,* "is the greatest luxury the soul of sensibility is capable of relishing." The kinds of pleasures with which Campbell is centrally concerned (the leisure activities of reading novels, window shopping, and the pursuit of fashion) were those, it may be inferred, enjoyed by both women and men. His analysis is also consistent with that distancing taste *The Spectator* exemplified and wished to foster along with the tea ceremony.[142]

The reconceptualizing of human nature corresponded to a reconceptualizing of God. Cambridge Platonists had rejected "the terrors of a fully deterministic Calvinism," accepting at least a part of the Hobbesian characterization Rochester set to verse:

> For Hell and the Foul Fiend that Rules
> God's everlasting fiery Jayles
> (Devis'd by Rogues, dreaded by Fooles)
> With his grim grisly Dogg, that keeps the Doore,
> Are Senselesse Storyes, idle Tales
> Dreames, Whimseys, and noe more.

This view of hell came under serious challenge after the Restoration.[143] Instead Cambridge Platonist Richard Cumberland's *Treatise of Human Nature* (1672) gave "a pre-eminent place" to "universal benevolence." His successors among Latitudinarians did not go so far as to sever ethics from God's will and the anxieties about eternity. They continued to maintain that a just God had made a "general judgement of universal damnation," but now God was susceptible to "the Softer Dictates and Whispers of Humanity" in contrast to the "hard and cruel Things" which expressed "the extremity of Justice." "The universe is reasonable and ordered because God is prompted by his feelings—the original and eternal benevolence of his nature—to exercise his power in a rational manner."[144] God was to be addressed as a benevolent, sympathetic parent rather than a "hard-hearted, arbitrary cruel tyrant." Over the course of the century, the "Father [was] reconceived in the image of the compassionate and mediatorial Son." That this bore a direct relationship both to familial and political ideology as well as to reform has been argued by others, who have also suggested its connection with literature.[145] God's intention, like that of reformed parenting, was not to "terrify humanity but to soften and improve it." Randall McGowen suggests that a relationship existed between such a view and England's commercial prosperity. "The progress in human knowledge, comfort, and behavior was taken as proof of God's character as a benevolent deity whose plans for the world included the progressive improvement of humanity." People had to feel more comfortable on earth and experience progress before they could attribute it to God.[146]

The allusion to "the extremity of Justice" in God signifies the continued existence of competing conception of God. McGowen has described a century-long "dispute over God's relationship to humanity." Traditional Anglican orthodoxy, carefully manifested, for example, at Assize sermons (the point where man's justice intersected with God's), presented the face of God as "necessarily grim." It was one of "unrivaled majesty of power," used, as a 1714 preacher said, "to fright men into heaven." By associating rituals of justice with divine authority, government intended to inspire terror in a human nature that orthodoxy continued to define as passionate, disorderly, rebellious, corrupt, and appetitive.[147]

"Feeling" was at the heart of the debate over the face of God. Latitudinarians and would-be reformers of criminal justice said that divine justice "should have no likeness to that narrow, unfeeling, vindictive spirit." William Whiston in 1740 defended the softened face of God, accusing his opponents of supposing God "to delight in cruelty and barbarity, the most savage cruelty and barbarity possible."[148] At the end of the century, a defender of the necessity of a frighteningly authoritarian God identified him with the hierarchic values of the writer's "rude forefathers" in contrast to the "more refined, more enlightened, and more liberal view." "Tenderness" had its place, but taken too far it could be profoundly "subversive." One orthodox preacher said in 1794 that "the new humanitarian spirit represented a severe threat to justice, and was perhaps more subversive than open warfare against society." This was the context for attributing the French Revolution to Rousseauistic sensibility. The vision of a barbaric and cruel God, worshipped by cruel forefathers, opposed to a benevolent and sympathetic one, worshipped by more refined and humane congregants, of people with "native Tenderness" in "their own bosom[s]" corresponded to the struggle between opposing definitions of manhood.[149]

Institutional circumstances had favored the emergence of an alternative view of God. The preaching of this sympathetic God and a corresponding view of humanity coincided with the reduction of Church of England's ability to enforce orthodoxy. A century of conflict had transformed the church "from a national church to a denomination in competition for adherents." Here was a parallel between eighteenth-century church history and the economic challenge to monopoly rationalized by the sentimentalist Adam Smith. Orthodox Anglicanism's most successful competitor emerged from its own ranks, and Methodism became "a major religious catalyst in eighteenth-century England," flourishing where Anglicanism had been weak, gaining "most from the expansion of the English population and economy." It sustained rapid expansion from 1740 to 1840, the period of the culture of sensibility's ascendance.[150]

Wesleyan theology, like the preceding "stages" in Anglican religious thought, was heir to the Cambridge Platonists, especially Henry More. Yet while Wesley shared the Latitudinarians' emphasis on feeling and their hostility to the Deists, he softened up their doctrine still further by rejecting the "absurd" opinion that God had by fixed decree determined one part of mankind be saved and one damned, assuring his audiences that all who received God's grace could be saved.[151] Wesley's mother, Susanna Annesley Wesley (educated by her dissenting father), was a decisive influence in this repudiation of predestination. The polarity between her husband's intellectual and physical engagement with a wider world and the domestic drudgery to which he confined his wife (who bore nineteen children) and his daughters, characterized the general relationship between male popular culture and laboring women's domestic lives.[152] Saying of young John, "I do intend to be more especially careful of the soul of this child," Susanna Wesley made sure that he was significantly "mother-identified." Like Richardson, Wesley would write "his best letters to women" and have "a natural ease in their company"—at least as long as it was sexually distanced. Wesley's mother and sisters were the ancestresses of "those great women of Methodism who together, in feminine bands, and singly, in savage homes were to bring sweetness and light to a brutal age of fierce masculinity."[153] Whatever its psychological origins, resting religion in the heart would be Wesley's central appeal, against what he called "formality . . . mere outside religion, which has almost driven heart-religion out of the world."[154]

Wesley and other revivalist preachers, eager "to reach the emotional core of masses of men and women," geared powerful techniques to penetrate the lower classes, from whom the upper strata, seduced by rationalism, had become increasingly divorced. His "manipulation of the media" was "especially suited to the age."[155] Above all, he appealed to the internal evidence which could be shared by all, an "argument so plain that a peasant, a woman, a child may feel its force," that is, he appealed to feeling, "the reasons of the heart." His insistence on feeling and on simplicity characterized one of Methodism's most powerful drives: to communicate intelligibly on what he took to be the "peasant's" and the "woman's" own terms.[156]

The first revolutionary technique used by Wesley, Whitefield, and their fellow evangelicals was, of course, preaching. Wesley used "matter-of-fact" preaching to produce emotional effects in his listeners. So, too, did Edwards. Whitefield wept at nearly every sermon, Tennent writhed and fainted. They wrought their spellbinding speech with a mastery of "stylized emotionalism."[157] Whitefield's oratorical "pathos," his ability to get his congregation sobbing, was admired by Garrick. Implementing very similar techniques in the theater now aiming to reform its audience by making them weep, Garrick invoked similar responses.[158] Similarly, Methodist preachers sought to break through what Wesley called his audience's "hardness of hearts" by telling precisely the same kind of stories Latitudinarians used. Whitefield strung tiny pathetic stories together, and Edwards, having read sentimental fiction, in his sermons used "all the weapons, conscious, and subconscious, verbal, emotional, and sensuous, of the [sentimental] author at his best."[159]

Whitefield was recorded saying to his audience, "Thus, I trust, some of you begin to feel . . . I see you concerned," "I see you weeping," and the first signs of his preaching's effectiveness on a group of coal miners' faces, were "the white gullies made by their tears, which plentifully ran down their black cheeks." An historian, in quantifying 234 cases out of Wesley's audience of 1739–43, found the whole number was suffused with tears, groans, and trembling.[160] Specific symptoms included feeling "as if a sword [was] running through them," as if "a great weight lay upon them," their "hearts swelled as if ready to burst."[161]

Sensational psychology supplied Wesley, his disciples, and his coreligionists with an explanation and a program for affecting his hearers' senses.[162] For example, in the sermon entitled "The Great Privilege of those that are Born of God" preached in 1748, explaining what spiritual rebirth meant, Wesley took Locke's account of the operation of the senses as his central explanatory device.[163] The unconverted person, he told his audience, which probably included many women (their attraction to Methodism a subject of Chap. 5, below), was like "a child which is not yet born," which neither feels, hears, nor sees: "it has no *senses;* all these avenues of the soul are hitherto quite shut up. Of consequence, it has scarce any intercourse with this visible world, nor any knowledge, conception, or idea, of the things that occur herein." By analogy, the person not yet "born of God" had "not yet those senses,—they are not yet opened in his soul, whereby alone it is possible to hold commerce with the material world." Once born, the child's senses were "awakened and flourished with their proper objects."[164] Wesley described the results of spiritual rebirth as "motion and sensation, all the senses of the soul now awake and capable of discerning good and evil." If Cheyne and the nerve doctors valued a "Degree" or a "Rank" of sensibility, Wesley characterized it as "Privilege."[165]

The other "revolutionary" technique in reaching a popular audience by way of emotion was the singing of hymns. The Wesleys published 6,500 of them in a cheap and portable collection, "a primer of theology for the Methodist people and a manual both for public worship and private devotions."[166] Wesley intended the music to draw on the same psychoperceptual resources as his sermons, transmitted via the auditors' strings to "raise" the proper "passions" in his auditors minds and to convert them.[167] Wesley explained these sensationalist assumptions in his 1779 "Thoughts on the Power of Music." The ancient Greeks had been "able to excite whatever passions they pleased" and had thereby played people as if they were instruments, varying their hearers' "passion just according to the variation of the music." They had done so with the simplest of instruments, a lyre, pipes, or a single harp, in contrast to complex modern instruments, the violin, oboe, and German flute. Modern, harmonic, and contrapuntal music did not have this power because it was "a contrast of various notes, opposite to, and yet blended with, each other."[168]

Here Wesley was facing a growing market for music, fostered by amateurs but still more notably by entrepreneurs, publishers, and professional musicians, presenting "more extrovert . . . and brilliant composition." Many Anglican organists were catalysts in galvanizing this popularization throughout the country. There was a "craze for French and Italian music." Handel's oratorios were the special target of early evangelicals because they were "played at Ranelagh and Vauxhall along with fireworks, fencing displays, and masquerades." Wesley's "Thoughts on the Power of Music" recognized that "modern" music's harmony and variety appealed "to the ear, to the imagination [and] the internal sense," that is to the auditor's sensory "pleasure" in music for pleasure's own, worldly sake. But Wesley's view resembled Cheyne's interpretation of the numbing overload of different kinds of international foods, all mixed by culinary art; Wesley also advocated "frugality and self-denial" in food. Similarly, *The Spectator* had wished to limit the stunning "variety of objects in a great city." All acknowledged the pleasures of variety available to unprecedented publics, and Wesley as much as Cheyne and *The Spectator* capitalized on the modalities of consumerism in marketing his new democratizable regimens and new forms of self-regard. Campbell suggests that Methodism contributed to the consumer "stream" in British bourgeois culture, a suggestion endorsed by what we have seen of the centrality of sensational psychology to Wesley's appeal. One notes the awakening and flourishing of the senses of his emblematic baby.[169]

Like *The Spectator,* Wesley offered his audience the kind of "indulgence" in the examination of their own feelings central to the consumerism of Campbell's thesis. Celtic peasants, said Wesley in the same essay, had retained the ability to play music consisting of melody alone, "composed not according to art, but nature—they are simple in the highest degree. There is no *harmony* . . . but there is much *melody.*" Hence listeners are "much affected." The melody "is not only heard but *felt* by all those who retain their native taste, whose taste is not biased (I might say corrupted) by attending to *counterpoint* and complicated music." It is not surprising that in publishing the music to his hymns, *Sacred Melody: or a choice of Psalm and Hymn Tunes,* "only the melody was given." A significant number were "Scotch and Irish airs." Presumably, Methodists could put them to the same use the ancient Greeks had, appealing to audiences who felt themselves closer to such "peasantry." Wesley had the same standards in mind in fostering the pleasures of reading. Having abridged *The Fool of Quality* and purged it of unsuitable passages, Wesley praised its capacity to invoke pleasurable pain. "The strokes are so delicately fine, the touches so easy, natural and affecting, that I know not who can survey it with tearless eyes unless he had a heart of stone."[170] The indulgences of singing simple hymns and reading cheap versions of sentimental novels corresponded to the circumstances and pockets of humbler, less sophisticated audiences than those who could appreciate Italian opera and classically informed learning, or afford exotic culinary art—but pleasures they were.

This connection with Campbell's thesis throws another light on "the pathos of the Protestant ethic," whereby an intensely ascetic self-discipline led to wealth and its tasteful expression in "goods," and worldly "love"—one kind of indulgence expanding into another. "Riches," in Calvin's phrase, brought "self-indulgence." Weber quoted Wesley as the epitome of this paradox.

> I do not see how it is possible, in the nature of things, for any revival of true religion to continue long. For religion must

> necessarily produce both industry and frugality, and these cannot but produce riches. But as riches increase, so will pride, anger, and love of the world in all its branches. How then is it possible that Methodism, that is, a religion of the heart, though it flourishes now as a green bay tree, should continue in this state. For the Methodists in every place grow diligent and frugal; consequently they increase in goods . . . Is there no way to prevent this—this continual decay of pure religion?[171]

By the 1790s Methodists were dominated by an elite of respectable, professionalized ministers, tightly linked to "substantial and reputable householders," the Methodist Society itself holding substantial property and with close and effective ties to the government. There was a powerful urge among the Methodist rank and file toward respectability and an eventual purging of radical elements. By then, historians suggest, society at large had come around to many of Wesley's terms.[172]

But at first Wesleyanism had been deeply disruptive, particularly to the domination by traditional males of agricultural areas and old municipalities, and it contributed to the competing representations of God described by McGowen. The very existence of Methodism as a style and an organization had threatened "the patriarchal authority of gentry and clergy alike," even if Wesley had not also threatened them "by his scorching critique of the 'polite world' and of the worldview of the 'carnal' clergy."[173] There is historical symbolism in the fact that a "clergyman and some local squires once used huntsmen and hounds to disrupt one of Wesley's outdoor sermons." Precisely the same contrast between irreligious, worldly, pleasure-seeking, hard males, and pious, otherworldly, tearful, feeling evangelical males, equalized in new communities of self-discipline and emotional release, has been described as male "culture and counter-culture" in eighteenth-century British Virginia.[174]

Symbolically, Wesley opposed the "mercurial elusive rake, John Wilkes" and his "bawdy, blasphemous," and antiauthoritarian movement. He opposed dueling and the whole masculine world symbolized by the tavern. One of his disciples seems to have persuaded a listener to go home and cut off the heads of his fighting cocks. The 1757 Society for the Reformation of Manners was able to draw its membership most strongly from the Methodists.[175] Methodists, Anglicans, Quakers, "rational dissenters," Baptists, and later evangelicals had common ground in their opposition to the "time-bound recreations" of cockfighting, cockthrowing, bearbaiting, and the other animal-killing sports;[176] to "drunkenness, bawdiness, rough music . . .

race-meetings," as well as the "wife sales" embedded in the same cultural tradition; and to profaning the Sabbath; opposition to fighting, gambling, to "alehouse people, fiddlers, harpers," and to "card-playing."[177] Garrick may have admired Whitefield as a rival, but Whitefield "denounced stage shows and stage players" to the extent that the feud between Whitefield and actors was caricatured.[178] Wesley said that he succeeded in "reclaiming" the drunkard and the whoremonger, the curser, swearer, miser, and sluggard, and that he opposed the traditional double standard of sexual behavior, calling for "male chastity."[179] His *Arminian Magazine* was aimed at "the deluge of depravity that has been pouring upon us" during a lifelong crusade against "irreligion and vice." The magazine propounded the replacement of coarse public behavior with the manners of reformed gentlemen. Langford suggests that part of the evangelical success lay in its appeal to the new elite of semi-industrial areas, not yet as confident of its politeness as the older ones.[180]

Wesley's efforts seem to have succeeded, at least on occasion. This is Wesley's account of Whitefield's effects in 1739 on the miners of Kingswood Hill, outside Bristol, where Wesley first learned "the techniques of mass evangelism" and where Whitefield had seen those tears streaking the coal-blackened faces. Wesley had returned to Kingswood after a year, finding the men drawn away from their popular culture of the streets.

> The scene is already changed. Kingswood does not now . . . resound with cursing and blasphemy. It is no more filled with drunkenness and uncleanness, and . . . idle diversions . . . wars and fightings, . . . clamour . . . wrath and envyings. Peace and love are there. Great numbers of the people are mild, gentle, and easy to be entreated . . . hardly is their "voice heard in the streets" or . . . their own wood, unless when they are at their usual evening diversion singing praise unto God.

An eyewitness described the submissive, supportive, pious, communal, behavior of "stout fellows" in a Yorkshire chapel, responding to a person "in distress" during a 1790s revival meeting.[181] The remarkable modification of raucous, riotous, appetitive, and brutal, public male culture even penetrated the sailor's world. "There was a set of fellows, called Methodists, on board the Victory, Lord Nelson's ship . . . They need to meet together to sign hymns and nobody dared molest them . . . They were allowed a mess by themselves; and never mixed with the other men."[182]

Under less patriotic circumstances, Methodist men had been associated with womanliness. Anti-Methodist prints characterized Methodist ministers as "unmanly." Whitefield's handkerchief was prominently featured. At the same time, from Methodism's early days, its ministers' very clear appeal to women was explained in those satiric prints as mutual sexual appetite, one Methodist ministers were also shown exploiting financially. One of the earliest, "Enthusiasm Displayed: or, The Moor-Fields Congregation" (1739) by George Bickham (1684–1769), shows Whitefield preaching while he stands literally on two women, who personify hypocrisy and deceit. He has attracted two more women, the most prominent of whom is young and scantily clad, and she is handing over a purseful of cash.[183] The same associations were made in the novels of Fielding and Smollett. They were preceded by a 1742 pamphlet in which an evil male protagonist was described joining the Methodists to reap "their alms and enjoy their women."[184] Presumably it was in response to such satire that in 1744 Wesley warned his preachers to "converse sparingly with women, particularly young women." Further evidence of Methodism's troublesome identification with women was Lord Littleton's dressing himself as a Methodist preacher for a 1769 masquerade and making a hit by "giving a very pathetic lecture to the ladies."[185]

It is not surprising, therefore, that Wesley asserted the manliness of his converts, although it was a reformed kind because of their expression of feeling and their opposition to what Smollett called the style of the "true-born Englishman."[186] Turning the point against his critics, one of Wesley's letters listed the damage that popular entertainments could do to young men, warning they could lead to "effeminacy."[187] Like other proponents of sensibility in men, Wesley made it clear that to bring men tearfully to Christ and to reform them was not to make them identifiable with women. He approved Gregory's *A Father's Legacy to His Daughters,* a book recommending that women cultivate "extreme sensibility," while warning that it could be deemed a "weakness" in men.[188] If those Methodist sailors sang hymns and did not curse, it was carefully recorded of them that "nobody dared molest them" and that in battle "they did their duty as well as any men." The battle was Trafalgar. Such males were well on the way to becoming the muscular Christian *paterfamilias* gracing "Victorian families."[189]

The Civilizing Process and British Commercial Capitalism

Eighteenth-century religion may well have contributed to the modification of the public manners of men. However, the godly's goals to reform popular culture met an existing appetite among "craftsmen and peasants" for "self-improvement." Both, it seems, were parts of a broader historical process. The word "process" is, of course, the historian's shorthand for the actions of many people over a long period of time. My previous use of the terms "manners" and "civilizing," as well as "process," have been intended to suggest a relationship between the history I am describing and the work of Norbert Elias. His model is amenable to the historian's disciplinary standards because it is so thoroughly in accord with eighteenth-century writers' own views of their society. Wollstonecraft's typical definition of "manners" as deep cultural characteristics, generated over time in the relations between family and society, is virtually the same as that of Elias. It could be said that eighteenth-century psychosociologists, from Mandeville to Smith and their followers, laid the groundwork for Elias and his more immediate predecessors.[190] Elias argues that the steadily increasing imposition of "standards of shame, delicacy, and self-control" over the period from the sixteenth through the nineteenth centuries resulted in adults being

> expected and their children taught to discipline all their appetites and desires, loves and hates, and the manifold gestures expressing them . . . eating . . . coughing, nose-blowing, scratching, breaking wind, urinating, defecating, undressing, sleeping, copulating, inflicting bodily pain on animals and [people].

The author of the 1727 *Dissertation on Drunkenness,* witnessing alehouse behavior, urged such changes, suggesting the means was "shame." The changes subsumed the split between what was permissible in public and what in private; sexuality (articulated more elaborately between men and women) was to be expressed in newly private and softened *sancta,* perhaps circumstances for repression or perhaps, one might point out, for greater freedom.[191] In medieval England "the most private acts," including sexual relations (more exposed because of the absence of room partitions), had been more subject to "community interest and control," penetrating this level of consciousness by way of confession.[192]

According to Elias, "manners,"—customs, behavior, and fashions—radiated outward from the court, penetrated the upper class, were imitated by the next class down, and so on, thereby motivating the higher "circles" to "further refinement" as a way of maintaining "distinction." Books of courtly behavior were crucial to this process, by definition depending on the spread of literacy. Their message was echoed and reechoed in still more popular literary forms, the genre of "apparition narratives," for example, described by McKeon. Typically, Defoe's contribution to them recommended "gentility," along with the qualities that would demonstrate its attainment, including sobriety, discernment, reasonableness, and piety, all of which he saw or advocated in an emergent middle class. Those statutes and proclamations, issued by Stuart and Hanoverian courts in order to foster the reformation of manners, also may be seen as conscious efforts to initiate the civilizing process. To promote "good manners" among Methodists and to draw them out of "the barbarous multitude," Wesley reprinted selections from an old etiquette book called *The Refined Courtier* (heir to Castiglione's work), advising against "such coarse practices as voiding in public, blowing one's nose vociferously, and breathing into another's face."[193] The eighteenth century offers copious examples of the concern to stimulate or to resist emulation of every kind of "manners" from above, from clothing to gestures, modes of display, to boarding school accomplishments. It can be inferred that eighteenth-century Britain (building on the revolution of the previous century) was a crucial chronological and geographical location for the process Elias describes because he emphasizes the importance of the bourgeoisie to it, and he symbolizes the significance of consumerism by emphasizing the dissemination of the fork.[194] Describing the "civilizing" of urban space, the subordination of educational and recreational initiatives to "moral censorship," as tantamount to "the Progress of Politeness," or the "embarrassment" caused "new sensibilities" by the brutal reality of slaughtering and preparing meat, recent historians of eighteenth-century England endorse Elias's view.[195]

The early origins of the civilizing process bore directly on the history of relations between men and women. Ninth- and tenth-century knights, spending most of their time among themselves, had shown "more or less contempt for women." Elias quotes one of them: "Go to your ornamented chambers lady, our business is war." There was "little talk of 'love'"—women "served to gratify [male] drives in their simplest form" and there was "scarcely a man with the patience to endure his wife." The men of this warrior society ruled their women with brute force. "Always the blow on the nose with the fist." We have seen other examples of men making their mark on this very visible and vulnerable center. The knight punching his wife on the nose till the blood flowed was "almost an established habit," to which the lady was to reply: "Most humble thanks. When it shall please you, you may do it again." Such dimensions of marriage were not limited to the elite. Bennett points out that wife beating in the Middle Ages, "as featured in both popular and sacred literature, was considered a normal part of marriage," whatever the extent to which "the banalities of everyday domestic life" transcended this norm. Differentiation from what would become an overlapping, archaic tradition began in the few large courts of the twelfth century "more closely attached to trade and money," requiring restraint for an "abundance of administrative and clerical" transactions. They were places where a greater variety of people—women and men—coexisted and that were able to support the minnesingers who promoted romance. Women played a crucial part in this process, imposing restraint, as we shall see, but Elias also insists on a relationship between its taking hold and men's transformation of economies, "the passage of goods from production to consumption, the growth of demands for unified mobile means of exchange."[196]

The criticism of public male street behavior described earlier; the attempts to repress the representation of violence on the stage, and the campaign against violent pastimes—bullbaiting, cockfighting, and the treatment of animals in general—may be seen as the further turning away from the medieval aggressiveness so vividly depicted by Elias. Under the Tudors, "the great bands of armed retainers were reduced," a development to be reflected, too, in the reduction of street gangs, some of them led by lords. Elias notes the state coming to monopolize physical violence: the concern over the state's replacement of the citizen-soldier by a paid soldiery (informed in Britain by old fears of a standing army) was a running theme of eighteenth-century political discourse, interpreted by the political outs as a sign of the effeminization of men. The English gentry resisted the creation of a professional police system because they associated the prospect with tyranny, the road to the curtailment of their "manly" independence.[197]

The history of the pressure against dueling, a facet of the eighteenth-century's campaign for the reformation of manners, also illustrates Elias's thesis. Collier denounced it in *Of Duelling* in 1698. From 1730, wearing a sword was largely replaced by the malacca cane as the badge of a gentleman, although dueling continued. Campaign and fashion signified a fundamental alteration in a powerful gender ideal, powerful because of its age and its association with the aristocracy. Dueling was opposed as "Gothic," the practice of "unlettered and feudal lords." It was "fierce, intractable and cruel."[198] Richardson campaigned against dueling in *Clarissa* and *Sir Charles Grandison,* although in the former, Colonel Morden's killing of Lovelace seems to illustrate the kind of ambivalence one also finds in other male critics of dueling, including Swift, Defoe, Fielding, Goldsmith, Hume, and Boswell. Dueling's latest historian, V. G. Kiernan, attributes the ambivalence to a "sense of manhood." In keeping with the tactic used by other reformers, Richardson showed in Sir Charles that reformed manners could be consistent with manliness. The same concern was expressed ironically by "Philautus," *The Pretty Gentleman: or, Softness of Manners Vindicated from the False Ridicule Exhibited under the Character of William Fribble, Esq.* (London, 1747).[199]

Late eighteenth-century sermons maintained evangelism's campaign against dueling, but, in the aftermath of a quarter century of warfare with France, the duel was revitalized, together with other expressions of Regency male appetites for "sport, horseflesh and women," and again such public violence was shared by lower-class males.[200] However, the French Revolution also had given a decisive push to the reputability of British evangelism. Antidueling associations were among the host of societies pushing the campaign for the reformation of manners onward into the nineteenth century. Upper-class men countered the "charge of effeminacy" not only by showing "pluck" in hunting but in "cold baths every morning" and "floggings in public schools." English gentlemen thus identified themselves with "nobility of the heart." Eventually disputes between them entered the courts to be resolved by money damages. The last recorded duel was fought in 1852. This story bore a clear relationship to alterations in "the face of battle" described by John Keegan. Feudal warriors had retained much of the ideal of "Homeric heroes," publicly proclaiming honor with the evidence of a trophy won in single combat which would "be concluded only by violent death—a death in which the victor exulted." At Waterloo, by contrast, death in battle was invested by gentlemen witnesses and even killers "with a tinge of Romantic regret, caught at goodness knows how many removes from Young Werther." Honor had become an "abstract ideal, a matter of comportment, of exposure to risk, of acceptance of death . . . of private satisfaction . . . at having fulfilled an unwritten code." Wellington's attribution of victory to the playing fields of Eton points to the successful implementation of the public school reforms advocated by Vicesimus Knox. This gentlemanly code, expressing "coolness and endurance, the pursuit of excellence and of intangible objectives for their own sake . . . learnt in game-playing," combined aspects of "feeling" with the "self-fashioning" now widely required by public male culture, a combination also discernible at Trafalgar.[201]

Elias's account of the gradual replacement of physical conflict in the relations between men by more "reserve and 'mutual consideration'" has been elaborated recently by other scholars intrigued by alterations in British manhood and their connections with individualism, with the operations of a commercial capitalism, and the associations of these phenomena with humanitarianism.[202] Elias suggested the importance of the Renaissance to the process he describes—disseminating new instruments, *The Courtier*, "the most representative book of the Renaissance," among them—for the "fashioning" of the individual. The freeing of the individual for transcendent self-expression is one climax of the civilizing process. McKeon has pointed to the "energy" emanating "from the autonomous figure of Castiglione's courtier himself," his "secular, present-centered, and self-authorized activity" and his "self-creative power."[203] Stephen Greenblatt sees the same Renaissance courtly culture as an important, proximate influence in the transformation of Englishmen. The Renaissance court had developed a new interest in the relationship between "the mask of persona" and some unchangeable identity beneath it. Castiglione's *Courtier* was urged "to bolster up his inherent worth with skill and cunning, and ensure that whenever he has to go where he is a stranger and unknown he is preceded by a good reputation" and that in turn he makes it "known" that "he is very highly regarded." This "fosters a certain unshakeable belief in a man's worth." In a cash economy such worth, a new version of honor, could be translated into "credit."[204]

Greenblatt describes the "intense individualism" of a group of talented and socially mobile males in sixteenth-century England, men who demonstrated "an increased self-consciousness about the fashioning of human identity as a manipulable, artful process." He terms it "self-fashioning." The word "fashion" came into "wide currency as a way of designating the forming of the self . . . quite literally, the imposition upon a person of physical form." The relationship between such consciousness and the possibilities manifested in literacy was a fundamental one, of which the campaign for the reformation of manners would be keenly aware. Self-fashioning "inevitably crosses the boundaries between the creation of literary characters, the shaping of one's own identity, the experience of being moulded by forces outside one's own control, the attempt to fashion other selves." And while Greenblatt concedes that cultural institutions—history—limit and shape the range open to self-fashioning, he also declares that self-fashioning expresses "the craving for freedom, and to let go of one's stubborn hold upon selfhood, even conceived as fiction, is to die."[205] Aspiring princes, courtiers, and those upper-class males closest to them socially, were perhaps the first and the most free to express the pleasures of self-fashioning. Rochester was emblematic of a court that reveled in the phenomenon. The earl of Shaftesbury, too, looking to classical precedents, found self-fashioning necessary and was influenced by *The Courtier;* indeed, his work was a how-to book for eighteenth-century men in this regard.[206]

Self-fashioning at first was very largely confined to the upper crust, permitting more popular expression only in the sharply demarcated reversals of Carnival masking; historian Burke suggests that the material deprivation of fixed, subsistence economies had an equivalent in "a kind of imaginative poverty,"[207] a phrase whose oversimplification is implicit and whose summary value is very useful. Referring to Greenblatt, Natalie Davis has suggested that the psychological values expressed by peasants in Carnival masking and in the self-fashioning of courtiers became more widely possible in the early modern period. The context for the increasing possibilities was the successful spread of Protestantism's aggrandizement of an individual's sense of private self, of the idea that one's "self" lay in one's own hands, to be shaped and presented publicly or not at will, in contrast to the enforcement of that hierarchy of limited and communal roles mediated by confession, a rite reaching deep into the individual's most private self. This, of course, is consistent with Tawney's brilliant demonstration of the "growth of individualism" in Protestant England between 1550 and 1640, suggesting the social penetration of self-fashioning along now more accessible routes. It is consistent, too, with Keith Wrightson's recent assessment of English society, 1580–1680, as one already "modern" in key respects, and "in the final analysis, based upon the individualistic pursuit of self-interest." Neither Rochester nor Shaftesbury can be seen detached from "the rise of capitalism" in England that was Tawney's subject. Like Tawney wishing to modify Weber, Campbell links Protestantism to consumerism along the lines suggested by Greenblatt and Davis—the capacity to take pleasure in one's own, private feelings. Tendencies toward self-fashioning and toward "autonomous hedonism" could be strengthened by popular efforts to emulate courtly manners, including those of "conspicuous consumption."[208]

The potentials here for the popularization of self-fashioning pointed to a later, much more democratic personification created by still more mobile men and mediated by the transatlantic personae of Benjamin Franklin, although rooted in the ancient tradition of "tall tales" and "lies" of travelers—stopping at inns—shaping the fantasies back of the earliest European expansion.[209] This archetypal figure registered the possibility of liberation from institutions and even from "the very ethos of community-based morality." Associated both with "merchant capitalism" and the transmutation of Puritan morality into mockery, the figure heralded "the facility with which ever new and unbounded identities could be put on and off, like masks, in explicit affirmation that all identities were masks, and that freedom grew therefore in the ability to present as many of them as possible."[210]

This freedom was associated with "the monied interest" arising amidst what Pocock points out was "a shattering collapse of civil authority" in mid seventeenth-century Britain—originating during the century before—where "pioneers of an entrepreneurial and market society" first appeared as "roving masterless men." They made their essential contacts in the elaborated culture of inn, alehouse, and tavern. The historian of the alehouse suggests it provided a stage for self-fashioning, as interpersonal transactions between its customers (and them and the alehouse keepers) were multiplied and extended over time and distance when separated from the medieval regulations and customs of market and churchyard. Conversely, men made it a nodal point in the economy they were transforming. The alehouse was, Clark concludes,

> quintessentially a neighbourhood theater in the widest sense, in which ordinary people could be actors and observers. Against the backdrop of its flickering fire men could gossip and rant, joke, laugh and posture, sublimate their miseries in drunkenness, applaud their own success in generosity and games. Their pots and tankards kept brimming by an explosive Mother Bunch or the serving wench . . . they could discover a further dimension of themselves and their lives.

It was the growing prosperity of skilled workers and tradesmen from the turn of the century that nurtured such individual discovery and, by the same token, "helped create a sense of group, if not class, awareness and identity." That exfoliating, more elaborately self-conscious identity was male.[211]

Apprehensively, Anthony Ascham called money "an invention onely for the more expedite permutation of things," facilitating "commerce" instead of "Community." Many men willingly hazarded themselves in furthering a market economy, freeing themselves, in McKeon's terms, "from the limitations imposed by traditional moral sanctions" and establishing market "equivalences between intrinsically disparate commodities," with the result that "the indulgence of imaginary wants appeared to produce not only more wants but also the means to their satisfaction." Donald Meyer has described the meanings of the "indefinitely transformative power" of money to the democratization of self-fashioning, in its "negotiable language of aspiration and salvation."[212] The speculator could be seen to constitute "a final, wonderful purification and parody of a Protestant logic—a man for whom all authorities had vanished and given to the limitless perpetuation of this vertiginous state . . . the last remnant of the relation of laymen to priest was purged." Eventually, in "a democratic capitalist society,"

> [l]and became money, ships, grain, wood, books, art, space, time, men themselves. Exchanges could be set up for translating the multifariousness of reality into a common language, enabling every man to venture, gamble, speculate, risk himself.

Meyer's speculators were heirs both to the credit making and wagering economic center of the alehouse and to the "Financial Revolution," which postrevolutionary Englishmen wrought in the 1690s, establishing the Bank of England and the Stock Exchange, "a system of public credit whereby individuals and companies could invest money in the stability of government and expect a return varying in proportion to the success of the government's operations."[213]

Commercial capitalists changed their own manners in fostering new modes of mass mannerliness among customers, both groups primed to change by appetite, by mobility, by religion, by successful rebellions and reactions, as well as by emulativeness and the other possibilities nurtured by alehouse culture. Pocock describes how the new mobile forms of property entailed the "construction of a new image of social personality," one "founded upon commerce: upon the exchange of forms of mobile property and upon modes of consciousness suited to a world of moving objects." In the view of contemporaries, this new image was brought about by the multiplying "encounters with things and persons"—including the cultural objectifications of print—evoking "passions and refining them into manners."[214] This new man wanted to be prepared for "an increasingly transactional universe of commerce and the arts . . . in which his relationships and interactions with other social beings, and with their products, became increasingly complex and various, modifying and developing aspects of his personality." According to Nicholas Barbon, writing in 1690, as man "aspires[,] his mind is elevated, his senses grow refined and more capable of delight. His desires are enlarged . . . for everything that is rare, qualify his senses, adorn his body and promote ease, pleasure, and pomp of life."[215]

These new roots of personality stood in contrast to those of "the farmer warrior" of the classical world, an image that continued to be idealized by eighteenth-century writers. However, "the resilient power of 'honor' to extend its tacit sway over the range of personality is lost" under the impact of the changes manifested by the Financial Revolution.[216] Langford's characterization of "the debasement of gentility"—the exchange of acquired for inherited quality—neatly invokes Greenblatt and McKeon: the significance of this "fundamental transformation" was "masked by the concern of those who counterfeited the currency of class to have it pass for sound coin." As McKeon suggests, this "loss" also held promise for the wider enjoyment of material pleasures. By 1748 a reporter on *The Present State of Great Britain* said that "the title of gentleman is commonly given to all that distinguish themselves from the common sort of people, by a genteel dress and carriage, good education, learning, or an independent station."[217]

The contrast with the old style of man put pressure on the new type to associate his development with "manners" in a redefinition of virtue: there was considerable apprehension that participants in the new economic world were inevitably "involved in dependence and corruption." The coming into existence of fully fledged commercial capitalism was greeted in some quarters not just with ambivalence but with "suspicion and alarm." This was true even of the Whigs who helped sponsor it and continued "to maintain public credit as well as the Hanoverian dynasty." The establishment's trumpeting of the need for public virtue and the reformation of manners marked its apprehensions over the triumph of "the monied interest." Despite their adherence to the Bank of England and the Stock Exchange, *The Tatler* and *The Spectator* presented moneymaking as ignoble. The ideology they embodied attempted to uphold "a single standard of ethical value—a standard embodied in the eighteenth-century conception of the landed patriotic gentleman-citizen." This standard claimed to be the same as that of the Greek and Roman republics, to which that gentleman-citizen had access by way of his privileged education. Yet *The Tatler* and *The Spectator* and their competitors also depended upon and fostered the new economic modes they seemed to denigrate. The same may be said of the novel which, McKeon believes, came into existence "in order to mediate" the reconceptualization of "virtue." Its origins lay with sixteenth- and seventeenth-century "histories of the individual."[218]

Pocock's phrase for the result of these changes (presumably including the internalization and mastery of ambivalence)—"an indefinite and perhaps infinite enrichment of personality"—stands in evident contrast to the "imaginative poverty" of the precapitalist, peasant personality of Burke's account. The transformation may be seen to correspond to the gradual replacement of subsistence, feast-or-famine psychology by a widening experience of daily pleasures, the transition from the brief ebullitions of Carnival role-playing to self-interested, longer-range psychology.[219]

Francesco Bartolozzi (1727–1815). *London Merchants in the Royal Exchange,* 1788. Engraving, after a drawing by J. Chapman, 15 × 21 in. Guildhall Library, Corporation of London.

Signs of the "mannerly" conduct necessary to business and credit included "courtesy." Such "a [p]resentation of self" was "a matter of economic survival," although the prospects of "unlimited acquisition and accumulation" also required a "transformation" in "the rules of civility, of politeness."[220] Larger ambitions and their implementation drew upon the mobilization of personal power and confidence in control over events, the expression of "sovereign" will and self-possession, including the mastery of a variety of roles. Andrew Marvell had seen that "commercial enterprise and Protestant ethics alike require[d] a systematic dependence on reputational credit and toleration of conscientious choice . . . a complex transformation in the way credit ha[d] traditionally been accorded and withheld." In Brewer's words, one "needed to be or at least to appear to be, a man" who kept up his "reputation" as reliably candid, affable, pious, fair, and generous "in order to carry on trade." Trade required the "presentation of self" and not necessarily self itself. In sum, the exponential growth of commercial capitalism worked hand-in-glove with the democratization of self-fashioning, albeit a cruder version than that enjoyed by Greenblatt's early exemplars.[221]

Mandeville, celebrant of commercial growth, illustrates its operation in the eighteenth-century market economy. He describes traders who, pretending "to more Honesty," were "Cunning Foxes," knowing that "those who have Money, get often more by being surly, than others by being obliging." This was one side of a transaction, the other the hopes of the customers who "imagine they can find more Sincerity in the sour Looks of a grave old Fellow, than there appears in the submissive Air and inviting Complacency of a Young Beginner." The coinage here—honesty, obligingness, sincerity, even naive submissiveness and complacency, and the play of the customer's imagination—expressed that softening of relations between men that Elias describes, qualities also advocated by eighteenth-century reformers of manners. On the grander scale of imperial interaction, Mandeville described the jockeying between an international trader in sugar and a "*West-India* Merchant," both pretending affability and candor, but with lines out to centers of international news and trade, including "Lloyds Coffee-House," each party calculating the rise and fall of sugar prices in order to profit at the expense of the other. All this "is called fair dealing." Mandeville wished his readers to face up to such transactions as the reality of trade in the context of ambivalence over the morality of a society now devoted to commerce.[222]

In broadening our understanding of how men transformed themselves during the early modern period, historians Borsay, Brewer, Clark, Earle, Haskell, Langford, and Thomas emphasize the interplay between individualism and cooperation in the behavior of self-fashioning capitalists. Shopkeepers, traders, and merchants bonded themselves into clubs and societies in order to escape their humiliating and economically constricting dependence for custom on aristocratic clientage. They turned instead to the possibilities of "a more broadly based and socially heterogeneous market." The aggregation of capital required men to cooperate on a large scale; growing "numbers of men . . . were involved in local business . . . [their] interest in international diplomacy, colonial war and politics generally was stimulated by the realization that they affected their business interests in different ways." Greater consciousness of "the underlying fragility of their economic position," a consciousness sponsored by the increasing time and interpersonal contacts at the alehouse, was one factor stimulating "craftsmen and small traders" to band together in clubs and societies.[223] Cooperation provided "protection against the vicissitudes of the open market," which the subversiveness of financial dealings at the alehouse had also helped to create. For very practical reasons, multiplying transactions required that "bonds of trust and confidence" be strengthened among men. They depended upon "regularity and punctuality based on some fairly strictly defined set of conventions." The larger "projectings" of international commerce and empire, the discovery of a "high time horizon," attached new meanings to the keeping of bargains and promises.[224]

Men further prepared themselves for wider horizons by assimilating print to their oral exchanges. From early in the eighteenth century, landlords supplied newspapers just as they had come to supply sports equipment. The alehouse was "improved" in other ways during the period 1660–1750 when it became the "public house."[225] The name was emblematic of its centrality to the expanding male sphere. Division into specialized rooms was evidence of improvement, as it was in the case of private houses, although "public houses" often had a large room where male organizations could meet. So, too, they were furnished with an increasing volume and range of chairs, tables, and a "profusion of types and sizes" of drinking vessels. There were "clocks, barometers, birdcages, mirrors, statues, Delft ware, prints . . . pictures," and even books. Sometimes the sports facilities showed similar elaboration, an alehouse in Milton, Kent, having built a nine-pin alley by 1732. A rising preoccupation with variety and fashion in what customers drank had been evident even prior to the Restoration, but variation was much more stimulated thereafter by "falling grain prices and the growth of larger, better-equipped breweries." Coming to London shortly before Cheyne, another Scot was dazzled by the "many strange kinds of drinks and liquors," including a huge range of flavored beers. The "lively demand for such drinks was a clear sign of the new willingness and ability of consumers to pay more for their liquor."[226]

As alehouses evolved into pubs they became more respectable, and alehouse keepers "appeared more substantial, more prosperous members of the community," even as they evinced "a more commercial approach to their business." Alehouses gained "broader social appeal." Or it could be said that the male culture they nourished became more respectable. The alehouse was ceasing to be "a focus for popular values conflicting with those of the elite . . . it was more a medium by which upper-class attitudes and fashions were being diffused down the social scale."[227] However, it had long been the wish of a wide social range of men gathering in alehouse culture to transform themselves, not merely to emulate the upper classes but to pursue their own economic and playful purposes. Among late seventeenth-century results was the creation of those large-scale, commercial breweries. Thereafter, large brewers joined reformers in the assault on disreputable alehouses, their intention to drive out of business those they could not "tie" to the retail of their beers. Here again, reformers' actions dovetailed with processes already under way. "By 1750 the alehouse problem was largely under control."[228]

Alehouse inventories included coffee-making equipment from the 1720s. In his *Journey through England and Scotland* (1722–3), John Macky remarked that some alehouses in Shrewsbury had begun calling themselves "coffee-houses" to give "a better air." In London there were about 20,000 coffeehouses by 1700.[229] The evolution of the alehouse into the pub overlapped with the rise of the coffeehouse as another growth center for the elaboration of public male culture. In the coffeehouse one could drink ale and liquor, along with coffee, cocoa, and even tea. A 1719 traveler recorded the conveniences of this increasingly popular setting for pleasure and self-improvement: "You have all manner of news there; you have a good fire . . . a dish of coffee; you meet your friends there for the transaction of business, and all for a penny." They have been called "The Penny University" because they provided the space for "clubs and discussion groups" central to the generating of politeness and commerce.[230]

Lloyd's coffeehouse became the institutional focus for the growth of insurance far beyond its precedents in the burial plans of medieval guilds. Thomas says of this growth after the 1680s that "nothing yields greater testimony to the new spirit of self-help." New forms of insurance were invented to help master the risks and horizons of economic growth (for example, "coverage of goods travelling over land by wagon or cart,") in addition to expanding "schemes designed to cushion sufferers from theft, fire, sickness or other disasters." Insurance was both "speculative business" and "one of the most basic sources of security for the English middle classes." The trend was expressed, too, in the proliferation of working-class friendly societies. There was "a great surge" in the establishment of friendly societies from the 1760s; by 1803 three-quarters of a million men belonged to nearly 10,000 such societies, headquartered in public houses. In addition to the formal protection they promised "the skilled man," they "buttressed his social self-confidence."[231]

During the eighteenth century, male-group profligacy, bibulousness, vandalism, and street marauding were formalized by clubs, eventually becoming more respectable leisure. After the Restoration, cricket had been transformed "from a folk game to a regulated, commercialized, and above all, fashionable pastime." From the 1690s landlords organized spectator sports in which heavy betting was crucial.[232] Later, pubs would begin catering to groups of men specializing in the regularized forms of the old male sports—horse racing, boxing, and wrestling. James Walvin has suggested these public male pastimes were to become less bloody and less cruel to animals. Men issuing out of taverns to participate in the "commercialized" and crowd politics symbolized by the Wilkitism of the 1760s represented a profound alteration from the earlier sallying forth for more inchoate mayhem. By the mid-eighteenth century, clubs of apprentices and artisans marked political anniversaries "by the breaking open of a hogshead of beer [rather] than by the breaking of heads. Feasting, entertainment, and present-giving replaced rapine and violence." The group of rakes, led by Sir Francis Dashwood from 1737 and known as the *Dilettanti,* over time called itself to a more serious and more sophisticated purpose. The group sponsored a scholarly study by two of its members, which resulted in *The Antiquities of Athens, Measured and Delineated by James Stuart and Nicholas Revett* in 1762, and from that date the group of erstwhile rakes "sent young artists to Rome, and . . . concerned themselves in the founding of the Royal Academy."[233]

In fact, such private cultural societies had been founded from the post-Restoration period; they were particularly interested in the pursuit of horticulture, which united fashionable interests in gardening and science, and which Defoe had picked out as a consumer fashion appealing to men. Early in the eighteenth century, meeting in taverns and coffeehouses, the elite established societies dabbling "in a whole range of . . . intellectual pursuits" for which they could call on itinerant lecturers. But increasingly the elite were joined in these pursuits by bourgeois and petit bourgeois groups of men. Another reason for the "upsurge in alehouse societies" created by "craftsmen and small traders" was to emulate "the fashionable practices of the well-to-do." New businesses specialized in "education for leisure," and some of them catered to "young ladies" as well as young gentlemen, eager to express "the most elegant and genteelest taste."[234]

By mid-century, businessmen had long recognized the value to them of cultivating refinement; it enhanced their reputation and their status. Their clubs and societies were established to encourage "mutual consideration," "mutual benevolence," and "friendly feeling" between men, generating what one club called "principles of Benevolence, Charity, and Humanity." According to Langford, most writers "were careful to make to clear that sentiment and hard business sense . . . readily went together." MacKenzie would point out in 1786 that the mental improvement required of such refinement of sensibility, "discernment . . . comparison of objects, distinction of causes" could "guide the speculation of the merchant, and . . . prompt the arguments of the lawyer."[235] This view would feed into a movement to further the spread of education endorsed by the Societies for the Reformation of Manners, tailoring it to the new circumstances of commerce and industry. Clubs and societies raised subscriptions for libraries and other "civic improvements" and "community charity." While Borsay characterizes that philanthropy as "an altruistic facade behind which to pursue self-centered ambition," it may be more accurate to see these as two among a variety of roles, both useful to the same end, or even enjoyed because of their variety. In dramatic contrast to the earlier male haunters of taverns, these men raised money to provide street lighting and night watchmen. The charity of male associations "acted as an evangelizing means of improving the social environment, making it a better place in which to trade, sell, borrow, and lend."[236]

All of this could be qualified by pointing out continuities from the earlier tavern-based male culture, "a retreat, as in earlier times, from the pressures of family life." Ritual drinking and, on occasion, ostentatious blasphemy, provide clues to an overlap with past associations, even if most male club rituals did not extend to the literal phallicism of the order of Beggars Bennison and the Whig Club, both of Edinburgh. (Public masturbation seems to have been the climax of the Beggars' initiation ceremony.) Brewer includes the Mohocks and a rake's club in the gamut of clubs he describes, and Wilkitism was nourished in this male tavern culture. That Wilkes was a famous rake and that his kind of masculinity was as central part of his appeal should remind us that these clubs identified themselves quite literally with masculinity, even though Wilkes also represented himself as a patriot citizen and was defended as a figure of virtue in distress. The "political nation" described by Brewer was composed of adult males.[237] There were "few distinctively female societies," and clubs were "almost by definition meant for men." While literature testifies to the existence of a few coffeehouses in resort towns where the sexes could meet and converse, by and large women were "excluded" from the social and political activities of coffeehouses and therefore "denied access to the most direct means of hearing and sharing news." As men elaborated their political and economic sphere, women continued to be excluded from it. Nothing would be more significant for political feminism than that democratic politics—manhood suffrage—was generated in these tavern associations. Here would be another very tangible expression of the limits of male refinement.[238]

Yet the call for manhood suffrage coincided with the renewal of the campaign against the alehouse in the last thirty years of the century. It expressed the ascendant power of evangelism, still focused on the public manners of men and capitalizing on the wishes of women, but now able to capitalize, too, on the social effects of industrialization and the fear of revolution in the 1790s. Increasing numbers of "petty" unlicensed alehouses were seen as conduits "between economic distress and social disorder." Along with the triumph of evangelism, strict "alehouse regulation became a cornerstone of local administrative policy." There was a sharp class dimension to this and later phases of the regulation of male alehouse culture, the magistracy allying itself with middle-class reformers. At the same time, however, "the new radical organizations . . . supported by many skilled workers from the 1790s . . . emphasized the need for sobriety." So new men continued to find their own reasons to reform their manners. While still bonding together in pubs, these men replaced "excess" with moderate drinking, their consumption moralized as it was in other cases where women's wishes coincided with men's.[239]

The ways in which self-reformed capitalists, looking "to maximize the availability of street space," had transformed the visible "social environment" of British towns between 1660 and 1770 evidently benefited consumers. With the extension of the market, retailing had been separated from manufacturing. Early shops had been "ramshackle . . . , little more than stalls or sheds encroaching on to the pavement in the front of houses." But by the end of the seventeenth century, Earle points out, shops were fully enclosed, "with glazed windows through which the prospective customer could admire the choicer goods." Throughout the country and in an incremental process of individual decisions by a wide social range of men, sustaining a coherent, cross-generational vision, civic leaders combined subscription with the exercise of political will to make streets, squares, and promenades, marked by a host of new public and private buildings in classical style, "islands of ordered elegance amidst a sea of vernacular idiosyncrasy." Straighter, broader, and paved streets in towns became essential for the increase of traffic pulsating along those national arteries. Open gutters were replaced "with less obtrusive drainage systems." Preston's Guild Orders of 1662 required all inhabitants to scrape the dirt in front of their houses and shops into the channel built for that purpose; and also to "carry away that dung or dirt into their backsides . . . out of the street." Commercial success was signified by an "invasion" of dirt, especially the sediments of industrial smoke and the excrement of draught animals and all of the other animals driven to market. We can note, too, that the processing of serge required soaking in urine, the result dried and stretched in the open air. The rapidly growing permanent and visiting populations added to excremental production. From the 1670s town authorities showed a remarkable inventiveness in "highway sanitation."[240]

Borsay also describes significant improvements in streetlighting from the 1680s to the 1730s, where the key innovation was "oil burning lamps, harnessed to a glass or reflector." The rebuilders constructed public parades or promenades and commercial pleasure gardens. Just as the streets were paved and kept clean for vehicular and pedestrian traffic, so, too, walks and gardens were "laid with gravel or paved with stone and brick" to "safeguard the footwear of strollers from mud and dirt" and they were sheltered from other natural and social intrusions by the planting of lines of trees.[241]

Similarly, from 1700, squares and circuses were made so orderly and civil they were "in effect, open-air rooms." Borsay's language in describing the purpose and results of this urban renaissance points to its manifestation of the psychology of self-fashioning. Ambitious men upgraded their town's "image," the new fashion for sash windows closing on the same plane as the now uniform facades; "elegant deception" and "cosmetic treatment" presented the appearance of "order and balance," excluding "any view of their rear." Quite clearly there was a relationship between this and the politeness seen to be inherited from Renaissance manners and the Augustan imagery of eighteenth-century politics. As we shall see, courteous self-discipline in men was seen to be enhanced by the presence and mannerliness of women; these classically proportioned, open-air rooms were designed for "socializing" and mutual display among both sexes.[242]

The distance between these architectural expressions of aspiration and prosperity, on the one side, and the residential and industrial places inhabited by the masses, on the other, was consciously "accentuated." If Bath's and Tonbridge's arbiter of manners, Beau Nash, wished to "civilize the rural gentry and rescue them from the uncouthness of rural living," his architectural match, John Wood, wrote that the square "ought to be separated from the ground common to men and beasts, and even to mankind in general, if decency and good order are to be maintained." Beasts and common men bore the dirt and smells from which the polite wished to raise themselves. Furthermore, "the sea of vernacular idiosyncrasy" expressed itself in other ways, and inevitably streets and other public places remained susceptible to intrusion from the impolite.[243] There were servants, tradesmen, and those who came just to "ogle" the range of fashionable novelties, let alone those who had more "nefarious" profiting in mind. If fashionability required being carried (for the reason Cheyne suggested or for the more plausible ones the historian could invoke), then muscular and "unruly" chairmen were equally required to be present in the new streets, two per chair. Wood described them as "turbulent," ready to defend themselves with their poles against the swords of gentlemen "usually" wishing to teach them manners; thereupon, "the danger of murder frighted the ladies to such a degree, that the public assemblies for diversion seldom ended without the utmost confusion."[244]

Reformers of manners recorded riotous men's "scouring" of the streets—the attacking of the increasing number of public marks of order and civility, merchant signs and streetlamps, for example, which scowrers, rakes, and others either blackened or smashed. On his grand tour in 1689 Shaftesbury had remarked "how well the streets [were] lighted at night" in Vienna, in contrast to London and its "nocturnal dangers." The 1693 rake recorded other "low Mechanic actions" of street disorder, identifying with "ye Court Hector" and wishing to distinguish his own feats from those of less elevated libertines, who indulged in "Frightening of Cullies, and Bombasting Whores / Wringing off Knockers, from Posts and Doors / Rubbing out Milk-Maids and some other Scores." The erasing of tallies for milk orders and other commercial reckonings amplified the possibilities for reminding women who had to work in the streets of their vulnerability, adding the confusing of milkmaids to the buttering of higgling women.[245]

Milk scores and door knockers shared with windows the larger demarcation between street and interior. Rochester described rakes smashing windows in assaulting women at home, even while their "Lords" were there. As permanent shops challenged the clutter of stalls in the street, weekly markets, and replaced fairs (also under attack by reformers of manners from early in the seventeenth century), the shop window became a crucial delineation for the new mercantile order and for the transmission of consumerism. The proverbial "bull in a china shop" perfectly represents the conflict between the old culture and the new. The same symbolic convergence was exhibited by a group of rakes taking a blind horse into a china shop, the kind of incident familiar enough for *The Spectator* to compare clumsy lady customers of a "top china woman about town" to a club of rakes "tumbling over my ware."[246]

The continued coexistence of old and new public spaces, all connected to each other, from narrow streets to the squares, parks, and new residential sections meant the shocking juxtaposition of young males who were drunk and prone to violence with the newly fashionable assemblies of the polite of both sexes wishing to display themselves in public. It could be said that fashionably accomplished and dressed women, en route to shops or concerts, visiting friends for tea, or promenading for display, were still more essentially the successful indicators of politeness and commerce than streetlamps. In 1764, "ladies of quality" in Vauxhall Gardens were repeatedly insulted during disorders by rampaging "bucks." A "place like Vauxhall with the dark sequestered walk, its wide spaces, and its universal popularity, was altogether at the mercy of these men of fashion." Their social inferiors showed the same interest in fashionable display and in turning the new circumstances to their own interest. The 1693 rake had complained that "the Park" was no longer attractive to "ladies" because it had become "the Rendezvous" of the "Mob," where "Footmen, with the Greasie Cook-Maids walk / And Low / priz'd Cracks in Masks, with Cullies talk." The key point, though, was that no longer was the public appearance of women confined to workers; startlingly frequent now was the entry of women of all conditions—above all, the womenfolk of the male elites building the towns—intent on shopping and otherwise patronizing the new sources of pleasure.[247]

And rakish males of all ranks were seen as threats to this dramatic feature of British life. This has been illustrated already, but one may add to the attacks in Vauxhall Gardens *The Connoisseur*'s 1755 variation of John Wood's 1740s wish to separate the polite from men and beasts. Its subject was "Men about Town"—rakes—and it defined their behavior as "whatever is in violation of all decency and order." The internalization of such order and its at least partial replacement of previous street strife was symbolized by the fact that, by 1737, "pedestrians normally kept to the right, and there were no more quarrels of punctilio about keeping to the wall side of the pavement." That form of "punctilio had expressed the more archaic code of male manners."[248]

The countryside was also a place where men displayed their transformation of manners. The boorish squire of Restoration plays, talking with a provincial accent and getting drunk, became a countertype to the new style of manhood, defining it and marking its advance.[249] Sir Roger de Coverley, who appeared throughout *The Spectator,* was an early prose version.[250] Sir Roger permitted *The Spectator* to express sharp criticism of the excesses of consumerism, but he was represented as an anachronism in his style of manhood, in contrast to the new style of reformed and tasteful manners advocated by *The Spectator* and by Shaftesbury. One of their successors was Lord Chesterfield who, writing from the city, characterized fox hunting and horse racing as rustic and old-fashioned. He opposed the "sottish drinking, indiscriminate gluttony, driving coaches, [and] rustic sports such as fox-chases and horse-chases," preferring "the honest and industrious professions."[251] Yet hunting itself was on the verge of being subjected to the civilizing process in the same way that alehouses were. Formal hunting had been a royal and aristocratic preserve; its object, pursued with bows and arrows, was the deer. The decline of the deer because of the loss of its habitat to commercial farming signified the social and political changes that accompanied its replacement by the fox, previously the verminous prey of the lower classes. Formal, leisure-hunting began to be organized as a regular and public activity. The new form required a new hound and new kinds of horses and horsemanship, including jumping over fences, the latter the marks of the accelerating rate of enclosure. "Vast amounts of experimental breeding" of hounds and horses coincided with the breeding of farm animals for commercial purposes, creating a science.[252] By 1771, fox hunting had been placed "firmly in the world of fashion," requiring particular forms of figure as well as of dress because men had to be slim enough for a horse to carry them over hedges. Chesterfield's scorn was countered by such famous fox-hunting fashion leaders as the third duke of Rutland and Paul Bedford, who were accomplished connoisseurs in art. Hunting could show the same trend in manners as the rakes' clubs in town.[253]

Hunting became a national sport rather than a local one, rich men traveling many miles to participate. No longer was it the exclusive privilege of the aristocracy. Eventually, new industrialists would sink their profits into landed estates and into the hunt, joining those country gentlemen who also spent their high profits from commercial farming on this country fashion. They emulated the uppermost reaches of the landed gentry who used the new form of the hunt as a source of patronage and male bonding in politics.[254] During the last third of the century farmers and local tradesmen banded together in subscription clubs, as their social equivalents did in the city, although their purpose was to pay for horses, hounds, servants, and the farmers' claims and the other fees fox hunting entailed. Like the petty capitalist clubs meeting in taverns in London and other towns, they dined, drank from communal punchbowls, and sang songs, all demonstrating their adherence to this new fashion. The "Hunt Club" became the "hub of social life" in the country, and we can be sure it established the same connections and honed "modern" interpersonal skills.[255]

Here, too, the wishes and presence of women played a part, even though upper-class women's presence in the saddle remained exceptional, and hunting and horse racing (and related interests) remained expressions of male consumer appetites. A painter of horses at Newmarket, Ben Marshall (1767–1835), observed, "I discover that many a man will pay me fifty guineas for painting a horse who thinks ten guineas too much for painting his wife." Conversely, criticism of these horsey male activities was a characteristic of women's fiction. The different perspectives could be internalized. The verses George Stubbs attached to a series of four paintings, "Two Gentlemen Going a Shooting" (1767–70), express ambivalence to hunting, referring to "the murderous gun" and, in the last verse, attributing opposition to the "slaughter" to a principle symbolized as female.

> Calm Eve's approach here bids the slaughter cease
> And gives the winged Tribes to rest in peace
> Health thus preserved coarse viands will regale
> Each night whilst they rehearse the oft told tale.

This Eve coexisted with a growing tendency to personify sensibility as a female goddess, one manifestation of which held a dying bird in its hand.[256]

Nonetheless, if "[h]orses and hounds occupied a place in many a gentleman's affections that was scarcely less important than that of his wife and family," this emblematic gentleman became as answerable to his wife's wishes as Barbauld's Mr. Homelove had been.[257] The towns on which the reformed and fashionable sports of hunting and horse racing centered created the same "social infrastructure" of public pleasures and "consumer facilities" as the spa towns. The excluded wife of Ben Marshall's horse-loving patron was able to enjoy the consumer pleasures of Newmarket, made as fashionable as Bath by royal and aristocratic favor. Borsay presents this story in fascinating detail, too, describing Leicester's hunt ball, for example, and the assembly rooms at York during race week, wherein were held daily concerts and recitals and heterosocial assemblies every evening. There, during the 1736 race week, Mrs. Wilson sold "tea, coffee, chocolate, orange chips, queen-cakes, gloves, and packs of cards." Or in 1725, at the lesser race week in Beccles, a jeweler from Bury St. Edmunds sold "all sorts of silverware of the newest fashion, and china, and Tunbridge ware." While the occasion for this retailing explains Wedgewood's depiction of hunting scenes and animals on his china, presumably appealing to the sex most directly enjoying those pleasures, it is apparent that he, the Bury jeweler, Mrs. Wilson, the builders of spa- and hunt-towns' social infrastructure, and of the urban renaissance as a whole, wished for and assumed the presence of women in redesigned public environments.[258]

Changed Environments and the New World of Parents and Children

Pocock's references to the personality-changing effects of "objects," "products," and "things" endorse Elias's view that objects of consumption, as well as the requirements of trade and production, played a very significant part in the civilizing process. The court of William and Mary threw its authority behind the reformation of manners, and it introduced consumer fashions, in the taste for china and calicoes, fine houses and gardens. Many of them were displayed and stored at home. Wedgwood developed Mary's precedent, deliberately drawing the highest of social circles into his showrooms and in other ways engineering the identification of the English and other European courts with his long line of fine china products (including "Queensware").[259]

Hence another vital site for the most affordable alteration of male manners was the private house. (Here it should be noted that the new architectural taste reached craftsmen by way of cheaper pattern books: in the case of domestic architecture, the influence was Dutch.) The improvement in the material culture of domestic space expressed the profiting of "the yeoman class" from "the commercialization of agriculture," as well as other "changing patterns of production," responding to the key factor of "home demand."[260] The result of the absorption of consumer goods into the home was that men began to find there more of the comforts they previously had found in the public house. What Golby and Purdue conclude of nineteenth-century male culture became true of sections of the male population during the previous century. Male culture was, "to some extent, tamed by a private and domestic culture when rises in real wages enabled home and family life to become more of a centre and focus for leisure life." Such a life was associated with the internalization of "respectability." At the same time, it was the "impoverishment of many labouring families" at the end of the century that led many to switch from beer to the cheaper tea. By then, tea drinking was strongly identified with home.[261]

The rate and extent to which consumer goods penetrated the homes of all classes, including the laboring poor, was subject to great regional and chronological fluctuations, but the widespread aspiration for "respectability" and "gentility" among all classes seems irrefutable. Recording these and other meanings of consumerism to women (the subject of Chap. 4), Mandeville noted the recurrence of two "comprehensive little adjectives," "neat and clean," "especially in the Dialect of some Ladies." They signified the absorption of consumerism into domestic space.[262] "Very ordinary households were affected by the characteristic combination of self-conscious taste working with money." Even people with very little money showed their preference for new consumer goods. Shammas concludes her study of the early modern period: "Paradoxically, the individual who drank tea in a teacup, wore a printed cotton gown, and put linen on the bed could be the same person who ingested too few calories to work all day and lived in a one-room house." The change in "the physical surroundings of the middle-class family . . . was immense." Carpets laid on improved wooden flooring replaced cheap boards, and plaster was covered with wainscoting. Gradually, and in the middle class first, housewives replaced the hours saved from the chores of clothmaking and tending livestock under inevitably dirty farm conditions with frequent, regular housecleaning. People painted and papered their better-lit and heated rooms into which domestic space was increasingly divided, therein creating orderly spaces to display as well as store their chinaware, books (purchased or borrowed from new libraries), their children's toys, and their fashionable clothing in walnut or mahogany furniture, contrasting with former cheap oak. Here, behind hardwood "doors embellished with brass locks," they dressed themselves, read, and wrote letters in newly private "closets," sitting on more comfortable chairs, activities and spaces historians see as the generators of individualism.[263] Self-conception could be literalized and more carefully shaped in reference to mirrors, "both numerous and elegant," objects entirely absent from peasant households. These changes are at the heart of what Langford defines as "the progress of politeness," from everyday routine to the meaning of possession, to taste, the timing and mode of dining, and all of the connotations of "marriage."[264]

Along with the proclivity for neatness and cleanness, for privacy, for greater individual self-expression and self-control went a new material culture for alterations in adult excretion and the toilet training of children. Again, the court had led the way, the first water closets, designed by Sir John Harington, being installed at the Queen's Palace in Richmond in 1596. Earthenware jerries were first made in the seventeenth century, nicely timed to coincide with the proliferation of "the Protestant ethic" and to herald the cleaning of excrement from straighter streets bordered to the "backsides" of houses and streets that were now shielded. Among the finer china items to be mass marketed in the eighteenth century were sinks and chamber pots. By mid-century the latter were being made of a fine glazed white ware, "durable, impervious, non-corrodable" and had "a smooth surface" which now could easily be cleaned and therefore "shown." It was in 1754 that "Mr. Sadler of Liverpool" first applied the decoration of transfer-print patterns to chamber pots. The upper crust applied the family crest to please the nether eye. In short, at the same time that the fork, that "embodiment of a specific standard of emotions and a specific level of revulsion" was mass marketed for the delectation of one end of the alimentary canal, an instrument embodying the same standard and level was mass marketed in tasteful form for the other. Inspired by these conditions in 1778, Joseph Bramah patented the first "Valve Closet" that maintained "a water seal to prevent cesspool smells from entering the room," although the mass adoption of water closets had to await the nineteenth-century distribution of piped water, an improvement initiated during the "urban renaissance." Recognizing this prospect would require more water-pumping engines, James Watt wrote in 1796 that "[p]eople now have such a rage for washing their b-ms," his euphemism illustrating a relationship between reforming linguistic and anal manners, both linked to profit and progress. Finally, "pot cupboards" for the proper domestic concealment and revelation of these fine new china chamber pots were also made fashionable, being cataloged by Hepplewhite's, together with other substantial and tasteful furnishings for toiletry, including bidets.[265]

Consumption was united with its complementary function. The emblematic Cheyne had concerned himself with both, and with giving them moral values. Now consumers could pursue the ever-receding chimera of purging themselves of the filth Mandeville pointed out was the sign of vital economic life. The Freudian will have noted the possibilities here for the democratic exercise of Campbell's "autonomous hedonism" and Haskell's "sovereign will." If porcelain was the preserve of the aristocratic bottom, certainly fine-glazed china was in the reach of an increasing public, albeit a private one. What could such possibilities in style and will mean for women? For each gender in toilet training? Whatever its nature, it was only a specific part of general and pervasive historical circumstances.[266]

Given the salience of an altered domesticity within the civilizing process, one must raise the issue of parents' actions in it, gentler, more ambitious, and self-fashioning fathers, and increasingly literate mothers, recognizing the potentials to fashion selves. Central to Elias's explanation of "the civilizing process"—heavily influenced by Freud—was a new style of childrearing.[267] Becoming more "civilized" was the outcome of an inseparable, spiraling dialectic between nature and nurture. The "pressure and coercion" of individual parents on children was "allied to the pressure and example of the whole surrounding world," including the cleaned and neatened environments. Changes in childrearing behavior are implicit in the history of the changes in adult behavior sponsoring England's commercial and consumer capitalism. The market reached down into "the depths of personal psychology" to modify "character," in turn meeting human appetites for pleasure and the exploration of "indefinite" possibilities enriching personality.[268]

Ariès's notion (in *Centuries of Childhood*) that the idea of childhood was "invented" from the seventeenth through the nineteenth centuries is dubious.[269] Nonetheless, inspired by Ariès, historians have endorsed the idea of a significant change in childrearing in the eighteenth century, linking it to the spread of the ideas of Locke and, later, Rousseau, whose views were popularized by fiction. By the mid-eighteenth century, an "older patriarchal family authority was giving way to a new parental ideal characterized by a more affectionate and equalitarian relationship with children." Indeed, Wrightson argues persuasively that such a tendency, accompanied by a parallel one in the marital relationship, was already evident in the seventeenth century. Parents came to embrace a more "humane" form of childrearing, including breastfeeding, the value of which was advanced by doctors and by fashion. This newer ideal, indeed, an ideology, can be seen in a great range of religious, political, and literary evidence: sermons, speeches, prints, poems, plays, and pedagogical works as well as novels.[270]

Parents' greater literacy, that primary mode for self-fashioning, was echoed by their children's, as commercial booksellers, freeing themselves from clientage, published and priced reading materials to reach all but "the very poorest families of unskilled labourers." A Lancashire yeoman, Richard Latham, spent hard-earned shillings in the 1730s on his children's schooling and books, including a "child's guide" in 1738. Booksellers published a vast quantity of literature to teach children to read and to entertain them. Reformers of manners joined their effort to these processes, struggling to control the shaping of selves. Reading was taught at home, in charity schools and in the private, commercial schools and academies which were to become ubiquitous between 1700 and 1770.[271] We can note that in all of these developments, home teaching, the commercialization of schools, and the publication of children's literature, women were increasingly prominent.[272] Parents also exposed children to the "marvels and curiosities" of exhibitions and museums, augmented by an "outburst" of leisure travel if they could afford it, which literally raised "the horizon." Later in the century, these possibilities coincided with children's exposure to a world being changed by "mechanical ingenuity, electricity, and science in general."[273]

In sum, childrearing was changed to fit children to the new middle-class world of adults being brought into being. The translation of childrearing ideas into material terms was tantamount to a "new world of children." On the one hand, this world incorporated how children were treated by parents: handled, spoken to, dressed, fed, cleaned, placed in rooms, and what proportions of mother/father/

servant/sibling made up a child's immediate personal environment; and on the other, it incorporated what the child found inscribed in these adults' features, skins, smells, gestures, and dress; together with the coming into being of the mass-produced items and experiences with which children's own bodies and activities could be invested: "clothes, pets, toys, education, sports, music, and art." Some eighteenth-century children became "luxury objects upon which their mothers and fathers were willing to spend larger and larger sums of money." Many children must have been luxuriating subjects too, imbibing "indulgence" from their parents as many eighteenth-century observers warned. In any case, and to state the obvious: the values mothers and fathers injected into their childrearing were those about which they themselves felt most keenly in their new world.[274]

THREE

The Question of Effeminacy

Male writers recognized the large changes commercial capitalism was bringing about in Britain and tended increasingly to advocate them as signs of the progress of civilization. Yet they had profound doubts, concerned as they were with the effects on hierarchy should everyone freely pursue worldly pleasure. A persistent and fundamental concern was the meaning of changed manners for manhood, traditionally bound up with classical and warrior ideals. The "degeneracy" to which the rise of the "monied interest" and the decline of the citizen-soldier was believed to lead had a gender-specific dimension, expressed in the widespread use of the term, "effeminacy." The 1675 anti-Stoical *Man without Passion* asked rhetorically, "Must we be guilty of effeminacy to perform Acts of Generosity? . . . can we not relieve those that are in misery, unless we mingle our Sighs and their Sobs and Groans?"[1] The question persisted while men attempted to formulate new meanings for themselves. Pocock has demonstrated that, at first, economic man was characterized by doubters as "a feminised, even an effeminate being" because, to let loose fantasies and appetites—associated with such "female goddesses of disorder as Fortune, Luxury, and Credit"—that is, to pursue passions and to be victimized by them, was traditionally seen as female. The "new speculative image of economic man was opposed to the essentially paternal and Roman figure of the citizen patriot." Those who warned Englishmen that effeminacy was the inevitable effect of luxury had the most powerful of all precedents in mind, the history of the degeneracy of Rome, from virtuous republic to luxurious empire.[2] Writers who recorded the changes in this way were, by definition, more "sedentary" in Cheyne's word than other men, more susceptible to ambivalence over the manliness of their lives, which were in sharp contrast to those led by classical farmer-warriors; but they were also in contrast with the lives of those entrepreneurs, implementing what writers saw as progress, men who could easily be represented as warriors, "ransacking the globe" to the outreaches of empire, where "social control" was "looser," often literally warring on native peoples, for the luxury that writers at home indulged. Increasingly, too, male writers found themselves competing with women.[3]

Shaftesbury

Historians of the rise of sensibility have read the third earl of Shaftesbury (1671–1713) as the originator and celebrant of the existence of an innate "moral sense" in human psychology, an intuitive, essentially emotional response, distinguishing good from evil and oriented toward social affection. For this reason Shaftesbury is called "the father of sentimental ethics" and "the earliest synthesizer of an ethic grounded in the ultimate goodness of men."[4] Shaftesbury's intellectual predecessors included the Cambridge Platonists. The term "moral sense" may have been originated by Henry More, the Cambridge Platonist who influenced Wesley toward the anti-Augustinianism Shaftesbury shared.[5] In Shaftesbury's words, the sense of right and wrong was "a first principle" "in our constitution," "implanted in our heart."

> No sooner are actions viewed, no sooner the human affections and passions discerned (and they are most of them as soon discerned as felt) than straight an inward eye distinguishes, and sees the fair and shapely, the amiable and admirable, apart from the deformed, the foul, the odious, or the despicable.[6]

While such a response was natural, it was not sufficient to the morality and taste it was Shaftesbury's aim to teach: " 'tis not instantly we acquire the sense by which [graces and perfections] are discoverable. Labour and pains are required, and time to cultivate a natural genius." Here, too, Shaftesbury echoed Anglican thought, Barrow's for example.[7]

It also can be argued that Shaftesbury's adult belief in a "moral sense" was the transmutation of the high evaluation of good nature he had learned in his childhood from Locke. Locke was the employee and close collaborator of the first earl of Shaftesbury.[8] Because of his son's degenerative illness, this Shaftesbury delegated to Locke the task of rearing his grandson, and Locke was thus enabled to implement the "permissive" childrearing precepts that followed logically from his sensational psychology.[9] The rejection of innate ideas and the creation of self from the environment meant that if one shaped the total environment of a child, one might shape the adult. Historians have suggested that Locke's views of childrearing, transmitted down the social pyramid, helped to effect a revolution in family dynamics and, therefore, in social, religious, and political history, the latter in the antityrannical thinking of Locke's political heirs.[10]

As a child Shaftesbury experienced the effects of the following advice, intended to make good nature correspond with fashionable manners:

> Be sure to keep up in him the principles of good-nature and kindness, and encourage them as much as you can, by credit, commendation, and other rewards that accompany that state: and when they have taken root in his mind, and settled there by practice, the ornaments of conversation and the outside of fashionable manners, will come of themselves.[11]

Presumably Locke, or rather Elizabeth Birch, Locke's delegate in rearing Shaftesbury, also warned the boy against the cruel treatment of "very young birds, butterflies and such other poor things." "For the custom of tormenting and killing of beasts will by degrees harden their minds toward men."[12] As an adult Shaftesbury combined this view with his criticism of Hobbesian psychology. Declaring "the peculiar joy and pleasure," the "delight" that "many tyrants and barbarous nations have" in "beholding torments and in viewing distress, calamity, blood, massacre and destruction," to be "inhuman" and the opposite of "civility," Shaftesbury suggested that such pleasure-in-distress was the sign of social regression. It is the characteristic of "tempers as have thrown off . . . a just reverence for mankind" and the natural tendency, which otherwise works against "the growth of harshness and brutality."[13]

In the same work, *Characteristics of Men, Manners, Opinions, Times* (1711)—the compendium of all of his writings—Shaftesbury was "very careful to stick closely to the psychological principles outlined in Locke's *Essay*."[14] Shaftesbury's assumption of sensationalist psychology is everywhere apparent in his use of such terms as "sensation," "tender senses," "susceptibility," and "delicacy of sensation," all of which assumed the mediation of the nervous system in consciousness and "pre" consciousness, whatever Shaftesbury adds in the way of a "moral sense."[15] At the same time, Shaftesbury hardly ever uses the term "nerve" at all, reflecting his antipathy to "physiologists and searchers of modes and substances . . . enriched with science above other men," including among them Hobbes. The absence is parallel to Locke's demurral on the same score in his *Essay on Human Understanding*. Still, both authors' views could easily be read to have elevated and popularized the significance of the nervous system.[16]

But Shaftesbury rebelled against Locke, whom he called his "foster-father."[17] Shaftesbury saw his "times" endangered by the "relativity of all morality" and the dizzying prospects potentiated by Lockean psychology.[18] In his late twenties Shaftesbury construed Lockean sensationalism as a metaphor for personal vulnerability. Shaftesbury wrote to himself:

> Thou hast engag'd, still sallyed out, & liv'd abroad, still prostituted thy self & committed thy Mind to Chance & the next comer, so as to be Treated at pleasure by every-one, to receive impressions from every thing & Machine-like to be mov'd & wrought upon, wound up, & governed exteriorly, as if there were nothing that rul'd within, or had the least control.[19]

It was this possible identification of sensational psychology with receptivity, susceptibility, passivity, and vulnerability that one finds absorbed and regenerated in its becoming a characteristic of the culture of sensibility. Significantly in this connection Shaftesbury's metaphor is one of female sexual vulnerability. Countering these strong and persistent tendencies to paranoia and to isolation from the world of action, Shaftesbury discovered something "that rul'd within," a self asserted against his charismatic tutor. Among Shaftesbury's resources for such an assertion was the "political heritage" of his grandfather, a given of Shaftesbury's very name and being. He had a "burning desire to vindicate his grandfather," an aristocrat who had died, banished, in political disgrace.[20] His political views, those of the arch-Whig Commonwealthmen, were his grandfather's, looking backward to some simpler, golden age of parliamentary "freedom," one utterly dominated by the small clique of landowning aristocrats intent on maintaining their inheritance of blood.[21] Shaftesbury made sure in one of his last acts that the Ashley-Cooper coat of arms was imprinted over the preface of his revised *Characteristics* (1714), his summa of what it was to be a gentleman—practitioner of "virtue," assuming the existence of innate—that is, heritable—ideas.[22]

Of course there was more to it, but we cannot ignore such a value for inherited selfhood when considering Lord Shaftesbury's chief accusation against the ideas of commoner Locke:

> *Virtue,* according to Mr. Lock, "has no other Measure Law or Rule, than *Fashion & Custome,* Morality Justice Equity, depend only as *Law Will* and God indeed is a perfect *free Agent* in his sense; that is, *free to any thing* however ill, for if he wills it, it will be made Good; Virtue may be Vice, & Vice Vertue in its turn, if he pleases. Thus neither *Right* or *Wrong, Virtue* or *Vice,*

> are any thing in themselves; nor is there any trace or Idea of em *naturally imprinted* on human Minds.[23]

Shaftesbury's apprehensions of the social dangers posed to the moral order led him to support the established church "as a hindrance to fanaticism and social disorder."[24] Opposing Locke, Shaftesbury necessarily wrote of a generic human nature. This would be crucial because it would allow his readers to interpret his idea of "moral sense" as generally applicable, even though Shaftesbury had been thinking of himself and his intellectual and class peers, taking "Society" for "society." He held that "only the very few who through intensive reading of the ancients have come to love virtue for her own sake may not need religion." Heterodox himself, Shaftesbury admired Cambridge Platonist Whichcote as a preacher of Stoic Christianity to people like Shaftesbury's servants, his tenant farmers, and "the great mass of mankind." At the same time, Shaftesbury reserved the right of aristocrats and intellectuals to use wit and take pleasure in the exposure of false systems of thought; because he repudiated the educated gentleman's "dependence upon the revealed will of God," and subjected it to the mockery that outraged serious reformers, he was quickly attacked "as the chief enemy of the traditional doctrine of retribution."[25]

Shaftesbury further bound the anxieties raised by Lockean potentials by suggesting that innate human goodness was part of an entirely harmonious universe, all of whose parts "operated according to unalterable law."[26] The vision of harmony and sympathy would be fundamental to the worldview of the ensuing culture of sensibility. So, too, was his vision of the contrast between the natural goodness of men and the "unnatural" evil which still existed in the world. The latter entered by way of "custom and education" and the "counterworking passions" of rage and lust. Hence the existence of suffering had its justification "as a necessary part of a whole that is fundamentally good."[27] Similarly, Shaftesbury's harmonizing aesthetic embraced the "faults of nature." "Even the rude rocks, the mossy cavern, the irregular, unwrought grottos and broken falls of water, with all the horrid graces of the wilderness itself, as representing Nature more, . . . appear with a magnificence beyond the formal mockery of a princely garden."[28] The paeans of Shaftesbury's character, Theocles (later parodied by Sterne), contained the other values that cultists of sensibility attributed to "Nature," in the rapturous language in which they were couched.[29] Theocles argues that Nature's wonders (above all, constellations of stars) excited the idea of "their author," God—indeed the vision is close to pantheism. In keeping with the classicism his name invoked, Theocles presented the fields and woods as a "refuge from the toilsome world of business," where the "happiest mortals" lived in peaceful innocence and need not fear solitude nor the pleasures of melancholy. In fact, it was impossible that the world as a whole not be contemplated "without ecstasy and rapture."[30]

If Shaftesbury warned against "immoderate love," and "over-great tenderness" and declared that "excessive pity renders us incapable of giving succor," he more than "allowed" a "fair and plausible enthusiasm, a reasonable ecstasy and transport," for example in response to architecture, painting, and music.[31] Shaftesbury showed Theocles' pupil, Philocles, to have been converted by Theocles' "protracted raptures."[32] Hence, in spite of Shaftesbury's determination to draw a clear line between true and false "enthusiasm," his own technique resembled that of the preachers also drawing on sensational psychology to convert their listeners.[33]

Shaftesbury wished to teach that men who did not cultivate themselves in the way he recommended constituted an "unthinking world." They simply enjoyed pleasures superficially, loving whatever they fancied. The virtuous mind refused to depend on "sense only" but enjoyed "in a nobler way" by cultivating reason.[34] Personality constructed on the basis entirely of sensation was potentially anarchic: "what is pain to one is pleasure to another, and so alternately." Men were separating the pursuit of "PLEASURE" from any kind of labor. Shaftesbury wished to confront the utter individualism of taste (being "pleased with what pleases us") with his lesson of what is "rightly" pleasing. He undertook "to recommend morals on the same foot with what in a lower sense is called manners."[35] A late expression of Shaftesbury's lifelong effort to teach manners to his fellow Britons ("the latest barbarous, the last civilized or polished people of Europe") was an essay instructing the painter from whom Shaftesbury commissioned a picture in classical style. It was "A Notion of the Historical Draught or Tablature of the Judgement of Hercules." It was printed in the second, 1713 edition of Shaftesbury's *Characteristics* along with a plate of the picture. According to the famous story told by Socrates, Hercules, "the greatest of all Stoic heroes," at a crossroads faced the choice between the hard, uphill road to Virtue and the soft, easy path to Pleasure. The case for each was made to him by the appropriate goddess-personifications of Virtue and Pleasure. Hercules judged the former to be persuasive. Shaftesbury's picture was to emphasize both this decision and the fact that Hercules had found it a very real struggle.[36]

We cannot ignore the historical context for Shaftesbury's elevation of such a choice, the emergence in Britain of a commercial society ruled by a new "monied interest," provoking the "renewed . . . assertion—particularly among Whigs—of the ideal of the citizen" looking back to classical models. Shaftesbury wished to reform the pioneers of consumer pleasure, "ladies, beaux, courtly gentlemen, the more refined town and country wits, notable talkers," enjoying the economic boom and witnessing the popularization of consumer pleasures among the audience identified by, for example, *The Spectator*.[37]

The paradox here must be emphasized. Shaftesbury himself helped to foster the prosperity on which the individual pursuit of sensual pleasure depended. Like his grandfather, he was deeply involved in the Whig political establishment. His activities included his own political domination of the part of the West Country where he had his family seat. There Shaftesbury was an improving "Lord of the Manor," teaching and requiring his tenant farmers to implement what he called "Bolder Husbandry": enclosure, crop rotation, penning sheep to manure the fields, shifting from clover to French grass, destroying rabbit warrens to increase the extent of his arable land, and expanding his water meadows. Consequently his lands sustained a palatial, "sumptuously decorated" manor where Shaftesbury could demonstrate the results of his austerely disciplined taste in a lifetime of conspicuous consumption: being waited on hand and foot, daily lavish meals washed down with choice wines, a grand tour in his teens and several years abroad to hobnob with other European intellectuals, and the collecting and commissioning of paintings on a huge scale. He gave one of his agents "*carte blanche* to buy books of reproductions of classical art." He was a patron of writers, and his counterrevolutionary tendencies are expressed in his attack on those who were beginning to escape patronage by appealing to the undisciplined pleasures of a large audience. He was able to sponsor and oversee the publication of his *Characteristics* without regard to expense.[38]

Of course, all this is to say that, as an aristocrat inheriting vast property and making it his business to use power to increase and improve it, Shaftesbury was able to indulge in conspicuous consumption as aristocrats have always been able to do. The conspicuousness has been part of their display of power, as Queen Elizabeth's clothing and cosmetics were. But Shaftesbury's circumstances were historically different: the psychological prospects rationalized by Locke corresponded to the prospects for the democratization of pleasurable consumption being opened up by the commercialization of publishing, fashion, and a whole array of domestic items, signifying new possibilities in self-conception.[39] Later in the century, Matthew Boulton, famous for his contribution to the steam engine and a "major figure in the process of commercialization," would write:

> We think it of far more consequence to supply the People than the Nobility only; and though you speak contemptuously of Hawkers, Pedlars, and those who supply *Petty Shops*, yet we must own that we think they will do more towards supporting a great Manufacturing, than all the Lords in the Nation.

Boulton opened his Birmingham factory to tourists, now pleasuring themselves much differently than Shaftesbury had on the Grand Tour. He manufactured a huge range of metal objects largely for domestic and personal use and decoration, that is, enabling hundreds of thousands of people to enjoy facsimiles of life's facilities previously monopolized by Shaftesbury's class. The British industrial capitalism advanced by men like Boulton had built on the agricultural and commercial revolutions furthered by many of that class (including Shaftesbury) and nourished by their postrevolutionary establishment of national financial institutions. Shaftesbury recognized that the process identified by Boulton, bypassing his class and intended audience, was in train in his own lifetime, motivated by the individual and popular choice of pleasure among whole new classes of consumers. What he could not know was that Boulton and his fellows would harness this motive and their production to the same process Shaftesbury wished to foster: Boulton was proud that, while a century earlier (he wrote in 1773), Birmingham inhabitants' pleasures had been "bull-baitings, cock-fighting, boxing matches, and abominable drunkenness. . . . The scene is now much changed: the people are polite and civilized . . . and we have made much progress in the liberal arts." To this it may be added the same change was one where the earlier "inhabitants" were almost exclusively men, whereas the latter "people" were both women and men.[40]

In fact, Shaftesbury's apprehensions embodied particular meaning for his notions of manhood. Shaftesbury idolized the Stoics, devoting himself to them as if in prayer. He wished to discipline his susceptibility to intense passions and emotions. He condemned what he called his own "Hottspurr Inclination," and gave vent to "consuming rage" in his role as a proprietor of Carolina. In his determination to marry, he showed an "unbelievable ardor" beneath his Stoical "mask," although not for sex. He was, his biographer writes, "the slave of his emotions" in those family matters that were at the core of his being. Shaftesbury also associated his sense of "the despotism of passion" with "a very powerful sense of sin . . . carried over from his early religious training." The struggle Shaftesbury wished to see depicted on Hercules' face as he chose Virtue over Pleasure was one he felt in himself.[41]

Physically, however, Shaftesbury was no Hercules. Shaftesbury's ideal was to work through a "field of study and [master] it like an athlete." The simile betrayed what Shaftesbury himself saw as a decline in manhood, toward the sedentary achievements contemporaries warned could make a scholar an invalid. In fact, Shaftesbury was virtually an invalid all his life. Attributing his illnesses to the effluvia brought by bad air, he timed his movements to coincide with the direction of the wind. The smoke-laden air of prospering London kept him from his courtship of the first woman he wished to marry in order to perpetuate his line. Shaftesbury faced the limitations of what he saw as his "broken Constitution." His "bitter depreciation" of the body, which he could rationalize as Stoicism, reflected such limitations. When at forty-two years old he gave his Herculean instructions, he was a dying man.[42]

Moreover, Shaftesbury modified Stoicism in the same way that the Cambridge Platonists had. He found that "the bond that unites men," the higher "natural affection," was "more emotional than rational." Therefore, in attempting to be a "preserver of the moral wisdom of the past," in attempting "to maintain these eternal and immutable verities," Shaftesbury backed into the future. Shaftesbury assumed that the "chief happiness" of the "reader" of *Characteristics* lay in "his liberty and his manhood." It was to those characteristics that all of his subjects were "related."[43] Struggling for his own "inner reformation," Shaftesbury earned a reputation as a type literally antithetical to the Restoration type epitomized by Rochester. Shaftesbury's conception of his transformation corresponded to the repression of male behavior expressed in Carnival: he personified his passions of anger, ambition, desire, eager and tumultuous joys, wishes, hopes, "transporting Fancyes, extravagant Mirth, Airy-ness, Humour, Fantasticallness, Buffoonery, Drollery," as masked, carnivalesque figures in the streets: "once any of these are let loose, when once they have broke their Boundaryes & forc'd a passage, what ravage & destruction is sure to follow? and what must it cost ere all be calm agin within?"[44] He recommended the debrutalization of public space as well as tastefully disciplined consumer spending. The erosion of Carnival included the aristocracy's withdrawal from their previous public intermingling with males of all classes, and its characterizing such withdrawal as refinement, polish, and a softening of manners.[45] Shaftesbury's enemies at court supposedly "gave out that he was too bookish, because not given to Play, nor assiduous at Court; that he was no good Companion, because not a Rake nor a hard Drinker, and that he was no Man of the World, because not selfish nor open to Bribes."[46]

Shaftesbury's intention in *Characteristics* was to make men neither "foppish" nor "licentious" in the "courtly style" nor of "the vulgar, enthusiastic kind" like the "fierce unsociable . . . modern zealots, those starched, gruff gentlemen, who guard religion as bullies do a mistress." Instead, Shaftesbury wanted men to be "all serene, soft, and harmonious." Wishing to reconcile a "manly liberty" with "the goodly order of the universe," Shaftesbury generated an ideal that looked back to Castiglione's *Courtier* and forward to *Sir Charles Grandison.* Such a paragon embodied "a mind subordinate to reason, a temper humanised and fitted to all natural affections, . . . a thorough candour, benignity and good nature, with constant security, tranquility . . . equanimity." This gentleman should be of "good breeding,' not "gross or clownish."[47] While Shaftesbury's purpose was to make gruff, barbaric bullies softer and to temper and humanize antisocial ferocity into social affections, he was equally concerned that such polish should not be at the expense of manhood. A man must not become a "person who has much of goodness and natural rectitude in his temper, but withal so much softness or effeminacy as unfits him to bear poverty, crosses or adversity." "Effeminacy" in Shaftesbury's book was a derogatory term, applied to men and coupled with cowardice and weakness.[48]

Shaftesbury's sexual values here would be typical of True Whigs throughout the century. They faced what Shaftesbury called "the enormous growth of luxury in capital cities . . . improvements . . . made in vice of every kind where numbers of men are maintained in lazy opulence and wanton plenty."[49] Shaftesbury epitomized the attempt to uphold the standard of the "landed patriotic gentleman citizen," along with the ambivalence that accompanied it. He regarded himself as such a citizen but, more strikingly, he aggrandized himself as a contemplative virtuoso; he was seen as a modern kind of male softened by literacy and consumerism. He felt acutely the difference between himself and those "busiest spirits" among men, seized with the idea of novelty, restless, ambitious, ranging sea and land and rifling the globe to its very entrails.[50] They did so in order to create the "luxury" on which virtuosity depended. Shaftesbury would have liked to unite in manly, harmonious health "the remote provincials, the inhabitants of smaller towns, and the industrious sort of common people" with "the mathematician who labours at his problem, the bookish man who toils, the artist who endures voluntarily the greatest hardships and fatigues." Shaftesbury's ideal, self-made Hercules "builds in a different matter from that of stone and marble" and "becomes in truth the architect of his own life and fortune, by laying within himself the lasting and sure foundation of order, peace, and concord." Such a self-conception was manifest in the urban renaissance then under way, its architecture intended like Shaftesbury's, to improve the character of those who inhabited it, much as domestic objects were to do.[51]

Self-evidently, however, there was a marked contrast between metaphorical building (albeit of a self-made man)—the toils of the bookish, the fatigues of the artist—and the physical industry of the common people, let alone between the sedentary philosopher-aristocrat and the manly fighting of his ideal and his predecessors. While "the future belonged to the humanist rather than to the feudal revival," writes McKeon of the heirs to Renaissance courtliness, "the pressure of social change now gave to the old questions of 'arms versus letters' new urgency," and those choosing the latter could be insulted as "carpet-knights." Formerly, Shaftesbury bewailed, youth were trained in "academic discipline" when "not only horsemanship and military arts had their public places of exercise, but philosophy too had its wrestlers" but, now, men wish to be rid of "academic examination" on the easiest terms. By 1711, men had become "too lazy and effeminate." The "real disadvantage of our modern conversations, [is] that by such a scrupulous nicety they lose those masculine helps of learning and sound reason." The "effeminacy" with which Shaftesbury was most concerned was that of learning and conversation. Modernity, civilization—Shaftesbury's own ineluctable circumstances—could threaten men like Shaftesbury with "effeminacy."[52]

It was "astonishing," he wrote, how "fast the world declined in wit and sense, in manhood, reason, science, and in every art when once the Roman Empire had prevailed and spread an universal tyranny and oppression over mankind." Falsity of morals and taste, of "language" itself, would follow naturally "after such a relaxation and dissolution of manners, consequent to the horrid luxury and effeminacy of the Roman court." This transformation would be the guiding metaphor for those True Whigs bearing the seventeenth-century's torch, as they watched "untrue" Whigs entrench themselves at court and ministries as securely as their predecessors had feared the Tories would. Without the support of his kind of political liberty, said Shaftesbury, a man found it necessary to follow "the general way of courts," that is, "to flatter the great, to bear insults, to stoop and fawn and abjectly resign one's sense and manhood."[53] In fact, as Shaftesbury saw in 1701, the Tories adopted "Country Party" ideology; the gender values I am describing came to permeate both parties.[54] Contemplating "The Foolish Methods of Education among the Nobility," Swift said of the "frequent extinction of aristocratic lines" that it was a "Remedy in the Order of Nature; so many great Families coming to an End by Sloth, Luxury, and abandoned Lusts, which enervated their Breed through every Succession, producing gradually a more effeminate Race."[55]

At the other end of the scale, but also defining Shaftesbury's gender aesthetic, were the "barbarian" manners "we allow to our own people" in their "gladiatorian and other sanguinary sports . . . the baitings and slaughter of so many sorts of creatures . . . for diversion merely."[56] Shaftesbury supported those he called "the *solemn* Reprovers of Vice," even though his emphasis there was intended to contrast their solemnity with his technique of ridiculing vice.[57] Shaftesbury's work must be seen as his intentional contribution to the national campaign for the reformation of manners, radiating outward from his own attempted transformation. His recommendation that the theater reform men was consistent with his long-lived scheme (rooted in classical precedent) for improving men through art. In Shaftesbury's view, the stage was and would continue to be the place where a wider slice of English youth would "draw their notion of manners" and of taste, more so even than from the "sacred oratory" of the pulpits with which the stage competed. The stage could reach the illiterate and the poor who could afford the price of standing in the pit more than the cost of a book, unless they wanted to read a free but edifying tract on how to reform. Unfortunately, one of the consequences of late seventeenth-century history was commercialization of theater and publishing. Our "modern penmen," said Shaftesbury, echoing his inmost sense of vulnerability, were debasing their work by "prostituting" it to the untutored taste of "the people." They were "turned and modelled (as they themselves confess) by the public relish[.] [T]hey accommodate themselves" to the "irregular fancy" and "current humour" of the world. This was in contrast to "the early poets of Greece" who had refused to comply with their nation's "appetite." Instead, they had "formed their audience, polished the age, refined the public ear and framed it right, that in turn they might be rightly and lastingly applauded."[58]

Shaftesbury's contemporary "stage poets," responding to the "British nation" as a whole, wrote plays resembling the people's "rude Olympics" and "trials of skill wholly of the body, not of the brain." Their "barbarous" works played "havoc" on "virtue and good sense." Because of their bestial and bloody representations, Shaftesbury grouped such plays with "sanguinary sports," presumably bearbaiting, bullbaiting, and cockfighting, sports that included the "slaughter" of "wild" creatures hunted by the populace at large. Shaftesbury held that dramatists had the means to extend his own notion of the cultivation of virtue to a popular audience, perhaps in the way he saw the Rev. Whichcote preach classized Christianity to his humbler congregants. The task was "to amend" the common stage not less than "the higher sphere." Included in his recommendation was that his "brother-authors" look inward to that Shaftesburian moral sense. In his proposal to dramatists, Shaftesbury maintained his emphasis on the "thorough diligence, study and impartial censure of themselves. 'Tis manners which are wanting.' Tis due sentiment of morals which can . . . give us the just tone and measure of human passion." This was Shaftesbury's definition of taste.[59]

The Spectator joined Shaftesbury in this branch of the campaign to reform manners, duplicating his argument for the reformation of the theater in an issue published the year following the first edition of Shaftesbury's *Characteristics. The Spectator* hoped that the writers and readers of its class and persuasion could "restrain the licentiousness of the theatre and make it contribute its assistance to the advancement of morality, and to the reformation of the age." The author of this issue was Addison, also the author of the sentimental play *Cato,* exemplifying the softened Stoicism widely preached from Latitudinarian pulpits and exemplified by Shaftesbury.[60] Bishop Berkeley added his voice in 1721, calling on the parliament to reform the theater so that it would give "fine lessons of morality and good sense." Seeing society permeated by licentiousness, scurrility, profaneness, and "scandalous libertinism," and lambasting British gambling, operas, and masquerades, Berkeley wished to put architecture, sculpture, and painting to the same use as Shaftesbury and *The Spectator.* He reserved particular hostility for women's luxury of dress. Berkeley's jeremiad was immediately triggered by the recent collapse of the South Sea Bubble, although he believed that "ever since the luxurious reign of King Charles the Second we have been doing violence to our natures." Yet, like his tastemaking predecessors, Berkeley did what he could to nourish the luxury-producing system; if he called for frugality, he was deeply committed to capitalist development, improving roads, navigable rivers, and the merchant marine, and giving premiums for investment and improvement in several key manufactures. The apparent paradox of the combination was to be mediated by the moral value implicit in "taste," as it was in the sensibility advocated by Shaftesbury and *The Spectator.*[61]

Reaching that point in his argument where he singled out educated youth-cum-sedentary-philosophers as particularly vulnerable to "effeminacy," Shaftesbury turned to the damaging intrusion of women's wishes into "modern" British life. (This reaction immediately followed women's appearance on the published, public stage, feminists among them.) It was, wrote Shaftesbury, "our" men's idea of what women want—that men leave aside learning and reason—which had contributed to a loss of masculinity. The "fair sex in whose favour we pretend to make this condescension may with reason despise us for it and laugh at us for aiming at their peculiar softness. 'Tis no compliment to them to affect their manners and be effeminate." Women were naturally soft and without reason, men naturally harder and reasonable. Shaftesbury illustrated the same assertion of gender hierarchy one finds in *The Courtier,* as well as in the views of his contemporary nerve theorists. "Our sense, language, and style, as well as our voice and person, should have something of that male-feature and natural roughness by which our sex is distinguished. And whatever politeness we may pretend to, 'tis more a disfigurement than any real refinement of discourse to render it thus delicate." Refinement should only go so far or it would become effeminacy. Shaftesbury specified the masculine qualities required by art and learning: a perfect work of wit required "boldness of hand"; a painting, "good muscling"; and discourse of great moment "strong reason" and the whole fund of scientific and historical knowledge. His instructions for the classical rendering of Hercules illustrated this ideal. It was to be in contrast to the "popish priesthood's" requirements that artists depict Christ as a "wretched Model" and "Barbarian."

> No form, no grace of shoulders, breast . . . no *Démarche,* Air, Majesty Grandeur, a lean uncomely Proportion & Species, a mere Jew or Hebrew (originally an ugly scabby people) both Shape and Phyz: with half beard, peaked not one nor t'other. Lank clinging Hair, sniveling face, hypocritical canting countenance & at best Melancholly Man & enthusiastical in the common and lower way.[62]

And Shaftesbury blamed "female saints" for this kind of "enthusiastical" perversion. They were "the greatest improvers of this soft part of religion," "quietists, pietists and those who favour the ecstatic way of devotion." Shaftesbury credited the rumors of the sexual operation of "amourous zeal . . . between the saints of each sex, in these devout ecstasies." Shaftesbury's generation looked back with horror to the women of the civil war sects, to the "late Commonwealth" when, in Clarendon's vision, "all ages, sexes, and degrees, would become reformers . . . [such confusion] intoxicated the brains of men." And it could be said that the memory and associations also shaped the reactions to women's attraction to the enthusiasm later revived by Methodism.[63]

Shaftesbury's notion of women's emotional susceptibility (the standard for his apprehensions and those of his contemporaries, who believed that their modernity, their links to a vicissitudinous market economy and its enervating products laid them open to "effeminacy"), also expressed itself in his declaration that the unreformed, market-oriented success of playwrights with "ribaldry and gross irregularities" depended chiefly on the female part of their popular audience. He said that women frequented these crude, violence-ridden plays, too, an observation borne out by recent scholarship. He was particularly offended by women's appearing on stage—"sometimes," he said, they were in the theater as "not spectators only, but actors in the gladiatorian parts." His "gospel" deemed women especially "susceptible" to depictions of "passion," and he wished to restrict them to the controlled sexuality of breeding the family line. Both he and his father regarded upper-class women's staying in London as their "ruination." His sister "violated some of Shaftesbury's most intense prejudices" when she borrowed his coach and six, drove into London, and picked up her sister-in-law for a trip to the theater.[64]

Shaftesbury deemed women naturally incapable of "strong reason" and the whole classical heritage, in spite of his tutoring by Elizabeth Birch. Whatever his standards of tough-mindedness and skepticism, Shaftesbury maintained it was "real humanity and kindness to hide strong-truths from tender eyes." At best, women were one among the "other beauties of Nature."[65] What women *were* naturally capable of in the way of culture was romance, which by 1711 Shaftesbury said was "sprung from the mere dregs of chivalry or knight-errantry." Such archaic "gallantry" now existed in "novels: those dear sweet, natural pieces, writ most of them by the fair sex themselves." Shaftesbury said of the chivalric code that it was "as impertinent and senseless as it was profane to deify the sex [and], raise them to a capacity above what Nature had allowed . . ." The novel's perpetuation of this whole "false, monstrous, and Gothic" "scheme of wit," in tandem with the moral sensibility of which Shaftesbury himself would be deemed one source, continued to elevate women to female sainthood.[66]

Reading was essential to the "formation of taste." Yet it was dangerously affecting: the "very reading of treatises and accounts of melancholy has been apt to generate that passion in the over-diligent and attentive reader." And Shaftesbury suggested that women readers were the most liable to be affected, to the extent that they deified the writer and turned themselves into tragic votaries, addicts, and cultists: "the very person of such relators or tale-tellers, with a small help of dismal habit, suitable countenance and tone, become sacred and tremendous in the eyes of mortals who are thus addicted from their youth. The tender virgins, losing their natural softness, assume this tragic passion, of which they are highly susceptible, especially when a suitable kind of eloquence and action attends the character of the narrator." The scene here is reading aloud. How women's private, individual reading to themselves might be controlled would be a century-long and unavailing preoccupation.[67]

Shaftesbury was faced by the misreading of his own ambiguous text immediately it was published. He expostulated against those who made "their humour alone the rule of what is beautiful or agreeable," that is, who accepted his idea of the innateness of a "moral sense" but ignored his adjuration for "the labour and pains of criticism." This would remain a note in the culture of sensibility but so, too, would Shaftesbury's emphasis on the moral sense and its aggrandizement of feeling in social relations and in relation to the natural world. Shaftesbury would have "deplored" the reading of his work as the unleashing of feeling as well as the democratization of taste.[68] But the notion of an inner sense, emotionally responding "to qualities as the physical sense responds to sensible characteristics," by definition could be read as something that all "humanity" shared, including women. It was this meaning that, Brett suggests, two or three generations "imbibed" from Shaftesbury, until "the headier brew of Rousseau became available."[69] In spite of his own gender values, Shaftesbury's treatise contributed to the shaping of the characteristics of women. They would turn his "sentimental ethics" to their own purposes, attempting to inhibit the freedom women saw men using against their persons and interests.

Mandeville

Bernard Mandeville (1670–1733) challenged Shaftesbury's vision, including his apprehension of "effeminacy." He had come to London right after the "Glorious Revolution" whereby the Whigs brought another Dutchman to England, establishing the political basis for England's economic take off.[70] Mandeville's immigration also coincided with the renewal of the puritan campaign for the reformation of manners. Mandeville homed in on the dramatic coexistence in England of the fantasy of perfect virtue and the reality of human appetite and ambition, what he called this "Contradiction in the Frame of Man." His origins and youth had sensitized Mandeville to discern in his adopted country the central cultural characteristic of the land of his birth. I referred earlier to Simon Schama's identification of the "embarrassment of riches" as a "syndrome," "a contradictory value system, a perennial combat between acquisitiveness and asceticism."[71]

> The incorrigible habits of material self-indulgence, and the spur of risky adventure that were ingrained into the Dutch commercial economy, themselves prompted all those warning clucks and solemn judgements from the appointed guardians of the old orthodoxy.

The Dutch, too, had their version of a campaign for the reformation of manners. Provoked by the English reformers who embodied the same "abstinence and indulgence" to be found in the Dutch, Mandeville's *The Fable of the Bees: or, Private Vices, Publick Benefits* was published as quite a brief poem, *The Grumbling Hive: or, Knaves Turn'd Honest,* in 1705, six years before Shaftesbury's work. In 1714 he reprinted the poem together with a lengthy prose gloss as *The Fable of the Bees.* Having "vindicated" it against the "aspersions" of a grand jury presentment in 1723, Mandeville added another lengthy gloss in 1729, this time in the form of a debate mirroring Shaftesbury's *The Moralists,* published as a part of his *Characteristics.*[72]

The Fable of the Bees reeks of the prosperity of early eighteenth-century London. From the preface we are plunged into London's filthy streets, the filth itself in Mandeville's view the healthy sign of "the Plenty, great Traffick and Opulency of that mighty City," of the constant supply of materials in its trades and handicrafts, the waste of all the food, drink, and fuel being consumed, the multitudes of horses, carts, coaches, carriages, and "above all the numberless swarms of People, that are continually harassing and trampling through every part of them." The filth was necessary to opulence and might, and it was absurd to wish the streets cleaner and free of bootblacks and scavengers—they all had their part. The "Smell of Gain was fragrant even to Night-Works," that is, clearing the streets of some of the excrement. Central to Mandeville's understanding was the fantastic irrelevance of wishing filth away and believing it could be abolished. The same people who sermonized against the vices of appetite were in fact indulging and profiting from them: a man raised in society by the success of a distilling business became a justice of the peace and thereafter the "scourge" of the criminal and poor from whom originally he made his profits. This representative J.P. attempted to spread "the Reformation of Manners throughout every cranny of the populous Town." He plagued sabbath-breaking butchers, and he terrorized the "Rioters and discontented Rabblers" in the streets.[73]

Mandeville's perspective on this apparent and emblematic polarity throws a great deal of light on the meaning to gender of prosperity and reform. Mandeville defended pleasurable life in "the world." To reformers, "world" connoted the old Christian notion of "Things Mundane and Corruptible" and the Augustinian tendency to repudiate all of it, reinforced by Luther's "excremental vision."[74] In fact, said Mandeville, whether we like it or not, "the real Pleasures of all Men in Nature are worldly and sensual, if we judge from their Practice; . . . How strange it is [Devout Christians] should all so unanimously deny it!" Facing such a reality himself, Mandeville returned again and again to that denial: "we hide even from our selves the vast Extent of Self-Love, and all its different Branches." Mandeville detected the same proclivity in his contemporaries, who projected their realism onto the past. While they conceded that "Pride and Luxury" had been "the great Promoters of Trade" in the "sinful nations" of history, they refused to own "the Necessity" for the same "vices" in their own age and country because they wished to claim they were more virtuous. Similarly, Mandeville punctured the fantasy of nostalgic pastoralism that was upheld as a moral standard by religious, sentimental, and political ideologies throughout the century. Mandeville lays out

> the Impossibility of enjoying all the most elegant Comforts of Life that are to be met within an industrious, wealthy and powerful Nation, and at the same time be bless'd with all the Virtue and Innocence that can be wish'd for in a Golden Age.[75]

It would be "an unspeakable felicity" to banish utterly "the Sin of Uncleanness," but Mandeville said that was impossible, as was "complete happiness."[76] Society would be benefited by facing up to the reality of human passions and appetites rather than prosecuting them.

In Mandeville's view, society was the result of a long historical process, not of the biblical fantasy of Genesis nor of some ascertainable social contract amidst a state of nature. "Human Wisdom is the Child of Time. It was not the contrivance of one Man, nor could it have been the business of a few Years." Mandeville was a "Cultural Evolutionist," imparting a persuasively complex vision of the origins of civilization.[77] History, said Mandeville, was rooted in the frailties, defects, appetites, and ingenuity of "human Nature itself." Drawing on this mixture, the European societies of which Mandeville wrote, above all Britain and Holland, had made the "slow advance from barbarism" to cultures sustaining "the most elegant Comforts of Life."[78]

Contributing to the civilizing process Mandeville described was the "unmix'd Prodigality of heedless and voluptuous Men" and, he made clear, of women. If frugality was a virtue, it was "a mean starving" one, "only fit for small societies of good peaceable Men, who are contented to be poor so they may be easy." It fell into the same category of irrelevant fantasy as a golden age because it was "an idle dreaming Virtue that employs no hands." Mandeville dismissed the apprehension that luxury led to effeminacy. He had "heard People speak of the mighty Figure the *Spartans* have made" but "the only thing they could be proud of, was, that they enjoyed nothing." Spartan simplicity and honesty were incompatible with being "an opulent, potent, flourishing, as well as a Warlike Nation" in eighteenth-century Europe.[79] Mandeville's target here was Shaftesbury. According to reformers of manners, said Mandeville, luxury "effeminates and enervates the People, by which the Nations become an easy Prey to the first invaders." Mandeville admits that when he was a schoolboy in Holland he had been susceptible to the "frightful Notion" of "Luxury's effeminating and enervating a Nation."[80] As an adult, however, he could dismiss this charge against luxury in several ways. It was simply inaccurate to personify a whole nation as effeminate. In every society some men would indulge in the vices attributed by reformers to luxury whether they were expensive or cheap. Moreover, clean linen, good wainscot, or a gilt chariot were "no more enervating than a cold floor or a Country Cart." Even if you granted that the luxurious lives of the rich made them "unfit to endure Hardships and undergo the Toils of War," so what? They could pay the taxes to support soldiers who were raised from the poor. And officers and generals were qualified by experience and knowledge rather than strong sinews and supple joints. They could be carried to battle in litters: the duc de Villars, "the best General the King of France has now, can hardly crawl along."[81]

In ringing the changes on his familiar argument that "consumption" worked to the common good, Mandeville registered the pervasiveness in early eighteenth-century London (as well as contemporary Holland) of specific kinds of appetites and the consumer goods that supplied it. The former were the "worldly and sensual" pleasures: taking "delight" in rich and fashionable clothing, voluptuousness, prodigality, pride, and vanity.[82] Mandeville recognized the force of emulation in the "various Shifting and Changing of Modes," which spurred industry and improvement. A "restless desire after Changes and Novelty" were valuable to society, in contrast to the supposed virtues of steadiness, content, frugality, and generosity.[83] The goods on which Mandeville's Englishmen and Englishwomen lavished such feelings included "Diet, Furniture and Dress," horses, coaches, and fine wines. In direct challenge to Shaftesbury, they "may call everything a Pleasure that pleases" them. The words "decency" and "conveniency" as well as "clean" and "neat" were being used to cover a multitude of consumer vices which had penetrated the middling sort. Thus the

> Goldsmith, Mercer or any other of the most creditable Shopkeepers . . . must have two Dishes of Meat every Day, and something extraordinary for *Sundays.* His Wife must have a Damask Bed against her lying-in, and two or three Rooms very well furnished.

Contributing to the "pleasure," "ease," and "comfort" that Mandeville celebrated were the arts of cloth making, brewing, and baking as well as watchmaking, shipbuilding, and navigation. He recognized "that good food, adequate drink, warm rooms and clean clothes are pleasant and desireable." In other words, while one can see the appeal to men of Mandeville's unmoralistic acceptance of "the delight in trade," the significance for women's "home demand" of the encouragement of the flow of technical improvements and comforting goods into domestic space is very clear.[84]

Accused by the grand jury of creating a plan "to debauch the nation," Mandeville in a later edition published its presentment and then tore it apart. Denounced by Bishop Berkeley, Mandeville parodied the bishop's sanctimoniousness in an irreverent prayer in the preface to his *A Modest Defence of Publick Stews.* He dedicated this defense of brothels "To the Gentlemen of the Societies," that is, Societies for the Reformation of Manners, telling them that their efforts to suppress "Lewdness" had only promoted it as pruning promotes the growth of a tree. He suggested that their claims to statistical success which were published in their attacks on John James Heidegger, the leading sponsor of commercial masquerades, reflected their desire for preferment.[85] Mandeville suggests, too, that "the mercenary Officiousness of Reforming Constables" was inspired by the portion of the fines they received. He opposed the reformers on every issue, from charity schools to dueling and from religious toleration to the benefits of drinking. In every case, Mandeville's standard was the reality of experience, of history.[86]

He described the clergy hypocritically wallowing in luxury and lust in *The Fable of the Bees,* where his satire resembles that of Swift, both echoing Rochester's.[87] In his *A Modest Defence of Public Stews* (1724) Mandeville described the various expressions of lust (including that of male homosexuals about whom he is also ecumenical) by ancient philosophers, whom he called the "great Reformers of the World," the "Reverend Schoolmasters of Antiquity." Referring to the treatment his contemporary male reformers of manners gave women for sexual offenses, that is, imprisonment and transportation but, most especially, being "Stripped Naked" and "flogged," Mandeville suggested not only that these "reverend schoolmasters" were employing a double standard but they were enjoying what we would call sadism. Furthermore, he said to them, the "Women, You say are weaker Vessels, and You are resolved to make them Submit; rightly judging, that if you cou'd make all the Females Modest it would put a considerable Stop to Fornication." Mandeville could be said to have pointed out the sexual prejudice in Burnet's representative view. He suggests too, that the reformation of manners depended at some level on the cooperation of middle-class, literate women and that these clerical gentlemen of the societies used women to implement their own puritanism.[88]

Mandeville recognized the kinship between Shaftesbury and the puritan reformers of manners. This "noble Author" endeavored "to inspire his Readers with refin'd Notions, and a Publick Spirit abstract[ed] from Religion." The gregarious and appetitive Mandeville was opposite in character to the rigid, aloof, and reclusive Shaftesbury, who sequestered himself on his country estate, away from what Mandeville relished as "the Bustle of the World." Franklin has left us a tiny picture of Mandeville in precisely the freewheeling, alcoholic, and masculine setting that so bothered the reformers. In 1726 a mutual acquaintance brought Franklin "to the Horns, a pale ale house in—Lane, Cheapside and introduced [him] to Dr. Mandeville author of *The Fable of the Bees* who had a club there, of which he was the soul, being a most facetious entertaining companion." One can imagine the soft spot Mandeville had for his own metaphor for the body politic, a bowl of punch, combining, for example, the valuable vices of both avarice and prodigality. Their very different styles, including Shaftesbury's elevation of refinement and Mandeville's of appetite, may be connected with the former's concern over "effeminacy" and the latter's dismissal of it.[89]

Mandeville explained that he and Shaftesbury were "diametrically opposite."[90] At the bottom of Shaftesbury's thought was the idea that "the most virtuous action" was "the result of the greatest self-denial," a view linked to his argument that human beings were entirely subordinate to a Platonic system coextensive with God's mind, "trifling parts in respect to the whole."[91] By contrast, Mandeville, whose thought was not "caged by theological prepossessions," emphasized that "individual Persons," shaped by history and pursuing their own pleasures and ambitions, made up society rather than some innate and selfless ideal of sociability.[92] In Mandeville's view, pity was as much "a frailty of our nature as Anger, Pride, or Fear," and not to be abstracted and hierarchalized according to some arbitrary scheme.[93] He said that most people reckoned it "poor pay" that the recompense for a virtuous action was the pleasure of doing it, and he doubted that the satisfaction of being good lay in the consciousness of being so. Pleasures for Mandeville were to be active and direct.[94]

Recognizing what he called distinctions of "class" as the result of historical exploitation (in which one of the most powerful instruments was religion), Mandeville extended his egalitarian psychology to all classes. He believed, in McKeon's words, that "self-originated activity is not the privilege of the few whose lineage justifies it." Gentlemen were just as lustful as lower-class men; they simply went about satisfying their lust differently and masked it with hypocrisy. Again opposing Shaftesbury, Mandeville wrote that "an *Englishman* may justly call every Thing a Pleasure that pleases him, and according to this Definition we ought to dispute no more about Mens Pleasures than their Tastes."[95] Shaftesbury had rewritten Locke in order to hold back the brutal hordes on this very ground.

Mandeville was Lear-like in describing the rich lolling in luxury and vice at home while publicly excoriating such sinfulness by lesser mortals. Although ridiculing the "Superstition and miserable notions the Vulgar were taught to have of God," Shaftesbury presented the same superstition as more "Sublime Ideas of the Supreme Being and the Universe." And commenting on Shaftesbury's invidious comparison between the opera and the bear garden, Mandeville wrote that "Vice and what is criminal are not to be confounded with Roughness and want of Manners, no more than Politeness and artful Behaviour ought to be with Virtue and Religion." Shaftesbury's beautiful scheme could not reach "the meanest Tradesmen," "Draymen, and [the] swillers of beer" whom Shaftesbury would "exclude" from his "generous Sentiments and noble Principles." What would help such persons—and the poor—bridge the social "chasm" Shaftesbury was fighting to maintain was the whimsical consumerism of the rich (which Shaftesbury exemplified), together with all the other appetites and needs that fueled commercial prosperity.[96]

His repudiation of Shaftesbury's standard of a classically informed, moralized taste exemplifies Mandeville's general opposition to that system of values espoused by the reformation of manners, including the political expression of the need for "public virtue" and extirpation of "private vice." That Mandeville was challenging and subverting any such moral standard explains the hostility he invoked: he was ready to accept the mentality of "continuous money making" and the corollary of consumer "hedonism."[97] Amidst the ambivalence marking the public response to the coming into existence of fully fledged commercial capitalism, Mandeville opposed "both the actual early eighteenth-century standard of value and the position that there is any such single correct standard." It was this denial of an authoritative standard of morality and taste that signified Mandeville's wholehearted acceptance of the spirit of capitalism and of consumerism. "Either everything (beyond bare subsistence—whatever that might be) counts as luxury, or nothing does."[98]

Included in Mandeville's acceptance of worldly pleasure was his positive view of sex. His *Defence of Public Stews* associated sexual appetite with "Wantonness of Fancy" and "a Luxuriousness of Pleasure." Sexuality, like the palate, looked to luxury in variety. Asserting that a man's appetite was natural, Mandeville's language came close to Rochester's. "The Gods have given us one disobedient and unruly member, which, like a greedy and ravenous Animal that wants Food, grows wild and furious, till, having imbib'd the Fruit of the common Thirst, he has besprinkled and bedewed the Bottom of the Womb." Mandeville was interested in recording the "Sensations" of "the Nerves," and he declared that among the "most exquisite" were those of a penis ready for orgasm. He rejoiced in physiological directness, puns, and other form of free and playful sexual speech.[99] A respectable maiden lady in one of his books matter-of-factly uses the term "bare-ass'd."[100] While in the end critical of masturbation because its practitioners do not "manage" it "prudently" enough, Mandeville acknowledged its attractions of "Safety, Privacy, Convenience, and Cheapness" as well as clearly describing that the "knack" lies in "the Agility of [the] Wrists." In sum, the urge for sexual pleasure was "born and bred with us; nay, it is absolutely necessary to our being born at all."[101]

Mandeville recognized women's bearing children as "the greatest and most extensive of all temporal Blessings that accrue from Society, on which all the Comforts of Life, in the civilis'd State," depend. In our terms, he recognized that reproduction was production. To the extent that women could be seen to operate as individuals free of sexism, their motives were the same as men's. A poor woman put her son to sweep chimneys not out of some high-flown sense of the public good but out of sheer economic need: "the great Business as well as perpetual Sollicitude of the Poor are to supply their immediate Wants, and Keep themselves from Slavery." This had nothing to do with being "virtuous." Similarly, the foundation of a woman's "Honour" was "Interest" in the historical circumstances in which she found herself.[102]

Mandeville's Dutch origins may have first exposed him to feminism, although Anna Maria van Schurman, perhaps the best known of seventeenth-century feminists, had died the year of Mandeville's birth. Her *The Learned Maid: or, Whether a Maid May Also Be a Scholar* was translated into English in 1659, during the first phase of English feminism. There were male feminists in the Netherlands, too, including the influential van Beverwijck, like Mandeville, a doctor. He argued that women were "capable of all things." In *The Fable of the Bees,* Mandeville's account of gender logically followed sensationalist psychology. "The Brain of a Child, newly born, is *Charte Blanche.*" Women were innately equal to men: "there is no Labour of the Brain, which Women are not as capable of performing, at least, as well as the Men." The apparent differences between women and men were the result of upbringing and history. The reason for the rarity of "sound Judgement" among women was simply their "want of Practice." The same was true of abstract thought. This was the case in the most fundamental way, that of body, despite what he had said in his treatise on nervous disorders. Women were "educated" into their "Weakness of Frame and Softness." Mandeville described the "inculcation" of "modesty"—in fact, "shame"—into a little girl before she was two years old so that, at six, "she'll be ashamed of showing her Leg, without knowing any Reason why an Act is blameable, or what the Tendency of it is." Such characteristics were the result of custom, as his examination of different countries showed. Shaming was part of the same interlocking gender system whereby men could express themselves directly while women must do so by a careful code of blushing and lowering of the eyes.[103]

It was the result of "Custom and Education" that women were put into tortuous binds over sex. Educated to abominate "unfashionable Denudations and filthy expressions" still, the "most Virtuous Young Woman alive will often have Thoughts and confus'd Ideas of Things arise in her Imagination, which she would not reveal to some People for a thousand Words." Mandeville's sympathy here is evident: "when obscene Words are spoken in the presence of an unexperienced Virgin, she is afraid that some Body will reckon her to understand what they mean, and that she understands . . . which she desires to be thought ignorant of."[104] Mandeville was uncompromising in his attack on the double standard, and he pointed out the distortions caused women's character by the identification of their "honour" solely with chastity, or rather the reputation of chastity.[105] He said that women were more courageous than men because throughout their lives they must face "all the Artillery of our Sex." Lower-class women were particularly vulnerable to being seduced and abandoned by a "Powerful Deceiver." Thus made pregnant, a woman's sorrows were "unspeakable" because she was attacked by "Shame" as well as by her employers and her relations. It was under those circumstances that she might make away with the child. On this issue, the sheer vulnerability of women to men, Mandeville was in agreement with the culture of sensibility.[106]

At the same time Mandeville stated unequivocally and repeatedly that women "lust" as men do. Sexual appetite is "innate both in Men and Women."[107] Again he marveled at the doublethink that such an appetite, as natural to human beings as hunger or thirst, should have been called "*Filthy* and *Abominable*." He was skeptical of the notion that people could be in love "without feeling any Carnal Desires," although he allowed the possibility. Their absence was unnatural, the result of "the force of Education" or of dissimulation or of sickness. In fact, "the more sublime and exempt this Love is from all Thoughts of Sensuality, the more spurious it is."[108]

Mandeville described the vagina's response to the intromitted penis in graphic detail and went on to explain the part played by the clitoris in "this handsome Disposition of the vagina." Woman's arousal was essential, and "all our late Discoveries, in Anatomy, can find out no other Use for the *Clitoris,* but to whet the Female Desire by its frequent erections," by "prior Titillation, to provoke a Woman." Here Mandeville extended his egalitarianism from the brain to the genitals: "those erections are doubtless, as provoking as those of, the *Penis,* of which it is the perfect Copy, tho' in Miniature."[109] Their roots in classical physiology, these views were refurbished during the Renaissance by Vesalius, who would help shape Mandeville's university studies. Women's capacity for orgasm and the notion that the clitoris was homologous with the penis was also a "commonplace" of "popular knowledge" in the seventeenth century. An "extraordinarily frank sex manual" in Dutch, *Venus Minsieke Gasthuis* (adapted from an earlier French medical work), had published this view while Mandeville was a student in Holland. Combining learned and popular knowledge, Jane Sharp's book of midwifery had published the same views in England in 1671. It was not reprinted after 1728, which may indicate the progress of the same reformation of manners that brought Mandeville before the grand jury. In any case, Mandeville observed that, taught the "Rules of Religion, Law and Decency," women had to "disown" their sexual "Appetite" and "linger, waste, and die, rather than relieve themselves in a lawful manner."[110]

Men's self-serving idealization of women "condemned [women] to inferiority, praising them as delightful but regarding them as a distraction to the pursuit of honour and virtue." According to Mandeville, men have kept women ignorant in order to maintain their domination. This included men's excluding women from history. A 1709 *Tatler* had listed twelve male heroes who had taken that Herculean path upward to virtue and fame by rejecting "the sirens of pleasure." Mandeville's *Female Tatler* took on this sexism by naming a large number of women who had exemplified just as great "magnanimity, fortitude, and learning."[111] In monopolizing "the Writing of History" men have made the exercise of political power the standard for inclusion. Speaking as a woman, Mandeville wrote, "Since Men have enslav'd us, the greatest part of the World have always debar'd our Sex from Governing, which is the Reason that the Lives of Women have so seldom been describ'd in History; but as this is only to be imputed to the Injustice and Tyranny of the Men, so it ought not to be of any Disadvantage to the Women."[112]

By contrasting the mere "outward shew" of Englishmen's "Respect and Tenderness" to Englishwomen with the economic independence or partnership enjoyed by Dutchwomen, Mandeville implied that Englishwomen should enjoy such economic status, too. "In *Holland,* Women sit in their Counting-houses, and do Business, or at least are acquainted with everything their Husbands do."[113] For years, English and other foreign observers had publicized the greater independence of Dutch wives, who had significantly more legal authority to engage in the business activity for which their childrearing had prepared them. Despite their "confinement within the household realm," to those famous Dutch interiors (the site for widely distributed material abundance), they managed "to alter somewhat the scale of sexual inequality." English traveler Joseph Shaw said in 1709 that "the great power and happiness" of the Dutch republic was in part owed to Dutch women. English feminists, preceding and contemporary with Mandeville, had drawn on these reports. Among them were Bathsua Pell Makin and Judith Drake, and Mandeville's observation here is a virtual quotation from Drake's *An Essay of the Female Sex,* first published in 1696, expanded in a third edition in 1697, and republished in 1721. In England, thought Mandeville, men separated their business from women, instead calling them "ladies" and sending them out to playhouses. According to him, the ascribed status of English wives masked greater economic and vulnerability and exploitation.[114]

The Virgin Unmask'd (1709), in which, like Rochester, Mandeville shows a "capacity for literary transvestism," is a blend of his own feminist views with his satire of those with which he disagreed, notably Mary Astell's repudiation of heterosexual relations.[115] His form is a series of one-sided dialogues between two virgins, the mature aunt Lucinda who, like Astell, chooses to remain unmarried, and her young niece Antonia, susceptible to sexual stimulation and romantic fantasy. (Here, Mandeville may have reflected his exposure to the Dutch moralists described by Schama, warning that young women's "allure, their weakness, their vigorous instincts, all exposed them to daily trials . . . [during] a period of prolonged and intense peril before safely installed in conjugal bliss.") Throughout, Lucinda represents the relations between women and men as essentially political. Lucinda's aim is to preserve a young woman's "liberty" in the face of men's design to "enslave" her in marriage. Mandeville said in his preface, "My Design through the whole, is to let young Ladies know whatever is dreadful in Marriage." In so doing via Lucinda he makes a powerful case for a woman's remaining single. Demonstrating learning, wisdom, tough-mindedness, and wit, Lucinda counters the stereotype of the old maid.[116] Like Astell, she notes the paradox of a man's courtship, begging "on his knees," matched by the woman's scorn and pride, "because she designs to make him her master." The metaphor of politics is appropriate because the true circumstances are those of warfare, with men as the attacking warriors and women the defenders, garrisoning their very selves. This would be a persistent eighteenth-century metaphor, notably in Lovelace's laying siege to Clarissa.[117]

So there was a double meaning to Mandeville's prefatory expectation, "I expect to be censured for letting Women talk of Politicks." Antonia asks Lucinda to teach her politics because "every Cobler and Tinker talk Politicks." Lucinda made Antonia "read the News, and look every Place in the Map." This was also a pun because Mandeville was reversing the message of Walter Map's "Discussion from Matrimony," an early thirteenth-century version of the ancient message warning men that all women are "monsters and vipers": "Friend, fear all the sex," wrote Map.[118] While Lucinda ostensibly refuses to talk politics because neither of them have the "universal knowledge," especially of the history necessary for its mastery, in fact she goes on to devote the two succeeding dialogues to a consideration of Louis XIV's achievements, between her account of the political economies of the French, the Dutch, and the English. While this allowed Mandeville to express his views of these histories, the analyses were also bent to his feminist purpose, in the first place by showing Lucinda, an unmarried, self-educated, older lady, perfectly capable of them and, second, by connecting these complex worlds of power, politics, and conflict to the lives women must lead amidst the perpetual assaults of men, what he calls in *The Fable of the Bees* "all the Artillery of our Sex."[119]

Lucinda tries to get Antonia to face up to the inevitable trials and tribulations of married life, in, for example, the real futures of one's children, from birth through adulthood. According to her, it was vital for women that the actual prospects of family life be faced no less realistically than courtship and marriage. Such understanding was as significant for women, given political reality, as his grasp of the political economies of Europe had been for Louis XIV; if this great king could be brought to terrible ruin, so could a woman who married under any illusions.[120]

Mandeville's most powerful illustration of this truth was what he calls "the History of Aurelia." It is a grim tale, taking up nearly a third of the book, anticipating a major political theme of the literature of sensibility and its intended effects on its readers. However, if Mandeville's purpose in *The Virgin Unmask'd* was to present to women the harsh realities of the sexual order from a feminist point of view, unlike Astell and unlike sentimental fiction, he was not interested in thereby making women morally superior, let alone paragons of virtue. All along he insists on their equality to men in regard to intelligence, motivation, sexual appetite, and the capacity for complex interrelations. Aurelia, Lucinda warns Antonia, got into the fix she did not out of some virtue or even naivete but because she became obsessed with her husband (capable "at the height" of her "Passion" of enjoying great "Wantonness' with him). Eventually she becomes a battered wife (here Mandeville provides a brilliant and sympathetic psychological analysis), her story a representation of a woman faced with the realization of the potential horror of eighteenth-century sexual politics in their own terms. No human being should be subject to this, whatever their misjudgments, which all human beings make. Recources against such vulnerability were self-knowledge, including one's own physiology; much better education; a thorough investigation of potential husbands; and wide knowledge of "the World," from politics and history to family psychology.[121]

The second long story in *The Virgin Unmask'd* reiterated the book's theme: the extent of the treachery of men required women to be on ceaseless guard. This had been as central to Astell's work as it had been to Dutch moralists, and it would be Richardson's message (further reprintings of *The Virgin Unmask'd* overlapped with Richardson's output), but Richardson upheld the entire standard of the reformation of manners, embodying it in the paragonic purity of Clarissa and posing that against the worldly values Richardson identified with Lovelace, with unreformed men, and with Mandeville. In *Clarissa,* Lovelace asks rhetorically "is it not natural for *all men* to aim at obtaining whatever they think will make them happy?" then associates this view with *The Fable of the Bees:* "I am entirely within my worthy friend Mandeville's assertion, *That private vices are public benefits*" and thereby justifies his continuing assault on Clarissa. Richardson, then, reversed Mandeville's style of feminism in the interests of the reformation of manners, just as Burnet reversed Rochester's.[122] The aspiration of novelists of sensibility was to convert rakes to puritanism and softness. By contrast, the "dumb signs" of grief, joy, wonder, and fear in the female exemplars of the cult of sensibility, to Mandeville signified childlikeness and a lack of education, and, one might say, a denial of the wish to enter the world as adults. Worldliness itself, Mandeville suggests, including his kind of feminism, would bring about the civilizing of men and greater equality between the sexes.[123]

Hume and Smith

The capstone of the historical progress celebrated by the creators of the Scottish Enlightenment was the "refinement of the arts" which they saw as the culmination of the same processes Mandeville had described. History allowed one to see, in Hume's words, "human society in its infancy, making the first faint essays towards the arts and sciences. To see the policy of government, and the civility of conversation refining by degrees, and every thing which is ornamental to human life advancing toward its perfection." Such refinement was the height of civilization. Sensibility—even "exquisite sensibility"—was the "character" most suitable to "the circumstances" of "one who lives in a very civilized society."[124]

Hume, Smith, and the Edinburgh Scots associated with them in the "Select Society," Henry MacKenzie, Lord Kames, David Fordyce, and William Cullen, among the best known, idealized sensibility in men and implemented their social affections among themselves. Their refinement extended to body, in a process to which nerve specialists like fellow Scot, Cheyne, had lent their expertise. Hume recorded the physiological distinctions of these men, congregating in the splendid new houses and public buildings of Georgian Edinburgh (their builders consciously creating the latter as symbols of "prosperity, humanity, and prestige," as their models were doing in England's urban renaissance), withdrawing from "the grimy vitality of old Edinburgh to the prim and properness of the New Town," just as the same men rejected "Scotticisms" for more civilized English speech. The "skin, pores, muscles and nerves of a day labourer are different from those of a man of quality, so are his sentiments, actions and manners." Respectable people left their customary taverns "to the craftsmen and shopkeepers." Such persons "of delicate feelings" also contrasted their new city with the "savagery" of the "barbarian" Highlanders among whom it was set.[125] The historian William Robertson, a member of the same "Select Society," described the rejection of the ancient mummers by the gentry in the countryside near Edinburgh: "As their rhymes were mere unmeaning gibberish, and their demeanour exceedingly boisterous, the custom became intolerable." Hume said that sensibility's cultivated incapacitating of the mind for "rougher and more boisterous emotions" was an "improvement." This was the psychological equivalent of the "improvement" implemented by aesthetician Lord Kames in his farming and gardening, following the precedent of Lord Shaftesbury, both efforts ultimately bound up with the commercialized agriculture spreading a better diet to a larger market. There was an obvious historical connection between these men's cultivation of sensibility and their material circumstances in Edinburgh.[126]

In the following discussion of Hume's evaluation of "effeminacy" we should note that he intended his *Essays* to reach a more popular audience than his *Treatise of Human Nature* had managed to do. Publishing that early work, Hume said he desired "to be absolutely independent and to seek no help from a patron or a list of personally solicited subscribers," in other words, he desired to escape the clientage resisted by his fellow writers and by tradesmen at large. Because the *Treatise* fell "dead born from the press," Hume then incorporated some of its views in a series of essays (including those on refinement, luxury, and "The Stoic") modeled on *The Spectator* and *The Craftsman.* The larger audience they were intended to reach was to be composed of women as well as men. (In addition to his calculations about his audience, Hume, like Richardson and Wesley, "took a particular pleasure in the company of modest women," and he said that they were receptive to him.) His *Essays* were "successful," selling out right away in London, Hume noted with pleasure.[127]

Hume referred to Mandeville's ideas throughout the 1742 essay which he first entitled "Of Luxury" and later "Of Refinement in the Arts." The difference between the moral connotations of "luxury" and "refinement" signified Hume's refinement of Mandeville's views. Hume, like Smith, acknowledged Mandeville's accuracy in evaluating human appetite as an engine for economic progress, but he attempted to distinguish between private vices which were tasteful and contributed to improvement and those that were not. He reproduced Mandeville's punchbowl metaphor, but he held that the "ingredients ought to be mixed in different proportions." "Innocent luxury" was to be separated from the "vicious luxury" which Hume suggested Mandeville advocated.[128] The latter included obsessive eating and too much culinary refinement, "drunkenness," and illicit sexual intrigue—in fact, all of the excessive appetites "nourished by ease and idleness." This was the kind of "ASIATIC luxury" which had led to Rome's loss of liberty and, Hume suggested, was the kind to which the contemporary British aristocracy tended, in contrast to "the middling ranks of men."[129]

Pursuit of "innocent luxury" by the middling ranks, that is, "refinement in the gratification of the senses," was the "spirit of the age," putting "the minds of men . . . into a fermentation on all sides" and carrying "improvements into every art and science." Hume specified how such economic progress produced "an increase of humanity," that is, humanitarianism. Knowledge flowed out from towns, permitting distant or remote persons to store up "a fund of conversation."

> They flock into cities; love to receive and communicate knowledge; to show their wit or their breeding; their taste in conversation or living, in clothes or furniture. Curiosity allures the wise; vanity the foolish; and pleasure both. Particular clubs and societies are everywhere formed. Both sexes meet in an easy and sociable manner; and the tempers of men, as well as their behaviour, refine apace. So that, beside the improvements . . . from knowledge and the liberal arts . . . they must feel an encrease of humanity from the very habit of conversing together, and contribute to each other's pleasure and entertainment.

The more men refined their pleasures, the less susceptible they were to indulge themselves in "beastly gluttony" and "drunkenness," and Hume wished that were also true of "libertine love"—clearly he shared values with the campaign for the reformation of manners.[130]

At the same time and like Smith, he acknowledged the way in which British economic development contributed to the same goals. Thus "private life" was beneficial to "*public*" life. Revealing this link between "*industry, knowledge,* and *humanity,*" Hume said it was characteristic of "the more luxurious ages." British history's economic success effected "refinement," the "encrease and consumption of all the commodities, which serve to the ornament and pleasure of life, are advantageous to society." Here Hume illustrates Pocock's account of the belief in the personality-changing effects of "products." He assumes throughout that production was bound up with "consumption." As a writer he had been made acutely aware of that connection. The volume of luxury was measured by the sheer numbers of people enjoying it, indulging themselves in refined feelings, conjoined with their pleasures in clothes, furniture, ornaments, and "decencies." They were tastefully mediated to a remarkable extent by women. We have seen that Hume attributed to women "a more delicate taste in the ornaments of life" and "the ordinary decencies of behaviour," and here he suggests that it is the easier and "sociable" intercourse men have with women, habitually conversing and considerate of each other, all in the context of a consumer society that reforms men's manners, civilizing them, making them more humane, and thereby contributing to the improvement of public life. This connection became a commonplace of an age attempting to combine politeness with commerce, to reconcile harmony with the individual pursuit of happiness. Thus William Enfield, in one guise, attempted to build young men's character by teaching them to become proper speakers, in another, celebrated Liverpool's rebuilding in 1773 as the manifestation of "humanity and public spirit." Borsay makes it clear that the same thirst for civilizing "sociability" was expressed in the urban renaissance as Mullan detects in the language of sentiment. And a crucial dimension to this conjunction of humanity and public spirit, one illustrated by Hume's account of the humanizing process, was that women join with men in the public social spaces for the "pleasure and entertainment" created in cities. The same developments humanizing men benefited middle-class women by drawing them into pleasurable, amplifying dimensions from which previously they had been excluded and within which reformed men behaved more considerately to women.[131]

In the same year, Hume published "The Stoic," which presented the male ideal created by the process of "refinement" described in the essay of that name, illustrating that sensibility was virtually synonymous with "humanity" as the product of this process. Like his English predecessors, Hume significantly modified the classical ideal of the Stoic, asking,

> Does he constantly indulge this severe wisdom . . . harden his heart, and render him[self] careless of the interests of mankind and of society? No; he . . . feels too strongly the charm of the social affections ever to counteract so sweet, so natural, so virtuous a propensity . . . bathed in tears he laments the miseries of the human race . . . What charms are there in the harmony of minds . . . What satisfaction in relieving the distressed, in comforting the afflicted, in . . . stopping the career of . . . cruel man in [his] insults over the good and virtuous! But what supreme joy in the victories over vice as well as misery.

Nonetheless, it was in its striking combination of toughness as well as tenderness that this masculine ideal resembles "the divinity." "The softest benevolence, the most undaunted resolution, the tenderest sentiments, the most sublime love of virtue, all of these animate successively his transported bosom." Like Shaftesbury, Hume advocated that "our" aesthetic "judgement," our "taste," should be "strengthened" by cultivation and exercise. Too delicate a passion and sensibility needed to be thus "cured." The Stoic's reward of this combination of virtues is "GLORY" and "an immortal fame among all the sons of men."[132]

Arguing in favor of capitalist ambition (in effect of the triumph of a pervasive "monied interest") and of the consumer luxury it produced, Hume said it need not lead to the effeminacy against which Shaftesbury had warned. The modern state benefited from men's industrious pursuit of happiness and prosperity because their acquirement of goods represented their social investment. On the grounds that prosperous societies could support fleets and armies, Hume dismissed the "fear, that men, by losing their ferocity," would be less vigorous in defense of their country or their liberty. The arts will have no such effect in "enervating the mind or the body." Industry "adds new force to both." The "effeminacy" of his contemporary Italians was not due to their luxury but to other historical circumstances. The "severe moralists" who ascribed Rome's "corruption" to its luxury and refinement were similarly ignorant of history. Yet it appears that this dismissal of the danger of effeminacy was on more ambiguous grounds than Mandeville's.[133]

Hume was capable of distinguishing between male requirements of a woman as a sexual creature and his recognition that women were "rational" beings. This is implicit in his account of men's and women's civilizing meetings and conversations. It is explicit in his thoughts on Queen Elizabeth:

> The fame of this princess, though it has surmounted the prejudices both of faction and bigotry, yet lives still exposed to another prejudice which is more durable because more natural . . . This prejudice is founded on the consideration of her sex. When we contemplate her as a woman we are apt to be struck with the highest admiration of her qualities and extensive capacity; but we are also apt to require some more softness of disposition, some great lenity of temper, some of those amiable weaknesses by which her sex is distinguished. But the true method of estimating her merit is to lay aside all these considerations, and to consider her merely as a rational being placed in authority, and intrusted with the government of mankind. We may find it difficult to reconcile our fancy to her as a wife or a mistress; but her qualities as a sovereign are the object of undisputed applause and approbation.

While somehow the requirements of men were "natural," they were also prejudices, the expression of sexual "fancy." That women should usually and characteristically show "more softness' ' and more "weakness" than men was evidently in part the result of their deference to male wishes. Their "original frame of mind" was usually reflected in greater "delicacy," but Elizabeth showed women were capable of precisely the firm Stoicism that Hume idolized: "[T]he force of the tender passions was great over her, but the force of her mind was still superior; and the combat which her victory cost her serves only to display the firmness of her resolution, and the loftiness of her ambition's sentiment." Like Mandeville and other eighteenth-century writers, Hume recognized that the corollary of sensational psychology was that women were "distinguished" by custom, that is, by men's sexual "prejudice." (This, presumably, is what appealed to Wollstonecraft, when she reprinted Hume's characterization of Elizabeth in *The Female Reader.*) Nonetheless, Hume still demonstrated the tendency of even enlightened men to claim that women were essentially creatures of sensibility, perhaps because he held that men depended on them for refinement.[134]

Smith criticized Mandeville at some length in his *Theory of Moral Sentiments* (1759). In this he was lining up with his teacher, Francis Hutcheson (1694–1747), whose major work had carried the flame of Shaftesbury's innate goodness idea to Smith and the whole school of Scottish "moral sense" by defending Shaftesbury against Mandeville. (Even so, Hutcheson also had incorporated "elements" of Mandeville's thought into his system.)[135] Smith accused Mandeville of having been locked in a time warp with the puritanical extremists he had been countering half a century earlier. He was, therefore, not refined enough in his definition of "vices." For example, Smith distinguished between the lavish prodigality—the "profusion"—of aristocratic consumer spending on "frivolous" amusements—on "a multitude of horses and dogs," say—and the useful, even "frugal" consumption of "necessaries and conveniences."[136] Mandeville had rejected such distinctions. Smith linked self-improvement to "vanity," "the desire to be observed, . . . to be taken notice of with sympathy, complacency, and approbation." This seems identical to Mandeville's view, but Smith's notion of vanity depended on the "natural" "class distinctions" of "refinement" which Mandeville had rejected as he had dismissed the hierarchalism of Shaftesbury's moral sense. Smith located the manners closest to nature and of which he approved most in "the middling" rank, as did Hume and Cheyne. Because such an evaluation followed Smith's criticism of the "licentiousness" of Charles II's court and that court's scorn for "puritan" virtues of "frugality . . . painful industry, and rigid adherence of rules," which Smith said were, in fact, social "virtues," it will be seen that, like Hume, Smith shared the goals of the reformation of manners in key respects. This, too, put him at odds with Mandeville.[137]

Still, Smith agreed that puritan asceticism "would be pernicious to society by putting an end to all industry and commerce." While Smith wished to refute Mandeville's "licentious system," he conceded the value to the British economy even of conspicuous aristocratic consumption, provided it was tasteful, and he included the pursuits of his mentor's mentor, Lord Shaftesbury: "a taste for the elegant arts and improvement . . . for whatever is agreeable in dress, furniture or equipage, for architecture, statuary, painting, and music." Such "luxury, sensuality, and ostentation" were "public benefits." But in *The Wealth of Nations* (1776) Smith points to the still more important consumer demand of "the inferior ranks of people" for "durable commodities," houses, and "many agreeable and convenient pieces of household furniture." He lists linen and woolen cloth, soap, salt, and candles, and he notes the greater availability and cheapness at that date of commercially grown and marketed food, turnips, carrots, and cabbages, for example, The result of the flow of these commodities down the social pyramid were "the common complaints that luxury extends itself even to the lowest ranks of people and that the labouring poor will not now be contented with the same food, clothing and lodging which satisfied them in former times." Against the complainants Smith argues that such, more democratized "luxury" is a public benefit. His vision here is the same one industrialist Boulton expressed, looking to the promulgation of "liberal arts" in the following year.[138]

It is apparent that women's home demand was as central to Smith's account of the "Causes" of the *Wealth of Nations* as it was in Mandeville's. Furthermore, Smith noted "the labour of the wife [included] her necessary attendance on the children."[139] Together, Smith's *Theory of Moral Sentiments* and his *Wealth of Nations* (linked by their concern for "bettering" the human "condition")[140] demonstrate his view that material conditions at home improved childrearing and thereby nourished "sensibility." Poverty, he said, was "extremely unfavourable to the rearing of children . . . the common people cannot afford to tend them with the same care as those of the better station." "No society can be flourishing and happy, of which by far the greater part of the members are poor and miserable." By contrast, Smith exclaims over the pleasure brought him by viewing the kind of feelings generated in a middle-class family, able to afford such psychological luxuries as careful childrearing as well as material ones.

> With what pleasure do we look upon a family, through the whole of which reign mutual love and esteem, where the par-

> ents and children are companions for one another, without any other difference than what is made by respectful affection on one side, and kind indulgence on the other; where freedom and fondness, mutual raillery and mutual kindness, show that no opposition of interest divides the brothers, nor any rivalship of favour sets the sisters at variance, and where everything presents us with the idea of peace, cheerfulness, harmony, and contentment.

In Smith's view, as in Hume's, history, including this family history, culminated in the "man of perfect virtue . . . he who joins to the most perfect command of his own original and selfish feelings, the most exquisite sensibility to the original and sympathetic feelings of others."[141]

Like Shaftesbury and Hume, Smith saw this refinement of feeling as the outcome of histories of "manners." He made an historical hierarchy, placing very high value on the most "cultivated" and "civilized" societies. They were founded upon "humanity," he said, whereas "savage" and barbarian societies were "habituated to distress." His illustrations of the latter included the Spartan and the North American "savage," who showed the extreme of self-command in being tortured ritualistically to death. Another distinction between civilized and savage societies was in the relation between the sexes. "The weakness of love, which is so much indulged in ages of humanity and politeness, is regarded among savages as the most unpardonable effeminacy."[142]

This points to the fundamental limitation that Smith placed on the civilizing of men. Smith insisted in the strongest terms that "our sensibility to the feelings of others" was not at all "inconsistent with the manhood of self-command." While Smith stressed the "extreme gentleness" of Hume's "nature" he went on to say that this feature "never weakened either the firmness of his mind or the steadiness of his resolutions."[143] Firmness and self-command still connected the most civilized of males with the utterly impervious Indian: "We" (in Edinburgh), Smith wrote, still give "our highest admiration" to the man, "who under the severest tortures allows no weakness to escape him." It was only "an entire insensibility to the fair sex [which] renders a man contemptible in some measure even to the men." Men's refined contact among themselves in some degree depended on how they treated women on heterosexual occasions, as it were, and clearly that pointed to the matrix of Smith's sympathetic family, a set of relationships that stood in sharp contrast to the "mere connexion" he said was made by savages. The recognition of women as human beings from whom one might learn more manners than those men taught each other was a mark of civilization. Women's "company should inspire us with gaiety, more pleasantry, and more attention."[144] Hume had said as much and suggested that women therefore specialized in fostering social affections. A later avatar of the Scottish Enlightenment suggested that women were "led to cultivate those talents which are adapted to the intercourse of the world, and to distinguish themselves by polite accomplishments that . . . heighten their personal attractions, and to exite [in men] those peculiar sentiments and passions of which they [women] are the natural objects."[145] For men, Smith implied, 'love" could be "weakness" and "indulgence." From the entirely masculine point of view of the savage, it was "effeminacy." This, presumably, was the basis for Smith's distinguishing "brothers" from "sisters," even in the most civilized and affectionate of families. David Fordyce, another fellow of Smith's in the Edinburgh elite, advocated the softening of male ferocity into a new male ideal in which "gentleman," "man of worth," and Christian "all melt insensibly and sweetly into one another." Marking out the same, refined, gender gauge, however, he said, "I do not mean that the men I speak of will become feminine." The qualification recorded a risk. In Smith's words, "the delicate sensibility required in civilized nations sometimes destroys the masculine firmness of character."[146]

Smith's subjects in both of his best-known books were men. Smith's civilized males were distinguished, on the one hand, from "the vulgar" by their "degree of sensibility which surprises us by its exquisite and unexpected delicacy and tenderness." The surprise was due to the fact that they were male. On the other hand, such refined males showed their "amazing superiority" to "the weak" by their degree of "self-command." Given his identification of such firmness with masculinity it is clear that those "weaker" beings included women. Presumably women were free to show still more delicate sensibility. Smith's ideal men, all those "we's," and "ours," and those represented by the passive voice of *The Theory of Moral Sentiments,* could extend their "pity" to such weaker beings without apprehending a loss of manhood. Such a sympathy's distinction, in fact its essential condescension in relation to such distress, was central to its definition. Smith's famous "spectator" at the core of his theory was a man.[147] Only the "most brutal and worthless" men would look on "the too tender mother" or "the too indulgent father" with "hatred and aversion" or "even with contempt."

> There is a helplessness in the character of extreme humanity which more than anything interests our pity. There is nothing in itself which renders it either ungraceful or disagreeable. We only regret that it is unfit for the world, because the world

> is unworthy of it, and because it must expose the person who is endowed with it as a prey to the perfidy and ingratitude of insinuating falsehood.

The latter sentence could be the plot of a sentimental novel.[148]

It was as if Smith was able to reconcile the standard of perfect humanity (which Mandeville had labeled fantasy) to the hard, appetitive world of reality—one depicted in *The Wealth of Nations*—by identifying the categories with gender. These categories were to be maintained, however softened or civilized men allowed themselves to become. Too much luxury of feeling destroyed a man's "masculinity." On the other hand, luxury "in the fair sex, while it inflames perhaps the passion for enjoyment, seems always to weaken, and frequently to destroy altogether, the powers of generation." A nation's becoming wealthy could challenge old sexual identities in fundamental ways.[149]

Henry MacKenzie

This tension between the high evaluation of refinement in men and the wish to square it with manliness permeated the eighteenth-century novel, whatever the sex of the writer. Richardson made softened manhood a central goal of his participation in the reformation of manners, saying in his own voice that "the man is to be honor'd who can weep for the distresses of others," at the same time making the sympathetic Sir Charles Grandison an emblem identical, in his firm, resolute Stoicism, to the ideals upheld by Smith and Hume.[150] (*Sir Charles Grandison* was published in 1753, between Hume's *Essays* and Smith's *Theory of Moral Sentiments.*) Fielding wrote to Richardson of *Clarissa,* "God forbid that the Man who reads this with dry Eyes should be alone with my Daughter when she hath no assistance within call."[151] This sign of a man's morality corresponded to a capacity for artistic sympathy: "no man can paint distress well which he doth not feel while he is painting it, nor do I doubt but the most pathetic and affecting scenes have been writ with tears."[152] Fielding joined Anglican divines in attempting to popularize this form of masculinity. Indeed, one of his exemplars of muscular yet feeling Christianity was a divine, Parson Adams, his "heart naturally disposed to love and affection." In the characters of Joseph Andrews and Tom Jones, Fielding further exemplified manly sympathy and moral weeping. At the same time, Fielding showed the vulnerability of such a style of manhood to charges of "effeminacy" in order explicitly to refute them; unless refuted and however moral, sympathetic weeping could be synonymous with being "unmanned."[153] Taken too far, sensibility in men disqualified them for worldly business: Squire Allworthy and Smollett's Matthew Bramble had to learn to toughen up in the face of reality, recover the firmness with which Shaftesbury, Hume, and Smith required male sensibility to be tempered in order to avoid "effeminacy."

"Effeminacy" in men was also presented as objectionable to female characters who were devoted to converting hard men to greater sensibility. *Clarissa* illustrates the point.[154] Charlotte Lennox illustrates it by way of Arabella, the "Female Quixote," whose identification with feudal "romance" allowed her to contrast the fashionable men she sees in eighteenth-century Bath—in its assembly, sauntering in public walks, and tattling over a tea table—with the romantic male adventurers of the feudal past, who fought glorious battles, took cities, and rescued ladies. Her view was that of her contemporary male politicians, concerned as they were with the contrast between "the monied interest" and traditional ideals of manhood. Contemporary males, wrote Lennox, had "figures so feminine, voices so soft, such tripping steps and unmeaning gestures," they were, in sum, "sunk in sloth and effeminacy."[155]

Popular novels written by men in the 1760s and 1770s were preoccupied with the meanings of sensibility for manhood. The "unfitness" of the oversensitized man for "the world" which excited Smith's pity and condescension in 1759 was the object of satire in the novels of Goldsmith, Sterne, and Smollett (as well as of Voltaire in *Candide*). The twentieth-century literary debate over whether such figures as Yorick and Harley were celebrations of or satires on "the man of feeling" reflects the eighteenth century's own ambivalence over the meaning of refining manhood.[156] The issue is complicated for historians by the competition among male and female writers who were self-consciously catering to a flourishing female readership. This ambivalence and its complication are clearly demonstrated in the work of another Scot who achieved immense fame in Britain, the novelist Henry MacKenzie (1745–1831).

MacKenzie lived in the Edinburgh of Hume and Smith and his novels preached the latter's theory of moral sentiments. Born to the city's elite, MacKenzie was educated at its high school and university. Thereafter he was articled in the law department of the Scottish Exchequer. Sir Walter Scott, MacKenzie's lifelong friend and the editor of his *Collected Works,* wrote that "to this profession although not perfectly compatible with his literary taste" he applied himself "with due diligence." That slight incompatibility was a sizable burr under MacKenzie's saddle. In 1765 he went to London to study the English Exchequer. Recognizing the market for sentimental fiction (Sterne's *Sentimental Journey* was published in 1768), MacKenzie published *The*

Man of Feeling there in 1771. He said that its hero's shyness was his own in London, where he felt a "martyr" to it. There, the ambitious and privileged Scot could feel an outsider and probably the prejudice experienced by Cheyne before him. MacKenzie returned to Edinburgh where he succeeded his law teacher as attorney to the Crown. Having gained the patronage of Pitt via his fellow Scot, Henry Dundas, MacKenzie got the lucrative job of Comptroller for the Taxes of Scotland. He married the daughter of a Scottish baronet and lived to see his eldest son become a Scottish Supreme Court judge.[157] MacKenzie combined this successful legal and governmental career with the literary life for which he also hankered. He joined a "Society of gentlemen . . . accustomed at their meetings to read short essays of their composition, in the manner of *The Spectator.*" Just as it inspired Hume's *Essays, The Spectator* inspired MacKenzie and his literary gentlemen friends to publish an Edinburgh equivalent, *The Mirror* (1779–80), and then *The Lounger* (1785–7), both of which were intended to contribute to that refinement of manners that was as deliberate a feature of Georgian Edinburgh as it was of London (and Georgian Philadelphia for that matter). MacKenzie was an active member of several other societies of gentlemen, including the new Royal Society of Edinburgh, again emulating English precedent.[158]

According to Scott, MacKenzie's principal, "direct and professed" object in his novels was "to reach and sustain a tense or moral pathos, by representing the effect of incidents, whether important or trifling, upon the human mind, and especially on those which were not only just, honourable and intelligent, but so framed as to be responsive to those finer feelings to which ordinary hearts are callous." This is a good definition of the purpose of writers of sensibility in general, including the combination of the "firm" and the "fine."[159] In the June 19, 1779, issue of *The Mirror,* MacKenzie, describing "The Effects of Religion on a Mind of Sensibility," praised his own prose for its "power of awakening the finer feelings, which so remarkably distinguish the composition of a gentleman." He devoted another issue to the description of his own exquisite feelings at the funeral of a young woman; he celebrated his sympathy for pain, above all. "It is by such private and domestic distresses, that the softest emotions of the heart are most strongly excited," and they should be preferred to the more material "pleasures" of "luxury." MacKenzie's representation of "domestic distresses" expressed the same value Smith placed on private life. Sympathetic "virtue" is excited "amidst the warmth of social affections and of social sympathy" where "the heart will feel the weakness, and enjoy the duties of humanity."[160]

MacKenzie's view of the limitation to be placed on feelings in a man was also derived from Smith's *Theory of Moral Sentiments.* He noted of his own feelings at Maria's funeral that his "sorrow was neither ungentle nor unmanly." MacKenzie recommended the "indulgence of pensiveness and sorrow" because such indulgence contributed to "virtue," to "the refinements" and "improvements of life," but it should be only "occasional." The next issue, "On the Effects of Sentiment and Sensibility in Happiness," illustrated "the danger in pushing [such] qualities too far." Books written with "those delicate strokes of sentimental morality, which refer our actions to the determination of feeling" were dangerously "captivating." MacKenzie's illustration of such dangers was the tragic life of a young woman named Emilia after Richardson's maddened heroine: she had "inherited from nature" a "certain delicacy and fineness of feeling" which "her earliest reading had tended to encourage and increase." That such "delicacy" was "natural" in a woman echoed Hume's typical view of the female frame, and the young woman whose literacy contributed to her excessive sensibility was a monitory stereotype in fiction.[161]

In *The Man of Feeling* MacKenzie shows a male whose feelings had "acquired such an ascendancy as to render him unfit for the business of life." This was in accordance with Smith's formula quoted earlier, declaring that "delicate sensibility" could destroy "masculine firmness of character." Sheriff's recent demonstration of MacKenzie's intention to satirize such unrestrained sensibility in a man is entirely persuasive, but, significantly for the history of the relations between gender and sensibility, the best-selling *The Man of Feeling* was "consistently misread" from the date of its publication as a celebration of the character "who relies on his feelings as if they were alone a guide to his virtue."[162] MacKenzie's view of the misreading of his novel would later become apparent in an essay in *The Lounger.* It was also expressed by MacKenzie's close friend, Scott, in commenting in his introduction to MacKenzie's *Collected Works,* on which he collaborated with MacKenzie. Harley's extreme "gentleness of temper" was not at the expense of his manhood: a couple of episodes in *The Man of Feeling* (a reaction to "impertinence" and a little "spirited indignation") had been "skillfully thrown in to satisfy the reader that his softness and gentleness of temper were not allied to effeminacy, and he dared, on suitable occasion, to do all that might become a man."[163]

Divided between the profession of the law and his "literary taste," MacKenzie wished both to refine businessmen and to establish the status of artists in the new world businessmen were shaping. Two issues of *The Lounger* illustrate MacKenzie's concern over definitions of manhood under such circumstances. One published on December 30, 1786, was entitled "Defense of Literary Studies and Amusements in

Men of Business." Its autobiographical opening referred to the "danger which is said to result from the pursuit of letters and of science, in men destined for the labors of business or professional life." Such pursuit of "fineness of mind," the "abstraction," the "speculations," and "the visionary excursions of fancy" were all "supposed to incapacitate a man for the drudgery by which professional eminence is gained; as a nicely-tempered edge, applied to a coarse and rugged material, is unable to perform what a more common instrument would have successfully achieved."[164]

In fact, MacKenzie argued, only a few of the writers-and-scholars category had failed in this way. Certainly his own well-cultivated success in the literary marketplace testified to the opposite. MacKenzie went on to defend the artist's manhood still more directly; finding their youthful "effervescence" tyrannized by the drudgery of their professional training, young businessmen—"men of the world"—looked for "amusement." Unfortunately, because their "fancy and feeling," their tasteful responsiveness to art and to "the beauties of pity" were undeveloped, "the amusements will generally be either boisterous or effeminate, will either dissipate their attention or weaken their force." "Boisterous" connects them to the vulgar entertainments of mumming and of the tavern; "effeminate" perhaps, because of its context, to an overindulgence in sex, against which Smith had warned, too. Rakish insensitivity and effeminacy were the Scylla and Charybdis for men heading for improvement. By contrast, the education of men of letters was "friendly to sober manners and virtuous conduct." They prepared men for "those avenues of more refined pleasure." "Cultivation of feeling" steered them to the refined but manly indulgence advocated by other members of Edinburgh's Select Society. MacKenzie went still further in his defense of the value of "the love of letters" to businessmen, articulating a rationale we have seen absorbed and promulgated in the taverns and coffeehouses of eighteenth-century London and Edinburgh. Refinement made men better at business itself as well as fostering "love and friendship." "Feelings of delicacy" and other characteristics of the culture of sensibility, the "direct, the open, and the candid," enhanced the reputation of businessman and professional and led them away from sharp practice. Moreover, "the improvement of our [men's] faculties" in the pursuit of arts and science, when applied to professional and business careers (those of the doctor, the merchant and the lawyer, MacKenzie said) were "the road to eminence and wealth." Cheyne had taken it from Aberdeen to London and Bath.[165]

A further advantage lay in the real social distinction refinement created and maintained, a way of getting the monied interest to make itself more mannerly. According to MacKenzie, "the influx of foreign riches, and of foreign luxury, which this country has of late experienced, has almost levelled every distinction but that of money among us." Aristocratic manners had given way to the "vulgar," a "tide of fortune which has lifted the low, the illiterate, and the unfeeling into stations of which they were unworthy." However, the cultivation "of knowledge, of fancy, and of feeling" gave to "the votary" a "real superiority in what he possesses." Here MacKenzie reproduced the softened Stoic ideal, perpetuating religion's and literature's contributions to civic humanism; the "love of letters was connected with an independence and a delicacy of mind" which was "a preservative against that servile homage which abject men pay to fortune." It was "the classical pride which from the society of Socrates and Plato, Cicero and Atticus, looks down with an honest disdain on the wealth-blown insects of modern times."[166]

Like Smith, MacKenzie suggests that there was a beneficial relationship between the businessman's expression of sensibility in his public work and the "softened feelings he experienced in his relations with women and children at home." Sensibility provided a man an elevating rationale, linking the public and the private. "In the more important relations of society, in the closer intercourse of friend, of husband, and of father, that superior delicacy and refinement of feeling which the cultivation of the mind bestows, heighten affection into sentiment and mingle with such connexions a dignity and tenderness which gives its dearest value to our existence." This *Lounger,* then, argued that the male writer had identical interests with the businessman, reconciling the different aspects of MacKenzie's own life.[167]

The second *Lounger* that addressed the male writer's status had been published six months earlier, June 18, 1785. This looked to the other end of MacKenzie's spectrum, as it were, the one much closer to women as writers and readers. Businessmen had shaped a world that included the mass marketing of novels to women whom, therefore, male writers could not afford to ignore in regard to style and subject. Here MacKenzie attempted to distinguish the kind of male novelist he was from a man of sensibility carried too far, the kind of sensibility Smith had said "sometimes destroys the masculine firmness of character," and the kind against which MacKenzie's Harley had warned. One particular reader whom he seems to have had in mind was Hannah More, who approvingly but mistakenly identified MacKenzie with his weepy hero in a sentimental poem she had published just the previous year.[168]

MacKenzie's premise was the sheer popularity of the novel, a popularity he desired and from which he had benefited. If the novel was popular because it could be understood by "the young and indolent" it was held in contempt by "the more respectable class of literary men." The "few novels which superior men have written" did not merit such a judgment, and we can guess whose novels our self-praised novelist here included. This grade of novel writing required a "degree of invention, judgement, taste and feeling, not much, if at all, inferior to the higher departments of writing." We can assume they were written with the compositional "power" of a "gentleman." Unfortunately, such works had been lumped with novels lacking such "genius." The superior novels "were meant to convey no bad impression but, on the contrary, were intended to aid the cause of virtue, and to hold out patterns of the most exalted benevolence." They were intended to promote "a certain refinement of mind as part of a moral code including the duty to parents; ties of friendship and of love; the virtues of justice, of prudence, of economy; the exertions of generosity, of benevolence, and of compassion." Perversely, however, inferior novels singled out the emotional, tender qualities from this list, that is, friendship, love, generosity, benevolence, and compassion, in order to contrast them favorably with the tough ones, duty to parents, justice, prudence, and economy. As we shall see, this moral contrast was a general subject of sentimental novels, including those written by women.[169]

There were other ways in which MacKenzie judged the novel to have been "debased." The "enthusiastic" authors of this "species" of novel (which MacKenzie here labeled "sentimental") separated "impulses and feelings" of a visionary kind from practical "good works." "Refined sentimentalists" had created a false religion of their own, one of impulses, feelings, visions, words, minds open to impressions, imaginary evils and distresses, imaginary blessings and enjoyments, and "a certain childish pride" of "superior delicacy," Here, too, MacKenzie probably had More's recent poem in mind because it literally had deified "Sensibility" in aggrandizing every quality on MacKenzie's list.[170]

Another reason MacKenzie gave for the debasement of the novel was that its subjects were "domestic scenes and situations in private life." On one hand, this opened superior novels "to the judgement of the people." Hence, presumably, the popular misunderstanding of *The Man of Feeling*'s message and manhood. On the other hand, it meant that "all whose necessities or vanity prompted them to write, betook themselves to a field, which, as they imagined, it required no extent of information or depth of learning to cultivate, but in which a heated imagination or an excursive fancy were alone sufficient to succeed." Fielding, too, had registered his sense of unfair competition from "foolish novels" by semieducated "scribblers." The tasteless, uncontrolled expressions of the imagination of the hoi polloi, especially of women, is what Shaftesbury, Steele, Johnson, and Richardson had apprehended. For that reason, MacKenzie complained, "men of genius and of knowledge, despising a province in which such competitors were to be met, retired from it in disgust, and left it to the unworthy." MacKenzie had published his last novel, *Julia de Roubigné,* in 1777, eight years previously.[171]

MacKenzie conceded that the superior level of novel, written by well-educated men, was capable of being misconstrued because such men attempted to communicate the "refinement of mind," including feeling. Aiming at refining "manners" they were confused with their debased and merely "sentimental" competitors. He further distinguished between even "some of the best of our novels" in which authors mistakenly thought it appropriate to depict heroes of mingled vice and virtue and "that common herd of novels (the wretched offspring of circulating libraries) which are proscribed for their immorality."[172] But, in practice, these distinctions were very difficult to maintain. If MacKenzie scorned "refined sentimentalists" because their refinement and distinction constituted "the enthusiasm of religion," he had himself earlier argued on behalf of religion "as a feeling, not a system, an appealing to the sentiments of the heart, not to the disquisitions of the head." How, then, could he accuse his imitators of "debasement" and "perversion" of deviating from "reason"? There were readers out there, some of them becoming writers, who would take from their reading the messages that suited them, above all, the message of the value and pleasure of simply feeling. Moreover, women readers could well prefer more "effeminate" men, a preference from which MacKenzie's sales had probably benefited. The writer could not control his readers.[173]

Politics and Boy's Literature: Thomas Day

The historical lesson held up by Rome—the subordination of republican manhood to tyranny, imperial ambition, the corruption of courtly manners, and the degenerative effects of luxury, all leading ultimately to effeminacy—had been a centerpiece of the mirror held up by Commonwealthmen and Tories alike to the power center they opposed from early in the century, and it continued to permeate British politics. Political historians have documented the presence of this theme in speech after speech and pamphlet after pamphlet.[174] The Scottish school's insistence on an historical progress toward humanity without effeminacy was also in part shaped by the wish to refute Roman history. That history was made still more authoritative in 1776 with the publication of the first volume of Gibbon's *The Decline and Fall of the Roman Empire,* wherein may be found the same connotations of decline articulated by earlier writers and corresponding to the experiences Gibbon described in his autobiography.[175] Definitions and redefinitions of gender had become highly valued counters in public and in private. Conversely, it may be said that the reformation of men espoused by a massive body of literature may be thought of as political.[176]

Caroline Robbins's roster of "eighteenth-century commonwealthmen" includes a number of novelists, Henry Brooke (1703–83), for example, whose sentimental *The Fool of Quality* so impressed Wesley. Published between 1764 and 1770, it was in Wesley's abridgement that it became known. Brooke's protagonists celebrate the "species of pleasure in the heart, a kind of soothing and deep delight, that arises with the tears which are pushed from the fountain of God in the soul, from the charities and sensibilities of the heart divine." Harry, its hero, advocates "the heroism of the heart as opposed to the heroism of martial or political prowess," yet he "duels, fights with his fists, and kills a mad dog." According to Clive Probyn, Brooke's novel "attempts to create a whole national psyche and vision of endless commercial expansion based on British Christian benevolence," a combination Mandeville would have recognized.[177] It also pointed to the dangers expressed throughout the century that the reformation of male manners could go too far. For that reason John Brand suggested in his *Observations on Popular Antiquities* (1777) that "innocent sports and games" should be revived among the common people. This was at a time, he wrote, when "the general spread of luxury and dissipation threatens more than any preceding period to extinguish the character of our boasted national bravery." Langford takes this as evidence of a deepening anxiety over the subversiveness of sentimentality, which reached a climax at the end of the 1770s. Clearly Boulton perpetuated the more confident spirit of the civilizing process at the same time, but there is evidence for Langford's point. Brand quoted another moralist, an older male writer, who suggested that "*open* pastimes in my youth being now suppress, worse practices within doors are to be feared." The significance of that change over time, from outdoor sports ("May-games, Mid-summer-eve rejoicings, etc. anciently used in the streets of London") to indoors, the world of home and women, is apparent. The association between the nation's loss of male bravery because of men now being more associated with women is barely veiled. It is not surprising that reformers would intervene in childrearing in order to make little boys tougher, too.[178]

One of the most popular and durable of proponents of this view was Thomas Day (1748–89), another of Robbins's "commonwealthman" novelists.[179] Day was an adherent of Lockean psychology at its Rousseauistic extreme, insofar as he believed that animals (heavily anthropomorphized) were as susceptible to being shaped by luxury or hardship as were human beings. Day's belief that working-class males were the most deserving voters was consistent with his view that their exposure to hardship made them tough-minded. Day's intention in *The History of Sandford and Merton* (1783–9) was to provide parents with the means to resist tyranny by educating sons to the manly hardihood required by the defense of liberty, although he was deeply prejudiced in favor of a paternalistic middle class.[180] His environmentalism was brought to earth only by his death. He was testing "that kindness alone could control an unbroken colt, when the colt threw him on his head."[181]

That *Sandford and Merton* continued the long effort to reform manners is illustrated by its attack on bullbaiting, the "diversion" of "a rude and illiterate populace."[182] The class values of the campaign for the reformation of manners are particularly evident, indicated by the ceaseless drip of qualifying "buts": houses "small but neat," "small but clean," "small but warm . . . furnished with the greatest simplicity, but managed with perfect neatness," all in keeping with the "Dialect" detected by Mandeville. Typically, Elizabeth Griffith's sentimental "The History of Louisa" (1780) said her heroine's "house, though small, was neatly furnished."[183] The link between such domestic spaces and the reformation of men can be illustrated by Day's depiction of "The Cottagers." Young Sandford and Merton have lost their way in the woods but they can rely on the virtuous poor for rescue. A ragged boy leads them to his home, where his father confesses to his visitors, "I was once an idle abandoned man myself, given up to swearing and drinking, and taking no thought of my wife and children." That is, he was a participant in that outdoor, popular male culture also diverting itself with bullbaiting. The agent in reforming his "life and manners" was Mr. Barlow, the minister who is Day's agent in teaching the spoiled Tommy Merton how to reform his manners, too. The book the reformed drinker is reading is the "Gospel of Jesus Christ," which he is now relaying to his children. His wife records the man's reformed treatment of her: "there is not now a better and kinder husband in the world: you have not wasted an idle penny or a moment's time these two years." He heads the kind of family economy Smith assumed, the wife and eldest daughter supplementing its income by spinning.[184]

Day also urged the reform of women. Men had to be reformed by weaning them from their traditional leisure and work habits, women from modern sources of corruption, that is, luxury and fashion. This was a typical contrast, echoing Smith's warnings of the dangers of luxury to women's fecundity. Day wished women purged of fashionable appetites and boarding school ambitions and returned to the traditional domestic and pastoral activities of milking, churning, baking, and "anything necessary in a family." (Just where they should now graze their cows in accordance with medieval economy he does not say.) Women should give up plans for "gentility" because it contradicted "industry." Such reformed women would be "adapted to produce and educate warriors." Day's "notable" female ideals are sentimental props, weeping as their properly educated young males stride off to war or being grouped as the background for a hardy African male "reposing by his door." It was "manly hardiness" that attracted "beautiful young virgins."[185]

Sandford and Merton popularized the male ideal of softened Stoicism we have seen in loftier forms. Young Harry Sandford, full of grit and the Protestant ethic, bursts into tears on realizing how cruel he has been to a cockchafer, but while Day's males of all ages frequently show "effusions of tenderness" and throw themselves into each other's arms, the reservations about such moments become dominant because of the intensification of the need to maintain manliness. One of Day's masculine exemplars declares there "are some philosophers who aspire to triumph over human feelings . . . as disgraceful weaknesses . . . I have indeed, opposed as criminal that habitual acquiescence in sorrow which renders us unfit for our duties: but while I have endeavoured to *act,* I have never blushed at *feeling,* like a man." The tendency is to urge males to feel for the distress of others but then to draw back from feeling as soon as it is expressed. "Here a tear started from his eye, wetted his manly cheek: instantly, however, he recollected himself . . . [and restored the] appearance of manly fortitude." In Day's case a century of ambivalence has tipped toward a preoccupation with the dangers of "effeminacy." There are other clues that this was a widespread reaction to the cresting triumph of sensibility.[186]

The most prominent feature of *Sandford and Merton* is its obsessively repeated contrast between the hardihood of males reared under Spartan circumstances and the enervation of those reared in luxury. (Rousseau's influence must have boosted this element in Day.) Spartans, Kamtschatkans, Scots Highlanders, American Indians, Greenlanders, Scythians, Bedouins, and Africans; yeoman farmers, common laborers, men shipwrecked or otherwise placed under the most extreme of natural conditions, or vastly outnumbered in battle, confronted by freakishly enormous beasts; a little schoolboy bullied by a cruel lad bigger and older than him; all of these illustrated the value of hard, physical activity and frugality in food, drink, and all living conditions. Such males were "men indeed."[187]

While there was a notable emphasis on a good heart, sympathy for the worthy poor, for virtue in distress, and for animals, one cannot avoid seeing the intensity with which Day coupled those qualities with his repeated warnings against effeminacy. Luxury made men "effeminate." By "luxury" he meant a room that was painted and ornamented (contrasted, say, with the great natural decorations of stars in the sky); fashionable clothes; all the pleasures produced by "barbers, cooks, confectioners, fiddlers, dancers"; indeed, Day intoned, "everything that is unmanly and unfit for war." Day repeatedly links this view to the century-old Commonwealth argument on behalf of hardily reared citizens successfully fighting a just war against mercenaries. Egypt was assimilated to other ancient, decayed civilizations to warn English lads of the dangers of luxury: "the ease and plenty which they enjoy enervate their manners, and destroy all vigour both of body and mind; no one is here inflamed with the sacred love of his country, or of public liberty; no one is inured to arms, or taught to prefer his honour to his life." Instead, the very children "catch the contagion from their parents; they are instructed in every effeminate art; to dance in soft, unmanly attitudes."[188]

Day made the same criticism of the rich directly, excoriating eighteenth-century English gentlemen "who cannot do anything for themselves" and who were, therefore, "weak and childlike." By the same token, the poor were to be envied because they learn to bear hardship; outdoor labor made "the common people" more resistant to the cold, for example. The presence of Highlanders in his series of males for boys to emulate, together with his relentless assaults on effeminizing luxury, illustrates how far from Hume and Smith Day had traveled, although MacKenzie's later writings—contemporary with *Sandford and Merton*—indicates the same tendency.[189] Highlanders had represented "barbarism" to reformers of male manners at mid-century; now they were aggrandized as repositories of masculinity. This was a powerful motive in romanticism's "rediscovery" of popular culture, in Scotland and other "uncivilized" places.[190]

Here one could compare the changes in Godwin's view of manliness. Long having shown his adherence to Richardson's notions of gender, when writing his grief-stricken *Memoirs* of Wollstonecraft Godwin illustrated the transformation that the culture said pain could bring about. "I hope to be made wiser and more human by the contemplation of 'the memory of a beloved object'; I find a pleasure, difficult to be described in the cultivation of melancholy. It weakens indeed my stoicism in the ordinary occurrences of life, but it refines and raises my sensibility." This was a change for which Wollstonecraft had hoped in giving him *Heloïse*. Her death and Godwin's reading of Hume seemed to reinforce it for a while, but beginning in 1799 his series of romantic novels (one subtitled *The New Man of Feeling*) showed Godwin's preoccupation with the avoidance of "effeminacy."[191] The ways in which romanticism absorbed and modified elements engendered by preceding and contemporary conflicts over sex is beyond my scope here, although I turn later to related aspects of the 1790s.[192]

Sandford and Merton was frequently reprinted in the nineteenth century. Harry Sandford's pluck and determination in eventually defeating the bigger, stronger bully, Mash, was recognizably like those of the protagonists of a thousand Victorian boy's stories, in fact those on which I cut my teeth in the 1940s and 1950s. Harry's "patient fortitude" had at first been mistaken for "cowardice." Mash hurled him to the ground. "Mash had superior strength . . . but Harry possessed a body hardened to support pain and hardship; a greater degree of activity, a cool unyielding courage, which nothing could disturb or daunt."[193] And while Day was thoroughly typical of the culture of sensibility in attacking another of its targets among the array of public male violence, the cruel, hard-riding, aristocratic squire, his imperatives led the animal-loving and "radical" Day to a position on manhood very close to that taken by Sir John Eardley-Wilmot, Bt., in this nineteenth-century rationale for fox-hunting:

> The manly amusement of fox hunting is entirely, and in its perfection, exclusively, British. Its pursuit gives hardihood, and nerve, and intrepidity to our youth, while it confirms and prolongs the strength and vigour of our manhood; it is the best corrective to those habits of luxury and those concomitants of wealth which would otherwise render our aristocracy effeminate and degenerate; it serves to retain the moral influence of the higher over the lower classes of society, promotes good fellowship among equals and is one of the strongest preservatives of that national spirit by which we are led to cherish, above all things, a life of active energy, independence, and freedom.[194]

The combination of sentiment with the wish to assert manhood which one finds in Day's book, and perpetuated in much subsequent boy's literature, was the one expressed both by gentlemen at Waterloo and Methodist sailors at Trafalgar. The "civilizing process," including its effects on gender, moved on, now engaged by the cogs of industrialization.

FOUR

Women and Eighteenth-Century Consumerism

Home Demand

Women were excluded from the gregarious "world of the tavern" except as workers in it. They had "always" been "excluded from much of the recreational culture of the labouring classes," one that denigrated women. From the Middle Ages and earlier, women's "social activities" had been "particularly narrow and oriented toward family members." They found the principle site of their lives in that largely comfortless home. Given the combination of childbearing and rearing with women's other essential work for the household's economy, it is not surprising that the historical ledger for a female public popular leisure culture appears largely blank compared to the male one. Speaking for women generally, Margaret Cavendish, duchess of Newcastle (1623–73), said in her "Female Orations" (1668), "we Live and Dye, as if we were produced from Beasts, rather than from Men; for, Men are happy and we Women are miserable; they possess all the Ease, Rest, Pleasure, Wealth, Power, and Fame; whereas Women are Restless with Labour, Easeless with Pain, Melancholy with want of Pleasures . . . they would fain bury us in their houses or Beds, as in a Grave."[1]

When unmarried and in their teens, women normally worked as servants, their hours "gruellingly long," and they were "hardly allowed [social] lives of their own." If much the same could be said of teenage males, they had the daily prospect of becoming "socially at ease in the community," joining in leisure activities as well as official "public functions" of an entirely different sort. These were adult prospects—in marriage and in work as well as in leisure—significantly different from women's. Marriage brought men "personal autonomy" and "full authority over the domestic economy." As adolescent daughters and, if they survived, as widows, women had greater legal independence but marriage, lasting most of their adult lives, brought them "a new kind of dependence." As soon as they were married, eighteenth-century women, no less than their medieval sisters, were "wholly *in potestate viri,* at will and disposition of the husband." Yet everything pressed women to marry, in order to gain "the strength, protection, status, and earning power of husbands." Of course, there was an important distinction between legal subordination and the particularities of daily marital relations; it has even been argued that the medieval English peasant household "was based firmly on the partnership of husband and wife." This is a complex issue I can only oversimplify here. It can be said, however, that, once married, women traditionally had faced "a bleak existence" of unrelieved work, its bleakness apparent in precapitalist England, despite recent theorists of "a golden age" who echo eighteenth- and nineteenth-century reformers' biases.[2]

In the medieval countryside, women's work had appeared never ending, in part because wives were always on call, their work seen as supplementary to the work of men. The peasant home was merely a "workplace," one its "huswif" rarely left. Sixteenth-century poets recorded the same endlessness, one praising the worthiness of woman because "she serveth a man both day and night"; another contrasted husbands' possibilities for "respite" with "huswives," whose "affaires have never an end."[3] Women's fieldwork was unskilled, heaviest during planting and harvesting, and consisting of breaking up clods, weeding, and collecting stubble. Most of their time was spent producing food and drink; women brewed, baked, grew vegetables and herbs, and, it must be stressed, cared for meat and dairy animals, making butter and milk.[4] Women's work also included "working wool and flax into cloth." Already in the fourteenth century, however, their work in "basic production" was being altered by the purchase of bread, ale, and cloth from England's growing market economy. But that economy remained subject to traumatic vicissitudes, and, in good times as well as bad, "women would be content with very limited roles."[5]

It was the subsequent loss of livestock (as a result of decisions taken by different levels of landed capitalists) that permanently affected women's work. That loss was fundamental to the changes on which Carole Shammas concentrates her account of the preindustrial consumer. Between the mid-sixteenth and the early eighteenth centuries, a half to two-thirds of the "low wealth" section of the population significantly reduced their production for home consumption, replacing it by the purchase of "groceries," cloth, and other commodities. This was no sudden and ubiquitous transformation, and it varied in accordance with wealth as well as in timing and geography. Moreover, many early modern women continued to work in the fields, both for their "own" households and as hired laborers. They went to market with home products, as Rochester's buttered victim was doing, although such victimization may have become more salient as the use of livestock became more specialized and commercialized.[6]

"Above all, women span, kept house, and raised children," Roy Porter writes of the eighteenth century. These priorities reflect some significant changes that had taken place in women's work. While spinning continued an age-old tradition, women largely ceased making cloth for home consumption, even though the regional putting-out system absorbed much of their "available labor" in making lace and mantuas, as did their "finishing" contribution to the newly established commercial, artisanal, production of cloth and clothing, and the related work of the burgeoning number of shops in the countryside.[7]

Keeping house meant cooking, of course, but that changed, too, in accordance with the new dietary pattern. As we saw, many laboring families of the early modern period were purchasing "nearly their entire diet," the "more prepared the better," albeit doing so in small amounts at a time. Middle-class women could purchase larger quantities of bread, beer, and meat, as well as equipment to prepare and serve it, far more readily than those laboring families. Their purchase of sugar led to the allotment of time and skill in preserving fruit and making jam. Weatherill's study of inventories made up between 1675 and 1725 suggests that few families were yet capable of "elaborate sauces, pies, and confections," but in 1733 Cheyne testified to the appetite among "all Ranks who can afford it" for such "inventions," "the most delicate and savoury possible." Middle-class women "were expected" to do as gentlewomen had done, themselves cooking or supervising cooking to satisfy this newly attainable appetite for domestic "sensual Pleasure." Shammas suggests that, over the course of the eighteenth century, a much wider social spectrum of women devoted "special attention" to their daily cooking, in place of the habitual pattern of hasty cooking and eating, broken by the communal preparation of feasts for special occasions. Many may have found burdensome the longer hours such cooking required, although it well may have seemed an improvement over previous labors of production. A growing number of women could read recipes in the proliferating books of domestic economy now addressed to housewives, replacing books of husbandry to which wives' instructions were an appendix. So more women could incorporate greater choice, literacy, skill, and control in the acquisition and preparation of food. Late in the century

Wollstonecraft observed women's strong wish "to keep a better table."[8]

If medieval women had made food preparation "relatively simple and fast," they also had devoted far less of their time to other "tasks associated with modern housewifery: childcare was a much less time-consuming matter . . . household possessions were minimal and required little upkeep." To take the latter subject first: the "severity" of earlier domestic environments can be symbolized by the Elizabethan William Harrison's record of his forefathers' use of "a good round log under their heads instead of a pillow." The previous generation had slept on mats or straw rather than the beds Harrison could observe replacing them, as pewter was replacing wooden spoons. Still, through most of the seventeenth century, "forks were non existent," and homes continued to be marked by "austerity" and a "sheer lack of possessions." The lower stratum of society used "crude planks" for furniture and wore the simplest of homemade clothes.[9]

However, bedding, linens, and some brass as well as pewter goods did begin to filter significantly into the houses even of the poorest during the sixteenth and seventeenth centuries. More homes were built of brick, there were chimneys and fireplaces and room partitions, so inhabitants could find privacy indoors, although houses generally remained without other furnishings and furniture, or the equipment for games or music.[10]

The "enhancement" of the domestic environment accelerated in the late seventeenth century, coinciding with a particularly heavy period of new building. Houses came to be much better lit because of the "near universality" of glass windows by the Restoration, making it easier for women to see what they were doing in their daily work. Rooms were increasingly differentiated. The tendency toward the greater comfort of domestic space—the greater reliability of warmth, privacy, and a comfortable bed—was augmented from early in the eighteenth century by the increased investment in other consumer goods. People may well have been better rested, in separate bedrooms and their beds, like their meal plates, now individuated. Shammas suggests that the comforting of domestic space coincided with the democratization and relocation of prayer and Bible reading as domestic, family rituals, rituals that persisted when their religious impulse waned. "By the mid eighteenth century all levels of society showed some traces of new secular, domestic" rituals, those traces including the material artifacts associated with eating and drinking, associated, that is, with manners. Family meals came to be shaped by the fork, by cheaper, lighter crockery and glassware instead of pewter, by the tea equipment noted by *The Spectator.*[11] The English manufacture of cheap editions of delft and, later, queensware, fostered their inroads into a much broader range of homes after 1730. A probate record from 1739 shows a significant comforting and softening of the domestic space even of a man whose total possessions were valued only at ten pounds.[12]

More items seemed to require more cleaning. By 1726 a French traveler found "inconceivable" the amount of water the English used, "especially in the cleaning of their houses." He linked it to the same moral characteristic which Schama has explored in the case of Dutch housewives.

> Though [the English] are not slaves to cleanliness, like the Dutch, still they are very remarkable for this virtue. Not a week passes by but well kept houses are washed twice . . . and that from top to bottom; and every morning more kitchens, staircases and entrances are scrubbed. All furniture, and especially all kitchen utensils, are kept with the greatest cleanliness. Even the large hammers and the locks on the door are rubbed and shine brightly.

Earle says of the middle class at this period that their "[h]ouses, clothes, bed linen, cooking equipment and furniture . . . seem to have been kept scrupulously clean." Not only some greater availability of water but also the new materials of which items were made—glass, china, and lighter fabrics, in contrast with wood, metal, and heavier woolens—facilitated cleaning.[13] Moreover, new, shop-bought items were associated with easier times, perhaps, and with status. Handling them (or supervising their handling) must have brought feelings of pride and pleasure, and they were invested, too, with the moralistic power of taste. The diminution of home production facilitated the implementation of new standards of cleanliness, the psychological meanings of which I have mentioned. This process was helped, too, by the improved supply of water in the rebuilt towns, which began piping it and installing public pumps, a symbol of the growing connections between inside and outside, for women as well as men.[14]

Wedgwood's "protean variety" provided mannerly materials for eating, excreting, drinking, washing, and playing, but it was on much more widely affordable, "humbler" versions of Wedgwood that the consumer revolution and "the civilizing process" depended. Like Wedgwood's, these were "aimed specifically at a female market," aimed, that is, at women now living and working in more specialized rooms as well as with more and more elaborate equipment.[15] And it seems that this most self-interested group responded. The "diffusion of tableware almost perfectly mimic[ked] the rise in tea consumption during the first half of the eighteenth century." The same may be said of a genre of teatime paintings, among them two significantly entitled "An English Family at Tea" (1720) and "Family at Tea" (1732). In both, as in the genre they represent, it is women who are literally central, serving themselves and each other, as well as men, and serving the viewer to display the proper gestures accompanying the new equipment. Men are ancillary, taking their cues from women in this recreational activity.[16]

Its ritualistic power—women's ritualistic power—is implied by the contemporary naming of teatime as the "unfortunate shrine of female devotion." Men who spent much time drinking tea with women ran the risk of effeminacy, such effeminate tea drinkers "stock comic characters" of the period.[17] The consumption of tea was identified with women and, by and large, tea-drinking was a domestic activity, even a domesticating one. Shammas suggests that the eventually ubiquitous stimulants of tea, coffee, and chocolate may have replaced the "morning draft gulped down at the alehouse," although men continued to patronize that institution as it evolved into the tavern and coffeehouse. (Tea became "the basic drink of the lower classes, its popularity advancing steadily from south to north.") On the other hand, tea also became the occasion for women to make visits, with men and by themselves; this new, leisure activity, one which allowed women to assert themselves at home and abroad, was associated with politeness and commerce.[18]

Traditional mealtimes were also transformed. More time was now devoted to the consumption of food as well as its preparation, nourishing greater familial "interaction" and even allowing "conversation between bites," conversation that increasingly could be informed by literacy. Previously, "the average meal was a hurried affair," food taken directly from a large vessel by way of a spoon, a knife, and fingers; in the eighteenth century it came to be served on an individual plate, probably at the direction of the woman who had prepared it.[19] From mid-century, women more frequently joined other members of the household at the table for meals, whereas formerly they had stood to serve. By 1797, Sir Frederic Eden could write in his *The State of the Poor* that sitting "together at a table is perhaps one of the strongest characteristics of civilization and refinement." The sitting down may be explained in several ways, not the least being the acquisition of chairs. (It may well be that women asserted themselves in shopping for furniture very early.)[20] Participating in literally more stimulating meals (which manifested more elaborate skill in preparation), perhaps recognized as more expert in the use of the new eating as well as new cooking equipment, women must have been seen—by children, say—not only as less unequal, less unskilled than men, but as more influential, even powerful players in the dispensation of food, the most fundamental form of production and consumption. The revival of breastfeeding among the fashionable may be placed in the same perspective, evidently a matter of choice. It may be noted that Wollstonecraft was among its proponents, and she represented it as integral to the "reformation of the manners" of both sexes advocated by the *Rights of Woman.* "Affections" were strengthened by this primal family feeding, the "habitual exercise of mutual sympathy."[21]

Of course, women had always labored in producing and rearing children, but from late in the seventeenth century a steadily increasing number of them could have a record of their feelings. "Women's letters harrowingly chronicle the fatigue, ill-health, and premature aging they suffered" in pregnancy and childbirth.[22] Between 1680 and 1800, the proportion of both sexes who never married dropped from 16 percent to 6 percent, and women's age at marriage dropped with it, increasing their production of children (especially after 1740), an increase crucial to industrial capitalism's take-off.[23] These demographic facts coincided with the transcendence of dearth and the falling price of food. Previously, dearth "had led to births not happening, to marriages being postponed or forgone altogether."[24] Whether more desirable or not, the high marriage rate (and consequent increase in children) conspired with other factors to encourage women to invest more in their domestic space.

The value to women of houses becoming primary "sites for consumption" seems indisputable, and Shammas argues that women were "a major force in promoting enhancements to the domestic environment."[25] Novelties in house construction, room arrangement and the objects inside them, in work patterns, and in daily family habits all carried a doubly pleasing message because they existed in a social world of sharp contrasts, one where those less well-off reminded newly middle-class women how far they had come. They also must have been grounds for hope. "The evolution of a house into a home made social interaction more accessible to women and put more under their control." These new, more abundant interiors may have been "a source of power and influence for the physically vulnerable and legally unequal woman of the early modern period."[26] It has been argued that wives' subordination to husbands' patriarchalism had been modified during the seventeenth century, en route to the more "companionate" marriage of the eighteenth. If mothers, as well as fathers, felt better about themselves, they could transmit that to their children, to whom they now devoted far more time. In previous ages, "people had exhibited respect and concern for one another by getting their work done rather than by attending to each other's personal needs."[27] Between 1580 and 1680, parents came to make "a material and a psychological investment in their children, which was both considerable and prolonged." This preceded the eighteenth century's creation of a "new world of children" described earlier. By the late seventeenth century "the whole system of childrearing was . . . well adapted to the 'putting forth' of children . . . into a highly individualistic and competitive environment in which they would have to stand on their own feet." That demand was most fully made of sons, but new kinds of parenting had the potential of sponsoring individualism in daughters. In sum, for many women work shifted to more "modern" housewifery tasks in the eighteenth century.[28] The changes described also opened up less ambiguous or, rather, more direct routes for self-expression.[29]

Women Become Literate, Women Write Novels

Bennet writes of her local, medieval subjects: "No sources reveal the thoughts and aspirations of women in Brigstock—whether they ridiculed the public world from which they were so often excluded, whether they valued protection over independence."[30] Shifting work patterns allowed more women to find more time for literacy. Moreover, since Watt's pathbreaking study, scholars have connected the transformation of domestic space with the rise of literacy in the seventeenth and eighteenth centuries and, therefore, with women's ability to leave the historian a record of their wishes on an unprecedented scale, albeit one still largely confined to the bourgeoisie. Wollstonecraft would point out that being alone was a resource for selfhood, for "strength of character." "Solitude and reflection are necessary to give to wishes the force of passions, and to enable the imagination to enlarge the object, and make it the most desirable." Prior to the seventeenth century, interiors had been "just a hall, where cooking, eating, working, sleeping, and general activities took place, and a loft." The division and specialization of domestic space into doored rooms was a class privilege first, but it was seized by increasing numbers of the lesser orders.[31] In the eighteenth century "a feature of the Georgian house" was a closet adjoining the bedroom, holding books and a writing desk. There, wrote Richardson, a young lady "makes her closet her paradise." The existence of such space and its literary equipment was the context for what Watt calls the eighteenth-century "cult" of letter writing, addressing "news and opinions about ordinary lives." Women who read epistolary fiction were themselves writing letters on a new scale. Reading and writing letters were embedded in the economic prosperity signified by literacy, privacy, and the invention of the penny post in 1680. Its national development during the next century gave England a postal system "unrivalled throughout Europe."[32]

While letter writing was associated with intimacy, privacy, and domesticity, it is also true that writing letters, reading novels, and the incorporation of purchased objects into domestic space very significantly elevated women's "horizons," in keeping with the elevation of consumerism's and capitalism's other "high-time horizons." They seemed to "move into a tantalizing world of apparent choice." Literacy contributed to the growth of personality, one's absorption of knowledge of self and other, and its transformation into one's own terms and purposes, including art. "The very privacy of reading opens up possibilities for independence of mind, freedom of thought, and deviance from the norm." Writers could feel "vanity" in their literacy, the pride that Clarissa described.[33] Writing and reading letters could express appetite, "to discover, defend, assert, and manufacture the self," in Spacks's phrase, echoing the notion of "self-fashioning." Readers wrote to each other with pseudonyms drawn from novels. The characters that readers met in real life they named for those they read about: for example, a 1766 colonial letter writer contrasted a "Clarissa" of modesty and sweetness with a woman whose discourse was "Rough and Indelicate," making up the name "Masculina" for the latter. In short, readers and letter writers could add to the worlds they exchanged with each other by peopling them with alternative senses of selves.[34]

That women first became literate in significant numbers is a profoundly important feature of seventeenth- and eighteenth-century history. The number of literate persons as a whole may have been relatively small, although the actual number is impossible to ascertain.[35] In the big picture, there was a general increase of literacy in Europe between 1500 and 1800. It increased in Protestant countries first and England may have had the highest literacy rate in Europe. While a gap between the number of male and female readers remained, it closed significantly over that period. It is, moreover, "very probable" that statistics "underestimate the number of women who were literate." Of the English population in the Middle Ages, 10 percent of men and 1 percent of women had been literate. By the mid-seventeenth century, those figures were at least 30 and 11 percent, respectively, hiding wide variations between classes and occupations. Perhaps 30 percent of women could read by 1675. The end of the seventeenth and early eighteenth centuries "saw a significant growth in the rates of female literacy, particularly in the cities."[36] By the 1690s, the urban figure for female literacy may have been 52 percent. Between the 1580s and the 1720s, London women's rate of illiteracy was halved from a high of 90 percent. There was also a decline in female illiteracy in the North, from 80 percent in the 1660s and 1670s to 72 percent in the 1680s and 1690s. It seems that by 1750 60 percent of men and 40 percent of women could read. Between 1754 and 1800, the rate of increase of literacy among women continued to be greater than that among men. If in 1754 one bride in three signed the marriage register and by the 1840s it was one in two, Hunter argues that more women than men among the population unable to sign could read.[37] Contemporaries could not help noticing that women were reading and writing in much larger numbers than earlier. Among them was Dr. Johnson; significantly he interpreted the development as competition with men. In his youth (the 1720s–30s), he said, a woman who could spell an ordinary letter was considered "all accomplished," whereas in 1775 "they vie with men in everything."[38]

The explanation for this growth lay in large part with Protestantism and the later historical transformation it helped unleash. Little girls and boys witnessed their Protestant fathers reading the printed Bible at home to the assembled household and, presumably, to themselves. Protestant women would capitalize on their equality of soul before God and emphasize, too, that his gift of reason distinguished humankind, not just men. English feminism originated in this tradition, emphasizing that women should be more admired for their minds (preparing them for salvation) than for their worldly and corrupt persons. Further improvement in women's education, as well as the acceleration in the literacy rate, awaited the investment in schools and in the production of books that were part of late seventeenth- and eighteenth-century England's embourgeoisement.[39]

Charity schools had been established from the sixteenth century, but their largest growth would come in the eighteenth, sponsored by the campaign for the reformation of manners and "popular where they existed." Dame schools and parish schools taught reading and writing for the girls of parents who could afford the small fees. Boarding schools for girls were established in quiet towns near London and in Exeter, Leeds, Manchester, and Oxford. The rapid increase of boarding schools for "young ladies" illustrates the relationship between women's education and embourgeoisement or, in the eighteenth century's terms, between women's "delicacy" and the advance of civilized manners. Teaching many thousands of young women to read, boarding schools aimed to acculturate them into gentility. Their *curricula* would emphasize "commercial subjects" for boys and accomplishments for girls. The latter geared women to the display of consumerism in deportment, music, and dance. They, too, could be "luxury objects," although their being taught to read potentially subverted all goals.[40]

Mandeville said in 1724 that boarding schools were established to make "fine ladies" out of middle-class girls.[41] Hence many schools set their fees to attract the daughters of "every description of tradesmen" and they succeeded in attracting a greater investment from lower-middle-class households than ever before. One scholar has suggested that the most important reason for the popularity of these schools was "social advancement through marriage," assuming that higher-class men wanted their homes graced by a fashionably educated wife. Clearly, the grooming of young women for fashionable society, learning "manners, deportment, religion, French, arts and graces and even cards," fitted them for a life of consumption. A necessary if not sufficient cause for social advancement, such education could also prepare women for teaching in the same kind of schools if they did not marry. With one of her sisters and a friend, Wollstonecraft opened a school first in Islington and then in Newington Green, country towns neighboring London in 1783, close enough to attract customers but far enough to be safe for young ladies to congregate and walk to church and to the shops. Like many such "venture schools" it did not long survive, but it led Wollstonecraft to her first book, *Thoughts on the Education of Daughters* (1787), launching her literary career.[42]

The commercialization of publishing was another engine increasing literacy among women.[43] It accelerated a tendency that had existed in the seventeenth century. Shammas has found while "in Tudor Oxfordshire almost no one had books (1%), by the Restoration in Worcestershire more than one in six probated decedents possessed a volume or more." By the late seventeenth century, books began to appear in urban and rural probate records in significant numbers and increased still more by 1725 in London and other towns. The first of these was probably a Bible or other pious works. The latter continued to be a requisite of a "lady's library," but among the upper class they were augmented by romances and by plays.[44] Books were themselves consumer items, bought or borrowed and placed in the home. The April 12, 1711, issue of *The Spectator* described a "lady's library" in which the books were "ranged together in very beautiful order," separated by "great china jars," "tea-dishes of all shapes, colours, and sizes," and "a thousand other odd figures in china ware." On "a little japan table" was a quire of gift paper and "on the paper a silver snuff-box made in the shape of a little book." There were other such "counterfeit books" serving as furniture. And fashion was among the reasons for the owner's choice of real books. A woman correspondent of Richardson's complained that "we are obliged to read every foolish book that fashion renders prevalent in conversation." Fashion fostered literacy among women and was ineluctably associated with it. In 1778 Dr. Johnson linked what he called "this teeming of the press in modern times" to consumer motives by admitting that "it obliges us to read so much of what is of inferiour value in order to be in the fashion." Nonetheless, that "teeming" meant that "we have now more knowledge generally diffused; all our ladies read now, which is a great extension."[45]

Those "engaged in the trades of manufacturing and selling the products of the printing press" addressed a new readership in an attempt to outflank the aristocratic patrons on whom previously they had been dependent. Booksellers and writers "exploited" all the possibilities in producing "a flood of print," finding a growing audience in a rising, consuming middle class, one in which "a hunger for culture could easily be induced."[46] No inducement may have been necessary because the "needs and desires" new kinds of people brought to their reading were already there. Class barriers to reading were brought further down by the "rapid spread" of circulating libraries after 1740. Their "main attraction" seems to have been novels, now within the reach of those who could not afford to buy them. Describing the general "boom in literacy," Stafford suggests that the novel, "more than any other product . . . helped democratize literacy." To regular editions, serialization, chapbook versions, subscription borrowings, free and unofficial borrowings between readers, and Wesley's publication of cheap abridgments can be added both the peddling of secondhand books and the remaindering of new books at half-price. The 1779 catalog of bookseller James Lackington had 12,000 titles, and in 1792 he said he sold "more than one hundred thousand volumes annually." He claimed that his half-price remaindering of books was "highly instrumental in diffusing that general desire for READING, now so prevalent among the inferior orders of society."[47]

Domestic service provided another route to female literacy. The huge numbers of unmarried women working as servants in more prosperous homes, some of them taught to read and write by the

Artist unknown. *Beauty in Search of Knowledge,* 1782. Mezzotint. 9 15/16 × 13 15/16 in.
Courtesy of the Print Collection, Lewis Walpole Library, Yale University.

burgeoning charity schools, were exposed to the incorporation of books in domestic environments. "They could have leisure and light to read by; there would be books in the house; if there were not, since they did not have to pay for food and lodging, their wages and vails could be devoted to buying them if they chose; and they were . . . peculiarly liable to the contaminated by the examples of their betters." In this way, suggests Watt, "Pamela may be regarded as the culture heroine of a very powerful sisterhood of literate and leisured waiting maids." While this may exaggerate the leisure allowed female servants, it is apparent that they shared exposure to fashionable literacy with those daughters of the lesser ranks who attended boarding schools. A 1747 cookbook attempted to capitalize on servants' literacy by addressing its recipes ("made Plain and Easy") to them directly, thereby saving "the Ladies a great deal of Trouble."[48] Lady Chudleigh said in 1701 that she wished to replace "that nauseous Jargon and those impertinent Stories with which our Maids usually entertain us in our younger Years" with Latin, Greek, history, and morality. One can imagine a connection between maidservants' knowledge of impertinent stories and the warnings that novels inspired the lower orders "to indulge in dangerous dreams of pre-eminence." Eighteenth-century children of both ladies and servants increasingly witnessed sisters and mothers reading at home; to other agents for female literacy must be added female kin—mothers above all—as perhaps the most influential.[49]

The success of the novelists in meeting the appetites and interests of an ill-educated if literate mass audience "made possible the remarkable independence of Defoe and Richardson" and a host of other novelists from "the classical critical tradition." This independence made a virtue of necessity in the case of most women novelists but they could "rise" under the new conditions in a way that had been impossible before. Perhaps women writers responded with greater fidelity to the wishes of their readers because fewer of them engaged in subscription publishing. In any case, writers were keenly aware that "readers' preferences steered the novel's progress" in accordance with the "law of the market-place." "So long as our British Ladies continue to encourage our hackney Scriblers, by reading every Romance that appears we need not wonder that the Press should swarm with such poor, insignificant productions." It seems to have been especially after 1740 that "novels were being specifically produced for a middle-class and . . . predominantly female audience."[50]

An "immediate best seller," *Pamela* was "the most popular novel of the century." In what today is a very familiar process, the book "spun-off" other consumer items, for example, the series of prints by Joseph Highmore, one of which is included in Chapter 1. Some items, "fans and flat straw hats," allowed female readers to express their identification with the heroine in very public, tangible ways. Upscale, "fashionable ladies displayed copies in public places, and held fans painted with pictures of its best-loved scenes. *Pamela* became a play, an opera, even a waxwork." It would be read from the pulpit.[51] The decisive popularity of Richardson's three novels reflected his responsiveness to the new audience of female readers, one he and his successors influenced and enlarged. Of course, Richardson had followed "a long line of epistolary fiction, much of it written by women." Recognizing women's appetite for literacy, Richardson had begun *Pamela* as "a popular guide to letter writing" for young women, a work he published the year after that novel.[52] His way of composing his novels (absorbing the responses of a number of close female collaborators) contributed to the deftness with which he located and spoke to literate women's interests.[53] He put to marvelous entrepreneurial use his capacity to sympathize with women; one striking common bond was his sense of having been denied what he called "the very great Advantage of an Academical Education."[54]

Richardson's novels had "a crucial effect" on the status of the novel, making it respectable as a form.[55] At the same time his work expressed the moral power of literate women and the potential conversion of men to the values for which women stood. This was the central thrust of the emerging literature of sensibility. The major truth that the correspondence between the rise of sentimental fiction and the laws of the marketplace expressed was that the themes of the fiction answered the interests of female readers. Women "were not only writing in greater numbers than ever before, they were not only reading more than ever before; [they and] some of their male counterparts were also questioning the patriarchal values of society itself, women's gender roles, and their economic status." This was "profound and revolutionary."[56]

Lackington testified that women's wishes in reading extended much further than novels, but he declared that novels were valuable because "the best" of them gave "a more genuine history of Man . . . than is sometimes to be found under the more respectable title of History, Biography, etc." Well over half of his total of "the best" authors were writers of sentimental fiction: Cervantes, Fielding, Smollett, Richardson, Burney, Voltaire, Marmontel, Sterne, Le Sage, Goldsmith, MacKenzie, Dr. Moor, Green, Charlotte Smith, the Gunnings, the Lees, Reeve, Lennox, and Radcliffe. Nine of these were women. Women (for example, Behn, Manley, Jane Barker, Haywood,

Aubin, and Mary Davys) "were popular novelists long before the arrival of Richardson" although they had to overcome the notion that writing was disreputable to them. At the same time, some were immensely popular—Manley's political novels of the first decades of the century, for example. By 1790 "a good many spinsters" supported themselves by writing. Women wrote history, treatises on education, political pamphlets, plays, moral essays, children's literature, and poetry (the first general collection of British poetry was published by Elizabeth Cooper in 1737), and produced translations and anthologies. But it was in the genre of the novel that women wrote and read most.[57] Moreover, the majority of novels published between 1692 and the end of the eighteenth century were written by women.[58] This was noted by contemporaries. In 1771 Smollett suggested that men had been driven out of writing novels: "that branch of the business is now being engrossed by female authors, who publish merely for the propagation of virtue, with so much ease and spirit, and delicacy, and knowledge of the human heart, and all in the serene tranquility of the high life, that the reader is not only enchanted by their genius, but reformed by their morality." Evidently women novelists bent their efforts to the campaign for the reformation of manners, too, a tendency illustrated by Penelope Aubin's career earlier in the century.[59]

That women should thus come to dominate a branch of literature as soon as they became literate in large numbers is another remarkable feature of eighteenth-century history. That it was the popular novel that was "feminized" reflects one obvious historical fact.[60] The novel was "a new and unexacting literary form, hedged round by no learned traditions, based on no formal techniques." When women had begun publishing in significant numbers during the seventeenth century, virtually "all . . . were ignorant of Latin, the language of professional and theological discourse." *The Spectator* coupled its observation that most books calculated to reach a male audience were written "with an eye to men of learning," with its recognition of women's greater appetite for romances (a recognition and an apprehension that went back to Dante and, of course, to the troubadours).[61]

The Spectator attempted to associate its standards of taste with classical authority, symbolically heading its papers with Greek or Latin mottoes; this attempt, however, coexisted with *The Spectator's* association of itself with the popularized consumerism symbolized by tea and china, and it addressed a readership drawn from both sexes. Fielding assumed that *The Spectator's* mottoes were intended to guard against "those scribblers who [have] no talents of a writer but what is taught by the writing-master," but he apprehended that "a swarm of foolish novels and monstrous romances will be produced, either to the great impoverishment of booksellers or to the great loss of time and deprivation of morals in the reader." His own "introductory chapters" to each Book of *Tom Jones* may have been intended to serve a similar elevating purpose as *The Spectator*'s mottoes, but he wrote them in English. Like his classically trained predecessors and successors, Fielding contributed to the dissemination of popular literacy and the cultivation of sensibility even as he decried its effects. In his *Elements of Criticism* (1774) Lord Kames translated his quotations into English "with a view to the Female Sex." Literate women had become an audience that authors and booksellers could not afford to ignore.[62]

Barbauld suggested in "On Romances" (1773) that sentimental fiction was popular because it appealed to those who could not reason: "few can reason, but all can feel." Furthermore, she suggested that emotional pain was the lowest common denominator among the writers and readers of the same kind of works Fielding had condemned as "monstrous." Here, she said, was illimitable potential: "Sorrow is universally felt." Debarred from the educational establishment and therefore from a knowledge of the ancient languages; excluded from the Royal Society, that powerhouse of scientific and intellectual life generally; and reading in a context where literature was considered a learned activity, women turned their hand to a form and subject they could master by themselves.[63] Women far down the social scale wrote novels. "Cook-Wenches" might become writers. *Virtue in Distress,* subtitled *The History of Miss Sally Pruen, and Miss Laura Spencer* (1772) was written "By a Farmer's Daughter in Gloucestershire." Elizabeth Inchbald, too, was a farmer's daughter. The poets Susanna Harrison and Ann Yearsley were, respectively, a domestic servant and a "Bristol milkwoman." The African-born, Massachusetts domestic slave, Phillis Wheatley, supported by the countess of Huntingdon because of evangelical common ground, had her poems published in London in 1773.[64]

The value of writing for a popular audience found its defenders, beyond the far greater number who in effect ignored the issue and wrote. Francis Coventry criticized the "pride and pedantry of learned men, who are willing to monopolize reading themselves, and therefore fastidiously decry all books that are on a level with common understandings, as empty trifling and impertinent." While he derided frothy romance, Richardson defended sentimental fiction on aesthetic grounds. He suggested that women could not help writing sentimental fiction, but he went on to say that it was superior to learned men's writing. Speaking through Clarissa, Richardson argued that "the pen, next to the needle" is the most proper employment for women, "best adapted to their geniuses."

> Who sees not . . . that those women who take delight in writing, excel the men in all the graces of the familiar style? The gentleness of their minds, the delicacy of their sentiments (improved by the manner of their education), and the liveliness of their imaginations qualify them . . . for this employment; while men of learning, as they are called (that is to say, of *mere* learning) aiming to get above that natural ease and freedom which distinguish this (and indeed every other kind of writing) when they think they have best succeeded, are got above, or rather beneath, all natural manners.

The "feminized" Richardson, aided by his circle of female discussants, was able to write in "the familiar style," but he could assume in accordance with the paradigm his language invoked that the very structure of women's brains and nerves, "improved" by education, naturally led them to it. The polarity Richardson describes between, on the one hand, gentleness, delicacy, imagination, freedom—all female associated—and, on the other hand, the unnatural ambition of learned men, was a characteristic of the sentimental novel. This contrast corresponded to the old polarities of street and home: men "assume a style as rough as their manners," their sublimity "in *words* not in *sentiment*," and they "call them MASCULINE." In reversing the values convention placed on women's writing, Richardson contributed to making the sentimental novel respectable, but the very serious danger in the defense was apparent as it hardened into definition. A reviewer of the anonymous *The History of Miss Della Stanhope* (1766) could tell a woman wrote it because of its "ease of the language, the vivacity of spirit, the delicacy of sentiment, the abundance of love and tenderness in the novel." A woman's style, said another reviewer, naturally exuded sensibility, "warmth, . . . tenderness, and . . . unaffected modesty."[65] In any case, if the "unexacting" requirements of the novel's language was seen to suit women's nervous system and education, it was also the form wherein they could best express their preoccupations with the gender arrangements governing their domestically focused lives.[66]

Not only did women readers become writers but they became great ones. Kirkham has described the "extravagant burgeoning of female talent at the end of the century," referring to Burney and Edgeworth, as well as to Wollstonecraft and Austen, but noting, too, the talent of the preceding generation. Spencer has laid out a splendid case for women writers throughout the eighteenth century. Her book's title, *The Rise of the Woman Novelist*, properly corrects Ian Watt's *The Rise of the Novel* of 1957, which first inspired critics and historians to grasp the importance of women readers.[67]

Here the individual, creative exuberance of selfhood in women writers capitalized on the potentials in literacy described earlier. In her dedication to her first novel, *Evelina,* begun in her youth and published when she was twenty-six, Burney's first and ironical sentence was this: "To the Authors of the Monthly and Critical Reviews. Gentlemen, The liberty which I take in addressing to You the trifling production of a few idle hours, will, doubtless, move your wonder and contempt." She thus made her own declaration of independence in 1778, two years after the more famous one. She declared she lacked "patronage" but thereby her freedom to reach a market in "the commerce of the world." Laying out the obstacles to a woman's writing which these "gentlemen" represented, Burney compares her "Courage . . . one of the noblest virtues of this nether sphere" to that of "the fighting hero" on "the field of battle." Her circumstances as a female writer entering this critical world were analogous to those of her own letter-writing heroine, Evelina, ready to delight in the public entertainments of commercialized London, yet under potential assault from men. In her diary Burney wrote that she was "frighted out of my wits from the terror of being attacked as an author." Therefore, she said, she "shirked" notice. She published *Evelina* anonymously. Yet Burney concluded her dedication by asserting her devotion to the modern deity of "EGOTISM,—a monster who has more votaries than ever did homage to the most popular deity of antiquity; and whose singular quality is, that while he excites a blind and involuntary adoration in almost every individual, his influence is universally disallowed, his power universally condemned, and his worship, even by his followers, never mentioned but with abhorrence." Her declaration is of individualism as well as independence.[68] In *Emma Courtney* Hays issued a similar challenge to Burney's, in which she reversed the values previously placed on asceticism and barbarism. "Man does right when pursuing interest and pleasure—it argues no depravity—Ascetic values are . . . barbarous."[69]

By the 1790s Austen was able to join in the battle fought by Burney by referring to the great novels achieved by both Burney and Edgeworth.

> Yes, novels—for I will not adopt that ungenerous and impolitic custom so common with novel writers, of degrading by their contemptuous censure and very performances, to the number of which they are adding—joining with their greatest enemies in bestowing the harshest epithets on such works, and scarcely ever permitting them to be read by their own heroine, who, if she accidentally takes up a novel, is sure to turn over its insipid pages with disgust.

Austen begins her challenge by acknowledging novelists' identification with the aggressor, "their joining their enemies" in censuring their own works, showing their readers heroines (themselves readers) who identified with the aggressor in the same way. Her stance toward these aggressors, "the Reviewers" who "abuse such effusions of fancy," resembles Burney's in *Evelina.* Like Burney, Austen feels embattled, she and other creators of reading heroines facing "foes almost as many as our readers." She suggests very strongly that this was a defense of women novelists against male reviewers or, at least, reviewers prejudiced against women novelists, in contrast to the favor they heaped even on hacks who merely anthologized male writers.[70]

"Pleasure" is Austen's first ground for defending women novelists, or novelists focusing their work on literate heroines.

> Let us not desert one another; we are an injured body. Although our productions have afforded more extensive and unaffected pleasure than those of any other literary corporation in the world, no species of composition has been so much decried.

Presumably Austen herself derived pleasure from the novels she was about to praise, and she testified to other women readers' pursuit of pleasure. Austen goes on to defend novels—novels written by women—on aesthetic grounds. Asked what she is reading, the female reader, showing the effects of the barrage of "disgust" just described, replies with "affected indifference, or momentary shame.—"

> "It is only Cecilia, or Camilla, or Belinda;" or, in short, only some work in which the greatest powers of the mind we displayed, in which the most thorough knowledge of human nature, the happiest delineation of its varieties; the liveliest effusions of wit and humour are conveyed to the world in the best chosen language.

Austen herself wrote masterpieces and implicitly declared them to be among several masterpieces women novelists had achieved.[71]

Women's Self-Expression in Fashion

From very early in the eighteenth century, observers suggested that women had a peculiar fondness for dress. It was "wives and daughters" of London citizens and tradesmen, provincial tradesmen and merchants, and of menfolk still deeper down the social pile who were the most avid consumers of fashion. Bourgeois women could now enjoy the predilection for fashion against which Elizabeth, wishing to monopolize it, had warned in 1597, concerned by "the confusion of all places being great where the meanest are as richly apparelled as their betters." In the sixteenth century sumptuary laws shifted their focus from food to dress, "the food battle perhaps being recognized as a lost cause." (Perhaps the now general transcendence of "crises of subsistence" debased the value of "the parade of wealth" on the tables of the aristocracy.) James I had made the same complaint as Elizabeth of the dressing up of women of the "Nobilitie and Gentrie" and clearly this was an appetite waiting to be unleashed.[72] Postrestoration, middle-class women "maintained a minimum of three complete outfits (and often much more)," and Earle illustrates the point by listing the quite staggering wardrobes owned in 1665 and 1675 by the widows, respectively, of a London grocer and a London apothecary. *The Spectator* criticized women for their adaptation "to sex than to their species" and illustrated its point by women "making the toilet their great scene of business," a function extended out into the new world of consumerism, as they made work of "sorting ribands" and exhausted themselves in shopping. Wollstonecraft would say that women were "continually talking" about clothes. Fiction voiced the same complaints, Sir Thomas Grandison noting the devolution of modes of appearance—fashion—from courtiers to the female bourgeoisie.[73]

This avidity for fashion is not surprising for several reasons, among them, perhaps, women's taking pleasure in now purchasing what in previous ages their ancestresses (and in their own, their poorer acquaintances) labored hard and long to produce themselves. Textile advertisements were aimed at women. "Many spent all they earned on 'Ribands, Ruffles, Necklaces, Fans, Hoop Petticoats and all those Superfluities in Dress.'" Mandeville recorded the demonstration of such appetite by women "almost of the lowest rank," who wore "good and fashionable clothes." They did so as part of the marking of public, popular leisure, that is, "in *Easter, Whitsun,* and other great Holidays."[74]

Mandeville provides us with further explanations of the value of this particular form of consumerism. On holidays, "respectable" women could be approached by strange men as Mandeville approached them.

> If coming to talk with them, you treat them more courteously and with greater Respect than what they are conscious they deserve, they'll commonly be ashamed of owning what they are; and often you may, if you are a little inquisitive, discover in them a most anxious Care to conceal the Business they follow, and the Places they live in.

Good and fashionable clothing allowed a degree of self-fashioning to women, transcending the daily anxiety and work of their homes.

Mandeville explained his interviewees' reticence in talking about their mundane lives.

> The Reason is plain: while they receive those Civilities that are not usually paid them, and which they think only due to their Betters, they have the satisfaction to imagine, that they appear what they would be, which to weak Minds is a Pleasure almost as substantial as they could reap from the very Accomplishments of their Wishes: This Golden Dream they are unwilling to be disturbed in . . . they hug themselves in their disguise.

Clothes available in the fashions assumed by the rich allowed women of "the meanness of Condition" to disguise themselves. They could take on an outward identity which invoked courtesy, civility, and "Esteem" from others, specifically a man. Fashionable clothes could bring them the courtesy due to "ladies," that is, the manners previously confined to the aristocracy.[75]

Second, according to Mandeville, women gained substantial pleasure from this approximation to fantasy, which presumably included wishes for daily mannerly treatment from men, although other parts of these women's "Dream" can only be imagined. Third, the very power of being able to assume a different identity in this new but accessible way was evidently the source of pleasure, despite the danger of detection. Not as protean in its possibilities as the masks of personality available to the new men of commercial capitalism, nonetheless, fashionable dress was a significant addition to women's repertoire. While it was the upper and middle classes who could first afford the new fashions, evidence of several kinds (retail stocks, prices, inventories, travelers' accounts, and fiction) suggests that they met the wishes of many lower-class women too.[76]

These kinds of female motives played a vital role in Britain's growing prosperity. "The variety of work that if perform'd, and the number of Hands employ'd to gratify the Fickleness and Luxury of Women is prodigious."[77] Fickleness stood for the combination of changeable taste and available goods essential to the undisciplined consumer pleasures against which moralists fulminated. Linking women's consumption to this whole scheme, Mandeville said that the loss of even the quarter of the consumer trade that went to the highest ranks would throw half a million people out of work, causing "a Calamity to such a Nation as ours." He also showed that "the worst of women and most profligate of the Sex . . . contribute to the Consumption of Superfluities, as well the Necessaries of Life," but it was on the consumer appetites of respectably married women of the "middling" ranks, "Prudent and Moderate in their Desires[,]" that trade depended most. Marriage was the fundamental source of disposable income, and Mandeville describes the wives and daughters of "creditable shop-keepers" (a class vastly increasing in accordance with the new consumption patterns) frequently buying new suits of clothes "especially to display" at church. Given that church had been virtually the only place respectable women went into public (except on working missions to market), it is not surprising that it figures prominently in moralists' accounts as the first site for women's display of fashion.[78]

But in 1714 Mandeville was able to report meeting fashionably dressed women in the street. Fashion demanded display, as well as purchase, and we have seen some the consequences of the emergence into public space of the whole social range of women. This was a topographical equivalent of the publication of their writings. Defoe called the "conversing by assemblies," (that is, the public, heterosocial intercourse later praised by Hume), "new-fashion'd" in the 1720s. Assemblies had begun to meet regularly in the earliest resort towns before the turn of the century, and soon weekly assemblies—for cards, dancing, and conversation—were being held in London and throughout the network of provincial towns.[79] Here were public nodal points for women (presumably discussing fashionable literature as well as discussing and displaying fashionable clothes) to formulate new cultural terms for themselves, part of the new personal skills required by public heterosocial groupings. "Women not only shared fully in the literary and recreational life of the day but seemed positively to dominate it." Women's public presence is widely illustrated in prints of the new streets and buildings.[80] The effect of these new opportunities for self-expression on the "ordinary lives" of the "Hanoverian middle class" was "striking." Over time, the "consequence of playhouses, assemblies and concerts," in the words of a contemporary Scot, was "a wonderful change upon female manners." In Scotland's no less than in England's previous history, women leaving the home on expeditions other than work had been confined to religious occasions. Previously, "the Scottish women made their most brilliant appearance at burials." The creation of a polite and commercial people entailed the transformation of each sexes' manners, although leisured women were excluded from the process going on among men in taverns, inns, and most coffeehouses.[81]

Tracing female consumption led Mandeville to consider the vital question of how married women were able to gain use of money, which their husbands controlled, a question we have seen Barbauld address in explaining how Mr. Homelove's wife and daughter got themselves to Bath.[82] Those "prudent" women wanting to look fashionable in church had to "plead." According to Wollstonecraft, it was "to preserve his own peace" that a "man of sense" let his wife "go to church in clothes made of the very best materials." Mandeville itemized methods married women used in order to express their own "desires" in consumer goods, to "pleasure their fancy." A "few men" had a real passion for their wives, were "fond of them without reserve" and therefore were "very lavish" to them. Husbands who did not care for them at all allowed their wives to spend "out of Vanity," taking pleasure "in the consciousness of an uncontrollable Possession" "as a Coxcomb does in a fine Horse." Notable in Mandeville's categorization of this crucial nexus for the economy were women's challenges to the husbandly purse: "a considerable Portion of what the Prosperity of *London* and Trade in general, and consequently the Honour, Strength, Safety and all the worldly Interest of the Nation consist in, depends entirely on the Deceit and vile Stratagems of Women." Mandeville detailed these "strategems." "It is incredible what vast quantity of Trinkets as well as Apparel are purchas'd and used by women, which they could never have come at by any other means, than pinching their Families, Marketing, and other ways of cheating and pilfering from their Husbands." Here was further subversion for consumer purposes, the expression of individual wishes. Other wives were more direct in technique, "conquering" even obstinate husbands by a combination of "teazing" and "assiduity." Others fell back on ancient stereotype for modern purposes, "scolding" and bullying "their tame Fools out of any thing they have a mind to," while other wives, especially "the Young and Beautiful," laughed at their husbands' denials for their wishes, then employed "the most tender Minutes of Wedlock to promote a sordid Interest."[83]

Mandeville compared the sexual transaction in marriage to that between prostitute and customer (as would Fielding), culminating in the wife's "Counterfeited Transports" when she watched "for the Moment when Men can least deny." Such a moment, a man at the point of orgasm, his wife thereby "extorting a Gift," was of more value to society than the prayers emanating from "Clergyman of all Sorts and Sizes." That moment illustrated the social value of widely available leisure, "when People are merry and doing of nothing."[84]

To Mandeville's explanation of how women gained control of income for consumption can be added the conclusion of historians that, in a wage economy, working-class women became the "financial managers." What has been said of the nineteenth century was also true of the eighteenth: because "even well-paid skilled workers spent most of their earnings on food" and "the wife" did such spending, her role "as a consumer was . . . central to the family's economic well-being." Women wished to ensure that a proportion of wages went toward their own goals. Mandeville assumed as much in describing women "pinching their Families [and] Marketing." Women played "a fundamental role in determining whether a family was respectable or non-respectable," a role to which historians of eighteenth-century evangelism also have pointed. Women were "more susceptible to the preachings" against traditional male recreations and "especially to demands for temperance." Women of the lower and middle classes made it clear that booze, betting, paying for sex, and other forms of prodigal spending could be a prime absorber of their own and their children's prospects. Women's decisive part in consumer spending in the interests of improved domesticity and, eventually, of "better child psychologies" promised "an empowerment of those in charge."[85]

Later observers recorded women's self-assertion in dressing fashionably. The author of a 1735 account of *A Trip through the Town* bemoaned the fact that "[o]ur servant wenches are so puffed up with pride nowadays that they never think they go fine enough. It is a hard matter to know the mistress from the maid by their dress." Defoe had suggested that servants—notably "girls"—were becoming "more sophisticated about . . . a proper work-load." During his lifetime, servants became "better paid and more independent. . . . They dressed well, enjoyed themselves in the myriad ways offered by London and regularly changed jobs to make the best of their excellent bargaining position." This provoked their employers in the familiar way. At the end of the century, however, one writer, satirizing Wollstonecraft's *Rights of Woman,* recognized that servants who "happily" rivaled their mistresses in dress could be interpreted as expressing "independent spirit" rather than "boldness and impudence." Implicit in that 1735 observation of puffed-up servants was the motive most commonly ascribed to women's appetite for fashionable clothing and other consumer items: emulation, the word standing for the spiral described by Mandeville, whereby "the poorest Labourer's Wife in the Parish . . . will half starve herself and her Husband to purchase a second-hand Gown and Petticoat . . . because . . . it is more genteel." As the lower ranks emulated the higher, the latter made "the contrivance of Fashion their Study that they may have always new Modes ready to take up, as soon as those saucy C[h]its shall begin to imitate those in being."[86] John Collett's 1750s painting, "High Life below Stairs," shows two young women dressed to the nines, one of them accompanying herself with a mandolin as she sings to a suitor, the other watching in her hand-held mirror as a hairdresser completes his attentions to her head. In 1755 *The World* complained that "every commoner . . . treads hard on the heels of the quality in dress." Wollstonecraft observed in 1792 that "one class presses on another," and its gender variation that "women all want to be ladies."[87] Moreover, the corollary of dressing fashionably was the wish to be seen "in public places." Entrepreneurs were delighted by this valuable emulation they deliberately fostered, including facilitating its display, and some historians have attributed great significance to it as the engine for the rise of a "consumer society."[88]

The social extensiveness of women's expression of wishes is as remarkable to historians as it was disturbing to higher-class complainants. Rather than being "deplorable exceptions to their class and station" women servants illustrated women's general addiction. Domestic service remained women's "largest single employment throughout the century," and, while permanent for many, was a stage through which many more passed en route to marriage and the employment of servants. The prestige of resort towns, attracting an expanding upper crust, meant the exposure of increasing numbers of servants to the same fashions and pleasures (they are described "pressing into the assembly rooms"), and this is another explanation for the "relatively high ratios of women to men generally found in these communities."[89] A servant's knowledge of the latest fashions extended from public gesture and speech to all the intimacies of a lady's toilet, and provincial tradesmen profitably stocked fashionable underwear. Servant women's tastes were susceptible to being "acculturated by their workplaces" in richer people's houses, and by the reformed urban spaces through which their work required them to travel. These circumstances embodied a wider world, a "Beau Monde," signs of which servant women could transpose into their own domestic interiors, learning "from their superiors to take snuff, drink tea, use sugar, and prefer white bread." In Nottingham at mid-century, the use of tea, coffee, and chocolate was observed to been made commercially accessible "to that Degree that . . . almost every Seamer, Sizer and Winder will have her tea in the morning . . . and even a common Washer woman thinks she as not had a proper Breakfast without Tea and hot buttered White Bread!" This was a common complaint among middle-class reformers, indignant that the markings of taste were breaking down and concerned, too, over the effects on working-class energy.[90]

Higher classes took different measures in an attempt to hold the line, including separate passages and staircases in both private and public buildings, or intensifying residential segregation by having servants "live out." Or they could deliberately expose prospective servants to consumer items with the same hegemonic purpose pursued by *The Spectator* in supporting the charity school movement. Lady Elizabeth Hastings encouraged her servants to attend school in order to imbue them with the Christian knowledge later exemplified by Richardson's fictional servant, Pamela. Along with other women, Hastings contributed to the founding of charity schools which, after teaching girls to read, directed them into domestic service. Hastings laid out money for her schools to purchase sets of pewter, "being designed rather for ye girls to learn to clean than to use." She also directed local vicars to "examine the girls on their learning and knowledge of the Christian Religion, and on their morals, behavior, and conduct." Evidently she and her vicars would be unable to control the effects of such exposure to domestic items on the aspirations of lower-class women, let alone their tastes in literature.[91]

Fiction recorded the percolation of consumer fashions to all social levels, from prostitutes to shopkeepers' daughters, but especially to mistresses and to the women who served them.[92] Clarissa willed her linen, unsold laces, and her book of extracts from the Bible to Mrs. Lovick and Mrs. Smith, with whom she had lodged in London and who had tended her in her last illness. In *Tom Jones,* Fielding describes the superiority claimed by Mrs. Western's maid over Sophy's maid, Mrs. Honour, on grounds that she had accompanied her mistress to London and therefore "seen more of the world." She would be ashamed to walk in St. James's Park with Mrs. Honour. In the ensuing argy-bargy, Mrs. Honour violently "brushed the hoop of her competitor with her own." Sophy's being encouraged by novels to show her sensibility by weeping was similarly emulated by Mrs. Honour. The public ball provided another point for the display and transmission of fashions across class lines, as women enjoyed yet another kind of pleasure with men outside home. Smollett's *Humphry Clinker* recorded a "Master of Ceremonies leading, with great solemnity, to the upper end of the room, an antiquated Abigail, dressed in her ladies cast [off]-clothes; whom he mistook for some countess just arrived at Bath." The masquerading abigail symbolized "the general mixture of all degrees assembled in our public rooms, without distinction of rank or fortune." Nonfictional records endorse this vision, Elizabeth Montagu recording, "The Rooms were prodigiously crowded with very uncouth figures most wonderfully dressed: those . . . who education made awkward, mantua-makers, tailors, friseurs, and milliners made monstrous[,]" a neat list of service workers directly exposed to fashion. It was said of a Portsmouth assembly that "rather than stand still, a Gentleman may dance with a Wench, who, the Morning before, sold him a Pair of Gloves." Such apparent social heterogeneity is comparable to the new and commercial mixing of foods and harmonies which Cheyne and Wesley saw as the corrupting effects of Britain's increasing "civilization."[93]

Smollett's novel also illustrates how literacy (valuably flawed from the point of view of the historian) provided servants with another way of transmitting fashion information to the country. Winifred Jenkins writes from Bath to Mrs. Mary Jones, her fellow servant, back at Brambleton-Hall. Describing the garment her master's daughter Lydia has handed down to her, Jenkins looks forward to the havoc she will make among "the mail sex" when it is combined with a "full foot of ga[u]ze, as good as new" which she had purchased in Bath: "Mrs. Patcher, my Lady Kilmacullock's woman," had "shewn me all her secrets and learned me to wash gaze, and refrash rusty silks and bumbeseens." She has become learned in such consumer skills, which she tells Mary Jones "is all Greek and Latten to you." To the face-to-face and letter-writing contacts between women may be added a large number of advertising, discount, and credit techniques revived or created by eighteenth-century producers and retailers to foster consumerism. And there was the "key distributive role of shops (bright, glass fronted and bow windowed), . . . enabling English householders to obtain goods from the length and breadth of the country" from early in the century. Additionally, the fashion doll was an effective method to connect "the wives" of "artisans, craftsmen, and even laborers" with the world of fashion. "Sophia," a mid-century feminist, complained that men "invented dolls and put them into girls' hands to confine us to trifles," a complaint renewed by Wollstonecraft.[94]

In Rochester's day as in James I's, countrywomen had the same wishes for fashionable life, which they might implement with Mandevillean strategy:

> Comes a fine Lady, with her humble Knight,
> Who has preval'd with her, through her own Skill,
> At his request, though much against his Will,
> To come to London.

She then sends him off to the tavern while she looks for the latest fashions.[95] The 1696–1709 account book of Rachel Pengelly, widowed and not subject to the expostulations endured by Shaftesbury's sister, took a coach from her home in Finchley to London, where she visited relatives after attending a religious "meeting" and stopped off at shops to buy "groceries, clothes, and many miscellaneous personal items." Increasingly over the next century, however, "metropolitan fashions were sucked into the provinces" along the improved roads, bringing "more remote areas into the hectic economy of consumption and emulation." Provincial towns were primary regenerating points for the consumer grid but young women in the country expressed "the most longing desires" to participate in London fashions. Of course, men did too, ploughboys and cowherds "deserting their dirt and drudgery" and swarming "up to London to wear fine clothes."[96]

Literate women could also follow London fashions every day without leaving home by way of advertisements in the provincial press. Moreover, *The Connoisseur* in 1756 observed that after

> the newest fashions are brought down weekly by the stage-coach, all the wives and daughters of the most topping tradesmen vie with each other every Sunday in the elegance of their apparel. The same genteel ceremonies all practised there as at the most fashionable churches in town.

Molly Seagrim was able to dress herself in a fashionable "sack," in order to hide her pregnancy, a dress the higher-class and charitable Sophy Western had donated to her out of sympathy. Molly also decked herself with "a new laced cap and some other ornaments" Tom Jones gave her. Molly thus displayed her "ambition and vanity" by way of fashion beyond her station, provoking the envious attack by other lower-class women at church.[97] If fiction recorded the penetration of rural countries across England, so did John Byng's diary: "met a milkmaid on the road with the dress and look of Strand misses." George Stubbs painted women wearing fashionable clothes while they worked in the fields.[98] Referring to other English artists and the observations of travelers that servants and agricultural laborers even in backward country areas wore plebeian versions of fashionable clothes, Perkin points out that England had become the only nation in Europe without a "national costume." A continuous stream of evidence, from a satirical rhyme of 1722 to Arthur Young's words at the end of the century, makes clear that the aspirations of boarding school tutored tastes and accomplishments also brought trained singing, printed music and, eventually, pianos into the domestic lives of many farming women and men.[99]

The pleasures of dressing up reached an apotheosis in the masquerade, prominent among the array of new consumer pleasures of eighteenth-century urban life. Literary scholar Terry Castle suggests that the "commercialization of popular culture" strongly influenced the development of the masquerade in the eighteenth century, although her declaration that they were also "a vestige of the ancient and powerful world of carnival" must be seriously modified.[100] The eighteenth-century masquerade's characteristics were in obvious contrast to the annual and cathartic explosions of carnivalesque appetite for food, sex, and violence described by Peter Burke, and perhaps deliberately so. As Castle herself points out, those earlier "festivals of misrule" had taken place outside, "in town streets or surrounding fields." They could lead to the masculinist riots targeting women. Eighteenth-century masquerades took place inside buildings, were put on as commercial ventures by impresarios who sold tickets to

George Stubbs (1724–1806). *Haymakers* 1785. Oil on panel. 35 1/4 × 53 1/4 in. Tate Gallery.

them, and advertised and reported in newspapers, were deliberately attended by women enjoying themselves, and supplied occasions for the display of literary allusions—dressing up as Clarissa, for example. Richardson characterized masquerades as "modern." For him and other moralists the masquerade was a metaphor for a life they saw as modern because of the vanity and sexual games-playing to which they believed a better past had degenerated. It was because the masquerade was a manifestation of eighteenth-century consumerism—one in which women asserted themselves in pursuing pleasure—that the criticism leveled against it was exactly the same as the criticism leveled at consumerism's other manifestations—novels, boarding schools, and wearing fashionable clothing.[101]

Nonetheless, Castle's book is extremely useful in describing the pleasures of masquerading, an occasion for newly heterosocial conspicuous indulgence.[102] At the masquerade, women "in particular enjoyed a conversational nonchalance not usually permitted them in public settings . . . cursing, obscenity, loud joking—were usurped by women masqueraders." Now both sexes frequently cross-dressed in contrast to the limited male transvestism and the still more "scanty" female transvestism of medieval Carnival.[103] (Among the cross-dressers was the sentimental novelist Inchbald, at first a successful actress; she attended a 1781 masquerade dressed as a man. While Wollstonecraft is reputed to have attended a masquerade in 1792 with the Fuselis and Lavater, it is not recorded what she wore.)[104] A 1721 pamphleteer on behalf of the campaign for the reformation of manners pointed out that once dress, "the distinguishing Mark of the Sexes," was exchanged, both sexes found "an Opportunity of conversing together with the most unlimited Freedom; and Shame . . . having here no Place, they greedily run into those Excesses, which otherwise they durst scarce have thought of." Another critic observed, "The mask secures the Ladies from Detraction, and encourages a Liberty, the Guilt of which their Blushes would betray when barefac'd, tell by Degrees they are innured to that which is out of their Virtue to restrain."[105]

The masquerade offered pleasure-seeking women the promise of "sensual self-determination." Sexual "liberty was only one aspect of the masquerade's . . . transfiguring relations of men and women . . . the overriding impulse was toward . . . perfect freedom—a state of intoxication, ecstasy, and free-floating sensual pleasure." It seems evident that women had to be more circumspect than that suggests. Nonetheless, the masquerade was for women as well as men a "safe zone, a locale in which impulses suppressed or veiled in everyday life could be acted on."[106] The masquerade temporarily elided other social distinctions in addition to the one based on sex. Upper-class masqueraders assumed "the dress of the working orders . . . dairymaids and orange girls, shepherds, and shepherdesses, millers, flower sellers, and soldiers and sailors." And for "every garter'd small-coal merchant" and duchess "crying sprats" there was "the hairdresser turned alderman, the apprentice in magistrate's robes." In 1725 a masquerade held by "Chamber-Maids, Cook-Maids, Foot-Men, and Apprentices" was subject to a "crackdown."[107] All masquerades could be seen posing the threat of social levelling. Sometimes entrepreneurs kept the price of tickets low to attract a wider audience but poor people could sneak into masquerades in disguise. Hence the masquerade "could lead to the revolutionary notion that rank itself could be altered as easily as its outward signs." A satirical "Essay on Masquerades," published in the *Lady's Magazine* of February 1777 (the postrevolutionary date is notable), referred to the masquerade's "tendency to diffuse a spirit of liberty, by reducing all men to equality . . . the noble peer is confounded with the ignorant peasant." This was one of the conventional criticisms made of boarding schools, fashionable clothing, and the novel.[108]

Indeed, the masquerade had much in common with the novel, another expression of the new world of fashionable consumerism and potential self-fashioning. Readers attended masquerades wearing disguises based on literature, blurring the boundaries between "real and unreal beings, living and fictive entities."[109] And like the masquerade, the novel made possible the expression of female wishes, the proliferation of self-conceptions and gender transformations, readers imagining selves as heroines, seeing heroes in the men they met, playing the part of heroines to each other by signing letters with aliases drawn from fiction. Moreover, the novel was a still safer "locale" than the masquerade for women's expression of egotistical will and creative freedom, one where they could mask themselves with anonymity, diffidence, and orthodox femininity. Women novelists and readers of novels were subjected to the same charges of sexual immorality as masqueraders.

Eighteenth-century writers, from political critics, like the authors of *Cato's Letters,* to sentimentalists, from Richardson to Edgeworth, made of the masquerade an ideal metaphor for the corrupt and duplicitious "world." The masquerade was the creation of a commercializing culture deeply self-conscious of role-playing, of the self-fashioning the new forms of capitalism required. The effects of entrepreneurial ambitions and the public response to them was to put the whole order into the apparently open-ended and everyday flux against which Elizabeth had warned, a flux in which social characters were as unrecognizable as they were in a masquerade. Fielding wrote in 1750 that trade had "subverted" the previous order, had "changed the manners, customs, and habits of the people especially of the lower sort. The narrowness of their future is changed into wealth, their frugality into luxury, their humility into pride, and their subjection into equality." Social aspiration led to the "confusion" of gentleman and nobleman, tradesman, and gentleman, and reached "to the very Dregs of the People." To N. Forster in 1767, "fashionable luxury" threatened to dissolve the "several ranks," as the "perpetual ambition" of inferiors to raise themselves" led one rank to "slide into" another. Fashion, he said, expressed a "spirit of equality" which held "uncontrolled sway" in British society.[110]

Smollett's representation of Britain's pursuit of the pleasures of fashionable disguise, while including the masquerade, was very significantly not limited to it. People, he wrote, entertained themselves, "disguised on their betters," at their own houses and at the tavern, as well as at "the court, the opera, the theater, and the masquerade." All of the "gayest places of public entertainment are filled with fashionable figures; which, upon inquiry, will be found to be journeymen taylors, serving-men, and abigails, disguised as their betters." He concluded, that "there is not distinction or subordination left—the different departments of life are jumbled together."[111]

Fielding's "confusion," Forster's "sliding," and Smollett's "jumbling" were very close to the masquerade scenes of "vertiginous, existential, recombination." In short, what Castle says of the masquerade was characteristic of fashion at large (including the pleasures created at the new urban resorts, where various effects to preserve exclusivity bore witness to permeability), seeming to overthrow "the hierarchy of rank and class, destroying distinctions between masters and servants, consumers and producers." An historian of fashion, not the masquerade, declares that the "urbanity of fashion masks all emotions, save that of triumph . . . Yet fashion does not negate emotion, it simply displaces it into the realm of aesthetics. It can be a way of intellectualizing visually about individual desires and social aspiration." Fashion has the capacity for irony, paradox, mockery; the unmasking of hypocrisy, elusive double bluffs, and "statements about the unnaturalness of human social arrangements." If day-to-day fashion was a less intense form of fluidity than the masquerade, it was, or would become, a much more widely accessible one, another "Dialect" that women could make their own. In his commentary on the meanings of the fashionable *Pamela,* McKeon refers to its analogy between words and clothing as modes of self-expression.[112] Instead of Castle's nostalgic view, one may suggest a positive interpretation of her notion that "the culture of the carnivalesque had been fragmented and diffused by the end of the eighteenth century." This coincided with the beginning of the industrial mass production of cloth and clothing and the further diffusion of fashion's daily disguises.[113]

Edgeworth's *Belinda* supports this view. In that 1801 novel the masquerade epitomized the modern world of fashion, one where, to the moralists' view, women joined the corrupt world of mere appearance, like Lady Delacour, perverted from their "true nature." The masquerade, however, was but one of other public entertainments where Lady Delacour introduced the country-bred Belinda to "the gloss of novelty." She planned to take her to the same kinds of "modern" places of public, heterosocial mixing against which Richardson had warned. They were "the Theatres, the Opera, and the Pantheon, the Ranelagh," as well as to "Phillips's exhibition of French china." Then there was "the ceremony of a morning visit," where Lady Newland wore her "ostentatious livery . . . Overdressed like a true city dame! . . . entangled in her bale of gold muslin and conscious of her bulge of diamonds!" Against this, Belinda dressed herself with "the most perfect simplicity." Her observers thought this was another way of dressing up—how could real simplicity be discerned when it became the fashion? The masquerade stood for all of the "art and affectation" manifest in this urban world of pleasure and fashion. The common factor is represented by Edgeworth's phrase, "the transformations of fashion."[114]

Fiction Records Women's Pleasure Seeking

The historian must sometimes view women's wishes for the pleasure of masking through the scrim of disapproval. Harriet Byron's being abducted by the rake, Sir Hargrave Pollexfen was, she confessed, in large part the result of her "presumptuous folly in going dress'd out, like the fantastic wretch I appeared to be at a vile, a foolish masquerade." Or one can refer to Fielding's chapter in *Tom Jones,* "Containing the Whole Humours of a Masquerade," promoted by "Heydegger," who, along with Theresa Cornelius, was the most famous among the masquerade's commercializers. There the country innocent, Tom Jones, accepts the sexual initiative of the corrupt pleasure seeker, Lady Bellaston. Inchbald's Miss Milner's refusal to subordinate her pleasures in the masquerade—including taking pleasure in her own sexual attractiveness—dooms her. And before Lady Delacour is persuaded of the folly of her ways she had delighted in being "Mistress of the Revels," presiding over the fashionable display and greater sexual freedom of the masquerade.[115]

Fiction's frequent moral message makes it clear that women's pleasure seeking was widespread. It accompanied fiction's representation of heroines indulging their feelings, including this expression of consumer psychology. The very existence of popular sentimental novels afforded women "extensive and unaffected pleasure," in Austen's phrase. In fact, fiction directly unveiled its heroines' wishes for public pleasures.[116]

Fielding's sentimental paragon, Sophia Western, "eagerly longed" to see London, "a place in which she fancied charms short only of those a rapturous saint imagines in heaven." To Lennox's Miss Glanville, London was "that seat of magnificence and pleasure" full of "new and surprising objects[,]" and she planned to take Arabella to "the Drawing Room, Park, Concert, Ranelagh . . . the Duchess of ——'s Rout, Vauxhall." To Miss Milner, London was "that gay metropolis—a wild rapturous picture of which her active fancy had often formed." During her tour of England in the 1690s, Celia Fiennes had not restrained her excitement over Bath's shops, its two coffeehouses, "two rooms for the lottery and hazard board" and the piazza outside them, paved "for the dry walking of the company in the rain."[117] By 1771, Smollett's Lydia found Bath "an earthly paradise," enjoying its unceremonious jostling, "a coffee-house for the ladies[,]" and "the booksellers shops, which are charming places of resort; where we

Thomas Rowlandson (1756–1827). *Vauxhall Gardens,* 1784. Pen and gray and gray-black ink and watercolor over pencil. 19 × 29 1/2 in. Courtesy of the Board of Trustees of the Victoria and Albert Museum.

read novels, plays, pamphlets, and newspapers, for so small a subscription as a crown a quarter." Thence Lydia visited other shops and Spring Gardens, "a sweet retreat, laid out in walks and ponds, and parterres of flowers; and there is a long-room for breakfasting and dancing." Lydia was equally delighted with London, her "imagination quite confounded with splendour and variety." London was a materialized prodigality which heretofore had only existed in her imagination, like "the Arabian nights." Lydia thought herself "in paradise" at Ranelagh, "the enchanted palace of a genie," with its profusion of decoration and golden lamps. The people, in turn, were gaily decorated in glittering richness and variety. Lydia took fine imperial tea in this visual paradise while she listened to the "ravishing delights of music." Then she went across the river to "the pleasures of Vauxhall" where the crowd was again a source of pleasure to her, all enlivened as it was "with mirth, freedom, and good-humour." Listening to a singer, her head ached "through excess of pleasure."[118]

This was the world Burney's Evelina wished to enter. In a series of letters to her anxious guardian in the country, Evelina reported the excitement she felt in London, "now in full splendour." Her first "entrance" to Ranelagh, she wrote, "made me almost think I was in some enchanted castle, or fairy palace, for all looked like magic to me." Like her fictional predecessors and like the "boarding school damsels" to whom Burney refers in her preface, Evelina has been prepared for this magical world by the romantic fiction which was itself a product of it.[119] Eager to visit Ranelagh, Evelina and another young woman "ran up stairs to dress." At the opera, she thought herself "in paradise," her response sharply contrasting with Wesley's. Of all entertainments, Evelina said the opera was "the sweetest, the most delightful. Some of the songs seemed to melt my soul." Sensibility intensified pleasure as well as pain. After the opera, Evelina "went into a place called the coffee-room, where ladies as well as gentlemen . . . walk about, and *chat,* with the same ease and freedom as in a private room." Women entered public space with men for pleasure in a process Hume described.[120]

Evelina went to a "ridotto," another public social assembly for women and men, including music and dancing, introduced into England in 1722, contemporaneously with the commercialization of the masquerade. She walked in Hyde Park and Kensington Gardens and visited the Pantheon. She went to the theater in Drury Lane, where Garrick's sentimental performance ("every look *speaks*") made her declare "in what raptures I am returned!" She visited Portland chapel, the Mall in St. James's Park, and she went "shopping, as Mrs. Mirvan calls it, all this morning, to buy silks, caps, gauzes and so forth." The shops were "very entertaining" and, "at the milliners," Evelina marveled at the speed with which the dressmakers worked "in these great shops, for they have promised one a compleat suit of linen against the evening." She described, too, having her hair dressed, her head "full of powder and black pins, and a great *cushion* on the top of it. I believe you would hardly know me, for my face looks quite different to what it did before my hair was dressed." If a hairdresser could turn alderman at the masquerade, he was capable of transforming his customers for a larger world of pleasurable representations of self.[121]

Evelina records the mingling of classes as well as sexes at the entertainments she attended and the radiation of them outward into suburban towns like Hampstead, the kinds of places where ladies' boarding schools were attractively established in comparative safety. And, of course, Evelina's meeting and eventual marriage to Lord Orville hinged on the existence of these public places, but even after the novel reaches its romantic denouement in Evelina's engagement, her wishes to implement her appetite for consumer pleasures remains open-ended. "The charming city of Bath delighted me."[122]

If it is essential that the historian recognize women's pursuit of pleasure in eighteenth-century Britain, she/he must acknowledge the moralists' point: writers from Addison to Wollstonecraft registered the fact that the new world of fashion could be seen merely as ways to put women on the marriage market, that is, to update their being bought and sold in marriages by assimilating traditional practice to modern commerce. Eighteenth-century moralists directed much of their fire on public pleasure occasions where the unmarried mingled. Both Borsay and Langford emphasize "the crucial mechanism" that marriage was in "the distribution and redistribution of wealth, power, and status," at the center of this polite and commercial society. It may be that the proportions between "parental" consent and "children's" choices were reversed over the century, but daughters generally remained more subject to "the ultimate sanction of . . . a father" than sons. The provincial resorts successfully supplied the demand for conditions under which partner selection could be made. On the one hand, that children, including daughters, were gaining an increasing say in such a process may be seen as another aspect of women's ability to express themselves on the other fronts described and manifest in the resorts. On the other, the latter may be seen as simply "larger, more cosmopolitan, and better appointed markets" equivalent to Britain's market expansion as a whole.[123] It was at a masquerade that Belinda learns how her Aunt Stanhope's introduction of her into the public world of fashion at Bath may be interpreted. She was, said a worldly male, "hawked about every where, and the aunt was puffing her with might and main. Belinda Portman, and her accomplishments, I'll swear, were as well advertized as Packwood's razor strops." Her aunt had intended to widen Belinda's prospects by sending her to the larger market of London's fashionable world, where George Packwood was an entrepreneur of advertising techniques, his innovations illustrating the "level of marketing skill, the ingenuity, salesmanship, the quality of promotional imagination" so important to the elaboration of Britain's consumer society. This overlapped with other reasons for sentimental fiction's preoccupation with the world of mere "semblance," wherein Christian and neo-Platonist traditions were adapted to women's experience of the dangers presented to them by experienced, worldly men.[124]

Ambivalence toward Women's Pursuit of Consumer Pleasures

From the second half of the seventeenth century a series of writers urged women to repudiate material, consumer pleasures in the world. If women were peculiarly liable to such pleasures, they were also peculiarly endangered by them. In her poem "The Introduction," Anne Finch, countess of Winchelsea (1661–1720), attacked those who, defending "the rights of men" and in the "name of Witt,"

> tell us, we mistake our sex and way;
> Good breeding, fas[h]ion, dancing, dressing, play
> Are the accomplishments we shou'd desire;
> To write, or read, or think, or to enquire
> Wou'd cloud our beauty, and ex[h]aust our time.

Lady Chudleigh asserted "that the Pleasures of the Mind are infinitely preferable to those of sense" and she advised women to replace "dull insipid Trifles" and "debasing Impertinencies" with rational thought. The frequent warning that "Beauty, with all the Helps of Art, is of no long Date" would be another aspect of this long-running resistance to identifying women simply with sensation, with materialism.[125]

This view had obvious roots in the Christianity refashioned by Puritanism, but it took on new meanings after commercial capitalism began its exponential flooding of women's lives with consumer pleasures and women responded with unmistakable appetite. Resistance to consumerism, the attempt to control it, and underneath the recognition of its pleasures and values, all came to characterize sentimental fiction. We can see these themes emerging in the writings of two more early feminists, Bathsua Pell Makin and Mary Astell.

In 1673, looking to patronage and customers at twenty pounds a head per annum, Makin (1612–74), who had been governess to Charles I's children, published an essay and a prospectus for a school for young gentlewomen just outside London. Women, argued Makin, were "capable of Improvement by Education." Makin recognized the argument the women had to make against their supposedly innate inferiority. "Custom . . . hath a mighty influence: it hath the force of Nature itself. The Barbarous custom to breed Women low, is grown general among us, it is verily believed . . . that Women are not endued with Reason, as Men; nor capable of improvement by Education, as they are." Makin illustrated the way in which sensational psychology could strengthen the case for women's being educated, that is, on the grounds of their mothering: "none have so great an advantage of making most deep impression[s] on their Children, as Mothers." Makin also advocated that unmarried women "that cannot subsist without depending on Servants" be "imployed in Nurseries; by their Conversation, to teach Tongues to children." Evidently the argument that the significance of mothering required the improvement of women's education preceded its dating by recent historians by at least a century.[126]

However, Makin did not say that all women should be educated. Education was neither necessary "to the subsistence, or to the Salvation of Women." Necessary to women's education was "liberty and opportunity" in their childhood, factors contingent on wealth. Unfortunately even privileged women were spending "the over-plus time of their youth" on the pleasures to which wealth also could be devoted. "Gentlewomen" were being taught "to Frisk and Dance, to paint their Faces, to curl their Hair, to put on a Whisk, to wear gay Clothes." They "spend their time" on "Toyes and Trifles." Uneducated, such women perpetuated "Play" when they became adults. They had "nothing to imploy themselves in, but are forced, to Cards, Dice, Playes, and frothy Romances." In such pursuits, young women infantilized themselves, "dressing and trimming themselves like Bartholomew-Babies, in Painting and Dancing, in making Flowers of Coloured Straw, and building Houses of stained Papers, and such like vanities." These habits led women to "polish their Hands and Feet . . . to dress and trim their Bodies," leaving them defenseless against "Seducers." Such pleasures converged with the rakish male's application to women of consumer delight in variety. Makin wished to control and redirect women's pleasures, to exchange adulterations of their bodies for "truly" adorning them. There was "no pleasure greater nor more su[i]table to an ingenious mind than what is founded in knowledge." Education would give women "something to exercise their thoughts about, which are busie and active." Forced to concede women's appetite for outdoor, material pleasures, Makin urged women to confine them by moral hierarchy and domesticity, a view consistent with Burnet's vision of sexual arrangements.[127]

Because women's destiny was "home," Makin recommended that their improvement should follow an earlier phase of domestic education, that is, "being competently instructed in all things now useful that concern them as Women." Thereafter, women's education was to be improved by extending it to the "Polite Learning . . . Religion, Arts, and in Tongues" monopolized by men. Makin's curriculum included the instruction of gentlewomen in "the Principles of Religion and in all manner of Sober and Vertuous Education." Her scheme either would work "to reclaim the Men; or make them ashamed to claim Sovereignty over such as are more Wise and Vertuous than themselves." Makin's vision aligned women's "improvement" with the goals expressed by the other critics of the Restoration's reaction to puritanism: "We cannot expect to prevail against the Ignorance, Atheism, Prophaneness, Superstition, Idolatry, Lust, that reigns in the Nation, than by a Prudent, Sober, Vertuous Education of our Daughters. Their Learning would stir up our Sons, whom God and Nature hath made superior, to a just emulation." If Mandeville's clergy wished to use women in the reformation of manners, their wish could converge with women's wishes.[128]

The purpose of Makin's plan bore directly on that separation of spheres whereby men left women and home for the greater pleasures of public gathering places. If, by the improved education, "some of this abused Sex" would be moved "to set a right value upon themselves," they also would "indear" themselves and their company "to husbands" and "make them admired by others."

> How many Families have been ruined by this one thing, the bad education of Women? Because the Men find no satisfactory converse at home, out of meer weariness they seek abroad; hence they neglect their Business, spend their Estates, destroy their Bodies, and often time damn their Souls.

Women should offer the pleasures of private, female-occupied, domestic space as an alternative to the attractive prodigality of outdoor pleasures. Women were to be polished in order to keep men more at home as well as to preserve the family and its reputation. Among the "entertainments" a better-educated wife would be able to offer would be the musical accomplishments taught at Makin's projected school. In addition, the husband's business vulnerability—or even his proclivity to wasteful spending—could be protected by the "Keeping Accounts" also to be taught at Makin's school. In cases of "debauched" husbandhood, a learned wife's "prudence" would supply the "defect."[129]

Despite her criticism of the pursuit of material pleasure, Makin's project was itself dependent on the prosperity that funded education and permitted women properly to adorn themselves. She makes it clear that women's contribution to the reformation of manners depended upon the softening materialism of an improved home and its more constant denizen. In short, she suggested that judicious consumerism could be an instrument of reform.

Astell, said to have developed Makin's educational ideas,[130] deepens our understanding of why a women's culture coming to be so imbued with consumerism should also appear so hostile to it. Astell had received her unusual education as a child in Newcastle at the hands of her uncle, Ralph Astell, a royalist curate who had himself sat at the feet of several Cambridge Platonists. She aspired to be a missionary, like Peter or Paul, to convert "the Infidel" abroad. She saw herself denied that by her "Sex," and in pursuing an equivalent goal at home, she abjured marriage, sex, and reproduction. "The whole World is a single Lady's Family, her opportunities of doing good are not lessen'd but encreased by her being unconfin'd." A lady justified choosing "the world" over marriage by confining herself to moral purpose. Astell became a pamphleteer for the Tory and High Anglican cause (she was a Jacobite sympathizer), like Makin, joining the campaign against the "Inundation of Faction, Libertinism, and Wickedness," which she believed to be breaking over England. Astell opened an SPCK school in Chelsea in 1709. Here and in her other efforts, Astell was patronized by several ladies of the aristocracy.[131]

Coming to London in 1687, Astell sought out an intellectual relationship with John Norris, "the last Cambridge Platonist," who published his attack on Locke in 1701, taking Locke to task for the small part left God by sensational psychology. Astell shared Norris's views here and, even though she attacked Shaftesbury as a "deistical liberal thinker," in effect was on the same side in posing Cambridge Platonism against the dangers embodied in the writings of Locke. Astell rejected Locke's politics in favor of passive obedience. She was opposed to political equality, to individual rights, and, nominally at least, any move toward social leveling. Her biographer finds in her work a "feminist critique of possessive individualism."[132]

In fact, Astell could not free herself from the sensational psychology Locke systematized anymore than Shaftesbury could. One can see the particular appeal of Locke's environmental explanation of mind to any female intellectual of this era. So despite her Platonic assertions of "imortal mind" and "Soul," Astell argued that women's defects grew in the first place from a faulty education, as had Makin and Poulain La Barre before her.[133] "Women are from their very infancy debar'd those advantages, with the want of which, they are afterwards reproached, and nursed up in those Vices which will hereafter be upbraided to them." Conversely, the "Superiority and Preeminence of Men" was due in the first place to the fact that "Boys have much Time and Pains, Care and Cost bestow'd on their Education, Girl's have little or none." Indignantly detailing the continuing disparity in education, Astell then ridiculed the claim that women were "born" intellectually inferior to men.[134]

The appeal of Cambridge Platonism to women also seems clear, albeit in the light of sensational psychology. Norris recommended "long and constant Meditation to free our Minds of that early Prejudice that sensible Objects do act upon our Spirits, and are the Causes of our Sensations." He claimed to discount "the influence of the appetites and the senses . . . so as to perceive and be guided by higher imperatives."[135] Astell applied Platonist categories in order to denigrate the power men based on sex, at the same time castigating Locke. "Most Men are so Sensualiz'd, that they take nothing to be Real but what they can Hear and See. Others who wou'd seem the most refined, make Sensation the fund of their Ideas, carrying their Contemplations no farther than these, and the Reflections they make upon the operations of their Minds when thus employ'd." Conversely, Astell saw the promise of freedom in Platonism. "The Mind is free, nothing but Reason can oblige it, 'tis out of the Reach of the most absolute Tyrant." The same postrevolutionary metaphor pervaded her contemporaries' feminism. One of Astell's critics, writing in *The Tatler,* understood the relation between Astell's Platonic critique of Locke and the claim to moral superiority it allowed women, even as the writer recognized the irony of Astell's adaptation of Lockean psychology to this purpose. Astell wished "to imprint true Idea's of Things on the tender Souls of her Sex so they might arrive at such a Pitch of Perfection, as to be above the law of Matter and Motion." The linking of sensationalism to male appetite is one clue in understanding the appeal of Cambridge Platonism and its derivatives in the ensuing sentimental culture of women, including its embrace of Shaftesbury and romanticism.[136]

According to Astell, women who attempted to devote themselves to immaterial reality were surrounded by self-fashioning wits, libertines, and tyrants. "It were endless to reckon up the divers Strategems Men use to catch their Prey, their different ways of insinuating which vary with Circumstances and the Ladies, Sometimes a woman is cajol'd, and sometimes Hector'd, she is seduc'd to Love a Man, or aw'd into Fear of him." Such a view was the complement of that of the rake and libertine Rochester, whose life Burnet had published when Astell was fourteen. Her well-known proposal for an all-female college for gentlewomen was a place where the Elizabeth Malets of the world would be safe from a Rochester's raping them away. "Here Heiresses and Persons of Fortune may be kept secure from the rude attempts of designing Men."[137]

Astell offered a place where women "shall suffer no other confinement, but to be kept out of the road of sin." Perry points to the sexual meaning of Astell's language describing this road. Instead of women's "capacities" being "filled" with "the froth of flashy wits," "Serpents" serving "their *own* base ends," they could "feast on Pleasures" not of "the World" but of "ingenious Conversation . . . real wisdom . . . instructive discourses," "seasonable Reproofs and wholesome Counsels."[138] In Astell's nunnery women would learn the same "disgust" for their own "appetites," which she felt for hers. At eighteen she had renounced "the trifling World," not daring "To dress my body," and renouncing the pleasures of "fashion, of wit, romance, . . . balls . . . and idle visits." At twenty-nine Astell demanded that women withdraw their "Minds from the World, from adhering to the Senses, from the Love of Material Beings, of Pomps and Gaieties" which "leave no room for Truth." Like Makin and Shaftesbury, Astell criticized women's addiction to French romances and wished to persuade them

> to pretend some higher Excellency than a well-chosen Petty-coat, or a fashionable Commode; and not wholly lay out their Time and Care in the Adornation of their Bodies, but bestow a Part of it at least in the Embellishment of their Minds, since inward Beauty will last when outward is decayed.[139]

Astell's "nunlike detachment from the world," spending two hours daily in meditation as her mentor Norris recommended, dining on bread, cheese, and herbs, seemed to epitomize the repudiation of the consumerism then aborning. Anticipating Cheyne, she saw herself "living thus according to Nature," choosing "the simplest refreshments" over the life of "the most study'd Appetite, that is always longing after what it has not." Some men, she said, "have writ of love, as if they knew nothing of it but what they learn from good Eating and like sensations." She died after contemplating her coffin in her room for two weeks.[140]

In this regard, Astell supplied a prototype for Clarissa. There were other ways in which Astell's life and her beliefs made her prototypical of the culture of sensibility's obsession with female "virtue in distress." Analyzing the hell marriage could be under tyrannical husbands, Astell advised women to avoid it. Because her political beliefs included the absolute sovereignty of the husband, Astell declared that marriage provided those women unable to live outside it the opportunity to demonstrate the "self-denying martyrdom" in virtuous "Passive Obedience." "There is not a surer Sign of a noble Mind than being able to bear Contempt and an unjust Treatment from ones Superiors evenly and patiently. For inward Worth and real Excellency are the Ground of Superiority." A line of her poetry declared her moral superiority in the same way: "I Love you whom the World calls Enemies / You are my Vertues exercise."[141]

It was this aspect of Astell's thought and life—her sexual repression and her claim therefore to moral superiority—that Mandeville had in mind in unmasking "Lucinda," despite his admiration for other aspects of her feminism. At the opening of *The Virgin Unmask'd* Lucinda criticized Antonia for baring her neck and breasts, "Obscene Parts" in her pursuit of "Fashion." Then, with irony, having Lucinda argue that women should study their own anatomy, including the physiology of pregnancy and birth, Mandeville shows Antonia provoked to one of a series of questions. They are, in effect, Mandeville's objections to Astell's position—entirely rejecting sex and marriage because of their dangers. "It is a wonder, that since you have been so curious, in examining all these things that belong to Men and Women, it never came into your Head to confirm your knowledge by Experience." She asks Lucinda "was you ever in love?" Lucinda answers she feared to marry but she concedes it was "unnatural, to deny by Appetite what my Reason told would hurt me." Mandeville held such denial to be perverse, indeed the expression of sexist childrearing. It is in this light one should read Lucinda's telling Antonia "Five Hundred Stories about Rapes of my own Invention" at that impressionable age when Antonia's desires are awakening. Antonia asks Lucinda, "What has Mankind done to you? Have they made War against You? How have they deserv'd your Hate?" Lucinda replies, "They have enslaved our Sex: in Paradise Man and Woman were upon an even foot; see what they had made of us since: Is not every Woman that is marry'd a Slave to her husband, I mean if she be a good Woman, and values her promise." We know that Mandeville thought such paradisial fantasies were self-defeating. At the same time, Mandeville's sympathy for women's need to defend themselves against the "Artillery" men brought to bear on them made clear that the representative issue between himself and Astell was not in the least a simple one.[142]

And if the real Astell rejected sex, she by no means rejected consumerism. She made the same assumption as Makin of the connection between female literacy and the creation of comforts in domestic space, promising to draw men away from outdoors male culture. A properly educated wife "will entertain him at Home when he has been contradicted and disappointed abroad"; she should "make it her Business, her very Ambition to content him." He need no longer "run into Temptation in search of Diversion Abroad." In this regard, Astell depended upon the results of what another 1690s writer, Dudley North, called "the exhorbitant Appetites of Man," their "main spur to . . . Industry and Ingenuity."[143]

Moreover, Astell herself sought diversion abroad. In spite of her moralism and asceticism, she was part of London's new commercializing culture, a writer gaining a public voice through the market. She had chosen to live in Chelsea, it seems, because it was known for its "great Number of Boarders, especially Young Ladies," attending its disproportionate number of fashionable boarding schools. That so many members of the aristocracy (including Shaftesbury) had houses in Chelsea made it "a safe enclave . . . a neighborhood with an unusual number of young unmarried women in the streets and shops." This population and level of consumer orderliness promised a base for Astell's career, either in self-supporting teaching and writing or else patronized by the aristocrats to whose defense her writings were devoted.[144] (The father of one of Astell's patrons, Lady Catherine

Jones—an improving landlady in her own right—created Ranelagh Gardens.) Like Jones and her other patrons, Astell was immersed in the new, pleasure-seeking, consumer culture, enjoying "teas, card parties, lotteries, musicals, and dinners." While restrained in her fashion, she experienced "the allure of choosing, matching, and arranging." The ostentatiously frugal Astell spent fifty or sixty pounds a year on the dress and linen required by the social life she chose, which included her regular attendance at fashionable St. Martin's-in-the-Fields. She was able to walk there from Chelsea. As the historian Browne has said, the "revulsion from finery, like revulsion for stereotypically feminine behavior, was all too clearly just the other side of intense attraction to it."[145]

Furthermore, the personal dimension she revealed in her pleasure in playing in card parties and lotteries Astell extended to the Stock Exchange, investing in the South Sea Bubble and watching the market with care and expectation of large profits. (The patrons who had contributed to Astell's educational projects made up her losses from the imperial profits of the East India trade.)[146] In her risk-taking play, Astell was by no means alone. Women, widows especially, were of "enormous importance" in the investment markets of Astell's London, and they "played a vital part in the provision of loan capital through the bond and mortgage markets." Moreover, respectable women like Astell could now participate in the equivalent dimension of leisure culture, formerly confined to men in their rakish extravagance of betting. Fiennes reported the formal presence in Bath of commercial "lottery and hazard board" during the 1690s, parallel to the national establishment of new forms of mobile property symbolized by the Stock Exchange. After 1694 national lotteries flourished as a method of raising venture capital.[147] As Bath, Tunbridge Wells, and all of the resorts like them (let alone London) increased their facilities for "unadulterated pleasure," women "particularly succumbed to gambling," although the full expression of such an appetite must have been very much inhibited by class. Gambling was not merely for pin money but, as Lady Bristol said, women engaged in "deep play."[148]

Borsay is surely right in suggesting of such gambling women that, disadvantaged "by their sexual position, the pastime allowed them to enjoy the unfeminine thrill of competition, engaged in monetary transactions, and compete on equal terms with men." He quotes Steele's 1713 characterization of this play as a "passion" for the "emulation of manhood" but it is apparent women were not emulating anyone; nor did they accord themselves with the femininity Steele and his fellow tastemakers urged on them. With irony, Steele told his readers "the gamester ladies have surmounted the little vanities of showing their beauty, which they so far neglect, as to throw their features into violent distortions and wear away their lilies and roses in tedious watching and restless lucubrations." Cards and dice were usual items on the roster of modern female consumer sins compiled by reformers of manners throughout the century. The same monitory ladies appeared in sentimental fiction—Mrs. Berlington in Burney's late-century *Camilla,* for example, insisting on pursing "her own course." Unmistakably, "deep play" provided women the opportunity to be entirely themselves, a selfhood including the pursuit of "will," from which the presence of men could be pleasurably, skillfully brushed off:

> Men oft-times sued in vain, with various arts,
> To seduce me from my charming ace of hearts,
> To no effect, I baffled all their skill,
> I scorned their offers, and pursued my will.[149]

Writers of sentimental fiction shared with early feminists an ambivalent response to commercial capitalism. It was an adaptation to women's circumstances and wishes of the ambivalence toward "the monied interest" expressed from early in the century by political theorists and other male writers.[150] As they did in the case of commercial masquerades, sentimental novels decried women's pursuit of consumer pleasures, even as the selfsame fiction recorded it and contributed to its seemingly inexorable advance. Richardson targeted "music, concerts, operas, plays, assemblies, balls, drums, routs, and the rest of the amusements of modern life," in addition to those "light and frothy" books "inflaming" spoiled young women. His tale of Sally Martin, one of Lovelace's victims, was the translation into fiction of the connections Astell had made between the materialism of consumerism, the giving-in to sensual appetite, and the consequent susceptibility to men. Brought up to follow fashion, Sally was included in "pleasure parties" from the age of nine; enjoying "luxurious living" with her parents quickened her appetites. At fifteen or sixteen, Sally "aped" the dress and manners of "the quality," and, wearing the richest silks of her father's shop, she was a leader in "public diversions," pushing herself forward at the theater, frequenting "public places," and familiarizing herself with men at Vauxhall, Ranelagh, and Marybone. With her parents she looked "to attract some man of rank" as a husband, but her "turn of education" and her "warm constitution" encouraged "appetites" she was not equipped to resist and her public indiscretion meant no man proposed marriage. Meeting Lovelace at a masquerade, she thought him just the aristocratic man she had read about in novels and longed to marry. She was, therefore, ripe for his plucking.[151]

Thomas Rowlandson (1756–1827). *A Gaming Table at Devonshire House,* 1791. Pen and watercolor on paper. 12 1/8 × 17 1/8 in. The Metropolitan Museum of Art, Harris Brisbane Dick Fund, 1941.

Richardson testified to women's appetite for public consumer pleasures at the same time that he tried to direct women to the pursuit of private virtue at home. His Charlotte Grandison found that of ten visits she attempted to make, she found "six of the ladies will be gone to sales, or to plague tradesmen, and buy nothing. Anywhere rather than home. The devil's at home is a phrase. All our modern ladies live as if they thought so." Here, too, Richardson followed Makin and Astell. By the 1740s the burgeoning attractions of shopping and commercialized entertainments drew women still more irresistibly out of the home into the newly ordered urban spaces. (There "were more shops per capita in the 1750s than in the industrial era.") This was the circumstance of Richardson's typically sentimental complaint against "a taste even to wantonness for out-door pleasure and luxury, to the general exclusion of domestic as well as public virtue." Part of his explanation seems to point to advertising and certainly to the socially dissolving effects of the pursuit of pleasure: the taste for "out-door pleasure," he wrote, was "industriously promoted among all ranks and degrees of people."[152]

Fielding included a similar list to Richardson's of "manners" and "fashions" pursued in what he noted as "the said world." In contrast, he offered the example of Mrs. Heartfree, who "confined herself mostly to the care of her family, placed her happiness in her husband and her children, followed no expensive fashions or diversions, and, indeed, rarely went abroad, unless to return the visits of a few plain neighbors, and twice a year afforded herself, in company with her husband, the diversion of a play, where she never sat higher than the pit." It is significant that this moral ideal still expresses the attraction and permissibility of consumer pleasures, albeit inexpensive ones. Charlotte Lennox favorably contrasted Arabella's pleasures in "solitude and books" with those of people who spent their time in "trifling amusements." She specified "dressing, dancing, listening to songs and ranging the walks" with other "thoughtless" people. If Smollett shows the attractions of Bath to the romantic young Lydia Melford, he also presents them through Matthew Bramble's eyes. The "rage of building" in the hands of commercial "adventurers" had given rise to a higgledy-piggledy "wreck of streets and squares" of badly constructed houses, without beauty or proportion, threatening to turn Bath into a "monster," overrun by the "upstarts of fortune." Smollett's description of women there, a tasteless, pleasure-seeking, surge of socially mobile "dregs," careless of traditional class barriers, reiterated the established "joke" expressed by Mandeville and Mrs. Barbauld. They were the "wives and daughters of low tradesmen, who like shovel-nosed sharks, prey upon the blubber of these uncouth whales of fortune, are infected with the same rage of displaying their importance; and the slightest indisposition serves them as a pretext to insist upon being conveyed to Bath." Bath was the present fashionable focus of an "irresistible torrent of folly and extravagance," but the "flood of luxury" would surge on to newly fashionable centers in England and, eventually, abroad.[153]

To the public expressions of this "rage" for display Bramble added the extravagant purchase of articles of "housekeeping," the symptom of a "contagious frenzy" which had "infected" "the very rabble and refuse of mankind." The pursuit of "extravagance and dissipation" had driven up rents and prices paid for "house-keeping" in town. Dress would cost much less if people were "delivered from the oppressive imposition of ridiculous modes, invented by ignorance and adopted by folly." Novelists Inchbald and Day maintained the same campaign against the fashionable and "gay world." "The world," said

Day, represented "pleasure and sensuality as the only business of human beings" and picked out "ladies" as the chief propagators of the fashion and deportment a young male must learn. The higher "rank" had been raised "only to waste, to consume, to destroy, to dissipate what was produced by others." Clara Reeve said that the "monster Fashion, extends her influence to the whole circle." Fashion had become "the arbiter of manners" in England, and she called for the revival of sumptuary laws targetting dress.[154]

For Smollett, as for novelists in general, London was the headquarters of fashion and of those other pleasures described as "modern" by Richardson. He recorded those conditions that had become more favorable to women's shopping and attending other pleasures than previously. London and Westminster were "much better paved and lighted than they were formerly. The new streets are spacious, regular and airy." But "notwithstanding these improvements, the capital is become an overgrown monster," and while Smollett registered its attracting villagers and small farmers he saw, too, that the commercialization of agriculture drove them off the land. Other novelists' representation of London's moral corruption did not include Smollett's kind of economic analysis; instead, they concentrated on the sense of sexual dangers. In London, heroines of feeling, as well as subsidiary female characters like Sally Martin, were exposed to abduction, seduction, rape, and the threat of these and other forms of violence and abuse. They included Clarissa, Harriet Byron, Sophia Western, Evelina, Inchbald's Miss Milner, Wollstonecraft's Maria, and Belinda.[155]

The woman dangerously addicted to the "taste" for "out-door pleasures" became a type in sentimental fiction, the "woman of the world," a kind of female equivalent of Voltaire's "Le Mondain" and MacKenzie's "Man of the World." (The same type of "promenading, spendthrift and modish" women appeared as a warning in Dutch culture, in Schama's account, drawing the line between "purity and pollution" which anthropologist Mary Douglas has described.)[156] The type affected "feeling" as a fashion, and she was absorbed in the urban consumer pleasures moralists warned could lead women to a disgraceful end. Richardson held Clarissa up as a kind of Medusa to the "modern ladies," whose time was "wholly spent in dress, visits, cards, plays, operas, and musical entertainments." Fielding's "affected" Lady Bellaston was an exemplar of the woman of the world. He described women "of the upper life" in general to be entirely made up of "form and affectation," in a world where "all is vanity and affectation. Dressing and cards, eating and drinking, bowing and curtsying, make up the business of their lives." Many "have been taught by their mothers to fix their thoughts only on ambition and vanity" rather than on love.

From the same ranks of fashion were drawn those now "distinguished by their noble intrepidity and a certain superior contempt of reputation" to follow their desires into sexual initiative.[157]

Presumably this last was not the case with the actual Elizabeth Montagu, whose worldliness was one of more respectable consumerism. Barbauld wrote her brother in 1778 that "Mrs. Montagu, not content with being the queen of literature and elegant society, sets up for the queen of fashion and splendour. She is building a very fine house, has a very fine service of plate, dresses and visits more than ever; and I am afraid will be full as much a woman of the world as the philosopher." There were sharp tensions (colored by class and religious differences) between women over the forms their self-expression should take; Wollstonecraft held up her former employer, Lady Kingsborough, as "Lady Sly," in her *Original Stories from Real Life.* Lady Sly spent her days visiting in a fine carriage, drawn by richly harnessed horses and attended by elegantly attired servants, but she felt no pleasure. Her face was wrinkled by suspicion which "arises from a knowledge of her own heart and the want of rational employments." Lady Sly was a fictional representation of those women Wollstonecraft described in the *Rights of Woman* who "have seldom sufficient serious employment to silence their feelings [instead] a round of little cares, or vain pursuits fritter[ing] away all strength of mind and organs."[158]

The transformation of women's lives by consumerism is a central theme in Wollstonecraft's *Rights of Woman,* one she placed in her vision of historical change. "Pleasure is the business of a woman's life, according to the present modification of society"; like Richardson, Wollstonecraft recognized that the pursuit of pleasure "detached" women "from domestic employments." She brought gender to Defoe's class perspective on this historical change. "Women, in general, as well as the rich of both sexes, have acquired all the vices and follies of civilization, and missed the fruit." Among the vices to which "civilized women" were susceptible were: "an immoderate fondness of dress," "visiting to display finery, card-playing, and balls . . . the idle bustle of morning trifling," "making caps, bonnets, and the whole mischief of trimmings . . . shopping, bargain-hunting," and, especially, reveling in sentimental novels. In sum, women pursued "a round of pleasures." Such "luxury" and "idleness" historically had been characteristic of the rich but, by the late eighteenth century, Wollstonecraft observed middle-class, urban women were "in the same condition as the rich, for they are born—I now speak of a state of civilization with certain sexual privileges." The commercialization of Britain made it possible for "middle-class" women to live as the rich always had, that is, as "vain and helpless," "weak artificial beings," instead of "rational creatures." "Women all want to be ladies. Which is simply to have nothing to do, but listlessly to go they scarcely care where for they cannot tell what." One quality of ladyhood to which women aspired was sensibility. Women were "made fine ladies, brimful of sensibility, and teeming with capricious fancies." Capricious fancies were identifiable with the "Fickleness and Luxury" of women, Mandeville had said; their desire to "pleasure their fancy" these writers recognized as a form of willfulness, although they sharply disagreed over its value. Like Astell, Wollstonecraft recognized the value of sensational psychology to women, attributing their apparently inferior mental accomplishments to their upbringing. But, also like Astell, Wollstonecraft spelled out the dangerous implications the paradigm could hold for women. Without the cultivation of reason, women become "the prey of their senses, delicately termed sensibility, and are blown about by every momentary gust of feeling." Sensibility made women "the plaything of outward circumstances." Therefore, they became the "prey" of men, "love alone" concentrating the "ethereal beams" of sensibility. In her view—and in this it was typical—such sensibility could be simply a fashion, and its spread down the social scale was integral with consumerism.[159]

Critical representations of "women of the world" (both in fact and in fiction), from parvenus to the duchess of Devonshire, symbolized "the growing tendency of women to travel, participate in outdoor leisure activities, and . . . exploit the opportunities offered by contemporary enthusiasm for family life in a social setting." Emblematically, some of these opportunities required "the widespread adoption of the male's riding habit, including the frock coats," provoking sharp debate over the meanings of femininity and masculinity. Masquerade wishes spread into daily fashion; their literary correlative was that of young heroines disguising themselves in male clothing "at the drop of a hat." Historian Langford connects women's public expressions in this and in other self-assertive fashions to the "sexual politics" they discussed in their written publications. By the 1770s, three decades' worth of "feminist tendencies" appeared, in the eyes of contemporaries, "to have developed into a full-blown revolution," provoking a "cultural crisis." Paintings and prints satirized women's participation in sport, and a "torrent of sermons and addresses" poured down on women in the 1760s and 1770s. Among them was Hannah More's *Essays Addressed to Young Ladies* (1777), in which she reacted to the new measure of freedom enjoyed by Englishwomen by advising them to be "exemplary in their general conduct." In fact, women expressing themselves faced reaction all along. Still, we may place the views expressed by MacKenzie and Day during the 1780s in this context and see it laying the groundwork for the century's final struggle over gender in the late 1790s.[160]

Taste

The evident fact of women's appetite for consumer pleasures had always gone hand in hand with attempts to control it. This is the perspective from which one must view the culture of sensibility's insistence on a tasteful relationship with the goods and services supplied by "bourgeois consumerism."[161] The possibilities in consumerism placed a growing number of women in the quandary anticipated by Makin and Astell. The value to women of the aggrandizement of feeling, the proliferation of personal pleasures, and the softening of domestic space were evident. But because they were all associated with sensationalism, the dangers to women who gave into feeling and who sanctioned appetite seemed clear. Men could see themselves endangered by the same potential "license." "Taste" represented one attempt to spiritualize or moralize the new possibilities or even to turn them to reform.

Shaftesbury had wished to strengthen the moral weight of "taste" by identifying it with morality and with divine power; but his description of this qualification as a "moral sense," discerned by the emotion of its expression and capable of being shorn of the gentlemanly education he assumed, opened the door to the possibilities he opposed. Later writers also insisted on the importance to taste of knowledge and practiced judgment. "Hume, Burke, and others [including Hogarth] tried unavailingly to fix the standard of taste as a reaction against the great variety of tastes they saw about them in the middle years of the century."[162] *The Universal Spectator* observed in 1747: "There are not only in every AGE, but almost every Year, *Words, Terms,* and *Expressions* which become the favourite mode of Speech, which make our Language have as many changes as our Fashions. . . . Of all our favourite Words lately, none has been more in Vogue, nor so long held its Esteem as that of TASTE." The old system of "hierarchical demand and distribution" of consumer goods, under assault from both new consumers and new producers, was in steep decline. The pursuit of fashion and other consumer pleasures, which producers met and further stimulated, unleashed a dynamic of competitive distancing and catching up, continuously threatening to overtake any fixed standard.[163]

In any case, all of these aestheticians absorbed Lockean psychology and the Newtonian nervous system, and therefore continued to place very high value on sensibility. Richardson, combining the conventional model of an eighteenth-century psychology with a consciousness of his female readership, taught that his kind of epistolary novel represented "those lovely and delicate Impressions, which *Things present* are known to make upon the Minds of those affected by them." Here was a point where women, whose public emergence was sharply identified with the emergence of the intensifying cycle of widening circles of fashion, could be identified/identify themselves with taste and, therefore, with the civilizing of men in public and private settings. Hume's account "of the standard of Taste" suggests the ease with which women could associate their supposedly naturally finer sensibility with taste. "Where the organs are so fine, as to allow nothing to escape them; and at the same time, so exact as to perceive every ingredient in the composition: This we call delicacy of taste, whether we employ these terms in a literal or metaphorical sense." Perception of "the most minute objects" was "the perfection of any sense" and "the smaller the objects which become sensible to the eye, the finer is that organ." Thus, said Hume, women had "a more delicate taste in the ornaments of life." Citing Hume among others, Ronald Paulson has very recently characterized the transformation of aesthetic values in the eighteenth century as a "feminizing" process.[164]

So "taste" was assimilated to sensibility as the expression of women's literate and consumer culture. Sentimental fiction held up a specific range of subjects with implicit aesthetic value: artfully produced informal and irregular gardens, wild landscapes, melancholy poetry, romance, the poetry of Ossian or paintings of Salvator Rosa, Gothicism, peasants, and banditti, the production and reproduction of which depended on the "world" against which sentimentalism appeared to pit itself. Two fundamental standards were those of simplicity and naturalness. There was a marked tendency to aggrandize a greater freedom of form and emotion.[165] But the clearest mark of taste as it was presented in sentimental fiction was the ability to respond to this particular range of stimuli and, even more, to the "trifles" of human interaction—that "family" of words and vocabulary of tears, blushes, and gestures—and to do so with great and shared emotions. Like sensibility, "taste" expressed distinction, not only from "the world" but above "the vulgar." Montagu's view of the monstrous intrusion of uncouth workers into assemblies—into what the upper classes viewed as "society"—is a perfect illustration. Taste became one expression of sensibility's codification of itself as a system of manners associated particularly with women and its definition of itself as a civilized culture.

Novelists taught the moral value of taste by contrasting tasteful heroines of sensibility with tasteless women of the world. Wollstonecraft's Mrs. Trueman is the countertype to Lady Sly. She has the essential, civilized qualities of "taste" and "elegant manners." Accomplished in music, drawing, and literature, the epitome of a "happy blend" of "understanding and a feeling heart," Mrs. Trueman is free "from vanity, and those frivolous views which degrade the female character." In contrast to Radcliffe's Emily, whose daily activities are a catalog of her tastefulness, Madame Cheron furthered her "inclinations . . . into a life of dissipation." Her world was one of envy, social climbing, and "selfish vanity," displayed in the same round of frivolous pleasures listed by Radcliffe's predecessors. Madame Cheron lacked taste as well as feeling; traveling with Emily over the Alps, she "only shuddered as she looked down precipices near whose edge the chairmen trotted lightly and swiftly . . . and from which Emily too recoiled; but with her fears were mingled such various emotions of delight, such admiration, and awe, as she had never experienced before." Radcliffe's message was that taste was the sign of the simple and natural feelings the culture of sensibility opposed to the complex, artificial, and unfeeling "world."[166]

Taste was identical with morality. "Virtue and taste," were, according to Radcliffe, "nearly the same, for virtue is little more than active taste." The failure to cultivate one's taste was a failure to discipline one's pursuit of pleasure, and it could lead to ruin. Lady Sly's only having one child was connected to her sterile life, as it would be in the case of Edgeworth's Lady Delacour. Lady Sly's husband married her for her money and neglects her. His son is "undutiful." Mme. Cheron's worldliness—her vanity—had led her to marry Montoni: both of their motives had been mercenary. Eventually he killed her. Lady Delacour's reveling in fashionable follies placed her in severe moral jeopardy.[167]

"Delicacy," virtually synonymous with sensibility and connoting the nerve structure assumed by the latter term (specifying its fineness), shaped a woman's taste more completely than it did that of a man. According to John Bennett in 1789: "Delicacy was a very general and comprehensive quality. It extends to everything where woman is concerned. Conversation, books, pictures, attitude, gesture, pronunciation should all come under its salutary restraints." As Hume's logic illustrates, a woman's taste was synonymous with her delicacy and, like "taste," delicacy connoted appetite and its simultaneous restraint, pleasure and morality. Smollett's competitive irony had expressed the same assumption as Bennett had in declaring that women's "engrossing of novel-writing" was naturally expressed with so much "spirit" and "delicacy" that the reader was "reformed by their morality." Perhaps women could be seen as embodiments or mediators of the "contradiction" observed by Mandeville. Bennett's two sentences, like

Hume's assumption of women's special tastefulness in "the ornaments of life," also invoked a gendered version of the eighteenth-century psychology described by Pocock to be shaped by "things," by "objects," and by "products." (Schama suggests that the outpouring of consumer items from prints to "engraved utensils and decorative items" and their use in "ceremonies," triggered a "collective allegiance" to key features of seventeenth-century Dutch culture, for example, that it was holy and free.) According to Wollstonecraft's analysis of gendered sensibility, "everything" that females saw or heard from their infancy served "to fix impressions, call forth emotions, and associate ideas, that give a sexual character to the mind." From childhood, females were acculturated by the "associations, forced on them by every surrounding object." Wollstonecraft's assessment of this process was that it perverted women's human capacities, a development of the view we have just seen she shared with Astell. Women "have their sensations heightened in the hotbed of luxurious indolence at the expense of their understanding."

> Novels, music, poetry, and gallantry, all tend to make women the creatures of sensation, and their character is thus formed in the mould of folly during the time they are excited, by their station . . . to acquire. This overstretched sensibility naturally relaxes the other powers of the mind, and prevents intellect from attaining the sovereignty which it ought.

To "their senses are women made slaves, because it is by their sensibility that they obtain . . . power." But this is what Pamela had advocated as she took the "dark leep" of subordinating herself to Mr. B in domesticity even as she succeeded in reforming him.[168]

Fashionable books of sentimental fiction celebrated their own emotional effects on properly sensitized readers. With conduct books like *The Compleat Housewife,* they registered that readers should have the same sensitized and tasteful relationship to fashionable "objects," selected from the increasing range of consumer items women wore, carried with them, or used to characterize domestic space. (As we have seen, such a code, perhaps administered immediately by women, was implemented by fork and plate in the relation of food to mouth.) Again Richardson's *Clarissa* was profoundly influential, although it was only advancing the banner hoisted by earlier reformers. Because she was unmarried and her grandfather made her his heir, Clarissa was able to bequeath land, a house, its "plain and neat" furnishings, and money. She left her apparel, including headdresses, ruffles, and a gown and petticoat she had made herself, jewels, a watch, pictures, the harpsichord, and the chamber organ. Richardson specified the feelings to be attached to these items by their new owners. Clarissa intended everything she left to invoke memories of her and the pain of her being dead. Most of the rings were of or incorporated her hair, a convention standing for widespread feelings toward the dead. Leaving her "woman's library" of books to her cousin, Clarissa said: "I know that she will take the greater pleasure in them (when her friendly grief is mellowed by time into a remembrance more sweet than painful) because they were mine." Here and elsewhere Richardson's novel supplied its reader with a recipe for a proper indulgence in a combination of pleasure and pain, one occasioned by books. It was incorporated in the tasteful, sensitive "familiar" style. All of the objects Clarissa bequeaths are accompanied with this style, standing for the legatee's painful/pleasurable relationship to them and embodying the moral lesson of Clarissa's life and death. And because Richardson's readers were the final legatees of Clarissa's final bequest, the "letters and copies of letters" from the middle drawer of her escritoire at Harlowe Place, he intended them, too, to find the same, appropriate feelings invoked in them by the mass-produced book they held in their hands.[169]

Lydia Melford, intended to typify the young, moral-reading women of feeling, conveyed "ready manufactured" bath rings to her dear friend, Laetitia Willis, wrapped in a sentimental letter, and intended both for Laetitia and to be distributed "among the young ladies, our common friends, as you still think proper—I don't know how you will approve of the mottoes; some of them are not much to my own liking; but I was obliged to take such as I could find ready manufactured—." This was in 1771, on the eve of an avalanche of "ready manufactured" items for personal and domestic use.[170]

Women writers continued to aggrandize the investment of those feelings that betokened sensibility in items worn or situated in domestic space. This tastefulness was an aspect of the emphasis that literacy and the increasing production of sentimental fiction was able to give domesticity at the end of the century. On one occasion, Inchbald's yearning Matilda visits the part of the house where her father lives and from which he had debarred her:

> In the breakfast and dining rooms she leaned over those seats with a kind of filial piety, on which [*sic*] . . . he had been accustomed to sit. And in the library she took up with filial delight, the pen with which he had been writing; and looked with the most curious attention into those books that were laid upon his reading desk.—But a hat, lying on one of the tables, gave her a sensation beyond any other she experi-

> enced on this occasion—in that trifling article of dress, she thought she saw himself, and held it in her hand with pious reverence.

The narrator of *Udolpho* reached off the page to suggest common ground with her readers on the basis of their recognition of this kind of sentimental investment. She appealed to those, "who know, from experience, how much the heart becomes attached even to inanimate objects." She assumed her readers would model their responses on the combination of painful and pleasurable feelings deliberately stimulated in the heroine by her contemplation of objects associated with her just-dead father:

> The chairs, the tables, every article of furniture, so familiar to her in happier times, spoke eloquently to her heart. . . . Not an object, on which her eye glanced, but awakened some remembrance, that led immediately to the subject of her grief. Her favourite plants, which St. Aubert had taught her to nurse; the little drawings, that adorned the room, which his taste had taught her to execute; the books that he had selected for her use, and which they had read together; her musical instruments . . . every object gave new force to sorrow. At length, she roused herself from this indulgence.

Tasteful objects and fine nerves are attuned in the same system. The heroine finds it impossible to repress her feelings in a domestic space stuffed brimful; "where, alas! could she turn, and not meet new objects to give acuteness to grief?" There, the heroine luxuriated in or "indulged" her feelings, making a virtue of necessity but fostering the psychology of consumerism.[171]

Hays's *Emma Courtney* suggested that refined consumerism was an inevitable dimension of female sensibility. In the library of her "deceased friend" the heroine recorded that "a mysterious and sacred enchantment is spread over every circumstance, even every inanimate object, connected with the affections." Like Radcliffe, Hays flatters the sympathetic readers—those who are not "strangers to these delicate, yet powerful sympathies,"—and criticizes those to whom the attribution of enchantment to inanimate objects "may appear ridiculous." The blend of defensiveness and self-aggrandizement is characteristic of the culture of sensibility. And even though Austen ridiculed the excessive indulgence of young women in feelings excited by sentimental novels like *Udolpho,* Austen's account of Fanny Price comes close to duplicating the passage just quoted from that novel.

> Her plants, her books—of which she had been a collector from the first hour of her commanding a shilling—her writ-

> ing desk, her works of charity and ingenuity were all within her reach; or if indisposed for employment, if nothing but musing would do, she could scarcely see an object in that room which had not an interesting remembrance connected with it.[172]

An increasing range of personal and domestic items were invested with a particular combination of the culture's feelings, that is, with taste. During the last thirty years of the century, fashion prints were published on a very large scale—"democratized"—in a host of magazines with "Ladies" in the title. They shared a constituency with the sentimental "ladies" magazines which were promulgating the literary fashion of sensibility. Literary periodicals, the *Novelists Magazine*, for example, illustrated their novels, short stories, and dramas with "sketches of fashionable life styles." (Burney's cousin, E. F. Burney, was an early designer of colored fashion prints in the 1770s.)[173] Commercially produced and advertised items included the famous smelling bottles, hartshorn drops, and handkerchiefs—in the phrase used by Wollstonecraft, Radcliffe, and Hays, "every inanimate object"—with which women were concerned. One symbol of the inevitable tears of sensibility was the cambric handkerchief at which MacKenzie (perhaps echoing anti-Methodist cartoons) had ambiguously poked fun in *The Man of Feeling* in 1771, coupling it with other familiar pieces of sentimentalized equipment—a chair associated with someone long gone and a lady's lapdog. Edgeworth's Miss Annabella "did all that could be done by a cambric handkerchief to evince delicate sensibility at [a] parting scene." An 1806 writer of the *Saturday Review* signified sensibility in this very precise way. "It is not our habit . . . to flourish cambric over the woes of any one." As a cultivated sensibility became a fashion, it was popularized as other fashions were. So the white linen originally from Cambrai—still purchased as such early in the eighteenth century, *The Spectator* records—was first imitated in a hand-spun cotton yarn and eventually democratized by being manufactured from power-spun flax. This was the kind of "humble" consumer item on which the industrial revolution rode, providing the means whereby women were able to implement the sentimental style.[174]

The new industrial manufacturers had to take note of women's wishes, given the centrality of home and fashionable demand to their purpose of reaching a mass market. Wedgwood and Boulton, emblematic of late eighteenth-century entrepreneurship, owed their success to marketing "as much as manufacturing."[175] They were as acutely conscious of women's tastes as writers and publishers had been since early in the century. So Wedgwood quickly absorbed news of "women's craze for bleaching their hands with arsenic," women intending thus to be more like "ladies," their skin signifying their distance from vulgar, outside work. Wedgwood's responsiveness on this occasion boosted the sale of "black basalt tea ware during the general down-turn in home demand in late 1772." Black provided a tasteful contrast during the tea-ceremony's civilities with which women were now identified.[176]

McKendrick calls Boulton and Wedgwood's skills in responding to or whipping up new fashions "stage-management" (and both men made "showrooms" for their work). The phrase accurately reflects his subjects' self-conceptions: Wedgwood said of himself that he scarcely knew "whether I am a landed gentleman, an engineer, or a potter, for indeed I am all three, and many other characters by turns," and Boulton exhibited the same versatility. They had this in common with Ben Franklin, with whom they were connected by the congeries of clubs and associations fostering it along with imperial and international trade. Self-fashioning was a pleasurable requirement of the vast geographical and social range of transactions undertaken by Boulton, Wedgwood, and their fellow innovators, employing their *personae* at all levels, from lobbying governments to selling to the home.[177]

And just as other self-fashioned leaders and participants in Britain's birthing of consumerism and rebirthing of towns identified their efforts with the reform of its exterior and interior environments' shaping character, so, too, did these new industrialists. Obviously they were capitalizing on preceding changes, the awakening of women prominent among them. Boulton identified the transformation he and his fellow manufacturers wrought with the campaign for the reformation of manners, that is, to repeat his words, the purging of cruel, animal-baiting sports and "abominable drunkeness." Of course, E. P. Thompson demonstrates that manufacturers thus had identified themselves from the earliest days, that is to say, from 1700. In Boulton's vision, those outdoor male activities were to be replaced by the heterosocial "scene" in which, implicitly, women could put manufactured objects to good use. This was the Smithian progress of "liberal arts," manufacturers' intentions interwoven with the civilizing process. Langford has recently emphasized the relationship between entrepreneurship and reform from the other angle, describing such philanthropists as Jonas Hanbury, Granville Sharp, John Howard, William Jones, Colin Milne, Thomas Gilbert, Robert Raikes, and Robert Young (the latter a promulgator of "social science"), as "entrepreneurs of charity, marketing philanthropy much as Wedgewood marketed porcelain." Wesley was an early exemplar. The successful among them exhibited similar skills to Boulton and Wedgwood, and they, too, linked moral with "material improvement." Another essential link was the recognition by philanthropists that their market "included men as well as women," and women like Hannah More and Catherine Cappe would be increasingly important fellow reformers.[178]

It is not surprising, therefore, that early industrial producers were widely seen as reformers by their contemporaries, bringing employment and other benefits to the poor, men, women, and children. Erasmus Darwin (devoted to the improvement of female education) said that Boulton's mechanization of coin pressing saved "many lives from the hand of the executioner," because they made forgery impossible. That is, they contributed to the virtuous and beneficial truthfulness with which the middle-class culture of sensibility identified itself. Similarly, the dramatic juxtaposition of industrial sites with the spectacular natural scenery in which they were often set were viewed as Gothic and picturesque, and we have seen that Boulton welcomed tourists to his factory.[179]

Thus producers wove their interests (including the "civilized" behavior of a well-disciplined work force) with the taste and manners of the prominent female market. The objectifications of sensibility spun off from *Pamela* (from clothing to a waxwork) had anticipated the production of porcelain figurines and mementos—and another waxwork—of Goethe's Charlotte, contributing fuel to the translated *Werther* "craze" in 1779. It is in the light of consumer wishes which assumed the personality-forming power of "products" that one must view Wedgwood's well-known 1787 china representations of a kneeling slave, its motto "Am I Not A Man And A Brother?" Here spin-offs included "cameos, coins, and medals," and consumers' humane feelings could be reinforced by finding the same supplicant on "commercially produced and marketed crockery." Circles of women translated the figure into needlework, which they sold to raise money for the antislavery cause. Subsequently, women designed a female equivalent asking, "Am I Not A Slave And A Sister?" The emblems' purpose was, in Franklin's words, "to have an Effect equal to that of the best written pamphlet." The "speechless agony of the fettered slave" was to "appeal to the heart," and there is testimony that it did so affect children who grew up to be abolitionists.[180] These figures asked the same question sentimental fiction asked on behalf of women, and stood for the possibility that sensibility expressed in the home could be an instrument of reform.[181]

It seems apparent that the artifacts transforming domestic space, including the volumes of sentimental and other literature explaining them, may be seen as "feminine" equivalents of the material culture associated with the preceding and accompanying transformation of men, recasting "a political nation." Consumerism marked the elaboration of two spheres, although males moved between both as boys became men, then husbands and fathers. Taverns, coffeehouses, pubs; the increasingly varied drinks and food they supplied; the equipment in which they were served, and newspapers and pamphlets, upgraded the comforts of the alehouse and were the sites, occasions, and means for the creation of manners required by the amplification of commerce, complementary to the effects of similarly upgraded homes and childrearing. Self-consciously forming clubs and societies to resist economic clientage and pursue "bourgeois aspirations" by way of more popular marketing, these men triggered "collective allegiance" publicly by way of emblems, insignia, and ceremony. The production and ceremonial consumption of feasts and toasts during the Wilkes affair, served in special versions of pewter pots, flagons, tankards, and plates, lit by similarly marked candles and candlesticks, and accompanied by specially designed tobacco pipes and a focused literature of newspapers, pamphlets, songs, prints, cartoons, and plays all helped create "a radical political style or culture centered on the club, tavern, and coffeehouse." Responding "swiftly to changes in taste and fashion" and "reaping considerable, albeit short-term profit," entrepreneurs of many kinds, including the ubiquitous Wedgwood and his imitators, supplied the culture with a huge array of artifacts in addition to those listed, and catering to "those of all incomes." They were marked with political emblems and/or mottoes. "Let not liberty be sold / For Silver nor Gold / Your votes freely give / To the brave and the bold."[182]

Wedgwood's kneeling male slave emblem illustrates the hope that male psychology be extended in feelings of sympathy and humanity (and represents, too, the reformation of male manners advanced on other fronts by public male culture). This could find common ground with women. On the other hand, that a complementary female version was manufactured and at the behest of women is telling.[183] Other feelings to be invoked in men by the items of their public acculturation were resistance, boldness, self-assertion, and sovereign will. Sometimes an item invoked a "creed," a secular faith in politics that was entirely "blasphemous."[184]

FIVE

A Culture of Reform

Antiworldview

Selected by people in accordance with the changing social circumstances of both sexes, elements of the nerve paradigm, of political thought, the campaign for the reformation of manners, the evangelical challenge to orthodoxy, of literacy and the commercialization of publishing—each integrally connected with the other and all to the establishment of a consumer society—sensibility became a culture. This chapter develops previous suggestions that it became a culture of reform.

Eighteenth-century fiction in general propagated a "new ideology of femininity" and of masculinity, in opposition to ideologies represented by coarser, less civilized figures of shrew and saint, by classical and feudal warriors, and by a harsher, more corporally punitive God, as well as by the new, hard man of the world.[1] Best known of the new ideology of sensibility is that its proponents posed "the social affections"—sympathy, compassion, benevolence, humanity, and pity—against selfishness. This was so from the Cambridge Platonists through late-century evangelicals, from *The Female Quixote,* where "tenderness and sympathy" are identified with that Shaftesburian "compassion which is implanted in us as an incentive for acts of kindness" to Radcliffe's heroine's observation of her father's tears which "often swelled to his eyes . . . the sympathy of her own heart told her their cause." Her "ready compassion" for the "suffering of others" stood in sharp contrast to the "cold heart that could feel only for itself." "[D]o not let my mind be stained with a wish so shockingly self-interested," she exclaimed. This was an antiworldview.[2]

Heroines of sensibility were held up as affection-seeking beings, imagining, like Harriet Byron, being an "affectionate wife . . . run[ning] with open-arms to receive a worthy husband after a long absence or an escaped danger." Emma Courtney fantasized "uniting" herself to a worthy man and perpetuating mingled virtues and talents in their offspring. "I would experience those sweet sensations, of which nature has formed my heart so exquisitely susceptible. My ardent sensibilities incite me to love—to seek to inspire sympathy—to be beloved!—" She referred with Smithian psychology to the fact that nature was "refined and harmonized by the gentle and social affections." They extended outward from their creation in the family, "the centre of private affections," to "the whole sensitive and rational creation."[3]

In keeping with the position represented by Burnet against Rochester, marriage was shown regenerating social affections in opposition to individualism, "happy social energy" in place of selfishness seen to have had a material basis in the "mutual attractive Virtue" of Newton's etherealized nerves. *Tom Jones* concluded with a vision of Tom and Sophy married in "the family of love," which Fielding repeatedly posed against the cut-throat world of Hobbesian competition on which he had focused in *Jonathan Wild.* Their respectable and sentimental domesticity is identical to that propounded by *Sir Charles Grandison.* Tom and Sophy preserved "the purest and tenderest affection for each other, an affection daily increased and confirmed by mutual endearments and mutual esteem." And so it went, through works by the reformed Eliza Haywood (*The Wife* and *The Husband* of 1756), to Susanna Cooper's *The Exemplary Mother,* and MacKenzie's *Man of Feeling:*

> As I approached our little dwelling my heart throbbed with the anticipation of joy and welcome. I imagined the cheerful fire, the blissful contentment of a frugal meal, made luxurious by a daughter's smile.

Radcliffe's *Udolpho* concludes as *Tom Jones* had, half a century earlier. Her heroine and hero,

> after suffering under the oppression of the vicious and the disdain of the weak, they were, at length, restored to each other—. . . to the securest felicity of this life, that of aspiring to moral and labouring for intellectual improvement . . . to the exercise of the benevolence, which had always animated their hearts; while the bowers of [their home] became once more the retreat of goodness, wisdom and domestic blessedness.

Edgeworth exemplified "domestic happiness" in the marriage of Mr. Percival and Lady Anne. Between them there "was an affectionate confidence, an unrestrained gaiety in this house," "a union of interests, occupations, tastes, and affection." Everyone therein appealed to the standards of "reason and the general good." Affairs were discussed openly, there were "no family secrets, nor any of those petty mysteries which arise from a discordance of temper or struggle for power." Subordinates—children—had a common "interest" in the general society of the household. They were "managed" by a combination of reason, example, and sympathy.[4]

At the center of these visions was the progenitrix of social affections, a woman and usually a mother, in Richardson's 1740 words, serving the "cause of Virtue and Religion." Clarissa referred to "that pleasing nest which the mother of well-nurtured and hopeful children may glory in." MacKenzie's perpetuation of fiction's maternalism was reinforced by his assumption of Smith's view that the sentimental family was vital to the civilizing process. Harriet's illegitimate baby in MacKenzie's *The Man of the World* "drew forth [her soul's] instinctive tenderness; she mingled tears with her kisses on its cheeks, and forgot the shame attending its birth in the natural meltings of the mother."[5]

Copying a picture of Lady Anne Percival and her family (a picture of "domestic happiness more interesting than that of all the . . . gods and goddesses," but evidently comparable to them), Belinda exclaimed:

> this is the natural expression of affection in the countenance of the mother . . . these children, who crowd round her, are what they seem to be—the pride and pleasure of her life!

Such affections, Lady Anne said, "arise from circumstances totally independent of our will." From mid-century, medical experts had contributed to the culture and its ideology in arguing that the "natural" mother nursed her children and thereby the growth of their affections, a view Wollstonecraft would stress.[6]

The obverse of this same vision was the literary convention of virtuous families shown severely distressed by the world's hardheartedness but drawn together in their pain. Fielding's Heartfree weeping with his family when they visit him during his unjust imprisonment or his depiction of a family in *Tom Jones* as a "Scene of Distress" illustrates the convention. In the latter case Mrs. Miller describes her cousin's family, near starvation yet still relishing the "sensibility and affection" of their child. Listening to the story of the pitilessly unjust treatment of a gardener who was devoted to the support of his "large, indigent family," Matilda was "drowned in tears," the story bringing a vision of her dying mother before her eyes. Wollstonecraft's governess in *Original Stories from Real Life* teaches her two aristocratic charges sensibility by exposing them to a series of "objects of distress" in such scenes. (The same lesson was publicized by William Redmore Bigg's painting, *A Lady and Her Children Relieving a Cottager,* exhibited at the Royal Academy in 1780 and popularized in the print reproduced below.) Tear-drenched scenes of revelations of kinship and consequent reconciliations fall into the same category—the elevation of social ties and affections—in contrast to the selfish and antisocial values of the world.[7]

These aggrandized domestic scenes, whether expansive or under siege, were set amid a fashion-conscious world of individual pleasure seeking, sponsored by what Edgeworth, in typical sentimental fashion, called the "votaries of avarice and ambition." Edgeworth admitted that her picture of the Percivals' "domestic happiness" could be supposed "visionary and romantic" and that its pleasures appeared "insipid," in contrast to those of "the world." Because of their virtue heroes and heroines seemed helpless in a world they depicted as wicked and corrupt. Clarissa said after her rape, "I knew nothing of the town and its ways." According to Smith's *Theory,* there was "a helplessness in the character of extreme humanity which more than anything interests our pity. There is nothing in itself which renders it either disgraceful or disagreeable. We only regret that it is unfit for the world because the world is unworthy of it." Alienated, the protagonists of sentimental fiction were connected to the "world" by their vulnerable dependence on it. In Burney's representation, persons of sensibility saw themselves as "the slaves of custom, [and] the dupes of prejudice," yet they could not escape the world's antithetical force, "the torrent of an opposing world."[8]

At a simple level, this polarity was that of women and men. It was women Smith saw at the extreme end of the spectrum of sensibility. It was women, therefore, who were far more likely to exhibit what he saw as that incapacitating but admirable morality and disqualification for action in the world, in contrast to naturally firmer men. In effect, the "world" for which the virtuous protagonists of sentimental culture were unfit or against which they were polarized, or which forced them to internalize conflict, was a masculine one. There were men of feeling like Harley, who tended to be bounced from victimization to victimization, like balls in a pinball machine. At first sight such men may seem as "unfit" or invalid as women but, in fact, Harley went to London in an attempt to settle a legal problem and MacKenzie expressly defended him as showing some masculine firmness of character, in contrast to women. In an important sense, fictional men of feeling represented those men, like Hume, who welcomed heterosociality in the facilities supplied by the urban renaissance. All men of feeling could enter "the world" without fear of rape in contrast to women, whose increased entry into the public world of pleasure threatened to expose them to the violence with which men had traditionally threatened them, from Clarissa's persecution at the hands of her father, her brother, and of Lovelace, through Emily St. Aubert's imprisonment in a fortress governed by men carousing, fighting, and threatening her with rape. "Virtue in distress" was archetypally female. Appropriately, therefore, women's vulnerability to the predatory world was a sexual one, their worldview corresponding to the system of home and street spaces, now being civilized for women's apprehensive entry. The extreme polarization between tender sensibility and hard world makes the best sense when one acknowledges its alignment with gender, even though very significant male writers shared the moral vision that criticized the culture of worldly men.[9]

Sentimental fiction's adherence to simple country values, the century's recurrent Horatian "dream," in contrast to the materialism and corruption of the city, has allowed it to be interpreted as "ardently anticapitalist." Richardson had *Clarissa*'s man of feeling, the Clarissa-converted Belford, declare that those who "take advantage of fellow creatures, in order to buy anything at a less rate than would allow them the legal interest of their purchase-money . . . are no better than robbers." To heighten "the distresses of the distressed" was no better than to "plunder a wreck or to rob at a fire." It was the duty of everyone to "relieve" such distresses, not to profit from them. In fact, Richardson, the reformer, was also the archetype of the bourgeois businessman, fostering the ideology of capitalism and catering to the new literary constituency. The downwardly mobile writer, William Combe, can be accused of sour grapes for telling Bristol's burghers in 1775: "Love of gain entirely envelopes all traits of feeling and delicacy of sentiment, . . . I bless heaven I am not a man of merchandize." MacKenzie was another sentimental author who at times seems critical of capitalists while in fact enjoying bourgeois success. He identified a long and specific list of hard exploiters in commercializing England, sharpers, creditors, an evil steward, and an "improving" landlord who purged tenants from his land, as well public agents of the state—a constable, the press-gang, and a Justice of the Peace—he describes, too, the social effects of bankruptcy and the "unlucky fluctuation of stocks," enabled to do so because of his masculine experience as a lawyer and public official. Yet, like most male writers among his contemporaries, he declared that "sentiment and hard business sense . . . went readily together." He, like Richardson and Combe, presented himself and his characters as men of feeling, literally mediating between "harder" male types and women, and, consequently, sometimes vulnerable to feelings or charges of "effeminacy."[10]

Certainly writers were picking up qualities in male behavior that might be seen as capitalistic excesses, although sentimental writers conflated these with or characterized them as traditionally misogynous behavior. Women writers were particularly critical of selfishness, duplicity, and extravagant materialism, the qualities epitomized by rakes, rather being "ardently anti-capitalist." Their elevation of the "tranquility of nature against the bustle of men of affairs" takes on a particular, gender-specific significance. Sentimental novelists criticized those aspects of "the men of the world" which affected them directly. That they did not present their readers with a clearly defined, well-informed account of the new operation of commercial production of the market from their permeable bastions of virtuous domesticity is not in the least surprising; nor is the fact that sentimental fiction is saturated with its authors' awareness of the consumer side of the economy.[11]

As Astell's views illustrate, the seventeenth- and eighteenth-century origin of sensibility's criticism of selfishness and materialism was the well-known Christian, Augustinian perspective, refreshed by the Reformation and by the widespread ambivalence toward the ascendancy of "the monied interest," and brought to bear on material developments in British culture by the campaign for the reformation of manners. Fielding contrasted the "poor pride arising" from all the "appearances of fortune," with the virtuous feelings celebrated by the culture of sensibility; "the warm solid content, the swelling satisfaction, the thrilling transports, and the exulting triumphs which a good mind enjoys in the contemplation of a generous, virtuous, noble, benevolent action." As we have seen, this Christian and Neoplatonic perspective was one reason for sentimental culture's obsession with the distinction between the true and the false. The obsession was fueled by new and increasing signs of wealth. Yet the absorption of consumer goods probably owed much to the self-same feelings of self-regard Fielding presents. This paradox intensified that obsession still further. Were not the critics of consumerism false to themselves?[12]

In any case, sentimentalists presented the "world" as essentially duplicitous and predatory. The view is illustrated by the manipulative Jonathan Wild's comparison of the good-natured person in the world to a little fish put in a pike pond to be preyed on. Clarissa opposed the inmost privacy and goodness of her "heart" to a manipulative Lovelace who reveled in a world "governed by appearances." Fiction perpetuated the view of the world articulated by Astell as one of the actively willed duplicity of men, intentionally manipulating innocent women. "Virtue in distress" meant women at the mercy of men depicted as liars, cheats, frauds, hypocrites, rogues, and sadists. Evelina wrote, "I cannot but lament to find myself in a world so deceitful, where we must suspect what we see, distrust what we hear, and doubt even what we feel." The simplicity of her terms points to an existential explanation beyond that of reiterating Neoplatonist Christianity and developing those early-century doubts about the intrusion of unabashed capitalism. It lay in women's exclusion from the world, symbolized by Clarissa's ignorance of "the town and its ways." Evelina's mistrust, extending at one point to an utter lack of self-confidence, can be explained by her sheer lack of experience. Evelina said she depended on others to guide her in "the world" because she was "unused to acting for myself." Her guardian asks her, "guileless yourself, how could you prepare against the duplicity of another?" To encounter the complexity of "the necessary and desirable social forms," through which people in the world "must find expression," challenged and bewildered that group which, by and large, had always been restricted to the household and denied participation in worldly business, yet who now had rising expectations encouraged by literacy and the public pleasures of heterosociality. While sentimental fiction publicized its private virtues, what good could they be in a public world unless women had the economic and political power advocated by Wollstonecraft? To be "experienced," a "woman of the world" like Lady Delacour, was grounds for moral condemnation.[13]

Another explanation for the culture's polarity and its anxiety over duplicity was the growing evidence of the alterations in men's characters. Reinforced in male culture centers outside the home, although also somehow generated within it, the variety of representations of selfhood, controlling feelings and manipulating features, matched the requirements of the increasing numbers and complexity of commercial transactions. Wollstonecraft wrote Imlay, "I do not admire your commercial face." It was a view of worldly men ceaselessly promulgated by sentimental fiction: Renaissance self-fashioning had lent itself wonderfully to the Elizabethan theater whence it had entered Restoration comedy. English drama's absorption and perpetuation of Renaissance self-fashioning was a powerful literacy source for its appearance in sentimental fiction, which reacted sharply against its playful and self-interested disguises.[14]

Where clearly "modern" men were able to move easily between "homosocial" worlds (of business, hunting, and race meets) on one hand, and heterosocial worlds of assemblies—or home—on the other, and where the ceaseless change of fashions also symbolized a new freedom of human self-expression, the culture of sensibility clung to the simpler notions of utter sincerity and the immediate legibility of gesture and expression. Sentimental novels repeatedly sounded the value of "openness of heart," "frankness," "candour," and "unequivocal sincerity." Told by a tavern host: "if you had travelled as far as I have, and conversed with the many nations where I have traded, you would not give credit to any man's countenance." Fieldings's Quixotic character, Parson Adams, offered to the world the values of a feeling heart, of "meekness, humility, charity, patience and all the other Christian virtues." Pamela contrasted what she called the "naked sentiments of my heart" against the duplicitous worldliness of Mr. B. Lennox's worldly Miss Glanville could not believe that Arabella would praise another woman "sincerely." Belinda's strength lay in her speaking "the simple truth," and Hays's Emma Courtney cried that the "sensible heart yearns to disclose itself." Her self-righteous impatience with the complex and therefore duplicitous world was typical of the culture. This fundamental polarity bespoke a very deep cultural conflict, one accompanying the awakening of women, their publicizing of their circumstances and wishes, and their entering a wider world.[15]

One response to this conflict and to the "torrent of an opposing world" was retreat. Having experienced "the baseness and ingratitude of mankind," Arabella's father in *The Female Quixote* "resolved to quit all society whatever, and devote the rest of his life to solitude and privacy." There he married, and reared Arabella in "perfect retirement," the conditions under which she immersed herself in romance and learned to complain of "the insensibility of mankind." MacKenzie's sentimental Annesley "looked on happiness as confined to the sphere of sequestered life . . . the pleasures of the affluent, he considered only as productive of turbulence, disquiet, and remorse; and thanked Heaven for having placed him in his own little shed . . . the residence of pure and lasting felicity." Men admired in sentimental fiction were those who chose the kind of space women inhabited. Radcliffe's *Udolpho* opens with the father of the heroine retiring from the "gay" and "busy scenes of the world" to "scenes of simple nature, to the pure delights of literature, and to the exercise of domestic virtues." He "disengaged himself from the world," one coextensive with "the intrigues of public affairs" and ambitions for "the attainment of wealth." The "vexations and tumults of public affairs . . . too frequently corrode the heart and vitiate the taste." This was the same rejection of politics one finds in Barbauld's poem, "The Rights of Woman," published two years earlier, repudiating the case Wollstonecraft made against such cultural segregation.[16]

Cultivators of sensibility retreated from "the world" in looking to the past, a widespread tendency encouraged in sentimental fiction by the "nostalgic feudalism" derived from earlier romances and women's aspirations toward the courtly manners of ladyhood as well as by classical pastoralism. The past provided safer opportunities for the indulgence of feelings. In her "Epistle to Dr. Enfield, On his Revisiting Warrington in 1789," Barbauld asked,

> Will not thy heart with mixed emotions thrill,
> As scenes succeeding scenes arise to view?
> While joy or sorrow past alike shall fill
> Thy glistening eyes with Feeling's tender dew.

Inchbald described and analyzed the same "mixed emotions" in *A Simple Story,* published two years later. The emotional effect "of returning to a place after a few years absence" is derived from the coexistence of two feelings, pleasure and pain. One observes "an entire alteration in respect to all the persons" of the neighborhood, "those left in the bloom of health are dead or beauty is faded, the rich made poor, the virtuous vicious." The pleasure of familiarity was combined with the pain of inevitable change toward decline and death. Emily returns to "the scene of her earliest delight" which, "after the first shock had subsided" (because of its association with her dead parents), was succeeded by "a tender and undescribable pleasure." In his *Memoirs* of the dead Wollstonecraft, the grieving Godwin tells his reader that in September 1796 he accompanied her on a visit to Barking in Essex, where she had lived as a child in 1765–8. He said of her response, "No person reviewed with greater sensibility, the scenes of her childhood." Childhood was celebrated in sentimental fiction because at that stage of life, the yet-to-be-distressed heroine had not entered the world. The hostile "world" was adult as well as male.[17]

The final place of privacy and retreat in the culture's worldview was the grave. The elevation of the significance of death which accompanied the devaluation of "the world," while intended as a warning against worldly indulgence, in the hands of sentimentalists tended in the opposite direction. Even Clarissa's protracted dying early in the last quarter of that novel was followed by extensive grief and nostalgia by all characters before its conclusion. Grief, combining pain and the relief of being alive, was one of sensibility's most frequent indulgences, drawing the cultist backward in time and place. The literary concern reaches back to the "graveyard poets," above all, to Edward Young and Thomas Gray, as well as to Richardson's elaborate recreation of the traditional rituals of death in *Clarissa.* In her sentimental *Letters from Sweden* Wollstonecraft registered the pleasure of invoking death:

> The imagination renders even transient sensations permanent, by fondly retracing them. I cannot, without a thrill of delight, recollect views I have seen, which are not to be forgotten,—nor looks I have felt in every nerve which I shall never more meet. The grave has closed over a dear friend, the friend of my youth; still she is present with me.

The emotions thus aroused slid easily into Wollstonecraft's feelings over her separation from and dying relationship with Imlay, to whom she was addressing these words. She continued: "why starts the tear, so kin to pleasure and pain?" If in depicting Marianne Dashwood's deliberate indulgence in the grief caused by the death of her father and her abandonment by Willoughby, Austen was putting her finger on a powerful characteristic consistent with a sea-change in Western attitudes toward death, it took on particular meaning when articulated by women of sensibility.[18]

Women and Humanitarian Reform

All of the suffering addressed by the humanitarian reformers of the later eighteenth century could be laid at the door of that masculine world against which the culture defined itself and which its advocates wished to enter and to change. The wide range of "obvious and pointless physical suffering" they protested came to include the cruel treatment of animals, the mistreatment of children, of the sick, and the insane; the corporal punishments of public flogging and executions; imprisonment for debt; dueling, war, and imperialism; the abuse of the poor, their economic exploitation unrelieved by charity; the press-gang and injustice generally; political corruption; and the slave trade and slavery. Langford has argued that sensibility's galvanizing of "public opinion" was fundamental to the remarkable legislative initiatives aimed at humanitarian reform during the last third of the century. The preoccupation of cultists of sensibility with "virtue in distress," and the central place that this trope gave pain and suffering in their worldview, oriented women and their sympathizers to areas of immediately recognizable human suffering. It has been claimed that sentimental fiction attempted "a brave argument for much-needed human compassion in a brutalizing world characterized by class privilege, and the kind of institutionalized cruelty depicted by Hogarth." There is little question that fiction represented a heightened awareness of suffering, a fundamental meaning of "sensibility."[19]

Historians have established connections between sentimentality and the beginnings of the antislavery movement, although there are few direct signs of this in the novels I have discussed. Wollstonecraft illustrated the capacity of antislavery writers to put themselves "in the Negro's place." In a brilliant simile, she compared woman's automatic subjection to man, her pleasingness—that is, "blind propriety"—to sugar, and asked:

> Is sugar always to be produced by vital blood? Is one half of the human species, like the poor African slaves, to be subject to prejudices that brutalize them, when principles would be a surer method to sweeten the cup of man?

Evidently the subject of this comparison in her *Rights of Woman* is the brutalization of women and the need for its reformation.[20] John Howard and his different audiences (from private readers to Members of Parliament) could draw upon the culture of sensibility, a culture nourished by Burke's philosophical language and the political tradition of civic humanism as well as by sentimentalism in novels. *The State of the Prisons* (1777) is an expression of the campaign for the reformation of manners and of the culture of sensibility. But while sentimental novels were concerned with imprisonment, it was obvious that their chief concern was with the real and metaphorical imprisonment of women by men, from Clarissa through Radcliffe's Emily and Wollstonecraft's Maria, rather than with the state of the prisons. Unsurprisingly, eighteenth-century, middle-class women's chief focus was on their own sufferings.[21]

The two sides of the culture of sensibility's orientation toward reform were the liberation of women from their internalized and brutally enforced limitations on one hand, and the reformation of men on the other. The former side included self-assertion of mind, feelings, and moral value. It is in this way that one can understand the criticism that sentimentalism's antislavery tended "to retreat from rational engagement with the ethical problems posed by Negro slavery," in favor of indulgence in the feelings aroused by slaves; or the very similar characterization of sensibility's reform orientation, that it had "far less to do with moralizing and teaching anything about the conditions which make its victims suffer than it does with validating the moral authority of those who look on with sympathy." In fact, this was a source of concern to sentimentalists themselves.[22]

It is apparent that there was an ongoing relationship between commercial capitalism and the general growth of "humanity," just as Hume had said there was. The coincidence of the rise of the culture of sensibility (subsuming literacy and consumerism) with the rise of humanitarianism is striking. Commercial capitalism fostered the victimizations addressed by reformers (slavery, for example), as well as the transformation of male manners, and, at the same time, led to the softening of domestic environments and the related modifications of parenting and childhood, and the increase in public heterosocial occasions for conversation, which women turned to their own advantage where they could.[23]

Sentimentalism and sentimental fiction were intended to generate "humanity." Behn's *Oronooko* had associated the "humane" with the "noble" as praiseworthy qualities of soul. The notion is to be found in Shaftesbury's work, too, and clearly had romantic and aristocratic antecedents. By 1720 "humanity" was synonymous with "good Nature," according to Latitudinarian preaching. "Humanity's" frequency of use accelerated with the rate of publication of sentimental fiction. In his history of sensibility, Brissenden notes the formation of the Royal Humane Society in 1776. The term is highly valued in *Evelina,* published two years later, where "humanity" was used synonymously with the emotional responsiveness and the vulnerability connoted by "sensibility." Evelina declares in thinking of the father she believes she must write off as a hardened rake, "I must be divested, not merely of all filial piety, but of all humanity, could I ever think upon this subject, and not be wounded to the soul." The virtues clustered under Evelina's "humanity" include the "benevolence" devoted to "the relief of indigent virtue," and her dauntlessness "in the cause of distress," where her "fortitude and firmness" have been combined with the "gentleness and modesty" which, her guardian tells her, "are the peculiar attributes of your sex." Inchbald, too, illustrates the value that the culture of sensibility placed on being "humane," associating the term with generosity and compassion. Radcliffe's Emily pleaded "the cause of humanity, with the feelings of the warmest benevolence," her plea to the rapaciously vengeful Montoni equivalent to "pity." In Wollstonecraft's view, sensibility was a necessary although insufficient cause of "humanity." Untutored by "reflection," it remained "selfish," self-indulgent. It required "sense to turn sensibility into the broad channel of humanity."[24]

The reader was exposed to the affecting scenes of this worldview for the same reason preachers attempted to move their audiences with stories. The advocacy of social affections extended to the self-conscious creation of a particular kind of relationship between writer and reader, one evolving into a constituency and an elemental culture in opposition to the "world" inhabited by those incapable of feeling pity. Even when abandonment or solitude were the lot of a sentimental heroine, she was connected to her reader. Pamela writes to her family—to her readers—from a position analogous to that of all cult heroines: threatened with rape, hiding in a walled garden, tempted to suicide, subjected to "more wretched confinement and usage," she "lay down, as you may imagine, with a mind just broken, and a heart sensible to nothing but the extremest woe and dejection." Her writing incorporated material evidence of her misery, as she tells her readers that her "miserable scribble [was] all blotted and bathed with my tears." She invites her readers whose ducts are thus stimulated to mingle their tears with hers. With the tasteful octave or palette of emotions brushed by sensibility's "family of words," such literary "scenes" were supposed to "soften the heart, like the notes of sweet music, and inspire that delicious melancholy which no person, who has felt it once, would resign for the gayest pleasures. They waken our best and purest feelings, disposing in to benevolence, pity, and friendship." Wollstonecraft placed this view in the long political tradition that attempted to link private virtue to public life, and she suggested that geniuses among writers produced that "subtle," electric, Newtonian fluid which, "concentrating pictures for their fellow-creatures," perhaps "embraced humanity."[25]

While clearly such teaching shaped the general milieu within which humanitarianism arose, it is obvious that the immediate purpose of sentimental fiction was to persuade men to treat women with greater humanity. This purpose was rooted in the sixteenth-century origins of the novel, in turn the heritage of still earlier romance.[26] That the nongendered term "humane" was elevated with this in mind is of considerable interest to the historian of gender. Clarissa expressly wishes to "reduce" Lovelace's explicit hard masculinity to "a standard of humanity." While Richardson opposes that kind of masculinity's expression in atheism, materialism, blasphemy, swearing, cruelty to servants, cruelty to animals, and dueling, most of all, his profoundly influential work opposed "the villainous aim of all libertines" to "triumph" over "the sex." In the same place where Wollstonecraft criticizes the popular leisure culture she terms "masculine," she says that "the talents and virtues" she wishes to claim for women and thus to amplify them, pertain to all "mankind." That is, their attainment "ennobles the human character and [therefore] raises females in the scale of animal being."[27]

Sentimental fiction's aspirations to reform men shared limitations of class with other humanitarian efforts. Among them was the hegemonic wish expressed in *The Spectator*'s and Lady Hastings's support for the charity-school movement. Madame Cambon's *Young Grandison*, a book whose translation from the Dutch Wollstonecraft rewrote and amended, illustrates the way in which the cultivation of sensibility could be thoroughly consistent with the maintenance of rigid class hierarchy. Day's *Sandford and Merton* further illustrates this characteristic. If one finds some examples in sentimental fiction of new kinds of writing "in touch in a real and personal way, with the degradation of poverty" and able to take seriously "the inner life of ordinary people," one can point with greater frequency to the well-known "sentimentalization" of the poor and the lack of a "serious attempt to find a literary language which would give such people an effective voice."[28] Frequently the representation of peasants in sentimental novels resembles their classically informed, pastoral representation in other forms, in painting, for example, some of them transferred to chinaware. Frances Brooke's description in *The History of Lady Julia Mandeville* (1769) is virtually prefabricated. "On a spacious lawn, bounded on every side by a profusion of the most odoriferous flowering shrubs, a joyous band of villagers was assembled; the young men, drest in green, youth, health, and pleasure in their air, led up their artless charmers, in straw hats adorned with the spoils of Flora." This is the kind of language Fielding had already parodied but it persisted through late eighteenth-century "idyllic" fiction and into the nineteenth. Radcliffe supplies numerous scenes of the "tasteful simplicity" of peasants. In her work, "peasants" are usually parts of the landscape who, in her phrase, "heightened the effect of the scenery."[29]

This perspective represented Radcliffe's class; as we have seen, the culture of sensibility depended upon the possession of or access to property for its literacy, consumerism, and self-indulgence, let alone its giving charity.[30] Approving neatness, cleanliness, decency, and piety in the poor, sentimental literature expressed a note of disgust for those who did not thus mirror the ideals of middle-class observers. The distancing pleasures the proponents of a cultivated sensibility derived from "pain" depended in part on the misery of others.[31] Sentimental fiction endorses the view that the novel embodies the values of an emerging middle class, and one of the most recent historians of that class's rise sees sensibility as the expression of its "need for a code of manners."[32] Writers who popularized sentimental values—Cheyne and Hume, for example—preceded Wollstonecraft in her view that "those in the middle class . . . appear to be in the most natural state."[33]

Significant to the history of women in this middle-class orientation toward reform was fiction's advocacy of the distribution of charity, another sign of women's aspirations to follow the *Ladies Calling*. Looking back to courtly culture, Jeremy Taylor had declared in his *Rule and Exercises of Holy Living* (1650), "Let the women of noble birth and great fortunes . . . nurse their children, look to the affairs of the house, visit poor-cottages, and relieve their necessities." Puritan reformers had urged that "visiting the sick, relieving the poor, and such like duties, duties of piety, charity and mercy," replace previous Sunday activities, with evidently a less privileged audience in mind. Influenced by Taylor and Puritan reformers, all of Richardson's novels gave heavy emphasis to women's specialization in charity, although it was to be distributed only to those poor people who had the proper qualifications.[34] Clarissa's will made provision for the temporary relief of "the honest industrious, labouring poor only; when sickness, lameness, unforeseen, or other accidents disable them from following their lawful callings." She felt this gave her "godlike" power. Pamela's dispensing alms demonstrated her "bountiful heart." One of the reasons for marrying was to get this "power" to do good. A lady's charity was dramatized by her leaving her home to visit poor cottages, although like other evangelized males, Howard also regularly visited the sick and aged among his villagers, distributing money.[35] In Ireland as a governess, Wollstonecraft visited the "cabbins" of the poor, experience she would incorporate in her *Original Stories.* According to Hays, sensibility was demonstrable in the distribution of charity, when it was accompanied by "kind accents, tender sympathy, and wholesome counsels" to the "indigent but industrious" cottagers. Emily's "employment" in relieving her tenants she found "the sweet antidote to sorrow," and all such scenes were intended to encourage readers to do likewise.[36]

In this regard, sentimental fiction contributed to the shaping of the reforms that would stream into the nineteenth century. That Hannah More devoted her efforts to the founding of charity schools, as well as writing unrelievedly didactic and sentimental stories to be used in them, demonstrates the relationship that existed between the gendered ideology of sensibility and the deep class-consciousness of its charitable efforts. She said in her 1799 book that was aimed at educating females into Christian ladies:

> It would be a noble employment, becoming the tenderness of their sex, if ladies were to consider the superintendence of the poor as their immediate office. They are peculiarly fitted for it; for from their own habits of life they are more intimately acquainted with domestic wants than the other sex; and in certain instances of sickness and suffering peculiar to themselves, they should be expected to have more sympathy; and they have obviously more leisure.

Again, whatever the beneficial effects of such efforts (in literacy, say, or in adding to the momentum for political reform), More's purpose here was the improvement of women reformers themselves.[37]

One detects in sentimental fiction the fantasy of class harmony—even "a feast of love"—in which hierarchy is fixed and accepted by

John Raphael Smith (1752–1812). *A Lady and Her Children Relieving a Cottager,* 1782. Mezzotint (after a painting by W. R. Bigg). 17 7/8 × 21 3/4 in. Collection, David Alexander.

the lower classes with joy.[38] The fantasy runs counter not only to the widening gulf between rich and poor, described by Barrell in his account of this fantasy in painting, but also to the class confusion and anxiety created by the powerful urges to emulation and social mobility which new levels of capitalism allowed more and more people to implement. The fantasy tended in sentimental fiction to be combined with scenes of domesticity, and they expressed the aspiration for gender harmony which was also characteristic of the culture.[39] Edgeworth's Lady Anne Percival sees in "her" peasants the domesticity she holds most dear. Radcliffe celebrates sentimental domesticity among peasants, but her heroine also envies the fantasied ability of peasant girls to "range at liberty." This last fantasy's significance lies in its enhancement of the novel's most evident preoccupation with a middle-class woman's entrapment, rape, and murder at the hands of men.[40]

Stalking Horses: The Campaign on Behalf of Victims of Male Barbarity

Eighteenth-century women writers put themselves "in the place" of animals more than they did in the place of peasants or African slaves. In the case of animals as well as slaves, prisoners, and peasants, sentimentalists were self-regarding, concerned first and foremost with women's brutalization. Keith Thomas presents the campaign against cruelty to animals, originating in seventeenth-century Puritanism and natural philosophy, as evidence for the emergence of the "cult of tender-heartedness." The "new emphasis on sensation and feeling as the true basis for a claim to moral consideration" consolidated the other intellectual sources for the reorientation toward the natural world.[41]

Prior to the Civil War, the attack on cruelty to animals "was concentrated on bear-baiting, cock-fighting, and the ill-treatment of domestic animals. Then, in the later seventeenth century, it widened out to embrace hare-hunting, vivisection, the caging of wild birds, brutal methods of slaughter, and the cruelties involved in gastronomic refinements." Cheyne illustrates the reaction to the latter form of consumption. The argument on behalf of the feeling "that men and beasts inhabited the same moral universe" was made by "those of the professional middle classes, unsympathetic to the warlike traditions of the aristocracy." Their opposition to animal sports, along with aristocratic duels, was part of the embourgeoisement of manners. At the same time, ladies' lapdogs, one expression of obsessive pet keeping, were marks of the trickling down of an aristocratic fashion, which had started in the late Middle Ages. To Wollstonecraft, ladies' coddling of lapdogs epitomized effete female sensibility.[42]

The new attitudes toward animals manifested the ambivalence toward consumerism shown elsewhere. The context was the growing "gulf" between "human needs on the one hand and human sensibilities on the other." Hogarth's *Second Stage of Cruelty* depicts cruelty to draught animals, to sheep destined for the table, to the target of bull-baiting (and refers to cockfighting) as well as cruelty to a child, amidst a street newly shaped by the classical facades of buildings. The gulf was dramatized in sentimentalization of the country life, for example, in MacKenzie's and Radcliffe's sentimentalization of trees.[43] In fact, it was the profits from commercialized agriculture—"the most ruthlessly developed sector of the economy"—that sustained the ostentatious, fashionable consumerism of the towns. Despite their "cult of the countryside" writers found that "the pleasures, the vitality and the economic opportunities of metropolitan life were irresistible." Kindness to animals was itself a "luxury which not everyone had learnt to afford."[44]

The new attitude's "modernity" was also expressed in the willingness to scientize the breeding of animals, most obviously in agricultural production and labor. Selective breeding was effected for other forms of consumption: horse breeding for hauling as well as hunting, homing pigeons, pets like goldfish and canaries, trees and plants—there "was scarcely a flower or a vegetable that lacked enthusiasts," eighteenth-century Britain's consumer addictions analogous to the "great tulip mania" in seventeenth-century Dutch culture. This widespread "manipulation" of nature, of God's creation, was a powerful sign of "the acceptance of modernity." The eighteenth-century's preoccupation with changes in the traditional human roles ascribed to sex and the widespread absorption of the idea that gender was the result of custom and education should be seen as part of the same phenomenon.[45]

The history of this revolution in attitudes toward animals demonstrates the existence of a relationship between the awakening of women and the rise of humanitarian reform. Traditionally women had been associated with animals (although, significantly, economic change was ending their cattle tending); like animals, women were confined to virtually ceaseless labor, including reproductive labor when not sported with by men, and, like animals, women had been deemed unconscious. Women, "like the brutes . . . were principally created for the use of man," wrote Wollstonecraft. From Margaret Cavendish through Frances Power Cobbe, women made the connection between men's treatment of animals and their treatment of women.[46] Cavendish described herself as "tender-natured," finding, she said, that the "groans of a dying beast strike my soul." She asked

William Hogarth (1697–1764). *The Second Stage of Cruelty,* 1751. Drawing, 1751. 13 7/8 × 11 15/16 in. Courtesy of the Print Collection, Lewis Walpole Library, Yale University.

in her *Dialogue Betwixt Birds* (1653), what right "did human beings have to shoot sparrows for taking cherries and then eat the fruit themselves?"[47] Cavendish, one of the earliest of feminists, "rejected the whole anthropocentric tradition, applying a sort of cultural relativism to the differences between the species and arguing that men had no monopoly of sense or reason."[48] She identified her own body with the tree attacked by the woodsman's axe. "You do peel my bark, and flay my skin, chop off my limbs." One sees immediately the use to which women could put the ambiguous meaning of "man" in describing his cruelty to and ignorance of the life of other kinds of being than himself. "Man may have one way of knowledge and other creatures another way, and yet other creatures' manner or way may be [as] intelligible and instructive to each other as Man's." Cavendish went on to suggest that "the ignorance of men concerning the creatures" was the cause of despising them and "imagining themselves as petty gods in nature." Elsewhere, Cavendish challenged

> the Car[e]less Neglects and Despisements of the Masculin Sex to the Femal, thinking it Impossible we should have either Learning or Understanding, Wit or Judgement, as if we had not Rational Souls as well as Men . . . so we are become like Worms, that only Live in the Dull Earth of Ignorance . . . or we are Kept like Birds in Cages, to Hop up and down in our Houses, not Suffer'd to Fly abroad.[49]

"Small boys were notorious for amusing themselves in the pursuit and torture of living creatures," and Thomas supplies many grisly examples. Locke made the case that young boys' tormenting and killing of young birds, butterflies, and other "poor things" by degrees hardened their minds in their treatment of human beings, a view we have seen echoed by Shaftesbury. The issue passed into sentimental fiction. Lovelace writes that when he was "a boy, if a dog ran away from me through fear, I generally looked about for a stone or a stick; and if neither offered to my hand, I skimmed my hat after him to make him afraid for something. What signifies power if we do not exert it?" Describing his approach to the conquest of women and rationalizing his treatment of Clarissa, Lovelace writes: "We begin, when boys with birds, and when grown up, go on to women; and both, perhaps in turn, experience our sportive cruelty."[50]

Throughout sentimental fiction men are depicted as savage hunters, trappers, and fishermen, with women as their prey, although Fielding's prosaic Blifil "looked on a woman as an animal of domestic use."[51] The literature represents men as predatory "wild beasts," hunting women, as goshawks, vultures, kites, and other birds of prey, seizing and destroying wrens, sparrows, jackdaws, crows, and wigeons; or as hunting dogs, joyfully in full cry, pursuing "the winding game." Lovelace is a "panther." To novelist Elizabeth Griffith, writing in 1782, a man was a "tyger," devouring the woman whom Griffith represented as a "lamb." All of those romantic and sentimental metaphors of wounding, especially by arrows and daggers, so characteristic of women's sense of themselves as vulnerable, can be considered from this perspective, whatever their classical and Christian antecedents.[52]

Conversely, writers and heroines anthropomorphized animals and identified with them, as Cavendish had and as Clarissa was shown doing. Radcliffe presented insects as she presented carefree peasants, the novel's second female lead composing a poem, "The Butterfly to His Love," just as Emily had written "The Glow Worm," and Mrs. Barbauld "The Caterpillar" as well as "The Mouse's Petition," written on behalf of Joseph Priestley's experimented-upon mice. Emily spoke in the glow worm's voice, wishing unavailingly to guide the benighted traveler "with my pale light." A creeping, shrinking, well-intentioned little creature, vulnerable to "terror," its suitability for female virtue in distress is evident. After her father's death, Emily found his dog acquiring "the character and importance of a friend." Seeing animals in this way was a mark of a proper degree of sensibility, and this was the standard whereby *Evelina*'s readers were to judge the vulgar and "unfeeling" Branghtons' cruelty to their cats. Several male writers, including Goldsmith, applied caustic wit to these expressions of female sensibility; one of them pointed out that God's real design for animal life resembled "a great slaughterhouse."[53]

Books addressed to women on this issue converged with those addressed to children—or rather, to parents—mothers—teaching them sensibility. That new world of children's literature gave the anthropomorphization of animals a prominent place.[54] It stressed the "avoidance of cruelty, violence, brutality . . . the development of . . . virtues which are obedience, sensibility, a love of nature, and therefore of reason, which naturally leads to industry, benevolence and compassion." Pet animals could take their domestic places alongside Wedgewood's kneeling slave as objects inducing pity, and one notes the value of the flourishing pet trade as well as specialized publishing to several of these childrearing goals. "Most detestable of all is cruelty to a mother bird by the taking or destruction of eggs," and the aggrandizement of "Moral Mothers" was a feature of this literature.[55] Such works as *Pity's Gift: A Collection of Interesting Tales, to Excite the Compassion of Youth for the Animal Creation: From the Writings of Mr. Pratt,* "Selected by a Lady" in 1798, abounded with "exquisite sensibility" and contributed to its deification: its "pathetic and instructive relations win their way to the heart, and make it melt at the shrine of Pity."[56]

The sensationalist assumptions of environmental psychology and the ductility of young and tender nerves made children's reading a logical route by which reform could be implemented. It was aimed particularly at little boys, prone to such things as bird nesting and therefore growing up to be cruel. One of the best-known of a whole subgenre of children's literature (much of it written by women) was Sarah Trimmer's *History of the Robins,* first published in 1786 under the more labored title, *Fabulous Histories, Designed for the Instruction of Children, Respecting Their Treatment of Animals.* As a sentimentalist and a founder of an Anglican Sunday school, Trimmer (1741–1810) was out of the same mold as Hannah More. After meeting with what she called the "truly respectable" Trimmer, Wollstonecraft mirrored Trimmer's work in her *Original Stories.* Its subtitle declared it was *Calculated to Regulate the Affections and Form the Mind to Truth and Goodness,* and therein she, too, campaigned against men's cruelty to animals, in part by anthropomorphizing them. She would move on to men's cruelty to women, five years later.[57]

The struggle between prey and hunters represented the struggle over women's consciousness which, under siege, was "sensibility." Women were saying that no longer would they be treated as animals. The writer of *The Freaks of Fortune* (1740) wished to expose her "pages" to "those who can feel for the distress of virtue, for innocence oppressed." She recognized they were open to the "callous" and ill-natured, who thus could find "amusement, in the misfortunes of mankind." This sense of vulnerability runs through sentimental literature, not the least in Burney's "[s]upplicating" "MERCY" from the "GENTLEMEN" reviewers, but anticipating that *Evelina* would be "cut" and "slash[ed] without mercy." Nonetheless, she declared not only the existence of female mind but its egotistical independence.

In other words, sentimental fiction's contribution to revolutionising attitudes toward animals was a kind of surrogate feminism.[58] It was expressed within the direct revolutionaryism of women's literacy and it was a part of direct feminism in its eighteenth-century form. As preceding chapters have illustrated, sentimental novels raised fundamental questions about the nature of each gender and the relations between them. They asserted the right of women to marry for love in accordance with their own wishes rather than to be parties to a marriage arranged for mercenary reasons.[59] Sentimental fiction warned of the dangers of simply following one's own heart, a major ground for urging that sensibility be tempered by reason: women therefore required a proper education. A daughter's having a marriage choice made "the tension between love and filial obedience" a preoccupation of women's writing.[60] Eighteenth-century novels challenged forced marriages, characterizing patriarchal authority as tyranny. Central to many of the novels is the struggle between daughters and fathers and this struggle was complemented by fantasied harmony and obedience to sympathetic fathers. The desire to soften and improve relations between parents and children is a related theme.[61]

A woman's relation with a husband as well as a father was of central concern. Lennox's Arabella shows that marriage ended her "adventures" and, in *Pamela,* Richardson describes a woman's profound apprehensions over getting married. One eighteenth-century woman called marriage a "dark leep." Belinda's "reflections . . . upon the miserable life this ill-matched couple led together, did not incline her in favour of marriage in general"; this can stand for the continuous expression of such a concern dating to the seventeenth century, at least. Sentimental fiction graphically answered the question raised by the unmarried Elizabeth Carter: "what might I not have suffered from a husband! Perhaps be needlessly thwarted and contradicted in every innocent enjoyment of life: involved in all his schemes, right or wrong, and perhaps not allowed the liberty of even silently seeming to disapprove them!" Fiction did so by describing

> the crowds of wretched souls
> Fetter'd to minds of different moulds,
> And chain'd to eternal strife.

Radcliffe's noting cases of wives being murdered by husbands simply extended the horrors of which sentimental fiction always warned: women were subject to seduction, rape, and abandonment. Sentimental fiction elaborated women's claim to enjoy public pleasures with men, without fear of such violent assault. Above all, women's literacy and women's fiction declared that women had minds and wishes of their own.[62]

Lovelace's treatment of women as unconscious animals expressed his representative opposition to the prospect of their having minds. Through Lovelace, Richardson published a catalog of the male stereotypes of women which continued the ancient tradition of separating and submerging them. Repeatedly he refers to women's "identicalness," a view with which his fellow rakes concurred. His "triumph" over Clarissa is "a triumph over the whole sex." All women were "below" him and inferior to all men. No women are fit for "independencey": "man is the woman's sun; woman is the man's earth." Women were made to bear pain.[63] The sex is "imbecile." They were "a confounded sly sex" and "no wickedness is comparable to the wickedness of a woman." "Cunning women and witches we read of without number. But I fancy wisdom never entered into the character of a woman." Women were incapable of friendship. "Apes, mere apes of *us!*" he writes to Belford. These views helped rationalize Lovelace's career of cruelty to and conquest of women, one he wishes to go down in "rakish annals," a celebration of unreformed male culture, which believed that rape was an instrument to discipline uppity women: "*once subdued, and always subdued.*"[64]

Lovelace's denigration of women accorded with what was self-evidently another male type, a declared "*marriage-hater.*" Not surprisingly, this was a general characteristic of sentimentalism's depiction of rakes and libertines. Marriage would singe the wings of Lovelace's liberty, a liberty which, like Rochester, he needed to pursue "frolics," and he depicted husbands as "manacled."[65] He apprehends wives will be so irrational as to misunderstand their natural inferiority to men and to be wickedly defiant. Moreover, "never was there a directing wife who knew where to stop; power makes such a one wanton—she despises the man she can govern." Such a wife would be like Lovelace, looking for "new worlds to conquer, . . . new exercises for her power." She is "manlike" whereas a "*wife*" should be all "meekness," sighing "with bent knee and supplicating hands, and eyes lifted up to [a man's] imperial countenance, just running over."[66]

Lovelace's idea of liberty extended consumer psychology to sexual pleasures and to women, as had Rochester's before him. In Lovelace's alternative marriage scheme, spouses would change every Valentine's Day and, therefore, "fresh health and fresh spirits, the consequences of sweet blood and sweet humours (the mind and the body continually pleased with each other), would perpetually flow in, and the joys of *expectation* the highest of all our joys, would invigorate and keep all alive." He concentrates largely (although not exclusively) on his own pleasures under such conditions, rather than the pleasures of his female partners, and he contrasts this excitingly tumultuous, innovative, and pleasurable relationship, where each person would be "always new to each other, and having always something to say," with that of a married pair "sitting, dozing and nodding at each other in opposite chimney-corners."[67]

There are deliberate echoes here of Rochester's debate with Burnet. If Richardson's picture of Clarissa is one of her stunning self-assertion, he also supports the laws of marriage. He judges Lovelace's Rochesterian vision of sexual freedom as a mere rationalization for the violent control and exploitation of women. In the social circumstances of the eighteenth century, and despite the great significance of the self-assertion of "women of the world," women's sexual freedom could never be more than a fantasy, untestable in conditions of sexual autonomy for women as well as for men. In fact, Lovelace was an explicit supporter of the double standard. The culture of sensibility's elevation of the value of marriage, of mothering, of the home, and of the whole of domestic life, were seen to correspond to the elevation of women.[68]

Other sentimental novelists also made a point of cataloging sexist views, putting them in the mouths of rakes, squires, and men of the world.[69] These males were the most egregiously prejudiced and therefore the clearest targets, perhaps the tips of an iceberg of male resistance to the rise of women, to the emergence of their consciousness, and to the expression of their wishes. Here is the clearest evidence that sentimental literature was part and parcel of the campaign for the reformation of manners and that a primary target of that campaign was men's brutalization of women.

The rake remained on the literary landscape from the Restoration through the novels of Thomas Holcroft, Robert Bage, Mary Robinson, and Charlotte Smith, as well as Radcliffe, Austen, Wollstonecraft, and Godwin.[70] Because I have devoted considerable attention to rakes already, I will confine myself to Burney's representation of them in *Evelina,* where they are combined with the figure of squire. Burney insists that women faced regular male assault in the new pleasure grounds intended for polite, heterosocial mingling. The vulgar Branghton youth had declared his pleasure in seeing the frequent "riot" at Vauxhall Gardens when "the women run skimper scamper." Reaching the end of a long, dark alley there, Evelina and the young Branghton women meet "a large party of gentlemen, apparently very riotous," "hallowing" and "laughing immoderately" they "seemed to rush suddenly from behind some Trees." The men encircled them, answering their screams with laughter, until one of them seizes Evelina, calling her "a pretty little creature." Terrified, she struggles free and flees toward the light, only to be grabbed by another group of men, who begin to assault her. One of them turns out to be the rake, Sir Clement Willoughby, who interprets her presence, alone in Vauxhall Gardens, as a sanction for sexual assault.[71] Evelina has a second "adventure" of this kind in Marybone Gardens, where she had gone to see a fireworks display and was accosted every "other moment by a bold and unfeeling man, to whom my distress, which I think, must be very apparent, only furnished a pretense for impertinent or free gallantry."[72]

Evelina's meeting with Merton, Coverley, and Lovel reverberated with the same assaultive tensions. In Bristol, walking to the pump room with Mrs. Selwyn, the two women were "very much uncommoded by three gentlemen, who were sauntering by the side of the Avon, laughing and talking very loud, and lounging so disagreeably that we knew not how to pass them. They all three fixed their eyes very boldly upon me," and they insulted Mrs. Selwyn with sexist remarks. Evelina and Mrs. Selwyn soon learn that the men were a rake and his gang. Merton's manners "evidently announced the character of a confirmed libertine." He "had already dissipated more than half his fortune: a professed admirer of beauty, but a man of most licentious character: that among men, his companions consisted chiefly of gamblers and jockies, and among women, he was rarely admitted."[73]

Captain Mirvan and Willoughby's cruel attack on Madame Duval resembles the public assault of rakes on women, properly named a "frolick" by Burney, who thereby connects this late-century phenomenon with its deep roots in carnivalesque behavior and rough-music.[74] Captain Mirvan called his "love of tormenting," "sport," and in Evelina's view, the "insatiable Captain would not rest, till he had tormented Madame Duval into a fever. He seems to have no delight but in terrifying or provoking her," and he was obsessed by "inventing" new "methods" to do so, seeing them as "exploits." Almost every word he uttered was accompanied by "an oath." Mirvan illustrates that the rakish violence against women was not in the least the preserve of the aristocratic Lovelace, Sindall, Merton, and Willoughby. (Emily apprehended being raped by the "ruffians" of Montoni's entourage, a recrudescence of the nobleman-led gang of earlier years.) Burney's whole novel makes clear that women entering the world apprehended public violence from all quarters.[75]

The hunting squire was the second representative of the male culture targeted by sentimental fiction, despite hunting's being subjected by men themselves to the civilizing process. The development of resort towns specializing in hunts and race meets *and* catering to women and to heterosocial facilities (assemblies, coffee shops, walks, and even masquerades) sustained and intensified the contrast between the homosocial culture of males and the expanding world entered by women together with more mannerly men. Evidently there were increasing numbers of more "civilized" men able to enjoy both homo- and heterosocial pleasures, presumably meeting the equivalent wishes of women. But some of the former—versatile, modern types—were ready to exploit the latter. Perhaps the simply uncouth squire persisted. There was a continuous literary tradition here, from Restoration drama and early eighteenth-century prose right through to the sentimental fiction of the early nineteenth century. To writers and readers the squire represented the insensibility of corporal violence and the hostility associated with the traditional male attitude to women, although his cultural trappings were updated in accordance with the "modernization" of hunting.

Fielding's Squire Western, introduced by his "slaughter" of whole "horse-loads of game," is representative of those "low orders of the English gentry," attending "horse-races, cock matches, and other public places." As in the case of its Virginian branch, this culture includes threats of castration, the Squire promising to "geld" Tom should he continue his courtship of his daughter. The Squire is an unreconstructed abuser of women, not in the least deferential to the new mealtime manners. It

> was a maxim with him that women should come in with the first dish and go out after the first glass. Obedience to these orders was perhaps no difficult task, for the conversation (if it may be called so) was seldom such as could ever entertain a lady. It consisted chiefly of hallooing, singing, relations of sporting adventures, b-d-y, and abuse of women and of the government.[76]

Fielding's account is comparable to other horrified descriptions of husbands' abuse of wives, including Mandeville's in *The Virgin Unmasked.* Apart from such mealtime encounters, Squire Western ignored his nameless wife the rest of the day, being "engaged all the morning in his field exercises and all the evening with bottle companions." When he "repaired to her bed he was generally so drunk he could not see, and in the sporting season he always rose from her before it was light." Presumably these were the conditions under which their daughter was conceived. That Squire Western's wife occasionally "remonstrated against his violent drinking" and that she entreated him to take her to London (he refused) worsened her circumstances by increasing her husband's "hatred" for her, although he also spread his misogyny thickly around him. His wife's terrible circumstances were, in part, Fielding says, the result of the mercenary reasons for which her father had arranged her marriage to Squire Western. They were the ones Sophia must challenge, in alliance with her feminist aunt and with Squire Allworthy, a man of feeling. This contrast between the brutal hunter and the sympathetic man was a typical theme in gender ideology.[77]

In *Humphry Clinker* Smollett presented the same contrast, between the "tender, generous, and benevolent" Charles Dennison, on the one hand, and his elder brother, "a fox-hunter and sot" who "insulted and oppressed his servants," on the other. Smollett contrasts another "mighty fox hunter" with the sensitive Matthew Bramble. When not hunting he insists on entertaining his guests at London's taverns. Like

Squire Western, he "hates his wife mortally" although he "truckles" to her. She is forced to put up with "the brute in him," which runs counter to her wishes for his manners. This brutal addict of hunting made his own domestic space resemble the public ones he preferred: it looked "like a great inn, crowded with travellers, who dine at the landlord's ordinary, where there is a great profusion of victuals and drink." The contrast between this and the softened domestic space inhabited by an educated wife and mother is apparent. The same spatial contrast is fundamental to Goldsmith's *She Stoops to Conquer.*[78]

MacKenzie presents a significant variation in his *The Man of the World* (1773), in deliberate contrast to *The Man of Feeling,* who was in turn marked off from "the common race of country squires." The title character, Sir Thomas Sindall, puts to evil use the versatility encouraged in the modernizing, provincial worlds described by Professor Borsay. Sir Thomas Sindall

> fashioned his behaviour to the different humours of the gentlemen in the neighbourhood, he hunted with the fox-hunters through the day, and drank with them in the evening. With these he diverted himself at the expense of the sober prigs, as he termed them, that looked after the improvement of their estates, when it was fair, and read a book within doors when it rained; and tomorrow he talked on farming with this latter class and ridiculed the hunting phrases and boisterous mirth of his yesterday's companions.

Perhaps the "sober prigs" had more in common with literate women, in their opposition to boozing squires, for example, and their estate improvement was fundamental to the creation of resort towns sponsoring women's pleasures. But the versatility, which towns—and, in effect, women—required, could be dangerous, as this duplicitous rake demonstrated.[79]

Taking violent and exploitative males very seriously is a distinguishing characteristic of wholeheartedly sentimental fiction. Here one may group the "femininity" of Richardson with the orientation of women writers. In the bet between Coverley (descendant of *The Spectator's* prototype) and Merton, Burney gets to the heart of the meaning of sentimental fiction's view of the male culture symbolized by "the hunting squire." Here the figures of rakes and squires overlapped, again representing the new combination of types found in the places—Bristol Hotwells and Clifton, for example—where Burney sets her scenes. Coverley and Merton lowered the sum they wished to bet from one thousand to one hundred pounds because they changed its object from horses to old women. The race embodied and feminized another element of the traditional carnivalesque, "some kind of competition" which sometimes was "a race for old men."[80] The scenario was also another version of men's victimization of women against which Evelina poses expressly "humane" values. The "two old women . . . looked so weak, so infirm, so feeble, that I could feel no sensation but that of pity at the sight." The women were treated as if they were horses or hounds: the "confused hallowing of '*Now Coverley!*' '*Now Merton!*' rung from side to side." The old women's sufferings were the cause of "inexpressible diversion." When finally one of the woman falls and was "too much hurt to move," "Mr. Coverley was quite brutal; he swore at her with unmanly rage, and seemed scarce able to refrain even from striking her." Merton, "giddy from wine and success" in winning the bet, begins to assault Evelina, "frequently and forcibly seizing my hand, though [she] repeatedly, and with undissembled anger, drew it back." The sequence of events, the competition and drinking, turning into an assault even on upper-class women, further resembles male behavior at Carnival, an old target of the campaign for the reformation of manners, but now felt to be a far more frequent threat in Bristol, Bath, and London.[81]

To the "dissipated conduct and extravagance of the gamble," Merton and Coverley added freedom in drinking. And, like Lovelace and Rochester, they and their fellow rake, Lovel, had "epicurean" appetites, too, a mark of their "modern" character; it would be very "difficult to determine whether they were most to be distinguished as *gluttons* or *epicures*." This is another dimension of reformers' reaction to excessive consumption, one linked to cruelty to animals in the way Cheyne illustrates and also perpetuating Astell's view of women as victims of male appetite. Wollstonecraft identified it in an amusing picture of the spendthrift husband's acting the gourmet in bossing the table, and Edgeworth, too, perpetuated the theme.[82]

The hunting squire type persisted in sentimental literature both in its simple form, the heroine's father in Wollstonecraft's *Mary*, or Squire Chase, for example, in Day's *Sandford and Merton*, and in the updated form, fused with the rake, in the way MacKenzie and Burney illustrate. Inchbald's Viscount Margrave, linked by name and modus operandi to Richardson's Sir Hargrave Pollexfen, expressed the same fusion, the polar opposite of Matilda's eventual husband, Rushbrook, a man of feeling.[83] Godwin presented this contrast in *Caleb Williams* (1794), between Falkland and Barnabas Tyrrel, whose name is painfully associated with "tyranny" throughout. Falkland's "acute sensibility" was rooted in "an extreme delicacy of form and appearance" and linked to his love of "the chivalry and romance." In contrast to "hard-favoured and inflexible visages," Falkland could not help showing "tokens of the most poignant sensibility," that is, "tears unbidden rolled down his manly cheeks" and he never lost sight of "humanity." "His polished manners were particularly in harmony with feminine delicacy." By contrast, Tyrrel "might have passed for the true model of the English squire." Although "boorish" and a votary of "beef and pudding," he was "an expert in the arts of shooting, fishing, and hunting," sagacious in "the science of horseflesh." Godwin said that the contrast represented "a revolution in sentiment." Thereafter, Falkland turns out to be a consummate hypocrite, like Sindall playing his audience's sentimentality as if it were his piano.[84]

Near-contemporary creations of Godwin's contrasting types were Austen's John Thorpe and Henry Tilney in *Northanger Abbey.* Thorpe is preoccupied with horses from the moment he is introduced to Catherine in Bath. He frequently adorns his words with oaths and he boasts of his drinking ability, superior, he tells her, to "the general rate of drinking" at Oxford. He has nothing to tell Catherine, to whom he proposes marriage, except news of horses, races, shooting parties, and fox hounds. Marriage to him would have been the same as Fielding's nameless gentlewoman's to Squire Western and, like Squire Western, Thorpe viewed women as "cattle."[85] By contrast, Catherine and Henry Tilney found common ground, chatting "on such matters as naturally arose from the objects around them" and going on to the subject of sex and writing. He remarks that in "every power, of which taste is the foundation, excellence is pretty evenly divided between the sexes." Their choice is heterosocial common ground, Humean "conversations" as it were, in contrast to the horsey pleasures to which Bath also catered.[86]

In *Belinda* Edgeworth contrasts Sir Philip Baddely with the sensitive Clarence Hervey in the same terms. Baddely boasts he could "make" Belinda "sing to [his] tune, if [he] pleased" just as Lovelace had boasted of his captured songbird, Clarissa. But with many an oath, Baddely puts aside the notion of putting Belinda in his marital cage: "Why, a man could have twenty curricles, and a fine stud, and a pack of hounds, and as many mistresses as he chooses into the bargain, for what it would cost him to take a wife." The context is the Bath marriage market for which Baddely correctly sees Aunt Stanhope had intended Belinda. He continues to be tempted to capture Belinda but only out of competition with Hervey.[87] Hervey is Baddely's antitype, a far more selective consumer, as it were, although he has to be weaned from the all-male culture he had earlier shared with Baddely. His distinction, however, had been prefigured by his lack of gluttony and by his avoiding running over a child in a foot race with Baddely. Significantly, too, Hervey's interest in books stands in sharp contrast with the Baddely gang's anti-intellectualism. From the first, Hervey had had a "quick feeling of humanity." Like Godwin, Edgeworth aligns the contrast between Hervey's civility and Baddely's lack of it with change over time, coinciding with the progress of evangelism: in a later edition she appended a note to Baddely's characteristic oaths: "The manners, if not the morals, of gentlemen, have improved since the first publication of this work. Swearing has gone out of fashion. But Sir Philip Baddely's oaths are retained, as marks in a portrait of the times held up to the public, touched by ridicule, the best reprobation."[88]

The characteristic versatility of updated squires and rakes explain their overlap with men of the world. The three types were united in their hostility to the interests of women. The connotations of the phrase "man of the world" combined the dangerous and selfish qualities of the unreformed male with the materialism and corruption of "the world" against which the culture of sensibility defined itself. His origins lay in earlier exemplifications of "the monied interest" and, later, may have owed something to Voltaire's "Le Mondain" (1736), a poem celebrating Mandevillian economics. The man of the world devalued or opposed the "domestic" qualities the cult aggrandized, instead expressing the most developed, ambitious, materialist, manipulative, "projecting" psychology which historians and sociologists describe furthering Britain's commercial and imperial economy. Richardson associated Lovelace with Mandeville, and Fielding's Latitudinarian Squire Allworthy remarked that "distress is more apt to excite contempt than commiseration, especially among men of business with whom poverty is understood to indicate want of ability."[89]

Jonathan Wild was an early prose version of the man of the world, a figure designed to contrast with the good-natured and domestically oriented Thomas Heartfree, a man of feeling. "Wild" signifies that the freedom of morality—"heartfree"—was not as free as the freedom enjoyed by the man of the world because the heartfree had chosen civilization, including domesticity and sexual convention. The innermost motive of the man of the world "was the inward glory, the secret consciousness of doing great and wonderful actions," a consciousness that is of "inward satisfaction" and "glorious appetite of mind." This motive impels him "to break openly and bravely through the laws of his country, for uncertain, unsteady, and unsafe gain." It carried over to his attitude toward women. Wild uses the phrase "like a woman" as an insult, applying it to a follower or even to himself when fear or scruples rear their heads. Fielding contrasts the selfish pursuit of ambition, gaining wealth for one's "own use only," to the actions of those yeomen, manufacturers, merchants, and "perhaps" gentlemen, who "employ hands" to improve the economy of the community in which they live. One could say that the challenge was how to inhibit the transformation of men or to moralize the "monied interest," one formulated already by Fielding's predecessors.[90]

According to the sentimental view, the man of the world controlled his feelings and/or masked them with his manipulation of feature, just as the rake did. He personified the duplicity with which we have seen sentimentalists characterize "the world" generally. The counterfeiting of virtue was prominent among Wild's fifteen Franklinesque maxims, his "steady countenance" the result of his "perfect mastery of his temper, or rather of his muscles, which is necessary to the forming a GREAT character as to the personating it on the stage." Lovelace was identical to Wild in this regard, and both could trace their pedigrees through Mandeville's Mincio to Machiavelli.[91] MacKenzie's men of the world illustrate the ability "to command their features," showing that "cool indifference, which is characteristic of him, who should always be possessed of himself, and consider every other man only as the sponge from whom he is to squeeze advantage."[92] Montoni repeatedly demonstrates his ability to "bend" his "passions, wild as they were, to the cause of his interest, and generally could disguise in his countenance their operation in his mind." Sentimental fiction emphasizes above all that men of the world, in their guise of rakes, used their manipulation of feature to seduce women, bending their versatile worldly skills of scheming and projecting to the consumption of those excluded from the world's toughening effects.[93]

Montoni's genuine "ardour" was politics. He "cannot feel" or, rather, his "cold heart could only feel for itself." Sentiment, he said, should yield to the consideration of "solid advantage," and he dismissed Emily's plea for "humanity" as the childish and "romantic illusions of sentiment." Like Lovelace, his "chief aim" was "power." He "imposed submission on weak and timid minds" "to make them instruments of his purpose." At the core of the novel was the virtuous Emily's being "in the power of a man, who had no principle of action but his will." Yet, perpetuating and adapting to heterosexual circumstances the ambivalence long expressed toward the new men, Radcliffe also shows Montoni's willful masculinity to have been a necessity in the "world" he mastered as well as the source of pleasure to him. Radcliffe's description seems to contain an element of admiration for Montoni's worldliness:

> His character, unprincipled, dauntless, cruel and enterprising, seemed to fit him for the situation. Delighting in the tumult and in the struggles of life, he was equally a stranger to

> pity and to fear; his very courage was a sort of animal ferocity . . .

Radcliffe said that life's difficulties, "which wreck the happiness of others, roused and strengthened the powers of [Montoni's] mind, and afforded him the highest enjoyments, of which his nature was capable." The reservation at the end of the sentence pales besides the positive contrast between appetite and vulnerability, the willful individualism enjoyed by a style men monopolized, and, on the other hand, the vulnerability and unhappiness of those who lacked Montoni's energies. At this point Radcliffe comes closest to Wollstonecraft's *Rights of Woman* of two years earlier, repeatedly demanding that women acquire virtue by their exercise of "mental powers," facing "*rough toils,* and useful struggles with worldly cares." But taking refuge in the unworldly moral superiority of feminized sensibility, Radcliffe concludes her novel with Emily and Valancourt holed up in domestic bliss.[94]

Sensibility's Goal: The Man of Feeling

Sentimentalists defined unacceptable masculinity; the corollary was their publicizing their ideal of manhood. In *The Fair Moralist; or, Love and Virtue* (1743), Charlotte McCarthy declared "it is not my Business here to describe both Sex [*sic*] as they really are but as they ought to be." Lennox's Arabella said that her romance "gives us an idea of a better race of beings than now inhabit the world." Evelina declared that Lord Orville was "formed as a pattern for his fellow-creatures, as a model of perfection" and we have seen that Edgeworth presented the Percival family as a "visionary" ideal.[95] The creation of men of feeling was the expression of "collective wish fulfillment," and of "deep need" on the part of women.[96] Men of feeling have been called "dream figures," an echo of the eighteenth century's own criticism of the effects of sentimental fiction on women—that it put them in fantasyland.[97] Aware of the female market, male writers publicized a very similar ideal to that publicized by women. Richardson directly reflected female wishes, in his words, "having been teased by a dozen ladies of note and of virtue, to give them a good man."[98] He "tells men what to be if they want to marry heroines."[99]

The new male ideal was identified with Christian piety and goodness, expressed early in the century by Steele's *The Christian Hero* and influenced by the courtly manners of the Renaissance. There was an obvious relationship between the idealization in sentimental fiction of men capable of virtuous suffering and the "feminized" figure of Christ, elevated by the campaign for the reformation of manners.[100] Sentimental heroes opposed gambling, oaths, drinking, idleness, cruelty to animals, and other elements of popular male culture.[101] It was also in keeping with the reformation of manners that Lord Orville respected the objection of "ladies" to the Restoration theater and, conversely, their preference for "the sentimental." Fictional heroes repudiated "incontinence" and the double standard.[102] Thus reformed, men were said to have "manners" or the "delicacy" expressing their politeness. Orville displayed "refined good breeding in his manners." Of his predecessor, Sir Charles Grandison's "manners," Harriet Byron remarked, "His good breeding renders him very accessible," that is, to women.[103]

Here was where women's wishes and men's converged in the civilizing process. Hume, and Smith, and other members of Edinburgh's Select Society believed that the company of women, in Fordyce's words, would "melt" and "soothe" the ferocious and forbidding aspects of male behavior, making men more "agreeable."[104] This served that Society's own purposes. By associating their targets quite frequently with the past—with the dueling warrior mentality of an earlier aristocracy and with the appetitive explosiveness of Carnival, as well as with barbarism, sentimental reformers made their wishes reconcilable with progress, visible in the manners men were to exhibit in the new public pleasure centers–cum–marriage markets. Fielding's Squire Western, MacKenzie's Sindall, and Burney's Sir John Belmont are "brutal," "inhuman," and "savage." Deeply depressed because Augustus Harley ignores Emma's offering herself to him, she calls him "*Barbarous, unfeeling, unpitying,* man!" "Humane" feeling "assimilates man to higher natures," wrote Barbauld. Men could show their civility by repudiating the brutal treatment of women. Novelists shared psychological and sociological assumptions with the Scots heirs of Locke, believing that men could change. Clarissa wrote Anna Howe that the black "passions which we used so often to condemn in the violent and headstrong of the other sex may be only heightened in *them* by *custom* and their freer *education.*"[105]

Because sentimental fiction's softened male was benevolent, compassionate, and humane, was literate and had "true taste," he would make a better husband. He wanted to do so because he placed a high value on a harmonious marriage and on domesticity. Burnet had transmitted this from still earlier Protestant tradition. It was the case from Fielding's Heartfree and Richardson's Mr. B through Edgeworth's John Percival, from Sir Charles Grandison's and Tom Jones's eventual uxoriousness through the blissful conclusions of *Udolpho* and Edgeworth's *Belinda.* In effect, the depiction of marital harmony on the basis of mutual sensibility symbolized women's right to assert such standards in the judgment of husbands.

Above all, and this cannot be too strongly emphasized, the man of feeling was shown to respect women and make common ground with them. Tom Jones's "obliging, complaisant behavior to all women in general . . . greatly distinguished Tom from the boisterous brutality of mere country squires," and it was this that made him very attractive to women. Evelina contrasts the "libertine," Sir Clement Willoughby, with Lord Orville, the man of feeling:

> the latter has such gentleness of manners, such delicacy of conduct, and an air so respectful, that, when he flatters most, he never distresses, and when he most confers humour, appears to receive it! The former *obtrudes* his attention, and forces mine; it is so pointed, that it always confuses me, and so public that it attracts general notice.

The forced, pointed behavior of a rake to a woman in public was now no longer acceptable.[106]

To be "admitted anywhere" (that meant the heterosocial congregating points of a polite and commercial society), a rake had at least to promise to "*reform.*" Not only had men to give up their physical harassment of women, they also were asked to be extraordinarily careful not to give women psychological pain. From Tom Jones and Hickman to Valancourt, the masculine ideal was shown taking women's feelings into account and deferring to their importance. Tom tells Sophy, "I know the goodness and tenderness of your heart and would avoid giving you any of those pains which you always feel for the miserable." Seeing Emily's grief, "Valancourt understood her feelings and was silent," and he weeps silently with her. It was as if women exaggerated their sensibility to try to get men to be this careful. The culture of sensibility wished to reform men, to make them conscious of women's minds, wishes, interests, and feelings, in sum, their sensibility. The sentimentalists' targets were men who were "hard," "hardened," "hard-hearted," and "unfeeling" to women, those who, like Clarissa's brother, thought "it proof of a manly spirit, to show himself an utter stranger to the gentle passions." "How delicate [is] his whole behavior!" exclaimed Evelina of Lord Orville's treatment of her, "willing to advise, yet afraid to wound me." By late in the century, "all writers' agreed that women were the arbiters of proper behavior in mixed company."[107]

There was one final general characteristic of the male ideal which sharply distinguished the hero from the heroine of feeling, and reflected the reality of the legal and economic disabilities of women. All of the heroes of sensibility were "in touch with reality . . . They exercise masculine authority in a world whose ways, even if sometimes distasteful, are comprehensible." Married or unmarried, sentimental heroes were shown free to enter or leave "the world" with an ease in sharp contrast to the experience of sentimental heroines. This was as true of Valancourt and Harley as it was of Sir Charles Grandison. Wollstonecraft criticized romantic manners on this basis, and Edgeworth, in describing male deference to female wishes for their manners, complained that such politeness placed a veil between women and reality.[108]

Sensibility's Method: Conversion

The specific means whereby sentimental fiction showed insensitive men transformed into men of feeling was conversion. Sentimental fiction perpetuated the same ambition as Burnet's *Life of Rochester* and gave it much wider circulation, but it was very significantly different from that earlier text. Sentimental fiction made women's role in men's conversion decisive. Beasley writes of Pamela that her "letters, meditations, and journal entries have upon Mr. B precisely the effect that Isaac Barrow and John Tillotson had claimed for the lives and histories of familiar Christian heroes and heroines, and presumably they are to have similar effects upon the reader." However, Barrow and Tillotson were not women, and women were not admitted to the Anglican pulpit. Women's public claim to the power of conversion reflected the interest of the constituency which read and wrote the bulk of sentimental fiction.[109]

Pamela makes a "convert" of Mr. B "from libertinism" even while he repeatedly tries to seduce and rape her. Her effects are those of a saint; seeing her praying upon her knees, Mr. B says that no picture was equal "to that which your piety affords me." Marrying Pamela will complete his conversion, a process Cheyne urged Richardson to elaborate. Reformed himself, like Belford Mr. B. preaches reformation to other rakes as well as to his sister, Lady Davers. "Egregious preacher! said she: What, my brother already turned *Puritan!*—see what marriage and repentance may bring a man to! I heartily congratulate this change!"

The religious conversion of men was identified with a conversion of their manners. Just as Mr. B comes to respect the word "wife," he comes to despise dueling and all of his former "libertine" "pursuits and headstrong appetites," replacing them with "the most delicate manner." He gives up rape and seduction in favor of pity, toleration, and concern. His new purity of language is in sharp contrast with his old, libertine style. "No light and frothy jests drop from his lips; no alarming railleries; no offensive expressions; no insulting airs, reproach and wound the ears." His "delicacy" recognizes and defers to

Pamela's vulnerability, even though he believes her tender "modesty" "over-nice." Her feminine "manner" is still more "delicate" than his, signified by her "colour" coming and going.[110]

Three points need to be emphasized. First, conversion was adapted to women's wishes and purposes to transform male treatment of women. Second, conversion did not challenge the male's powerful legal authority as husband and father. In fact, Richardson criticized himself on this point in a 1749 letter. "It is apparent by the whole [tenor] of Mr. B's behavior, that nothing but such an implicit obedience, and slavish submission, such as Pamela shewed to all his injunctions and dictates, could have made her *Tolerably* happy, even with a *reformed* rake." Wifely deference remained a feature of popular fiction, reflecting "economic necessity sublimated by wifely ideals." The maintenance of crucial aspects of male authority can be connected to the third point to be emphasized. Typically, Pamela's power of conversion was derived from a female gender style manifest in tearfulness, fainting, and physical weakness—that is, her distinctively susceptible nervous system. This style was presented as women's refinement of manners, linking women together as well as promising to maintain their subordination. It signified their apparent power to refine and civilize men, while contributing to the reassurance of men that their greater delicacy was still "manly."[111]

In *Clarissa,* Richardson contradicted the conclusion of *Pamela* "that a reformed rake makes the best husband." His recantation was a grand one since he attributed his first, highly publicized conclusion to "the author of all delusion," identifying himself with the devil.[112] But the notion—that a reformed rake makes the best "husband"—remained a preoccupation among eighteenth-century writers because it encapsulated the great reform goal characterizing the culture of sensibility. The question of making "the best husband" assumed that women's interest was fundamental. That the conversion of rake to husband was laden with religious and moral values stemming ultimately from Protestantism was signified by the word "reformed." It also connoted the possibilities for dramatic personality change. The appeal of this idea, "empowering" women, to use Richardson's own term in *Pamela,* must be connected to that novel's great popularity. And while Clarissa's attempt to convert Lovelace literally fails, she has the entire moral victory over him. The novel of which Clarissa is the heart symbolized the same aspiration as *Pamela.*

From beginning to end, Clarissa expresses her wish to reform Lovelace, "to be able to reclaim such a man to the paths of virtue and honour; to be a secondary means [God being the primary], if I were to be his [wife], of saving him."[113] Clarissa is depicted as a goddess, a divinity, God's instrument, while Lovelace is "the instrument of Satan," presented as such with a wealth of imagery. The ancient Christian moral struggle is thereby dramatically and insistently gendered. Religious power is literally "feminized" and traditional masculinity diabolized.[114] Other literary rakes and brutal husbands are presented in the same way, sustaining Astell's Neoplatonic, Christian view of male treatment of women. During her resistance to the rakish gang in the public setting of Bristol, Burney's feminist Mrs. Selwyn retorts to Merton's insults by telling him he will be visiting "the dominions of the devil." Satanic costumes were popular at masquerades, presumably mocking moralism and the reformation of manners.[115]

Lovelace frequently shows signs of potential conversion at Clarissa's hands. On one occasion, he was "so very much affected for trying to check my sensibility, it was too strong, and I even sobbed."[116] Later hardened rakes had similar potential. Of Montoni, Radcliffe writes that "the divinity of pity, beaming in Emily's eyes, seemed to touch his heart. He turned away, ashamed of his better feelings."[117] Lovelace is tempted to convert to marriage by his vision of Clarissa-as-mother, suckling twin Lovelaces:

> I now . . . behold this most charming of women in this sweet office; her conscious eye now dropped on one, now on the other, with a sigh of maternal tenderness; and then raised up to my delighted eye, full of wishes, for the sake of the pretty varlets, and for her own sake, that I would deign to legitimate; that I would condescend to put on the nuptial fetters.

Lovelace had associated Clarissa's "divinity" with her maternal power earlier in the novel, too. It converted him both to the wish to marry her, and reduced him to rebirth and to infancy:

> Clarissa!—O there's music in the name,
> That, soft'ning me to infant tenderness,
> Makes my heart spring like the first leaps of life![118]

One can tie this vision to Richardson's ascription of Lovelace's obsessive desire to conquer women to his overindulgence in infancy by his mother; this psychological diagnosis pointed to a danger in the general elevation of female parenting and domestic power to which sentimental writers (including Richardson) generally subscribed.[119]

Instead of welcoming his conversion and spiritual rebirth, that is, interpreting Clarissa's power as secondary to God's, Lovelace interprets it as Clarissa's own power as a material being, as a woman. Belford tells Lovelace that his "senses have been so much absorbed in the WOMAN in her charming person, as to be blind to the ANGEL that shines out in such full glory in her mind." Belford wishes to teach Lovelace to see beyond Clarissa's sexuality, asserting that gender differences were due to "education." He wishes to convey to Lovelace "the more exalted pleasure in intellectual friendship, than ever thou couldst taste in the gross fumes of sensuality." Belford said that, on his own part, he would find it impossible, were Clarissa "as beautiful, and as crimsoned over with health as I have seen her, to have the least thought of sex, when I heard her talk."[120]

Richardson's women readers wished him to bring about a "happy ending" by "reforming Lovelace, and marrying him to Clarissa." While Richardson refused them that, he did present Belford's undergoing successful conversion. This is a major topic of *Clarissa,* although it is dimmed by the greater vitality and conviction in the heroine's unsuccessful struggle to convert Lovelace. Prior to Clarissa's converting Belford, he had been "a profligate . . . one who lived a life of sense and appetite." Immersed in "vices" and therefore dying in agony, Belton tells Belford: The "excellent Miss Harlowe has wrought a conversion in you."[121] The converted Belford resolves to "look upon my past follies with contempt; upon my old companions with pity. Oaths and curses shall be for ever banished from my mouth; in their place shall succeed conversation becoming a rational being and a gentleman." In atonement for past evils he will become "a universal benefactor," exchanging "pagan authors" for the Bible. Another text Belford resolved to read whenever he wished to firm up his abhorrence of his "former ways" was Clarissa's posthumous papers, that is, the novel the reader holds in her/his hands. *Clarissa,* Richardson's great, seminal, sentimental novel, is to be immortalized as a handbook of reform efforts against rakish "annals," one embodying biblical authority. Richardson, like his heroine, is to be an instrument of God.[122]

The obstacle to conversion is men's own, willful power which Lovelace illustrates they take as central to their masculinity. It is in contrast to the receptivity required in the acceptance of "grace." Little "do innocents think . . . what portion of Divine Grace is required . . . when it is considered that it is not in a man's *own power* to reform when he will." In effect, the renunciation of willfulness was exemplified by a virtuous woman "free" of the temptation of world because, in Richardson's view, she gives up public pleasure for domestic happiness. The gendering of virtue raised the question whether men can ever be as fully converted as women: because women are excluded from "the world" even the converted male must mediate it. (This is consistent with Richardson's defense of men's legal superiority.) Belford's "securing" his conversion, beyond reading the Bible, or even rereading *Clarissa's* letters, depended on his securing "a virtuous and prudent wife." She would fortify "him against the apostasy" of reverting to rakery, secure in her moral superiority, won at the expense of a life beyond home. Such security would also gain the converted husband the "pleasure" accruing to those of a moralized taste, in contrast with the "deviation" of "sensuality."[123]

Taking pleasure in virtue links Richardson's heroes to Fielding's. At the same time Fielding points out to his male readers that "goodness of heart and openness of temper" would "by no means—alas!—do their business in the world." Life required "business"—legal and economic realities—to be conducted in the public world. Fielding advised his male readers: "It is not enough that you design . . . that your actions, are intrinsically good; you must take care that they shall appear so." This was a major message of the novel, an emphasis distinguishing it from more unworldly, more sentimental works.[124]

The message has the effect of modifying Tom Jones's moral conversion, although it is not intended to undercut it altogether. Falling on his knees before Allworthy, Tom declares that his sins have been "follies and vices" rather than "gross villainy" but still sufficient ones "to repent." It is consistent with Sophia's female sensibility that she should still hold Tom a "libertine." The language between the couple can be read at least in part as Fielding's parody of the conversion motif of sentimental "scribblers." Tom throws himself at Sophy's feet, declaring his repentance sincere, but it is suffused with sexual feeling, as are her replies. She relents immediately Tom takes her in his arms and kisses her, giving an archly ambiguous reply to Tom's declaration of the distinction he has always made between penile love and heart love. "I will never marry a man," replies Sophia very gravely, "who shall not learn refinement enough to be as capable as I am of making such a distinction." Paying lip service to the view expressed by Astell and Richardson, Tom then declares that "the first moment of hope that my Sophia might be my wife taught it me at once, and all the rest of her sex from that moment became as little the objects of desire to my sense as of passion to my heart."[125]

The conversion theme appears in the work of later male sentimentalists appealing to a female audience, for example, in MacKenzie's Sir Thomas Sindall's being converted by Harriet, "his saint, his guardian angel."[126] Men's conversion, however, is dramatically more central and more equivocal in later novels by women. Burney's unsentimental feminist, Mrs. Selwyn, takes up Belford's warning to women not to trust a "confirmed libertine" who promises to reform. A woman who agrees to marry a man "under that notion" is a "fool." The man in question is the squire, Merton, and the woman, Lady Louisa Larpent, underage, pretty, with a large fortune and an invaliding sensibility.

The "foolishness" of a woman's marrying a rake is central to *Evelina's* plot. Evelina's mother, Caroline Evelyn, had escaped a forced marriage by marrying Sir John Belmont, "a very profligate young man," known for his "libertinism." Her marriage was rash because it was done privately and without a witness. Like Clarissa, when she knows she is dying, Caroline Evelyn wonders if her death will convert the rake who has abandoned her. She imagines that he will be reading her letter when "the kind grave has enbosomed all my sorrows," and she offers him another "ray of consolation" in the afflictions she is certain are coming. In her angry fantasy of the future, their powers are reversed. She will be able to give him something he will desperately need, her pity, her prayers, and the recollection of the love she once bore him.[127]

When eventually father and daughter are reconciled in a typical sentimental scene of kneeling and weeping, Belmont's "bitterness of grief" turns to "frantic fury," because "owning" his daughter as his wife required "humbles" him as a father. He alternates between bidding Evelina begone and abasing himself. He offers "to crawl upon the earth,—I would kiss the dust,—could I, by such submission, obtain the forgiveness of the representative of the most injured of women." The time is ripe for Evelina to reveal her mother's undelivered letter. Hastily reading it, he exclaimed, "Yes! thou art sainted!—thou art blessed!—and I am cursed for ever!" He has Evelina play the forgiving mother to him. Sinking on his knees before her and addressing her as "dear resemblance of they murdered mother!" he begs, "Oh . . . thou representative of my departed wife, speak to me in her name, and say that the remorse which tears my soul, tortures me not in vain." All this is consistent with the feminized iconography of the culture of sensibility. Evelina forgives him, but Belmont remains permanently vulnerable to Evelina's reminding him of the woman he has wronged. He hurries from the room leaving Evelina to the sure prospect of marrying Lord Orville, who also had promised to "revere" her. Unlike Belmont, Belford, and Mr. B, Orville has not had to be converted. He has been unambiguously a man of feeling all along, identifying himself thoroughly with the reformation of male manners. Belmont's permanent emotional rending suggests that guilt for rakery cannot be fully expiated and/or that a rake's reform is shot through with conflict. Burney thus identifies herself with the view she expressed through Selwyn: better it would be if men never became rakes at all.[128]

Conversion is at the heart of Inchbald's *A Simple Story.* For much of the first volume, Dorriforth/Lord Elmwood seems to be as perfect a man of feeling as Lord Orville, a man of "delicacy" as well as "exquisite sensibility." Dorriforth's exquisite sensibility makes him deeply susceptible to "love"—in effect, susceptible to women and to sexuality.[129] Nonetheless, he exercises self-control for several chapters and attempts to teach the equivalent prudence to the excessively sensitive Miss Milner (although his apparent "firmness of mind" turns out to be a fault, liable to become "implacable stubbornness"). So the first conversion is Miss Milner "teaching him to love," her "sensibility" converting the man she fantasizes as "the grave, the sanctified, the anchorite Dorriforth" to "the veriest slave of love." It was a perversion of reformation because Miss Milner's motives were, like Lovelace's, to enjoy her lover's "submission." She was playing a dangerous game. Lord Elmwood was confused over the distinction between feeling passionately and losing control, a confusion with which his willful manhood was implicated. There was anger and even vengefulness, perhaps, in Miss Milner's call for his "submission" to her, and Inchbald presents it as a big mistake to construe conversion as humiliation, the sign of victory in a power struggle, a construction Lovelace and Belmont also mistakenly gave it. Certainly, women should not admit such motives. Instead, conversion should be the basis for a more mutual and harmonious relationship between the sexes, although one in which women must still subordinate themselves.[130]

Miss Milner had been incapable of recognizing the full force of such a man's feelings and therefore of managing them, that is, of repressing her own feelings in the interests of managing the marriage. In penetrating Dorriforth's vulnerable guard in order to convert him, Miss Milner unleashed his capacity to focus his sensibility on her. His emotional force was only contained by his returning to his willful shell after her adultery and consequent banishment with the resulting illegitimate daughter. That this shell was a reversion to masculine culture is indicated by Lord Elmwood challenging his wife's lover, the rake, Lord Frederick, to a duel, in which Lord Elmwood maimed him and defaced him with scars. Lord Elmwood acquires the "character" of "unplacable stubbornness" warned against in the first volume.[131]

The result of Lord Elmwood's repression of his sensibility is that Lady Matilda's challenge duplicates her mother's. She, too, must break through Lord Elmwood's masculine firmness in order to teach him how to love, but this time the penetration will not be complicated by sex. Not only is this because of the difference of generations and the incest taboo; Matilda herself, unlike her mother, has been "properly educated" to purge her sensibility of sexual desire. Her conversion succeeds. The first appeal of Matilda's virtue in distress "unmanned" Lord Elmwood, that is, it broke through his obstinate repression of the qualities Inchbald advocates. When Matilda is then abducted by another rake, "her deliverer" proves to be her father, who is then finally converted. Men have the capacity to be converted by women, Inchbald shows twice, but, to be effective, such a conversion must be deserved by a virtuous and self-governing female.[132]

Other late-century sentimental novels by women illustrate the same powerful urge to convert men as well as a significant degree of ambiguity over conversion's value. Emerging from the urban culture of gaming, dissipation, and sexual "flirtation," Valancourt asks Emily to be "willing to hope for my reformation." His regaining "virtues" is dependent on being "nurtured" by Emily's "affection," a dependence that invoked the characteristic fusion of maternal and divine power. Emma Courtney's "dearest ambition" was to be Augustus Harley's wife, supplying him with "domestic comforts." He seemed an "inflexible, impenetrable man," and her offering herself to him was "to soften, and even elevate his mind." He admits, when dying, her "tenderness early penetrated my heart." "I had not only to contend against my own sensibility, but against yours also." As a male he is able to withstand full penetration, whereas Emma Courtney is held up as an example of the inability of a woman to exercise such self-control. Ambiguously, though, this is also the source of her feminized moral superiority.[133] In *Belinda* Lord Delacour's reformation accompanies his wife's. His getting dead drunk had become a daily ceremony; when intoxicated, he treats a female servant violently, with "brutal oaths, dragging" her out of his way. Prior to taking to drink he was obsessed with his racehorses, and he regularly eats out with his boon male companion. Still, he only takes to drink as the result of the power struggle with his wife. At bottom Lord Delacour is "a humane man," with a "good-nature," capable of being moved by an appeal, possessing the "delicacy" of being more jealous of his wife's mind than her person. Lady Delacour unbends and reformation immediately follows. Lady Delaçour's challenge in firming up this conversion is to add other tasteful pleasures of "home" to "dining" and to "sentiment." Fortunately, Lord Delacour has "talents"—drawing and "a very pretty taste for music"—that a cultured, sentimental, and domesticated wife can elicit, in substituting the sanctioned heterosocial comforts of home for the popular male pleasures abroad.[134]

Thus the culture of sensibility published the wish-fulfillment that may be traced back to the late seventeenth century, to monarchist Astell as well as to the implications of the Commonwealth call for private virtue. Looking back to such origins, Smith and the other founders of modern sociology had urged that the home should become the generator of the social bond rather than merely of individualism. This tendency required the curtailment of women's expression of willfulness or, perhaps, its greater focus on domesticity at the expense of moralizing their willful pursuit of pleasure abroad that had become so striking (and troubling) a feature of eighteenth-century Britain.

The Cult of Sensibility

A distinct worldview, infused with religious values and claiming to reform a fallen population by conversion, raises the possibility that sensibility did in fact comprise the "cult" that so many literary critics and scholars have termed it.[135] In describing nineteenth-century "sentimentality," the continuation along still more popular lines of a phenomenon created out of the literacy, religion, consumerism, and gender values of the previous century, Meyer refers to it as "a pseudo-religion in a passive mode."[136]

From its beginnings, Protestantism had replaced "the sacrament of the real presence on one's knees in church [by] encounter with the Holy Spirit in the familiar language of men on the printed page of the sacred text." The Protestant faith in the power of the Bible's word to make converts was compounded by the belief in sensational psychology to make character. "Because it assumed that the impressions made by fiction are as real to the mind as those made by other experience, sensationalist epistemology radically intensified the cultural anxiety over the influence of fiction." Anxiety over literacy's effects on nervous systems and morals was coextensive with its spread to a mass audience.[137] Steele had worried that the techniques used by his "Contemporaries the Novelists" gave "great Disturbance to the Brains of ordinary Readers." Dr. Johnson said written narrative had power "to take possession of the memory by a kind of violence and produce effects without the intervention of the will." By the same token, however, reading could reform readers, when its power was turned to moral ends. In Lord Kames's view, reading about an act of gratitude would dispose the reader to perform a similar act.[138] The measure of a narrative's effectiveness was its capacity to make an impression on "almost" the "hardest heart."[139] The more impressionable the reader, the more responsive to less crude nuances, particularly of a character's pain or embarrassment. In this way the sense of intimacy between reader and writer was built up and the reader's own sense of being qualified was endorsed. By definition, those qualified by their special degree of sensibility constituted themselves a special group, self-conscious in its capacity for feeling and virtue—"privileged" in Wesley's cognate vision—in opposition to the unfeeling and vice-ridden world from which they were distinguished.

Beasley argues that the literature of sensibility was part and parcel of eighteenth-century English religious history, entitling one section of his book, "*Pamela* and *Clarissa:* Fiction as Devotional Literature." Eighteenth-century literature referred to its own writings, the distresses of its characters, and the feelings aroused by them, as "sacred."[140] Richardson described the belief that readers generally brought to fiction as a kind of "Faith." Fielding remarked that one of his female characters in *Tom Jones* (named Arabella as Lennox's misguided heroine would be) divided her time "between her devotions and her novels," but such irony was rejected by the "true" cult. Moreover, Fielding compared his own purpose to preaching a superior kind of "sermon" and to "inculcate" a "doctrine." Richard Griffin records his grandmother poring over *Pamela* as if she were reading her Bible, a connection that was in perfect accord with Richardson's express intention to bring about a "reformation" by conveying "the great doctrines of Christianity" by way of the novel. Redirecting the century's widespread belief in the power of reading, sentimental novelists presented their texts as agents of conversion, just as sentimental dramatists did. If Rousseau "opened up his soul to those who would read him right," his French readers brought a religious purpose to reading him and other writers as they read the Bible, "in order to reach heaven" and "to improve their manners." The same may be said of eighteenth-century English readers and writers, their novels consciously intended to contribute to the campaign for the reformation of manners.[141]

Writers made the effects of reading a subject for their readers. For example, Fielding entitled one of his chapters "Containing a Dialogue Between Sophia and Mrs. Honour, Which May a Little Relieve Those Tender Affections Which the Foregoing Scene May Have Raised in the Mind of a Good-Natured Reader." After remarking on the "lasting impression" left on a "thoughtful mind" by "returning to a place after a few years absence," Inchbald told her reader she would attempt to create the same "sensation" in "him." Characters throughout the fiction of sensibility were shown by their authors to be deeply affected by reading. A very obvious example is Arabella, the "Female Quixote," whose constantly reading romances "roots" romantic heroism "in her heart." It had become "her habit of thinking, a principle imbibed from her education." Austen's concern with such effects on women readers in *Sense and Sensibility* and *Northanger Abbey* are well-known culminations of a century's concern over the influence of their reading on newly literate women.[142]

And real readers were so affected. The Fielding parodying Richardson's *Pamela* as *Shamela* became the emotional votary of Richardson's "homilectic" second novel. He was literally converted by Clarissa, although it is clear Fielding had long held sensibility's values. His description of the emotional sequence through which reading *Clarissa* brought him resembles the morphology of the conversion experience through which a properly prepared Protestant hoped to pass. Having being thunderstruck and melted by reading of Clarissa's rape, Fielding wrote, "here my Terror ends and my Grief Begins which the Cause of all my tumultuous Passion soon changes into Raptures of Admiration and Astonishment." The "masculine" Fielding, converted by Richardson through the godlike Clarissa, writes to his "feminine" fellow artist, "Let the Overflowings of a Heart which you have filled brimfull speak for me."[143] Burney recorded herself "sobbing" over *The Vicar of Wakefield;* Lady Louisa Stuart recalled her mother and sister weeping over MacKenzie's *Man of Feeling,* "dwelling upon it with rapture." Godwin implied to his readers in a book intended to rack their sensibility that he fell in love with Wollstonecraft by reading her *Letters from Sweden.*[144] Godwin and Wollstonecraft's contemporaries and opponents, the Anti-Jacobins, demonstrated in their fiction, in political essays, and in cartoons that they shared such a view of reading's power by attributing the French Revolution to it, in addition to female sexual revolutionaryism. Burke interpreted the novel as "part of a systematic scheme by Rousseau to destroy all social and family relationships, thus enabling the French revolutionaries to take power."[145]

Novelists advocated a set of virtues and condemned corresponding vices by way of characters they intended as exemplars and symbols, ones we have seen they invested with wishes, dreams, and visions. According to one eighteenth-century writer, literary characters were to be "patterns" transcending the reality of "pleasure and vice," shaping young readers "before they are well entered into the world."[146] Writers intended that readers think of their characters as religious icons. In *Jonathan Wild* Fielding had warned that no fictional character was a "proper object for adoration" but we have seen the effect that *Clarissa* had on him six years later. If Richardson depicted Pamela and Clarissa as saints, one of the worldly characters in *The Man of Feeling* said of Harley, "you might have sworn he was a saint" and, whatever MacKenzie's intention, we have seen his readers capable of responding with weeping "rapture." Rousseau noted the growth of the cult of Julie's memory in *Heloïse* and Hays described Emma Courtney's "weeping over the sorrows of the tender St. Preux." The portrait of the son of Emma Courtney's benefactress reminded her of St. Preux and Emile rolled into one, and stimulated her to an irresistible, lifelong passion for him. Hays's heroine also modeled herself on

Rousseau, the actual male "confessor," like him revealing her sexuality. She was a kind of fictional-cum-autobiographical equivalent of Rousseau's reader, Jean Ranson, described by Professor Darnton. The poses, language, and emotions of the cult's idols were essentially religious, signs of grace entwined with Christian piety throughout the century. Evidently influenced by Richardson's heroines and those succeeding them, Radcliffe's Emily registered "the finest emotions of the soul . . . [her] eyes filled with tears of admiration and sublime devotion, as she raised them . . . to the vast heavens." Her still "rapture" put her in touch with a music unheard by others, the emanation of an "unfeigned sensibility." Her inspiration included "the genius, the taste, the enthusiasm of the sublimest writers."[147]

Writers often extended the dimensions of their fictional characters beyond the page (if their readers didn't do it for them), mystifying them into greater reality by identifying character with authorship. Anne Donnellan, one of Richardson's correspondents, assumed a correspondence between his fictional characters and his own "character." She wrote to him, "Tom Jones could get drunk, and do all sorts of bad things in the height of his joy for his uncle's recovery. I dare say Fielding is a robust, strong man." Johnson recorded that "Richardson used to say, that had he not known who Fielding was, he should have believed he was an ostler." Sterne was most playful with these possibilities. As the Rev. Laurence Sterne he delivered the same sermon to a congregation in York Minster that had appeared in *Tristram Shandy*. He published a collection of his actual sermons under the name of his fictional Yorick, that name itself connoting further fictional mysteries beyond the grave. One of MacKenzie's male characters explains how he created a relationship with an author he conjured up.[148]

No wonder, then, that sentimental writers were turned into "tutelary deities," in Brissenden's phrase. The convention of educated aristocrats visiting the graves of artists as Rochester did reverence at Ariosto's was popularized under eighteenth-century circumstances—the proliferation of literacy and of easier travel. Rousseau's grave at Ermenonville was a shrine for this "unofficial religion," and Mrs. Barbauld described "the fashionable," visiting "the banks of the Avon with all the devotion of enthusiastic zeal." (Emblematically, they could take in Boulton's neighboring Soho works at the same time.) She wrote her brother that "we" British idolize Shakespeare too much. Fashionable devotees also kissed "with pious lips the sacred earth which gave a Hampden or a Russell birth." Godwin proposed a national scheme for the enshrinement of such figures.[149]

Yorick's tongue-in-cheek apostrophe to the god "Sensibility" was in contrast to Emily's serious rapture, but it illustrates the phenomenon: eighteenth-century observers thought of sentimentalism as a cult very largely based on literature. MacKenzie propounded it, profited from it, and persecuted it. He distinguished between the true religion "of sentiment not theory" laid out in his story of La Roche—the "true religion" in which he believed—and the "superstition" preached by popular novels, written by his inferiors. Here he may well have been alluding to Barbauld's 1773 defense of "superstition" as an aspect of what she defined as a "religion" of sensibility, in the face of the scorn of "superior natures" as well as the upsurge in Methodism.[150] As we saw, in 1785 MacKenzie sought to distinguish his own fiction (distinct in its masculine firmness) from that of the immoral, uninformed, and vulgar sentimentalism disseminated by circulating libraries. He associated the latter spurious religion with "enthusiasm," the by-now traditional term for an emotional and disreputable sect of which Hays was less unambiguously critical.[151] 1790s writers and artists also identified sensibility as a cult. In an Anti-Jacobin novel of 1797, a "Mr. Sympathy invented a new religion." In a 1798 cartoon entitled "The New Morality," James Gillray depicted sensibility as a "hag" enshrined above a crowd of revolutionaries. Hazlitt and Coleridge discerned a kinship between Methodism and sentimentalism at the same time.[152]

To name as a "cult" the form in which a story was told and received is to suggest one of the culture's innermost origins and its proselytizing power. Its sacred beings were deified authors and factualized characters, its rituals expressed by a system of signs, gestures, and words, at first responses to the figures on the page, read in a closet, perhaps aloud to oneself, like prayers, the page often held tremblingly or bedewed with tears. Then these rituals were carried out into the relations between cultists, or, hesitatingly, in the expectations of courtship, then more assertively in marriage and childrearing. Explicitly embracing Protestant pietism, the cult combined this with the "natural religion" illustrated by Shaftesbury's apostrophes. Sterne's famous parody could be read as the sincere kind of prayerful invocation of nature, of God, or of authors, which were incorporated into works of unambiguous sensibility. It was the cult of a group of people enjoying literacy, privacy, intimacy, servants, and other distancings from economic distress, and free to concentrate on their own emotional pleasures and pains in their vaunted distinction from the world.[153]

If sensibility was a form of religion, the evidence suggests it was overwhelmingly a religion of women. Women's minds, bodies, and domestic spaces were its sanctums (one "shrine" therein was the tea table), where it could be consolidated and developed into self-consciousness and authoritative convention, before issuing outward in demands for heterosocial politeness and, eventually, reform. Its fundamental intention was to reshape men, although each sex was to be softened and sensitized. Male and female paragons were held up to "serve as major devices to establish value judgments, creating and controlling the reader's attitudes and opinions." The novel was intended, in the 1744 words of Eliza Haywood's *The Fortunate Foundlings,* "to encourage Virtue in both Sexes."[154] *Pamela*'s intention was to teach "religion and morality" by giving practical examples "worthy to be followed in the most critical and affecting cases by the virgin, the bride, and the wife." Richardson's friend, the poet Edward Young (his work also popularized by Wesley), praised the novel, *Pamela,* by calling it a conduct book, "The Whole Duty of Woman" the counterpart of Richard Allestree's *The Whole Duty of Man* (1658–60).[155] Pamela, then, still more, Clarissa, required an updated male counterpart, which Richardson supplied in *Sir Charles Grandison.* This hero's predecessor, the converted Belford, wishing Lovelace to read "*grace* from my pen," exclaimed:

> O Lovelace! What lives do most of us rakes and libertines lead! . . . little do innocents think, what a *total revolution* of manners, what a *change of fixed habits,* nay, what a *conquest of a bad nature,* and what a portion of *Divine* GRACE is required to make a man a *good husband,* a *worthy father,* and *true friend,* from principle.

After reading Rousseau, merchant Ranson had written him, "I will follow your lessons in order to form them [his sons] into men—not the kind of men you see everywhere around you, but the kind that we see in you alone." Emma Courtney attempted to rear her son to Rousseauism, too, as Wollstonecraft attempted to convert Godwin by giving him Rousseau's novel.[156]

John Gregory said that heroines were to function like goddesses "in order to be at once the greatest incitement to love, and the greatest security to virtue," and this recommendation was quoted approvingly by Reeve in her *Progress of Romance.* Pamela, Clarissa, Arabella, Matilda, Emily, Emma Courtney, and all of the other heroines of sensibility engaged in proselytizing men could be extended to what must have appeared to a reader as a series of icons, almost infinite because they became predictable. Their overlapping characteristics blurred into a single female ideal, charged with moral power. Sophia Western was a queen of sensibility receiving "adoration" and Clarissa a Christian goddess, "[t]rapped in the body of an earthly woman." In the melancholy moonlight, Radcliffe's Emily had "the contour of a Madonna with the sensibility of a Magdalene." This series of ironic heroines, all emblematic of female virtue, contributed their effects to the deified figure of "sensibility" emerging in the last quarter of the century. A 1776 piece in *The London Magazine,* signed "Rosaline," described "The Birth of Sensibility" as the birth of a goddess. To Emma Courtney, sensibility was a "sublime enthusiasm" to which she carried all of her other human values as "offerings carried to its shrine," while to Gillray, it was that witchlike "hag."[157]

The tendency toward the deification of female figures of sensibility is striking. "Niobe is a favorite figure in the 'Age of Sensibility.'" In 1780 Anna Seward answered her own question of Captain Cook, "What Pow'r inspir'd his dauntless breast to brave, / The scorch'd Equator, and th' Antarctic wave?" with "Nymph Divine! Humanity." Poems written by two other famous female poets, Hannah More and Helen Maria Williams, illustrate the same tendency. More appended "Sensibility: A Poem" to her *Sacred Dramas* in 1784. It had been inspired by the death in 1779 of her close friend, Garrick, a leading exponent of the drama of sensibility. More hailed "Sensibility" as "the melancholy Muse," a female deity, also called "tender Sorrow," which "has her pleasure too." Sensibility is that "quick'ning spark of Deity." More allows for the appearance of sensibility in men but she dismisses Sterne's "feeling" as spurious, preferring the desexualized MacKenzie, whom More confused with her version of his most famous character, *The Man of Feeling.* She does not place male writers under the muse of "Sensibility," reserving this position for her fellow Bluestockings, Frances Boscawen, Elizabeth Carter, Hester Chapone, Frances Walsingham, and Mary Delaney, and paying tribute to the "Virtues and Muse" of "Much lov'd Barbauld."[158]

"Sensibility" inhered in the female nervous system that More assumed was finer than a man's. It exists where

> . . . fine-wrought spirit feels acute pains:
> Where glow exalted sense, and taste refin'd,
> There keener anguish rankles in the mind:
> There feeling is diffus'd thro' ev'ry part,
> Thrills in each nerve, and lives in all the heart.

Sensibility gives "immortal Mind its finest tone," and while More says sensibility "eludes the chains / of Definition," she defines it repeatedly, in terms representing its origins, modified and popularized by sentimental fiction and More's friend, Burke.

> Sweet Sensibility! thou keen delight!
> Thou hasty moral! sudden sense of right!

> Thou untaught goodness! Virtue's precious seed!
> Thou sweet precursor of the gen'rous Deed!
> Beauty's quick relish! Reason's radiant morn . . .

More prizes sensibility's thin-skinned reactiveness to the "trifles" she sees making "the sum of human things,"

> The hint malevolent, the look oblique,
> The obvious satire, or implied dislike,
> The sneer equivocal, the harsh reply,
> And all the cruel language of the eye;
> The artful injury, whose venom'd dart,
> Scarce wounds the hearing while it stabs the heart
> Small slights, contempt, neglect unmix'd with hate
> Make up in number what they want in weight . . .

Such a view made a virtue of consciousness of that "sneer" James Lackington observed men gave women's reading. It was symbolic of the consciousness of hostility to themselves—"the noble few"—which women were articulating on a wide front.[159]

While Williams was a Dissenter and her politics took a very different turn from More's, she, too, represented sensibility as a goddess, to whose "shrine" she brought her ode, "To Sensibility" (1786), characterizing it in precisely the same way More did. (We have seen elsewhere that "Pity" conventionally had a "shrine" in such literature.) Like More, Williams welcomed the pain of sensibility: "No cold exemption from her pain / I ever wish to know; tis Sensibility that lights the melting eyes," "prompts the tender marks of love," is "Of every finer bliss the source!" The idolization welcomes dependence and self-effacement and provides the same references to quick nerves, susceptibility to wounds, and the assertion of superiority to "vulgar minds." Like More's, Williams's sentimental poetry was "fashionable" and remarkably "popular." Fashion and the market applauded and sustained the deification of sensibility by women writers.[160]

Barbauld joined More and Williams in deifying sensibility, her occasion, Wollstonecraft's attack on it in the *Rights of Woman.* Immediately following Wollstonecraft's observation that the identification of women with "instinct" and "sensuality"—that is, with sensibility—leads women to manipulate men by "wit and cunning," she criticized Barbauld's poem, "To A Lady With Some Painted Flowers," in which Barbauld had compared a lady to flowers, "SWEET, and gay, and DELICATE LIKE YOU . . . YOUR BEST, your SWEETEST empire is—to PLEASE." This is where Wollstonecraft commented, "So the men tell us; but virtue, says reason must be acquired by *rough* toils, and useful struggles with worldly *cares.*"[161] Barbauld's poem, "The

Rights of Woman," was published very soon after the November, 1792 publication of the *Rights of Woman* and was evidently a reply to Wollstonecraft.[162] Declaring that woman herself is "the courted idol of mankind," Barbauld urged "injured Woman" to assert her right by resuming her "native empire o'er the breast"—"native" referring to Wollstonecraft's sarcastic "instinct." Barbauld directly restates the "SWEETEST empire" that Wollstonecraft had just challenged. According to Barbauld, woman's weapons in this resumption of right were "Soft melting tones," "Blushes and tears."

> Thy rights are empire: urge no meaner claim,—
> Felt not defined, and if debated lost;
> Like sacred mysteries, which withheld from fame,
> Shunning discussion, are revered the most.
>
> Make treacherous Man thy subject, not thy friend;
> Thou mayst command, but never canst be free.
> Awe the licentious and restrain the rude;
> Soften the sullen, clear the cloudy brow;
> Be, more than princes' gifts, thy favours sued;
> She hazards all, who will the least allow.

Woman's "rights" are defined by her gender; they are feelings she can neither articulate verbally nor defend against male argument; they are hidden in the female breast to avoid being lost. Barbauld rationalized and aggrandized this hiding as "sacred," identifying her empire of feeling with the private, the innermost mysteries, which "shun" exposure, and are withheld from the publicity of fame. Idolized woman's "angel pureness" is posed against licentious and rude males, woman's "rights" entirely absorbed by the deified figure of sensibility. Woman's innate superiority of moral feeling sponsors her claim to mitigate and even to reform male licentiousness and rudeness. The vision corresponds to the century's larger effort to reform male manners, posing softened domesticity and heterosocial manners against the world of male power in street and tavern.[163]

Methodism and the Culture of Sensibility

The literary deification of sensibility coincided with a tendency of women acting in more specifically religious circumstances. Women of all denominations wrote religious tracts, pamphlets, and missionary letters. Launching religious magazines, women edited and translated, and "popularized . . . letters from the dead to the living, and poured forth a steady stream of hymns and devotional verse." All of these expressions promulgated sensibility. Women's hymns contributed to the movement for the softening of God's face and the elevation of the suffering Son over the grim Father. The Baptist Anne Steele, called the "mother" of English hymn writers, depicted Christ as a man of feeling, with "lovely melting eyes."

> Those healing hands with blessing fraught,
> Nail'd to the cross with pungent smart!
> Inhuman deed! Could no kind thought
> To pity move the ruthless heart?

Steele also published sentimental poetry. Women's hymn writing in the last decades of the century was full of "fainting hearts, distressed souls, drooping spirits," and "low and languid states." Among women hymn writers were More, Williams, and Barbauld, worshippers of the supradenominational "Sensibility" as well as adherents of Anglicanism and Dissent. Barbauld portrayed "her ideal Christian as a Man of Feeling":

> Blest is the man whose softening heart
> Feels all another's pain;
> To whom the supplicating eye
> Was never raised in vain.
>
> Whose breast expands with generous warmth
> A stranger's woes to feel;
> And bleeds in pity o'er a wound
> He wants the power to heal.

There are other cult elements in Barbauld's hymns, for example, their assertion of the transcendent value of identification with the pain of those whose "hearts, whose faith are one! / Their streaming tears together flow."[164]

It was Methodism that seems most to have resembled the cult of sensibility, a resemblance noted by contemporaries. Wesley himself encouraged the convergence by his publication of sentimental novels and poems, albeit properly edited. In publishing his selection of *Moral and Sacred Poems* in 1744, Wesley declared, "There is nothing therein contrary to virtue, nothing that can offset the chastest ear, or give pain to the tenderest heart." A reviewer of MacKenzie's *Man of the World* summarized its *denouement,* wherein a previously unrecognized daughter, Harriet Annesley, about to be raped by her rakish, brutal father, converts him. The reviewer summarized it thus: the good characters, by revealing the truth, "turn the heart of Sir Thomas; who, in the stile of the Methodists, is converted, and prays, and goes to heaven."[165]

Adherence to both Methodism and the cult of sensibility was demonstrated by the capacity to feel and to signify feeling by the same physical signs—tears, groans, sighs, and tremblings, both depending on and furthering the nerve paradigm. Scenes of pious group weepings in fiction and reform-minded audiences responding to Garrick-like actors performing sentimental drama may have resembled Methodist meetings. Both movements spread literacy, a vital force for upward mobility and for the exponential possibilities of self-expression, as Wesley's attempted control of it illustrates. This coincided with the drive to respectability, and with the sexual moralism one finds in both Methodism and the culture of sensibility. Both phenomena incorporated a striking combination of a rigid code and intense emotional release.[166]

Wesley followed Richardson as well as William Law in attacking the diabolical Mandeville's advocacy of private vices.[167] Sentimentalism and Methodism ostentatiously rejected the worldly pursuit of fashion and other consumer goods and entertainments, sometimes sharing an "almost morbid preoccupation with death." Whitefield scorned "fashionable worldlings," and Wesley said in his instructions: "I do not advise women to wear rings, earrings, necklaces, laces, or ruffles . . . Neither do I advise men to wear coloured waistcoats, shining stockings, glittering or costly buckles or buttons either on their coats or in their sleeves."[168] Wesley later added bans on "Calashes, High-heads, or enormous Bonnets," presumably keeping pace with his congregants' temptations to consumer sins. Baptists also denounced ostentatious personal decorations, the males, for example, cutting off their hair and giving up such "superfluous forms and Modes of Dressing . . . [as] cock't hatts." Presumably, too, congregants gave occasion for these denunciations.[169]

Nonetheless, Methodist austerity in dress became its own distinctive fashion, the "serious" among Methodists recognizable "by their dress, hairstyle and physical detachment from the world of revelry, sports and dancing."[170] Characters in sentimental fiction were intended to exemplify a similar simplicity of costume, the renunciation of material "luxury," in favor of the "luxury" of grief and other forms of morally superior feelings; but inevitably such simplicity could itself become a "stile" popularized by commercially published novels (some of them serialized in magazines displaying fashion prints, too) and exemplified in the simple gestures, diction, dress, hairstyles, and clothing of Harriet Annesley, Evelina Belmont, Emily St. Aubert, or Belinda Portman—displays influencing the trend toward neoclassicism or neopeasant with which some heroines explicitly identified themselves. That sensibility could be false, assumed like a dress or a masquerade costume, indeed, that it was merely a fashion, was a running preoccupation of sentimentalists, as, indeed, it became one. Wesley, too, apprehended that his auditors could pretend feeling.[171] The apprehensions betrayed the interweaving of both movements with consumerism, not the least in their fostering of consumer psychology, as Campbell suggests. They depended on the commercializing world they seemed to reject, on the publishing of cheap Bibles, hymn books, and novels, for example, seeing themselves addressing a market.[172]

Wesley and Methodism took a "fervent, unsophisticated approach to politics," expressly adjuring any formal connection at all. Wesley opposed speculation, bribery, and corruption but his standards were based on the politicians' moral failings, "covetousness, ambition, pride, and resentment."[173] These features, too, were characteristic of sentimental literature's stance toward the world of politics. Another obvious parallel between Wesley's views and those expressed in sentimental fiction lay in views of the poor and oppressed. Rich men, Wesley said, hardly ever entered heaven. The majority robbed God, "embezzling and wasting their Lord's goods." They also robbed "the poor, the hungry, the naked; wronging the widow and the fatherless."[174] Wesley said, "I love the poor." In "many of them I find pure genuine grace, unmixed with paint, folly, and affectation." As with other sentimentalists, there was a strong "note of condescension" in Wesley's view. Like the heroines and heroes of sentimental fiction, Wesley visited the cottages of the poor, distributing money he had begged for their necessities and holding readings and prayer meetings there, in weepy scenes duplicated in sentimental novels. Similarly, Wesley extended his compassion to the criminal and outcast, welcoming all to his congregations. He and his fellow members of the Holy Club had visited the prison in Oxford and Methodism and made it a requirement of membership that prisoners be visited or helped. Methodism extended Protestantism to African-American slaves. Wesley attacked slave owners, press-gangs, and the "merciless cruelty" of the English who were plundering "the desolated provinces of Indostan."[175] In these respects he shared sympathies with Whitefield and other evangelicals. Wesley initiated reforms by opening a dispensary, a home for widows, and a school for poor children, all precedents for Victorian reformers.[176]

Above all, the resemblance between the cult of sensibility and Methodism lay in their identification with the interests of women. The countercultural polarity symbolized by the scene of the squirearchy hallooing into a field where the pious had gathered may be augmented by the historical record of mobs of men encouraged by the traditional hierarchy to attack Methodist gatherings and target Methodist women for "sexual assault or indecent behaviour."[177] Conversely, Methodism opposed men's brutal treatment of wives, just as the cult of sensibility did. A summary in Wesley's *Journal* of the reasons for expulsions from the Newcastle Methodist society was a mirror image of a popular male culture opposed to women's interests.

> Two for cursing and swearing
> Two for habitual Sabbath-breaking
> Seventeen for drunkenness
> Two for retailing spirituous liquors
> Three for quarreling and brawling
> One for beating his wife.[178]

Prominent among the "pleasures and amusements" Methodists were said to "hate" was "punchinello," that powerful symbol of popular male culture.[179] Evangelism as a whole "disavowed public pleasures. What recreation was permissible should take place within the family and home, and should dovetail with piety and prayer." In Methodism, the center of worship first shifted "from the parish church to the hearth of outlying farm kitchens."[180]

Very significantly, women themselves preached the same message, joining their voices to the preaching of women novelists. They may be seen as heiresses of the prophetesses of the English Civil War period, grasping the potential of the priesthood of all believers.[181] Quaker women would mediate this tradition to nineteenth-century feminism; parallel to it was the eighteenth-century feminist argument, rooted in Protestant tradition and made from Astell to Wollstonecraft, that women had souls equal to men's. Challenged by Sarah Crosby, a female exhorter (that is, preaching without a text), in 1761, Wesley reluctantly sanctioned her and then, recognizing the effectiveness of women preachers, allowed women "with an extraordinary call" to preach but not to be itinerants. Because women became so prominent in encouraging rebirth, they were satirized as "obstetrical saints." One reason given for the effectiveness of Methodist women preachers was their seizing the freedom "to devise their own methods of proclaiming the Gospel." Women preachers of other evangelical sects in their early stages were notable for their "unthought out theology." It was women's preaching that could be depended on "to sustain communal fever" in local societies. They grasped Protestantism's legitimization of "private emotional upheaval" as "accessible material" for "the immanence of the spirit." "Whenever women have moved into the visible church leadership, the relative importance of Scripture and tradition has been reduced and the legitimacy of personal religious experience has been enhanced."[182] The same may be said of the eighteenth-century novel. Hester Ann Rogers, Mary Fielden, Elizabeth Ritchie, Mary Tatham, Mary Barritt, and Ann Cutler were among the recorded female Methodist preachers.[183] Their preaching seems to have inspired other women to preach, and early Methodism saw the creation of "mutually supportive networks of female co-workers." One can imagine the impact made by a female Wesleyan preacher like Ann Carr as she was described by her fellow evangelist, Martha Williams: a

> woman of extraordinary firmness and decision of character. . . . The fervency of her religious enthusiasm was calculated to work powerfully upon uncultivated minds, putting a strong check upon the developments of licentiousness in its grosser and more revolting form.

The Methodist women who played a leading role in Sunday school teaching, using the literature and hymns described, imparted the same message.[184]

The appeal of Methodism to women must have lain at least partially in the sharp contrast between, on the one hand, their being offered a heaven of love and soft feeling, and, on the other, a popular culture denigrating them and wasting the household's money. It could also sustain women in efforts to convert their menfolk. The context for the disaffection between husbands and wives caused by adherence to Methodism (and other evangelical groups) was its unforgiving view of popular male leisure culture, including wife beating. (Contemplating the high ratio of unmarried women to unmarried men, Hempton suggests that women found chapel more appealing than marriage.) There is evidence, from the end of the eighteenth century through the early nineteenth, that women of the middle and lower classes in America were the successful agents of evangelical ministers in converting their menfolk. In England at the same time, the "most important agents in the spread of Evangelical religion among the upper classes seem to have been the female members of their families." Davidoff and Hall describe the increasing importance to evangelism of the middle-class clergyman's wife. At its best, Methodism was "a religion of family commitment, thrift and charity."[185] Such a vision squares with the economic worldview of lower-class women, managing the family purse, agents for the family's prospects for "respectability."[186]

So Methodism tapped into a female market just as sentimental literature did. In fact, already after the Restoration women were attending the Anglican church "more frequently than men," providing the congregations to which some ministers appealed with the softened doctrines of Latitudinarianism long before Wesley began competing with it.[187] Scholars have coined the phrase the "feminization of religion" for the tendency they discern in eighteenth-century religious history.[188] (That others have referred to the "feminization" of literature at the same time was noted in the previous chapter.) If the majority of consumers of fiction were women, so, in all likelihood, were "a substantial majority" of Methodism's adherents. Local studies of British Methodists suggest that women made up from 55 percent to 70 percent, comparable to "the persistent female majority of between 60 and 70 percent" of American Methodists between 1750 and 1825 (this was a figure they shared with other American denominations). A significant proportion was unmarried. This was probably connected with the youth of many converts. Many of these young, unmarried women must have been servants because service was unmarried women's usual work.[189]

A large proportion of Methodist women also must have been class or blood kin to the "craftsmen" who made up 47 percent of the ranks of Methodist men, "more than twice as numerous as in the country as a whole." Probably they included those artisans turning from agriculture and from livestock as Shammas describes. According to Clive Field, Methodism's "influence on the unskilled masses was weak," although, because Field ignores gender, that question also needs to be asked of the category of "unskilled" servant women.[190] Impressionistic evidence suggests both that many Methodist women came from the same social strata as the men and that they included a wider class selection. Of the two women shown victimized by Whitefield in that 1739 print, one seems to be a domestic servant because she is carrying utensils and wearing a spotty apron; the other, well-shod and well-clothed (albeit scantily), and handing over the cash, is middle-class, at least. The Countess of Huntingdon "was as much a head of her Connection as Wesley was of his."[191] Horace Walpole attended a Wesleyan service in Bristol and reported that the congregation "was very mean," excepting the presence of some "*honourable women.*" His emphasis may have been intended to carry the sexual innuendo so frequently leveled at Methodist women as a way of explaining their prominence in the sect. More likely, though, it carried both meanings. Some unmarried women inherited enough property to support themselves and donate it to the society. Martha Williams was described as "a young lady of culture and refinement." In 1792, Wollstonecraft made it clear that she thought that women attracted to Methodism were urban and middle class.[192] Fictional representations from the 1740s through the end of the century emphasized that

Methodism's "enthusiasm" was attractive to women, and to women of a range of ranks and conditions.[193]

At the end of the century, after Wesley's death and capitalizing on the British reaction to the French Revolution, Methodism would become deeply enmeshed in politics in order to protect its substantial establishment and to foster its respectability. That context would include new prospects for manhood suffrage, one which coincided with the purging of female preachers from Methodism.[194] By 1792 it was said that Wesleyans were sending "their children to boarding schools where music, dancing, and finery were introduced." They, too, produced "ladies" in accordance with that urge toward respectability and the civilizing of domestic space noted earlier. "In the nineteenth century the well known institutionalization of Methodism brought the movement more firmly into the male world of professional ministry, chapel finance, business meetings and local courts." Methodist women joined other respectable evangelical women in formal reform societies, expressions of "Victorian womanhood."[195]

The differences between the two phenomena are less apparent. The cult of sensibility may have depended more on the private operation of its gods and goddesses, although private devotion was also characteristic of Methodist behavior. There were probably strong class differences (susceptible to changes over time), to which the literacy rate corresponded. Eventually "respectable" women Methodists converged with other middle-class women. Yet even in this respect, women servants probably made up a significant proportion of both constituencies for a long time previously. In any case, it is reasonable to suggest that Methodism (and probably evangelism generally) and the cult of sensibility were two branches of the same culture, nourished by the same roots in the awakening minds of eighteenth-century women.

Just how a cult and a denomination may be said to comprise parts of a still larger culture in the making is suggested by Barbauld's 1773 "Thoughts on Devotional Taste, and on Sects and Establishments," its latter section hypothesizing a morphology whereby a sect grows into an established church. She seems to have had Methodism and Anglicanism in mind (she was herself a Dissenter).[196] She characterized each as a "mode of religion" and introduced them by way of a definition of religion that transcended—or could underlie—such fashions.[197] This was "religion . . . considered as a taste, an affair of sentiment and feeling." Hindsight might see Barbauld's essay as a herald of turn-of-the-century romanticism (she claimed that the "warm and generous emotions" she celebrated were scorned as "romantic" by "cold-hearted philosophy"), but, of course, like all historical statements, hers was about her present and drew upon her sense of the past, including attitudes taken toward earlier romance, enthusiasm, and female-associated sensibility. Barbauld effectively identified religion with that "family of words" Brissenden describes, popularized by way of Locke, Newton's *Opticks,* the Latitudinarians, Shaftesbury, *The Spectator* and its imitators, Cheyne, Wesley, Hume, Smith, and Burke, but, above all, by the novels addressed to women and/or aiming at the reformation of men.[198]

According to Barbauld, true religion, trusting to "our genuine feelings implanted in us by the God of nature," "has its source in that relish for the sublime and the vast, and the beautiful, by which we taste the charms of poetry and other compositions that address our finer feelings;" it is "nourished by poetry and music," and even "the regions of chivalry and old romance." Thus nourished, its tasteful devotees hear, pray, speak, and write with a "delicacy" sheltered from the "indecent . . . coarse, and vulgar language" of sectarian and establishmentarian men doing combat with one another. Against such "freedom of speech" and disputatiousness, Barbauld's devotees posed "sympathy" and "silence." These sensitive, sentimental, silent, and sympathetic creatures of fine feeling, their "hearts" giving way "to honest emotion," were liable to the "ridicule" and "sneer" to which their post-Restoration ancestors also had been subjected by the libertine likes of Rochester. In fact, Barbauld expressed her admiration for "the puritans in the reign of Charles the Second" because they "seasoned with wholesome severity the profligacy of public manners." The "extreme delicacy" of Barbauld's devotees leads them to "indulge themselves freely" only when in solitude or sustained "by the powerful force of sympathy."[199]

In place of the remote, disinterested God of Newtonian philosophers, whose manifestations of "power" and "dominion" left worshippers with "a deep and painful sense of abasement," Barbauld presents her God in that feminized version promoted by her forebears and contemporaries, personifying the traits women wished to see in reformed men. She is quite clear in telling us that she fashioned this picture to suit her:

> I may paint him too much in the fashion of humanity; but . . . [t]oo critical a spirit is the bane of every thing great or pathetic . . . in composition addressed to the heart, let us give freer scope to the language of the affections, and the overflowing of a warm heart.

She wants a God "open to feelings of indignation, the soft relentings of mercy, and the partialities of particular affections." That is, her "Deity" is to have a "common nature . . . on which to build our intercourse"—to resemble "us"—us women, together, presumably, with men of feeling like the Reverend Rochmont Barbauld. Mrs. Barbauld also provides further definition of the softened deity's devotees: their tastefulness is "in a great degree constitutional," their "religious affections in a great measure rise and fall with the pulse," in keeping with the nerve paradigm, the material sensibility defined by Dr. Johnson and criticized by Wollstonecraft and others, constituting the delicate bodies beneath religious fashions. Barbauld illustrates her own constitutional proclivities by declaring that God has "impressed me with the idea of trust and confidence, and my heart flies to him in danger" and confessing "I melt before him in penitence"; her deity, she says, fulfills all of her wishes.[200]

The place for this softened intercourse with a personal deity (evidently identifiable with the "idol" Barbauld shared with More and Williams) is the "altar" of the "heart." Its religious taste is represented and inspired by pictures of "home views and nearer objects" rather than of outdoor, "unbounded views," those pictures corresponding to the remoteness of men's philosophy and an impersonal God. The "warm and pathetic imagery" of the former paintings or sketches seem to be hung on the walls of private rooms, which Barbauld implies also contain properly sentimental books, tastefully played musical instruments, as well as painting or drawing equipment (their users perhaps prepared by boarding schools). These are among the refined "pleasures" and "personal benefits" Barbauld assumes widely exist in British middle-class homes. Characterizing her religion of refined taste as "generous, liberal, and humane," Barbauld acknowledged it was made possible in Britain because "the social affections have full scope in the free commerce and legitimate connexions of society."[201]

In sum, the devotee of "humanity" was created by moralized taste, a "feminized" selection from the products, objects, and things ("trifles" even) that eighteenth-century psychology from the beginning had believed built selves.[202] Such a wish informed all of those fictional representations of roomfuls of tasteful objects suffused by appropriate feelings, quoted at the conclusion of my previous chapter. It was on this ground, the dynamic potentials in reshaping homes and selves in them, augmented by the "outdoor rooms" of polite public spaces, that cults, sects, denominations, and establishments broadened into culture. Having transformed themselves, and sanctioned by men's wishes for civilizing conversation, women could attempt to transform men, adult men perhaps, but more hopefully sons. Autobiographies praised their authors' mothers for taking "all opportunities to instruct and instill good principles of religion and moralls into us her children." Perhaps their identical terms reveal the significant existence of formulaic expression.[203] Such female efforts converged with changes originated by British capitalists' furthering their own increasingly various ends, improving their outdoor environment and the flow of goods into the domestic environment. Hence women, exercising a significant degree of power over the new "supplies of domesticity" could promise themselves new power in converting men and especially so in the "naturalized" power of mothering.[204] The material creation of "domesticity" and its potentials provided the circumstances where "men and women waged a silent power struggle in the home."[205]

Central to the purpose of the culture of sensibility was the aggrandizement of the affectionate family and, at its heart, mothering, because it generated traits (the happy energy of social affections) that society needed. (Bennett writes that late "medieval artists increasingly emphasized the loving interaction of Virgin and Child, but the elevation of ordinary motherhood to a praised occupation awaited both the Protestant reformers and the Victorians.") With Locke, Richardson had allowed that "the first parts of Education . . . might be under a Mother's Eye," a view he enthusiastically spelled out in *Pamela.* But, by the same token, in the darker vision of *Clarissa,* with all of its warnings against the pursuit of consumer pleasures in the town, Richardson said that motherly indulgence had helped make Lovelace a rake, his chief characteristic also indulgence, that is, the willful pursuit of individual pleasure. Here Richardson popularized a warning heralded in *The Rake* of 1693, which also attributed the rake's self-indulgence to his mother's indulgence of him as a child. Rochester had made pleasure his principle, although Burnet had not blamed his mother for it. Later, Shaftesbury blamed the "public disturbances" of too rough, carnivalesque manners on the failure of "parents" to restrain "frolicsome mischievousness" in "the nursery," and he blamed excessive "motherly love" for "effeminacy," both unacceptable alternatives to the disciplined, Herculean pursuit of tasteful pleasure. Mandeville had worried about "the indulging care of Mothers," which could "totally spoil" children, in a book otherwise encouraging the unrestrained indulgence of appetite.[206]

Parental self-indulgence (taking different forms in accordance with sex) explained the disablingly "excessive" "indulgence" or "sensibility" of such heroines as Wollstonecraft's Mary and Hays's Emma. Lady Delacour's preoccupation with worldly pleasures led her to the total neglect of her daughter, even though Lord Delacour was similarly

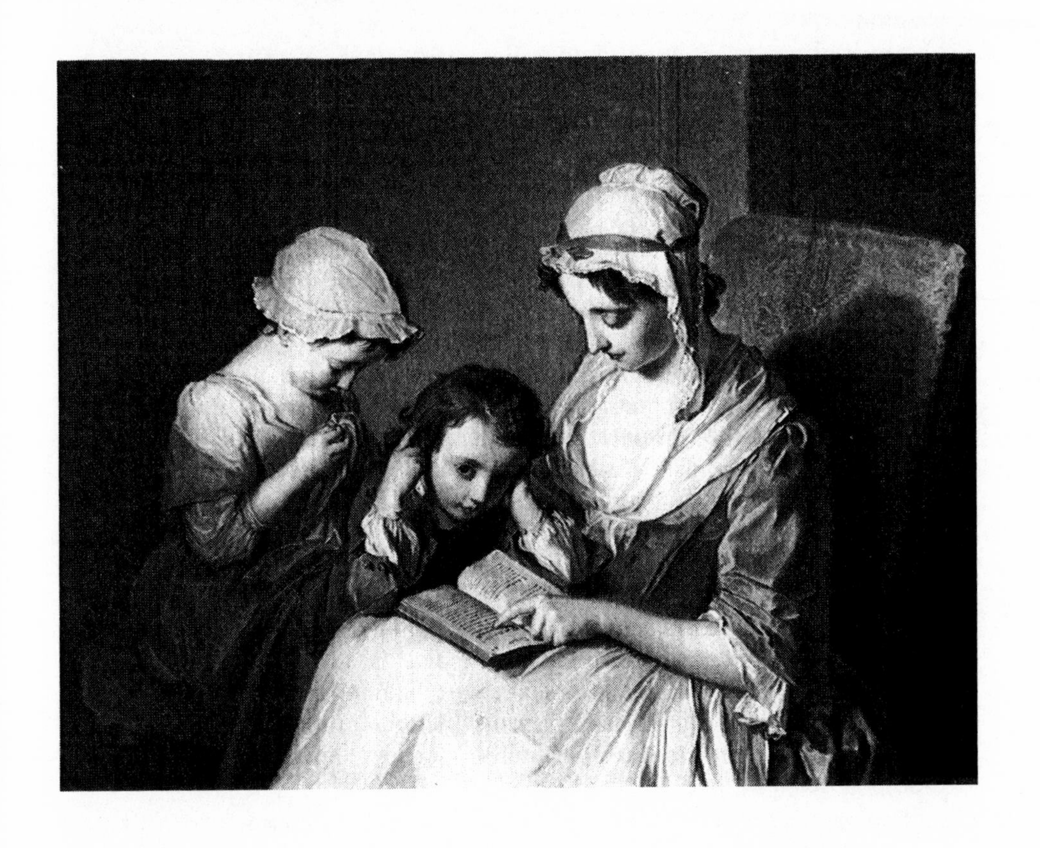

Philipp Mercier (1689[?]-1760). *Bible Lesson,* 1743. Oil on canvas. 37 1/2 × 50 1/4 in. Collection, Myles Hildyard, Photograph, Courtesy of the Paul Mellon Center for Studies in British Art, London

irresponsible. (In novels by women, it seems fathers' indulgence of children collaborated with or even replaced mothers' indulgence, resulting in the production of "women of the world," like Inchbald's Miss Milner, willfully pursuing the fashionable pleasures of "the town," in her case Bath and London, pleasures which tended to the same sexual willfulness as the rake.)[207] By late in the century, childrearing literature and other advice books joined sentimental fiction in expressing concern over the effects of mothers "indulging" their children. The counterpart of the "excessive social mixing of the sexes" to which *Female Government* (1779) ascribed current social problems was the new quantity of intimacy between husbands and wives at home; it recommended that a boy be sequestered from his mother after weaning, "and by no means suffered to see that dangerous parent, until by a masculine and proper education he may be judged to be superior to the contagion of effeminate manners." Day, too, warned against the mothers' rearing of effeminate sons. The obverse was a strong emphasis at several levels of discourse on women's capacity to rear "manly" sons—citizens eventually—for the good of the nation.[208]

This powerful theme reflected widespread apprehensions over childrearing or, one might say, the future, under circumstances where, in a complex process, mothers had gained more power, where both parents had their own reasons for placing a high value on sensitizing their children, and, above all, where politeness and commerce required the willful pursuit of pleasure by huge numbers of the population. In sum, it required the creation of consumer psychology subsumed by "sensibility."

Reformers were preoccupied with the contradiction noted by Mandeville, and they wished to reconcile the pursuit of pleasure on which they depended with morality, identifiable with sexual restraint, sexual orthodoxy. Salient results of the excessively willful pursuit of pleasure included the creation of sexual deviants in eighteenth-century terms, daughters who became women of the world or solipsistic, childless invalids, and sons who became rakes or effeminates. In fact, the dynamics we have seen to be at the heart of British consumer capitalism (the abstraction standing for the individual wills I have described) continuously advanced the changes symbolized by these deviant figures, drawing women toward self-expression and outdoor, heterosocial pleasures (albeit entwined with the marriage market), making them vulnerable to rakes as well as accusations of bad mothering; and bringing men closer to women, in more comfortable homes or those irresistibly fashionable, public places. Both tendencies were perceived to make women and men characterologically more like the other. The same circumstances attended the elevation of the common standard of "humanity" and Wollstonecraft's challenge to the notions that reason was masculine and feeling feminine.

Wollstonecraft wished to show the contribution of both parents (indeed, gender arrangements as a whole) to the exaggerated effeminizing of women. How excessively sentimentalized women, shaping themselves in accordance with the desires of men, then acculturated daughters to excessive sensibility, was a running theme throughout her work. She also said in the *Rights of Woman* that boys grew up "vain and effeminate" in part as a result of "the anxiety" expressed by most mothers on the score of "manners." Eager to teach sons "the accomplishments of a gentleman" (this included the courtly but, in Wollstonecraft's view, disabling treatment of women, of which Mandeville's consumers and writers of sentimental literature dreamed), mothers "stifle, in their birth, the virtues of a man." She said that "tyranny and indulgence" were "the extremes that people of sensibility fall into;" here she may have had the faults of fathers and mothers, respectively, in mind. But "women of sensibility," that is, of a sensibility unchecked by reason, "are the most unfit" for rearing children "because they will infallibly, carried away by their feelings, spoil a child's temper. The management of the temper, the first, and most important branch of education requires the sober, steady eye of reason." This accorded with the chief thrust of her feminism. Children learn by example; women—mothers—must be able to manage themselves but, Wollstonecraft implied, they were angry as well as self-indulgent and consequently would make their children angry, above all, at their mothers. Somehow the cycle had to be broken, so that "the child will not have, as it grows up, to throw off all that its mother, its first instructor, directly or indirectly taught." In the eighteenth-century's rewriting of the previous age's "manners," "the sins of [the] fathers'" had become the "weakness of the mother visited on the children." By the same token, however, the power of childrearing to reshape society and history, Wollstonecraft believed women could reshape themselves and exercise their new, materially based, domestic power to reform sons as well as daughters.[209]

The Rights of Woman and the Reformation of Manners

Wollstonecraft called for a vastly improved education of women, to replace the entire absorption of their capacities by sensibility and to prepare them for economic independence. She suggested that women be granted political rights, calling for women's freedom "in a physical, moral, and civil sense." All this would improve the relations between women and men in general, between husbands and wives, between mothers and children. Reason "is absolutely necessary to enable a woman to perform any duty properly, and I must again repeat, that sensibility is not reason." Reason was essential to self-management and the development of self.

> Connected with man as daughters, wives, and mothers, their moral character may be estimated by their manner of fulfilling these simple duties; but the end, the grand end, of their exertions should be to unfold their own faculties.

Such individuation would be expressed in a woman's capacity for flexibility and self-assertion in those familial relations, very much to the benefit of all concerned:

> in every circumstance of life there is a kind of individuality, which requires an exertion of judgement to modify general rules. The being who can think justly in one track will soon extend its intellectual empire; and she who has sufficient judgement to manage her children will not submit, right or wrong, to her husband, or patiently to the social laws which make a nonentity of a wife.

Wollstonecraft laid claim on behalf of women to the open-ended "education" that some in her age saw nurturing individualism. Of course, individualism existed in a dialectic with "general rules." Furthermore, Wollstonecraft's vision incorporated that romantic/sociological tension noted earlier; she wished to impose a different set of social laws, albeit equalizing ones and capable of generating individualistic subversion. The *Rights of Woman* declared throughout that its aim was "the reformation of manners." And because of the eighteenth-century insistence on the relation between the manners generated by the family and the character of society, women were in a key position to bring about historical change. "It is time to effect a revolution in female manners . . . and make [women] as a part of the human species, labour by reforming themselves to reform the world." Wollstonecraft said that her intention in her projected second volume was to enlarge "on the advantages which might reasonably be expected to result from an improvement in female manners towards a general reformation of society."[210]

Mothering was central to women's contribution to this reformation of manners. The responsibilities of mothering were important grounds for improving women's education:

> As the care of children in their infancy is one of the grand duties annexed to the female character by nature, this duty

> would afford many forcible arguments for strengthening female understanding, if it were properly considered.

In a mother's power lay "the formation of the mind" which "must be begun very early." Immersed in novels and pursuing material pleasures, mothers lacked "reason in their affections" and they ran "into extremes, and either [were] the most fond or most careless and unnatural mothers."[211] Woman's freedom was to be used to strengthen her reason in order to make her "comprehend her duty, and see in what manner it is connected with her real good."[212]

The state was to sponsor women's freedom and education and, in turn, the state would derive support from the improved children reared by educated women: "If children are to be educated to understand the true principle of patriotism, their mother must be a patriot." That women's education would be valuable to the nation had been an argument made by seventeenth-century feminists. Mothers linked public morality to private virtue, a connection preoccupying politics since the same period, along with profound ambivalence over the effects of commerce on the sexual character. Like Barbauld, Wollstonecraft was part of the "Commonwealth" tradition. "Public spirit must be nurtured by private virtue," she said in the *Rights of Woman*.[213]

It seems an austere vision for mothers, having to put aside the consumer pleasures to which they had been oriented by their cultivation of sensibility. In fact, Wollstonecraft was not advocating the entire purgation of sensibility from woman's character; to the contrary, its proper cultivation in its proper setting was central to her program for reform.

Throughout her life, Wollstonecraft placed a very high value on a fine sensibility, a source of distinction that placed its possessor in touch with the sublime. It was automatically responsive to the culture's other marks of taste, quickly sympathetic with the poor and oppressed among humankind and animals. The distinction Wollstonecraft attempted to maintain was between sensibility combined with reason, and the entirely ungoverned and emotional kind characterizing the fashionable, conventional rearing of females. "We ought to be aware of confounding mechanical instinctive emotions that reason deepens and justly terms the feelings of *humanity*. This word discriminates the active exertions of virtue from the vague declamations of sensibility." She idealized male artists, "poets, painters, and composers." "Men of these descriptions pour sensibility into the compositions, to amalgamate the gross materials; and moulding them with passion, give to the inert body a soul." This was the ideal to which she laid claim on behalf of women, too. The challenge lay in getting the balance right: "perhaps, in the education of both sexes, the most difficult task is so to adjust instructions as not to narrow the understanding, whilst the heart is warmed by the generous juices of spring . . . ; nor to dry up the feelings by employing the mind in investigations remote from life." Her advocacy of balance here reminds one of Hume and was, rhetorically at least, the position taken by all of the advocates of sensibility.[214]

Hence Wollstonecraft celebrated sentimental motherhood, which she intended to be a primary agency for the reform of men. Reformed mothers, together with the kind of national system of schools Wollstonecraft proposed, would teach the "tenderness" which was widely advocated in the didactic children's literature of her age, a literature to which Wollstonecraft contributed. Wollstonecraft adapted Locke's criticism of the "habitual cruelty" of boys' sports in tormenting miserable brutes by developing the argument that the "transition, as [boys] grow up, from barbarity to brutes to domestic tyranny over wives, children, and servants is very easy." Wollstonecraft joined the cry against outdoor, male leisure culture represented by men's "ardour in hunting, shooting, and gambling," and the related abuse of oversensitized, inexperienced, and irrational women by "rakes" and "libertines" who treated women as if they were birds or animals.[215] Instead, she wished childrearing and education to generate more "humanity," more humane men and women, by teaching "children" "to love home."[216]

In sentimental, familiar prose, Wollstonecraft described the pleasures granted a man by the vision of a mother implementing an approved form of "sensibility," including a properly focused "sensuality."

> Cold would be the heart of a husband, were he not rendered unnatural by early debauchery, who did not feel more delight at seeing his child suckled by its mother than the most artful wanton tricks could ever raise.

Suckling was a central focus of the proper sentimental domestic scene. This "natural way of cementing the matrimonial tie, twisting esteem with fonder recollections" was parallel to the natural tie between mother and child. A woman's "parental affection scarcely deserves the name, when it does not lead her to suckle her children, because the discharge of a duty is equally calculated to inspire maternal and filial affection . . . affections must grow out of the habitual exercise of a mutual sympathy." Woman-as-mother was the common figure to each of these latter dyads. The social bond taking its origins in this kind of familial relationship (either by way of the impression made on the suckling child or by the impression made on the warmed heart of the observing husband) was one route to a reformation of manners generally.[217]

Wollstonecraft suggests that the "maternal solicitude of a reasonable affectionate woman is very interesting" to the husband who is receptive to it. Perhaps recalling Lovelace's arousal by the thought of Clarissa suckling his twins, Wollstonecraft hastens to add that "the chastened dignity with which a mother returns the caresses that she and her child receive from a father who has been fulfilling the serious duties of his station is not only a respectable, but a beautiful sight." A man's appreciation of this mother-centered domesticity was the mark of respectability as well as the occasion for esthetic pleasure. The attractions of a better-educated wife and mother, drawing a husband home from a man's homosocial outdoor pleasures, was by now a century-long argument made by feminists and sentimental novelists.[218]

At this point, Wollstonecraft, the narrator, joins the scene she has created in order to illustrate its sentimental effects and to place "domestic affections" within the value system of the culture of sensibility:

> after being fatigued with the sight of insipid grandeur and the slavish ceremonies that with cumbrous pomp supplied the place of domestic affections, I have turned to some other scene to relieve my eye by resting it on the refreshing green everywhere scattered by Nature. I then viewed with pleasure a woman nursing her children, and discharging the duties of her station.

Wollstonecraft presented her appreciation of the sight of a nursing mother as the reassertion of "domestic affections," themselves part of Nature's fecundity. While influenced by her sometimes Rousseauistic view, this passage reflects the one quoted earlier from Smith's *Theory of Moral Sentiments,* beginning, "With what pleasure do we look upon a family, through the whole of which reign mutual love and esteem," but Wollstonecraft, the feminist spectator, adapts it to her own purposes. She singles out the power of the wife/mother, and she purges the distinction Smith made between brothers and sisters.[219]

Elaborating her account of her feelings, in keeping with the increasing range of activities of the figures (now increased in number) in this domestic space, Wollstonecraft continues:

> I have seen her prepare herself and children, with only the luxury of cleanliness, to receive her husband, who, returning home in the evening, found smiling babes and a clean hearth. My heart has loitered in the midst of the group, and has even

> throbbed with sympathetic emotion when the scraping of the well-known foot has raised a pleasing tumult.

The phrase, "only the luxury of cleanliness," is intended to stand in contrast to the more expensive consumer luxuries Wollstonecraft had described elsewhere, but cleanliness was itself a luxury. Wollstonecraft tells us that this mother has "merely a maidservant to take off her hands the servile part of the household business." This may have included hauling the ashes from the hearth and scrubbing food residues from cooking pots with water, which the servant had also hauled. One has to imagine what else the "luxury of cleanliness" stands for, distinguishing what was made possible by the servant from what was made possible by purchase of consumer goods.[220] Her husband's biography of her provides some further clues; Godwin tells us that when Wollstonecraft established herself as a successful author in 1791, she moved to "a more commodious apartment," close to the most fashionable part of London. There she "added to the neatness and cleanliness which she had always scrupulously observed, a certain degree of elegance, and those temperate indulgences in furniture and accommodation, from which a sound and uncorrupted taste never fails to derive pleasure."[221]

Wollstonecraft's ideal family scene in the *Rights of Woman* was "natural" in the sense that she had written the "middle class" was the most natural state. Its members were raised "sufficiently above abject poverty not to be obliged to weigh the consequence of every farthing they spend, and having sufficient to prevent their attending to a frigid system of economy which narrows both heart and mind." Wollstonecraft's account of the possibilities here links her implicit alternative—that is, a comfortless home to which a husband was loth to return, one without a servant and, conversely, with a dirty, exhausted, and illiterate wife—to the "imaginative povery" which accompanied comfortless peasant houses, void of the material culture of beds, chairs, easily cleaned dinnerware, and forks. By contrast, the "luxury" of this 1792 domestic space permitted its inhabitants to be happy and "respectable," those qualities evident in "a taste for literature," "a little variety and interest [in] social converse and some superfluous money to give to the needy and to buy books." Those qualities, that taste, are also expressed in the inhabitants' and the narrators' appreciation for "Nature" and for the moral and aesthetic value in the mother's suckling, and for "domestic affections" in toto. There is an intergenerational psychological process here because such parenting will generate such sensibility. Wollstonecraft's *Original Stories* presented the same arguments by way of Mrs. Trueman. Her "cultivated mind" may have made her pleasures "independent of prosperity," but it is essential to recognize that her successful functioning, from her charity to her fashionably simple and clean clothes, her musical instruments, and her tastefully stocked bookcase, all depended on a critical level of consumer spending for domestic space. Because she was an exemplar of properly balanced sensibility in this comforting house, she was beloved by her children. She extended her humanity beyond her home by caring for the poor and, evidently, both she and Wollstonecraft's other exemplary mother also entered respectably disciplined and pleasurable public space to shop (for books at least) and even to enjoy "variety in social converse."[222]

The full development of sensibility, Wollstonecraft argues very directly in the *Rights of Woman,* was contingent on a certain level of prosperity:

> For it is not pleasant when the heart is opened by compassion, and the head active in arranging plans of usefulness, to have a prim urchin continually twitching at the elbow to prevent the hand from drawing out an almost empty purse, whispering at the same time some prudential maxim about the priority of justice.

Humanity follows prosperity, implicitly the effect of commercial capitalism, as Hume had argued it did. These connections were assumed—or in Barbauld's case, made explicit by her linking sensibility with "free commerce"—in fiction's representation of tasteful homes. And if the domestic luxury of this couple enabled them to express the values of sensibility to each other, to the "needy," and in their rearing of humane sons and daughters, it also allowed the observer's "heart" to enter the group and throb with sympathy. As Wollstonecraft said of her response, "my benevolence has been gratified by this artless picture."

In sum, in spite of Wollstonecraft's harsh criticism of women's frivolous, obsessive consumerism and their exaggerated sensibility, she still assumed that women were to be identified with consumerism and sensibility. Those qualities were at the heart of women's "reformation," providing the base from which they were to reform children and men. Her apparent ambivalence toward consumerism is easily explained by seeing that Wollstonecraft distinguished between good sensibility and bad sensibility, good consumerism and bad consumerism—good taste and no taste. The distinction, arising with the origins of feminism, corresponded to the one made by male writers—especially Hume and Smith—between "frugal," tasteful consumption and frivolous extravagance and amusements, but shaped very much by women's own most pressing concerns.[223]

Good consumerism was shaped by reason. Reason, wrote Wollstonecraft, was "the simple power of improvement, or, more properly speaking, of discerning truth. Every individual is in this respect a world in itself." Women had the same capacity to reason that men did, the same capacity for full consciousness—sensibility and reason—and consequently for "egotism," for individualism. Here Wollstonecraft restored the tough-minded part to Shaftesbury's view, the part that sentimentalists forgot if they merely celebrated feeling: "can that soul be stamped with the heavenly image that is not perfected by the exercise of reason?" On this point, Wollstonecraft cites Lord Monboddo, another member of the Edinburgh school and of the "Select Society." It will be seen that Wollstonecraft's recommendations for women's improvement coincided with that school's hopes for men. She quoted and paraphrased Smith, Monboddo, and Hume in the *Rights of Woman,* and she quoted Hume and Robertson in *The Female Reader,* the former in making the case that Elizabeth had met Hume's standards for consciousness, despite her sex. Wollstonecraft's vision of a reformed family, generating the social bond of sympathy as well as individualism, resembles Smith's very closely, although Wollstonecraft's earlier writings show she had her own reasons to repudiate a familial experience of brutality and partiality.[224]

It is not in the least surprising that Wollstonecraft shared Smith's famous view of the relationship between the liberation of individual talent, commercial prosperity, and the health of the state. She wrote that "the prosperity of a state depends on the freedom of industry; that talents should be permitted to find their level; that the unshackling of commerce is the only secret to render it flourishing." Moreover, if prosperity was essential to women's capacity to reform manners, Wollstonecraft also assumed it could sponsor women's becoming individual worlds in themselves. "I will take it for granted that she was not created merely to be the solace of man, and the sexual should not destroy the human character." To appropriate Meyer again, women could find promises in the prosperous family's "more complex, stimulating, and intense relations between children and grownups" for the development of their own talents, their individualism, too.[225]

SIX

Women and Individualism: Inner and Outer Struggles over Sensibility

The Sentimentalizing Process

Women's reformation of men is central to Elias's vision of the civilizing process. Where military functions receded, replaced by the proliferation of administrative functions and interpersonal relations at great twelfth-century courts (those same courts growing wealthy by their close attachment to the developing "network of trade and money"), women's "social importance" increased. Court ladies emerged from those "ornamented chambers," to which previously they had been banished by nose-punching knights, to pursue the "luxury interests" sponsored by and sponsoring trade and courtly power. They were the first, Elias suggests, to be "liberated for intellectual development, for reading." They had a "more refined" education than men. One could say they were the first women at this phase of history to enjoy a leisure culture. They attracted "poets, singers, and learned clerics." Identified with "the cult and ideal" of romantic love, they compelled "socially inferior and dependent men . . . to constrain [their] drives and to impose control on them." Of course, women's power to "compel" other men had to be in conformity with the wishes of women's male peers and superiors. Furthermore, Elias refers to "the pressures on the libidinal life of women" which "throughout western history" were "considerably heavier than men of equal birth." [1]

The new male ideal of the Renaissance, representing the acceleration of the civilizing process, was accompanied by the questioning of the role of woman, a "commonplace" of Renaissance culture. The Urbino Court, in which *The Courtier* was generated, was shaped by the personality of its duchess. Castiglione recognized the apparent wish that "every women" had, "to be a man," really expressed women's desire "to gain their freedom and shake off the tyranny men have imposed on them." The influence of *The Courtier* on Elizabethan courtly culture and its passage thence into literature (Spenserian romance onward), as well as more immediate experience, lay behind Rochester's representation of "Amaçoa."[2]

The Courtier suggested that, without women, men would be "more uncouth and savage" than wild beasts. Castiglione conceded that female and male courtiers had qualities in common and that "many virtues of the mind are as necessary to a woman as to a man." Those virtues included prudence, sagacity, magnanimity, and continence, as well as "letters and temperance." He advocated women's education in those accomplishments that would be diffused later among bourgeois ladies, their subsequent skill at "conversation" thence improving male manners in the way reflected by Hume. Castiglione insisted on some crucial differences between the sexes, however, the most apparent being that woman was to be "fashioned" by men rather than by herself. Second, Castiglione makes it clear that the newly educated woman would have "the qualities that are common to all classes of women," specifically "the ability to take good care, if she is married, of her husband's belongings, and the virtues belonging to a good mother." (Makin, associated with the Stuart court, inherited the same priority.) Third, precisely because her distinctive courtliness seems to require some common virtues with men, a courtly woman "should no way resemble a man as regards her ways, manners, words, gestures, and bearing." While "a man should display a certain robust and sturdy manliness," a woman should "have a certain soft and delicate tenderness, with an air of feminine sweetness in her every movement." Her "sweet gentleness" is sweeter and more gentle than that of even the most civilized male courtier.[3]

She must be more "circumspect" than men because she must guard herself against them. If it happens that she is exposed to "improper conversation," she cannot run off because that might suggest she was hiding something about herself. Instead, she should listen to the improprieties "with a slight blush of shame." A civilized woman's "honesty" is identified with her chastity and her sexual "reserve." This separates her from those women who "display their lack of shame" with "wanton laughter, loquacity, brashness, and scurrilous behavior." A woman's becoming civilized not only marks her transcendence of a barbaric past and the barbarian present embodied in the lower classes: it distinguished her from the inevitably greater hardness of even the courtliest of males.[4]

Addressing the "destabilization of social categories in England" during the late seventeenth and early eighteenth centuries, McKeon suggests that as the notion of "honor as virtue" was detached from "male aristocratic honor, it simultaneously encourage[d] its relocation not only among commoners but women," who came to "embody the locus and refuge of honor as virtue." The potentials for women in courtly precedent became much more salient when women's claim to shape manners began to be placed on revolutionary new bases. During the seventeenth century, "honor" shifted its meaning from "title of rank" to "goodness of character," a shift corresponding to the evolution of the fluidity of sensational psychology, but corresponding, too, to the promises Protestantism and its sequelae (as well as civic humanism) held for women. Clarissa would tell Lovelace "you know not how to treat with a mind of the last degree of delicacy, notwithstanding your birth and education." Clarissa, unlike a courtly lady, is Lovelace's social inferior in traditional terms. Her introduction of the word "degree" in this context illustrates that delicacy and sensibility manifested an alternative hierarchy of values to those of inheritance and birth, one based on morality. In 1771 Dr. John Armstrong recognized that servants were often born with "as delicate Sensations as their Superiors," the subversiveness of which Langford notes. As we have seen, however, this fluidity was also sharply defined by the values associated with gender. So, for example, Miss Rogers's *History of Miss Temple* (1777) suggested that the female heart experienced "the delicate sensibilities of the tender passion, in a degree of refinement of which the rougher sex is seldom capable." This, too, was an inheritance from *The Courtier.*[5] The tradition expressed in *The Courtier* was popularized in those conduct books mentioned previously, disseminating a courtliness infused with English Protestant values. The title of one of them, *The Ladies Calling* (1673), a sequel to *The Gentleman's Calling* (1660), demonstrates this fusion. It was frequently reprinted in the next century, and the years 1760–1820 "might be called the age of the courtesy books for women."[6]

One of their aims was the control of appetite; indulgence in one led to indulgence in others, and *The Ladies Calling* warned that "she who is first a prostitute to Wine, will soon be to Lust also." Increasingly conduct books urged "good taste" in the preparation of food and other forms of "domestic display" rather than mere "frugality." In 1711 *The Spectator* presented a letter aimed directly at the kind of habits Elias has in mind and written in the voice of a "gentleman" whose "taste" was "delicate," in contrast to that of the young woman he describes "daily committing faults" to the extent that he threatens not to marry her. She

> either wholly neglects, or has no notion of that which polite people have agreed to distinguish by the name delicacy. After

> our return from a walk the other day she threw herself into an elbow chair, and professed before a large company, that she was all over in a sweat. She told me this afternoon that her stomach ached; and was complaining yesterday at dinner of something that stuck in her teeth. I treated her with a basket of fruits last summer, which she ate so very greedily.

The recent change in manners, now being spread to more of the middling ranks by new means of communication and a new availability of private interiors, of armchairs, and the formal presentation of food, added up to a new social standard of "politeness" named "delicacy," "délicatesse" in its courtly French precedent. It included restrained movement (not throwing oneself into a chair), not naming the body's functions (sweating) or even parts (stomach and teeth) in public. Significantly, the condition of these parts were connected with appetite, of which the young woman's last faux pas (eating greedily) was the clearest example. (And was the author hinting that the greedily eaten fruit had an affect even further down the digestive tract?) Moralists pushed inexorably against women's uninhibitedly expressing appetite. John Gregory was horrified about overeating in women. "It is a despicable vice in men, but in your sex it is beyond expression indelicate and disgusting."[7]

Cleanliness was another sign of the tendency toward "civilization" with which women were particularly identified, again one made more possible by commercialization. Ladies' creation of a special dialect of neatness and cleanliness expressed their adoption of the process. James Fordyce observed in 1766 that women's achievement of both "cleanliness and finery" was still frequent enough, and he exclaimed, "A dirty woman—I turn from the shocking idea." Shocking ideas depended on shocking language; words, too, were evidently suffused with shock value and therefore subjected to the civilizing process. Lady Mary Wortley Montagu warned her daughter in 1752 that Richardson's Lady Charlotte used "coarse jokes and low expressions as are to be heard only among the Lowest Class of People." In an earlier phase, it seems, a middle-class woman looking for a larger house had been able to use a Northern expression and say she "wanted a canny hole of her own to fart in," while "even fashionable ladies habitually swore." In *The Fable of the Bees* Mandeville referred to the clearing of excrement from the streets and also, in that work as well as in his defense of "stews," he described sexual transactions, physiologies, and pleasures without euphemism. In this presentation of sex, Mandeville expressed popular convention. By 1759, Adam Smith, proponent of the civilizing process, termed Mandeville's speech "coarse." In its stead he advocated the spread of properly expressed sensibility and domesticity. The internalization of delicate manners by women marked their upward advance toward ladyhood. Smollett had recorded the wish of "the wives and daughters of low tradesmen" to be "delicate," aspiring to manners above those of the "vulgar."[8]

Mrs. Thrale recognized the national historical change in "female manners" which had occurred since that 1711 issue of *The Spectator.* Her reading it aloud in 1782 to her eleven- and twelve-year-old daughters made them burst out laughing; "even the maid who was dressing my hair" joined in the laughter at the idea. A 1791 piece in the *Gentleman's Magazine* joined Mrs. Thrale in noting the change, euphemism replacing archaic and direct forms of speech. It, too, suggested the social meaning attached to the change by suggesting that only "the lowest class" now used the word "sweat." Speaking of both sexes, the writer linked his vision of this national process to delicacy, virtue, refinement, and politesse, albeit with irony. "We are every day growing more delicate, and, without doubt, at the same time more virtuous; and shall, I am confident, become the most refined and polite people in the world." The "refinement and delicacy" of the "well-bred female" distinguished her, wrote Mary Anne Radcliffe in 1799, from the "poor and abject" who were ignorant of the manners subsumed by those terms.[9]

Wollstonecraft registered this trend by reacting in part against it. She opposed the convolutions required of women's "delicacy of sentiment," even as they aimed at the sexual goal of marriage; instead, she referred to "the common appetites of human nature." Declaring "I have conversed, as man with man, with medical men on anatomical subjects, and compared the proportions of the human body with artists [one of them presumably Henry Fuseli], yet, with such modesty . . . that I was never reminded by word or look of my sex," she said the sexualization of "modesty" was "absurd," "a Pharisaical cloak of weakness." She recommended that children be told the truth about the physiology of sex and pregnancy—"that their mothers carry and nourish them" in the same way as the cats children could not help observing. She scorned women's displaying "the care not to let their legs be seen" and the warning that modest women not put their hands "by chance under [their] neck-handkerchief."[10] While she went along with the belief that women "[a]s a sex are more chaste than men," her purpose was to turn that to women's own interest by urging the development of women's minds. "Men are not always men in the company of women, nor would women always remember that they are women, if they were allowed to acquire more understanding." She urged that women's chastity depend on a modesty arising, like men's, from "pursuits purely intellectual" rather than "sexual" ones. Purity of mind "or that genuine delicacy, which is the only virtuous support of chastity, is near akin to that refinement of humanity, which never resides in any but cultivated minds." It is evident that her standard here remained the progress of civilization in the minds of both sexes, that is of "humanity," and that such refinement required modesty, chastity, purity, and delicacy. It must be reiterated that the *Rights of Woman* was devoted expressly to "the reformation of manners." Wollstonecraft wished to modify that process by equalizing its claims on each sex as much as possible. Denying the "existence of sexual virtues," she advocated "one eternal standard" for men and women, a single set of "the virtues that should clothe humanity." [11]

If she argued that women had power as mothers to inculcate virtue into their children, she also declared, in opposition to a strong tendency in eighteenth-century prescription, that women were not "created . . . to save [man] from sinking into absolute brutality, by rubbing off the rough angles of his character." And she reversed the emphasis in Fordyce's disgusted judgment of women's gluttony. Not only were men "more depraved" than women, "by unbridled indulgence and the fastidious contrivances of satiety" that "luxury" had introduced (here Wollstonecraft perpetuated Cheyne's view of the effects of consumerism): men compounded their "beastly" "gluttony" by indulging it in the presence of others and then by complaining about its corporeal effects. Wollstonecraft emphasized that it was only "[s]ome women, particularly French women, [who] have also lost a sense of decency in this respect; for they will talk very calmly of an indigestion." Here Wollstonecraft's euphemisms illustrate the success *The Spectator* and *The Dissertation on Drunkenness* had hoped for: she mentions neither "stomach ache" nor "belching" or "breaking wind." By the same token, Wollstonecraft shared Castiglione's view of women's public expression of sexual feelings.

> The shameless behaviour of the prostitutes, who infest the streets of this metropolis, raising alternate emotions of pity and disgust . . . They trample on virgin bashfulness with a sort of bravado, and glorifying in their shame, become more audaciously lewd than men ever appear to be.

Wollstonecraft was deeply puritanical in her opposition to masturbation, against which she held that open sexual talk was a weapon, and in her view of menstruation, calling it "an insult to humanity." If she assumed that most women would show "decency" in not mentioning indigestion, she urged in the interests of "delicacy" that women repress the "nasty custom" of talking about "so very disgusting" a "part of the animal economy," even to each other. The "disgust" also aroused in Wollstonecraft by physical "deformity" was identical to that expressed by Barbauld (or Mark Akenside, for that matter), in turn inspired by Shaftesbury's expression in his *Characteristics*, quoted earlier. Even so, Wollstonecraft's call for explicitness in naming sexual parts was interpreted by a reviewer as a sign of her masculine mind and she was advised to return to the "female" state.[12]

Evidently the civilizing process was applied to women's bodies, an application illustrated by the gendering of the nervous system, which Cheyne named "delicate." It was illustrated, too, by Fielding's characterization of the six-foot Mrs. Western as "masculine," and by Edgeworth's labeling a woman's "masculine arms" freakish, a "freakishness" defining feminine norms throughout the century. Gregory recognized that men's desire that women have delicate manners extended to their desire that women's bodies correspond.

> We so naturally associate the idea of female softness and delicacy with a corresponding delicacy of constitution, that when a woman speaks of her great strength, her extraordinary appetite, her ability to bear excessive fatigue, we recoil at the description in a way she is little aware of.

The obverse of the strength, appetitiveness, size, muscularity, self-assertiveness, and even belligerence of the antitypes held up by sentimental literature, were delicately refined heroines exemplifying body type, use, and gesture. Educated by her mistress to be a "lady's" maid, the upwardly mobile Pamela could "make a fine figure" with her singing and dancing. Paraded at last before her future husband's "ladies," Pamela received their praise, she wrote, "upon my complexion . . . my eyes, my hand, and, in short, upon my whole person and behaviour." That included her god-given delicacy of constitution, which allowed her to faint at crucial moments. Fielding associated greater delicacy of bodies, minds, and morals as well as language with greater femininity, although his novels showed women of all classes having sexual appetite and expressing it. They showed, too, women of the lower classes with developed musculature, capable of fighting, their skins and muscles toughened by their ceaseless and arduous work in the fields and in kitchens. By contrast, his heroines, typical in this regard of sentimental fiction, were extremes of physical delicacy, paleness, and sensibility.[13] The heroine of Frances Brooke's 1763 novel, *Julia Mandeville,* manifested a femininity of body that corresponded to her soul. "Her whole form is delicate and feminine to the utmost degree . . . her complexion . . . often diversified by blushes . . . strongly expressive of the exquisite sensibility of her soul." Shammas's work suggests there was a circular relation between nutritional change and physically less demanding work. The less women worked in the fields and tending livestock the less they were able to do so because of the drop in their calorific intake, the whole change perhaps eventually contributing to the general reshaping of women's bodies.[14]

Commerce provided women the means more elaborately to ritualize the intake of food and tea and to adorn their domestic spaces and their persons, and it contributed to their wishes to color and shape their bodies. A 1777 print demonstrated that, despite the fact that women of all classes wore fashionable caps, ribbons, shoes, buckles, and bows, lower-class women still had heavier musculature and less refined features. However, women aspiring to delicacy and ladyhood could buy "Trents Depilatory"; "arsenic to whiten the hands"; "Witmer's Sicilian Bloom or Youth Beauty"; teeth cleansers, artificial teeth, and other devices to enhance the attractions of the properly mannered female body. Men, too, wore false calves and dressed their hair elaborately; perhaps the concentration on a smoother shave was linked to their desire for greater refinement and a less barbarous, more civilized appearance, betokening cultivated manners and minds. This may have corresponded to women's wishes for a softened manhood.[15]

However, men's refinement was not designed to go so far as women's, and it could not be enforced in the same way women's could. As Gregory's warning to women indicated—telling them that their overeating was beyond expression "disgusting"—women were required to internalize male wishes. To the psychic controls internalized by all those subjected/subjecting themselves to the civilizing process were superadded the pressures men exercised against female habits. Women could not afford to ignore such pressures, as *The Spectator*'s gentleman's threat not to marry intimated. Whatever those feelings were—"shock," "disgust," "recoil," or their appetite for female "delicacy"—men could invest them with sexual and economic power. The power of men's wishes was incorporated into the engendering of improved manners in eighteenth-century British homes and the deeper psychic changes sponsoring them, although women, too, including Wollstonecraft, wished sons to be "manly." Boys emerged from transformed homes ready to assume the "harder" values and innovativeness required by the "world." The relationship between childrearing and the transformation of manners was not (and never can be) a closed one, as we shall see a bit later in this chapter.

Sentimental fiction—indeed, fiction generally—embodied and extended this gendered civilizing process in language Wesley said could not "offend the chastest ear." That passage in *Clarissa* in which Richardson identifies a feminine style with "gentleness" and "delicacy of sentiments" had echoed Castiglione's definition of an ideal lady. Among his sources for the exemplary *Clarissa* were those female-conduct books derived from *The Courtier* and its English Puritan descendants. Courts and aristocratic manners sustained a continuing influence by way of their fictional representation. Ladyhood's delicacy was composed, according to Richardson's compendium, of "a multitude of punctilios and decorums." Gregory wished "romance" to be perpetuated because its heroines were distinguished for "modesty, delicacy, and the utmost dignity of manners," and, late in the century, Clara Reeve endorsed him.[16] The language of "courting" in the literature of sensibility was the archaic and romantic language of court (or pseudocourt) etiquette proliferated in the bourgeois form of the novel by a bourgeois infrastructure (mass publication, marketing, libraries), all in the bourgeois context of consumerism, which the novels and conduct books also recorded.[17] Clarissa says, "Our sex must expect to bear a—uncourtliness shall I call it—from the *husband* whom as a *lover* they let know the preference gave him to all other men." Lord Fellamar in *Tom Jones* applies the same standard in his judgment of Sophia Western's manners. "I should swear she had been bred in a court; for besides her beauty, I never saw anything so genteel, so sensible, so polite." Sophia had learned courtly manners far away from court, although her citified aunt reinforced them. One of her sources was reading novels.[18]

The depiction in the fictive world of sensibility of deferential gestures was derived from the romantic or feudal past. Most apparent are the kneelings and other postures of super- and subordination, expressing a range of meanings: supplication, gratitude, and distress, for example. Such postures permitted the extravagant expression of emotions because of their subordination to form. To these must be added the myriad of subtler signs which can be aligned with Elias's history of manners: from a single brimming tear to torrents of weeping, sighings, blushes, tremblings, eye lowerings, silences, and degrees of swoonings. They encoded a specific system of emotions along the very border of the most private-public split imaginable, that is, the body. Such a system was subtle enough to reach even the interoceptors of the nervous system, increasing still further, therefore, the reaches of personality. Courtly elements were thus combined with the psychoperceptual paradigm, pietistic values, and adherence to a moralized taste in consumerism. Together, the culture's language of gesture and word became a system defining female propriety and attempting to define "the sex" as "ladies." Sensibility marked a "bourgeoisified" courtly status remote from the blatant, noisy, and smelly nose pickings, scratchings, belching, and farting which signified the "vulgar" but one to which, it seems, large numbers of the vulgar aspired.

The literacy extended by novels to a gendered audience furthered the bowdlerization of language, especially female language, already discernible in *The Spectator.* Aphra Behn, admirer of Rochester, Restoration wit, playwright, and novelist, had depicted women's longing to make love and referred to their expertise in its "wanton Arts."[19] Her heiresses, Mary Manley and Eliza Haywood notable among them, were Restoration playwrights as well as novelists, and Manley trod the boards herself. Spacks has called their sentimental fiction "semi-pornographic." It had been written in the first three decades of the century, but by the 1730s their more explicit sexuality was being purged from English fiction.[20] The reformation of manners showed itself in other ways, too. Very conscious of his audiences and his competition in the 1740s, the personally scatological Fielding recorded with some circumlocution the direct bodily slang of "country gentlemen" and "the low orders of the English gentry." This was the same kind of language found "vile" and "obscene" by the 1727 *Dissertation upon Drunkenness.* It was a language with which Fielding said men "bespattered" each other at "horse-races, cock-matches, and other public places," and it stood in sharp contrast to Sophia Western's courtly, sentimental diction. The coming into existence of ever stricter demands "for propriety in language and society" kept pace with the proliferation of sentimental fiction.[21] In 1751 Richardson would categorize writers Behn, Manley, and Haywood with several women notorious for their sexual acts.[22]

By the 1760s, we have seen, male writers were treating sentimentalization with a great deal of ambiguity, some of it clearly satire. (Similarly, courtly conduct books for men "mutated" into satire by mid-century, in contrast to those addressing women.)[23] The ambiguities, double-entendres, and other satirical elements were purged from the versions of Sterne's *A Sentimental Journey* (1768) when it was popularized for the female market.[24] One anthology representing his sentimentalization was *The Beauties of Sterne, Including All His Pathetic Tales and Most Distinguished Observations on Life, Selected for the Heart of Sensibility* (1782) which went through thirteen editions by 1799.[25] Another anthology including a wide variety of authors and one on which Wollstonecraft would draw in 1789 for yet another, was the Rev. William Enfield's, which simply "recruited the 'pathetic' elements of Sterne."[26] Sterne's sensibility was publicly extracted at the expense of his eroticism. *The Beauties of Sterne* were those purged of sex, selected "for the *chaste* part of the world," for those who "with some reason" objected to "the obscenity which taints" Sterne's writings.[27] Symbolically, the "avowed first principle" of the *Sentimental Magazine,* its first issue (1773) "A Sentimental Journey through Life" in imitation of Sterne, was "Chastity of Sentiment."[28] It declared in 1773, "What was caviare to the last century will promote disgust in this. As we have increased in politeness, we have likewise increased in the chastity of our literary productions . . . Our ancestors placed their amusement in laughter, we place ours in chastity of sentiment. If they were more witty, they were less modest, than us."[29] This change in many authors' voices, away from satire and eroticism and from the Restoration values connoted by "witty," toward an evangelized seriousness, was characteristic of the relationship between writers and an increasingly female audience throughout the century.[30] According to her brother, Austen ranked Fielding lower than Richardson because "she recoiled from every thing gross. Neither nature, wit, nor honour, could make her amends, for so very low a scale of morals." Educating her readers' taste and defending women's achievement, Austen contrasted the novels by Edgeworth and Burney favorably to essays even in *The Spectator.* In keeping with Mrs. Thrale's judgment, she said that *The Spectator*'s "matter" and "manner" would "disgust a young person of taste," and its language was "frequently so coarse as to give no very favorable idea of the age that could endure it."[31]

The theater was subjected to the same process, moved in the direction indicated by the divines, by Shaftesbury, and by *The Spectator.* In the words of Dr. Johnson, "Collier lived to see the reward of his labour in the reformation of the theatre."[32] Those moral values of "good nature," preached by Collier and other Latitudinarian divines, were represented in plays written and performed contemporaneously with their sermons. The authors of *The Spectator* contributed several plays. Against those naughty titles listed earlier were posed *The Constant Couple* and *The Married Philosopher.*[33] The trend was subject to the same challenges and reservations as fiction was, Goldsmith expressing his in both genres. At first George Colman "resisted demands for a serious improving stage" with such "robust satires" as *The Jealous Wife* (1761), but even he "eventually succumbed to the needs of polite audiences." In sentimental drama as in *Clarissa,* "women become touchstones of morality and fetishized centres of the plot." Representations of domestic tragedy and sentimental comedy in terms of sensibility "possessed great appeal" for eighteenth-century audiences. The traditionally Stoic hero of classical precedent had been "extravagantly transformed" into "a tearful and penitent Christian Man of Feeling."[34]

In performance, sentimental drama emphasized the emotion-laden gesture of which the "modernizing" Garrick, Whitefield's admirer, was the most famous exemplar. According to Gibbon, Garrick invoked "exquisite feeling and discernment" in his audience. Sterne said Garrick had "some magic irresistible power," which was "released 'feelingly' on stage with the vibrations of 'every Fibre about your Heart' "; his gestures touched "the nerves." While thus aligned with the civilizing process, it should be noted that this emotional appeal was also linked to a subversion of language and a diminution of the deepest of traditional aesthetic standards, characteristics of sentimental fiction and of cognate evangelical theology: "—And how did *Garrick* speak the soliloquy last night?—Oh, against all rule, my Lord,—most ungrammatically! . . ." Garrick replaced grammatical agreement with "expression of attitude or countenance." At the same time, like preaching, such drama embodied moral, Christian purpose, audiences attending "the theatre to cry to be improved."[35]

Some writers, notably Pope, judged the sentimentalism of drama to be "a breakdown" of traditional aesthetic standards, because they saw it, in Janet Todd's phrase, as "an unfortunate feminization of culture." Such "feminization"—liquifying the Stoic male, purging Restoration sexuality, and making women the moral focus—can be seen as the effect of the reformation of manners and the civilizing process, vehicles, as it were, for women's wishes because these changes all assumed that women were in the new audiences. They were accompanied by more mannerly men, and they were acting on the appetite for public pleasures they expressed in fiction and in their other choices, able to use the streets to attend plays written and put on by entrepreneurs conscious of the possibilities. Civic leaders built theaters in the fashionable provincial towns (York in 1734, Bath in the 1740s, and Liverpool in 1772), dedicated to "polite and thinking" audiences of women and men together. Theatrical inaugurations declared their Shaftesburian purpose to promote "decency and regularity."

> A graceful ease and polish to impart,
> Refine the taste and humanize the heart

Sentimental drama coexisted with theaters catering to other tastes—pantomime, animal acts, Punch and Judy, the "robust" entertainments shading into music hall as well as into sentiment as in the cases of Goldsmith and Colman. Performances of Restoration drama continued too; if Evelina refused to see Congreve's *Love for Love* a second time because it was "too extremely indelicate," she had seen it once to find out what she did not want. Consequently, the struggle of sentiment against "robustness" persisted, too, Hannah More keeping her nose to the grindstone with the sentimental moralistic play, *Earl Percy*, which Garrick produced in 1777, a few years before More dedicated her *Sacred Dramas* to him.[36]

"Indelicacy" connoted sex. That sentimental literature carried a sexual code is one of its most salient features. Clarissa warned Anna to show affection to Hickman before marriage so that affection afterwards would not be "construed as a compliment to a *husband* made at the expense of the *wife's delicacy*." One notes Richardson's acknowledgment of women's sexual feelings and that they could be part of the social affections intensified by marriage.[37] The sexual code was most frequently named "delicacy." While it could be synonymous with "sensibility" (both words denoting nerve quality), "delicacy" represented a wished-for, built-in inhibitor of the sexual dangers inhering in sensibility itself, the automatic responsiveness of material physiological processes. "Delicacy is often a kind of regulator of sensibility, checking it when it is excessive or verges on impropriety." Women were accused in a 1735 issue of *The Prompter* of thinking that any sentiment that seems "involuntary and out of power not to feel, more true and *genuine* than a *Sentiment* formed upon Principle and born of Reflection." This was consistent with the association of ideas and sensibility's identification with the nerve paradigm. Somehow, sensibility's dangerous manifestations were to be "completely in accordance with the strictest code of decorum." The "immediate expressiveness" of the sentiment was simultaneously, it was hoped, "scrupulous propriety." Griffith said in *The Delicate Distress* that "there is everything to be expected from *sensibility and delicacy* joined; but indeed, I have scarce ever known them separated, in a female heart." We have seen John Bennett's definition of a gendered, female delicacy as "salutary restraint." "Delicacy" gave particular meaning to the "moral sense" hypothesized by the Cambridge Platonists and Shaftesbury. When implemented, the code of delicacy mediated a complex power struggle, one which took on new meaning because of women's widespread participation in "recreational life" for the first time during the eighteenth century and their fuller expression of wishes in the marriage market. A premature avowal by a woman "was generally requited with insolence and contempt: whereas the confessedly obliged man would be all reverence and gratitude." The most crucial circumstances for this struggle were those that could be construed as premarital. For a woman the outcome was either reputability and some economic security, or else disaster. *Clarissa* was a guidebook for this code. It suggests both the vital importance of delicacy to women and its fragility.[38]

Traditional, patriarchal male control of female sexuality seems to have been basic to shaping the code of delicacy. MacKenzie followed Richardson in arguing both against the damaging effects on a daughter of a tyrannical father's control of her marriage choice and for maintaining the father's right to enforce the sexual code against her wishes. MacKenzie called the latter "that delicate concern." Evelina recognizes that her observation of the code is derived from her de facto father:

> so strong is the desire you have implanted in me to act with uprightness and propriety, that, however the weakness of my heart may distress and afflict me, it will never, I humbly trust, render me willfully culpable. The wish of doing well governs every other, as far as concerns my conduct,—for am I not *your* child?—the creature of your own forming?—Yet, oh Sir, friend, parent of my heart!—my feelings are all at war with my duties.[39]

Radcliffe, too, justified a father's implementation of the sexual code, made especially necessary because of the recognition that sensibility made a daughter vulnerable. Women had to manifest this sexual code continually, because it identified them with being civilized in a particular way. In her 1777 sentimental novel, *The Excursion,* Frances Brooke attributed "half of their virtue" to women's "grace, manner [and] decorum in morals."[40]

Strengthened by what Inchbald called "A Proper Education," reason could come to the aid of the less reliable delicacy in enforcing the code and repressing sensibility's sexual potentials. Lavinia, the heroine of Elizabeth Ryves's *The Hermit of Snowden* (1793), was left waiting by her lover. Her

> passions were warm, and her bosom tremblingly alive to every touch of joy or sorrow; yet her reason was sufficiently strong to regulate not only her conduct, but her wishes; and though she felt the thrills of sensibility, she always preserved an absolute dominion over herself.

Evidently women had to distinguish among the myriad of clues ("every touch") that a female nervous system was particularly oriented toward registering. Conversely, the operation of sensibility's characteristic responsiveness revealed the existence of reason's archetypal opponent. Writing in 1736 to the "mainly homosexual" man she pursued, Lady Mary Wortley Montagu said, "One must have a Heart filled with a strong passion, to be touched by trifles which seem of such little importance to others." Her "trifles," her clues, were very different from those Hannah More's "Sensibility" gloried in picking up, half a century later, although each woman's system brought great suffering, Lady Mary recognizing that she loved "to the degree that I love without hope of return."[41] Indeed, her apprehensions, in Spacks's account, "implicitly recognizes 'a degree of insanity' in the predominance of passion over reason." How far would the association of ideas take a woman's wishes? Without strengthened reason, a woman could be left "at the mercy of wayward Sensibility," according to Burney. Vicesimus Knox warned that many a "connexion," begun "with a fine sentimentality which Sterne has recommended and increased, has terminated in disease, infancy, madness, suicide, and a gibbet."[42]

The quotations from *Evelina, The Hermit of Snowden,* and Lady Mary Wortley Montagu's letter illustrate the existence of severe conflict over the patriarchally enforced code, a conflict women insisted on expressing in their novels. It had been laid out, too, by Richardson's account of Clarissa's anguish over her resistance to her father. Lennox's Arabella adhered to romance's code in that she could not be alone with prospective lovers, could not allow them to write to her, and could not talk to them about love. Yet Arabella also illustrates the internal struggle implicit in the very notion of a sexual code. She pronounced Glanville's name in front of her maid with a sigh which "involuntarily forced its way" through her otherwise strictly codified lips. One of Spacks's illustrations of this psychic conflict is Burney's comment on Mrs. Thrale's faulty technique in trying to repress her passions for Piozzi. "Her fault and grievous misfortune was, not combating them in their origin; not flying even from their menace." The same conflict between spontaneous wish and a code of manners is clear in *A Simple Story,* where Miss Milner was forced to "infringe [a] delicacy, of which she had so proper a sense" in wishing to see a man she loved before he left but after he had formally taken his leave of her. Recovering from her surprise in seeing Valancourt again, Radcliffe's Emily "answered him with a tempered smile; but a variety of opposite emotions still assailed her heart, and struggled to subdue the mild dignity in her manner." Her successful struggle to maintain her "manner" is but one of a larger number in which this exemplary heroine of sensibility "always endeavoured to regulate her conduct by the nicest laws, and whose mind was finely sensible, not only of what is just in morals, but whatever is beautiful in the female character." The tension between feeling and code was intended to sharpen the emotional effect on the sensitive reader who, presumably, experienced the same conflict herself. It must be noted that Emily's "uncommon delicacy" was an expression of her "too exquisite . . . sensibility." Doubts about "excessive sensibility" in women had been expressed by

Richardson and would intensify in keeping with the increasing manifestations of women's minds and feelings in sentimental fiction.[43] The conventional formula of "excessive sensibility" permitted criticism while continuing to sanction the sensibility that had become the defining characteristic of eighteenth-century femininity.[44]

Conflict over the value of the code—and of sensibility—was also expressed outwardly, between women, as the definition of being female reached another critical stage late in the century. Reeve's *Plans of Education* (1792)—written in the form of an epistolary and sentimental novel—accepted that women stood "in need of protectors in every stage of their journey through life" and praised male ideologues of the code, including Addison, Richardson, Fordyce, and Gregory, for standing "forth in behalf of the defenseless part of our sex." On the other hand, Wollstonecraft was one among many writers critical of "women who have fostered a romantic unnatural delicacy of feeling," and she cited "the herd of Novelists" as examples of such women. Austen was ironic about the Richardson rule that a woman wait for a man to declare his love. Hays attributed the "force" Emma Courtney allowed a "first impression" to Emma's "immature" judgment, and even to a "fanaticism" derived in large part from her reading romantic, sentimental novels. And Edgeworth put into the mouth of an exemplary character in *Belinda* the view that the "belief in the inextinguishable nature of a first flame" was a "pernicious doctrine," "dangerous to domestic happiness."[45]

"Whence arises the easy fallacious behaviour of a courtier?" Wollstonecraft asked, and she answered from his need of "evasively feeding hope with the chameleon's food": women "likewise acquire from a supposed necessity, an equally artificial mode of behaviour." The notion that "all the power that they obtain must be obtained by their charms and weakness" was derived from romance. (This was *The Courtier*'s other-directed fashioning of female behavior). What could "save such beings from contempt; even though they be soft and fair[?]" "So ludicrous do these ceremonies appear to me that I scarcely am able to govern my muscles when I see a man start with eager and serious solitude to lift a handkerchief or shut a door when a *lady* could have done it for herself." Wollstonecraft insisted on the connection between romance and the crippling exaggeration of a female sensibility by saying that those who argued on behalf of man's superiority had softened the argument "with chivalrous generosity." Their chivalry was expressed by the argument that "man was made to reason, woman to feel." Her attack on the code was identical with her attack on the gendering of sensibility.[46]

The code of delicacy was symptomatic of the danger posed by women's acculturation to the civilizing process. In effect, Wollstonecraft argued that, because middle-class women were proscribed from work, defined hereditarily, and imbued with aristocratic habits of consumerism and display, they perpetuated feudalism amidst a dynamic, progressive culture that had been put in ferment by middle-class men's increasing individuation of themselves. Middle-class women spread "the seeds of false refinement, immorality, and vanity previously shed by the hereditarily great." By aspiring to become ladies, "brimful of sensibility," women exchanged the possibilities for a fully individuated humanity in "the world" for a rationalization of exclusion and subordination, of which they were to make their very bodies the symbols.[47]

Egotism and Opposition

Wollstonecraft warned women against dismissing that wider world so far monopolized by men.

> The world cannot be seen as an unmoved spectator; we must mix in the throng and feel as men feel, before we can judge of their feelings. If we mean, in short, to live in the world, to grow wiser and better, and not merely enjoy the good things of life, we must attain a knowledge of others at the same time we become acquainted with ourselves. Knowledge acquired any other way only hardens the heart, and perplexes the understanding.

While Wollstonecraft associated women's progress with "the good things of life," sustaining her advocacy of that prosperous, tasteful environment that sponsored good parenting, female literacy, and the prospects for a woman becoming an "individual . . . world in herself," she also emphasized the dangers of the same circumstances, the narrowing effects of identifying women only with a gendered sensibility in withdrawn self-indulgence, segregated from the wider world where it now seemed possible to experience life with men, sharing the feelings there that men had been able to experience. (Griffith, too, had recognized in 1782 that the "neatly furnished" home could become not merely a prison but the altar whereon heroines become sacrificial victims.) Wollstonecraft applied the male apprehension of civilizing effects on themselves—"effeminacy"—to women. "Effeminacy" meant degeneration through "luxury" and "idleness." How much more was that true of women's subjection to the civilizing process! This had been the starting point for the *Rights of Woman*. Her breakthrough had been made in her previous book, where she had called for a life that would "unfold the mind and inspire a manly spirit of independence."[48]

Some modern scholars could be said to have followed this aspect of Wollstonecraft's criticism of sensibility, referring to the "sentimental" innocent's radical inhibition of "individuality." The sentimental heroine's innocence and chastity represent "the self unrealized and inexperienced." (We have just seen that Knox warned that one of sentimentality's disastrous outcomes was to terminate life in "infancy.") The "retreat to the 'simple life' is also the withdrawal to the 'inner life' and its celebration of . . . childhood involves a radical inhibition of all experience." Eighteenth-century fiction and autobiography expressed women's longing "for the emotional freedom of a child." The heroine reduces herself "to a victim whose only experience is suffering and death." To such a view may be added that notable "passivity of the experiencing mind," in other words, the reflexive and suffering cast the culture of sensibility so frequently gave Lockean psychology. (Construing selves as "ceaselessly bombarded" by "the forces of externality" can "invite the passivities of mere consumption.") Sensibility's language tells of nervous disorder and ambiguous susceptibility, including constant vulnerability to one's own "involuntary" feelings.[49] "Submissiveness" was at the core of sentimental novels,—praise for "submission, long-suffering, forgiveness, and self-abasement." This was identification with a feminized Christ, a figure shaped and elevated by the long-suffering women among the followers and hymn writers of heart religion. The repression of sexuality and the martyrdom of wifehood were readily available resources for moral superiority.[50]

All of this seems fair enough: but it is inadequate. The culture of sensibility itself, in its moralizing efforts to shape women and repress their wishes, testifies to the existence of an opposite impulse in the lives of women; indeed, fruitfully torn, the culture incorporated the wishes of assertive, pleasure-seeking women. One should bear in mind those "gamester ladies" Steele described in Bath, neglecting "the little vanities of showing their beauty," and, instead un–self-consciously throwing "their features into violent distortions." Burney tells us they were still going strong in the 1790s. Wollstonecraft also testified to the culture's nourishing prospects for female individualism. Retreats and solitude had their psychological equivalent in the "belief in the sanctity of individual judgement," publicized by way of sentimental heroines from Clarissa to Emma Courtney and Belinda Portman. Once again, a truism about eighteenth-century literary history—the "unprecedented claim" made by the novel for "the validity and significance of the individual experience" in opposition to society—takes on particular meaning when one recognizes its value for each sex. Of the previous world, Laslett writes that almost "no woman ever belonged to England as an individual, except it be a queen regnant . . . or a noble widow and heiress or two, a scattering of relicts of successful merchants and yeomen." Presumably, in this respect, too, "process" was rooted in family psychologies, sponsored by individualizing parents.[51]

Evelina's subtitle, *A Young Lady's Entrance into the World,* indicates that Villars's wishes did not come true. The plot hinged on Evelina's entering the gay and dissipated "world," and we have seen the pleasure she took in it. Lady Howard draws Evelina out from Villars's paternalistic wing by asserting that it was "time that she should see something of the world." Her reason was to get Villars to face up to the reality of "young people's"—young women's as well as young men's—appetites for pleasure, and then to have young people themselves face up to the reality of "the world." Implicitly exposing women to experience of the world was intended to enable them to make the proper moral choices.

> It is time she [Evelina] should see the world. When young people are too rigidly sequestered from it, their lively and romantic imaginations paint it to them as a paradise of which they have been beguiled; but when they are shown it properly, and in due time, they see it such as it really is, equally shared by pain and pleasure, hope and disappointment.

This view of "the world" suggests that Villars's sequestering youth from it was inadequate to the development of selfhood. For whatever reason one did so, to leave home was to see the world "as it really is," experience vital to the development and individuation of human consciousness.[52]

The idea of entering the world is a striking one because it connotes birth or, because of the age of the entrant, rebirth. It suggests that in this eighteenth-century view, "woman" had been fetal as well as childlike—("infantile" in Wollstonecraft's analysis)—in her previous phase of individual life and of history. The parallel to Wesley's metaphor of the awakening of the unborn sinner to a spiritual life is not fortuitous. The century's revolutionary possibilities shaped themselves in accordance with the Lockean vision of psychology, to which the original, unlettered blankness of the child was fundamental. Spacks suggests that it was women's childlike and imaginative awakening of "hidden parts of the personality," previously "concealed" from the "waking adult mind," and their assertion of "the autonomy of the inner self" against "the claims of all mankind," that pointed with special meaning to what the twentieth century has come to understand by "Romanticism." Of course, the same impulse can be found in eighteenth-century male writers, but Spacks suggests that their conflicts could be more "largely self-created." The prospects of awakening and entering the world were especially frightening to women because they were new and because women felt their resources to be tender. It was still more frightening because the environment they wished to enter was dominated by men who were at best ambivalent and, at worst, traditionally hostile to women's entrance. Men embodied material, "sensational" dangers, the most material and sensational of all being sexual ones. Nonetheless, women entered it for reasons of pleasure and egotism, and thereby were able to draw its resources into their homes. Vulnerability, passivity, and self-effacement contradicted themselves to a significant extent by their very articulation and publication. (Even the conduct books demonstrated the unstoppable emergence of female minds.) In their literacy, women left a record of heroism in the face of the hostility they chose to risk. Reading and writing were expressions of individualism, the accompanying self-doubt reflecting the version of individualism that, of necessity, women had to grasp. Literacy might seem to promise women the same possibility for "self-fashioning" that it offered men; but eighteenth-century women tell us in their novels (just as their seventeenth-century predecessors had in their writings) that if women wished to express egotism in entering the world—by publishing—they faced difficulties men did not. Women risking their "honor" by entering the world seemed analogous to the risk taken by women going to market. Their self-fashioning would be limited by this, indeed, would have to incorporate it, in Greenblatt's terms as an additional "institutional" burden of history.[53]

Women's egotism had to cope with constant pressure to keep women segregated from direct experience of "the world." So, for example, *The Spectator* brought pressure to bear against women's behavior as consumers. Its subject was what it called the entire "female world" of the new leisured classes it wished to educate to a level above that of the female past but subordinate to that occupied by men. *The Spectator* refers to its female readers as "ordinary women," existing below those of "a more elevated life and conversation," but it is clear that it was being entirely ironical. It aimed to define "proper employments and diversions for the fair ones[,]" in place of going shopping, making their toilet "their great scene of business," and dressing their hair "the principal employment of their lives." Testifying to such consumer appetites among women, *The Spectator*'s observation was a variant of that expressed by Makin, Astell, and other early feminists, indeed, they could all be said to have anticipated Wollstonecraft. "Their amusements seem contrived for them rather as they are women, than as they are reasonable creatures; and they are more adapted to the sex than the species." The public acknowledgment of women's capacity for reason—of women's minds—was forced on *The Spectator* by its wish to sell itself. It conveyed to all of its readers the significance of Lockean and Newtonian science, hoping to use it to impart the internalization of hierarchy, as it had in its support of literacy for the lower orders.[54]

If *The Spectator* attempted to popularize a distancing aesthetic among all of its readers, it insisted that women's "female world" be constituted still more remotely. Its male readers lived "in the world," even if they also enjoyed the new domestic tea ceremony or regularly distanced themselves from it, to "refine and civilize" their "nature," their hearts softened by the "contemplation of distresses." Prominent in the paper's designated male audience were out-of-work politicians. But women had become self-conscious adherents of party politics, too, along with entering the world as shoppers and consumers of entertainment. Their participation in "public political activity" has been dated precisely to 1641, when they first petitioned Parliament, as participants in the Puritan revolution,[55] a public participation they perpetuated by way of their published writings. Astell illustrates the continuity of women's publishing political views into the eighteenth century. Similarly, Behn's *Oronooko* (1688) had been a serious political novel, like some of the subsequent novels of Manley and Haywood. The *Female Tatler* had posed itself against the politics of Steele's male *Tatler* (1709–11). "Polite urban culture" was "readily exploited" for the promotion of partisan causes by women as well as men.[56]

It is in that context we must regard Addison's reporting in *The Spectator* that, in the winter of 1710, he had witnessed a political demonstration by female Whigs and Tories at the opera. Calling them "Amazons," Addison tried to persuade women to abandon politics. (Middle-class women as well as men had shown extraordinary interest and excitement in the record number of general elections that had followed the Triennial Act, above all in the elections of 1710 and 1713.) Instead of identifying themselves with partisan politics, Addison advised women to subordinate themselves as an unpoliticized, undivided group, their common ground opposition to such male conflict, expressed in female "tears and entreaties," signs of their powerlessness. His illustration of this gendered, apolitical grouping was women's interposition and prevention of battle between Roman and Sabine men. The Sabine women, raped and kept by the Romans, had been no longer identifiable as distinct nationalities but, instead, as the sex characterized by subordination, weakness, and domesticity. "We recommend this noble example to our British ladies, at a time when our country is torn with so many unnatural divisions," the most evident being politics:

> our English women . . . should endeavour to outshine [other nations] in all other accomplishments proper to the sex, and to distinguish themselves as tender mothers, and faithful wives, rather than as furious partizans. Female virtues are of a domestic turn. The family is the proper province for private women to shine in.

Forced to acknowledge women's strong wish to show "their zeal for the public," *The Spectator* complained "let it not be against those who are perhaps of the same family, or at least of the same religion or nation, but against those who are the open, professed, undoubted enemies of their faith, liberty and country." Of course, one of the concerns here was the religious dispute subsumed by the politics of Whig and Tory, whose ancestors had broken out comparatively recently into "civil war and bloodshed." *The Spectator* satirized "the rage of party," against which it posed "good nature, compassion, and humanity," to be adopted by all its readers, but it urged that these terms—political and nonpolitical—take on special meaning according to sex. The Civil War had also heralded the rise of feminists and *The Spectator*'s contemporary feminists were pointing out that, within "their country" and within their families, women confronted political enemies to their "liberty." Those enemies were men, like the Sabines, fathers and brothers, like the Romans, husbands and sons.[57]

Unless *The Spectator* applied itself to "the due regulation of female literature," as one of its putative male correspondents begged, he would not be able to tell the difference between "a gentleman that should make cheesecakes and raise paste, and a lady that reads Locke, and understands the mathematics." Hence, despite its apparent sympathy for women, *The Spectator* articulated serious qualms over its own promulgation of potentially subversive literacy and of revolutionary Locke.[58] Calling for women's withdrawal from the kind of fashionable and political life they had now entered, *The Spectator* chivalrously identified women with a sensibility more "exquisite" than that of men. In keeping with its courtly forebears, but in an entirely new setting, *The Spectator* recommended that women should always show "that gentle softness, tender fear, and all those parts of Life, which distinguish her from the other Sex; with some Subordination to it, but such an Inferiority that makes her still more lovely." *The Spectator*'s twin goals for the reform of gender styles were "to recover the manly modesty in the behaviour of my men readers, and the bashful grace in the faces of my women." Number 231 recommended a "due proportion" of modesty in men—soldiers and orators—as well as in women, but it personified "quick and delicate feeling in the soul" in which modesty exists as female, and made it synonymous with "exquisite sensibility as warns her to shun everything which is hurtful." It was naturally "the characteristic of their sex." It was a quality that "seldom fails to raise a benevolence in the audience toward the person who speaks." All this was consistent with that short-circuiting of the nerve paradigm by gender described in Chapter 1.[59]

Borsay suggests that in the period soon after Addison's appeal "fashionable town culture developed an apolitical, even anti-political complexion," although what part heterosociality may have played in this is not clear. Did men—husbands, fathers, brothers—attempt to make nonpartisanship a prerequisite for taking their women to resorts? In any case, women continued to show "zeal" for public life as well as for undisciplined consumer pleasures. It is important to recognize that unmarried women in the eighteenth century—widows and heiresses—owned more than a sixth of all property, with "unlimited access to the social privileges which property brought," and there was a "growing tendency" for middle-class men to protect themselves and their heirs by providing their wives with legal rights and legal instruments, a tendency historians also have detected in the nascent capitalisms of seventeenth-century Holland and early nineteenth-century America.[60] Historians are beginning to readdress the question of just how women exercised these and even political rights and there are intimations that women participated in local politics more than has been thought. They participated in political campaigns, voted in local elections, and they published political pamphlets and other works, most notably, perhaps, Catherine Macaulay's great Whig *History of England.* All this was within circumstances where only a tiny proportion of men voted. It was not until the idea of the vote's being democratized was popularized in the last third of the century that it was also gendered as "universal manhood suffrage." This direction dovetailed with the triumph of the sexual ideology laid out by *The Spectator,* Barbauld in effect identifying "The Rights of Woman" with sorrow being "universally felt." In *Pamela,* Richardson had endorsed the apolitical nature of the culture of sensibility, the converted Mr. B declaring he thought "the distinction of *whig* and *tory* odious." We have seen the frequency with which other wished-for men of feeling were shown abjuring politics still more strenuously in favor of domestic life with morally superior women of feeling, even though they retained an essential foothold in the public world.[61]

If the literature of sensibility contributed to the triumph of this particular sexual ideology, fiction was also the subject of the struggle between women's wishes and men's attempt to shape them. Adapting its own purposes to the views expressed by the first feminists, *The Spectator* had attempted to guide women away from reading romance. Richardson held up the contrast between the exemplary Clarissa's Bible and the "inflaming novels and idle romances," which "turn girls' heads," putting them in the reach of "common seduction." Facing what he saw as an inexorable tide in women's appetite for sentimental and romantic fiction, Dr. Johnson declared:

> I have often wished (since novels *will* be read) that . . . this species of composition, no longer perverted to the worst purposes, by an abandoned pace of scribblers, might be monopolized by men of genius who have abilities and inclinations to *make* . . . the passions *move at the command of virtue.*[62]

MacKenzie would echo him. While all sentimental writers at the very least paid lip service to this Johnsonian goal, all thereby distinguishing themselves from those who did not, gender was of vital significance to the distinction, or, rather, it was really its subject. The inescapable context was the rise of the popular novel from the very early eighteenth century, written by women against the traditional male monopoly of literacy, learning, and publication, another way of seeing the persistence of the conflict between romance and classicism. Women novelists personified the male imperative to dominate women's literacy in figures like Manley's guardian Duke in *The New Atlantis,* shaping and reshaping Charlot's reading; or Lennox's Glanville, making it his business to "produce a reformation" in Arabella's reading, ridding her of "romantic notions"; Inchbald's Lord Elmwood "warning" Matilda against some authors and selecting others; and Austen's Henry Tilney teaching Catherine Moreland the dysfunctional effects of romance.[63]

Hence, while Burney, Hays, and Austen made declarations of independence, their modes reflected the strength of their opposition. Burney's irony and anonymity were linked in this respect to Hays's presentation of her adherence to the pursuit of pleasure in a heroine ostensibly crazed by an overdeveloped sensibility. Henry Austen noted Jane Austen's ambivalent feelings about her work's reception on the public stage. Despite the gratification of the "applause" which occasionally reached his sister from discriminating readers, he wrote,

> so much did she shrink from notoriety, that no accumulation of fame would have induced her, had she lived to affix her name to any productions of her pen . . . In the bosom of her family she talked to them freely, thankful for praise, open to remark, and submissive to criticism. But in public, she turned away from an allusion to the character of an authoress.

Her "real characteristics" were those of "cheerfulness, sensibility and benevolence." Of all Austen's traits, the most important was that she was orthodox—"thoroughly religious and devout; her opinions accorded strictly with those of the Church of England."[64]

It was within what Barbauld called the "bounds of female authorship" that the culture of sensibility was expected to flourish. Women were urged to keep their experience of the world vicarious. Hume noted women's "aversion to matters of fact" in favor of their "appetite for novels and romances." He recommenced the study of history to "the ladies" especially, as a way of transcending the same "trifling pastimes" for which *The Spectator* had taken women to task, but doing so safely. Here Hume was recharging the advice given "young Ladies" by *The Ladies Library* of 1714; history supplied "illustrious Patterns of Virtue, which will make Stronger Impressions on their Minds . . . and give them a Contempt for the common Amusements of the Sex." They would be thus enlarged and elevated; "let them not have so mean an Opinion of themselves as to think they are incapable of improving by [reading history]." Studying history, Hume said, allowed women to "see all the human race, from the beginning of time, pass as it were, in review before" them. The exposure would maintain proper distance between person and experience. It acquainted women "with human affairs, without diminishing in the least from the most delicate sense of virtue." This was of profoundly ambiguous value. The study of history amplifies one's knowledge of human beings in a way that nothing else can. It can nourish the potential for self-fashioning and, as Mandeville suggested by way of Lucinda, the invaluable exercise of personal power in private relationships. On the other hand, to study history as a substitute for actual engagement with the wider world on the grounds of maintaining virtue could rationalize segregation and powerlessness.[65]

Following Hume, Austen suggested in *Northanger Abbey* that women readers' undisciplined pleasure in sentimentalism found history antipathetic; it was all about the remote acts of authoritarian men. In her unreformed state, Austen's Catherine Morland defended sentimental fiction and said she could not be interested in "tiresome," "solemn" history, "the men all so good for nothing, and hardly any women at all." She was corrected by Eleanor Tilney, who illustrated her argument by referring expressly to Hume. History in such an historian's hands could be "as much depended on . . . as anything that does not actually pass under one's own observation." Here, Elinor and her brother persuaded Catherine of the value of greater tough-mindedness, in fact, of the need for more rigorous "taste" in the consumer pleasures of literacy, but Elinor's opportunity to learn such a lesson depended on the arbitrary fact of her having a sympathetic brother. Henry had "entered on" his "studies" at Oxford, while Elinor, as he said to her, was "a good little girl working your sampler at home."[66]

The drive to segregate women in domesticity could make particularly invidious the "vicarious experience" Peter Burke notes of literacy's possibilities. The argument was made, at least from the 1670s, that novels led women away from "the real world" and substituted for it a "dangerous view of life." David Fordyce said that novels stimulated "extravagant desires and notions of happiness alike fantastic and false" to the extent that "the whole system of life seems converted into romance." Barbauld defended the contribution of tales of chivalry to the religion of sensibility, but elsewhere she recognized the dangers in sentimental "romances," criticizing "fictitious sorrow" for its vicariousness. "We" readers of "romances," she wrote, "are induced to acquiesce with greater patience in our own lot by beholding pictures of life," pictures, that is, of people worse off than the reader. The segregated watchers of Hume's parade of life could turn inward on themselves. Burney suggested that if "wayward Sensibility" could impel "to all that is most disinterested for others" it could also "forget all mankind, to watch the pulsations of its own fancies." Barbauld's metaphor for the pleasure of sympathizing with distress is literally one of consumption, even self-consumption: "we take upon ourselves this burden of adscititious sorrows in order to feast upon the consciousness of our own virtue." This self-conscious theme in the culture of sensibility was a reflection on its distancing aesthetic and an indication of further inner conflict.[67]

Campbell presents the eighteenth-century appetite for sentimental novels, filled with "indulgence" in the "luxury of grief," as an illustration of consumer psychology—"dream play" permitting "autonomous hedonism." "Literacy, in conjunction with individualism," was the key development in emotional self-determinism "because it grants the individual a form and degree of symbolic manipulation which was previously restricted to groups." His insistence on the possibilities for autonomy in these pleasures suggests one reason why novels and the "dream-play" of consumerism proved so attractive to women, but dangerous in the eyes of self-doubters and unambiguous critics of both novel reading and fashionable women. Typically sentimental novelists praised "an imagination which is desirous of cultivating melancholy ideas." It is not surprising that a person whose imagination was excessively cultivated in such a direction could fall in love with a picture, as Emma Courtney fell in love with the portrait of her landlady's son. Virginia, a character in Edgeworth's *Belinda,* also fell in love with a portrait. Virginia's "imagination," wrote Edgeworth, "exalted by solitude and romance, embodied and became enamoured of a phantom."[68]

Literacy's other pleasures also could be ambiguous for women. One of them was "relief," one of *The Spectator*'s distancing pleasures. By definition, relief assumed a prior condition of pain. Clarissa's abused mother wrote "My heart is full: writing may give some vent to my griefs, and perhaps, I may write what lies most upon my heart." One acknowledges the psychological value of such expression but must see, too, its reactive, limited quality for selfhood. Emma Courtney concluded a letter, in which she had described how "*exquisitely wretched*" she was (becoming a Rousseauistic "poor solitary wanderer"), by telling her correspondent that while "pouring itself out on paper, my tortured mind has experienced a momentary relief." She went on to say that such unrestrained pouring out of feelings was intended to awaken "tender sympathies." Distress was the posture and subject of women who said they were writing to relieve it. In Emma Courtney's case, intended by Hays to illustrate the effects on women of "excessive sensibility," the whole world of experience impinged on her with unbearable pain. Lockean sensationalism could be a metaphor for near total vulnerability, a sense that Shaftesbury and some of his contemporary males, expressing their sense of vulnerability to new "market forces" even if they created them, had associated with being female. More specifically, Hays said, consciously echoing Wollstonecraft and linking her ambiguity to a process of internalization, the distress women suffered was derived from the fact that they operated in a world dominated by men.[69]

Presumably writers of fiction who declared that writing about distress brought relief were being autobiographical. Wollstonecraft demonstrates as much. She wrote to a friend in 1786: "I scarce know what I write, yet my writing at all, when my mind is so disturbed, is proof to you that I can never be lost so intirely in misery as to forget those I love." She was subject to chronic depression. Her surviving letters suggest that it was in the period from the fall of 1787 to the spring of

1793 (from when she had begun her first book through the publication of her masterpiece in late 1792) that she was least subject to its effects.

> Many motives impel me besides sheer love of knowledge, which however has ever been a predominate mover in my little world, it is the only way to destroy the worm that will gnaw the core—and make that being an isolé, whom nature made too susceptible of affections, which stray beyond the bounds reason prescribes.

Developing her mind—her individuality in her own conception—was her answer to what she saw as the destructive effects of an overdeveloped, albeit natural, sensibility, according to her analysis decisively compounded by the rearing and acculturation of females and their acquiescence to male demands. Maria, the autobiographical heroine of Wollstonecraft's fictional sequel of the *Rights of Woman,* found writing the only way "to escape from sorrow, and the feverish dreams of ideal wretchedness of felicity, which equally weaken the intoxicated sensibility." In the largest perspective of the kindred phenomena—women's literacy and women's publishing novels, whose collective voice expressed women's feelings about gender under the conditions Wollstonecraft described—one may see the historical meaning of the enormous "relief," which, in Radcliffe's words, was "the relief which an overburdened mind finds in speaking of the subject of its interest."[70]

The struggle drew women together, their literature evidence of common ground among the growing number of literate women; this clearly was crucial to the rise of a culture. Sentimental novelists told their distresses to their readers—often in epistolary novels—as if the readers were correspondents, participants in family secrets conveyed by the family code, a family based on sympathy rather than blood or marriage. Writers suggested that the understanding they shared with readers was so mutual it could be left implicit. Fielding had alluded to this convention when he avoided describing his heroine Sophia's "sensations." The "reader's heart if she or he have any will better represent [them] than I." Without any of Fielding's irony and therefore with more typical sentimentality, Radcliffe declared: "It is unnecessary to say with what emotion Emily . . . watched the declining sun . . . sink towards the province which Valancourt inhabited." To leave implicit was, of course, an abjuration of consciousness. At the same time, the notion also assumed the existence of common ground, a pervasive assumption expressed by a variety of conventions, especially invidious ones. A reviewer of *The Man of Feeling* said "the reader that weeps not over some of the scenes it describes has no sensibility of mind." Radcliffe aggrandized readers in telling them, that "the fire of the poet is vain, if the mind of the reader is not tempered, like his own, however it may be inferior to his in power." A 1776 writer thought that women writers seemed to be animated by the wish to "vindicate the honor of women in general rather than for acquiring to themselves the individual reputation of great accomplishments." As useful and as comforting as the common ground may have been to women, it could also be a boundary and, again, a source of conflict with which egotism had to cope.[71]

The Reality of Heroism and Romance

That women's revolutionary literacy had to contend with powerful, reactionary pressures helps explain the most obvious characteristics of the female protagonists of sentimental literature. They were literate and they were heroic. "This girl is always scribbling," said Mr. B of Pamela. Her letters and her journal are a record of the "dreadful trial" through which she passed, which proved Pamela's wit, sincerity, and innocence. These "fruits" of her heroic pen were tantamount to Pamela's writing a "novel," of which she was the heroine, under circumstances where she had to conceal pen, paper, and manuscript, secreting them from the hostile vigilance of a powerful, rakish man and his agents. Belford said of Clarissa, "there was never a woman so young who wrote so much and with such celerity." She thereby left a record of her own heroism. She compared her own deathbed behavior to that of the "great Duke of Luxemburgh, the conqueror of armies and subduer of nations." Clarissa had defeated the military strategies of General Lovelace, her correspondence triumphing over his "rakish annals."[72]

The heroism of women's reading is the subject of Lennox's *Female Quixote.* In *Don Quijote,* Cervantes had satirized a man who projects onto reality the "romance" he derived from reading, but he also depicted Don Quijote as admirable in his idealism, in some respects a hero, too. From her very title Lennox asserted her own literary ambition and her heroine's equality in reading as well as in folly. Arabella's "foible" was to model herself on "all the heroines" of the romances she had read. Identifying herself with the heroines of romance, she can resist her father; the ambiguity of Lennox's form allows the reader to think the narrator sympathizes with romances that call "the remonstrances of parents' persecutions," and resistance to those persecutions, "constancy and courage." Arabella is prepared by her reading to defend women generally against men's calumniating "the sex." In her reading, whatever its misguided subject, Arabella has shown herself capable of "Herculean labour." Not only did Arabella's mastery of romance make her in understanding "superior to most" women; her "extensive readings" gave her "the superiority" to men who affected "great reading" but whose knowledge was "superficial." She declared that it was "the perusal of books from which all useful knowledge may be drawn; which gives us the most shining examples of generosity, courage, virtue, and love; which regulate our actions, form our manners, and inspire us with a great and noble desire of emulating those great, heroic, and virtuous actions." In apparently joining the century-long criticism of women's substitution of fantasy for reality, Lennox demonstrated women's heroism even in reading fantasy, and she illustrates Lackington's view of the value of "Romances" for "utilitarian self-education," which specified a list that began with Cervantes and included Lennox.[73]

In sum, if heroines were most ostentatiously writers and readers, then writing and reading was seen as heroic by those who created or identified with them. Wollstonecraft, looking explicitly to Clarissa, Lady Grandison, and Sophie for her lineage, called the autobiographical Mary "the Heroine of this Fiction." She was a heroine because she "displayed" the "mind of a woman who has thinking powers." In "a fiction, such a being may be allowed to exist whose grandeur is derived from the operations of its own faculties, not subjugated to opinion, but drawn by the individual from the original source." This was also a declaration of individualism. Given the obstacles women faced: reared against developing their minds; denied learning or, if they achieved it, being called "monstrous"; forced to square their urge for self-expression with accusations of sexual impropriety and worse; finding their authorship ridiculed as "scribbling" and novels sneered at; feeling in their reading that they were subject to sadistic pressure; in the teeth of all of this, achieving literacy, women novelists presented women's writing and reading as heroic, and created heroines with whom their woman readers could feel themselves especially qualified to identify. This was one way in which women's ostensibly romantic fiction was realistic.[74]

The heroism of sentimental fiction was shaped in part by its legacy from romance as well as sixteenth- and seventeenth-century antiromance, of which *Don Quijote* is the best known, although it looked back to *Orlando Furioso*.[75] The assault on romance had been "to some degree internalized by romances as self-criticism" during the seventeenth century. Because they ran the risk of inheriting the mockery still accorded romance and because they faced the continuing vitality of a backward-looking, aristocratic ideology, eighteenth-century novelists continued to distance themselves from romance.[76] (Wollstonecraft's opposition to women's perpetuation of feudal manners, which she linked to their reading romantic/sentimental novels, also perpetuated this theme.) Yet, in rejecting what Defoe called romance's "Errors," "Inconsistencies," and "Contradictions in the Fact," the novel also depended on "romantic elements." The difference was one of "degree rather than kind." The complexities of romance/antiromance illustrate literature's "dialectical gesture of recapitulation and repudiation" described by Mikhail Bakhtin, but, again, a phenomenon takes on fresh meaning when one introduces considerations of sex, in this case the revolutionary and conflicted circumstances created by the emergence of women writers and opposition to them.[77]

Sentimental-antisentimental novels extended the overlapping romantic/antiromantic dialectic. Mr. B had called Pamela's moral values, her letters, her representation of their plots and counterplots, and her refusal to barter her "honour" for gold mere "romantic folly." Once moved by her sentimental power and her "tale," however, he discovers they are real. She epitomizes the "redefinition" and "relocation" of honor in women.[78] *The Female Quixote* also shows the continuities between the romances Lennox parodies and the culture of sensibility then coming into flower; this is the case, for example, in its representation of women. A letter of John Kemble to Inchbald illustrates the same conflation. When Inchbald first began *A Simple Story* in 1778, Kemble asked her, "Pray how far are you advanced in your new novel?—what new characters have you in it—what situations? how many distressed damsels and valorous knights? how many prudes, how many coquettes? what libertines, what sentimental rogues in black and empty cut-throats in red?" Eliza, the neglected young wife obsessed with sentimental novels in Wollstonecraft's *Mary*, saw her fantasized lover as both man of feeling and as a "knight-errant."[79]

Sentimental fiction was "pervaded" by romance throughout the century. Other women writers, in addition to Lennox, agreed with Makin, Astell, Shaftesbury, *The Spectator*, Johnson, and Hume that romance held a profound appeal for women. Burney acknowledged women's addiction to it in the preface to *Evelina* and went on to "condemn" the romances which led young boarding school ladies to construe themselves as "damsels." Burney conceded that her emphasis on reason, sober probability, and the simplicity of nature would disappoint, or at least moderate, her readers' appetite for more extreme and transporting pleasures of the fantasy, the luxury, and the marvelous associated with "Romance."[80] This contrast was identical with the distinction generally made by the literature of sensibility between a sensibility tempered by reason and the "excessive" kind, given over entirely to "feeling" and to romance, a variation of the ambiguous struggle between romance and antiromance personified in the contrast between the Countess and Arabella in *The Female Quixote.* It was reiterated in conflicted heroines or in doubled sets of women characters throughout the century, permitting novelists simultaneously to perpetuate sentimental and romantic values and to satirize their being taken to an extreme. If Evelina exemplifies reason, simplicity, and tasteful pleasures, she is also a "heroine" from the beginning, constantly under siege from masculine dragons, until finally elevated above them by virtue and her noble rescuer. Her captures and rescues represent one set of romantic themes, and the fact that her tale is the "progression of the life of a young woman of obscure birth but conspicuous beauty" represents another, "the quest, the rise and progress of a low-born or apparently low-born hero" now made a heroine.[81]

In the Gothic novel, a variant within the sentimental genre,[82] "the spirit of romance" broke out in full force. Radcliffe's *Udolpho* was typical. It was set in the late sixteenth century but its heroines, already thus "romanticized" in time, were feudalized still farther back. One of them, named Blanche, like a famous medieval queen, had been immersed in "reliques of romantic fiction" and "antient Provencal romances." Approaching an "antient mansion" with "gothic features," she fancied herself approaching a castle, from whose battlements knights looked out on "some champion below, who, clothed in black armor, comes . . . to rescue the fair lady of his love from the oppression of his rival." Yet even *Udolpho* pays lip service to antiromantic, antisentimental values. All of the Gothic apparitions and mysteries are carefully given rational explanations. The chief female protagonist is modern insofar as she is always accompanied by her books, tangible products of eighteenth-century commerce. Most significantly in this antiromantic regard, Radcliffe tells the reader that Emily's chief problem is that she has a "too exquisite" "degree of susceptibility," reflecting her "uncommon delicacy of mind." Her father wished "to strengthen her mind; to enure her to habits of self-command, and to look with cool examination upon the disappointments he threw in her way." Radcliffe's apparent wish to teach women of her era to check their outflow of sensibility with the firmness of reason is the same as Burney's, Austen's, and Wollstonecraft's, all parallel to Hume and Smith's goal in holding up modified Stoicism as a male ideal.[83]

The ambiguities in the culture's refrain that sensibility and romance be tempered by reason reflected the circumstances of writers and readers, including the conflict between their wishes and their needs as they became more conscious of their ability to express them. The social rise of Cinderellas like Pamela and Evelina, marrying princes, represents the adaptation of romance's structure to a "greater conformity with ordinary experience" and, one may add, to the wishes of a newly literate group. While ostensibly writing "On Romances," in fact, Mrs. Barbauld presents her subjects as those of "common life." Romance transformed by the novel was fundamentally the expression of the needs and wishes of eighteenth-century women readers.[84] Earlier tales of chivalry—of El Cid or Guy of Warwick, for example—had shown their knights' main interest to be in "not love but war," corresponding to the behavior described by Elias. Under the influence of the transition to the *minnesang* and then seventeenth-century French culture, romances came to depict what Congreve in 1692 called "the Constant Loves and Invincible Courages of Hero's, Heroines . . . where lofty Language, miraculous Contingencies and impossible Performances, elevate . . . the Reader into a giddy Delight . . . [in] Knights success [in relieving] their Damosels Misfortunes." As we saw in the last chapter, central to the eighteenth-century sentimental novel were the most salient of these themes—courteous, mannerly males, governed by a deeply internalized code of sexual morality, making the relief of distressed and reverenced women their highest purpose, fighting off monstrous and bestial figures who capture and assault women.[85]

So sentimental fiction's romantic themes corresponded to women's historical reality in an obvious way, that is, in women's real or potential relationships with men. Dr. Johnson had poured scorn on romance and called for his contemporary writers to incorporate the "experience" they derived from "accurate observation of the living world." He wanted "men of genius" to take over the novel because he had strong doubts about women's capacity for judgment. Novels should be "conduct books," their moral purpose "to teach the means of avoiding the snares which are laid by Treachery for Innocence." Burney, too, in this regard a Mandevillean, saw "experience" as the cure for romance.[86] Yet if the disabling effects of preferring fantasy for reality must be seen as one profound historical danger tempting women, it is also true that the "avoidance of snares laid by Treachery for Innocence" corresponded to women's "experience" of men. The psychological analyses, the representations of family dynamics, inheritance law, material culture, urban life, and so forth are densely realistic in *Clarissa* but so, too, are the relations between the heroine and her pursuer. Lovelace, his ostensible purpose to help the beautiful, naturally noble young daughter to escape her tyrant-father, asks "was ever a hero in romance (fighting with giants and dragons excepted) called on to harder trials?" If he was depicted as a serpent, the irony of this self-fashioning man of the world allowed this to be antiromance, too.[87] Wollstonecraft's adaptation of Gothicism to depict "the Wrongs of Woman" at the hands of husbands who prostituted their wives or committed them to madhouses—indeed, a whole system of laws merely expressing male domination—was realistic. "Was not the world a vast prison and women born slaves?"[88]

The same may be said of *Northanger Abbey,* in which, like Wollstonecraft, Austen challenged the meanings of "heroine" to women readers. (Austen admired Lennox's *The Female Quixote.*)[89] Catherine Morland's expectations of "Northanger Abbey" were shaped by her reading of such novels as Radcliffe's *Udolpho.* Her addiction to sentimental Gothic fiction had led her to apprehend that Henry's father, General Tilney, had murdered his wife. In puncturing Catherine's fantasy, Henry referred her to "English" and "Christian" reality, and he asked her to consult her own "observation of what is passing around you—Does our education prepare us for such atrocities?" The next day, Catherine takes Henry's advice, but in so doing she begins to rekindle her doubts of the general: "in the central part of England there was surely some security for the existence even of a wife not beloved, in the laws of the land and the manners of the age." The delicate irony of "surely" reminds us that in English law, marriage "incapacitated" a woman, although some changes in the law must have further fueled expectations rising with literacy and Britain's consumer society. The general prevents Elinor from marrying the man she loves to keep her a virtual prisoner, serving his domestic needs. Elinor will say to Catherine, "you must have been long enough in this house to see that I am but a nominal mistress of it, that my real power is nothing."[90]

In fact, General Tilney is a modernized tyrant. That he is a big political power in that "central part of England" is manifest from the "postilions handsomely liveried and numerous outriders properly mounted," to the grounds and buildings of Northanger Abbey itself, outside and inside demonstrating "all the profusion and elegance of modern taste"—the general's taste, that is. His acres adjoining the house, surrounded by "countless" walls, with "a village of hothouses," are worked by "a whole parish" and "unrivalled in the kingdom." Inside, the "General's improving hand had not loitered" even in the kitchens, where "every modern invention" facilitated "the labour of the cooks." He was himself an inventor of such labor-saving devices. Sweeping away the feudal characteristics which Catherine had anticipated, General Tilney had put up a new building next to the abbey for "offices." Filled with workers "constantly appearing," the general's house and its support system epitomized the economic focus "the big house" was in the eighteenth century, but anticipated, too, the factory.

Its master's interests included his immersion in "the affairs of the nation" and his purchases were carefully made "to encourage the manufacture of his country." The attentive consumer could learn that the general's Staffordshire breakfast set was as elegant as those made in Dresden or at Sêvres. The general ran his family as he ran his domains, "always a check upon his children's spirits, and scarcely anything was said but by himself." He was like a despotic industrialist to his children; Elinor and Catherine found General Tilney "pacing the drawing room, his watch in his hand, and having, on the very instant of their entering, pulled the bell with violence, ordered "Dinner to be on *table directly.*"[91]

Discovering that Catherine is not an heiress, the general dismisses her cruelly; he "acted neither honourably nor feelingly, neither as a gentleman nor a parent." Austen reminds us of the romantic mode that earlier she had parodied. "I bring back my heroine to her home in solitude and disgrace." One outcome was that Catherine came to feel "that in suspecting General Tilney of either murdering or shutting up his wife she had scarcely sinned against his character." The doubt expressed in her first postdisillusionment thought (that there was "surely" some security for the existence of a wife) has grown into the realization that unfeeling, "grossly uncivil" masculine tyrants really existed, perhaps more dangerous than ever with their adaptation to modern politics and "improvement." The "fancied" Gothic terror of masculine abuse of women is brought into relationship with the abuse that certainly was possible "in central England." This was part of the world's reality to which Austen wished to awaken readers further, enabling women to regard them "without curiosity or terror."[92]

Subversive Potentials in Women's Developing Minds: Marriage and Class

The revolutionary nature of women's literacy also raised disturbing issues about marriage and class. Feminists from Astell to Wollstonecraft justified female education on the grounds that it would improve relations between wives and husbands, but the persistence of such an argument testified to the strength of the opposite belief.

On this issue, as on the others registered by women's first mass literacy, the evidence of fiction and fact endorse each other. *The Spectator* claimed to print the complaint of a young shopkeeper that his wife's preference for learning over "the affairs of the house" threatened to ruin him.[93] The disparity between a literate and even learned woman and her spouse—or potential spouse—played a fundamental part in the plot of *Clarissa.* The "extraordinary" Clarissa, more intelligent and better educated than her university-learned brother, protests to one of the male enforcers, her uncle Antony (who held that literacy was "too much" for young girls' "judgements"): "if I *am* to be compelled, let it be in favor of a man that can read and write—that can *teach* me something: for what a husband must that man make who can do nothing but command; and needs himself the instruction he should be qualified to give?" Conversely, she writes of Solmes, the husband planned for her: "what a degree of patience, what a greatness of soul is required in the wife, not to despise a husband who is more ignorant, more illiterate, more low-minded than herself?" She refused to bear such a husband who would rule her merely in virtue of "the prerogatives" of being male, treating her merely as a physical creature. "He has not the least delicacy. His principal view in marriage is not to the mind." He would not notice if Clarissa did not show him "tenderness." In short, there is a huge disparity between Solmes and Clarissa in terms of sensibility, that is, consciousness in mind and feeling.[94]

During the 1750s and 1760s Grace Growden Galloway wrote sentimental poems expressing her desperate unhappiness with her husband. Her daughter explained it by telling her children, "Your Grandfather was a good man, but your G[ran]dmother . . . had great sensibility." Wollstonecraft suggested that the disparity between a woman's positive development of mind and a man's derogation of it and all other expressions of her sensibility sharpened the effects of "matrimonial despotism."

> I cannot suppose any situation more distressing, than for a woman of sensibility, with an improving mind, to be bound to such a man as I have described [exploitative, despotic, brutal, and without sensibility] for life; obliged to renounce all the humanizing affections, and to avoid cultivating her taste, lest her perception of grace and refinement of sentiment, should sharpen to agony the pangs of disappointment.

Here she expressed in fiction the running theme in her letters to Imlay, the contrast between her own "romantic" qualities of delicacy and sensibility and his "brutal insensibility," which she associated with his "hard-headed" money getting. Wollstonecraft acknowledged that it corresponded to a literary motif going back to Vanbrugh's *The Provoked Wife*'s complaints against Sir John Brute.[95]

There are frequent scenes in sentimental novels where men are shown hostile to women's development of their minds, in *Sir Charles Grandison* and in Burney's *Evelina,* for example, and another in Hays's *Emma Courtney.* In the latter, during a discussion in which the heroine compares the position of women to slaves, one of her interlocutors asked rhetorically, "what have *servants,* or *women,* to do with *thinking?*" One man suggests that "the elegant and tasteful arrangement of ornaments" requires ladies to think, but Emma "coolly" declares that "some of the gentlemen present should object to a woman's exercising her discriminating powers, is not wonderful, since it might operate greatly to their disadvantage." This was the application to women of the argument made on behalf of the development of male minds—recently by MacKenzie but going back to very early in the century. Emma wittily defends rationalism in both sexes, resulting in one of her adversaries admitting that "of all things I dread a female wit."[96]

There is some suggestion in eighteenth-century fiction that the educated woman threatened to subvert the class system as well as male authority in marriage. In *Tom Jones* Fielding described the uppity servant, Jenny Jones, "spending all her time in reading," thereby becoming "greatly superior" to her master.[97] The "scribbling" Pamela is the most striking and influential illustration of the potential mobility of literate women in fiction. Pamela's aristocratic husband avowed, "I have preferred her to all of her sex, of whatever degree." It is well known that Richardson tempered the apparent social disorder in this by insisting it could be squared with the male prerogative. According to this view, men remained distinguished as a hierarchy; women must subordinate themselves in a category defined solely by their gender and their sexual honor. Making a virtue of necessity, women could construe this as common ground.[98]

Another location for the struggle over women's awakening was the boarding school, increasing in numbers throughout the century, and directly associated with female consumerism and their enjoyment of public, heterosocial pleasures. London's newly fashionable suburbs and the other resort towns were "ideal settings" for boarding schools because parents could combine business with pleasure in checking on their daughters there and enjoy "the full round of public recreations into which the young belles were to be initiated." The ability of lesser orders to disguise their offspring's origins by sending them to boarding schools provoked a stream of outrage. In 1759 it was said that "every description of tradesmen sent their children to be instructed not in the useful attainments necessary for humble life, but the arts of coquetry and self-consequence, in short of those of a young lady." The "self-consequence" learned at boarding schools was akin to the "independent spirit" of servants "dressing up" like their mistresses, and even the egotism declared by Burney.[99] While depending on the increase in female literacy and purchasing power, the *Sentimental Magazine* maintained its snob appeal by complaining in 1772 about the equalizing tendencies of all those young ladies' boarding schools which had sprung up in villages near London. "The expense is small and hither the blacksmith, the ale-house keeper, the shoemaker, etc. sends his daughter, who from the moment she enters these walls becomes a young lady." The "plan" of these schools ought to have been distinguished from those intended for the daughters of the gentry and nobility, in order to prepare their pupils for their "stations in life." Instead, the boarding school curriculum was the same everywhere, "and the daughter of one of the lowest shopkeepers at one of these schools is as much miss and young lady as the daughter of the first viscount at the other." [100]

In offering her own *Plans of Education,* Clara Reeve complained that "children of farmers, artificers and mechanics" are taught "to act out the part of young ladies" and disdain "to match with their equals." "All degrees are blended together in these schools, to the utmost disadvantage of all the parties concerned." Such a concern with the social confusion generated by commercial and consumer society overlapped with the widespread concern over the effects of fashion and with the "dissolution" of all boundaries in the masquerade. Reeve may have been influenced here by Day's sentimental *Sandford and Merton.* She combined the same refrain with Day's vision of the sexual decline of men and his contrast between the 1780s obsession with "conveniences" and fashions and a putative golden, peasant age "when we were all happy and healthy and our affairs prospered," when, too, it might be said, men were men and women were women. In 1789, however, farmers' daughters in general expressed sheer willfulness in their fashions. They

> must have their hats and feathers, and riding habits; their heads as big as bushels, and even their hind quarters stuck out with cork or pasteboard; but scarcely one of them can milk a cow, or churn, or bake, or do any one thing that is necessary in a family.

This corresponds to Stubbs's painting of women harvesters, although clearly they were able to combine fashion with work. What "we" need, Day said, was the government "to send them all to their new settlements," where the golden age was in full swing, and in return "to bring us a cargo of plain, honest housewives, who have never been at boarding schools."[101]

Inchbald's purpose in *A Simple Story,* published the year before Reeve's *Plans of Education,* was the advocacy of "A PROPER EDUCATION" for women. Among the improper kind was that given its heroine, Miss Milner, by "a Protestant boarding-school" (Inchbald was a Catholic) which taught her "merely such sentiments of religion, as young ladies of fashion mostly imbibed," along with "all the endless pursuits of personal accomplishments . . . [and] left her mind without one ornament." This education for consumerism and the marriage market contributed to Miss Milner's sexual disgrace.[102] Other late-century critics included More, Trimmer, and Wollstonecraft. In fact, the marital expectations with which the education of increasing numbers of middle- and even lower-class daughters were invested were believed to have contributed to a glut on the market. In 1781 John Howlett explained the high proportion of unmarried daughters among the urban lower class as a result of

> a certain pride of station; a shame and fear of descending beneath it; a superior, perhaps, a false, refinement of thought; a luxury and delicacy of habit; a tenderness of body and mind, which rendering formidable the prospect of poverty, and thereby checking the impulses of nature, frequently prevent matrimonial connections.

The argument that the education of women's minds came at the expense of their "nature," destined for subordination to reproduction, would be a familiar one in the future, along with a romanticized view of female health in a pastoral age.[103] The attack on boarding schools as promulgators of frivolous accomplishments continued into nineteenth-century reform and feminism, accompanying the continuation of the boarding school enterprise and the ambitions that sustained it.[104]

The sins of boarding school education included its encouragement of sentimental novel reading. The sentimental, novel-reading, boarding school young lady became a type, as Burney assumed in the preface to *Evelina.* In contrast to her brother John, a student at Oxford, Smollett's Lydia Melford had been placed in a boarding school, where she remained "remarkably simple and ignorant of the world." John and his uncle apprehended that Lydia's boarding school accomplishments had made her "deficient in spirit, and so susceptible—and so tender forsooth!—truly, she has got a languishing eye, and reads romances." Lydia viewed herself as a romantic heroine, seeing Bath's buildings as enchanted castles. She was led by her reading "romances" to substitute fantasy for reality and to become sexually "inflammable." A character in Edgeworth's *Belinda* (1801) was the same type, the mother of an illegitimate child who had been "scarcely sixteen when [her lover] ran away with her from a boarding-school; he was at that time a gay officer, she a sentimental girl who had been spoiled by early novel-reading." In 1802, saying that female boarding schools were a "substantial part of the market for pornographic literature," the Society for the Suppression of Vice prosecuted some tradesmen for "selling pornographic snuffboxes to girls' schools." Its groundwork had been laid by the associations between boarding schools, novel reading, and sexual subversiveness.[105]

Why did sentimental novels condemn boarding schools when, it seems, those institutions played an important part in creating an audience addicted to sentimental novels? Perhaps the paradox can be explained as a kind of compromise formation. Women insisted on writing effectively uncontrollable letters to each other; they publicly foreswore "clandestine correspondence," in potentially subversive and immoral fiction which itself was simultaneously raising serious questions about male authority and deferring to that authority's claim to control female literacy. Condemning the dangerous effects of boarding schools while continuing to benefit from them was a branch of the same phenomenon. Such a dialectic marked the revolutionary innovations of literacy, novel writing, novel publishing, and women's expression of consumer wishes generally. One finds women's shaping themselves by expressing their own wishes combined with their necessary awareness and internalization of the powerful wishes of men.[106]

Still More Subversive Potentials: Sensibility and Sex

Women's literacy dramatized the reality of women's secret wishes and private wills. Women used clandestine correspondence and consequent elopement to escape authoritarian families. There was a relationship between such realities and the popularity of clandestine marriage as a theatrical theme in the period, 1677–1714, whence it entered the novel.[107] The subversiveness of servant Pamela marrying up and the subsequent literary reactions to the novel were, among other things, signs of the concern over uncontrollable marriages. Lawrence Stone describes the crystallization of responses to subversiveness and clandestinicity in the Hardwicke Marriage Act (1753). Women's ability to write and read letters contributed decisively to their sexual self-assertion in elopement and clandestine correspondence, a frequent subject of sentimental fiction. So, too, did reading novels. Richardson's account of "giddy creatures . . . who . . . without any regard to decorum, leap walls, drop from windows, and steal away, from their parent's house to the seducer's bed" was informed by earlier warnings that these were the effects of women's reading novels. Elizabeth Carter blamed the example of Julie, in Rousseau's *La nouvelle Heloïse,* for the elopement of Kitty Hunter with the married earl of Pembroke, and Anna Laetitia Aikin's brother attributed her succumbing to the "unstable Frenchman"—thereby becoming Mrs. Barbauld, theologian of sensibility—to the same novel.[108]

Even with no particular prospects of elopement, women could be sexually aroused by reading novels, thereby readied for seduction. This was a powerful note in the attack on women's reading. In 1709 Mandeville described Antonia's reading "plays and romances," letting her fancy rove; sometimes as she did so, she "passionately" threw herself backward, Lucinda told her, "clapping your Legs alternatively over one another [to], squeeze your Thighs together with all the Strength you had, and in a quarter of an hour repeat the same." Two years previously, John Marshall's *The School for Love* had been prosecuted for publicizing such female masturbation techniques, and it seems likely Mandeville was challenging this prosecution.[109] Haywood's *Love in Excess* (1719) agreed that novels "prepared the reader's mind for 'Amorous Impressions.'" Throughout the century writers warned that novels turned women on.[110] According to George Colman,

> 'Tis NOVEL most beguiles the female heart.
> Miss reads—she melts—she sighs—
> Love steals upon her—
> And then—Alas, poor girl!—good night, poor Honour!

MacKenzie suggested that prostitution was the horrible end to a course of events initiated by plays, novels, and "those poetical descriptions of the beauty of virtue and honour, which the circulating libraries easily afforded." When an "alarming increase of prostitutes" was detected in 1790, it was blamed on novels. Medical experts supported the connection, translating it into diagnosis: the 1775 translation of a French work on "nymphomania" suggested that malady, too, could be caused by reading novels.[111]

From the preliterate age and overlapping with the rise of women's literacy, popular and scientific belief held that "lascivious words," spoken *by a man,* prepared a woman for the orgasm in copulation with him that ensured conception. (The belief would persist through the nineteenth century.)[112] A woman reading lascivious words for herself was a different matter, providing a further explanation for the frequent representation of men's attempting to control women's reading. It also seems possible that critics of women's novel reading sexualized the responses they saw in readers for the same reason that prints mocking Methodist women's appetite for religion interpreted it as sexual; bewildered by the strength of the women's wishes, critics interpreted them according to the standard whereby women had been traditionally repressed.

At the same time it seems reasonable to believe that reading love stories did stimulate women's sexual fantasies. Applying Locke and insisting on a connection between women's literacy and their sexual arousal, eighteenth-century writers anticipated "the fundamental discovery of modern psychologies that the most powerful sex organ was the brain." Spacks has argued persuasively that eighteenth-century women writers shared with men the understanding that imagination "is . . . actually the source of sexual feeling."[113] While it is particularly difficult to generalize about sex, it seems possible that for many intercourse mirrored "prevailing relationships" where women were denigrated by men, constantly apprehended brutalization, and where, of course, intercourse held the dangers of pregnancy and disease. (Stone has suggested that prior to recent history, foreplay was scanted. Bennett takes an opposite view.)[114] By contrast, fictional heroes were in the reader's control; they were shown respecting women's feelings—indeed, respecting women's definition of masculinity—and responding to them in the ways women wanted. It seems likely that some reformed men did accord themselves to women's wishes.

Wollstonecraft details the sexual fantasy that reading novels aroused in women. In her own sentimental/antisentimental and autobiographical novel, *Mary* (1788), the heroine's father, Edward, is a "vicious fool," but his wife, Elizabeth, readily "submitted to his will." (These were the names of Wollstonecraft's parents.) During the appropriate season they resided amidst the country's "delightful . . . beauties." Unconscious of them, however, the "brute," Edward, "sought amusements in country sports. He hunted in the morning, and after eating an immoderate dinner, generally fell asleep . . . digest[ing] the cumbrous load; he would then visit some of his pretty tenants." His *gourmand* appetite preferred their "vulgar . . . spirits" to Eliza's "sickly die-away languor," the expression, in turn, of "her delicacy," her "relaxed nerves." She had fashioned herself in accordance with her reading sentimental novels, which supplied her with fantasies while she was making her hair the object of her attentions in front of the looking glass. Thus pleasuring herself, "she ran over those most delightful substitutes for bodily dissipation, novels."[115] Those pleasures, Wollstonecraft insists, were "bodily" or "animal" ones, "addressed to the senses." They offered themselves "to the shrine of false beauty." The consequence of Eliza's reading sentimental novels like *The Platonic Marriage* was "the development of the passions." Eliza constructed at her introjected shrine a vision of a new kind of "knight errant," a "lover." She imagined him doing what her husband refused: loving her, sitting by her side, squeezing her hand and looking "unutterable things."[116]

That Eliza's pleasures in her novels were "substitutes for bodily dissipation" allowed her to remain "chaste according to the vulgar acceptation of the word, that is, she did not make any actual *faux pas;* but then to make amends for this seeming self-denial, she read all the sentimental novels, dwelt on the love scenes . . . accompanied her lovers to the lonely arbors and would walk with them by the clear light of the moon." Wollstonecraft's qualifications in this passage tell us she did not regard Eliza's gratifying sexual fantasizing as adequately chaste. In Wollstonecraft's view, Eliza's romantic fantasies could "force the sweet tears of sensibility to flow in copious showers down beautiful cheeks," beautiful but unchaste, so perhaps they were the displaced lubrication of sexual arousal—if not, orgasm can bring tears of pleasure. In the *Rights of Woman,* Wollstonecraft, referring to the effects of "dangerous pictures" penned by "exalted fervid imaginations," reveals "the sheer sensuality under the sentimental veil." She held that a person of sensibility could "sink into sensuality" even while talking of "sentiment."[117]

To her analysis of the sexual effects of reading on women can be added Wollstonecraft's Smith-like prognosis that such substitutive pleasure seeking had dire effects on women's reproductive systems, a connection that seems to have been implicit in Howlett's criticism of lower-class "luxury and refinement" which led to the frustration of "the impulses of nature." Eliza "brought forth" one "feeble babe" who survived, but her others "all died in their infancy." Eliza's "milk-fevers brought on a consumption," surely a resonant term for her disease. She became the well-known sofa-lying stereotype. The physical decline whereby Eliza's autonomous sexual sins had drastic effects on her sexual system were precisely analogous to that prognosticated by other masturbation phobes in their warnings to the young of both sexes.[118]

Some historians have suggested that late eighteenth-century middle-class women responded to their usual sexual circumstances by being "passionless."[119] Astell had advocated as much in self-defense against men. The warning that sentimental literature carried against its own immoral sexual effects, of which Wollstonecraft's were typical, if more explicit, also suggests the powerful attractions of sexual fantasizing to women and some form of autoeroticism, activities with which reading could be integrated in the ways Mandeville, Wollstonecraft, and others said that it was. The historical phenomenon of masturbation phobia (directed against both sexes) coincided with the sharp rise in literacy. *Onania or the Heinous Sin of Self-Pollution, and All Its Frightful Consequences in Both Sexes Considered* was published in London circa 1710, one among the avalanche of "dissuasives" against other "vices" which were printed in the campaign for the reformation of manners. In the ensuing half century, *Onania* sold 38,000 copies. Masturbation phobia seemed to go from strength to strength for another century and a half at least.[120] To previous speculations explaining masturbation phobia one may add the notion that masturbation became a sexual expression of consumer psychology, whatever cultural meanings it had previously. "Autonomous hedonism" was the capacity freely to take pleasure in one's own feelings, aroused by fantasy, in the privacy of one's own imagination, enjoyed under the new conditions of literal privacy—feelings, fantasy, and privacy all sponsored by the rise of commercial capitalism. Campbell's account of the interweaving of consumerism with Protestantism suggests the rich possibilities for guilt, anxiety, and repression, as consumers pursued the productive fantasy of purity, of transcending "uncleanness" in their bodies as they did in their houses and streets.[121]

Concern over the sexual effects of reading was a specific expression of the broader apprehension of reading's power, its capacity, in Dr. Johnson's phrase, "to produce effects without the intervention of the will." And Johnson was one who intimated the connection between "sexual passion" and the "Dangerous Prevalence of the Imagination" deplored in *Rasselas*. We have also seen that Fielding praised *Clarissa* for causing "tumultuous Passion" in him and then relieving it. By definition, sentimental fiction was intended to stimulate readers to feel. Moralists wished to capitalize on this power, just as dramatists did, to moralize arousal into the proper channels, to turn it to reformation rather than allow it to further the individual pursuit of pleasure. Privately, Richardson acknowledged sexual "Passions" to be part of "Human Nature" for both "Ladies" and "Men." Neither can "be kept in Ignorance," so the trick was to "properly mingle Instruction with Entertainment so as to make the latter *seemingly* the *View,* while the former is *really* the End." In writing novels, he said, one must guard against "sensual Finishings" but like the "Tragedy-writer," intermingle "love-scenes." He had "in View, to avoid inflaming Descriptions; and to turn even the Fondness of ye Pair, to a kind of intellectual Fondness."[122]

This effort against sex and sensuality was located at the key moment in the long trend characterized by Quinlan as "Victorian Prelude." The public acceptance of women's eroticism by Behn, by Rochester, by Mandeville, and by novelists Manley, Haywood, and Mary Hearne became "morally indefensible in the later eighteenth century." In the 1730s Haywood, said Clara Reeve, "repented of her faults and employed the latter part of her life in expiating the offenses of the former." Those words of Burney, Lennox, Lady Mary

Wortley Montagu, and *The Hermit of Snowden* quoted earlier illustrate the conflict women experienced in attempting to repress their sexual feelings, which we have seen their sensibility could be expected to register and even stimulate. Referring to those words and others, Spacks has argued that, despite their discouragement "from acting like sexual beings," middle- and upper-class women "thought of themselves as sexual beings, or expended a lot of energy avoiding such thoughts, and their writing testifies to the energy and complexity of their sexual attitudes." Still, Astell's views rather than Mandeville's gained the upper hand in accordance with the process described earlier.[123]

There were women writers like Jane Austen, "like Burney and [Charlotte] Smith, who could also encompass life and manners, wit and satire." Yet they did so by being "properly feminine" and "without losing the morality and modestly required of women." Those exceptional women writers had in common with authors of "mere sentimental fiction" a fundamentally serious attitude toward sex. They also had a fundamentally serious attitude toward mind, which many also saw endangered by the identification of women merely with a gendered sensibility, with feeling, an apprehension which also went back to the early feminists.[124]

Of course, women had good reason to be more serious about sex than men. Declaring their opposition to popular misogyny and capitalizing on the greater consciousness represented by the cultivation of sensibility, women had to fend off accusations that the latter was tantamount to sexual arousal, even if it did include such an element. From the beginning, critics had warned that the sentimental novel set women up for seduction. In 1698, Behn had referred wittily to the association: "Women enjoy'd are like Romances read."[125] The strength of women's wish for lovers sensitive to them made women easy marks for men who pretended sensibility in order to seduce them. Kitty Hunter and Mrs. Barbauld demonstrate the existence of "cases" of this kind of vulnerability along with "cases" of "women of the world." Women of "excessive sensibility" were by definition especially susceptible. When Miss Milner (as Lady Elmwood) gave in to her propensity for willful indulgence, she easily found "the dangerous society of one, whose every care [was] to charm her." Wollstonecraft argued in the following year that "Rakes know how to work on [women's] sensibility."[126]

Wollstonecraft's statement followed a series of such poseurs being held up in sentimental fiction as warnings to women.[127] Such posing goes back to Satan's offering Eve the apple but the Renaissance gave self-fashioning fresh meaning. Castiglione devised a complex code to help a woman "distinguish between those [men] who are pretending and those who love her sincerely." He wished to teach her a new system of the "safest signs by which she can distinguish true love from false" because "nowadays men are so cunning that they are always making false demonstrations of love, and sometimes they are quite ready to cry when they really want to burst out laughing." This deceitfulness had been a major reason for Astell to warn women not to marry, and it had been the chief burden of Mandeville's Astellian Lucinda in warning Antonia not to marry. His most developed cautionary tale described the downfall of Leonora who, in her youth, had been prevented from marrying Cleander. Arbitrarily separated from him by her father and then pursued by a rake in the form of a duke, Leonora shrewdly put herself under the protection of his wife, who arranged a practical marriage to a skilled artisan. Like Wollstonecraft's Eliza, Leonora's taste in lovemaking was at odds with that of her husband. "A Palate like hers could not relish the coarsest Food of love, unless it had been season'd with that obliging softness, and anxious Regard, in which the Delicacy of the Passion consists." Leonora wanted a refined man, a man of "exquisite Sense." This was the part Mincio plays—he was an "incomparable counterfeit." "No Mimick could ever assume so many Forms as himself, and he could act more different Parts than any lawyer in the Universe." His name and his characterization connect him with Machiavelli and with self-fashioning.

Mincio had become the incomparable "dissembler" by way of his father's wish that he be able to "shift and live in . . . and understand the World"—the world Mandeville and Lucinda know so well. This was Mandeville's adaptation to his feminist point of the early eighteenth-century "social psychology" Pocock has described, whereby "virtue was redefined" into manners. It "was pre-eminently the function of commerce to refine the passions and polish the manners." Mincio's father takes him away from Westminster School at twelve and puts him successively running errands at a tavern; working for a sleazy lawyer and then for "a broken Goldsmith turned Stock Jobber," by which time Mincio has become "an arch rogue," ready therefore to be "a Nobleman's Page." After a moneymaking stint in the West Indies, Mincio is given a final polish by way of some time at Oxford and the European tour. All this training was necessary to tackle Leonora, who had resisted the less polished romancing of a returned Cleander. It illustrates that seven or eight years of education of which, Lucinda has said, men can avail themselves, in contrast to women. If these manners were to be the reality of commerce, they looked very different in their application to "the marriage market," and of the new heterosocial conditions created by the pursuit of consumer pleasures.[128]

Jonathan Wild counterfeited the language of the eyes in his attempt to seduce Mrs. Heartfree. Lovelace claimed that he had "an undesigning heart," but his whole game was deception. "A feeling heart, or the tokens of it given by a sensible eye, are very reputable things when kept in countenance by the occasion." The culture operated according to such "tokens." Harriet Byron corrected Lucy Selby for believing John Greville was in love with her, with irony exclaiming, "And did he not weep when he told you so? Did he not turn his head away, and pull out his handkerchief?—O these dissemblers! The hyaena, my dear was a *male* devourer." Sophia Western's cousin, Mrs. Fitzpatrick, had been persuaded to marry Mr. Fitzpatrick because he had "put on much softness and tenderness, and languished and sighed abundantly." Once married, his "barbarity" was "indescribable." He had reverted to the male culture of dogs, horses, and drinking. Nonetheless, Mrs. Fitzpatrick had to have sex with him, and her relation resembles Mandeville's Aurelia's with *her* Irish husband. Sophia comforted her by saying "you need not be ashamed . . . for sure there are irresistible charms in tenderness, which too many men are able to affect." This profound danger—of marrying a man who turns out to be a brutal exploiter of women—gave tangible meaning to the culture's obsessions with distinguishing between the true and the false, the genuine and affected.[129]

Lennox's Arabella, a figure of extreme romanticism, is too easily "deceived" by a man's mastery of "the art of making himself agreeable to the ladies by a certain air of softness and tenderness." "Fraught, therefore, with the knowledge of all the extravagances and peculiarities" in romances, her would-be seducer "resolved to make his addresses to Arabella in the form they prescribed," thus using "her foible to effect his designs." Lennox had been preceded by Richardson and Fielding in suggesting men could use printed words to seduce women. Observing the "great use" he had been able to make in seducing "the reading part of the sex" by his knowledge of "their books," Lovelace stocked the library of the room in which he trapped Clarissa with books that would appeal to her "taste" and "sensibility." Cheyne told Richardson that because of his (Richardson's) mastery of "feminine" qualities, if he had "wanted women . . . [he] might had had [his] choice." Richardson used this mastery to sell women sentimental novels, capitalizing on the insight that "Instruction" could be mingled with sexual "Entertainment," and marking the evident connection between the emergence of women's consciousness and the sexual bogeys it provoked.[130]

Tom Jones elaborates the theme of young men's "spreading every net in their power" by "wishing, sighing, [and] dying." Their guides in this seductive technique were women's novels. When an Irish gentleman went to Bath to "try his luck with cards and the women," he prepared himself by "reading one of Mrs Behn's novels; for he had been instructed by a friend that he would find no more effectual method of recommending himself to the ladies than the improving his understanding and filling his mind with good literature." MacKenzie's Miss Atkins had prepared herself for seduction by absorbing "those warm ideas of an accomplished man which my favourite novels had taught me to form," and her seducer calibrated his opinions to match hers. She had been warmed up, in accordance with the traditional belief in the physiology of female arousal, by a combination of oral and literate culture. Mr. Winbrooke "asked my opinion of every author, of every sentiment, with that submissive diffidence, which showed unlimited confidence in my understanding. I saw myself revered, as a superior being." Miss Atkins "interpreted every look of attention, every expression of compliment, by the passion [she] imagined him inspired with, and imputed to his sensibility that silence which was the effect of art and design." Winbrooke argued that "genuine love should scorn to be confined" to marriage. Sindall behaved in precisely the same way to Harriet Annesley, disguising himself with "the semblance of tender feelings" as he argued for the transcendence of lover over marriage. Burney's Evelina is assaulted by the same type in the guise of Sir Clement Willoughy, able to exploit fashionable public places in addressing her from the first with the "nonsense" taken from "Romance." Even though Evelina has read Willoughby right, his skill at the game of sensibility, his "interest" in her "distress," engages her and for a moment she is led to "trust" him. Sir Clement improves the occasion by attempting to abduct her as Sir Hargrave Pollexfen abducted Harriet Byron and as Inchbald's Lord Margrave would abduct Matilda, throwing himself at her feet before he attempted to rape her.[131]

In *Sense and Sensibility* Austen named her male exploiter of excessive female sensibility "Willoughby." This was in tribute to Burney, but it indicates the persistence of the danger sentimental fiction warned that men posed, especially to the women of "excessive" sensibility Marianne Dashwood and her mother exemplified. Excessive sensibility let imagination "outstrip the truth." It led to the kind of fantasied wish fulfillment with which cultists had been charged for many years: "what Marianne and her mother conjectured one moment, they believed the next: that to them, to wish was to hope and to hope was to expect." Austen catalogs the extreme language and aesthetic conventions of exaggerated sensibility. Use of such language and identity of "taste" were vital tests in Marianne's conception of a lover; it was an exaggeration of that yearning for greater closeness and even certain forms of equality between women and men that was expressed everywhere by the culture. "I could not be happy with a man whose taste did not in every point coincide with my own. He must enter into all my feelings; the same books, the same music must charm us both." He must acknowledge her version of that culture of things described earlier. The excess in Marianne's sensibility includes her readiness to express sexual wishes: "his person and manners must ornament his goodness with every possible charm."[132]

Marianne and Willoughby's first impressions of each other are literally physical. When Marianne falls, twisting her ankle, Willoughby had "taken her up in his arms . . . and carried her down the hill." Of "manly beauty," his "person and air were equal to what her fancy had ever drawn for the hero of a favourite story," and Austen emphasizes Willoughby's "manly" and "exterior attractions" to the excessively passionate Marianne. Holding the distressed but conscious Marianne against him, Willoughby, in turn, registered her "striking form" and her other physical charms. This is Austen's version of the sexual expression of uncontrolled sensibility. Their attraction and their taste at first seem spontaneously identical, as Marianne had anticipated, but Austen lets us know that Willoughby is able to adapt his taste to Marianne's as he goes along because Marianne gives him all the clues he needs to calibrate his presentation of self to her "examination," just as Winbrooke had done with Miss Atkins:

> her favourite authors were brought forward and dwelt upon with so rapturous a delight that any young man of five and twenty must have been insensible indeed not to become an immediate convert to the excellence of such works, however disregarded before.

Austen's intimation is that Willoughby had disregarded them before. It is in accordance with sensibility's creed that Marianne fits what she learns of real people to the form of sentimental fiction, establishing "everything" "in the most melancholy order of disastrous love." When Willoughby parts from Marianne she combines her real sorrow with the feelings she believes she should have as a cultist of sensibility, "feeding and encouraging" her "violent sorrow" as a "duty." Thereafter, Willoughby drops Marianne to marry someone else for her money. Elinor points out that the very terms of the culture of sensibility—its short-circuiting of reflective thought—could lead to self-deception of drastic proportions, drastic, that is, to women. Sensibility had no formal power to override the double standard and men's power in the marriage market. Austen shows that Marianne's feelings, transcending legal covenant (as self-interested rakes like Winbrooke and Sindall argued), made her the ideal target of a male exploiter of women.[133]

It turns out that, despite Willoughby's earnest and convincing display of the sensibility on which she based her belief, at the very time of their passionate and tasteful mutuality he had kept hard-nosed, financial considerations in mind. In his presentation of himself to Marianne as a man of feeling, Willoughby had been "acting a part." He later confesses that thinking of his "own amusement" he had endeavored by every means in his power to "make myself pleasing to [Marianne] without any design of returning her affection."[134]

Even had Willoughby married Marianne after all, she would have faced "the worst and most irremediable of evils, a connection for life with an unprincipled man." Austen's position here was the same as Inchbald's, Burney's, and, of course, the Richardson of *Clarissa.* It looked back to Burnet's argument against Rochester. The culture of sensibility elevated the standards for marriage to love and compatibility but implementing them in the real world of power, including the use of the disguise that complex relations in the "World" required, ran fearful risks. In the words of Edgeworth's Belinda, "it was certainly very dangerous, especially for women, to trust to fancy in bestowing their affections." In reply, Lady Anne gave another version of Burney's ascription of women's vulnerability to their lack of experience. "And yet it is a danger to which they are much exposed in society. Men have it in their power to assume the appearance of every thing that is amiable and estimable, and women have scarcely any opportunities of detecting the counterfeit." Her solution was not to urge women to face a man on his terms. A woman, she said, should have an "opportunity of seeing her lover in private society, in domestic life," that is, on her turf, a place now naturally associated with the feelings. Provided "she has any sense, and he has any sincerity, the real character of both may perhaps be developed." It is hard to see that trusting to "sincerity" would be more reliable than trusting to "fancy," although the hope reveals the strength of the belief in domesticity's power—Edgeworth herself acknowledged in the same novel that her domestic hopes were "visionary." Perhaps women had developed ways of implementing their wishes for male treatment of themselves more effectively at home, but Lady Anne's stipulation here suggested, too, that there was no place where women could simply fall back on the moral superiority of "sincerity."[135]

The evidence also suggests a further dimension to this issue, the wishes of women for rakish men. It was not simply that some unusually naive or excessively sensitive women could be duped. It seems that a very large proportion of women were decisively attracted by "rakes." From Pope at the beginning of the century to Wollstonecraft at the end, writers warned, in Lovelace's version, that "half the female world [is] ready to run away with a rake," an opinion Anna Howe repeated: "how pleased half the giddy fools of our sex" were with Lovelace. The "nicest" of "your sex," wrote Lovelace, "will prefer a vile rake," and he noted the "mass of contradictions in you all." Lady Bradshaigh wrote Richardson after reading the earlier sections of *Clarissa* that "you must know (although I shall blush again) that if I were to die for it, I cannot help being fond of Lovelace . . . why would you make him so wicked, and yet so agreeable?"[136] Richardson repeatedly footnoted Lovelace's actions to underline their villainy because he apprehended that his female readers were inclined in Lovelace's favor: "many of the sex (we mention it with regret) who on the first publication had read thus far, and even to [Clarissa's] first escape, have been readier to censure her for over-niceness, as we have observed in a former note, than him [Lovelace] for artifices and exultations not less cruel and ungrateful, than ungenerous and unmanly." And Richardson shows the feminist, Anna Howe coming close to succumbing to Lovelace's "manly" charms.[137]

Both Fielding and MacKenzie intimated that women were partial to rakes and libertines, the former even suggesting via Lady Bellaston that women interpreted "rape" as the sign of a manly spirit. Like her predecessors, Inchbald wished to get women to give up their fatal attraction to rakes. Miss Milner exclaims, "What, love a rake, a man of professed gallantry? impossible.—To me, a common rake is as odious, as a common prostitute is to a man of the nicest feelings . . . 'Strange,' cried Miss Woodley, 'that you, who possess so many follies incident for your sex, should, in the disposal of your heart, have sentiments so contrary to woman in general' . . . Miss Woodley smiled at an opinion which she knew half her sex would laugh at . . ." But Miss Milner's excessive sensibility leads her to fall victim to the charms of a rake, anticipating Marianne Dashwood's fate.[138]

The literature (in part following the view expressed by Astell) suggested that women's attraction to rakish men could have lain in a kind of addiction to suffering. Frances Greville pointed out in her "Prayer for Indifference" (published c. 1756–7),

> Nor ease nor peace that heart can know,
> That, like the needle true,
> Turns at the touch of joy or woe,
> But, turning, trembles too.

Far as distress the soul can wound,
'Tis pain in each degree;
Bliss goes but to a certain bound,
Beyond is agony.

This was a celebrated and popular poem, revealing serious doubt over the cultivation of sensibility. However, More (who, like Astell, did not marry) and other celebrants of extreme sensibility rejected Greville's criticism—in fact, More interpreted it as an expression of the very mode it challenged. Instead, she relished gendered sensibility's self-directed, emotional pain significantly presented in metaphorical corporality: "the feeling heart / shapes its own wound, and points itself the dart." While she sometimes resisted the tendency, Wollstonecraft, relished her "sensibility" and "delicacy" in contrast to Imlay's hardness, the context for assessing her well-known words to him: "I leaned on a spear, that has pierced me to the heart." Dr. Johnson referred to "the fashionable whine of sensibility." Acknowledging the unhappiness that distinguished "sentimental folks" as a group, Hugh Kelly declared that "the devil take this delicacy; I don't know any thing it does besides making people miserable: And yet somehow, foolish as it is, one can't help liking it."[139]

Mrs. Barbauld's 1773 essay, "An Inquiry into Those Kinds of Distress Which Excite Agreeable Sensations," provided cultists of sensibility with a refreshed version of *The Spectator*'s rationale for the "pleasures of the imagination." Barbauld contrasted the "exquisite pleasures" experienced by "persons of taste and sensibility," their "nerves" registering "finer feelings," as they read of the distress of others, the prose "managed" so that it avoided "extremes." Her readers existed on the same historical and social continuum represented by *The Spectator,* their pleasures—sustained by their level of civility—more refined than the disgusting "tortures" delighting past kings (here Barbauld's historical vision corresponds to that of Elias). Her readers' pleasures in pain depended on knowledge of "the extremes of wrechedness" at the same time that knowledge was "kept out of sight" or comfortingly mitigated. (The pain may have been real but the wounds were metaphorical.) It depended, too, on their repeated "transition from a pleasurable state of mind to tender sorrow," and I have suggested that this may have expressed the wish to recapitulate the middle-class transition from subsistence to consumerism. The apotheosis of the distress enjoyed by Barbauld's cultists was represented by their reading *Clarissa.* Here is where she is distinguished from *The Spectator.*

> Amidst scenes of suffering which rend the heart, in poverty, in a prison, under the most shocking outrages, the grace and delicacy of her character never suffers . . . : [her] charm prevents her from receiving a stain from anything that happens; and Clarissa, abandoned, and undone, is the object not only of complacence, but veneration.

"Outrages," "stain," "anything that happens," all refer to the fact that Clarissa's sufferings include being raped. As we have seen, Wollstonecraft judged a woman's "dreams of ideal wretchedness or felicity" to be the expression of a feverishly toxic "sensibility."[140]

It was women's liability to this kind of toxicity that Austen presented in the figure of Marianne, who "courted . . . misery." (Presumably Austen named her after Marivaux's *Vie de Marianne,* then enjoying "an enormous circulation" because its translation had been republished in magazine form.)[141] Hurt to the quick by Willoughby, Marianne followed sentimental fiction's "order" in rejecting her sister's appeal to a more individualized, tougher-minded consciousness, crying, "No, no, . . . they who suffer little may be proud and independent as they like, may resist insult or return mortification, but I cannot. I must feel—I must be wretched—and they are welcome to enjoy the consciousness of it that can." While Marianne will learn "sense" eventually, in her present frame of mind she shows excessive sensibility's orientation toward welcoming suffering, setting women up as prey for men willing to exploit it.[142] In a sense, however, the issue here—for Greville, Kelly, and More, as well as Austen—was over what kind of "consciousness" to "enjoy," rather, say, than "masochism." The preoccupation with women's "excessive sensibility" expressed the possibility of women's being able to enjoy any consciousness they liked, controlled neither by taste, by morality, by men, in short, by anything but themselves. After all, that is what Lovelace wanted (literally following Mandeville's celebration of appetite), and that is what the bugbear of "libertinism" literally meant.

Hence the coexistence of the opposite explanation—the search for pleasure, not pain—for women's attraction to rakes: Richardson's power derives in part from the fact that he had embodied *both* the Lovelace-wishes and the Clarissa-wishes of women. He registered women readers' attraction to Lovelace by his attempts to counteract it. Anna Howe, representing a branch of female assertiveness that Richardson wished to condemn, shared Pope's view expressed by Lovelace that "every woman is a rake at heart." That was Lovelace's explanation for "ladies'" preference for the style of manhood he represented: women, too, would look to sexual pleasure they defined individually, beyond any bounds if they could. He added that women "always love cheerful and humorous fellows," whom he contrasted to "blubbering types." Influenced by Richardson (indeed, on this point, paraphrasing him), Wollstonecraft described the common ground that rakes and women of overcultivated sensibility found in pleasure. "With respect to superficial accomplishments the rake certainly has the advantage" over other men, she said in the *Rights of Woman,* for rakes are on women's own "ground." "They who live to please—must find their enjoyments, their happiness, in pleasure!" Both parties rested their "love" in the "grosser fuel" of sex. Wollstonecraft made her case on the same basis that previous moralists had made against consumer pleasures throughout the century. Women who chose to pleasure themselves with rakes lacked "taste." Implicitly, then, sensibility and conversion were linked to female sexuality. Women's ability to express greater consciousness under more comfortable circumstances, their awakening, could include the sexual fantasy and self-pleasuring observed by Mandeville and Wollstonecraft and apprehended by a host of critics between. If women should taste all of the world by feeling "as men feel," why not taste sexual freedom, too?[143]

Other eighteenth-century writers also suggested that rakes represented the attractions of "the world," of prodigality, playfulness, and sexual pleasures to women, who expressed the same attraction directly, too. In other words, rakes were symbols of women's own potential sensual liberation. Lady Mary Wortley Montagu knew teenage girls who declared that "if they had been born of the male kind they should have been great Rakes, which is owning they have strong Inclinations to Wh——ing and drinking, and want only Oppertunity and impunity to exert them vigorously." And a "Miss W" told Burney "the reason men are happier than us, is because they are more sensual." Women's possibilities, however, existed in a world where men still monopolized most power, power they could invest in their sexuality. We may align these suggestions with other explanations for the attractiveness of rakes to women. One is the taunt made to Clarissa by her cruel sister, Bella, "Call in your rake to help you to an *independence upon* your parents, and *depend* upon him!" The taunt was sharpened by its partial truth and recalls the larger eighteenth-century expression of the wish to escape parental direction and, instead, to marry for love.[144]

The continuing attractiveness of this style of manhood to women can also be explained by the apparent inadequacy of men of feeling or, rather, by the unfathomed question of their sexuality. To advance men's sensibility was to bring them closer to women. To make men more sensitive, more delicate, was, in the eighteenth-century's own terms, to run the risk of making them too "effeminate" or "feminine." Tom Jones's face had in it "the most apparent marks of sweetness and good nature" and included "spirit and sensibility in his eyes." These qualities, together with "a very fine complexion," gave his face "a delicacy almost inexpressible, which might have given him an air rather too effeminate had it not been joined to most masculine person and mien." Fielding insists on this qualification. In addition to his "leaping over five-barred gates and other acts of sportsmanship," including his accompanying Square Western in hunting, Tom Jones was a man of explicit sexual desires.[145]

Richardson's manly ideal also deviated physically from the conventional notion of manliness. Sir Charles Grandison's "slender" physique corresponded to his characterological sensibility. Harriet Byron noted that his "complexion seems to have been naturally too fine for a man: But as if he were above being regardful of it, his face is overspread with a manly sunniness." He has "an easy, yet manly politeness." Richardson repeatedly reassured his readers that the man of feeling was "a man indeed," to quote More's "Sensibility." In the eyes of epicurean, gambling, and horse-racing males, Burney's well-mannered Orville, sensitive to women's wishes, was "an old woman." But his qualities made Evelina love him. "I could have entrusted him with every thought of my heart, had he deigned to wish my confidence; so steady did I think his honour, so *feminine* his delicacy, and so amiable his nature!" Of Rushbrook, Inchbald remarked a "lover's fears are like those of women." But, like Richardson, women novelists combined their advocacy of a more feminine male with the reassurance that heroines regard him as "manly."[146] Moreover, sentimentalists declared him to be more manly than the types who brutalized or terrorized women.[147]

The reformation of men in order to bring them closer to women raised the difficult question of essential, irreducible difference, that is, of sex. This corresponded to the greater permeability of the old barrier between men's public leisure space and women's private work sphere, as the former was entered by significant numbers of women, sharing pleasures with men, and the latter attracted men into it for pleasure. Writers and reformers, addressing the sexual meanings of these changes, registered the concern over "women of the world," shaped, perhaps, by memories of respectable women who only went out to church, and the concern over "effeminacy," shaped by their awareness of past standards of manhood (and in the case of male writers, their greater remoteness from the new, worldly male producers). Brissenden suggests that Sterne was preoccupied with "the problem of impotence." Other scholars, recognizing the century's preoccupation with effeminacy (complemented by the century's concern with "masculine" women), link it to the greater proximity of male and female standards.[148] The goal of ending men's sexual brutalizing of women and of curbing the dangerous proclivities of women of the world tended to combine reform with the desexualization of both.[149] Hence Evelina began her potentially dangerous admission that she could have "entrusted Orville" with her inmost self with the desexualizing declaration, "As a sister I loved him." She thereby avoided the slippery slope embarked on by Miss Milner when she had admitted her sexual feelings for the sensitive Dorriforth.[150]

Another way of avoiding the difficult issue of reconciling sensibility with male sexuality was in the creation of the ideal male at a safe generational remove. Edmund Burke had remarked the feelings grandchildren had for their grandfathers, "where the weakness of age mellows into something of a feminine partiality." Evelina's guardian, Villars, resembles Matilda's guardian, Elmwood, in this respect, and in *Udolpho,* the Count de Villefort replaces Emily's desexualized and dead father to play a similar role. What the remove was a guard against is illustrated by the sexual relationship that grows up between Miss Milner and her "deputed father," Dorriforth.[151] Surrogates for fathers who had not yet been made safe, Villars and Sandford can help bring about the reconciliation between their wards and their real fathers, who then become nearly as much men of sensibility as their surrogates. All represent the female wish that men be softened, reformed fathers, too, shorn of dangerous power and sexuality. Sentimentalized fathers would cease to force marriage on their daughters. They would foreswear the still darker possibilities of incest embodied in the figures of Lovelace, Sir Thomas Sindall, Emily's "bad" guardian Montoni, as well as Dorriforth, a tendency pointing to the incest celebrated by de Sade.[152]

The problem of sexuality is illustrated in another, more direct way by Valancourt, one of Radcliffe's several "almost feminine" heroes. At first, Emily had noted "the manly grace" of Valancourt's figure: alone, she fantasizes Valancourt, "his countenance glowing with the poet's fire, pursuing his way to some overhanging height." But so sensitive does Radcliffe make him, so self-indulgent in his feelings, that Valancourt berates himself in the following way: "I have felt only for myself!—I! who ought to have shown the fortitude of a man, who ought to have supported you, I! have increased your sufferings by the conduct of a child! Forgive me Emily!" And she, therefore, has to act "with more than female fortitude."[153]

Radcliffe's doubts about the man of feeling's manhood explain in part the clear attraction of the hard Montoni to Emily. His mood swings, his sensitivity to slight, and his "quick intelligence" are qualities of sensibility, although he remains relentlessly aggressive toward Emily and women in general. Emily expresses her liking for "the chivalric air of his figure," and she responds with emotion to Montoni when the "fire" she had fantasied in Valancourt actually appears in Montoni's eye, along with "proud exultation" and "bold fierceness" as well as his alternation of gloom and "flashing energies of soul," when he is "roused" for "enterprise." Her response is "deep interest and some degree of awe, when she considered she was entirely in his power." Admiring a group of traditionally masculine martial figures, including the dexterous, graceful, commanding, and heroic "figure" of Cavigni, Emily hoped to see Montoni among them, "she scarce knew why." Count Morano has suspected she was in love with Montoni. Thinking Montoni "conquered" when the castle is attacked, Emily "grew faint as she saw him in imagination, expiring at her feet." The fantasy of this heroine of sensibility—a valiant, romantic, rakish hero at her feet—perfectly illustrates Wollstonecraft's scornful description (written two years previously) of the infantile aspirations of women excessively inculcated with sensibility.

> They want a lover, and protector; and behold him kneeling before them—bravery prostrate to beauty! The virtues of a husband are thus thrown into the background, and gay hopes, or lively emotions, banish reflection till the day of reckoning come; and come it surely will, to turn the sprightly lover into a surly suspicious tyrant, who contemptuously insults the very weakness he fostered.

Radcliffe telescopes the vision, showing a thoroughly emotional heroine actually living with the tyrant who fosters her weakness but fantasizing he is really the romantic lover.[154]

The heroines of nearly all of these novels, like Evelina, end in "the arms of the best of men." This demonstrated women's wish for sexuality but, with a male rigorously tested for civility, gentleness, and mutuality, under the most sanctified and guaranteed of circumstances possible, what kind of sexuality could this be? And who could write about it when a governing factor of the sentimentalizing process was a gendered literary market and the bowdlerization of women's reading? Women could make clear that they could do without the duplicity, violence, and cruelty in the male treatment of women, but beyond ridding themselves of those negative features, how to make sexual a new relationship built on mutual sensibility remained a problem. Wollstonecraft wished to desexualize relations between women and men, except the physical relations between lovers, but she did not explore the latter subject. Once they were married, however, she said unambiguously that the "master and mistress of a family ought not to continue to love each other with passion. I mean to say that they ought not to indulge those emotions which disturb the order of society, and engross the thoughts that should otherwise be employed."[155] Sexuality betokened inevitable difference, and therefore conflict, continually to be renewed and resolved, when sensibility's most basic fantasy had become final harmony, reflecting women's sheer inexperience of the world's "reality," in Burney's phrasing. In a sense, that reality had to be brought to bear on the sincere but segregated and necessarily defensive antiworld of domesticity, rather than the other way round, if both women and men were to realize the particularity of their deepest selves, and women "to feel as men feel."[156] Presumably a gentler manhood could be compatible with the pleasurable difference of sex—including conflict. But the culture of sensibility generated a continuing spiral of hard but sexual rakes and sensitive but nonsexual men of feeling in reaction to them, both expressions of women's wishes.

If women looked to their reading for clues to different kinds of sexuality than one based on their weakness and dependence, they would find them hard to come by. *The Spectator,* teacher of more civilized manners, said that "gentle softness" and "tender fear" were sexually attractive distinctions, the author implying that such "Inferiority" aroused him. "Delicacy" invoked as a code of female self-repression in large part because of the aggrandizement of feeling in women, as well as a protection against men, itself became sexual provocation to men in general. Richardson's Mr. B told Pamela that her watchfulness over her virginity (also called her "delicacy") "increased" his "passion" for her. Fielding would parody Pamela by suggesting that she made conscious use of what she recognized as her aphrodisiacal delicacy. Lovelace's response to the signs of Clarissa's sensibility and delicacy, her languor, her tears and her submissive posture anticipated Sterne's smacking his lips over Maria's stimulating tears in *A Sentimental Journey:* "How lovely in her tears! . . . her lifted up face significantly bespeaking my protection." He takes "delight" in "a woman's tears." Clarissa's appeal to delicacy as a way of resisting him, her placing her "assemblage of beauties" at his feet, only stimulates Lovelace "to do [his] worst," that is, to rape her.[157]

Fielding endorsed the notion that genuine virtue in distress sexually aroused men. This he had shown in *Jonathan Wild* in a series of encounters between Mrs. Heartfree and men who pretend to help her. In *Tom Jones,* "the agonies which affected the mind of Sophia rather augmented than impaired her beauty; for her tears added brightness to her eyes, and her breasts rose higher with her sighs. Indeed no one hath seen beauty in its highest lustre who hath ever seen it in distress," a view Fielding repeated. At the same time, men like Blifil, willing to act on the sexual stimulus they derived from a virtuous heroine's distress, were to be condemned. Fielding was acute in showing the aggression in Blifil stimulating himself with the fantasy of "obtaining absolute possession" of Sophia. Blifil's desire was not "at all lessened by the aversion which he discovered in her to himself. On the contrary, this served rather to heighten the pleasure he proposed in rifling her charms." One recalls the sadism Mandeville detected in male reformers, hypocrites all. Mackenzie's Harley was sexually aroused by female tears, and MacKenzie himself presented the heroine of *The Man of the World* as "lovely in her grief." MacKenzie virtually plagiarized from *Clarissa* and *Tom Jones,* as well as *A Sentimental Journey,* in describing the effects of Harriet Annesley's "assemblage" of beauties on the man who was intent on seducing her.[158]

Refinement of delicate nerves made women liable to sickness; so this liability of sensibility also became a sexualized characteristic, like other signs of vulnerability—kneeling, say—one arousing men. (Sterne describes "a tale of misery" told by "such a sufferer"—one who turned Yorick on, as "sickening.") This is suggested by the pervasive description of women as "languid," a deeply ambiguous term connoting both attraction and symptom. Again, Lovelace illustrates the point: Clarissa's "emotions were more sweetly feminine after the first few moments; for then the fire of her starry eyes began to sink into . . . languor. She trembled . . . She was even fainting, when I clasped her in my supporting arms. What a precious moment that!" Another male author wrote in 1780 that the "feeblenesses to which the tender frame of women is subject, are, perhaps, more seducing than her bloom. The *healthy* flower looks superior to protection, and expands itself to the sun in a kind *independent* state; but in *nursing* that which *droops* (sweetly dejected) and is ready to fall upon its bed, our care becomes more dear, as it becomes more *necessary.*" In the *Rights of Woman* Wollstonecraft registered the male requirements for this form of seductiveness, which she called both "sickly delicacy" and "languor," and she suggested that men's taste for it was that of a jaded "epicure." At the same time, her voice and the 1780 male's language also points to a salient factor continuously accompanying this male appetite for female delicacy: the female self-assertion which the very existence of a culture of sensibility could not but help express. Men were turned on by women's making themselves dependent.[159]

The Rev. James Fordyce conveyed the same message in a book Wollstonecraft said in 1792 had long been "a part of a young woman's library." His *Sermons to Young Women* (1766) summarized the courtly and enlightened view that women's greater delicacy should be used to help civilize men. He tells his audience that men of feeling—friends of women, as well as their rakish "enemies"—"desired" women to shape themselves into creatures of sensibility: "every woman" should show men "soft features . . . a form not robust . . . a demeanor delicate and gentle."[160] With characteristic irony, Wollstonecraft expands the picture of the exaggerated and sexualized style of sensibility Fordyce presented: written in sensibility's "rant," Fordyce's *Sermons* should be "drawled out in a whining voice," the phrase corroborating Dr. Johnson's phrase, "the fashionable whine of sensibility" as evidence for how such language was spoken. Mrs. Thrale's diary described other facets of the implementation of a sexualized, feminine sensibility:

> Mr. Thrale is fallen in Love *really* & *seriously* with Sophy Streatfield—but there is no wonder in that: She is very pretty, very gentle, soft & insinuating, hangs about him, dances round him, cries when She parts from him, squeezes his Hand slyly, & with her sweet Eyes full of Tears looks up fondly in his Face—& all for *Love of me* as She pretends; that I cannot help laughing in her face.
>
> A Man must not be a Man but an *It* to resist such Artillery.

This is nice testimony for women self-consciously fashioning their behavior in hopes of power in the face of the heavier "artillery" Mandeville and Richardson pointed out men brought against women. It is consistent with Barbauld's recommendation for women's employment of "Soft melting tones" and "Blushes and tones" in her reply to Wollstonecraft. Whether self-conscious or not, it was a dangerous game. With more irony Wollstonecraft went on to petition Fordyce's friends of women:

> oh do not take advantage of their weakness! Let their tears and blushes endear them . . . is it possible that any of you can be such barbarians, as to abuse it? Can you find it in your hearts to despoil the gentle, trusting creatures of their treasure, of their native robe of virtue? Curst be the impious hand that would dare to violate the unblemished form of chastity!

Such sentimental clichés are in fact, says Wollstonecraft, "indecent," her explication of the Reverend sermonizer here Mandevillean. Nonetheless, whatever forms women's wishes might have taken (and clearly they generated alternatives) they could not avoid facing male desires for their weakness and delicate subordination. "The sexual attention of men particularly acts on female sensibility, and this sympathy has been exercised from their youth."[161]

According to Wollstonecraft's social psychology, women had little choice but to internalize these very clear wishes.

> Men, for whom we are told women were made, have too much occupied the thoughts of women; and this association has so entangled love with all their motives of action and, . . . having been solely employed either to prepare themselves to excite love, or actually putting their lessons into practice, they cannot live without love.

This passage is taken from her chapter describing the childhood acculturation of females to sensibility, the time when little girls learned to blush. In eighteenth-century Britain, Wollstonecraft argued, women were prevented from growing up. Her first book, *Thoughts on the Education of Daughters,* had remarked that women "always retain the pretty prattle of the nursery, and do not forget to lisp, when they have learnt to languish." It was a view she developed when she expanded her subject in the *Rights of Woman.* Denying girls sufficient exercise in youth and confining them "until their muscles are relaxed and their powers of digestion destroyed," men required women to show "infantile airs." Women's "strength of body and mind are sacrificed to libertine notions of beauty." It was the logical result of this process that lisping, languishing, prattling, weakened creatures of sensibility, preoccupied with love, should orient themselves to "rakes." Until women "are led to exercise their understandings, they should not be satirized for their attachment to rakes; or even for being rakes at heart, when it appears to be the inevitable consequence of their education." Defined materially, ("sensationally") by an entirely sexualized rearing, women want material, sexualized partners. "Half the sex, in its present, infantile state, would pine for a Lovelace; a man so witty, so graceful, and so valiant can they *deserve* blame for acting according to principles so constantly inculcated?" Women's entirely reflexive and "pampered desire of pleasing beyond certain lengths" makes them literally complementary to men who live to abuse them, and here Wollstonecraft presents the tableau quoted earlier of the beauty prostrate before a tyrant.[162]

Incorporated in Wollstonecraft's explanation for what she, like Edgeworth and others, presents as a general appetite among men for excessively feminized women was her development of that pervasive apprehension that "civilisation" tended to make men effeminate. It had been a striking feature of the recently published *Sandford and*

Merton, which Wollstonecraft reviewed and the influence of which on the *Rights of Woman* she acknowledged.[163] She suggests that men's infantilizing of women, their doing what they can do to mold females into forms of perversely exaggerated delicacy, was the result of men's own effeminization. "Bodily strength from being the distinction of heroes is now sunk into such unmerited contempt that men, as well as women, seem to think it unnecessary." Men want to be "gentlemen" instead, and we have seen mothers' joining them in rearing effeminate sons. And, the softer men, the softer they required women to be. "Men who are inferior to their fellow men, are always most anxious to establish their superiority over women." In 1788, Alexander Jardine had given a similar interpretation to men's invidious shaping of women:

> Many of those female weaknesses which we term delicacy, etc., and pretend to admire, we secretly laugh at;—or when our taste is so far vitiated as to really like them, it is chiefly for their being symptoms of inferiority and subordination, that soothes and feeds our pride and domineering spirit.[164]

According to Wollstonecraft's metaphor, the "sword" had worn out the "scabbard" to the extent that "something more soft than women is sought for; till in Italy and Portugal, men attend the levees of equivocal beings, to sigh for more than female languor." However, the more general British male taste, she said, was for oversoftened women—the kind of creature men could create by arresting female development and keeping women permanently infantilized. One could say that a female child was more "equivocal" sexually than a mature woman; not only did mature women have developed secondary sexual characteristics—they had minds. This factor was the shaping force, one that Wollstonecraft's book epitomized, complementing male concern over the transformation of the classical warrior ideal.[165] Eighteenth-century women insisted on mind, on consciousness, thereby reducing the crucial dimension of the distance between themselves and men, whether men were more or less effeminate.

In adding the troublesome obstacle of mind to her explanation for why men demanded women become creatures of excessive sensibility, Wollstonecraft was considering men's view of sexual pleasure, even copulation: "men do not allow [women] to have minds, because mind would be an impediment to gross enjoyment." Men preferred women to lack reason and moral virtue, "lest pain should be blended with pleasure, and admiration disturb the soft intimacy of love." Men posed their own sexual pleasure against women's assertion of mind.[166] Similarly, Austen said in *Northanger Abbey* (begun within two years of Wollstonecraft's observations), that "though to the larger and more trifling part of the male sex, imbecility in females is a great enhancement of their personal charms, there is a portion of them too reasonable and too well informed themselves, to desire anything more in a woman than ignorance." Edgeworth, too, writing in 1795, suggested that men preferred in women "a certain degree of weakness both of mind and body." She would develop this idea in *Belinda,* where Clarence Hervey attempts (and fails) to create a woman entirely of mindless, dependent, reflexive sensibility, as a condition of marrying her. Edgeworth based this episode on Day's actual Rousseauistic project of adopting and rearing two young girls into creatures of feminine sensibility. Because of Day's remarkable obsession with men's becoming effeminate, we can see this as an illustration of Jardine's or Wollstonecraft's observations of "negative self-identification." [167]

Wollstonecraft characterized heterosexual relations as those of human hunters and animal prey, as well as pedophiliac and child. This was an insistent convention of sentimental literature, as we have seen. The idealization of women as heroines of sensibility and delicacy, asserting mind through literacy and fantasizing that their virtuous distress will empower them to tame male predators, shades into the diabolical hunter, Lovelace, raping St. Clarissa, an arrow in her breast, and enjoying her pain while doing so. Identified merely with sex, sensibility was read by men as provocation to victimization. According to Wollstonecraft, the sexualization of "virtue"—the materialization of sensibility—was "captivating to a libertine imagination." Novelist Manley had recognized long before Richardson that "this carefully created female innocence" was "itself the trigger for men's desire to destroy it." Miss Milner's sexily masquerading as the Goddess of Chastity made the same point. That Wollstonecraft had been provoked to develop it in part by Rousseau's naive view of gender suggests that her analysis of the sexualization of the maldistribution of power between women and men should also be compared with the observations of her contemporary, de Sade. He wrote, "We always find that a libertine is rarely a sensitive man—and that for the single reason that sensibility is a sign of weakness and libertinism a sign of power." [168]

De Sade presented the hard, exploitative rake as the logical sexual partner for the helpless, oversensitized female who identified her "virtue" with helplessness and distress, and whose sensations of pleasure were so "exquisite" they bore "along with" them "the sensations of exquisite pain." [169] Brissenden has made the case for a relationship between Austen's early work and de Sade's *Justine* (and further, between *Clarissa* and de Sade's *La philosophie dans le boudoir*). [170] De Sade as well as Austen was concerned to expose "the weakness of sensibility and the danger of trusting completely to it." If Wollstonecraft responded to Rousseau's sentimentalization of women, de Sade responded to his sentimentalization of men, and Laclos to the sentimentalization of both sexes.[171] Citing *Evelina*'s subtitle, Brissenden links the common subject of a young lady's entrance into the world to eighteenth-century feminism and to the emergence of a female audience for novels. Such an emergence exposed women to that worldly, improving knowledge of "others" that Wollstonecraft said made men what they were; at the same time, it exposed women to the still greater risk of sexual abuse, even sadism. Austen and Laclos, as well as Wollstonecraft and de Sade, made clear the inadequacy of women's appeal to sensibility as preparation for a fuller life, including relations with men as they really were.[172] Roberts has established that Austen drew on *Les liaisons dangereuses* for her unfinished *Lady Susan,* probably in the year after Wollstonecraft had described infantilized women "running after a Lovelace." That was immediately prior to Austen's criticism in *Sense and Sensibility* of a woman of unrealistic, incomplete consciousness, matching herself with a hard, exploitative man and, in *Northanger Abbey,* urging women to face up to a reality that included tyrannical males as well as men capable of realistic love.[173]

The polarity between, on the one hand, knowledgeable, individualistic, and sometimes duplicitous men who could make "great use" of women's appetite for wider horizons and, on the other, emergent, literate but naive women who bore largely opposite values was there in sentimental fiction all along. If "the threat and possibility of rape lurk in the background of most sentimental novels," symbolizing a young woman's apprehensions of entering the public world, that is because rape and other forms of the physical control of women had long been characteristic of the manners of men, previously aligning definitions of gender with definitions of the public sphere. Wollstonecraft knew the dangers and said what they were. She also said that it was only by entering the world that women would grow as men had been able to grow. The price of growth—in effect, of growing up—was labor and the risk of real sorrow.[174]

SEVEN

Wollstonecraft and the Crisis over Sensibility in the 1790s

Amazons at the Boundary

Wollstonecraft's public display of her powers of mind made her vulnerable to the charge of having a "masculine understanding." In the *Rights of Woman* she declared, "From every quarter have I heard exclamations against masculine women." Nonetheless, she went on to claim those talents and virtues men monopolized but that properly belonged, she said, to both sexes. Public challenges by women writers were a dangerous game in the eighteenth century, when the stereotype of the Amazon lay in wait.[1]

The Amazons were a mythic race of female warriors, their existence recorded by those who saw themselves as the male descendants of the Amazons' Greek adversaries. The Amazons were "always situated on the borders" of the "known world." They defined and maintained themselves by separating themselves from men, meeting them only to conceive. While they kept the resulting female children, they got rid of or disabled the boys. They were depicted in short tunics and sometimes scythian trousers. "Their occupations were hunting and fighting, their weapons . . . the bow and the 'Amazonian' crescent shaped shield . . . axe and spear, all used on horseback." Their rejection of women's customary role was signified by their destroying "the girls' right breasts to prevent them from getting in the way in battle." The fundamental importance of this transformation is marked by its originating the Greek word "amazon."[2]

During the century between Rochester's naming his feminist warrior-queen "Amaçoa" and Wollstonecraft's being stigmatized as Amazon, the term became the "Augustan code word for female pride and gender crossing." The Amazons had "deeply appealed" to Rochester's admirer, Aphra Behn, and Swift had called her "Afra the Amazon, light of foot." Swift may have had a narrower purpose in mind, but in general the term marked the revolutionary challenge in women's literacy. To many male writers, the Amazon was a bogey, embodying their fears and intended as a warning to women who crossed the "bounds of female authorship." Women's self-assertion in writing was a declaration of war, threatening to disable men. To female writers, however, the Amazon was a figure of remarkable ambiguity, one to which they were attracted and one from which they attempted to distance themselves.[3]

Anne Finch, countess of Winchelsea, challenged those men who saw "a woman that attempts the pen" as "an intruder on the rights of men," a person who mistook her "sex" (1713). She argued that in ancient fables woman had sung: "She fights, she wins, she tryumphs with a song / Devout, Majestick, for the subject fitt / And far above her arms, exalts her witt." Nevertheless, in the same poem Finch identified with a trapped bird, as would women writers from the duchess of Newcastle through the middle-class Wollstonecraft. Finch declared that the woman poet "wou'd Soar above the rest . . . with ambition" but "Debarr'd from all improve-ments of the mind / And to be dull, expected, and dessigned" must "with contracted wing, / To some few friends . . . sorrows sing." Because she wrote and she published, *The Tatler* called Astell "Amazonian," along with two of her contemporaries, Manley and Elizabeth Elstob. Elstob, "one of the foremost Saxon scholars in England," had written an Anglo-Saxon grammar (1715) "in order to put the 'mother tongue' within reach of those (mostly women) who knew no Latin." She also helped transmit the romantic values of Madeleine de Scudéry's *Essay on Glory* by translating it in 1708. Unable to raise subscriptions for her last Anglo-Saxon project, Elstob seems to have taken the same course as Astell, running a boarding school in Chelsea. To such Amazonianism may be added the activities of those women who in 1710 inscribed their dress with the signs of party politics and were therefore called Amazons by *The Spectator.*[4]

Fielding presented a number of Amazons in *Tom Jones,* a book expressing the author's sense of competition with "monstrous" scribblers. Among the audience at which they aimed, he suggests, was the explicit feminist, Mrs. Western, who had considerably improved her mind by study. Prominent in her "modern" reading are "romances" and "most of the political pamphlets and journals published in the last twenty years." Her "masculine person, added to her manner and learning, possibly prevented the other sex from regarding her . . . in the light of a woman."[5] In Fielding's view, her feminism was simply the reversal of the masculine contempt for women epitomized by Squire Western. At one point, Mrs. Western successfully opposed her brother's imprisonment of his daughter. "Have I not often told you that women in a free country are not to be treated with such arbitrary powers? We are as free as the men, and I heartily wish I could not say we deserve that freedom better." Fielding, too, opposed the barbarous treatment of women represented by Squire Western but, conflating the masculine feminist with monstrous scribblers, he invoked the ancient borderline across which such egalitarian claims were to be pushed back by men. "Thus she spoke with so commanding an air . . . that I question whether Thalestris at the head of her Amazons ever made a more tremendous figure." Against such a figure Fielding upheld the paramountcy of the "feminine" as the culture of sensibility defined it, in the "extremely delicate" figure and "amiable" personality of the "sublime" Sophia Western.[6]

Referring ironically to the sickly stereotype of femininity already established in novels, Fielding said that Molly Seagrim's beauty had "very little of the feminine in it, and would at least have become a man as well as a woman; for . . . youth and health had a considerable share in the composition." (He later refers to "that delicate race of women who are obliged to the inventions of vehicles for the capacity of removing themselves from one place to another"—a similar vision to Cheyne's—and favorably contrasts Mrs. Waters's limbs being "full of strength and agility," as well as her mind of "animated spirit," to the extent that she can fight off a rapist and keep pace with Tom Jones.) In any case, Molly Seagrim was an "Amazonian heroine." Uneducated and lower-class, she fought physically, like other women called "Amazonian" in the book—Susan, the "robust and manlike chambermaid," Mrs. Partridge, who fought her husband back, or Goody Brown, a leader of the group fighting Molly's troops in the church courtyard, that singular public place for women's display of fashion. If literacy had helped sponsor Mrs. Western's Amazonianism, the ambition, vanity, envy, and competition in dressing fashionably, even among countrywomen, helped spark Amazonian fighting on this occasion; their dress signified women's participation in a wider, commercializing world, just as women's reading scribbled romance did. The Amazonian feminist Mrs. Western was the outspoken defender of the new, self-assertive, urban-focused world of fashion.[7]

Dr. Johnson's *The Adventurer* in 1753 identified female writing with the threat of war against men. Part of this "epidemical conspiracy" was "a generation of Amazons of the pen, who with the spirit of their predecessors have set masculine tyranny at defiance, asserted their claim to the regions of science, and seem resolved to contest the usurpations of virility." Twelve years previously Johnson had published "A Dissertation on the Amazons," in which he had depicted the "revolt of the Amazons against the male warrior" as "an evil analogous with the Christian myth of the fall." Johnson's later phrase, "usurpations of virility," perhaps expressed some dawning sympathy for women writers' point of view, as Johnson did become "increasingly enlightened about the moral status and education of women." He may have been influenced by Charlotte Lennox. For thirty years Johnson was Lennox's champion, calling her writing "superior" to that of Burney, Carter, and More. In addition to praising her work, on occasion Johnson helped her do it, contributing a chapter-length "General Conclusion" to Lennox's 1760 translation of *The Greek Theater of Father Brumoy.* Lennox must have found this support vital. She lived a "Grub Street existence." Fielding said Lennox was "shamefully distressed." She spent the last years of a long life "in extreme poverty" and died destitute. Johnson's high praise for Lennox's work, promulgating virtue and ostensibly upholding gender orthodoxy, has been attributed to his approval of her "moral purpose."[8]

Johnson literally played a part in the moral conclusion to Lennox's *The Female Quixote,* wherein the "cure" of Arabella's "mind" from its absorption by romance is put into the charge of a "good divine." The chapter presenting this cure is entitled, "Being, in the Author's Opinion, the Best Chapter in This History," a tribute to Johnson. Even if he did not write it, the diction is very like his. The divine is a "doctor," accustomed to "speak to scholars with scholastic ruggedness." Early in the chapter, the "pious and learned Dr. ———" rejects Arabella's "contemptuous ridicule," which, he said, she was "pleased to exercise upon my opinion, not only of fictions, but of senseless fictions; which at once vitiate the mind and pervert the understanding." However, if this was the message Dr. Johnson wished to impart to the female reader of *The Female Quixote,* Lennox managed to bootleg other messages into it.[9]

The Female Quixote was published three years after *Tom Jones* and one year before Johnson's 1753 *Adventurer.* Arabella told her lover that Thalestris, queen of the Amazons, was not so "contemptible" an antagonist as he thought because a man as valiant as Orontes was "cut to pieces by the sword of that brave Amazon." A third figure in this conversation, representing orthodox femininity, said she would "be afraid to look at such a terrible woman. I am sure she must be a very masculine sort of creature who . . . must have the heart of a tiger." Arabella challenges this characterization by presenting a compromise figure: "Thalestris, though the most stout and courageous of her sex, was, nevertheless, a perfect beauty; and had as much harmony and softness in her looks and person, as she had courage in her heart and strength in her blows." She challenged men on behalf of her sex and defeated them in conversational battle, but she still had an "inexpressible grace" in all of her motions. Arabella was consistent with Lennox's at least ambiguous defense of romantic fiction.[10]

Naively, it turns out, the "Female Quixote" defends the "masculine" Miss Groves. Made masculine by the "unpardonable neglect of her mother," she is another deviant who is thus explained. Her deviation was expressed in her "riding about the country, leaping over hedges and ditches, exposing her fair face to the injuries of sun and wind; and by these coarse exercises, contracting a masculine and robust air not becoming her sex." Miss Groves's worldliness extended to conversations with "a young sportsman," who was part of the same "train," and when, for that reason, she was kept at home, her unrestrainable appetite for "adventures" led her to "a lover in the person who taught her to write." Her literacy and her adventurousness connect her with Arabella, particularly because of the novel's subtitle, *The Adventures of Arabella*. Surely, too, its main title invokes a woman on horseback, albeit a nag. The ancestresses of Arabella and Miss Groves, as well as the other Amazons of eighteenth-century fiction, included Spenser's Britomart and Tasso's Clorinda and "the line of noble women warriors," the sexual inversion of whom, Natalie Zemon Davis argues, both clarified social structure and marked conflict within it. They had "the potential to inspire a few females to exceptional actions and feminists to reflect about the capacities of all women." She refers to the labeling of Mary Wood's horse-riding band of recusants in seventeenth-century Britain (sharing coordinates with their Puritan opposite numbers) as "apostolic Amazons." These ambiguously monitory female figures were preceded and succeeded by real women who rode and hunted, attempting the same options for characterological versatility allowed men by eighteenth-century developments. In 1709, Steele had curled his lip at such women by way of "Mrs Alse Copwood, the Yorkshire huntress, who is come to town lately, and moves as she were on a nag, and going to take a five-bar gate." Soon after publication of *The Female Quixote* Stubbs was painting ladies who rode and hunted and, late in the century, Rowlandson recorded the fashionability of combining the display of dress and horsewomanship in town. That women also "widely" adopted "the male's riding habit" as well as the frock coat, in order to travel and "participate in outdoor leisure activities," has been noted, together with fiction's frequent representation of young women's cross-dressing and the "sensitivity" such "emulation" aroused among men, as did the Amazonianism women expressed in their writing.[11]

Burney's *Evelina* linked literary warfare to her challenge to masculine physical assaults on women. In the novel's dedication Burney

Thomas Rowlandson (1756–1827). *Showing Off in Rotten Row,* c. 1785–90. Pen and ink and watercolor over pencil. 12 1/8 in. diameter, circular. The Museum of London.

presents herself as a "hero," taking the "field of battle" against the male literary establishment. The "masculine" Mrs. Selwyn is a vehicle for Burney's exploration of that female egotism the dedication expressed as well as for her doubts over the adequacy of Evelina's exemplary sensibility. Burney based her on Frances Greville, her godmother and namesake. Greville, too, was the poet who challenged the value of sensibility in favor of "indifference." To "outsiders" Greville appeared "pedantic, sarcastic, supercilious; to her own circle, kind and good-humored." Burney described her as having fine "feminine" features and a "masculine" understanding.[12]

Mrs. Selwyn, a woman with an "unmerciful propensity for satire," is "masculine," too. Evelina introduces her thus:

> She is extremely clever; her understanding, indeed, may be called *masculine;* but, unfortunately, her manners deserve the same epithet, for, in studying to acquire the knowledge of the other sex, she has lost all the softness of her own. In regard to myself, however, as I have neither courage nor inclination to argue with her I have never been personally hurt at her want of gentleness; a virtue which, nevertheless, seems so essential a part of the female character, that I find myself more awkward, and less at ease, with a woman who wants it, than I do with a man.

Evelina sees cleverness taken to a certain degree as "masculine" but the two words following that notion ("but, unfortunately") suggest that extreme cleverness in a woman could be as admirable to the writer as kindness and attentiveness. It is masculine "manners," their hardness, "want of gentleness," and lack of mercy to which Evelina objects. So the writer preserves the validity of a woman studying to acquire "the knowledge of the other sex" (a nice ambiguity), provided she does so while preserving feminine "manners." Evelina has preserved her own virtuous softness because she lacks both "courage and an inclination to argue." She admires Mrs. Selwyn but she feels more essentially female, her gentleness a quality identifiable with "virtue" and laden with moral superiority. The ambiguous values here betoken conflict, helping us to understand Evelina's awkwardness described in the last sentence of the quotation, which also returns us to Mrs. Selwyn's masculinity.[13]

Mrs. Selwyn is called an "Amazon" by that group of dissolute, unreformed males, Merton, Lovel, and Coverley. The scene is set by an assault on the feminine and virtuous Evelina by another rake, Willoughby, by whom she has been beset throughout her entrance into "the world." The "wildness of his manner terrified me." Willoughby's exit is followed by Mrs. Selwyn's entrance and challenge to the rakes, demonstrating the "courage" Evelina lacks but admires. Saying he was averse to argument, Merton backs off, subjected to Mrs. Selwyn's sarcasm: "O fie, my Lord, a senator of the nation! a member of the noblest parliament in the world!—and yet neglect the art of oratory." She is not prepared to cut herself off from politics. At first seconded in her opinion by Mr. Lovel (an M.P.), Mrs. Selwyn adds that she "had supposed that a peer of the realm and an able logician, were synonymous terms." However high a man's rank and whatever his political power, he can be illogical, in fact, less logical than a woman. The scene gets hot, "monstrous hot," and Merton contrasts Mrs. Selwyn unfavorably with Lady Louisa, the other woman present, a weak, sofa-lying, aristocratic creature of sensibility: "your Ladyship is merely delicate,—and devil take me if ever I had the least passion for an Amazon." All of the men join him in this characterization of Mrs. Selwyn, and Lovel, "looking maliciously" at her, declares he has "an insuperable aversion to strength, either of body or mind in a female."

> "So would every man in his sense," said Lord Merton; "for a woman wants nothing to recommend her but beauty and good nature; in everything else she is either impertinent or unnatural. [I do not] wish to hear a word of sense from a woman as long as I live."

This provokes Mrs. Selwyn to "unmerciful satire."

> "It has always been agreed," said Mrs. Selwyn, looking round her with the utmost contempt, "that no man ought to be connected with a woman whose understanding is superior to his own . . . To accommodate all this good company, according to such a rule, would be utterly impracticable, unless we should choose subjects from Swift's hospital of idiots."

This "unbounded severity," writes Evelina, "excites" Mrs. Selwyn's male "enemies," the word denoting her acceptance of the sexual warfare to which the dispute has been raised by their branding her an Amazon. That this warfare between Mrs. Selwyn and the rakish gang is part of the same scene wherein Willoughby physically assaults Evelina links physical with mental assault. Clarissa had been assaulted in mind and body by Lovelace. One of Harriet Byron's inquisitors over the question of university education was Sir Hargrave Pollexfen, who then abducted her. Such juxtapositions were the counterpart of the persistent link men and convention made between a woman writer and her sexuality.[14]

With these themes in mind, we can return to *Evelina's* dedication. Burney had suggested via Mrs. Selwyn that masculinity was unmerciful. In presenting *Evelina* to the gentlemen literary authorities, Burney appealed "to their MERCY," at the time admitting her tenderness: "No hackneyed writer, inured to abuse, and callous to criticism, here braves your severity." She expressed the same fear in her diary, being "frightened out" of her wits "from being attacked *as an author.*" She prayed that "Heaven may spare me the horror irrecoverable of personal abuse! Let them criticise, cut, slash without mercy my book, and let them neglect me; but may God avert my becoming a public theme of ridicule." For a woman to publish a book, to send an Evelina out to make an entrance into the world, was to invoke the horrors of male assaults on women in public. Yet, at the same time, Burney wrote privately that she envisioned a "splendid success" as a writer, that is, as a woman with a splendid voice, capable of extreme cleverness, a heroine of healthy egotism, conceiving her writing as fighting a heroic battle against the unmerciful opposition of men as she entered the public, published world. She recognized men's authority in "knowledge" in that same ambivalent paragraph where her heroine shows she has internalized the conventional categories of gender by calling Mrs. Selwyn "masculine" and finding herself more at ease with similarly masculine men. This suggests that Burney's "shirking" public notice by anonymity was the effect of identification with the aggressor. Yet again, concealed in Evelina Anville's name is that of Greville, and there are phonetic as well as anagramatic elements in Selwyn, too. Burney's view of her battle and her admiration for Selwyn/Greville suggests that Burney knew she ran the risk of being called "Amazon."[15]

Wollstonecraft, Hays, and the Conflict over Sensibility

Sentimental fiction continued to be extremely popular through the rest of the century. *Udolpho* illustrates how authors could tip their hat to its apparent dangers but publish still more extreme forms anyway. And no one could prevent readers from identifying themselves with figures the author intended as warnings against sensibility's "excesses." In 1799, the *Lady's Monthly Museum* had a writer exclaim that her daughter "reads nothing but novels . . . from morning to night . . . One week she will read in the following order: *Excessive Sensibility, Refined Delicacy, Disinterested Love, Sentimental Beauty,* etc." Nonetheless, the ambiguous values of sensibility to women and men, present throughout the century, became critical problems for many writers during its last fifteen years. The French Revolution intensified and popularized earlier apprehensions: the representation of Wollstonecraft as both an exemplar of excessive sensibility and as an Amazon would crystallize them.[16]

At first, the fall of the Bastille was widely heralded in Britain. Wollstonecraft saw it ushering in the social reforms with which she identified the positive, humanitarian aspects of the culture of sensibility, although she wished such expressions to be controlled by "manly" reason. The September Massacres of 1792 and the execution of Louis XVI in January 1793 had a traumatic effect on British politics. The French government declared war on Britain in February 1793 and the "political climate" in Britain "was completely transformed." Henceforth British writers would be caught up in war hysteria, the radical and reforming side—called "Jacobins"—vulnerable to charges of treason by the counterrevolutionary or "Anti-Jacobin" side. Their ideological warfare fostered "mass political literacy." Marilyn Butler, Gary Kelly, and Warren Roberts most recently have demonstrated that any historical account of this warfare must be extended to include novels.[17]

Because in Britain the definition of gender was seen to be fundamental both to the Jacobin prospects for reform and to the Anti-Jacobin attempt to maintain the natural order, the debate over sensibility became a key issue in British politics. Women writers—novelists in particular—came under still more severe attack for subverting the natural ordering of the sexes.[18] Charlotte Smith recorded in *Desmond* (1792) that novels were being accused of inspiring a range of immoral behavior. "Novels, it is decided, convey the poison of bad example in the soft semblance of refined sentiment. One contains an oblique apology for suicide; a second, a lurking palliation of conjugal infidelity; a third, a sneer against parental authority; and a fourth, against religion." This was six years prior to Godwin's revelations of Wollstonecraft's exemplifying all of these in his *Memoirs of the Author of the Rights of Woman.* Following his 1785 attack on the irresponsibility and even revolutionaryism in sentimental novels by women, in 1792 MacKenzie declared his Anti-Jacobin sympathies. He was, in the words of Sir Walter Scott, "one of those literary men who contributed some little occasional tracts to disabuse the lower orders of the people, led astray by the prevailing frenzy of the French Revolution." The especially draconic treatment of Scottish Jacobins by the British government has been described by E. P. Thompson.[19]

MacKenzie's, Inchbald's, and Austen's criticism of excessive sensibility were part of a spate of such criticism cresting in the late 1780s, some of it in novels with titles that anticipated Austen's *Sense and Sensibility: Excessive Sensibility* (1787), *The Illusions of Sentiment* (1788), *Arubia: The Victim of Sensibility* (1790), *Errors of Sensibility* (1793). Their ostensible purpose was the same as Austen's. According to the *British Critic:* "the object of [*Sense and Sensibility*] is to represent the effects on the conduct of life of discreet, quiet good sense on the one hand, and an over-refined and excessive sensibility on the other." This was in 1813. Butler describes a series of novels of "education," published throughout the period of the French Revolution until 1814, in which progressive as well as conservative writers were "inflexibly severe towards self-indulgence; both denounce the passions." In addition to *Sense and Sensibility, A Simple Story,* and *The Mysteries of Udolpho,* Butler lists Jane West's *A Gossip's Story* (1796), Burney's *Camilla* (1796), Edgeworth's *Vivian* (1812) and *Patronage* (1814), and Mary Brunton's *Self-Control* (1812) and *Discipline* (1814). Many of these novels personified the contrast defined by the *British Critic* in the way Inchbald's Miss Milner and Matilda did. They supply the historian with an invaluable context for Wollstonecraft's *Rights of Woman,* wherein she, too, explicitly contrasted the lives of two hypothetical women, one reared to excessive sensibility, the other to a sensibility checked by reason. In fact, the implicit but clear alternatives Wollstonecraft presented throughout are between a woman reared to cripplingly exaggerated sensibility, utterly dependent and subject to emotional binges, and herself, the writer, capable of reasoned analysis, physically strong, independently minded, yet inspired with the positive warmth of sensibility.[20]

It is not the case that all of these works were "inflexibly severe towards self-indulgence"; in fact, *Udolpho* contradicts Butler's judgment on this point. With the exception of Wollstonecraft (and even she was ambivalent), all of these works upheld the notion that sensibility was a positive female characteristic when it was combined with mind and with will, albeit will for self-governance. Typically, Austen argued that women—writers especially—were able to combine good sense with sensibility and still be female. It was this idea that was under sharp challenge. So Austen declared that "Elinor's disposition was affectionate, and her feelings were strong, but she knew how to govern them; it was a knowledge which her mother had yet to learn, and which one of her sisters [Marianne] had resolved never to be taught." Like Hume's tempered Stoic, Elinor "possessed a strength of understanding and coolness of judgement," qualities Wollstonecraft also prized.[21]

Women's publication of so many works personifying sense and sensibility in characters who struggled for readers' minds suggests the widespread existence of conflict within women, parallel to the attacks made on them by men, between a sensibility governed by reason and a sensibility dangerously given over to fantasy and the pursuit of pleasure. This had been a dynamic that characterized the culture of sensibility all along, two parts of wished-for selves, capitalizing on literacy and consumerism to make sense of women's new social circumstances and their attempts to improve them.

As we have seen, Wollstonecraft was capable of distinguishing very clearly between these two versions of sensibility. Her adherence to sensibility's value and her insistent aspiration to modify sensibility with reason was, in many respects, a more passionate and developed version of a well-known view among her contemporaries, one to which both sentimental and antisentimental writers subscribed.[22] Wollstonecraft's distinction was to take "Sense" further in her defense of woman's mind, and to be still more damning in her analysis of the damage an exaggerated "Sensibility" could do to women. Moreover, in addition to her advocacy of the softening influence of mothers in improved domestic surroundings, Wollstonecraft insisted that women toughen themselves by fully entering the world and subjecting themselves individually to all of the experiences possible to men. Basing her call for women's rights on the "Commonwealthman" ideal of a *populo armato,* Wollstonecraft invoked a picture of women warriors, capable of burnishing their arms as well as their reason. To become "real" heroines of "public virtue" (in contrast to fiction's segregated fantasies), women should actually take "the field" to "march and counter-march like soldiers, or wrangle in the senate to keep their faculties from rusting." Women were capable of this range of roles, from sentimental yet tough-minded wife and mother to Commonwealth patriot and warrior.[23]

Despite the clarity with which Wollstonecraft distinguished between the good and bad versions of sensibility, she was also torn between them. Her demand that women subject sensibility to reason expressed her deepest personal struggle, evident throughout her published works and her letters.[24] The conflict can be discerned even in the *Rights of Woman,* where on occasion she used the same sentimental clichés that elsewhere are her target as "sentimental rant," and "turgid bombast"—the "sentimental jargon" induced in women by their reading sentimental novels. This had always been a major target in her reviews of novels.[25] But Wollstonecraft's ambivalence is much more dramatically evident in the contrast between the *Rights of Woman* and the *Letters from Sweden,* written four years later. She declared in the latter that she would allow "feeling to be my criteria" most of the time. She had decided to "let my remarks and reflections flow unrestrained," in order to give "a just description of what I saw by relating the effect different objects produced on my mind and feelings while the impression was still fresh." The book contains frequent examples of the culture of sensibility's characteristically passive variant of sensational psychology's operation.

> Nature is the nurse of sentiment,—the true source of taste; yet what misery as well as rapture, is produced by a quick perception of the beautiful and sublime, when it is exercised in observing animated nature, when every feeling and emotion excites responsive sympathy, the harmonized soul sinks into melancholy, or rises to extasy, just as the chords are touched, like the harp agitated by the changing wind.[26]

Of course, Wollstonecraft was writing this on a public, business trip, unaccompanied by a man, and she included a series of tough-minded reports on the economics, politics, and histories of the towns and regions she visited, reports that were reprinted in several British journals. In fact, her secret mission was a very difficult piece of political business, trying to recoup something from the disastrous losses incurred by one of Imlay's naive, pro-French Revolutionary enterprises.[27] In addition, Wollstonecraft sustained her criticism of the oppression of women in the countries she visited and referred to her own oppression. Nevertheless, extensive stretches of the book are passages like the one just quoted, unqualifiedly sentimental—"romantic" according to Wollstonecraft's own standard, which she laid out in her earlier and ironic picture of a "romantic" young woman, "tremblingly alive all o'er." In *Letters from Sweden* Wollstonecraft presented herself as romantic heroine, "virtue in distress," like one of Radcliffe's heroines. The reason is clear: Wollstonecraft was writing *Letters of Sweden* to her lover. Imlay had commissioned her to go to Sweden in part to ditch her. Godwin said that the *Letters from Sweden* "was a book calculated to make a man fall in love with its author." We know how aware Wollstonecraft was of what kind of femininity appealed to men and, conversely, how in her words "the sexual attention of man particularly acts on female sensibility." With a lover, a woman's "sensibility will naturally lead her to endeavour to excite emotion, not to gratify her vanity, but her heart."[28]

Wollstonecraft's private letters show her awareness of this deep conflict. She had not mastered the presentation of herself as a woman of sensibility as one of a repertoire of roles, comparable, say, to the ability she saw in Imlay to present a "commercial face," an ability she condemned in accordance with sensibility's values. She wrote him privately what she demonstrated publicly in *Letters from Sweden,* that "those affections and feelings" which "seem to have been given to vivify my heart" were in fact "the source of so much misery." "That being," said Wollstonecraft, "who moulded my heart thus, knows that I am unable to tear up by the roots the propensity to affection which has been the torment of my life."[29] She knew that "an accumulation of disappointments and misfortunes seem to suit the habit of my mind." She connected her adult misery to her own father's treatment of her as a child, but she also explained it as the result of the conventional rearing and education of middle-class females, their sensibilities developed at the expense of reason, their ambitions confined to love and marriage. She said that educated, middle-class women in general were subjected to the same "continual conflicts" between sensibility and reason. Precisely because Wollstonecraft showed herself able to make the most radical analysis of the dangers the culture of sensibility posed to women, her difficulty in disentangling herself from them dramatized the power of its hold.[30]

Nearly all of the reviews of the *Rights of Woman* had endorsed its largely familiar argument against the incapacitating effects on women of an overcultivated sensibility and its corollary, the advocacy of the cultivation of reason.[31] At the same time, the reviewers' approval was combined with expressions marking the fact that they judged Wollstonecraft's work on the basis of her sex. She was "our fair authoress." After quoting a considerable extract, the Jacobin *Monthly Review* remarked, "This subject is still farther pursued with a degree of freedom which may perhaps be thought singular in a female, but with a philosophical air of dignity and gravity, which precludes every idea of indecorum and almost prohibits the intrusion of a smile."[32]

The sole negative review was that by the Tory *Critical Review.* It raised the cry reviewers of Godwin's *Memoirs of Wollstonecraft* would take up six years later. Insisting there was "sex in mind," it accused Wollstonecraft of "indelicacy" and "immodesty" in discussing "anatomical subjects and the proportions of naked statues," reasserting the gendered modesty we have seen Wollstonecraft attacked in the passage to which the *Critical Review* referred. The review warned that if women were to follow Wollstonecraft's doctrines, they would be left "spinsters." Hence the reviewer sarcastically advised Wollstonecraft to adopt precisely the mode of behavior she was challenging: "dear young lady . . . endeavour to attain 'the weak elegancy of mind,' the sweet docility of manners,' 'the exquisite sensibility,' the former ornaments of your sex; we are certain that you will be more pleasing, and we dare pronounce that you will be infinitely happier." The reviewer's quotation marks signify the convention, the gendered culture of sensibility, and the kind of behavior that men had long demanded.[33]

By the same token, reviewers praised Wollstonecraft's *Letters from Sweden.* True, it expressed heterodox Jacobin views—on religion, for example—and criticized Pitt's paranoid crackdown. Wollstonecraft reasserted the position she had taken in her 1794 book devoted to the French Revolution, that it would have the generally positive effect of arousing "public spirit" by making politics a "subject of discussion," thus enlarging "the heart by opening the understanding." However, referring specifically to the "general discussion" in England of Robespierre's rationale for "tyranny"—that it was a political "necessity"—Wollstonecraft expressed her opposition to him, calling him a "monster," and referring to "the horrors [she] had witnessed in France." While they ignored this, Anti-Jacobin reviewers were mollified by Wollstonecraft's manifestation of sex. *The British Critic* praised Wollstonecraft for now showing she was

> capable of joining to a *masculine* understanding, the finer sensibilities of a female. An heart exquisitely alive to the beauties of nature, and keenly susceptible of every soft impression, every tender emotion . . . that delicacy of feeling which is the peculiar characteristic of the sex.

The reviewer attributed this to Wollstonecraft's having become a mother and a wife, not realizing she was unmarried. This reviewer was invoking the standards of feminine prose, emanating from a gendered nervous system, with which Richardson had defended "familiar," sentimental writing. Style and "person" were conflated as a boundary. It is this the historian must bear in mind in examining women writers' efforts to defend women's mental capacities on one side while insisting they were still female on the other.[34]

In the same year, 1796, Hays made still more direct the sexual self-assertiveness implicit in women's public awakening of consciousness. The heroine of her novel, Emma Courtney, falls in love with a man whose name, Augustus Harley, refers to MacKenzie's *Man of Feeling;* Harley does not return her passion, and Emma pursues him monomaniacally, even proposing sexual intercourse. This pursuit, her bludgeoning him with self-pity, and her attempts to induce guilt add up to the most convincing if painful aspect of the novel, perhaps because of its autobiographical nature. Hays interpolates the deterministic psychology of her friend Godwin's *Political Justice* throughout the novel, along with the associationist psychology of her friend Wollstonecraft's *Rights of Woman,* frequently quoting both books. Thus her heroine can claim that she was led "irresistibly" to her passion: it is the result of that sentimentalizing process of civilization Wollstonecraft had recently uncovered, one rooted in childrearing.[35] Ostensibly she presents her heroine, Emma Courtney, "as a *warning*" to her readers of the consequences of "one strong indulged passion." Her passion and its errors were "the offspring of sensibility." Hays's intention is to illustrate Wollstonecraft's general diagnosis of the causes of excessive sensibility in women with the case study of Emma Courtney.[36]

However, instead of grasping the balanced solution Wollstonecraft offered, Hays slides into the aggrandizement of extreme, feminine sensibility which seems genuine, not merely symptomatic. Or it might be said that Hays cobbles together the culture's celebration of feminine sensibility with Wollstonecraft's devastating critique of it. Wollstonecraft showed the same tendency, but it was a problem she recognized far more explicitly and therefore came much closer to mastering than Hays. Emma emphasizes "those sweet sensations, of which nature has formed my heart too exquisitely susceptible" and adheres to the notion that this is a laudable, female characteristic. "Nature has formed woman peculiarly susceptible to the tender passions," and here Hays quotes the sentimental orthodoxy of John Aikin, Barbauld's brother. Emma welcomes,

> The thousand soft sensations
> Which vulgar souls want faculties to taste,
> Who take their good and evil in the gross.[37]

All this was intended as a defense against charges of immorality, Hays appealing to the "feeling and thinking few" from the very beginning. Emma Courtney has been "enslaved by passion" and has become a "victim" of her own "ardent passions" and "mistaken tenderness," like Wollstonecraft, a "martyr" to her "propensity to attachment." She asks, "Is it virtue then, to combat, or to yield to, my passions?" It seems clear that "yield" is the correct answer. Emma confessed that she loved Harley, "not only rationally and tenderly, but *passionately*," and her love became "a pervading and a devouring fire!" Arguing against the "forcible suppression" of "these natural sensations and affections," against the "polluted" streams flowing from "monastic institutions and principles," Emma declared to Harley, "*My friend—I would give myself to you.*"[38] It had been Emma's "sensibility," the "tender, yet chaste, caresses and endearments of ineffable affection," a "complication of generous, affecting, exquisite emotions," that "impelled" her to make this "one great effort." Hays combined her Godwinian, Jacobin opposition to "custom" and a "false system of morals" with the old, Neoplatonic claim that sensibility was the moral sense. Unlike a "corrupt heart," sensibility was naturally virtuous. The heart is "compelled by the touching sympathies which bind, with sacred, indissoluble ties, mind to mind!"[39]

Hays openly declares that woman's sexual freedom is the natural extension of her sensibility. Her heroine's "ardent sensibility" incited her "to love." The awakening of women signified by "sensibility" included sexual wishes as well as mind. Moreover, Hays coupled her expression of sexual wish with her declaration of individual will and consciousness in the "pursuit" of a happiness founded in "nature." This, too, had long been implicit in the culture of sensibility, along with an opposite characteristic.

> I have ever spoken, and acted, from the genuine dictates of a mind swayed, at the time, by its own views and propensities . . . "Let the coldly wise exalt, that their heads were never led astray by their hearts." I have all along used . . . the language of sincerity.

The quotation within that paragraph was excerpted from Godwin's *Political Justice*.[40]

Despite this declaration of independence and of egotism, Hays also expressed "the shame of being singular," and the other aspect of sensibility, its assertion that it was synonymous with "social sympathy," the projection onto social arrangements of Newtonian vibrations. In Hays's words, "energetic sympathies of truth and feeling—darting from mind to mind . . . with electrical rapidity," could spread from the Smithian family, "the center of private affections," to "embrace . . . the whole sensitive and rational creation." This was the inflation of Newton's physics to a social, reformist vision the *Rights of Woman* had also invoked. Edgeworth would invoke it, too. Both elements, individualism and the wish for social harmony, would flow into Victorian conceptions of "separate spheres."[41]

Hays claims that Emma's sexual passion for Harley is "modest" and "principled" because "*it was individual*—it annihilated in my eyes every other man in creation." She writes that "*the individuality of an affection constitutes its chastity*." Thus Hays follows sensibility's precedent of arguing that her heroine's spontaneous outflow of feeling was accompanied by moral control. Her "delicacy would require assurance of [Harley's] present individual affection" as a condition of her giving herself to him. It seems like marriage in all but name but it was not, and Hays made it clear that the arrangement was the result of her sense of freedom, the moral control the result of her own choice. "The world may do its will—but I will never be its slave . . . I am determined to preserve my freedom, and trust to the general candour and good sense of mankind."[42]

Emma Courtney "was read as condoning sexual license for women, and as such attracted more remonstrance than any other individual revolutionary novel." If in her youth Hays had been inspired by Clarissa, she also compared her heroine to Rousseau's Julie, as well as to

Rousseau himself, a dangerously charged reference in 1796. The Anti-Jacobin *Critical Review* accused Hays of arousing "the contagious and consuming fever of perverted sensibility." Hays had associated female sensibility with the expression of individual sexual will: Hannah More stood for the jettisoning of the latter in the interests of preserving the former. The same reviewer of Hays praised More and Barbauld as "monuments of well-directed genius," who will be "deservedly admired when all the impassioned imitations of Rousseau and Diderot shall cease to be remembered." Barbauld's "The Rights of Woman," another response to the *Rights of Woman,* surrendered both sexual and intellectual autonomy in favor of the stereotype of feminine sensibility. Within two years but in the same counterrevolutionary context, Godwin erected his salutory monument to the "Author of a Vindication of the Rights of Woman."[43]

Wollstonecraft Becomes Amazon

Wollstonecraft's argument in the *Rights of Woman* had been virtually unobjectionable in 1792. It was only generally condemned after 1798. Part of the explanation lay with intensifying counterrevolutionary circumstances. Following the detection by a Parliamentary "Committee of Secrecy" of a "PLOT" to destroy the British constitution under the pretext of reform, the government staged a series of treason trials in 1794. Godwin published a pamphlet that was decisive in the acquittal of some of the defendants. Government repression increased as it faced food riots and evidence of widespread support for the radical cause in 1795.[44] The "Two Acts" of that year broke organized radicalism "in pieces." But the government remained "haunted" by the nightmare of French invasion. In her *Letters from Sweden* (1796) Wollstonecraft referred to Pitt's "crushing at home, plots of his own conjuring up."[45] The paranoia intensified in the year of her death, fed by mutinies at the Nore and Spithead, Napoleon's conquest of Switzerland, the French invasion of Pembroke, and then, in early 1798, of Ireland, accompanying an Irish rebellion. In England these events, spies, and rumors fostered belief in a widespread Jacobin plot: "The sense of crisis generated a formidable witch-hunt."[46] Godwin supplied the witch.

He published his *Memoirs of the Author of the Vindication of the Rights of Woman* late in January 1798, after Wollstonecraft's death in childbed the previous September. Godwin revealed that Wollstonecraft had been thwarted in her attempt to have an affair with Henry Fuseli, a married man; she had then consummated an affair with Imlay, by whom she had a child out of wedlock; in spite of the existence of this child and contrary to law and religion, she attempted suicide twice; she became pregnant by Godwin out of wedlock; finally, she had ignored religion on her deathbed. These were the sins on which the subsequent debate focused.

Godwin also reminded the opposition of a connection between Wollstonecraft and a juicy sex scandal of 1798, simply by describing her brief stint as a governess to the daughters of Lord and Lady Kingsborough. He wrote that while Lady Kingsborough "had imposed upon her daughters a variety of prohibitions . . . Mary immediately restored them to their liberty, and undertook to govern them by their affections only . . . they were uneasy under any indulgence that had not the sanction of their governess." This last phrase was echoed ironically in a review of the *Memoirs* because, four months prior to its publication, Mary King, the Kingsborough's eldest daughter, had eloped with her uncle, Colonel Henry Fitzgerald. He was the illegitimate half-brother of her mother, and a married man to boot, so this was incest as well as adultery. Fitzgerald was killed by Mary King's father and brother. There was a sensational trial in the House of Lords in 1798, during which it was rumored that Mary King's baby by Fitzgerald had been murdered by her family. While Mary King had been only eight at the time of her contact with Wollstonecraft, the latter was blamed for indoctrinating her pupil with sexual immorality. Noting Godwin's silence on the issue and summarizing the scandal as "the misconduct of one of her pupils, who has lately brought disgrace on herself, death on her paramour, risk to the life of her brother and father, and misery to all her relatives," the *European Magazine* explained it as the result of Wollstonecraft's "system of education." An Irish bishop preaching on the affair linked it to the French Revolution by associating the names of Wollstonecraft and Voltaire, the latter one of the philosophers whose ideas were held to have caused the Revolution. Sexual revolution was political revolution.[47]

Prior to Godwin's publication of the *Memoirs,* the public had known little of Wollstonecraft's life. One of them said, "I know nothing of Miss Wollstonecraft's character or conduct, but for the Memoirs of Godwin."[48] Wollstonecraft herself had been careful to conceal her conduct, maintaining she was "Mary Imlay," married to the father of her child, until it was impossible not to reveal the truth.[49] It was for this reason that the *British Critic*'s reviewer of *Letters from Sweden* had assumed she was married. After Godwin's revelations, critics could use the life to condemn the work. Their usual references to the theory or philosophy of Jacobinism referred to Godwin's *Political Justice,* which had been criticized in 1796 for advocating "the promiscuous intercourse of the sexes." Now Godwin's Wollstonecraft became the central emblem of the philosophy of English Jacobinism "in action," threatening "the destruction of domestic, civil, and political society." Godwin had introduced the *Memoirs* not only by asking "sympathy" for "Mary's" fate but by suggesting that doing justice to her included making her life "the fairest source of animation and encouragement to all who would follow." In the words of the *Anti-Jacobin Review,* the *Memoirs* was "intended by him for a beacon, [but] it serves as a buoy." In other words, this was understood as an ideological conflict by its participants.[50]

Godwin's chief purpose was to defend Wollstonecraft against what he seemed to be revealing. In fact her obituaries had already made public the most glaring of Wollstonecraft's sexual improprieties. Godwin's marriage to "Mary Imlay," unmediated by divorce, revealed that she had been an unmarried mother. At that time, pregnant by Godwin, Wollstonecraft had been between the devil and the deep blue sea; had she not married Godwin, she would have had a second child out of wedlock (specifically, out of legal British wedlock). Her correspondence shows her very practical awareness of this problem. Several of Wollstonecraft's friends did drop her because of what the marriage revealed. And now her September 10 death in childbirth following an August 30 birth and a March 29 marriage showed that Wollstonecraft had again engaged in unmarried sex. Because these facts were included in her obituaries, the cat was out of the bag, revealed not only to her personal acquaintances but to anyone who could read the newspapers. So Godwin's more extensive revelations (adding less serious sins to those already revealed) were a preemptive strike, welding revelation with explanation.[51]

Godwin's defense was to make Wollstonecraft a heroine of sensibility, the kind of female icon with which his readers were deeply familiar. Godwin had modeled all of his female characters on Richardson's in the novels he wrote prior to his biography of "Mary," and he would continue to do so in the stream of novels he wrote after the *Memoirs.* It has been fairly observed that Godwin's *Memoirs* of Wollstonecraft reads "like a passionate sentimental novel."[52]

That Godwin took for granted his readers' familiarity with Wollstonecraft's *Rights of Woman* is apparent from his title. In a single paragraph he puts his finger on the premise of the book: Wollstonecraft had stood forth "in defence of one half of the human species . . . degraded [by the other half] from the station of rational beings, and almost sunk . . . to the level of the brutes." Yet this might seem remarkable for its cursoriness, especially because Godwin's own assessment of the book, his praise for its genius, is strikingly qualified in sexual terms, as we shall see in a moment. True, his second edition revised the conclusion of the *Memoirs* to include what might also be a summary of Wollstonecraft's book. One sex, he wrote

> is accustomed more to the exercise of its reasoning powers and the other of its feelings. Women have a frame of body more delicate and susceptible of impression than men, and in proportion as they receive a less intellectual education, are more unreservedly under the empire of feeling.

Godwin, however, expresses these observations entirely as if they were his own, quite separate from his comments on the *Rights of Woman*. They were the cliché of his era, and Godwin only hints in the sparest way that Wollstonecraft's achievement had been to develop them on the Smithian, psychosociological scale I have mentioned. In place of such an account, Godwin concentrated on a particular presentation of Wollstonecraft's personality, that is, as a woman of extreme sensibility. Wollstonecraft was "endowed with the most exquisite and delicious sensibility," her mind was almost "of too fine a texture to encounter the vicissitudes of human affairs, to whom pleasure is transport and disappointment is agony indescribable." This was a misleading half-truth, a tempting self-conception which, unmistakably to a reader of the *Rights of Woman,* Wollstonecraft wished to teach women to resist. But Godwin's cursoriness, his qualifications, and misrepresentation must be attributed to his defensive purpose as he gauged his audience as well as to his own deeply held views; the latter incorporated Godwin's concern over the "effeminizing" effects of sensibility on men, noted in Chapter 3. In this he represented the widespread concern among other eighteenth-century male writers, not just Day and MacKenzie, and their predecessors but also apparent among several of Godwin's peers in the 1790s, including Coleridge.[53]

In addition to his Richardsonian models, Godwin's defense of Wollstonecraft in the *Memoirs* also may have been influenced by Hays's defense of a heroine of feeling in the recently published *Emma Courtney.* Godwin attributed to Wollstonecraft "sentiments as pure, as refined, and as delicate, as ever inhabited a human heart!" She exemplified the good side of the division between "the genuine march of sentiment" and "overflowing of the soul," and "the established rules and prejudices of mankind," between the "most sacredly private" and the values of "the vulgar." This could be a paraphrase of *Emma Courtney.* Moreover, like Hays's sentimental heroine, Godwin's Wollstonecraft believed that "the gratification of the senses" could be squared with purity by enjoying gratification "only as the consequence of an individual affection." Of course, if Hays's *Memoirs of Emma Courtney* influenced Godwin's *Memoirs* of Wollstonecraft, Hays had made it very clear that she had been influenced by Godwin's *Political Justice*. Furthermore, in Godwin's 1794 novel, *Caleb Williams*, Falkland had successfully defended himself on sentimental grounds against the charge that he had committed murder. These similarities and connections were all grist to the Anti-Jacobin mill.[54]

So, too, was Godwin's associating Wollstonecraft with Goethe's sexually subversive Werther. Godwin assimilated his sentimental stereotype to this current romantic symbol, a male hero who had indulged an illicit passion with a married person as Wollstonecraft had with Fuseli, and who had succeeded in the suicide Wollstonecraft had attempted. Godwin repeatedly presented Wollstonecraft as a "female Werter." (*The Female Werter* was the title of a 1792 novel capitalizing on the Werter craze.) He organized the events of Wollstonecraft's life around her sorrows, virtually ignoring her intellectual work in favor of her relationships with others, with her parents, with Fanny Blood, and, above all, with Fuseli, Imlay, and himself. In all of these relationships "Mary" demonstrated her capacity for exquisite feeling. His preface to Wollstonecraft's letters to Imlay, which he also published as part of her *Posthumous Works*, also identified "Mary" with Werter.[55]

Godwin insisted on this comparison between Wollstonecraft's real life and Werter's fictional one, and he suggested the former was superior to the latter because it was true. His introduction to the *Memoirs* explained that he told the complete truth about Wollstonecraft because it would more effectively arouse sympathy for her. In other words, Godwin appealed to the culture of sensibility just as Hays had. Setting the stage for his revelations of what convention would see as Wollstonecraft's fornication with Imlay and bearing a bastard to him, Godwin enumerated all the "evils" Wollstonecraft had suffered to that point in her life. Conceding that they might not appear to be "the heaviest in the catalogue of human suffering," he argued that "evils take their rank less from their own nature, than from the temper of the mind that suffers them." He argued, subtly and persistently, that Wollstonecraft's conduct was "reconcilable to the strictest rectitude." That was the culture of sensibility's claim to transcendence, its adherence to the higher law of sincerity and feeling, expressed in both romanticism and evangelical reform.[56]

Godwin's attribution of Wollstonecraft's sexual unconventionality to her excessive sensibility, already a preoccupation of critics of women's public expression of conscious willfulness, published at a crucial counterrevolutionary moment, forced his opponents to reemphasize the culture's sexual puritanism and its compatibility with sexual orthodoxy, because they shared the same, gendered view of sensibility with Godwin. Hays's connection of Emma Courtney's sexual heterodoxy to the radical politics of Godwin and Wollstonecraft contributed to the same effect. Hays and Godwin were but two among a significant number of provocative Jacobin writers whose defenses of greater female freedom only intensified Anti-Jacobin hostility. They were caught in the counterrevolutionary engine the British government, fearing domestic revolution at the same time that it was at war with revolutionary France, set in motion.

To be able to associate Wollstonecraft with sexual revolution was an invaluable weapon in the hands of the Anti-Jacobins. While they were eager for a witch hunt in 1797–8, they had found very "little contemporary evidence of real Jacobin feeling" and had gone back to the era of Godwin's publication of *Political Justice* in order to renew their attack on Godwin as "a powerful bogey." Henceforth, his revelations about Wollstonecraft were centerpieces of the Anti-Jacobin representations of "JACOBIN MORALITY."[57]

Godwin's defense of Wollstonecraft backfired. In a 1799 review which was intended to tar Jacobin writer Mary Robinson with Wollstonecraft's brush, Dr. Bisset said that Wollstonecraft "could plead her feelings in justification of her concubinage and her attempted suicide . . . We doubt not, that even Newgate is full of victims of sensibility . . . [Although agreeing] that sensibility is necessary to virtue and to happiness, we cannot help thinking that sensibility inculcated much farther than is beneficial [is] hurtful to its votaries." This, of course, was very close to what Wollstonecraft had said, but she had a very different purpose in mind. The long-running concern over "excessive sensibility" was thus given a final push by Godwin's figure of Wollstonecraft. He was understood to have justified her sexual freedom on the basis of what he called "the most exquisite and delicious sensibility," the "peculiar strength" and "warmth" of her feeling, perhaps stirring up the belief being outmoded that "warming" women prepared them for orgasm. Like Hays's Emma Courtney, Godwin's Wollstonecraft had merely taken one step further in expressing her feminine sensibility. This had been a fear generated by women's expressing their feelings all along. From now on, Godwin's Wollstonecraft became the vehicle for those apprehensions over the willful and sexual possibilities in female "sensibility"—female consciousness—now seen to have run rampant. After she had sex with Imlay, according to the *British Critic,* Wollstonecraft's "senses were so *completely awakened* that she could not exist without their gratification."[58]

The *Rights of Woman* was reread in light of Godwin's revelations. Wollstonecraft was now interpreted as the embodiment of intellectual and personal "license." She confirmed the apprehension that "ev'ry woman is at heart a rake." "A woman who has broken through all religious restraints, will commonly be found ripe for every species of licentiousness." (The word reminds us that Rochester, too, was "outlawed" finally in 1806.) Critics apprehended that Wollstonecraft was a "philosophical wanton" and that the Jacobin philosophy for which she stood, "by leaving women to the exercise of . . . their natural and social rights, . . . would take away powerful restraints on the promiscuous intercourse of the sexes . . . dissolve the tie of marriage, one of the chief foundations of political society, and then promote Jacobinical politics."[59] In the *Rights of Woman,* Wollstonecraft herself had condemned the "manners" that, she said made "men and women" "alternately timid and ferocious slaves of feeling." Looking to place virtue on the basis of a tougher-minded "education," she had condemned the rearing and teaching that made "weak woman . . . the slave of sensibility." Now Godwin's account of her relationships made her vulnerable to the charge of being, in the words of Thomas Matthias, "Fierce passion's slave, [who] veered with very gust."[60] Among the cornucopia of Jacobinical publications over which the deified figure of "Sensibility" presided in Gillray's 1798 cartoon was Wollstonecraft's recently published *Wrongs of Woman.* Apprehending willfulness, men claimed women lacked will. Wollstonecraft was a "voluptuary and a sensualist." Her constitution was "very amorous."[61]

Even Wollstonecraft's defenders increased the danger of women's identification with mindless sensibility by repeating and amplifying Godwin's tactic. The Jacobin *Analytical Review,* apparently criticizing Godwin's line of defense, in effect adopted it as its own.[62] Most striking in this regard is the "abridgement" of the *Memoirs* in the *Monthly Visitor.*[63] The anonymous author defended Wollstonecraft by arguing that Godwin had not gone far enough in identifying her as a heroine of sensibility: *The Rights of Woman,* Wollstonecraft's "most celebrated production" had brought her "fame," but fame "could not fill the heart of female sensibility."[64] The writer is able to bolster her/his depiction of Wollstonecraft as the figure of virtue in distress by quoting nine pages of the most sentimental passages from her private letters to Imlay. (Godwin had included all of them in the four volumes of *Posthumous Works* he published along with the *Memoirs.*)[65] Godwin, the *Monthly Visitor* argued, had failed to detect Wollstonecraft's signs of distress during the Fuseli affair, and even when uncovering them while writing the *Memoirs* the rational philosopher had shown himself a cold-hearted "sceptic" (a man who measures "the affections of the heart" rather than a man of feeling—again, Godwin himself had supplied the ammunition in the *Memoirs*), by suggesting that Wollstonecraft's feelings for Fuseli had been heightened by her celibacy. By contrast, Wollstonecraft's sensibility, the *Monthly Visitor* asserted, was free of sexual desire as well as reconcilable with strict morality. Thus Wollstonecraft could be reclaimed for the opposition to Jacobinism, that "New School," which Godwin embodied in his *Memoirs*. "Mrs. Godwin was not a member of the New School."[66]

"L. M.," the apparently female author of another response to the *Memoirs,* took the same tack. Prior to Godwin's publication, L. M. had brought "veneration" to Wollstonecraft because of her "revolution in principles," rescuing women's "minds" from oppression. She said that Wollstonecraft articulated "a theme which had long dwelt on my tongue." Wollstonecraft's writings had demonstrated that she was capable of experiencing and resisting "those darts of anguish, which a sensibility fostered at the expense of reason and discretion, can sharpen to agony." Godwin, however, revealed that Wollstonecraft had lost religion. The writer was "shocked" at the "licence" Wollstonecraft allowed "to the unrestrained indulgence of feelings." L. M. accepted Godwin's argument that Wollstonecraft had let her "reason" sleep. Wollstonecraft became, "after a season of torturing conflict, the self-devoted victim of ungovernable sensibility." She was a real Marianne Dashwood, as it were. Nonetheless, L. M. could fall back on Wollstonecraft's letters to Imlay, just as the *Monthly Visitor* had. Reading them changed her. They brought L. M. relief because they enabled her to retain her positive view of Wollstonecraft's heroic and victimized feminine sensibility: "By her letters to the monster of insensibility [Imlay], who deceived and abandoned her, the severity of my decision was softened, and my aversion converted into sympathy. From those letters, the purity of her heart appears to be incontestible." Of course, this was how Wollstonecraft had often presented her relationship to Imlay to him, to herself, and, presumably to Godwin, but it was only part of her fierce, unceasing struggle with her "sensibility." In any case, while L. M. went along with the Anti-Jacobins' condemnation of Wollstonecraft's "license," she rescued both the female culture of sensibility and women's exercise of wakeful reason by linking them with purity. Such a defense was capable of jettisoning Wollstonecraft entirely.[67]

The Anti-Jacobins pressed their attack through the opening Godwin had supplied, as if they could get women to reduce themselves merely to embodiments of reflexive feeling, the danger of which writers from Astell to Wollstonecraft had warned. They did so by saying that Wollstonecraft, showing "alarming eccentricities," was "unsex'd," and went on to suggest all women showing independence of consciousness in mind or body were also "unsex'd," that is, not women at all. The Reverend Polwhele's heavily annotated poem, *The Unsex'd Females* (1798), represents this mode of attack. It persistently contrasted Wollstonecraft's strong-mindedness unfavorably with that of weak, feminine sensibility, the standard the *Critical Review* had urged on Wollstonecraft in reviewing the *Rights of Woman.* Polwhele declared that "the crimsoning blush of modesty, will always be more attractive than the sparkle of confident intelligence."[68] Polwhele dramatized his wish in terms that linked it to the war with revolutionary France. He reminisced that "natural" woman,

> From sullen clouds relieve domestic care
> And melt in smiles the withering frown of war.
> Ah! once the female Muse to NATURE true
> The unvalued store from FANCY, FEELING drew.

This natural femininity was, he said, by "modest luxury heightened and refined[,]" understanding the relationship between the promulgation of the culture's ideal of femininity and Britain's economic history. The phrase illustrates, too, Polwhele's reading of the *Rights of Woman,* where Wollstonecraft had argued that women "should not have their sensations heightened in the hot-bed of luxurious indolence, at the expense of their understanding."[69]

Polwhele feared that, under the inspiration of Wollstonecraft and women like her, all women would give up sensibility's feminine ideal:

> Soon shall the sex disdain the illusive sway,
> And wield the sceptre in yon blaze of day;
> Ere long, each little artifice discard,
> No more by weakness winning fond regard,
> Nor eyes, that sparkle from their blushes, roll,
> Nor catch the languors of the sick'ning soul,
> Nor the quick flutter, nor the coy reserve,
> But nobly boast the firm gymnastic nerve;
> Nor more affect with Delicacy's fan
> [Instead,] Blend mental energy with Passion's fire,
> Surpass their rivals with the power of mind
> And vindicate the *Rights of Womanhood.*

Polwhele quoted Godwin's *Memoirs* to illustrate the transformation his verse describes, one that, he argued, unsexed women: Wollstonecraft "possessed a firmness of mind, an unconquerable greatness of soul; by which, after a short internal struggle, she was accustomed to rise above difficulties and sufferings." In fact, this could be a description of Elinor Dashwood or other tough-minded heroines, from Clarissa to Evelina.[70]

On one hand, the Anti-Jacobins asserted that Wollstonecraft and other female embodiments of excessive sensibility were tinged with Rousseauistic revolutionaryism and therefore veered mindlessly in the direction of lust. On the other, they reacted against women whose display of powers of mind was evidence that they were "unsex'd," that is, "masculine." The common ground was willfulness and consciousness. The *Anti-Jacobin Review* emphasized that Wollstonecraft had passed "for a young woman of extraordinary strength of mind." Polwhele sought to beat back women's "power of mind" in favor of that very gendering of extreme sensibility Wollstonecraft struggled against. This had long been women's own, external and internal fight. His sexual wish closely resembles King Lovelace's lip-smacking fantasy of a wife, crimsoned o'er, all "meekness," "sighing with bent knees and supplicating hands, and eyes lifted up to [a man's] imperial countenance, just running over." Polwhele's fantasy invoked the sexual dyad that both Wollstonecraft and de Sade understood. Polwhele's express fear that all women would discard little artifices, winning weakness, blushes, rolling eyes, sickening languors, quick flutters, coy reserve, and "Delicacy," in favor of the firm gymnastic nerve, mental energy, passion, and the powers of mind, combined the expression of men's wishes with the warning to women that they must conform themselves to them. Summoning the power of the century's own gendered, historical process, the *European Magazine* declared of the *Memoirs:* "It will be read with disgust by every female who has any pretensions to delicacy."[71]

The warning was attached to the symbol of the Amazon. Here, too, Godwin's *Memoirs* was significant, even if in the *Rights of Woman* Wollstonecraft herself had invoked a vision of women becoming public heroines and armed, marching as soldiers. It must have been just such a passage in the *Rights of Woman* that Godwin had in mind when he said in the *Memoirs* that readers of the *Rights of Woman* expected the author was in person "a sturdy, muscular, raw-boned virago." (These are the qualifications in Godwin's praise to which I just referred.) This "person" was appropriate to a book in which, Godwin said, "many of the sentiments are undoubtedly of a rather masculine description. The spirited and decisive way in which the author explodes the system of gallantry, and the species of homage with which the sex is usually treated, shocked the majority," including, it seems, Godwin himself. There were "occasional passages of a stern and rugged feature," and the author "scorned" to qualify what she thought at any given time. This manifested "a rigid and somewhat amazonian temper." It was Godwin who had expected that the author of masculine sentiments, rugged descriptions, and amazonian temper would be a "virago," a synonym of Amazon. He wished to dramatize the female character he preferred. Wollstonecraft's "essential character" was expressed, Godwin said, in other parts of the *Rights of Woman:* they showed Wollstonecraft's "luxuriance of imagination and a trembling delicacy of sentiment." Accordingly, when Godwin actually met the author, he found "a woman lovely in her person, and in the best and most engaging sense, feminine in her manners." Wollstonecraft's "person" was consistent with her being a heroine of sensibility and with what he saw as the best of her prose.[72]

Godwin's virago-amazonian-masculine characterization gave the Anti-Jacobins yet another stick with which to beat Wollstonecraft and the strong-minded, "unsex'd" women for whom she stood. In Polwhele's words, Wollstonecraft refused to heave,

> one female sigh;
> Arm'd with proud intellect, at fortune laugh'd,
> Mock'd the vain threat, and brav'd the envenom'd shaft.

She was "the intrepid champion of her sex," asserting "the sovereign claim" over "humbled man." He described the "chosen train" over which Wollstonecraft was "the plum'd chieftain":

> A female band despising NATURE's law
> As "proud defiance" flashes from their arms,
> And vengeance smothers all their softer charms.
> I shudder at the new unpictur'd scene
> Where unsex'd woman vaunts the imperious mien
> Where girls affecting to dismiss the heart
> Invoke the Proteus of petrific art.

This public parade of defiant women brought a shudder to Polwhele, threatening to turn him to stone, when he wished only to see women in melting privacy. At this precise point his vision shades into his picture of "girls" prepared to follow fashions in French dress as well as Revolutionary ideas:

> With equal ease, in body or in mind
> To Gallic freaks or Gothic faith resign'd,
> The crane-like neck, as Fashion bids, lay bare,
> Or frizzle, hold in front their borrow'd hair;
> Scarce by a gossamery film carest,
> Sport, in full view, the meretricious breast;
> Loose the chaste cincture . . .

The source of this fashion, he explained, was "among prostitutes—among women of the most abandoned character." (Did his recording their "petrific art" stand for the reverend's sexual arousal? Mandeville suggested as much of Polwhele's predecessor's attacks on women.) Polwhele's vision connects his other anxieties over sex with the continuing reactions we have seen stirred by women's public and willful pursuit of the subversive pleasures of consumerism.[73]

Polwhele footnotes his phrase, "A female band despising NATURE's law": "The Amazonian band—the female Quixotes of the new philosophy." The language associates revolutionary women on horseback with the popular novel as figures deluded by romance. Polwhele goes on to list the members of that female band of Amazons, all responding to Wollstonecraft's leadership. He included Hays, the "veteran Barbauld," Mary Robinson, Charlotte Smith, Helen Maria Williams, Ann Yearsley, and the painters Emma Crewe and Angelica Kauffman. "Angelica Kauffman's print should accompany Mary Wollstonecraft's instructions in Priapism . . . by way of illustration. This, and a little plant adultery, would go great lengths, in producing among girls, the consummation so devoutly wished."[74]

Polwhele might have derived this from Salzman's *Elements of Morality,* which Wollstonecraft had translated in 1790. It had argued that the best method of counteracting the "dreadful evil" of masturbation was "to speak to children of the organs of generation as freely as we speak of the other parts of the body, and explain to them the noble use which they were designed for." Most likely, however, Polwhele referred to Wollstonecraft's challenge in the *Rights of Woman* to the view that a lady might not be taught "the modern system of botany" on grounds of "female delicacy," in addition to her declaring that children should be taught that mothers "carry and nourish" their young. During the reaction provoked by Godwin, the *British Critic* accused Wollstonecraft of urging "the propriety of making young persons, particularly girls, intimately acquainted with certain parts of anatomy." This had the effect of invoking the long-standing connection between "excessive delicacy" and masturbation, a link Wollstonecraft had made in *Mary* but only to oppose it.[75] That Wollstonecraft had been a teacher and a governess, in addition to the author of such published views, added to the dangers of their being disseminated. Polwhele was appalled that "a woman of such principles," an irreligious fornicator as well as implicitly a masturbator, should have superintended "the education of young ladies." He "intimated" her effectiveness as an instructor of "Priapism" by referring to the fact "that Miss W. was a governess of the daughter of Lord Kingsborough."[76]

Against his list of Amazonian, sexually arousing women artists, sympathetic to the French Revolution, Polwhele arrayed a band of approved women writers who displayed Christian virtue: Elizabeth

Montagu, Elizabeth Carter, Hester Chapone, Anna Seward, Hester Piozzi, Burney, Radcliffe, the illustrator Diana Beauclerk, and, of course, Hannah More. (Radcliffe had quoted More's *Sacred Dramas* in the conservative and extremely sentimental *Mysteries of Udolpho.*) This wealth of divergent talents endorses the view expressed in other ways that the fundamentally important provocation for the furious onslaught on Wollstonecraft's revolutionaryism was the inescapable emergence of women's willfully published consciousness.[77] One of Polwhele's immediate inspirations for this attack on Amazonian writers, Matthias's *The Shade of Alexander Pope* (1798), expressed the same wish to reduce women to sensibility's weakening stereotype, praising Carter, More, Smith, and Radcliffe for their "varied excellencies." "But" he wrote, "when female writers forget the character and delicacy of their sex" they unloose "the spirit of gross licentiousness," wreaking moral and political havoc.[78]

On the other side of the ideological fence, Hays was able in 1793 to quote Jacobin poet George Dyer's celebration of "the respectable names of Macaulay, Wollstonecraft, Barbauld, [Ann] Jebb, Williams, and Smith." Such listings of exemplary women had its roots in the medieval collections of the lives of female saints, noted for their capacity to withstand suffering. Protestants had continued this exemplary form during that upsurge in the demand for improved education for women; in 1688 William Crouch published *Female Excellency: or, The Ladies Glory.* We saw Mandeville challenging *The Tatler*'s list of the historically important with his own list of notable women. John Duncombe's *The Feminiad: or, The Female Genius* (1751) was followed by the most ambitious of all, George Ballard's *Memoirs of Several Ladies of Great Britain Who Have Been Celebrated for Their Writings or Skill in the Learned Languages, Arts and Sciences* (1752; reprinted in 1775). (Elstob had suggested the idea to Ballard.) The trend in these exemplary works was to replace the emphasis on women's capacity for faith amid suffering by their capacity for intellectual achievement. Ballard declared "that prejudice of the supposed incapacity of the female sex, is what these memoirs in general may remove." Among the prejudices Ballard said he faced in this enterprise were those "which come from the Hunting Tribe." Fielding's emblematic Squire Western was the exact contemporary of this remark.[79] A significant proportion of Ballard's subjects were aristocrats; the differences in the lists made at the end of the century included their subjects' generally lower social rank and the fact that many of them were writers with a popular following.

Dyer argued that women were "more uniformly on the side of liberty" than men because of their own sense of oppression:

> the modes of education, and the customs of society are degrading to the female character, and the tyranny of custom is sometimes worse than the tyranny of government. When a sensible woman rises above the tyranny of custom she feels a generous indignation; when turned against the exclusive claims of the other sex, is favourable to female pretentions; when turned against the tyranny of government, it is commonly favourable to the rights of both sexes. Most governments are partial, and more injurious to women than to men.

Women, then, were primed for revolution and evidently they were becoming more conscious of the "tyranny of custom," particularly along the boundaries of authorship, but in a myriad of other ways, in the pursuit of which some of them adopted "male" riding habits. This notion—long underpinning women's challenge to traditional definitions of gender—was central to Jacobin political views. Hays's Emma Courtney proudly declared that she had "totally disregarded the customs of the world[,]" characterized the law as "chicanery," and judged herself innocent of "any crime." In 1806 Edgeworth was to suggest that Jacobin doctrines of "perfectibility" were especially attractive to "weak and enthusiastic women" who thereby become "zealots in support of their sublime opinions."[80]

The *British Critic* asserted that Wollstonecraft's "proselytes" were few. Still, while trusting that Godwin's Wollstonecraft "will obtain no imitators of the heroine in this country," the Anti-Jacobin *European Magazine* found it necessary to hold it up "as a warning to those who fancy themselves at liberty to dispense with the laws of propriety and decency and who suppose the possession of certain perverted talents will atone for deviations from rules long established for the well government of society and the happiness of mankind." In fact there are signs that sympathy for both Wollstonecraft and her views persisted. During the 1790s letters debating the *Rights of Woman* were published in several journals. The editor of the sympathetic *Monthly Magazine*, referring to a 1796–7 controversy in his column over the applicability to women of Locke's environmental emphasis in his explanation of the evolution of mind (which an opponent called "a monstrous doctrine"), said, "The Controversy concerning the Talents of Women has proved to be so prolific, that we must beg leave to decline inserting any farther letters on the subject." Nonetheless, the correspondence continued to be published.[81] Private and public expressions of praise and sympathy for the *Rights of Woman* survived even the calumny heaped on it after the publication of Godwin's *Memoirs*. Letters to editors agreed with the arguments of the *Rights of Woman* or pointed out that Godwin had misrepresented Wollstonecraft's views. Anti-Jacobin writer Jane West said in 1801 that Wollstonecraft's name had obtained "a lamentable distinction," because her "doctrines" had been "circulated with uncommon avidity," "loaded with extravagant praise," and "insinuated into every recess." Other opponents also testified to Wollstonecraft's appeal and her influence among women. Defenses of Wollstonecraft were to be published on both sides of the Atlantic until well into the first decades of the nineteenth century. The full story of the reception of *Rights of Woman* remains to be told.[82]

"Man Was Made to Reason, Woman to Feel"; Compromise

The alternatives offered to women in the 1790s—the approved vision of mindless sensibility or the outlawing bogey of the strong-minded Amazon—can be seen as a parody of the conflict represented by Marianne and Elinor Dashwood. As Wollstonecraft recognized, the conflict existed both within women, and between women and the surrounding male and female authorities, telling them what it was to be female. It is in that light that we may read Austen's well-known defense of women novelists in *Northanger Abbey.* While Austen seems to have begun *Northanger Abbey* in 1794, she added the very serious purpose of the "Gothic" sections late in 1798 and thereafter. (Austen worked intensively on the integrally related *Sense and Sensibility* "until the end of the summer of 1798.") Her sister said that Austen was writing *Northanger Abbey* in "98 & 99."[83] Austen's text refers to *Belinda,* which was published in 1801; and in her "Advertisement" she tells her readers that she "finished" the work in 1803. In short, Austen was writing *Northanger Abbey* at the height of the enraged attacks on Wollstonecraft and other women novelists. (Her defense could well be paraphrasing Polwhele's characterization of Burney.)[84] Austen expressed her apprehension of male "enemies" to women writers, enemies who responded to them with sexually prejudiced and "contemptuous censure." They were equivalent to what Austen's much admired Burney had called "Public Censors." Austen suggested that such censure succeeded in forcing women to internalize the "slights" and "disgust" with which their works were received, but, she declared, novels written by women "displayed" "the greatest powers of the mind." This is the unqualified, ungendered, human mind. Polwhele's *The Unsex'd Females* had attacked women who "Blend mental energy with Passion's fire / Surpass their rivals with the power of mind / And vindicate the *Rights of Womankind.*" Responding to the position Polwhele represented, Austen vindicated women's power of mind. In this she was at one with Wollstonecraft, who in her novel *Mary* of 1788 had aimed to display "the mind of woman."[85]

This always remained an insistent value in Austen's work. While in her last novels Austen may have shown a "continued retreat from the feminism of her earlier ones," that was not the case in respect of this fundamental point. Anne Elliott, the heroine of *Persuasion,* was faced by the full weight of previous male literary authority's asserting that women are fickle. Captain Harville tells her:

> all histories are against you, all stories, prose and verse . . . I could bring you fifty quotations in a moment and I do not think I ever opened a book in my life which had not something to say upon women's inconstancy.

To these he adds the weight of oral folk tradition. "Songs and proverbs all talk of women's fickleness." Yet Captain Harville is forced to recognize that women challenge all of this on the grounds that it simply expresses men's prejudice against women: "perhaps you will say that these were all written by men." Anne Elliott, who has insisted on the greater tenderness of women's feelings earlier in this conversation, turns Harville's dubious concession to her own purpose:

> Perhaps I shall—Yes, yes, if you please, no reference to examples of books. Men have had every advantage of us in telling their own story. Education has been theirs in so much higher a degree; the pen has been in their hands. I will not allow books to prove anything.

In other words, the heroine entirely dismisses male authority in defining women, going on to describe how each sex builds its view of the other on the foundation of "a little bias" and effectively claiming women's right to tell their own story.[86]

Roberts suggests that it was only uneasily that Austen came to approach the political position represented by More. Polwhele had said in his *Unsex'd Females* that "Miss Hannah More may justly be esteemed, as a character, in all points, diametrically opposite to Miss Wollstonecraft; excepting, indeed her genius and literary attainments." The exception stands for the mode of the danger Wollstonecraft presented. More was emblematic, said Polwhele, quoting More's own statement of the "distinction" that "sex" made to "mind," that is, a gendered "sensibility and good taste." We have seen that More had deified "Sensibility" in her *Sacred Dramas,* one of the masterpieces cited by Polwhele, and had expressed her qualms over women's apparently growing freedom still earlier.[87] More followed Polwhele in the attack on Wollstonecraft by way of her *Strictures on the Modern System of Education* (1799), her title perhaps referring to the subtitle of the *Rights of Woman: With Strictures on Political and Moral Subjects.* In any case, each author could be lined up on either side of the polarity defined by the *British Critic,* contrasting Wollstonecraft's "system of morality" with "the purity of female virtue and the precepts of our holy religion." More's *Strictures* "went through 13 editions and sold 19,000 copies."[88]

More repeated her earlier argument, summarized approvingly by Polwhele, that mind was gendered: men had not only "a superior strength of body" but "a firmer texture of mind . . . a higher reach and wider range of powers." Women "possess in a high degree . . . delicacy and quickness of perception." Their minds do not "seize a great subject with so large a grasp" as men. Power, range, grasp; these terms connoted a kind of muscularity of mind More identified with reason and with men, as had Shaftesbury, her predecessor in counterrevolution. By contrast, said More, women operated in the way that other proponents of sensibility said they should, short-circuiting the mind. Women

> have a certain *tact* which often enables them to feel what is just more instantaneously than they can define it. They have an intuitive penetration into character, bestowed on them by Providence, like the sensibility and tender organs of some timid animals, as a kind of natural guard to warn off the approach of danger, beings who are often called to act defensively.

More's simile again posed powerlessness as a defense against the men who hunt them, just as Pamela had done so long ago, and stands for More's perpetuation of the masochistic definition of woman she had published in "Sensibility."[89]

More recommended that women's minds be strengthened but not so that they could exercise the same reasoned grasp as men. This was something they could never do because they lacked the capacity for reflection, Locke's second source of understanding, which Wollstonecraft wished to restore to women's education. More argued that while women had equally to men,

> the faculty of fancy which creates images, and the faculty of memory which collects and stores ideas; they seem not to possess in equal measure the faculty of comparing, analyzing, and separating these ideas; that deep and patient thinking which goes to the bottom of a subject.[90]

Disagreeing with Wollstonecraft that women's inability to concentrate was the result of their biased acculturation, More argued that "the female" lacks "steadiness in her intellectual pursuits" and "is perpetually turned aside by her characteristic taste and feelings." (Here the reactionary More joins hands with Rousseau.) Women's minds were to be strengthened for defensive purpose, to prevent their "natural softness" from degenerating into "imbecility of understanding." She said that women ran the risk of that imbecility because of their "indulgence" and "the general habits of fashionable life." Here at least was some common ground with Wollstonecraft, the recognition of women's appetite for consumer pleasure.[91]

More could not entirely avoid the environmental explanation for gender differences, a particularly vibrant issue during the Jacobin/Anti-Jacobin debate. Wollstonecraft based her explanation for gender differences (aside from "physical superiority," which she conceded to men) on sensational, associationist psychology. More raised the issue in order to dismiss it. She accepted the differences as a given, however they were induced, and on that basis she claimed the separate-but-equalizing power conferred by the feminization of religion:

> Whatever characteristical distinction may exist [between the sexes]; whatever inferiority may be attached to woman from the slighter frame of her body, or the more circumscribed powers of her mind; from less systematic education, and from the subordinate station she is called to fill in life; there is one great and leading circumstance which raises her importance, and even establishes her equality. Christianity has exalted women to true and undisputed dignity . . . equally with men redeemed by the blood of Christ.[92]

In fact, argued More, the gendering of sensibility and even the apparent deficiencies in education, rather than crippling the female personality, sponsored a special propensity in women for the Christianity that empowered them. It was natural, rooted in women's slighter frame and, implicitly, all of More's terms assume, in their distinct nerves. Women's access to heaven was therefore "less obstructed" than men's.

> Their hearts are naturally soft and flexible, open to impressions of love and gratitude; their feelings tender and lively; all these are favorable to the cultivation of the devotional spirit . . . They have in the native constitution of their minds, as well as from the relative situations they are called on to fill,

> a certain sense of attachment and dependence which is peculiarly favorable to religion . . . Christianity . . . comes in aid of their conscious weakness, and offers the only true counterpoise to it. "Woman, be then healed of thine infirmity," is still the heart-cheering language of a gracious Saviour.

Here, again, More was directly countering Wollstonecraft, who had said in the *Rights of Woman:*

> Women, weak women, are compared with angels; yet a superior order of being should be supposed to possess more intellect than man; or in what does their superiority consist? . . . they are allowed to possess more goodness of heart; piety and benevolence. I doubt the fact, though it be courteously brought forward, unless ignorance be allowed to be the mother of devotion.

Instead, Wollstonecraft had argued, virtue depended on knowledge, on consciousness, not just feeling. In characterizing the presentation of the opposite view (the mere aggrandizement of feeling) as "courteously brought forward," Wollstonecraft repeated the sense of the phrase "with chivalrous generosity" she had used earlier in the book to make the same argument against identifying women entirely with sensibility and men with reason. Suggested in these phrases was the fantasied heterosexual relationship which More here insisted upon. The relationship between a sympathetic but still male Christ and the woman of sensibility had been depicted in heart-religion throughout the century (exemplified previously in the essay on devotional taste by More's "belov'd" Barbauld), and echoed by those earthly relationships in which men were attracted by weak, dependent, even sickly women, the power of their minds undeveloped, which Wollstonecraft wishes to transform.[93]

Provoked by Godwin's Wollstonecraft and then by their rereading of the *Rights of Woman,* some conservatives attempted to overwhelm the power of women's consciousness by asserting that feminine sensibility required the surrender of their minds. Provocation and reaction provided the inspiration for Edgeworth's *Belinda,* which must be read as both a part of this debate and the culmination of the century's less intense versions which had preceded it.

Like Evelina, Belinda goes to London to be introduced to "the world," under tutelage of Lady Delacour. With an "incomparable taste in dress" and a mastery of "knowledge of the world," the witty and beautiful Lady Delacour plays "Mistress of the Revels" to that fashionable world and to its microcosm, the masquerade. It is a world of "pleasure and frolic," that had been accompanied by evangelical assault since its beginning.[94] Lady Delacour tells Belinda to "dry up your tears, *Keep on your mask,* and take my advice"; in "the world," "every body must paint." Against such a vision, Belinda poses the truthfulness and sincerity of the culture of sensibility. She accords her appearance with the neoclassical lines of the era as they are applauded by the man she loves, the fashion representing the cultural triumph of sensibility:

> Give me a look, give me a face,
> That makes a simplicity a grace;
> Robes loosely flowing, hair as free
> Such sweet neglect more taketh me
> Than all th' adulteries of art,
> That strike mine eyes, but not mine heart.[95]

Soon after Belinda arrives in the Delacour household she "began to see through the thin veil with which politeness covers domestic misery." At its heart is a secret associated with Lady Delacour's body. Letting fall "her mask," and wiping the paint from her face, Lady Delacour showed Belinda that no trace of youth or beauty remained: her countenance was "death-like." She is a *memento mori*—but one combined with the figure of the Amazon. "As yet you have seen nothing—look here," she tells Belinda, "and baring one half of her bosom, she revealed a hideous spectacle." The diseased breast has a moral counterpart: "my mind is eaten away like my body by incurable disease . . . remorse for a life of folly—of folly which has brought on me all the punishments of guilt." The next morning, however, she retracts the declaration that her diseased breast is killing her. To the contrary, she tells Belinda that she means to live as an Amazon: "There certainly were such people as Amazons—I hope you admire them—"[96]

There are further revelations of the "domestic misery" symbolized by Lady Delacour's diseased-breast-cum-Amazonianism. She had married Lord Delacour to provoke another man she really loved and because she thought she "should have no trouble in governing him." When Lord Delacour finds this out, Lady Delacour decides to remedy his ensuing "obstinacy" by playing the "coquette" with Colonel Lawless. Like Burney's "Lovel," his name is an echo of "Lovelace" as well as of the same kind of character named Lawless in the anonymous anti-Wollstonecraftian *Robert and Adela* (1795). His name also connoted the anarchism of Godwin and signified Lawless's association with the disreputable, immoral world beyond the pale, inhabited by Amazons. Another symptom of her domestic perversity was Lady Delacour's rejection of mothering while she was in her Amazonian phase. Her first child, a male, was born dead. She suckled her second, a girl, only for a while, and only because it was "the fashion at this time." Heartily sick of the business of suckling, Lady Delacour saw this sickly daughter die, and she put her third child out to nurse in the country for three years, under a governess for three or four more, and finally sent her to boarding school. She was called an "unnatural mother." She had never heard of household "economy." Instead, Lady Delacour took up her life of worldly "dissipation." "You see I had nothing at home, either in the shape of husband or children, to engage my affections. I believe it was this 'aching void' in my heart which made after looking abroad some time for a bosom friend, take such a prodigious fancy, to Mrs. Freke." The friend whom she thus took to her bosom was the cause of its near destruction.[97]

The "wild oddity" of Mrs. Freke's countenance reminds one of the final insult offered by Lovel to the "masculine," Amazonian Mrs. Selwyn, which was that she was "*oddish.*" Like Mrs. Selwyn, Harriot Freke has a "masculine" understanding. While typically "disguised as a man," Freke accosts Colonel Lawless and Lady Delacour. "Who am I? only a Freke!" Mrs. Freke's frequent cross-dressing, her winning a bet that she would get into the gallery of the House of Commons, her "bold masculine arms," her swearing, and her rejection of "the morality of her own sex," all this showed the meaning of her name. She was a "*man-woman.*"[98] Here and elsewhere are deliberate allusions to other Anti-Jacobin writings, although the kind of masculinity to which Freke tended was the long familiar target of sentimental fiction: Freke engaged in a "frolic," loved bloodshed, including duels, and she "supported the character of a young rake with such spirit and *truth,* that I am sure no common conjuror could have discovered anything feminine about her." Hence her association with the rakish Lawless-Lovelace. But Lady Delacour found that Freke had "more assurance than any man or woman I ever saw." She loved her for her "dashing audacity," her "frankness," and her "unbounded freedom on certain subjects." In Edgeworth's terms, however, the danger Freke marked for women was a precipice.[99]

Edgeworth carefully associated Freke's feminism with "Mrs. W——," that is, Mary Wollstonecraft, whom Freke takes Lady Delacour to meet. Both Mrs. W. and Mrs. Freke are modern dealers in "magic"; Mrs. Freke turns out to be a "false prophetess." The Anti-Jacobin Matthias had compared Wollstonecraft to the "priestess of an ancient religion," two years before *Belinda* was published. These are phrases connoting the association between women and religious radicalism threading through the reaction to women writers and readers back to the Civil War.[100]

In a chapter Edgeworth entitled "Rights of Woman," she has Freke parody Wollstonecraft's attack on the culture of sensibility. Freke's being called "vindictive" is another allusion to the title of Wollstonecraft's now notorious book. From the first, Freke has made it a tenet of her religion to "abjure the heresies of false delicacy." Arguing with Mr. Percival, who upholds "Female delicacy" and the values for which the culture of sensibility stands, Freke declares in a paraphrase of a passage from the *Rights of Woman:* " 'This is just the way you men spoil women,' cried Freke, 'by talking to them of the *delicacy of their sex,* and such stuff. This *delicacy* enslaves the pretty delicate dears.' " Freke rejects the sentimental writings of Barbauld, as Wollstonecraft had. If the rejection of delicacy, of feminine modesty, and of sensibility is freakish according to Edgeworth's argument, then those qualities must pertain naturally to being a woman. (The subtitle of the Anti-Jacobin, anti-Wollstonecraftian *Robert and Adela* to which Edgeworth referred was *The Rights of Woman Best Maintained by the Sentiments of Nature.*) Freke cites other ideas from Wollstonecraft's *Rights of Woman,* for example, that their oppression makes women "cunning." Similarly, Freke would have "both sexes call things by their right names," as Wollstonecraft wished of sexuality. She expressed the Jacobin view that "the present system of society is radically wrong," and she represents Wollstonecraft's early enthusiasm for the French Revolution.[101] Edgeworth refers to Wollstonecraft's writing career and self-education by way of the books she reviewed for the *Analytical.* Quizzing Belinda, Mrs. Freke exclaimed "as she reviewed each of the books on the table, in their turns, in the summary language of presumptuous ignorance, 'Smith's Theory of Moral Sentiments—milk and water!' " The reference to Smith—paramount theorist of sensibility—appears to be another dig at Wollstonecraft's thoroughgoing repudiation of gendered sensibility.[102]

But it is important to recognize that Edgeworth rejects the extreme, ungovernable figure of feminine sensibility opposed by all of her 1780s and 1790s predecessors as she rejects the mindless extreme of deferential sensibility urged on women by the Rev. Polwhele. In *Belinda,* Edgeworth parodied this male wish by way of Virginia, whom Clarence Hervey reared from childhood in Rousseauistic fashion, intending to marry her, an episode modeled on that episode in the life of Day. Belinda teaches Hervey the superior attractions of a female sensibility tempered by a woman's reasoning power, in contrast to the infantilized Virginia, who "had been inspired by romances with the most exalted notions of female delicacy and honour!" Edgeworth's Virginia and Belinda are the equivalents of Austen's Marianne and Elinor. Of course, Edgeworth rejects the systematic, Jacobinical analysis of sexism of which Wollstonecraft made this a part but, on the fundamental point, Edgeworth's view resembles Wollstonecraft's. Edgeworth made it under very different circumstances, those shaped by Godwin's *Memoirs* and the reaction to them.[103]

Edgeworth's familiarity with that notorious work, published just two years before she wrote *Belinda,* is signified by Lady Delacour's quotation of a passage from it. Edgeworth also attributes to the Wollstonecraftian Freke the opposition to marriage Godwin had attributed to Wollstonecraft.[104] But the most significant connection between the books is Edgeworth's association of Wollstonecraft's feminism with Godwin's characterization of it as "amazonian" and its author as a "virago." Edgeworth's intention is to preserve strong-minded sensibility from the Polwhelean assaults provoked by Godwin's Wollstonecraft.

This intention is most clearly developed in the struggle between Mrs. Freke and Belinda over Lady Delacour's heart. Mrs. Freke wants her for Amazonian feminism and Belinda wants her for domesticated sensibility, albeit the strong-minded kind. Following Freke's Wollstonecraftian scorning of Barbauld's sentimentalism, she barks to Belinda, "Do you hunt?" and urges the heroine into coming riding with her, attempting to corrupt her into mannish behavior as she had corrupted Lady Delacour. When Belinda declines, Freke "strode" to the window, "threw up" the sash, and called to her groom, "Walk those horses about you blockhead." She thrusts out her hand to a male character saying, "Shake hands and be friends, man!" In the *Rights of Woman,* Wollstonecraft herself had criticized women's pretending weakness as men picked up their handkerchiefs or opened doors for them, and Godwin's *Memoirs* had said that she had exploded "the system of gallantry, and the species of homage with which the sex is usually treated." Hence Mrs. Freke declares, "I think all our politeness hypocrisy."[105]

Attracted by the free and self-assured Mrs. Freke, Lady Delacour acts to redeem the "independence" of which her husband had deprived her; he had used his legal position to swindle her of the inheritance she had brought to the marriage and to lose it on the horses. Edgeworth recognizes that marriages can be disastrous. Women have the alternative of devoting themselves to them, especially to making a good companion of a husband, or of following Mrs. Freke's road to independence, but Edgeworth presents the latter as unnatural. It is also sexual anarchy; the Freke pushes Lady Delacour to drop her husband in favor of "a Lawless Lover" or at least to marry him after divorcing Lord Delacour: both Freke and Lawless are "encouraged" by Mrs. W——.[106] Because of Freke's propensity to noise scandal abroad (again this is Godwin's Wollstonecraft),[107] Lord Delacour kills Lawless in a duel. Lady Delacour first experiences the "dreadful sensation" of having Lawless's blood on her hands but she then blames Lord Delacour. Egged on by Freke, she actively supports Freke's cousin in contesting a parliamentary seat with Lord Delacour. He, in turn, is supported by another cross-dressing woman, Mrs. Luttridge. Wollstonecraftian feminism wished to engage in the world of politics; hence "Harriot and I made our appearance on the hustings, dressed in splendid party uniforms." Lady Delacour's caricature of Mrs. Luttridge provokes her to wish "to be a man" that she might challenge Lady Delacour to a duel. Lady Delacour dresses "in male attire" and, seconded by Freke, rides out to the dueling ground.[108]

In short, Edgeworth associates Wollstonecraft's feminism not with the kind of individual freedom Wollstonecraft advocated, but with the assumption of the male manners targeted by the campaign for their reformation, including, in addition to dueling, swearing, hunting, drinking, betting, frolicking, and taking sexual advantage of women. She also associates them with the morally dubious masquerade. Such manners were the consistent target of sentimental fiction but they were Wollstonecraft's target, too. Recognizing that women's self-assertion was branded "masculine," Wollstonecraft had carefully distinguished her encouragement of women's development of their "human" talents from "masculine" appetites for hunting, shooting, and gambling. Moreover, in certain key respects, improved mothering, for example, Wollstonecraft's solution was the same as Edgeworth's.[109] In *Belinda,* Edgeworth combined elements in the *Rights of Woman* that differed from her own feminism with the sexual immorality revealed by Godwin, in order to characterize Wollstonecraft's attractions as the magic of a "false prophetess." *Belinda,* however, was also Edgeworth's attempt to maintain some "true" sense of female self-assertion in the face of the reactionary circumstances brought to a head by Godwin's *Memoirs.* Edgeworth's novel caricatured and repudiated Wollstonecraftian feminism but it also caricatured and repudiated the extreme, mindless feminine sensibility men asked of women by discrediting Hervey's fantastic construction of Virginia, bred up merely to his sexual taste.[110]

Edgeworth believed that women's self-assertion should be expressed within domesticity, within a reformed marriage, as More said it should be. This was in accordance with Edgeworth's fundamental belief in the identification of women with the sensibility epitomized by Belinda. Her ideal combined mind with a gendered sensibility, focused entirely on marriage: Freke's warning associated a life outside marriage with an inability to feel. Wollstonecraft, on the other hand, holding that women and men had talents and virtues in common, linked sensibility and mind to an individual, independent life for women outside marriage, as well as within it, like the lives led by male artists (not rakes), and certainly one that embraced politics. By 1801, history seemed on the side of Edgeworth.[111]

Dressed as a man and dominated by the feminist Freke's "masculine" understanding, Lady Delacour receives that wound to her breast, "the consequences of which you have seen." The progress of the blow into dangerous disease leads to the apparent need for an "amazonian operation." Lady Delacour represses her "real" problem, which to Edgeworth is her aching domestic void. This is where Belinda enters, in order to challenge Freke's sway. Lady Delacour recognizes that Belinda will "enjoy the office of censor" to her behavior. The task Belinda and her ally, the sensitive Hervey, set themselves is to make Lady Delacour "as happy in domestic life as she *appeared* to be in public." It is not too late because, unlike Harriot Freke, she does not lack "sensibility." As her name suggests, she can "return to her natural character."[112]

Belinda and Clarence are assisted by the "pattern" of Lady Anne Percival, who has taken on the responsibility of raising Lady Delacour's neglected third child, Helena. Lord Delacour is converted into a man of feeling and Helena returns to invoke Lady Delacour's maternal feelings. Belinda tells her that to engage such domestic prospects will be to "have the courage to live for yourself." The message is reinforced by a chaplain's bringing "the consolation of a mild and rational piety." Piety thus is united, More-like, with a woman's natural sensibility, and both qualities flow into Lady Delacour's restored "Domestic Tête-à-Tête" with her husband, flowing, too, into the nineteenth century. Lady Delacour repudiates feminism and the world of fashion, rejects being a "coquette" in favor of being a "prude." Here are further shades of More. Having resolved to publicize this resolution as a print stuck up in a shop window and entitled "The Reformed Amazon," Lady Delacour finds her breast is restored.[113]

In *Leonora* (1806) Edgeworth continued her effort to distinguish the combination of sensibility and strength of mind from the sexual Jacobinism represented by Godwin's Wollstonecraft. The Wollstonecraft character in *Leonora* combines Amazonianism with excessive sensibility, precisely as she was represented by Godwin, Polwhele, and More; she is "masculine" *and* she "begs to be pitied" because of her "more than female tenderness of heart." This is to defend "tenderness of heart" as a proper female quality when not taken to the "excesses" of Wollstonecraft, Hays, and other Jacobins. Edgeworth defends Anti-Jacobins against the Jacobin charge that they are insensible by attributing to the Jacobins the notion that "those who have yet yielded to their passions are destitute of sensibility," again referring to Godwin's Wollstonecraft. Jacobins would have you believe, she continues, that the

> sacrifice of the strongest feelings of the human heart to a sense of duty, is to be called mean or absurd; but the shameless phrenzy of passion, exposing itself to public gaze, is to be an object of admiration. These heroines talk of strength of mind; but they forget that strength of mind is to be shown in resisting their passions, not in yielding to them.

Significantly, Edgeworth here recognizes that Jacobin and Anti-Jacobin women speak the same language, both intent on asserting women's "strength of mind."[114]

In fact, said Edgeworth, Jacobins do not respect the code of sensibility that they claim to be upholding. Nothing deters them from "the gratification of their passions. Do you think that the gossamer of sentiment will restrain those whom the strong chains of prudence could not hold?" Or it could be said that heroines like Godwin's Wollstonecraft have read sensibility's possibilities as Miss Milner did, pursuing individual, unmoralized pleasures, even to "autonomous hedonism." Edgeworth was reiterating one of the clichés of Anti-Jacobinism in attributing to Jacobins the belief "that the general good of society is their immutable rule of morality, and in practice they make the variable feelings of each individual the judge of this general good." This, of course, had been a pre-Jacobin criticism of the cultivation of sensibility. It can be linked to Shaftesbury's early warning against the tasteless, democratic pursuit of pleasure, but now the dangers had been spelled out publicly by the Amazonian heroine of feeling. Thus women's achievement of the ability to express mind was preserved by women's clear opposition to sexual passion[115] and willfulness, their potential individualism blunted by their adherence to a sharply feminized sensibility. In her heyday between 1800 and 1814 Edgeworth "was undoubtedly the most commercially successful and prestigious novelist" in Britain, and one suspects that her success was linked to her orthodoxy as well as her talent.[116]

Francis Jeffrey said in his review of *Leonora* that Edgeworth's battle was already won. "Conjugal duty" had triumphed over "affected sensibility" and the crisis of the last years of the 1790s had been passed. Its focus had become the subject of humor. "The evil we think, is scarcely of so urgent a nature as to make us set any extraordinary value upon the remedy." The affectation and indulgence of excessive sensibility, now clearly identified with sexual immorality, "is no longer the vice of our countrywomen; they have been pretty well laughed out of it."[117]

One source of the demotion and the ridicule of the issue was its popularization. "The fashion" of sensibility, wrote Jeffrey, "has gone down to the lower orders of society; and we dare say there is still a good deal of raving about . . . overwhelming emotions, and narrow prejudices, among the abigails and dealers in small millinery, who read novels, and sip ratafia on the borders of prostitution." More recorded that, not "only among milliners, mantua-makers, and other trades where numbers [of women] work together, the labour of one girl is frequently sacrificed that she may be spared to read these mischievous books to others." Inevitably the dissemination of novels would continue to expand popular literacy among women, along with the culture of sensibility, once the terrible stages of the industrial revolution were passed. It continued to be attacked on the same grounds it had over the preceding century, as would the other expressions of women's consumerism. In 1856 George Eliot would classify one order of the whole "genus" of "Silly Novels by Lady Novelists" as "the *mind-and-millinery* species." One characteristic was that "men played a very subordinate part" by the typical heroine's side and another, that "[r]akish men . . . are touched to penitence by her reproofs." She said of her, too, that "her sorrows are wept into embroidered pocket handkerchiefs, and her fainting form resides on the best upholstery."[118] More, perpetuating sensibility's moralism along with its consumer psychology, had urged "ladies" to superintend "the instruction of the poor and of making it an indispensable part of their charity to give them moral and religious books." So if Jeffrey criticized Edgeworth for continuing to preach what, in his view, was a laughable message to the women of the middle and upper classes, Edgeworth could claim it was necessary to preach the same moral message as her predecessors.[119]

The 1790s was the culmination of a struggle over definitions of gender that had originated well over a century earlier, when religious, political, and economic revolutions launched profoundly successful efforts to transcend "natural" and God-given categories. The "GREAT" More[120] and the prestigious Edgeworth may be seen presiding over the reformed culture of sensibility as it entered the nineteenth century. Out of the final 1790s fusion of evangelism with a sensibility made unequivocally respectable would emerge the flood of reform organizations rooted in a middle-class, female constituency.[121]

They manifested the degree of tough-mindedness with which so many late eighteenth-century female writers had insisted that sensibility be tempered. The stereotypes of false, merely fashionable sensibility, and of sofa-lying, excessive sensibility also remained, characteristic of nineteenth-century fiction. Across this spectrum, the "naturalizing" of women's finer sensibility—connoting nerves and morality—continued to bedevil and aggrandize women's self-conceptions.

Symbolically, More's torch was passed to the woman who gave the next age its name. In 1838 young Victoria permitted the filiopietistic biography of the recently dead More to be dedicated to her. The Victorian age extended the curious "Contradiction" of reform and luxury identified by Mandeville. Its emblem of consumer success was the comfortable, middle-class Home, with Mother at its heart. The elaboration of the economy—the triumph and distress of industrial capitalism—was accompanied by the further elaboration of the culture of sensibility.[122]

Notes

Introduction

1. C. J. Rawson, "Some Remarks on Eighteenth-Century 'Delicacy,' with a Note on Hugh Kelly's *False Delicacy* (1768)," *Journal of English and Germanic Philology* 61, no. 1 (January 1962): 1–13, 1n.1; J. M. S. Tompkins quotes a writer's wish in the *Monthly Review* (August 1789) that novelists "would sometimes inform us what ideas they annex to the word sensibility," *The Popular Novel in England, 1770–1800* (Westport, Conn.: Greenwood Press, 1976 [1961]), 93. R. F. Brissenden has best summarized this breadth of meaning (subsuming "sensibility" under the tradition of sentimentalism) in *Virtue in Distress: Studies in the Novel of Sentiment from Richardson to Sade* (New York: Harper and Row, 1976), 16; see also 9, 20–21, 137, 140.

2. Because this is a truism one may find it everywhere in literary history, for example, Walter Francis Wright, *Sensibility in English Prose Fiction* (n.p.: Folcroft Press, 1970 [1935]), passim; Ian Watt, *The Rise of the Novel: Studies in Defoe, Richardson and Fielding* (Harmondsworth, Middx.: Penguin, 1957), ch. 6; or most recently, Janet Todd, *Sensibility: An Introduction* (London: Methuen, 1986); Clive T. Probyn, *English Fiction of the Eighteenth Century 1700–1789* (London and New York: Longman, 1987), ch. 7 and passim.

3. Harold Perkin, *The Origin of Modern English Society, 1780–1880* (London: Routledge and Kegan Paul, 1972), 11.

4. Patricia Meyer Spacks, "Ev'ry Woman Is at Heart a Rake," *Eighteenth-Century Studies* 8 (1974): 31; Donald Meyer, *Sex and Power: The Rise of Women in America, Russia, Sweden, and Italy* (Middletown, Conn.: Wesleyan University Press, 1987), 313.

5. I use the term "awakening" in the same sense as Meyer, *Sex and Power*, xiv–xv and passim. His use invokes Kate Chopin's great 1899 novel of that name, as well as Simone de Beauvoir's thesis in *The Second Sex* (1949).

6. Claire Cross, "'He-Goats before the Flocks': A Note on the Part Played by Women in the Founding of Some Civil War Churches," in *Popular Belief and Practice: Papers Read at the Ninth Summer Meeting and the Tenth Winter Meeting of the Ecclesiastical History Society*, ed. G. J. Cuming and Derek Baker (Cambridge: Cambridge University Press, 1972), 195.

7. Keith Thomas, "Women and the Civil War Sects," *Past and Present,* no. 13 (1958): 55; Patricia Crawford, "Women's Published Writings, 1600–1700," in *Women in English Society, 1500–1800,* ed. Mary Prior (London: Methuen, 1985), 212, 213.

8. John Mullan, *Sentiment and Sociability: The Language of Feeling in the Eighteenth Century* (Oxford: Clarendon Press, 1988), 15. See too J. M. S. Tompkins, *The Popular Novel in England, 1770–1800* (Westport, Conn.: Greenwood Press, 1963), 4.

9. Brissenden, *Virtue in Distress,* 20; Wright, *Sensibility,* 24.

10. Illustrations of this very common phrase are Arthur M. Wilson, "Sensibility in France in the Eighteenth Century," *French Quarterly* 13 (1931): 40; Bertrand Russell, *A History of Western Philosophy* (New York: Simon and Schuster, 1945), xxi, 676; Tompkins, *Popular Novel,* 148; Rawson, "Delicacy," 11; Brissenden, *Virtue in Distress,* 5; Todd, *Sensibility,* 4; Claudia L. Johnson, review of Todd, *Sensibility, Eighteenth-Century Studies* 22, no. 1 (Fall 1988); 111–3; Paul Langford mentions "fashionable worshippers at [the] new shrine of sensibility" and in that context writes that Sterne's *Tristram Shandy* "attained the status of a cult for a time," in *A Polite and Commercial People: England 1727–83* (Oxford: Clarendon Press, 1989), 433. For a working definition of "cult," see J. Milton Yinger, *Religion, Society, and the Individual: An Introduction to the Sociology of Religion* (New York: MacMillan, 1957), 154–5. Jerry C. Beasley's *Novels of the 1740s* (Athens: University of Georgia Press, 1982) must be credited with the most explicit identification of the essentially cultic nature of the phenomenon under consideration. In addition, Norman Fiering refers to the "inward and affective" "Shaftesbury-Hutcheson gospel," in *Jonathan Edwards' Moral Thought in Its British Context* (Chapel Hill: University of North Carolina Press, 1981), 356–7. Martin Green has described a literary "cult" in similar terms in *Children of the Sun: A Narrative of "Decadence" in England after 1918* (New York: Basic Books, 1976), 6–7, 14–16, and passim.

11. Erik Erämetsä, *A Study of the Word "Sentimental" and of Other Linguistic Characteristics of Eighteenth-Century Sentimentalism in England* (Helsinki: Helsingin Liikekirjapaino Oy, 1951), 70; Colin Campbell, *The Romantic Ethic and the Spirit of Modern Consumerism* (Oxford: Basil Blackwell, 1987), 14; Brian Vickers, "Introduction" to Henry MacKenzie, *The Man of Feeling* (Oxford: Oxford University Press, 1970 [1771]), x; Rawson, "Delicacy," 11; Brissenden, *Virtue in Distress,* 25, 259.

12. Perkin, *Origins of Modern English Society,* 99, 4.

13. Compare Meyer on de Beauvoir, *Sex and Power,* xx.

14. Daniel Defoe, *Robinson Crusoe* (New York: New American Library, 1961 [1719]), 9–10. For an account of the "middle station" assumed by Defoe, see Peter Earle, *The Making of the English Middle Class: Business, Society and Family Life in London, 1660–1730* (London: Methuen, 1989). The process Earle describes "has never been reversed and lead inexorably to the even more middle-class middle class of the nineteenth century and today" (334). He reminds us that this process was defined against the beginnings of a proletariat; the greatest social barrier and "one that was getting higher was that between the poor and the middle station" (331).

15. Peter Laslett, *The World We Have Lost: England before the Industrial Age*, 3d ed. (New York: Charles Scribner's Sons, 1984), 147. See too Carole Shammas, *The Pre-industrial Consumer in England and America* (Oxford: Clarendon Press, 1990), 121.

16. Peter Clark, *The English Alehouse: A Social History 1200–1830* (Longman: London, 1983), 203; Roy Porter, *English Society in the Eighteenth Century* (Harmondsworth, Middx.: Penguin, 1982), 27. See too Perkin, *Origins of Modern English Society*, 74–5.

17. J. M. Golby and A. W. Purdue, *The Civilisation of the Crowd: Popular Culture in England 1750–1900* (New York: Schocken, 1985), 26; Perkin, *Origins of Modern English Society*, 53, 125–7, 132. For the classic account of enclosure as "class robbery" see E. P. Thompson, *The Making of the English Working Class* (New York: Vintage, 1963), 217–20.

18. Clark, *English Alehouse*, 203–4; Perkin, *Origins of Modern English Society*, 75–175.

19. Peter Borsay, *The English Urban Renaissance: Culture and Society in the Provincial Town, 1660–1770* (Oxford: Clarendon Press, 1989), 22, 23. For a careful assessment of the influence of towns in spreading consumption see Lorna Weatherill, *Consumer Behaviour and Material Culture in Britain 1660–1760* (London: Routledge, 1988), ch. 4.

20. Neil McKendrick, "The Consumer Revolution of Eighteenth-Century England," in *The Birth of a Consumer Society: The Commercialization of Eighteenth-Century England*, by McKendrick, John Brewer, and J. H. Plumb (Bloomington: Indiana University Press, 1985), 21; Perkin, *Origins of Modern English Society*, 100.

21. Borsay, *Urban Renaissance*, 18–19.

22. Ibid., 15–16, 17.

23. M. M. Goldsmith, *Private Vices, Public Benefits: Bernard Mandeville's Social and Political Thought* (Cambridge: Cambridge University Press, 1986), 128; P. G. M. Dickson, *The Financial Revolution in England: A Study in the Development of Public Credit, 1688–1756* (London: MacMillan, 1970); Golby and Purdue, *Civilisation of the Crowd*, 26; Porter, *English Society*, 26–7; M. L. Bush, *The English Aristocracy: A Comparative Synthesis* (Manchester: Manchester University Press, 1984), chs. 10 and 11; Christopher Hill, *Reformation to Industrial Revolution: The Pelican Economic History of Britain*, vol. 2 (Harmondsworth, Middx.: Penguin, 1969), 173–4, 163, 224, 174, 171. See also Perkin, *Origins of Modern English Society*, 65, 38–56, 75–9, 11.

24. Joan Thirsk, *Economic Policy and Projects: The Development of a Consumer Society in Early Modern England* (Oxford: Clarendon Press, 1978), 179; Keith Thomas, *Religion and the Decline of Magic* (New York: Charles Scribner's Sons, 1971), 650; Borsay, *Urban Renaissance*, 31. 117.

25. Weatherill, *Consumer Behaviour*, 13–14. Historians emphasize the significance to the eighteenth-century spread of consumption in a middle class composed of "closely packed layers," nourishing emulation and the prospects of mobility, a social structure capitalized on by merchants and manufacturers. McKendrick, "The Consumer Revolution," 20; Perkin, *Origins of Modern English Society*, 18–23.

26. Borsay, *Urban Renaissance*, 303; see too Shammas, *Pre-industrial Consumer*, 111, and passim. For a discussion of the meanings of "consumption" and its cognates see Rosalind H. Williams, *Dream Worlds: Mass Consumption in Late Nineteenth-Century France* (Berkeley: University of California Press, 1982), 5–6.

27. Weatherill, *Consumer Revolution*, 39–41.

28. Perkin, *Origins of Modern English Society*, 22.

29. Borsay, *Urban Renaissance*, 17; Perkins, *Origins of Modern English Society*, 19.

30. Clark, *English Alehouse*, 252; Perkin, *Origins of Modern English Society*, 138.

31. Perkin, *Origins of Modern English Society*, 135; William Stafford, *Socialism, Radicalism, and Nostalgia: Social Criticism in Britain, 1775–1830* (New York: Cambridge University Press, 1987), 15; Thompson, *Making of the English Working Class*, passim.

32. Perkin, *Origins of Modern English Society*, 3.

33. Shammas, *Pre-industrial Consumer*, 111; Perkin, *Origins of Modern English Society*, 93.

34. Shammas, *Pre-industrial Consumer*, 41, 29, 3.

35. Ibid., 43–4, 17–18; Perkin, *Origins of Modern English Society*, 31.

36. Hoh-Cheung Mui and Lorna H. Mui, *Shops and Shopkeeping in Eighteenth-Century England* (Montreal: McGill-Queen's University Press, 1989); Shammas, *Pre-industrial Consumer*, 227–259, 145, 173, 181–6.

37. *The Spectator*, no. 10 (12 March 1710–11), in Joseph Addison, Richard Steele, et al., *The Spectator*, 8 vols. (London: T. Hamilton and R. Ogle, 1808), 1:42; Shammas, *Pre-industrial Consumer*, 181, 185.

38. Shammas, *Pre-industrial Consumer*, 26–7, 31, 98, 235.

39. Ibid., 259, 96, 295, 98, 100; Hill, *Reformation to Industrial Revolution*, 163; McKendrick, "Consumer Revolution," 16; Borsay, *Urban Renaissance*, 26; Langford, *Polite and Commercial People*, 69.

40. Daniel Defoe, *A Tour through the Whole Island of Great Britain* (Harmondsworth, Middx.: Penguin, 1971 [1724–6]), 175.

41. Perkin, *Origins of Modern English Society*, 58, 61, 59. Thompson uses the phrase "nascent industrial capitalism" in "Time, Work-Discipline, and Industrial Capitalism," in *Essays in Social History*, ed. M. W. Flinn and T. C. Smout (Oxford: Clarendon Press, 1974), 56. Simon Schama refers to preindustrial "nascent capitalisms" in Europe, see below, n.66.

42. Defoe, *Robinson Crusoe*, 8, 9; Watt, *Rise of the Novel*, 63.

43. Colin Campbell, *The Romantic Ethic and the Spirit of Modern Consumerism* (Oxford: Basil Blackwell, 1987); Stephen Greenblatt, *Renaissance Self-fashioning: From More to Shakespeare* (Chicago: University of Chicago Press, 1980).

44. Judith Bennett, *Women in the Medieval English Countryside: Gender and Household in Brigstock before the Plague* (New York: Oxford University Press, 1987), 198.

45. Meyer, *Sex and Power*, xv. Leonore Davidoff and Catherine Hall call

"separate spheres" the "nineteenth-century inheritance," in *Family Fortunes: Men and Women of the English middle class, 1780–1850* (London: Hutchinson, 1987), 33.

46. Porter, *English Society,* p. 97; Perkin, *Origins of Modern English Society,* 91.

47. Shammas, *Pre-industrial Consumer,* 185; McKendrick, "Consumer Revolution," 23. See too Neil McKendrick, "Home Demand and Economic Growth: A New View of the Role of Women and Children in the Industrial Revolution," in *Historical Perspectives: Studies in English Thought and Society,* ed. McKendrick (London: Europa, 1974), 152–210.

48. See Roland Barthes, *Mythologies,* selected and trans. by Annette Lavers (New York: Noonday Press, 1972 [1957]), 127–8, 129–31.

49. Compare Thomas Laqueur, "Orgasm, Generation, and the Politics of Reproductive Biology," *Representations* 14 (Spring 1986): 1–41.

50. Langford, *Polite and Commercial People,* 654; cf. Keith Wrightson, *English Society, 1580–1680* (London: Hutchinson, 1982), 220–1.

51. Wollstonecraft to William Roscoe, 16 October 1791, *The Collected Letters of Mary Wollstonecraft,* ed. Ralph M. Wardle (Ithaca: Cornell University Press, 1979), 202–3. This is still the most complete collection of Wollstonecraft's letters available, although more have been uncovered since 1979. Marilyn Butler and Janet Todd, eds., *The Works of Mary Wollstonecraft,* 7 vols. (London: W. Pickering, 1989), recommend that Wardle's edition be used because they include only the letters Godwin published shortly after Wollstonecraft's death. *Works,* 1:29.

52. Mary Wollstonecraft, *Vindication of the Rights of Woman* (New York: Penguin, 1975 [1792]), 118, 117, 80, 91, 98. The edition of Wollstonecraft's *Works* cited in the previous note appeared after I had prepared the Wollstonecraft aspect of this book. I have used widely available editions.

53. Wollstonecraft, *Rights of Woman,* 150, 98, 148, 93, and see 95.

54. Ibid., 220, 221, 271, 141.

55. Ibid., 102, 220.

56. Ibid., 144, 150, 80, 142, 104, 119. For the origins and context of this aspect of her thought see Barker-Benfield, "Mary Wollstonecraft: Eighteenth-Century Commonwealthwoman," *Journal of the History of Ideas* 50 (1989): 95–115.

57. Wollstonecraft, *Rights of Woman,* 101, 104, 116, 150–1, 141.

58. Ibid., 99, 148, 81.

59. Wollstonecraft to Joseph Johnson, c. late 1792, *Collected Letters,* 220–1.

60. Wollstonecraft to the Reverend Henry Dyson Gabell, 13 September 1787, *Collected Letters,* 162; Wollstonecraft to Everina Wollstonecraft, 4 September 1790, *Collected Letters,* 194. Emily W. Sunstein, *A Different Face: The Life of Mary Wollstonecraft* (Boston: Little Brown, 1975), 175.

61. Wollstonecraft to Joseph Johnson, 13 September 1787, *Collected Letters,* 159; Wollstonecraft to Everina Wollstonecraft, 7 November 1787, *Collected Letters,* 164; Wollstonecraft, *Rights of Woman,* 122.

62. Wollstonecraft, *Rights of Woman,* 85.

63. Simon Schama, *Citizens: A Chronicle of the French Revolution* (New York:

Knopf, 1989), 149–62, 133–7, 180–2; Jane Abray, "Feminism in the French Revolution," *American Historical Review* 80 (February 1975): 45–62; Williams, *Dream Worlds,* chs. 2 and 3; Perkin, *Origins of Modern English Society,* 91.

64. Langford, *Polite and Commercial People,* 467.

65. Fiering, *Jonathan Edwards' Moral Thought,* 15; Schama, *The Embarrassment of Riches: An Interpretation of Dutch Culture in the Golden Age* (Berkeley: University of California Press, 1988), 403, 541, 407.

66. Schama, *Embarrassment of Riches,* 323, 326, 49, 8; Ann Douglas, *The Feminization of American Culture* (New York: Knopf, 1977). Tocqueville described the increasing sensibility of his age in Europe and America, and he linked it to the rise of democracy. Alexis de Tocqueville, *Democracy in America,* trans. Henry Reeve, ed. Phillips Bradley, 2 vols. (New York: Vintage, 1945), 2:172–7. There are strong signs of the culture of sensibility in the American colonies during the eighteenth century.

67. Defoe, *Robinson Crusoe,* 9; Manchester, "Cobbler" quoted in Perkin, *Origins of Modern English Society,* 88–9.

68. Edith Birkhead, "Sentiment and Sensibility in the Eighteenth-Century Novel," in *Essays and Studies by Members of the English Association,* ed. Oliver Elton (London: Wm. Dawson, 1966 [1925]), 11:92–116; Jane Spencer, *The Rise of the Woman Novelist: From Aphra Behn to Jane Austen* (Oxford: Basil Blackwell, 1986).

69. Todd, *Sensibility;* and Mullan, *Sentiment and Sociability.*

70. Michael Foucault, *The History of Sexuality,* vol. 1: *An Introduction,* trans. Robert Hurley (New York: Pantheon, 1978), 10–12. A valuable guide to the history of critical theory sympathetic to Foucault's views is Terry Eagleton's *Literary Theory: An Introduction* (Oxford: Basil Blackwell, 1983). For a persuasive critique of deconstruction in literary criticism see Tzvetan Todorov, "All against Humanity," *Times Library Supplement* (4 October 1985): 093–4. J. Paul Hunter suggests that "the privatizing strategy for texts now seems, fortunately, on the wane." *Before Novels: The Cultural Contexts of Eighteenth-Century Fiction* (New York: Norton, 1990), xii. See also David Lehman, *Signs of the Times: Deconstruction and the Fall of Paul de Man* (New York: Poseidon Press, 1991). The debate over deconstruction has heated up among historians: Joan Wallach Scott, *Gender and the Politics of History* (New York: Columbia University Press, 1988); and Bryan D. Palmer, *Descent into Discourse: The Reification of Language in the Writing of Social History* (Philadelphia: Temple University Press, 1990). See also John E. Toews, "Intellectual History and the Linguistic Turn: The Autonomy of Meaning and the Irreducibility of Experience," *American Historical Review* 92, no. 4 (October 1987): 879–907.

71. Meyer, *Sex and Power,* 463, see too 558, 619–20. In his review of Lehman's recent book criticizing deconstruction, Malcolm Bradbury declares that "criticism must offer a portrait of creativity and of authorship as existential self-declaration." "Signs of the Times," *New York Times Book Review* (24 February 1991).

72. Thompson, *Making of the English Working Class,* 9; Robert William Fogel and G. R. Elton, *Which Road to the Past: Two Views of History* (New Haven: Yale University Press, 1983), 77–8. Despite the evident outdatedness of its view of

social history (including sexuality), R. G. Collingwood's *The Idea of History* (New York: Oxford University Press, 1956 [1946]) is still the noblest definition of the historian's discipline.

73. Stone, *Family, Sex and Marriage*, 247, 238, and ch. 6, passim; Keith Thomas, *Man and the Natural World: A History of Modern Sensibility* (New York: Pantheon, 1983), 16, 173ff; Thomas L. Haskell, "Capitalism and the Origins of the Humanitarian Sensibility, Parts 1 and 2," *American Historical Review* 90 (April and June 1985): 339–61 and 547–66; Earle, *English Middle Class*, 336; Langford, *Polite and Commercial People*, ch. 10; Norbert Elias, *The Civilizing Process*, trans. Edmund Jephcott, 2 vols.: *The History of Manners*, vol. 1, and *Power & Civility*, vol. 2 (New York: Pantheon, 1982 [1939]).

Chapter 1. Sensibility and the Nervous System

1. Mary Wollstonecraft, *Vindication of the Rights of Woman* (Harmondsworth, Middx.: Penguin, 1975 [1792]), 79, 161.

2. Ibid., 154. In this widely used edition, "essence" is misprinted as "offence."

3. Ibid., 154–5.

4. Ibid., 80, see too 142–3; Knox quoted in Paul Langford, *A Polite and Commercial People: England, 1727–83* (Oxford: Clarendon Press, 1989), 478–9. Recent scholars who have outlined a relationship between eighteenth-century science's view of the nervous system and a cult of sensibility include R. F. Brissenden, *Virtue in Distress: Studies in the Novel of Sentiment from Richardson to de Sade* (New York: Harper and Row, 1974), 37–48; G. S. Rousseau, "Nerves, Spirits, and Fibres: Towards Defining the Origins of Sensibility," *Blue Guitar* 2 (1976): 125–53; G. S. Rousseau, "Science," in *The Context of English Literature: The Eighteenth Century*, ed. Pat Rogers (London: Methuen, 1978), 153–207 (and see Thomas Hankins, *Science and the Enlightenment* [Cambridge: Cambridge University Press, 1985], ch. 5); Christopher Lawrence, "The Nervous System and Society in the Scottish Enlightenment," in *Natural Order: Historical Studies of Scientific Culture*, ed. Barry Barnes and Steven Shapin (Beverly Hills and London: Sage Publications, 1979), 19–39; Barker-Benfield, "Mary Wollstonecraft's Depression and Diagnosis: The Relation between Sensibility and Women's Susceptibility to Nervous Disorders," *Psychohistory Review* 13, no. 4 (Spring 1985): 15–31; John Mullan, *Sentiment and Sociability: The Language of Feeling in the Eighteenth Century* (Oxford: Clarendon Press, 1988), ch. 5.

5. Marlene Legates, "The Cult of Womanhood in Eighteenth-Century Thought," *Eighteenth-Century Studies* 10, no. 1 (Fall 1976), 26; Katherine Rogers, "The Feminism of Daniel Defoe," in *Woman in the Eighteenth Century and Other Essays*, ed. Paul Fritz and Richard Morton (Toronto and Sarasota: Samuel Hakkert, 1976), 22; Lawrence Stone, *The Family, Sex and Marriage in England, 1500–1800* (New York and London: Harper and Row, 1977), ch. 8.

6. In addition to the works cited in the Introduction, nn. 6 and 7, see Hilda Smith, *Reason's Disciples: Seventeenth-Century English Feminists* (Urbana: University of Illinois Press, 1982); Jerome Nadelhaft, "The Englishwoman's Civil

War: Feminist Attitudes toward Men, Women and Marriage, 1650–1740," *Journal of the History of Ideas* 43 (October 1982): 555–79; Christopher Hill, *The World Turned Upside Down* (New York: Viking Press, 1972), ch. 15; Stone, *Family*, 337–40.

7. Peter Burke, *Popular Culture in Early Modern Europe* (New York: Harper Torchbooks, 1978), 164–5 and Natalie Zemon Davis, "Women on Top," in *Society and Culture in Early Modern France* (Stanford: Stanford University Press, 1975), 124–51; Susan Moller Okin, "Women and the Sentimental Family," *Philosophy and Public Affairs* 2, no. 1 (Winter 1982): 72; Ian Watt, *The Rise of the Novel: Studies in Defoe, Richardson, and Fielding* (Berkeley: University of California Press, 1967 [1957]), 65, 117; Katherine Rogers, "Feminism of Defoe," passim; J. Paul Hunter, *Before Novels: The Cultural Contexts of Eighteenth-Century Fiction* (New York: Norton, 1990), 268–71.

8. Okin, "Women and the Sentimental Family," 72, 65, 68–72; Alice Browne, *The Eighteenth Century Feminist Mind* (Brighton: Harvester, 1987), 9, 82, 115; Nadelhaft, "Englishwoman's Civil War," 564. See also Melissa A. Butler, "Early Liberal Roots of Feminism: John Locke and the Attack on Patriarchy," *American Political Science Review* 72 (March 1978): 141–50.

9. The "benefits of liberal instruction" passage is quoted in Katherine Rogers, *Feminism in Eighteenth-Century England* (Urbana: University of Illinois press), 33; in eighteenth-century Britain, the "new social, literary, and sexual confidence of polite women" provided a "broad base" for the Blue Stockings, but with still wider-ranging "repercussions." Langford, *Polite and Commercial People*, 112; Edward Gibbon, *The Decline and Fall of the Roman Empire*, 3 vols. (New York: Modern Library, n.d. [1776]), 1:262–3; Wollstonecraft, *Rights of Woman*, 80–1, 219.

10. James Sambrook, *The Eighteenth Century: The Intellectual and Cultural Context of English Literature, 1700–1789* (London and New York: Longman, 1986), 50; see too Jay Fliegelman, *Prodigals and Pilgrims: The American Revolution against Patriarchal Authority, 1750–1800* (Cambridge and New York: Cambridge University Press, 1982), 14, and passim.

11. Michael MacDonald, "The Secularization of Suicide in England 1660–1800," *Past and Present*, no. 111 (May 1986): 86. MacDonald is quoting Henry Halliwell, *Melapronea: or, A Discourse of the Polity and Kingdom of Darkness* (London, 1681), 77–8; Pocock suggests that such a hankering—and its expression in science as the separation of spirit and matter—may be seen as a conservative reaction expressing "the ruling elite's horror of religious fanaticism." J. G. A. Pocock, *Virtue, Commerce, and History: Essays on Political Thought and History, Chiefly in the Eighteenth Century* (New York: Cambridge University Press, 1985), 52.

12. Rousseau, "Origins," 135, 136, 159–40, 129; Rousseau, "Science," 191; of course, Bacon began his method with "the simple sensuous perception," and at the opening of *Leviathan* Hobbes wrote: "there is no conception in a man's mind, which has not at first totally, or by parts, been begotten upon the organs of sense."

13. John Locke, *An Essay Concerning Human Understanding*, edited by Peter H. Nidditch (Oxford: Clarendon Press, 1975), bk. 2, ch. 1, secs. 2, 3, and 4.

14. Locke, *Understanding*, bk. 2, ch. 3, sec. 20; bk. 2, ch. 33, sec. 5; see

Ernest Lee Tuveson, *The Imagination as a Means of Grace: Locke and the Aesthetics of Romanticism* (New York: Gordian Press, 1974 [1960]), 33–5.

15. Walter Jackson Bate, *From Classic to Romantic: Premises of Taste in Eighteenth-Century England* (New York: Harper and Brothers, 1946), 130.

16. Quotation in I. Bernard Cohen's introduction to Sir Isaac Newton, *Opticks, or the Reflections, Refractions, Inflections and Colours of Light* (New York: Dover Publications, 1979 [1730 ed.]), xx; Locke, *Understanding,* bk. 1, ch. 1, sec. 2; see Sambrook, *Eighteenth Century,* 50–1, see also 202.

17. Sambrook, *Eighteenth Century,* 4–7; G. S. Rousseau, "Science," 136, 191; Stanley W. Jackson, "Force and Kindred Notions in 18th-Century Neurophysiology," *Bulletin of the History of Medicine* 54, no. 5, (September–October 1910): 397–410 and no. 6, (November–December 1970): 539–554; pt. 1, 401–2.

18. Newton, *Opticks,* xxix, xxxi–ii, 345, 353, 351, 352, 398. See too Eric T. Carlson and Meribeth M. Simpson, "Models of the Nervous Systems in Eighteenth-Century Psychiatry," *Bulletin of the History of Medicine* 43 (1969): 101–15, esp. 108–9, 105. The doctrine of the hollow nerve persisted through most of the century. Edwin Clarke, "The Doctrine of the Hollow Nerve in the Seventeenth and Eighteenth Centuries," in *Medicine, Science, and Culture: Historical Essays in Honor of Oswei Temkin,* ed. Lloyd G. Stevenson and Robert P. Multhauf (Baltimore: Johns Hopkins University Press, 1968), 128, 123; Carlson and Simpson, "Nervous System," 103–4, 112, 104, 106–7, 112, 105.

19. Newton, *Opticks,* 353–4.

20. Newton, "General Scholium" to the *Principia,* quoted in Sambrook, *Eighteenth Century,* 6–7; Newton, *Opticks,* 370, 403, 405–6; Sambrook, *Eighteenth Century,* 3, 8–10, 29; V. K. Kiernan, "Evangelism and the French Revolution," *Past and Present* 1 (1952–3): 46. For this tendency toward natural religion see Sambrook, *Eighteenth Century,* 6, 27, 200; Norman Fiering, "Irresistible Compassion: An Aspect of Eighteenth-Century Sympathy and Humanitarianism," *Journal of the History of Ideas* 37 (1976): 198. For Newton's place in the debate over the Christian community and for this contribution to the "argument from design" see John Redwood, *Reason, Ridicule and Religion: The Age of Enlightenment in England, 1660–1750* (Cambridge, Mass.: Harvard University Press, 1976), 94–97. For another useful perspective on "Religion versus Science" in this era see Michael McKeon, *The Origins of the English Novel 1600–1740* (Baltimore: Johns Hopkins University Press, 1987), 73–76.

21. Newton, *Opticks,* xxxiv; Fliegelman, *Prodigals and Pilgrims,* 272n.19; Sambrook, *Eighteenth Century,* 28–29. J. H. Plumb, "The Commercialization of Leisure in Eighteenth-Century England," in Neil McKendrick, John Brewer, and Plumb, *The Birth of a Consumer Society: The Commercialization of Eighteenth-Century England* (Bloomington: Indiana University Press, 1982), 269 and 284; for example *The Spectator,* no. 565 (9 July 1714), in Joseph Addison, Richard Steele, et al., *The Spectator,* 8 vols. (London: T. Hamilton and R. Ogle, 1808), 8:38–9. Addison made sure to couple his quotation of Newton with a quotation from the Bible.

22. Marjorie Hope Nicolson, *Newton Demands the Muse: Newton's Opticks*

and the Eighteenth-Century Poets (Princeton: Princeton University Press, 1946); Sambrook, *Eighteenth Century,* 30–1; Rousseau, "Science," 93–4; "James Thomson" in *The Oxford Companion to English Literature, New Edition,* ed. Margaret Drabble (Oxford: Oxford University Press, 1985), 979.

23. Rousseau, "Science," 194.

24. Brissenden, *Virtue in Distress,* 20–1, 37.

25. H. M. Sinclair and A. H. T. Robb-Smith, *A Short History of Anatomical Teaching at Oxford* (Oxford: Oxford University Press, 1950), 29–30; Carlson, "Introduction," in George Cheyne, *The English Malady: or, A Treatise of Nervous Diseases of All Kinds, as Spleen, Vapours, Lowness of Spirits, Hypochondriacal and Hysterical Distempers, Etc.* (Delmar, N.Y.: Scholars Facsimiles and Reprints, 1976 [1733]), xiii–xiv; Bernard Mandeville, M.D., *A Treatise of the Hypochondriack and Hysterick Diseases in Three Dialogues* (London: J. Tonson, 1730 [1711]); Rousseau, "Science," 189.

26. Lawrence, "Nervous System and Scottish Enlightenment," 25–28.

27. Sambrook, *Eighteenth Century,* 16; Carlson, "Introduction," *English Malady,* viii.

28. *The Letters of Doctor George Cheyne to Samuel Richardson* (1733–1743), edited by Charles F. Mullett, University of Missouri Studies no. 18 (Columbia: University of Missouri Press, 1943).

29. For brief biographies of Cheyne see Carlson, "Introduction," *English Malady;* Mullett's n. 23 in his edition of the *Letters to Richardson,* 17; R. S. Sindall, "George Cheyne, M.D.: Eighteenth-Century Clinician and Medical Author," *Annals of Medical History* 3, no. 4 (1947): 95–109.

30. Cheyne, *English Malady,* vii, 134–5, ix, 42–6; Carlson cites and quotes Cheyne's *Philosophical Principles,* in "Introduction," *English Malady,* vi; Sindall, "George Cheyne," p. 104; Cheyne describes his addition of "Gospel" religion to natural philosophy's argument for God in *The English Malady,* 226–8; Carlson, "Introduction," *English Malady,* vi.

31. Cheyne, *English Malady,* 3–4; see too 61 and 48.

32. Ibid., 42–6, 11–12, and 52–3.

33. Ibid., 49.

34. Ibid., 48–9, 46. In a letter posthumously published in 1744, Newton suggested the variation of aether by "degrees." Quoted in Newton, *Opticks,* xxix.

35. Rousseau, "Science," 195; Lawrence, "Nervous System and Scottish Enlightenment," 28, 29; Samuel Richardson, *Clarissa: or, the History of a Young Lady,* 4 vols. (London and Toronto: J. M. Dent, 1932 [1748]), 4:160.

36. Cheyne, *English Malady,* 71.

37. Ibid., 3, 253. See too Tuveson's quotation of Alexander Gerard's *Essay on Taste,* in *Imagination,* 148, to illustrate how the system could mean immediate and instinctive taste. Cf. too Brissenden's quotation of J. P. Marat, *Virtue in Distress,* 44.

38. Cheyne, *English Malady,* 223–56.

39. Ibid., 254.

40. Quoted in Sindall, "George Cheyne," 99.

41. Langford, *Polite and Commercial People,* 327–8; David Hume, *Essays,*

Moral, Political and Literary, 2 vols., ed. T. H. Green and T. H. Grose (London: Longmans, Green, 1875), 1:35–6. For MacKenzie, see Ch. 3, below; V. G. Kiernan, *The Duel in European History: Honour and the Reign of Aristocracy* (Oxford: Oxford University Press, 1988), 177.

42. Cheyne, *English Malady,* 222; Cheyne to Richardson, 23 December 1741, *Letters to Richardson,* 26–7.

43. Cheyne, *English Malady,* 222, 229–31.

44. Carlson, "Introduction," *English Malady,* viii; Cheyne, *English Malady,* 226, 240; Cheyne to Richardson, 23 December 1741, *Letters to Richardson,* 77; Cheyne to Richardson, 5 September 1742, *Letters to Richardson,* 109.

45. Cheyne to Richardson, 14 March 1742, *Letters to Richardson,* p. 88; Donald Meyer, *The Positive Thinkers: Religion as Pop Psychology from Mary Baker Eddy to Oral Roberts,* 2d ed. (New York: Pantheon, 1980), 60–1.

46. Cheyne to Richardson, 2 February 1742, *Letters to Richardson,* p. 83. In *The English Malady,* Cheyne describes himself going through "Purgation," 248.

47. Cheyne to Richardson, 22 June 1742, *Letters to Richardson,* 100.

48. Cheyne, *English Malady,* 34, 121. For an enlightening discussion of this eighteenth-century literary theme see Raymond Williams, *The Country and the City* (London: Hogarth Press, 1985), ch. 9 and passim.

49. Simon Schama, *The Embarrassment of Riches: An Interpretation of Dutch Culture in the Golden Age* (Berkeley: University of California Press, 1988), 158–9, 165. Cheyne, *English Malady,* 35, 39; Carlson, "Introduction," *English Malady,* vii.

50. Cheyne, *English Malady,* 108–9.

51. Ibid., 35ff. Carlson quotes the "martyrs" phrase in his "Introduction," xi. Consumers were "martyring" themselves because, in living "voluptuously," it was "the miserable Man himself that creates his Miseries and begets his Torture." *English Malady,* 20; *The Compleat Housewife* quoted by Nancy Armstrong, *Desire and Domestic Fiction: A Political History of the Novel* (Oxford: Oxford University Press, 1987), 70. See too Lorna Weatherill, *Consumer Behaviour and Material Culture in Britain 1660–1760* (London: Routledge, 1988), 146.

52. Cheyne, *English Malady,* p. 36.

53. Ibid., 37, 15.

54. Ibid., 38–9.

55. Ibid., 5, 9, 10–11, 117–8.

56. Carlson, "Introduction," *English Malady,* viii–ix; Sindall, "George Cheyne," 99, 104; Cheyne to Richardson, 26 April 1742, *Letters to Richardson,* 92.

57. Rousseau, "Science," 194–5.

58. In addition to Brissenden, *Virtue in Distress,* 16, 31, 39–43, 46–7, see Lawrence, "Nervous System and Scottish Enlightenment," 19–39; Rousseau, "Science," 192–3; and Donald D'Elia, "Benjamin Rush: Philosopher of the American Revolution," *Transactions of the American Philosophical Society* (September 1974): 23–25, 35.

59. Rousseau, "Science," 194.

60. Wollstonecraft, *Rights of Woman,* 219–20.

61. Richardson, *Clarissa,* 2:434; Edmund Burke, *A Philosophical Enquiry into the Origin of our Ideas of the Sublime and Beautiful,* ed. James T. Boulton (South Bend: University of Notre Dame Press, 1958 [1957]), 137; Tobias Smollett, *The Expedition of Humphry Clinker* (New York: New American Library, 1960 [1771]), 181; Ann Radcliffe, *The Mysteries of Udolpho* (Oxford: Oxford University Press, 1982 [1794]), 25; Mary Hays, *Memoirs of Emma Courtney* (New York: Pandora Press, 1987 [1796]), 174. Occasionally the old meaning of "nervous" as vigorous or strong appears. See for example Henry Fielding, *The History of Tom Jones: A Foundling* (New York: New American Library, 1979 [1749]), 413.

62. Richardson, *Clarissa,* 2:398; *The Spectator* 4:122. Believing his faculties rusted by "town smoke" and confinement with Clarissa, Lovelace hoped to "brace up . . . the relaxed fibres of my mind, which have been twitched and convulsed like the nerves of some tottering paralytic" (3:475).

63. Burke, *The Sublime and Beautiful,* 135; Cheyne, *English Malady,* 139; Smollet, *Humphry Clinker,* 176; Elizabeth Inchbald, *A Simple Story* (New York: Pandora Press, 1987 [1791]), 103–4, see too 81.

64. Fielding, *Tom Jones,* 655; Henry MacKenzie, *The Man of the World* published in a combined volume with *The Man of Feeling* (London: George Routledge, n.d. [1773]), 176. In MacKenzie's "Man of Feeling," "ideas" are "produced" by "sensations." MacKenzie, *The Man of Feeling* (London: Oxford University Press, 1967 [1771]), 17.

65. Burney's *Juliet* quoted in Rousseau, "Science," 154; Warren quoted in Linda Kerber, *Women of the Republic: Intellect and Ideology in Revolutionary America* (Chapel Hill: University of North Carolina Press, 1980), 83; Radcliffe, *Udolpho,* 46; Hays, *Letters and Essays Moral and Miscellaneous* (New York: Garland Publishing, 1978 [1793]), 110.

66. Richardson, *Clarissa,* 2:80; Richardson, *The History of Sir Charles Grandison,* ed. Jocelyn Harris, 3 vols. (London: Oxford University Press, 1972 [1753–4]), 1:17; Inchbald, *Simple Story,* 217; Hays, *Essays,* 115; Locke, *Understanding,* bk. 2, ch. 9, secs. 2–4.

67. See for example Aphra Behn, *Oroonoko: or, The Royal Slave* (New York: W. W. Norton, 1973 [1688], 19; Fielding, *Tom Jones,* 168; Inchbald, *Simple Story,* 79; Richardson, *Clarissa,* 1:446; Smollett, *Humphry Clinker,* 74, Thomas Day, *The History of Sandford and Merton* (Philadelphia: n.p., n.d. [1783–89]), 316.

68. Joseph Priestley, *Hartley's Theory of the Human Mind, on the Principle of the Association of Ideas . . .* (New York: Arno Press, 1973 [1775]); Burke, *Sublime and Beautiful,* 130 (although see Boulton's "Introduction" to the work, xxxiv and xliii). Hays, *Emma Courtney,* 176–7 (see too Hays, *Essays,* 79); Radcliffe, *Udolpho,* 580.

69. Richardson, *Pamela: or, Virtue Rewarded* (New York: W. W. Norton, 1958 [1740]), 440; Richardson, *Clarissa,* 1:23.

70. Richardson, *Clarissa,* 4:285; Richardson, *Pamela,* 109, 150; Richardson, *Sir Charles Grandison,* 3:70.

71. Richardson, *Pamela,* 310.

72. Ibid., 357; Jane Austen, *Sense and Sensibility* (New York: New American Library, 1961 [1811]), 190.

73. Richardson, *Pamela,* 353; Fielding, *Tom Jones,* 482; Richardson, *Clarissa,* 1:290; Richardson, *Pamela,* 28.

74. Smollett, *Humphry Clinker,* 139; MacKenzie, *Man of the World,* 333; Radcliffe, *Udolpho,* 24, 324, 500.

75. Richardson, *Sir Charles Grandison,* 1:133; Richardson, *Clarissa,* 2:175, 1:299.

76. Richardson, *Clarissa,* 1:439.

77. For example, Radcliffe, *Udolpho,* 423, 453, 479. Radcliffe and Hays use the phrase "harassed mind," in *Udolpho,* 324 and *Emma Courtney,* 133, respectively.

78. Richardson, *Clarissa,* 4:173. Compare the doctor's diagnosis, when Clarissa says, "My spirits have been hurried" (3:468).

79. Cheyne, *English Malady,* 120; Fielding, *Tom Jones,* 633; Richardson, *Pamela,* 422; Richardson, *Clarissa,* 1:387; 3:180, 416, 447; 4:212, 293; Richardson, *Sir Charles Grandison,* 1:135; Burke quoted in Boulton, "Introduction," xx; Radcliffe, *Udolpho,* 423; Anon., *Robert and Adela: or, The Rights of Women Best Maintained by the Sentiments of Nature,* 3 vols. (London: G. G. and J. Robinson, 1795); Maria Edgeworth, *Belinda* (London: Pandora Press, 1986 [1801]), 185.

80. *Collected Letters of Mary Wollstonecraft,* ed. Ralph M. Wardle (Ithaca: Cornell University Press, 1979), passim.

81. Richardson, *Clarissa,* 3:499; Richardson, *Pamela,* 308; Richardson, *Clarissa,* 2:200, 1:334, and see 1:325; Smollett, *Humphry Clinker,* 221, 182.

82. Richardson, *Clarissa,* 2:176; Cheyne, *English Malady,* 134–5; Mandeville, *Treatise,* 269–70.

83. Jonathan Swift, "A Tale of a Tub," in *Gulliver's Travels and Other Writings,* ed. Mariam Kosh Starkman (New York: Bantam, 1962), 279–94, 366–77; Smollet, *Clinker,* 103, 105.

84. *The Spectator,* no. 115 (12 July 1711), and no. 216 (7 November 1711) in *The Spectator,* 2:135–8, and 3:196–9; Daniel Defoe, *The Fortunes and Misfortunes of Moll Flanders* (New York: New American Library, 1964 [1722]), 168–225.

85. Richardson, *Sir Charles Grandison,* 2:324; Richardson, *Clarissa,* 1:203. Other illustrations of the stereotypical use of "vapourish" are Richardson, *Pamela,* 472, and *Clarissa,* 2:266 and 284.

86. Cheyne, *English Malady,* 134; Richardson, *Clarissa,* 2:401; 4:123; 2:169, 264; and 4:211.

87. Burke, *Sublime and Beautiful,* 140, see too 137; Radcliffe, *Udolpho,* 100, 292, 318; Hays, *Essays,* 115.

88. Phillis Wheatley quoted in Charles Scruggs, "Phillis Wheatley and the Poetical Legacy of Eighteenth-Century England," *Studies in Eighteenth Century Culture,* vol. 10 (Madison: University of Wisconsin Press, 1981); More, "Sensibility, A Poem," in *Sacred Dramas, Chiefly Intended for Young Persons: The Subjects Taken from the Bible* (Worcester, Mass.: American Antiquarian Society, 1963 [1787]); Wollstonecraft, *Letters Written during a Short Residence in Sweden,*

Norway, and Denmark (Lincoln: University of Nebraska, 1976 [1796]), 59; Radcliffe, *Udolpho,* 250, see too 287; Glanville quoted in the O. E. D.; Akenside quoted in Tuveson, *Imagination,* 145; Hays, *Emma Courtney,* 155.

89. Cheyne, *English Malady,* 3; Richardson, *Clarissa,* 1:417–8, 3:45.

90. Hume, *A Treatise of Human Nature* (New York: Penguin, 1985 [1739–40]), 626–7, bk. 3, pt. 3, sec. 1; see too his essay "The Stoic" in *Essays* 1:208–9; Radcliffe, *Udolpho,* 168.

91. Brooke quoted in Erik Erämetsä, *A Study of the Word 'Sentimental' and of Other Linguistic Characteristics of Eighteenth-Century Sentimentalism in England* (Helsinki: Helsingin Liikekirjapaino Oy, 1951), 65; Wesley quoted by E. P. Thompson in "Time, Work-Discipline, and Industrial Capitalism," *Essays in Social History,* ed. M. W. Flinn and T. C. Smout (Oxford: Clarendon Press, 1974), 62–3.

92. Quoted by Brissenden, *Virtue in Distress,* 8; see too Inchbald, *Simple Story,* 254.

93. Radcliffe, *Udolpho,* 318, 100.

94. Richardson, *Clarissa,* 4:420; J. H. Plumb, "The Commercialization of Leisure in Eighteenth-Century England," in Neil McKendrick, John Brewer, and Plumb, *The Birth of a Consumer Society: The Commercialization of Eighteenth Century England* (Bloomington: Indiana University Press, 1982), 271–2. Plumb describes the enormous spread of music from the early eighteenth century, both to be played at home and listened to at concerts in newly established concert halls. The "rapid development and specialization of musical-instrument makers" met "the ever increasing demand," 278–90.

95. MacKenzie, *Man of Feeling,* 71; Sambrook, *Eighteenth Century,* 63.

96. Baldesar Castiglione, *The Book of The Courtier,* trans. George Bull (New York: Penguin, 1976 [1528: trans. into English 1561]), 17, 223; Barker-Benfield, "Wollstonecraft's Depression and Diagnosis," 21.

97. Thomas Laqueur, "Orgasm, Generation, and the Politics of Reproductive Biology," *Representations* 14 (Spring 1986): 1–4, 18. Laqueur refers briefly to the nerves and sensibility, 22, 24. His argument is parallel to Barker-Benfield's suggestion of the relation between revolution, physiology, and antifeminism in *The Horrors of the Half-Known Life: Male Attitudes toward Women in Nineteenth-Century America* (New York: Harper and Row, 1976), ch. 6 and passim.

98. Cheyne, *English Malady,* 179, 180.

99. Ibid., 66, 67, 14; significantly, he says that all females are subject to nervous disorders as they pass through menarche, 153.

100. Ibid., 134, 154, pt. 3 passim.

101. Ibid., pt. 3, 116ff.

102. Barker-Benfield, "Wollstonecraft's Depression and Diagnosis," 21. Another Dutch doctor, J. van Beverwijck, held that women were more "delicate than men, linking that to their "weaker" tissues. Schama, *Embarrassment of Riches,* 400.

103. Like Cheyne, Johnson frequently lapsed into alcohol, and eventually he gave up both tea and punch, replacing them with water and lemonade. James Boswell, *Life of Johnson,* ed. R. W. Chapman (London: Oxford Univer-

sity Press, 1970 [1791]), 222; W. Jackson Bate, *Samuel Johnson* (New York: Harcourt Brace Jovanovich, 1975), 135–6, 358, 348, 409.

104. See below, 293–4, 344–9.

105. Bernard Mandeville, *A Treatise of the Hypochondriack and Hysterick Diseases in Three Dialogues* (London: J. Tonson, 1730 [1711]), 246, 247.

106. Quoted in Mullan, *Sentiment and Sociability,* 221–2.

107. Ibid., 209; Hume, *Essays,* 1:92.

108. Richardson, *Clarissa,* 3:303, 63. Fielding, *Tom Jones,* 168; Horace Walpole, *Memoirs and Portraits,* ed. Matthew Hodgart (New York: MacMillan, 1963), 232; Sarah Trimmer, *The Oeconomy of Charity: or, An Address to Ladies; Adapted to the Present State of Charitable Institutions in England,* 2 vols. (London: J. Johnson and F. and C. Rivington, 1801 [1787]), 1:19; Fanny Burney, *Camilla: or, A Picture of Youth* (Oxford: Oxford University Press, 1983 [1796]), 347; Austen, *Sense and Sensibility,* 264. For further illustrations see MacKenzie, *Man of the World,* 275; Inchbald, *A Simple Story,* 5, 198, 219, 241, 259; Radcliffe, *Udolpho,* 75; Hays, *Emma Courtney,* 5, 78, 130.

109. Richardson, *Clarissa,* 1:319; John Gregory, *A Father's Legacy to His Daughters* (London: W. Strahan, T. Cadell, 1781 [1774]), 27; Brooke's *Emily Montague* quoted in J. M. S. Tompkins, *The Popular Novel in England, 1770–1800* (Westport, Conn.: Greenwood Press, 1976 [1961]), 97.

110. *Letters to Richardson,* 82; Cheyne, *English Malady,* 34; Smollett, *Humphry Clinker,* 287–8.

111. Fielding, *Tom Jones,* 513, 94; Adair quoted in Rousseau, "Science," 184; and see Ida MacAlpine and Richard Hunter, *George III and the Mad-Business* (New York: Pantheon, 1969), 287. The interweaving of fashion and diagnosis is also apparent in the seventeenth century. Melancholy had been "à la mode in Jacobean England and the rage for this fashionable affliction popularized medical ideas about emotional distress." Michael MacDonald, *Mystical Bedlam: Madness, Anxiety, and Healing in 17th-Century England* (Cambridge: Cambridge University Press, 1981), 113, and see 151.

112. Williams, *Country and City,* 93–4; a good illustration of the view in the work of a later and very middle-class writer is Day, *Sandford and Merton,* 201.

113. Langford, *Polite and Commercial People,* 106–7, 261; Peter Borsay, *The English Urban Renaissance: Culture and Society in The Provincial Town, 1660–1770* (Oxford: Clarendon Press, 1989), 241, 31.

114. Langford, *Polite and Commercial People,* 105–6; Borsay, *Urban Renaissance,* 261–2, 33; for a detailed account of Bath's rebuilding see Borsay, *Urban Renaissance,* 31–2, 100–1, 134, 164–8, 241–2.

115. Langford, *Polite and Commercial People,* 103; Mandeville, *Treatise,* 269–70.

116. Anna Laetitia [Aikin] Barbauld, *The Works of Anna Laetitia Barbauld,* 2 vols. (London: Longman, 1825), 2:297.

117. Thomas Clarkson, *Portraiture of Quakerism* (London: New York, Samuel Stansburg, 1806), 44–5. I am grateful to Professor Randall McGowan for this reference.

118. Men of feeling also suffered from nervous disorders; see for example MacKenzie, *Man of Feeling,* 126; Brissenden, *Virtue in Distress,* 248; Mullan,

Sentiment and Sociability, 208; and G. A. Starr, "Only A Boy: Notes on Sentimental Novels," *Genre* (Winter 1977): 501–27; to the actual cases of Cheyne, Richardson, Hume, and Sterne can be added Dr. Johnson's, in spite of his heroic efforts to change his diet. Boswell, *Life Of Johnson,* 48–9, and passim. These were all Cheyne's "sedentary" types, perhaps feeling that if the pen was mightier than the sword, its value in comparison to business and invention was equivocal, a subject taken up in Chapter 3.

119. Richardson, *Pamela,* 213–4.

120. Ibid., 187; Fielding, *Tom Jones,* 774, 75, 158. Smollet, *Humphry Clinker,* 72; William Godwin, *St. Leon: A Tale of the Sixteenth Century,* 4 vols. (New York: Garland Publishing, 1974 [1799]), 3:49.

121. Richardson, *Clarissa,* 1:438, 3:91, 1:482, 2:186–7. See too Richardson, *Sir Charles Grandison,* 1:335.

122. Richardson, *Clarissa,* 1:22, 412; 3:522; 3:522, 4:349–53.

123. Radcliffe, *Udolpho,* 354, 589; Wollstonecraft, *Rights of Woman,* 112; Barker-Benfield, "Wollstonecraft's Depression and Diagnosis," 17.

Chapter 2. The Reformation of Male Manners

1. Peter Laslett, *The World We Have Lost: England before the Industrial Age, Further Explored* (New York: Charles Scribner's, 1984), 73; Judith M. Bennett, *Women in the Medieval English Countryside: Gender and Household in Brigstock before the Plague* (New York: Oxford University Press, 1987), 6, 188. Bennett goes on to qualify this somewhat, but later she writes, as "a rule, the social activities of women were particularly narrow and oriented towards family members . . . men [had] opportunities for neighborliness that were unavailable to most women," 7–8, 37, see too 136–8, 139, 177; review of *The Exemplary Mother* quoted in Jane Spencer, *The Rise of the Woman Novelist* (Oxford: Basil Blackwell, 1986), 21.

2. Graham Greene, *Lord Rochester's Monkey, Being the Life of John Wilmot, Second Earl of Rochester* (Baltimore and New York: Penguin, 1974), 40; John Redwood, *Reason, Ridicule and Religion: The Age of Enlightenment in England, 1660–1750* (Cambridge, Mass.: Harvard University Press, 1976), 40; Vivian de Sola Pinto, *Enthusiast in Wit: A Portrait of John Wilmot Earl of Rochester, 1647–1680* (London: Routledge and Kegan Paul, 1962), 34, 6–7; Greene, *Rochester's Monkey,* 32.

3. Redwood, *Reason and Religion,* 9–10; 220; Pinto, *Enthusiast,* 33; Lawrence Stone, "The New Eighteenth Century," *New York Review of Books* 31, no. 5 (29 March 1984), 45.

4. Pinto, *Enthusiast,* 34; Gilbert Burnet, *Some Passages of the Life and Death of John Earl of Rochester* (1680), in *Rochester: The Critical Heritage,* ed. David Farley-Hills (New York: Barnes and Noble, 1972), 49–50.

5. Clarendon quoted in Pinto, *Enthusiast,* 113; the other quotation is in Michael McKeon, *The Origins of the English Novel 1600–1740* (Baltimore: Johns Hopkins University Press, 1987), 68.

6. The "taboo" phrase is Jeremy Treglown's in his introduction to *The Letters of John Wilmot, Earl of Rochester* (Oxford: Basil Blackwell, 1980), 3; Pinto, *Enthusiast,* 115, 28–9; Burnet, *Rochester,* 57.

7. Pinto, *Enthusiast,* 58; Burnet, *Rochester,* 89.
8. Quoted in Pinto, *Enthusiast,* 109–10.
9. Aphra Behn, "On the Death of Lord Rochester" and "To Mrs. W[harton]. On her Excellent Verses (Writ in Praise of Some I had made on the Earl of Rochester) Written in a Fit of Sickness," in Farley-Hills, *Rochester,* 101–4, 105–6; Anne Wharton, "To Mrs. Behn on What She Writ of the Earl of Rochester" and "Elegy and Lines," in Farley-Hills, *Rochester,* 104, 107–8;
10. Rochester, "A Very Heroicall Epistle in Answer to Ephelia," and "How Perfect Chloris, and How free," in *The Poems of John Wilmot, Earl of Rochester,* ed. Keith Walker (Oxford: Basil Blackwell, 1984), 113, 40.
11. Pinto, *Enthusiast,* 144. Cf. William Empson, *Using Biography* (Cambridge, Mass.: Harvard University Press, 1984), viii.
12. For example "A Letter from Artemiza in the Towne to Chloe in the Country," in Rochester, *Poems,* 83–90; "Satire on Man," in Rochester, *Poems,* 90–1; Rochester, *Letters,* 3; Pinto, *Enthusiast,* 80–1, 125, 86–7, 106.
13. Burnet, *Rochester,* 51; Greene, *Rochester's Monkey,* 123; Pinto, *Enthusiast,* 72–3.
14. Greene, *Rochester's Monkey,* 168; see too Pinto, *Enthusiast,* 167n.1.
15. Pinto, *Enthusiast,* 123; Rochester to Savile, October 1677, in Rochester, *Letters,* 159; Samuel Butler, "Dildoides," in Pinto, *Enthusiast,* 73.
16. A contemporary account is quoted in Green, *Rochester's Monkey,* 106.
17. Quoted in Greene, *Rochester's Monkey,* 144. Pinto relegates this story to "gossip," *Enthusiast,* 147n.5.
18. Greene, *Rochester's Monkey,* 42. See Pinto, *Enthusiast,* 35–38.
19. Pinto, *Enthusiast,* 43–4.
20. Burnet, *Rochester,* 51; Pinto, *Enthusiast,* 147.
21. Quoted in Greene, *Rochester's Monkey,* 120–1.
22. Burnet, *Rochester,* 57, 72.
23. Quoted in Pinto, *Enthusiast,* 66–7.
24. Ibid., 169, 229.
25. Burnet, *Rochester,* 88; McKeon, *Origins of Novel,* 94.
26. Burnet, *Rochester,* 82, 83.
27. Pinto, *Enthusiast,* 206–7; Burnet, *Rochester,* 75; Burnet, *Rochester,* 75, 57–8.
28. Pinto, *Enthusiast,* 151; Burnet, *Rochester,* 75; Rochester's "A Very Heroicall Epistle in Answer to Ephelia," in Rochester, *Poems,* 112.
29. Burnet, *Rochester,* 75, 57.
30. "The Reformation of Manners" quoted in Farley-Hills, *Rochester,* 7; Behn, "To Mrs. W.," 105; Burnet, *Rochester,* 87, 91.
31. Burnet, *Rochester,* 85, 50, 41, 88–9.
32. Ibid., 86, 88, 85, 83; Pinto, *Enthusiast,* 145–6.
33. Pinto, *Enthusiast,* 88; Louis C. Jones, *The Clubs of the Georgian Rakes* (New York: Columbia University Press, 1942), 50; Jerry C. Beasley, *Novels of the 1740s,* Athens: University of Georgia Press, 1982), 98, 131–2.
34. Anon., *The Rake: or, The Libertine's Religion. A Poem* (London: R. Taylor, 1693), 13, 2, 12, preface, 10, 7, 13, 2, 12.
35. Samuel Richardson, *Clarissa: or, The History of a Young Lady,* 4 vols. (Lon-

don: J. M. Dent, 1932 [1748]), 3:483–4, 1:145; Lawrence Stone, *The Family, Sex and Marriage in England, 1500–1800* (New York: Harper and Row, 1977), 136.

36. Farley-Hills's account of Rochester's reputation, *Rochester,* 1–26, includes the 1806 quotation, 2.

37. Peter Burke, *Popular Culture in Early Modern Europe* (New York: Harper Torchbooks, 1978), 27, 104.

38. These two works are Jones, *Georgian Rakes,* and a 1923 article which attempted to provide the authority of historical precedent to the good ol' boys of the KKK, Thornton S. Graves, "Some Pre-Mohock Clansmen," *Studies in Philology* 20, no. 4 (October 1923), 395–421.

39. Peter Borsay, *The English Urban Renaissance: Culture and Society in the Provincial Town, 1660–1770* (Oxford: Clarendon Press, 1989), 176–80; Jones, *Georgian Rakes,* 5; typical illustrations of the culture of sensibility's view of "gaming" are Henry MacKenzie, *The Man of Feeling* (Oxford: Oxford University Press, 1970 [1771]), 27–8; and Ann Radcliffe, *The Mysteries of Udolpho* (Oxford: Oxford University Press, 1980 [1794]), 182.

40. Borsay, *Urban Renaissance,* 202; J. M. Golby and A. W. Purdue, *The Civilisation of the Crowd: Popular Culture in England, 1750–1900* (New York: Schocken, 1985), 49; Graves, "Clansmen," 410, 413n.43; Defoe quoted in McKeon, *Origins of Novel,* 219.

41. Jones, *Georgian Rakes,* 2; Paul Langford, *A Polite and Commercial People: England 1727–1783* (Oxford: Clarendon Press, 1989), 88; Burke, *Popular Culture,* 41, see too 184, 189, 191; *The Spectator,* no. 324 (12 March 1711–12), in Joseph Addison, Richard Steele, et al. *The Spectator,* 8 vols. (London: Hamilton, Ogle, etc., 1808), 5:11–12; Keith Thomas, "Age and Authority in Early Modern England," Raleigh Lecture on History (London: British Academy 1976), 16, 19.

42. Graves, "Clansmen," 393, 401–2, 418; Jones, *Georgian Rakes,* 11, 21, 28; Thomas, "Age and Authority," 18–19; Pinto, *Enthusiast,* 7; Burnet, *Rochester,* 48.

43. G. Elsie Harrison, *Son to Susanna: The Private Life of John Wesley* (Nashville: Cokesbury Press, 1938), 93; Edward Gibbon, *Memoirs of My Life* (New York: Penguin, 1984 [1788–93]), 83; Coleridge quoted in V. G. Kiernan, *The Duel in European History: Honour and the Reign of the Aristocracy* (Oxford: Oxford University Press, 1988), 185.

44. See for example Henry Fielding, *The History of Tom Jones, A Foundling* (New York: New American Library, 1979 [1749]), 382; Henry MacKenzie, *The Man of Feeling* and *The Man of the World* published in a combined volume (London: George Routledge and Sons, n.d. [1773]), 186, and chs. ix and x; Jane Austen, *Northanger Abbey* (New York: Penguin, 1985 [1818]), 83.

45. James Hurdis, "The Modern Rake's Progress," in William Enfield, *The Speaker: or, Miscellaneous Pieces, Selected from the Best English Writers,* etc. (Gainsborough: Henry Mozley, 1814 [1st ed. 1774]), 71–3.

46. Jones, *Georgian Rakes,* 147–8; Greene, *Lord Rochester's Monkey,* 191; *Spectator,* no. 324, 5:11; Rhys Isaac, *The Transformation of Virginia, 1740–1790* (Chapel Hill: University of North Carolina Press, 1982), 95.

47. Graves, "Clansmen," 420–1; *Spectator,* no. 324, 5:11; Jones, *Georgian Rakes,* 12, 26; Graves, "Clansmen," 414, 412. Fielding, *Tom Jones,* 750–2.

48. Graves, "Clansmen," 404–6, 411; *The Connoisseur* 54 (6 February 1755), 145.

49. Graves, "Clansmen," 398–406; Jones, *Georgian Rakes,* 21; Pinto, *Enthusiast in Wit,* 182–83.

50. Thomas, "Age and Authority," 19; Graves, "Clansmen," 409–10, 412n.31, 413; Langford, *Polite and Commercial People,* 158.

51. Pinto, *Enthusiast,* 171; Burnet, *Rochester,* 49; Rochester, "The Imperfect Enjoyment," in *Poems,* 31.

52. Burke, *Popular Culture,* 188; Rochester, "The Disabled Debauchee," in *Poems,* 98; *Spectator,* no. 324, 5:11.

53. Burke, *Popular Culture,* 202; Peter Clark, *The English Alehouse: A Social History, 1200–1830* (London: Longman, 1983), 233.

54. Quoted in Jones, *Georgian Rakes,* 16; Milton, *Paradise Lost,* bk. 1, line 5; *Spectator,* no. 324, 5:11.

55. Jones, *Georgian Rakes,* p. 20. Richardson demonstrates the impatient Lovelace's habitual insensitivity with a metaphor conjuring up this apparently notorious public treatment of women by rakes: "I can fancy that, to pink my body like my mind, I need only to be put into a hogshead stuck full of steel-pointed spikes, and rolled down a hill three times as high as the Monument." *Clarissa* 3:451. John Gay referred to "matrons, hoop'd within the hogshead's womb / [And] tumbled furious thence, the rolling tomb / O'er the stones, thunders, bounds from side to side." Quoted in Jones, *Georgian Rakes,* 18. A group of Mohawk chieftains visiting London shortly before the Mohocks came into existence must have inspired its name, symbolizing its freedom from "civilized" restraint; European travelers reported that Miami, Ottawa, and Illinois husbands cut off the noses of adulterous wives. James Axtell, ed. *The Indian Peoples of Eastern America: A Documentary History of the Sexes* (New York: Oxford University Press, 1981), 76, 79, 81; Anon., "Women," *Encyclopedia Britannica,* 29 vols. (New York: Encyclopedia Britannica, 1911): 783.

56. *Connoisseur,* 145; Ruth Rosen, *The Lost Sisterhood: Prostitution in America, 1900–1918* (Baltimore and London: Johns Hopkins University Press, 1982), 4; Greene, *Lord Rochester's Monkey,* 174; *Connoisseur,* 147; Jones, *Georgian Rakes,* 22.

57. Graves, "Clansmen," 413; Bernard Bailyn, *The Peopling of British North America* (New York: Vintage Books, 1988), 11–13.

58. George Sandys to John Ferrar, in *The Records of the Virginia Company of London,* ed. Susan M. Kingsbury (Washington, D.C.: Government Printing Office, 1906–35), 4:23; Society for the Propagation of the Gospel missionary quoted in Peter Wood, *Black Majority: Negroes in Colonial South Carolina: From 1670 through the Stono Rebellion* (New York and London: W. W. Norton, 1974), 133n.7.

59. Quoted in Julia Cherry Spruill, *Women's Life and Work in the Southern Colonies* (New York: W. W. Norton, 1972 [1938]), 9; see too Wood, *Black Majority,* 98; and Edmund J. Morgan, *The Puritan Family: Religion and Domestic*

Relations in Seventeenth-Century New England (New York: Harper Torchbooks, 1966 [1944]), 27, and see too 145–7.

60. Bailyn, *Peopling,* 112ff; William Bradford, *Of Plymouth Plantation* [1620–1647], ed. Samuel Eliot Morison (New York: Alfred A. Knopf, 1970) 204–6. Referring to the dynamic, individualistic, fluidly commercial colonies on the Chesapeake and the patriarchal, puritanical colonies in New England, Greene writes that between "1607 and 1660 the English emigration to America . . . produced . . . two simplified experiences of contemporary English society." Jack P. Greene, *Pursuits of Happiness: The Social Development of Early Modern British Colonies and the Formation of American Culture* (Chapel Hill: University of North Carolina, 1988), 26.

61. Evelyn quoted in Graves, "Clansmen," 413n.43; *The Rake,* 5; Graves, "Clansmen," 396, 398–9; Jones, *Georgian Rakes,* 27; *Connoisseur,* 145; Golby and Purdue, *Civilisation of the Crowd,* 35–36; Burke, *Popular Culture,* 109–10. See too Clark, *English Alehouse,* 153, 158.

62. Quoted in Graves, "Clansmen," 395; see too 405.

63. *A Brief Defence of the several Declarations of King James the First and King Charles the First, Concerning Lawful Recreations on Sundays,* 1708, quoted in Golby and Purdue, *Civilisation of the Crowd,* 28.

64. Keith Thomas, *Religion and the Decline of Magic* (New York: Charles Scribner's Sons, 1971), 17, 19, see too Clark, *English Alehouse,* 232; Golby and Purdue, *Civilisation of the Crowd,* 87, 22–23.

65. The alehouse was "the product of villages and smaller towns and did not [usually] supply accommodation for travellers." The inn was "primarily a hostelry for travellers, though . . . it also sold wine and beer to the inhabitants of the district." The tavern "or wine-shop . . . seems to have been more especially found in the larger towns [and] specialized in the selling of wine . . . for consumption on and off the premises, but also . . . provided cooked meals." R. F. Bretherton, "Country Inns and Alehouses," *Englishmen at Rest and Play: Some Phases of English Leisure, 1558–1714,* ed. Reginald Lennard (Oxford: Clarendon Press, 1931), 151. See Peter Earle, *The Making of the English Middle Class: Business Society and Family Life in London, 1660–1730* (London: Methuen, 1989), 51–7.

66. Burke, *Popular Culture,* 39–40; Bennett, *Women in the Medieval English Countryside,* 6, 139.

67. Bretherton, "Country Inns," 147; Clark, *English Alehouse,* 152; Golby and Purdue, *Civilisation of the Crowd,* 35.

68. Clark, *English Alehouse,* 115, 132, 148.

69. Golby and Purdue, *Civilisation of the Crowd,* 25; Carole Shammas, "The Domestic Environment in Early Modern England and America," *Journal of Social History* 14, no. 1 (Fall 1980): 11; see too Lorna Weatherill, *Consumer Behaviour and Material Culture in Britain, 1660–1760* (London: Routledge, 1988), 157.

70. Clark, *English Alehouse,* 148.

71. Bretherton, "Country Inns," 200; Clark, *English Alehouse,* 154–5.

72. Clark, *English Alehouse,* 138–9, 156, 157; W. P. Baker, "The Observance of Sunday," *Englishmen at Rest and Play,* 140–2. Laslett writes that alehouses

were "famous in popular history as the poor man's parliament." *World We Have Lost,* 73.

73. Quoted in Clark, *English Alehouse,* 341.

74. Ibid., 148, 115, 84, 205, 206, 148–50.

75. Ibid., 115, 131; Bretherton, "Country Inns," 188, 163–4, 199.

76. Clark, *English Alehouse,* 131, 225, 226, 311, 148, 86. The first alehouses had been simply private houses, where women—alewives—sold home brew. Their steady decline as keepers of alehouses coincided with the latter's elaboration on centers of male culture. Bennett, *Women in the Medieval English Countryside,* 120–4; Clark, *English Alehouse,* pp. 78–9, 30.

77. Baker, "Observance of Sunday," 86, 102, 110, 111, 85.

78. Natalie Zemon Davis, "Women on Top," *Society and Culture in Early Modern France* (Stanford: Stanford University Press, 1975), 141.

79. Barnsley visitor quoted in Baker, "Observance of Sunday," 121.

80. Bennett, *Women of the Medieval English Countryside,* 40, 129, 7; Laslett, *World We Have Lost,* 73; Gareth Stedman Jones, "Class Expression versus Social Control? A Critique of Recent Trends in the Social History of 'Leisure,'" *History Workshop* 4 (1977): 162; Golby and Purdue, *Civilisation of the Crowd,* 9, and see 14 and 48. While the 1931 collection claims it is an "attempt to depict" the "leisure hours" of "English men and women," its account of the latter is mostly confined to the aristocracy, and its title makes no bones about its subject, *Englishmen at Rest and Play,* v.

81. Golby and Purdue, *Civilisation of the Crowd,* 142; similarly McKeon refers to "the timeless battle of the sexes—. . . a traditional and harmless form of sexual conflict," *Origins of the Novel,* 224.

82. "Ballad of the Tyrannical Husband" quoted in Barbara Hanawalt, "Peasant Women's Contribution to the Home Economy in Late Medieval England," in *Women and Work in Pre-industrial Europe,* ed. Hanawalt (Bloomington: Indiana University Press, 1986), 9; Burke, *Popular Culture,* 164–5; Bennett, *Women in the Medieval English Countryside,* 140, 45; 1639 reformer quoted in Clark, *English Alehouse,* 148.

83. Patricia Crawford, "Attitudes to Menstruation in Seventeenth-Century England," *Past and Present* 91 (May 1981): 47–73; Davis, "Women on Top," 124–7.

84. Shammas, *The Pre-industrial Consumer in England and America* (Oxford: Clarendon Press, 1990), 198; Bennett, *Women in the Medieval English Countryside,* 40.

85. Verse quoted in Bennett, *Women in the Medieval English Countryside,* 37; Burke, *Popular Culture,* 164–5.

86. Burke, *Popular Culture,* 234, 18, 186, 190, and ch. 7, passim.

87. Shammas, "Domestic Environment," 11; Burke, *Popular Culture,* 246.

88. Simon Schama, *The Embarrassment of Riches: An Interpretation of Dutch Culture in the Golden Age* (Berkeley: University of California, 1988), 187–8. Schama suggests a nice connection between seventeenth-century Dutch representations of the Battle of Carnival and Lent and Hogarth's moral series, 152–5.

89. Quoted by Gamini Salgado in his introduction to *Three Restoration Comedies* (Harmondsworth, Middx.: Penguin, 1968), 11.

90. Clark, *English Alehouse,* 168–9, 166; Stuart Andrews, *Methodism and Society* (London: Longman, 1970), 69; Burke, *Popular Culture,* 223, 240, 208; Clark, *English Alehouse,* 166, and see ch. 8, passim.

91. Redwood, *Reason and Ridicule,* 190; Mrs. Barbauld wrote to her brother in 1786, "I am afraid there is a good deal of coarseness in the mirth of the vulgar and of licentiousness in the gaiety of the rich." *The Works of Anna Laelitia Barbauld,* 2 vols. (London: Longman, Hurst, Rees, Orme, Brown, and Green, 1825), 2:47. See too Stone, "The New Eighteenth Century," 46; and McKeon, *Origins of the Novel,* 3.

92. Christopher Hill, "Clarissa Harlowe and Her Times," *Essays in Criticism* 5, no. 4 (October 1955): 326–7; Maurice J. Quinlan, *Victorian Prelude, A History of English Manners, 1700–1830* (Hamden, Conn.: Archon Books, 1965 [1941]), 15; E. P. Thompson, "Time, Work-Discipline, and Industrial Capitalism," in Flinn and Smout, *Social History,* 59; Redwood, *Reason,* 189, 218; 1705 indenture quoted in Laslett, *World We Have Lost,* 3; Thomas, "Age and Authority," 10ff; Greene, *Pursuits of Happiness,* 37; R. W. Tawney, *Religion and the Rise of Capitalism* (West Drayton, Middx.: Penguin 1938 [1926]), 211–27.

93. M. M. Goldsmith, *Private Vices, Public Benefits: Bernard Mandeville's Social and Political Thought* (Cambridge: Cambridge University Press, 1984), 21.

94. Alan D. Gilbert, *Religion and Society in Industrial England: Church, Chapel and Social Change, 1740–1914* (London and New York: Longman, 1976), 18–19, 55; Quinlan, *Victorian Prelude,* 14–17; Redwood, *Reason,* 218, 263; T. C. Curtis and W. A. Speck, "The Societies for the Reformation of Manners: A Case Study in the Theory and Practice of Moral Reform," *Literature and History,* no. 3 (1976): 45–64; Langford, *Polite and Commercial People,* 128–30; Clarke, *English Alehouse,* ch. 8.

95. Goldsmith, *Private Vices,* 22; Redwood, *Reason,* 176, 190, 203; Quinlan, *Victorian Prelude,* 14; Jones, *Georgian Rakes.* 26, 41–2; Andrews, *Methodism,* 9.

96. Golby and Purdue, *Civilization,* 51–2; Langford, *Polite and Commercial People,* 499; Andrews, *Methodism,* 69–70; Gilbert, *Religion,* 85; Michael Hennell, "Evangelicalism and Worldliness, 1770–1870," *Popular Belief and Practice,* ed. G. J. Cuming and Derek Baker (Cambridge: Cambridge University Press, 1972), 229–36; Clarke, *English Alehouse,* 254–7.

97. Goldsmith, *Private Vices,* 3, 9, and ch. 1, passim; James Sambrook, *The Eighteenth Century: The Intellectual and Cultural Context of English Literature, 1700–1789* (London: Longman, 1986), 87–8; McKeon, *Origins of the Novel,* 209; Bolingbroke quoted in Sambrook, *Eighteenth Century,* 169.

98. Goldsmith, *Private Vices,* 14, 27, 84, 24; Jocelyn Harris, *Samuel Richardson* (Cambridge: Cambridge University Press, 1987), 1–3, ch. 4; Goldsmith, *Private Vices,* 13; Peter Earle, *The Making of the English Middle Class: Business, Society and Family Life in London, 1660–1730* (London: Methuen, 1989), 237.

99. Borsay, *Urban Renaissance,* 119; Greene, *Rochester's Monkey,* 38; Redwood, *Reason,* 188; Alice Browne, *The Eighteenth Century Feminist Mind* (Brighton, Sussex: Harvester Press, 1987), 82; Salgado, "Introduction," 28–36. In "1655 the first actress appeared in the Amsterdam theatre, strengthening the

clergy's view that it was the sink of the vilest iniquity." Schama, *Embarrassment of Riches,* 408.

100. Redwood, *Reason,* 187; Greene, *Rochester's Monkey,* 38.

101. Quoted in Redwood, *Reason,* 187.

102. J. H. Plumb, "The Commercialization of Leisure in Eighteenth-Century England," in *The Birth of a Consumer Society: The Commercialization of Eighteenth-Century England,* by Neil McKendrick, John Brewer, and Plumb (Bloomington: Indiana University Press, 1982), 275–7; Redwood, *Reason,* 185.

103. William Haller, *The Elect Nation: The Meaning and Relevance of Foxe's Book of Martyrs* (New York: Harper and Row, 1963), 52; see too McKeon's discussion of this issue, *Origins of the Novel,* 443–5.

104. Clive Probyn, *English Fiction of the Eighteenth Century 1700–1789* (London and New York: Longman, 1987), 24nn.7, 5; Ian Watt, *The Rise of the Novel: Studies in Defoe, Richardson and Fielding* (Berkeley: University of California Press, 1967 [1957]), 35–8; McKeon, *Origins of the Novel,* 51.

105. J. Paul Hunter, *Before Novels: The Cultural Contexts of Eighteenth-Century English Fiction* (New York: W. W. Norton, 1990), 65–6, 72, 76, 79, 77; Clark, *English Alehouse,* 202; Raymond Williams, *Communications* (Harmondsworth, Middx.: Penguin, 1968), 14; Borsay, *Urban Renaissance,* 128–30.

106. Redwood, *Reason and Ridicule,* passim; Probyn, *English Fiction,* 6–7; Burke, *Popular Culture,* 252; Richard E. Brantley, *Locke, Wesley and the Methods of English Romanticism* (Gainesville: University of Florida Press, 1986), 118–9.

107. Quoted in Probyn, *English Fiction,* 5; Langford, *Polite and Commercial People,* 92; Probyn discusses the relation between the cost of a book and its potential readership, as does Watt, *Rise of the Novel,* 40–2.

108. Quinlan, *Victorian Prelude,* 20–1; Hunter, *Before Novels,* 86–5; Thomas, *Religion and the Decline of Magic,* 650. Redwood, *Reason,* 193, 26; Bernard Mandeville, *The Fable of the Bees: or, Private Vices, Publick Benefits,* 2 vols. (Oxford: Clarendon Press, 1924), 1:232. See too Burke, *Popular Culture,* 270. The Restoration period had seen the first publication of pornography in England. Browne, *Feminist Mind,* 82.

109. Redwood, *Reason and Ridicule,* 184; Richard Altick has said that "the democracy of print" was a "revolutionary concept." Quoted in Probyn, *English Fiction,* 4.

110. Ruth Perry, *The Celebrated Mary Astell: An Early English Feminist* (Chicago and New York: University of Chicago Press, 1986), 234.

111. Borsay, *Urban Renaissance,* 297, 110. See too Langford, *Polite and Commercial People,* 130–3.

112. *The Spectator* no. 294 (6 February 1711/12), 4:174–7; Goldsmith, *Private Vices,* 6, 24–7, 47; *The Spectator* no. 10 (12 March 1710–11), 1:42. See too Quinlan's quotation of Steele's *The Guardian,* intended to rescue the age "out of its present degeneracy and depravation of manners." *Victorian Prelude,* 20. See too Watt, *Rise of the Novel,* 51.

113. *The Spectator,* no. 294 (6 February 1711/12), 4:177, 176.

114. T. J. Jackson Lears, "The Concept of Cultural Hegemony: Problems and Possibilities," *American Historical Review* 90, no. 3 (June 1985): 567–93;

The Spectator, no. 294 (6 February 1711/12), 4:176–77. For concise critiques of "hegemony" see Golby and Purdue, *Civilisation of the Crowd,* 12–13; Jones, "Class expression versus social control?" passim; and Schama, *Embarrassment of Riches,* 6, 576ff.

115. *The Guardian* quoted in Watt, *Rise of the Novel,* 48; *The Spectator* no. 417 (28 June 1712): 6: 52, 63; see too Watt, *Rise of the Novel,* 56.

116. Cf. Watt, *Rise of the Novel,* 48–9.

117. Shammas, *Pre-industrial Consumer,* 203; *The Spectator,* no. 411, 6: 92.

118. *The Spectator,* no. 411 (12 June 1712), 6:63: *The Spectator,* no. 418 (30 June 1712), 6:97; no. 413 (24 June 1712), 6:71; no. 416 (27 June 1712), 6:86.

119. *The Spectator,* no. 465 (23 August 1712), 6:289.

120. *The Spectator,* no. 418, 6:98–99; see William Stafford, *Socialism, Radicalism and Nostalgia: Social Criticism in Britain, 1775–1830* (Cambridge: Cambridge University Press, 1987), 41.

121. *The Spectator,* no. 397 (5 June 1712): 6: 8; Shammas, *Pre-industrial Consumer,* 146. Clark, *English Alehouse,* 214.

122. Langford, *Polite and Commercial People,* 69; Borsay, *Urban Renaissance,* 13–14, 18; *The Spectator,* no. 416 (27 June 1712), 6:87; no. 413, 6:71. Rosalind H. Williams suggests that it was the distance of the eighteenth-century French court from peasant life that enabled courtiers to play at it. *Dream Worlds: Mass Consumption in Nineteenth-Century France* (Berkeley: University of California Press, 1982), 45.

123. Probyn, *English Fiction,* 9, 22; see too John Mullan, *Sentiment and Sensibility: The Language of Feeling in the Eighteenth Century* (Oxford: Clarendon Press, 1988), 15.

124. Probyn, *English Fiction,* 8, 5.

125. *Watt, Rise of the Novel,* 49; Probyn, *English Fiction,* 5, 12, 16–17, 22; Rita Goldberg, *Sex and Enlightenment: Women in Richardson and Diderot* (Cambridge: Cambridge University Press, 1984), ch. 1; J. M. S. Tompkins, *The Popular Novel in England, 1770–1800* (Westport, Conn.: Greenwood Press, 1976 [1961]), 20; McKeon, *Origins of the Novel,* 268–9, and passim; Hunter, *Before Novels,* passim.

126. Beasley, *Novels of the 1740s,* 138, 134; Spencer, *Woman Novelist,* 86, 1.

127. Richardson, *Clarissa,* 4:553; Samuel Johnson, *The Rambler,* no. 4 (31 March 1750), in *Selected Essays from the Rambler, Adventurer and Idler,* ed. W. J. Bate (New Haven: Yale University Press, 1968), 11; McKeon, *Origins of the Novel,* 216; Sambrook, *Eighteenth Century,* 278; Probyn, *English Fiction,* 180, 153.

128. Thompson, "Work-Discipline," 67; see too David Hempton, *Methodism and Politics in British Society, 1750–1850* (Stanford: Stanford University Press, 1986), 49, 37; Kathleen Walker MacArthur, *The Economic Ethics of John Wesley* (New York: Abingdon Press, 1936); 100, 59; and Gilbert, *Religion,* 86. The "Protestant ethic" labels a behavioral style not limited to one religion, although probably linked to religion. See Harold Perkin, *The Origins of Modern English Society 1780–1880* (London: Routledge and Kegan Paul, 1972), 13–14; and Donald Meyer, *The Positive Thinkers: Religion as Pop Psychology from*

Mary Baker Eddy to Oral Roberts (New York: Pantheon Books, 1980 [1965]), 373n.1. Because Weber's phrase has come into popular usage in this more general way, I have continued to use it.

129. Gilbert, *Religion,* 83; Golby and Purdue, *Civilisation,* 60, 11, 43; Neil McKendrick, "Home Demand and Economic Growth: A New View of the Role of Women and Children in the Industrial Revolution," *Historical Perspectives: Studies in English Thought and Society,* ed. McKendrick (London: Europa, 1974): 152–210; Golby and Purdue, *Civilisation of the Crowd,* 18.

130. Golby and Purdue, *Civilization of the Crowd,* "Introduction," 77, 76.

131. Clark, *English Alehouse,* 147; Langford, *Polite and Commercial People,* chs. 3 and 12, and pp. 652–5; Borsay, *Urban Renaissance,* 201–2 and ch. 11.

132. Burnet, *Rochester,* 87, 89.

133. R. S. Crane, "Suggestions toward a Genealogy of the 'Man of Feeling,'" *English Literary History* 1, no. 3 (December 1934): 205–30; Donald Greene suggests that the ideas Crane attributed to a particular group of Anglican divines were in fact "nothing more than the general Protestantism of the time." "Latitudinarianism and Sensibility: The Genealogy of the "Man of Feeling Reconsidered," *Modern Philosophy* 5, no. 2 (November 1977): 180. Greene has criticized Crane's argument in other works, too. For a fair assessment, concluding that Crane's and Greene's conclusions "are not necessarily contradictory," see John K. Sheriff, *The Good-Natured Man: The Evolution of a Moral Ideal, 1660–1800* (University: University of Alabama Press, 1982), 104–5n.8.

134. Crane, "Genealogy," 214–5, 217, and see 215; Ian Donaldson, "Cato in Tears: Stoical Guises of the Man of Feeling," in *Studies in the Eighteenth Century,* ed. R. F. Brissenden (Toronto: University of Toronto Press, 1973), 377–95; David Hume, *Essays, Moral, Political, and Literary,* 2 vols., ed. T. H. Green and T. H. Grose (London: Longmans Green, 1875), 1:203–10.

135. Crane, "Genealogy," 213, 221, 222; Sheriff, *Good-Natured Man,* x. Among the Cambridge Platonists Crane includes are Benjamin Whichcote, Richard Cumberland, and Henry More.

136. Norman Fiering, "Irresistible Compassion: An Aspect of Eighteenth-Century Sympathy and Humanitarianism," *Journal of the History of Ideas* 37 (1976): 201; Crane, "Genealogy," 207, 209, 214.

137. Crane, "Genealogy," 217; Fiering, "Irresistible Compassion," 200.

138. Fiering, "Irresistible Compassion," 199; Margaret C. Jacob, *The Newtonians and the English Revolution* (Ithaca: Cornell University Press, 1976) (see too McKeon, *Origins of English Novel,* 71–5); Rousseau, "Science," 160n.3.

139. Crane, "Genealogy," 215, 225, 224, 228; More quoted in Ernest Lee Tuveson, *The Imagination as a Means of Grace: Locke and the Aesthetics of Romanticism* (New York: Gordian Press, 1974 [1960]), 12. For a brilliant account of the operation of the nervous system, including interoceptive and exteroceptive modes, see John Bowlby, *Attachment and Loss,* 3 vols. (New York: Basic Books, 1969), vol. 1, passim.

140. Crane, *Genealogy,* 223.

141. Jacob, *Newtonians,* 51; Colin Campbell, *The Romantic Ethic and the Spirit of Modern Consumerism* (Oxford: Basil Blackwell, 1987), 31, 26–7, 88–9.

142. Thistlethwaite's novel quoted in Brissenden, *Virtue in Distress,* 85; see Campbell, *Romantic Ethic,* 141–2, for other typical illustrations. For examples of the extremes of inward and voluptuous pleasures (albeit in being and doing good) preached by Latitudinarian divines, see Crane, "Genealogy," 225, 228.

143. Redwood, *Reason and Ridicule,* 50; Rochester, *Poems,* 51; D. P. Walker, *The Decline of Hell: Seventeenth-Century Discussions of Eternal Torment* (Chicago: University of Chicago Press, 1964), 45, 69.

144. Fiering, "Irresistible Compassion," 200; Sheriff, *Good-natured Man,* 4, 5; Crane, "Genealogy," 208, 213; Jay Fliegelman, *Prodigals and Pilgrims: The American Revolution against Patriarchal Authority, 1750–1800* (Cambridge and New York: Cambridge University Press, 1982), 154–64 and passim; Brissenden, *Virtue in Distress,* 49.

145. Fliegelman, *Prodigals and Pilgrims,* 168, and passim; Edwin G. Burrows and Michael Wallace, "The American Revolution: The Ideology and Psychology of National Liberation," *Perspectives in American History* 6 (1972): 167–301. For the persistence of a "masculinized " God over the century see Randall McGowen, "'He Beareth Not the Sword in Vain': Religion and the Criminal Law in Eighteenth-Century England," *Eighteenth-Century Studies* 21, no. 2 (Winter 1987–8): 192–211. See too Fiering, "Irresistible Compassion," 215–6, 208.

146. Randall McGowen, "The Changing Face of God's Justice: The Debate over Divine and Human Punishment in Eighteenth-Century England," *Criminal Justice History: An International Review* 9 (1985): 63–98. See too Thomas, *Religion and the Decline of Magic,* ch. 22.

147. McGowen, "Changing Face," 65, 72, 71, 70, 68, and see pp. 79–80 for a good illustration of the view that God's "terrors" should "be strong and powerful."

148. Whiston quoted in McGowen, "Changing Face," 77.

149. Quoted ibid., 77, 87, 84; see Fliegelman, *Prodigals and Pilgrims,* 174; "native . . . bosoms" quoted in McGowen, "Changing Face," 87.

150. Gilbert, *Religion,* 12; Robert Currie, Alan Gilbert, Lee Horsley, *Churches and Churchgoers: Patterns of Church Growth in the British Isles since 1700* (Oxford: Clarendon Press, 1977), 24, 25; Michael J. Crawford, "Origins of the Eighteenth-Century Evangelical Revivals: England and New England," *Journal of British Studies* (October 1987): 378; Hempton, *Methodism and Politics,* 22, 16. For a full layout of the statistics, see Currie, et al. *Church and Churchgoers,* 139–45.

151. Gerald R. Cragg, *The Church and the Age of Reason, 1648–1789* (New York: Penguin, 1960), 167; Andrews, *Methodism,* 6, 22, 62; Campbell, *Romantic Ethic,* 107–18.

152. Andrews, *Methodism,* 61–2; Harrison, *Son to Susanna,* ch. 3, and pp. 49, 42.

153. Harrison, *Son to Susanna,* 21, 50; Langford points out that Wesley's

relations with women were "not happy" when they were sexualized, *Polite and Commercial People,* 271. This, too, points to mother-identification.

154. *The Works of John Wesley,* ed. Albert C. Coulter (Nashville: Abingdon Press, 1984), 1:106.

155. Gilbert, *Religion and Society,* 8–11, 53; M. Crawford, "Evangelical Revivals," 379; Sambrook, *Eighteenth Century,* 41; Burke, *Popular Culture,* 274; Colin Campbell, *Romantic Ethic,* 109; Quinlan, *Victorian Prelude,* 28; Langford, *Polite and Commercial People,* 248.

156. Wesley quoted in Andrews, *Methodism,* 7. See too John Walsh, "Origins of the Evangelical Revival," in *Essays in Modern English Church History in Memory of Norman Sykes,* ed. G. V. Bennett and J. D. Walsh (New York: Oxford University Press, 1966), 151.

157. Andrews, *Methodism,* 41; Robert Glen, "Methodist Women Mocked in Eighteenth Century England" (paper presented at the Annual Meeting of the American Society for Eighteenth-Century Studies, Cincinnati, 23 April 1987), 4; Gary Nash, *Urban Crucible: Social Change, Political Consciousness, and the Origins of the American Revolution* (Cambridge, Mass.: Harvard University Press, 1979), 207–9; Isaac, *The Transformation of Virginia,* 168.

158. Horton Davies, *Worship and Theology in England: From Watts and Wesley to Maurice, 1690–1850* (Princeton: Princeton University Press, 1961), 163; John Vladimir Price, "Religion and Ideas," in *The Context of English Literature: The Eighteenth Century,* ed. Pat Rogers (London: Methuen, 1978), 138; Hume noted that in the theater "every movement . . . is communicated, as it were by magic, to the Spectators." Quoted in Mullan, *Sentiment and Sociability,* 36.

159. Wesley quoted in Sydney G. Dimond, *The Psychology of the Methodist Revival: An Empirical and Descriptive Study* (London: Oxford University Press, 1976), 130; Davies, *Worship,* 164; Ruth H. Bloch, "The Gendered Meaning of Virtue in Revolutionary America," *Signs* 13 (1987): 103; Edwin H. Cady, "The Artistry of Jonathan Edwards," *New England Quarterly* 22 (1949): 61; Harriet Vincent Temps, "From Compromise to Sovereignty: Edwards's Response to Eighteenth-Century Rational Theology" (M.A. thesis, Department of History, State University of New York at Albany, 1991), 43–4. See too Burke, *Popular Culture,* 132. Protestant culture had been "sermon" culture since the sixteenth century, congregations then "exclaiming, sighing, or weeping," in response. The seventeenth-century preacher was said by a contemporary to act "much with his hands, striking them together or beating his breast, or flinging them about in a rapturous manner." Crawford, "Evangelical Revivals," 392; Burke, *Popular Culture,* 226, 102; Hempton, *Methodism and Politics,* 33. But to many eighteenth-century observers whose context was the astonishing spread of rationalism and commerce and orthodoxy's repudiation of "enthusiastic" puritan traditions, the dramatically affecting preaching techniques of Wesley and Whitefield, drawing mass audiences, "transformed the pulpit and religious life" in the Anglo-American world. Davies, *Worship,* 123; Crawford, "Evangelical Revivals," 382.

160. Davies, *Worship,* 171, 147; Dimond, *Psychology of Methodist Revival,* 127.

161. Davies, *Worship,* 154; Dimond, *Psychology of Methodist Revival,* 131; see too Andrews, *Methodism,* 41, for the stabbing imagery.

162. Andrews, *Methodism,* 37, 54; Hempton, *Methodism and Politics,* 24. Wesley's chief source for his Lockeanism and its attempted reconciliation with faith was Peter Browne, *The Procedure, Extent, and Limits of Human Understanding* (1729). Brantley, *Locke, Wesley,* ch. 1, and 126, 17.

163. Wesley, *Works,* 1:431–43.

164. Wesley, "Privilege," 433.

165. Ibid., 434–5.

166. Crawford, "Evangelical Revivals," 380; *The Works of John Wesley,* vol. 7, ed. Franz Hildebrandt and Oliver A. Beckerlegge (Oxford: Clarendon Press, 1983), 28; see too 29, 55; Sambrook, *Eighteenth Century,* 42.

167. Crawford, "Evangelical Revivalism," 382; Wesley, *Works* 7:62.

168. Wesley, *Works,* 7:766–9.

169. Borsay, *Urban Renaissance,* 124–7; Hennell, "Evangelicalism and Worldliness," 230–1; Campbell, *Romantic Ethic,* 181–2, 185.

170. Quoted in Probyn, *English Fiction,* 153.

171. Max Weber, *The Protestant Ethic and the Spirit of Capitalism,* trans. Talcott Parsons (New York: Scribners, 1958), 175; see too Wesley's words on Methodists' success in business, quoted in Andrews, *Methodism,* 16. For "the pathos of the Protestant ethic" see Meyer, *The Positive Thinkers,* 132; Currie et al., *Church and Churchgoers,* 61; Perry Miller, *New England Mind,* 2 vols. (Boston: Beacon Press, 1961), 1:ch. 3; compare too Schama, *Embarrassment of Riches,* 124–5 and ch. 5, passim; Schama quotes Calvin on "self-indulgence" as the epigraph for his ch. 5. He also suggests how the paradox was relieved by still more consumerism. The successful entrepreneur's "moral discomfort"—his "embarrassment"—was "only made more tolerable by acts of conspicuous consumption on both pious and personal objects," *Embarrassment of Riches,* 335.

172. Hempton, *Methodism and Politics,* 71, 99–100, 47, 91; V. G. Kiernan, "Evangelicalism and the French Revolution," *Past and Present* 1 (1952): 44–56; Campbell, *Romantic Ethic,* 185.

173. Langford, *Polite and Commercial People,* 253; Walsh, "Methodism and the Mob in the Eighteenth Century," *Popular Belief and Practice,* 218; Gilbert, *Religion and Society,* 73; Langford, *Polite and Commercial People,* 264, 271.

174. Gilbert, *Religion and Society,* 79; Langford, *Polite and Commercial People,* 265; Isaac, *Transformation of Virginia,* chs. 7 and 8.

175. Hempton, *Methodism and Politics,* 45, 48; Langford, *Polite and Commercial People,* 266; Quinlan, *Victorian Prelude,* 15.

176. Keith Thomas, *Man and the Natural World: A History of the Modern Sensibility* (New York: Pantheon, 1983), 159; Golby and Purdue, *Civilization,* 54–5; Quinlan, *Victorian Prelude,* 35.

177. Hempton, *Methodism and Politics,* 29; Dimond, *The Psychology of Methodist Revival,* 215; Walsh, "Methodism and the Mob," 72; see too Andrews, *Methodism,* 72; and Langford, *Polite and Commercial People,* 266–7.

178. Davies, *Worship,* 176–7; Walsh, "Mob," 220.

179. Quoted in Roy Porter, "Mixed Feelings: The Enlightenment and Sexuality in Eighteenth-Century Britain," in *Sexuality in Eighteenth-Century Britain,* ed. Paul-Gabriel Boucé (Manchester, N.J.: Barnes and Noble, 1982), 10.

180. Cragg, *The Church and the Age of Reason,* 151; Porter, "Mixed Feelings," 14; Quinlan, *Victorian Prelude,* 25; Langford, *Polite and Commercial People,* 253.

181. Wesley quoted in Andrews, *Methodism,* 123; Yorkshire eyewitness quoted in Hempton, *Methodism and Politics,* 93; see too Langford, *Polite and Commercial People,* 266.

182. Andrews, *Methodism,* 123–4.

183. Glen, "Methodist Women Mocked," 3–8, 5, 4. A print of Bickham's engraving is in the Lewis Walpole Library. Walsh points out that the Methodists' "private, intimate meetings" were fantasized in "the popular imagination" to be "cover for obscene practices." "Methodism and the Mob," 224–5.

184. Fielding, *Shamela* (1741) (in an edition combining *Joseph Andrews* and *Shamela*), ed. Martin Battestin (Boston: Houghton Mifflin, 1961), 311; Fielding, *Tom Jones,* 849; Tobias Smollett, *The Expedition of Humphry Clinker* (New York: New American Library, 1960 [1771]), 144, 145, 258, 259, 342; Beasley, *Novels of the 1740s,* 94.

185. Wesley quoted in Andrews, *Methodism,* 45; Terry Castle, *Masquerade and Civilization: The Carnivalesque in Eighteenth-Century English Culture and Fiction* (Stanford: Stanford University Press, 1986), 63.

186. Humphry Clinker, for a while combining sentimentality with Methodism and imprisoned with his mutually blubbering converts, was accused by the turnkey of betraying the traditional manliness of "a true-born Englishman," who would have been able to play to the crowd even on his way to execution rather than "snivelling in the cart" with Methodistical repentance. Smollett, *Humphry Clinker,* 155.

187. Wesley quoted in MacArthur, *Economic Ethics,* 84.

188. Wesley, *Works,* 7:767n.3; John Gregory, *A Father's Legacy to His Daughters* (London: W. Strahan, 1781 [1774]), 22.

189. Andrews, *Methodism,* 123. The 1808 reporter, Robert Ingram, is, of course, echoing Nelson's famous admonition. This picture of evangelism's reformed manliness accords with the one given in Leonore Davidoff and Catherine Hall in *Family Fortunes: Men and Women of the English Middle Class, 1780–1850* (London: Hutchinson, 1987), 111–4.

190. Burke, *Popular Culture,* 207; Norbert Elias, *The History of Manners,* vol. 1 of *The Civilizing Process,* trans. Edmund Jephcott (New York: Pantheon, 1978).

191. This is John F. Kasson's admirably succinct summary of Elias's thesis in "The Rituals of Dining: Table Manners in Victorian America," in *Dining in America: 1850–1900,* ed. Kathryn Grover (Amherst: University of Massachusetts Press; and Rochester, N.Y.: Margaret Woodbury Strong Museum, 1987), 114–41; 118–19 (this piece has been reworked as part of Kasson's *Rudeness and Civility: Manners in Nineteenth-Century Urban America* (New York: Hill and Wang, 1990).

192. Bennett, *Women in the English Medieval Countryside,* 7. Elsewhere Bennett suggests that, together with medieval literature and people being fined by manorial courts for illicit sexual intercourse, penitentials reveal that "English peasants . . . took considerable pleasure in sexual play." *Women in the Medieval English Countryside,* 103. Of course, this could be true, but the appearance of sexual confessions in penitentials also could mean that people

were at least deeply ambivalent, their sexual playfulness perhaps inhibited by hierarchy's penetration to the innermost sense of self.

193. Elias, *History of Manners,* 100; McKeon, *Origins of the Novel,* 85; Quinlan, *Victorian Prelude,* 35. Sharing the same eighteenth-century assumptions, Wollstonecraft wrote that "Louis XIV . . . spread factitious manners, and caught . . . the whole nation in his toils." *Vindication of the Rights of Woman* (New York: Penguin, 1975 [1792]).

194. The same could be said for the seventeenth-century Dutch culture Schama describes in *Embarrassment of Riches.* Rosalind Williams has linked the history of French consumerism to Elias's civilizing process, recording the smaller, more dependent eighteenth-century French bourgeoisie's emulation of courtly manners. *Dream Worlds,* 8, 23–5, 33–4.

195. Elias, *History of Manners,* 126–9, and passim; Thomas, *Man and the Natural World,* 301; see too Roy Porter, *English Society in the Eighteenth Century* (New York: Penguin, 1982), 33; and Tompkins, *The Popular Novel,* 93.

196. Elias, *Power and Civility,* vol. 2 of *The Civilizing Process,* trans. Edmund Jephcott (New York: Pantheon, 1982), 78–85; Bennett, *Women in the Medieval English Countryside,* 103. This view is consistent with Emmanuel Le Roy Ladurie, *Montaillou: The Promised Land of Error,* trans. Barbara Bray (New York: George Braziller, 1978), 192–3.

197. Elias, *History of Manners,* 191–205; McKeon, *Origins of the Novel,* 183; see too J. G. A. Pocock, *The Machiavellian Moment: Florentine Political Thought and the Atlantic Republican Tradition* (Princeton: Princeton University Press, 1975), 394, 313, 411–12; Barker-Benfield, "Mary Wollstonecraft: Eighteenth-Century Commonwealthwoman," *Journal of the History of Ideas* 50, no. 1 (1989): 97–100, 105–6.

198. Stone, *Family, Sex and Marriage,* 93–94, 234; Kiernan, *The Duel,* 172; Phillip Cunnington, *Costume in Pictures* (London: Herbert Press, 1981), 75; the characterization of dueling as "Gothic," etc., quoted in Kiernan, *The Duel,* 165.

199. Richardson, *Clarissa,* 4:519–31; Kiernan, *The Duel,* 173–6, 178; Richardson, *The History of Sir Charles Grandison,* 3 vols., (London: Oxford University Press, 1972): 1, 206, 242, 255; Browne, *Feminist Mind,* 110.

200. Kiernan, *The Duel,* 181, 178, 192, 212–3, 206, 196. The classic upper-class, male vision linking "women and horseflesh"—both of which are vehicles perpetuating aristocratic bloodlines—is perpetuated in J. W. Fortescue's, *History of the British Army* (1963) quoted in Kiernan, *The Duel,* 205.

201. Kiernan, *The Duel,* 216, 220, 199, 218; Ian Bradley, *The Call to Seriousness* (New York: MacMillan, 1976), 152; John Keegan, *The Face of Battle: A Study of Agincourt, Waterloo and the Somme* (New York: Penguin, 1978), 193–4.

202. Elias, *History of Manners,* 201.

203. Ibid., 70–84; McKeon, *Origins of the Novel,* 184–5. Renaissance manners also found their way into "Dutch family manuals." Schama, *Embarrassment of Riches,* 158ff.

204. Natalie Zemon Davis, "On the Lame," *American Historical Review* 93, no. 3 (June 1988): 602; Baldesar Castiglione, *The Book of the Courtier,* trans. George Bull (Harmondsworth, Middx.: Penguin, 1976 [1528]), 12, 13, 141

(see too Niccolò Machiavelli, *The Prince,* in *The Portable Machiavelli,* trans. and ed. Peter Bondanella and Mark Musa (New York: Penguin, 1979 [1532]), chs. 15–19, and 128). Greenblatt distinguishes Machiavelli's less developed version of self-fashioning from the more complex form of his later, English exemplars. Stephen Greenblatt, *Renaissance Self-fashioning: From More to Shakespeare* (Chicago: University of Chicago Press, 1980), 14–15. For an account of the operation of credit in London, 1660–1730, see Earle, *English Middle Class,* 115–20.

205. Greenblatt, *Self-fashioning,* 46, 2, 4, 3, 256–7. Of course, Tocqueville credited himself with inventing the term "individualism" in his description of nineteenth-century American men. Alexis de Tocqueville, *Democracy in America,* trans. Henry Reeve and ed. Phillips Bradley, 2 vols. (New York: Knopf, 1945) 2:104. Others have attempted to trace "individualism" back to postconquest England and even to the preconquest origins of the English. McKeon, *Origins of the Novel,* 35; and Alan D. MacFarlane, *The Origins of English Individualism: The Family, Property, and Social Transition* (New York: Cambridge University Press, 1979). The Foucauldian feminist literary critic, Nancy Armstrong, asserts that "the modern individual was first and foremost a woman," pointing to eighteenth-century texts to do so. *Desire and Domestic Fiction: A Political History of the Novel* (New York: Oxford University Press, 1987), 8. While women first expressed the individualism associated with literacy and self-fashioning in large numbers in the eighteenth century, it is not the case that they were the first to do so.

206. Characteristically self-fashioning caused Shaftesbury to doubt the solidity of his personality. He wrote to himself: "And first as to COUNTENANCE: that this be suitable and remember how much depends on it; how instantly a Chang[e] here is follow'd by an absolute Chang[e] of the Mind. And hence it is that Mimickry & Imitation in speech is at all times very dangerous." Quoted in Robert Voitle, *The Third Earl of Shaftesbury, 1671–1713* (Baton Rouge and London: Louisiana State University Press, 1984), 92.

207. Davis, *The Return of Martin Guerre* (Cambridge, Mass.: Harvard University Press, 1983), 40; Burke, *Popular Culture,* 176.

208. Davis, *Martin Guerre,* chs. 4 and 5, and 102–3. See too Stephen Greenblatt, "Psychoanalysis and Renaissance Culture," in *Literary Theory/Renaissance Texts,* ed. Patricia Parker and David Quint (Baltimore: Johns Hopkins University Press, 1986), 210–24. Tawney, *Religion and the Rise of Capitalism,* 178–96; Keith Wrightson, *English Society, 1580–1680* (London: Hutchinson, 1982), 58; Campbell, *Romantic Ethic,* 4–11. Relevant too are Karl J. Weintraub's observations in his introduction to *The Autobiography of Johann Wolfgang von Goethe (Aus meinem Leben: Dichtung und Wahrheit),* trans. John Oxenford, 2 vols. (Chicago: University of Chicago Press, 1974), 1:xv–xvi.

209. John William Ward, "Who Was Benjamin Franklin?" in *Retracing the Past: Readings in the History of the American People,* 2 vols., ed. Gary B. Nash and Ronald Schulz (New York: Harper and Row, 1990), 1:175–83; McKeon, *Origins of the Novel,* 100.

210. Donald Meyer, *Sex and Power: The Rise of Women in America, Russia, Sweden and Italy* (Middletown, Conn.: Wesleyan University Press, 1988), 256–

7, and see 507, 559. See too Constance Rourke, *American Humor: A Study of the American National Character* (Tallahassee: Florida State University Press, n.d. [1931]), passim.

211. Pocock, *Virtue, Commerce, and History: Essays on Political Thought and History, Chiefly in the Eighteenth Century* (Cambridge: Cambridge University Press, 1985), 108, 106, 53; Clark, *English Alehouse,* 341, 238.

212. McKeon, *Origins of the Novel,* 204; Meyer, *Sex and Power,* 254; see too Isaac, *Transformation of Virginia,* 21.

213. Meyer, *Positive Thinkers,* 139; Meyer, *Sex and Power,* 254; Pocock, *Virtue, Commerce, and History,* 108; and, in connection with the meanings of the Dutch bourse, Schama, *Embarrassment of Riches,* 343, 348, 351; see too McKeon, *Origins of the Novel,* 229; and Fliegelman, *Prodigals and Pilgrims,* 112.

214. Pocock, *Virtue, Commerce, and History,* 111, 109, 49; McKeon, *Origins of the Novel,* 222.

215. Pocock, *Virtue, Commerce, and History,* 48–9; Barbon quoted in Porter, *English Society,* 276.

216. Pocock, *Virtue, Commerce, and History,* 114–5, 48, 49; McKeon, *Origins of the Novel,* 162–3, 166.

217. Langford, *Polite and Commercial People,* 66; *The Present State of Great Britain* quoted in Borsay, *Urban Renaissance,* 327.

218. Pocock, *Virtue, Commerce, and History,* 48–9; M. M. Goldsmith, *Private Vices, Public Benefits: Bernard Mandeville's Social and Political Thought* (Cambridge: Cambridge University Press, 1985), 133–5; McKeon, *Origins of the Novel,* 21, 22, ch. 3, and passim; Clark, *English Alehouse,* 235.

219. Pocock, *Virtue, Commerce, and History,* 49.

220. John Brewer, "Commercialization and Politics," in *The Birth of a Consumer Society: The Commercialization of Eighteenth-Century England* by Neil McKendrick, John Brewer, and J. H. Plumb (Bloomington: Indiana University Press, 1982), 197–262; 214; Pocock, "Clergy and Commerce: The Conservative Enlightenment in England," *L'età dei lumi-studi storici sul settecento europeo in onore di Franco Venturi* (Napoli, 1985), 1:525–62, cited in Marc Raeff, "Literacy, Education and the State in 17th-18th Century Europe" (Eighth Annual Phi Alpha Theta Distinguished Lecture on History, State University of New York at Albany, 1988), p. 4.

221. Thomas Haskell, "Capitalism and the Origins of the Humanitarian Sensibility, Part 2" *American Historical Review* 90, no. 3 (June 1985), 552–3; Marvell quoted in McKeon, *Origins of the Novel,* 198; Brewer, "Commercialization and Politics," 213, 214;

222. Bernard Mandeville, *The Fable of the Bees: or, Private Vices, Publick Benefits,* 2 vols., ed. F. B. Kaye (Oxford: Clarendon Press, 1924), 1:81, 62–3.

223. Earle, *English Middle Class,* 134–5; Brewer, "Commercialization and Politics," 198, 216; Clark, *English Alehouse,* 235.

224. Brewer, "Commercialization and Politics," 200, 213; Haskell, "Capitalism and Sensibility, Part 2," 552, 555, and passim; Haskell, "Capitalism and the Origins of the Humanitarian Sensibility, Part 1," *American Historical Review* 90, no. 2 (April 1985): 346. The phrase "high time horizon" is Alexander

Gerschenkron's, quoted by Raeff, "Literacy," 4. See too Pocock, *Virtue, Commerce, and History,* 112ff, and Earle, *English Middle Class,* 136.

225. Brewer, "Commercialization and Politics," 215–7; Clark, *English Alehouse,* 314, 195. The date of the OED's first illustration of the modern usage of "public house" is 1669.

226. Clark, *English Alehouse,* 197–8, 199, 225, 209–10.

227. Ibid., 201, 205, 195, 221, 238.

228. Peter Mathias, "An Industrial Revolution Is Brewing," *The Transformation of England* (New York: Columbia University Press, 1979), ch. 11; Clark, *English Alehouse,* 184, 236–4, 195.

229. Clark, *English Alehouse,* 214; Macky quoted in Borsay, *Urban Renaissance,* 145.

230. Clark, *English Alehouse,* 214; 1714 quotation in Borsay, *Urban Renaissance,* 145–6. A less sympathetic contemporary description is quoted in Brewer, *Party Ideology and Party Politics at the Accession of George III* (Cambridge: Cambridge University Press, 1976), 148.

231. Thomas, *Religion and the Decline of Magic,* 651–4; Clark, *English Alehouse,* 320.

232. Jones, *Georgian Rakes,* passim; Borsay, *Urban Renaissance,* 175; Clark, *English Alehouse,* 233.

233. Golby and Purdue, *Civilisation of the Crowd,* 64; James Walvin, *Leisure and Society, 1830–1950* (London: Longman, 1978); Brewer, "Commercialization and Politics," 247; Jones, *Georgian Rakes,* 94–5.

234. Borsay, *Urban Renaissance,* 136–7; Clark, *English Alehouse,* 235; Borsay, *Urban Renaissance,* 138.

235. Brewer, "Commercialization and Politics," 223, 219; Golby and Purdue, *Civilisation of the Crowd,* 35–6; Jones, *Clubs,* 129; Langford, *Polite and Commercial People,* 465; MacKenzie, "Defence of Literary Studies and Amusements in Men of Business," *The Lounger* (30 December 1786): 172.

236. Brewer, "Commercialization and Politics," 225, 228–9; Borsay, *Urban Renaissance,* 252. Occasionally this middle-class, public, male culture criticized "sexual malpractice among the aristocracy." Furthermore the political journals issues by this culture contrasted "the toadying footman, the venal customs official, the cruel bum-bailiff and the favour-seeking tradesmen . . . stereotypical courtiers and conservatives" with "the impecunious yet independent bricklayer [and] the decrepit blind old man." Such sympathies coincided with the sermons and the literature of sensibility. Brewer, "Commercialization and Politics," 257, 232.

237. Clark, *English Alehouse,* 236; Jones, *Georgian Rakes,* 175, 184–9, 197; Brewer, "Commercialization and Politics," 217, 200; see too E. P. Thompson, "Eighteenth-Century English Society: Class Struggle without Class?" *Social History* 3, no. 2 (May 1978): 133–65, esp. 142; Brewer, *Party Ideology,* 17, ch. 9, and pp. 141, 151–60; John Sainsbury, "John Wilkes: the Debtor as Hero" (paper delivered at the Forty–first Annual Meeting of the New York State Association of European Historians, State University of New York at Albany, September 21 1991).

238. Brewer, "Commercialization and Politics," 218; Hunter, *Before Novels,* 378n.22; Langford, *Polite and Commercial Society,* 101. Jerome Nadelhaft suggests that while men enjoyed a burgeoning culture of clubs, they opposed women assembling in the same way. "The Englishwoman's Sexual Civil War: Feminist Attitudes towards Men, Women and Marriage, 1650–1740," *Journal of the History of Ideas* 43 (1987): 575–76.

239. Clark, *English Alehouse,* 254–6, 260, 309. This was the context for the leveling off of tobacco consumption in the later eighteenth century noted by Carole Shammas. She links it to the "decline" of the alehouse, where men "brought most of their pipes and tobacco." Smoking was "largely the preserve of adult males." *Pre-industrial Consumer,* 81.

240. Earle, *English Middle Class,* 45; Borsay, *Urban Renaissance,* 53, 99, 65, 60, 69–70, 43, 70–1, 66.

241. Ibid., 72, 162–72, 74–9, 168.

242. Ibid., 273, 13, 51–9, 150.

243. Ibid., 294, 261, 295. This suggests the answer to the question raised by Golby and Purdue, whether "riots were more frequent or more serious in the eighteenth century than previously or whether respectable society was simply more worried by them and less patient of them." *Civilisation of the Crowd,* 49.

244. Borsay, *Urban Renaissance,* 292, 294.

245. Voitle, *Shaftesbury,* 34; *The Rake,* 6; Jones, *Georgian Rakes,* 12; Graves, "Clansmen," 416, 417; *Connoisseur,* 145.

246. Pinto, *Enthusiast,* 120; Borsay, *Urban Renaissance,* 68, 107; Burke, *Popular Culture,* 111, 112; Golby and Purdue, *Civilisation of the Crowd,* 38–7; Porter, *English Society,* 206; McKendrick, "The Commercialization of English Fashion," in McKendrick et al., *Birth of a Consumer Society,* 78–79 and 85; *The Spectator,* no. 336 (22 March 1712), 5:72–3.

247. Weatherill, *Consumer Behaviour,* 164–5; Jones, *Georgian Rakes,* 19, 25; *The Rake,* 9.

248. Langford, *Polite and Commercial People,* 109; *Connoisseur,* 148; Stone, *The Family, Sex and Marriage,* 94.

249. Philip Mason, *The English Gentleman: The Rise and Fall of an Ideal* (New York: William Morrow, 1982), 68. The caricature owed something to Whig pamphleteering against the "backwoods Tory," as Fielding illustrates in Squire Western, who is in fact a Jacobite. Raymond Carr, *English Fox Hunting: A History* (London: Weidenfeld and Nicholson, 1976), 41; Fielding, *Tom Jones,* 231–32, 284.

250. *The Spectator,* no. 2 (2 March 1710/11), 1:6–12; no. 6 (7 March 1710/11), 1:26–30; no. 116 (13 July 1711), 2:139–44; no. 119 (17 July 1711), 2:152–5; no. 118 (16 July 1711), 2:148–52.

251. Quoted in Mason, *English Gentleman,* 68.

252. Carr, *Fox Hunting,* 18, 33, 36, 37, 16, 53–54; J. H. Plumb, "The Acceptance of Modernity," in Neil McKendrick et al., *Birth of a Consumer Society,* 319–25.

253. Carr, *Fox Hunting* 40–1, 64, 55, 59, 57.

254. Walvin, *Leisure,* 11; Carr, *Fox Hunting,* 46–9, 53–4, 50.

255. Carr, *Fox Hunting,* 52, 58, 59, 46.

256. Marshall quoted in Carr, *Fox Hunting,* 41; Judy Egerton, *George Stubbs, 1724–1806* (London: Tate Gallery Publications; Salem, N.H.: Salem House, 1985), 108–11.

257. Borsay, *Urban Renaissance,* 173.

258. Ibid., 179, 195, 187, 179, 192–3.

259. McKendrick, "Josiah Wedgewood and the Commercialization of the Potteries," in McKendrick et al., *Birth of a Consumer Society,* 100–45.

260. Borsay, *Urban Renaissance,* 50; Nikolaus Pevsner, *An Outline of European Architecture* (Harmondsworth, Middx.: Penguin, 1968), 316; Burke, *Popular Culture,* 246–7; McKendrick, "Home Demand and Economic Growth," passim.

261. Shammas, "Domestic Environment," 8; Golby and Purdue, *Civilisation of the Crowd,* 87; Clark, *English Alehouse,* 295, 297.

262. Golby and Purdue, *Civilisation of the Crowd,* 141 (see too 85); Mandeville, *Fable of the Bees,* 1:107.

263. Langford, *Polite and Commercial People,* 70; Shammas, *Pre-industrial Consumer,* 299; see, too, Earle, *English Middle Class,* 290–6; Watt, *Rise of the Novel,* ch. 6; Elias, *The Court Society,* trans. Edmund Jephcott (New York: Pantheon, 1983), ch. 3 and 114–6; Isaac, *The Transformation of Virginia,* 302–5, 309–10.

264. Langford, *Polite and Commercial People,* 70–1; Davis considers the meaning of the absence of mirrors from peasant households. *Martin Guerre,* 38.

265. Lawrence Wright, *Clean and Decent: The History of the Loo* (London: Routledge and Kegan Paul, 1980), 88, 84; Witold Rybczynski, *Home: A Short History of an Idea* (New York: Viking, 1986), 128–30. Watt quoted in Perkin, *The Origins of Modern English Society,* 96.

266. In his "Character and Anal Erotism" (1908) Freud postulated the existence of a particular set of characteristics in a person fixated on the anal stage of early childhood and attributable to the history of his or her toilet training. The "anal character," which corresponded to Weber's capitalist type, influenced Elias and was rigorously explored in Norman O. Brown's *Life against Death: The Psychoanalytical Meaning of History* (Middletown, Conn.: Wesleyan University Press, 1985 [1959]), especially in pt. 5, "The Excremental Vision." More recent psychoanalytic research bears out the existence of such a character constellation, although researchers have modified the cause. Indeed, vol. 1 of *Attachment and Loss* by John Bowlby, cited in n.139, above, persuasively refutes the theory of an economy of the libido on which Freud based anality, as well as much of the rest of his work. Nonetheless several scholars have discovered a relationship between the "anality" of adults (including a preoccupation with "neatness" and the characteristics associated with "the Protestant ethic") and "the intensity of anal attitudes present in their mothers." It is reasonable to assume, it is argued, that "a mother's anal traits"

> continue to affect her offspring, not only during the toilet-training period but also throughout her contacts with him [or her] . . . the

> effect of her anal traits would [still] be maximal during the toilet training period, when she was confronted by so many experiences that vividly highlight anal themes, thus stirring up anxiety and eliciting extreme forms of response from her . . . her anal attitudes might be profoundly mobilized during the pretoilet training period, when she was confronted by a child with no control over its anal sphincter . . . the . . . phase would be more threatening to an anally oriented mother . . . because she would have less capability . . . of exerting control over the "dirty" behavior of her child. (Seymour Fisher and Roger B. Greenberg, *The Scientific Credibility of Freud's Theories and Therapies* [New York: Basic Books, 1977], 164)

For an illustration of an eighteenth-century urban housewife's association of "over" anxiety with the new possibilities for cleanliness and orderliness see Mary Beth Norton, *Liberty's Daughters: The Revolutionary Experience of American Women, 1750–1800* (Boston and Toronto: Little Brown, 1980), 22. Again, the golden age of Dutch culture, attempting to reconcile Protestant morality with material success, expressed comparable dimensions. "It was mothers who patrolled the dangerous frontier, between the dirt of the street and the cleanliness of the home." Schama links housewives' ritualistic and even obsessive cleaning to the attempt to impose "domestic virtues" in a culture "that otherwise would have been inevitably soiled by materialism." *Embarrassment of Riches,* 393, 388.

267. For example, Elias, *History of Manners,* 129, and see 140; here as elsewhere, Elias is paraphrasing Freud.

268. Elias, *History of Manners,* 160, 127; Haskell, "Capitalism and Sensibility, Part 2," 550; Pocock, *Virtue, Commerce, and History,* 49.

269. Linda Pollock, *Forgotten Children: Parent-Child Relations from 1500 to 1900* (Cambridge: Cambridge University Press, 1983); James Walvin, "Seen and Heard: Historians and the History of Childhood" (Seventh Annual Phi Alpha Theta Distinguished Lecture in History State University of New York at Albany, 1987). Pollock's challenge to Ariès is itself challenged by Earle, *English Middle Class,* 233–37.

270. Fliegelman, *Prodigals and Pilgrims,* 1–3, 9–12, and passim. The history to which Fliegelman refers is Stone, *The Family, Sex and Marriage;* see too Plumb, "The New World of Children in Eighteenth-Century England," McKendrick et al., *Birth of a Consumer Society,* 286–315, esp. 287–9; Wrightson, *English Society,* ch. 4. For breastfeeding see Stone, *Family,* 426–32.

271. Watt, *Rise of the Novel,* 54–6; Plumb, "New World of Children," 300–301; Isaac Kramnick, "Children's Literature and Bourgeois Ideology in the Later Eighteenth Century," in *Culture and Politics from Puritanism to the Enlightenment,* ed. Perez Zagorin (Berkeley: University of California Press, 1980), 203–40; Mitzi Myers, "Impeccable Governesses, Rational Dames, and Moral Mothers: Mary Wollstonecraft and the Female Tradition in Georgian Children's Books," in *Children's Literature* 14, ed. Francelia Butler, Margaret Higonnet, and Barbara Rosen (New Haven: Yale University Press, 1986), 31–59; Geoffrey Summerfield, *Fantasy and Reason: Children's Literature in the Eigh-*

teenth Century (Athens: University of Georgia Press, 1986); Langford, *Polite and Commercial People*, 502–3.

272. P. J. Miller, "Women's Education, 'Self-Improvement,' and Social Mobility—a Late Eighteenth-Century Debate," *British Journal of Education Studies* 20 (1972): 302–14.

273. Plumb, "New World of Children," 308, 307.

274. Ibid., 312, 310. Compare Schama, *Embarrassment of Riches*, 484–6, and ch. 7 passim.

Chapter 3. The Question of Effeminacy

1. "Man without Passion" quoted in R. S. Crane, "Suggestions toward a Genealogy of the 'Man of Feeling,'" *English Literary History* 1, no. 3 (December 1934): 216.

2. J. G. A. Pocock, *Virtue, Commerce, and History: Essays on Political Thought and History, Chiefly in the Eighteenth Century* (Cambridge: Cambridge University Press, 1985), 114. See too John Brewer, "Commercialization and Politics," in *The Birth of a Consumer Society: The Commercialization of Eighteenth-Century England*, by Neil McKendrick, John Brewer, and J. H. Plumb, (Bloomington: Indiana University Press, 1985), 213; Michael McKeon, *The Origins of the English Novel 1600–1740* (Baltimore: Johns Hopkins University Press, 1987), 205. The Dutch version of Fortuna was "Queen" or "Dame" Money. Simon Schama, *The Embarrassment of Riches: An Interpretation of Dutch Culture in the Golden Age* (Berkeley: University of California, 1987), 373–4.

3. Norbert Elias, *The History of Manners*, vol. 1 *of The Civilizing Process*, trans. Edmund Jephcott (New York: Pantheon, 1978 [1939]), 192. Unfortunately I came across Ronald Paulson, *Breaking and Remaking Aesthetic Practice in England, 1700–1820* (New Brunswick: Rutgers University Press, 1989) too late to incorporate its findings. Salient in its account of the transformation of eighteenth-century aesthetics is male artists' "feminizing the hero." (168–192)

4. Robert Voitle, *The Third Earl of Shaftesbury, 1671–1713* (Baton Rouge and London: Louisiana State University Press, 1984), 115, 113. The best concise introduction to Shaftesbury's ideas is James Sambrook, *The Eighteenth Century: The Intellectual and Cultural Context of English Literature, 1700–1789* (London: Longman, 1986), 53–5 and 203. See too John Vladimir Price, "Religion and Ideas," ch. 3 of *The Context of English Literature: The Eighteenth Century*, ed. Pat Rogers (London: Methuen, 1978). Several students of sensibility's history have emphasized Shaftesbury's influence: see for example Louis I. Bredvold, *The Natural History of Sensibility* (Detroit: Wayne State University Press, 1962), 11–18; Janet Todd, *Sensibility: An Introduction* (London and New York: Methuen, 1986), 24; Norman Fiering, "Irresistible Sympathy and Humanitarianism," *Journal of the History of Ideas* 27 (1976): 202; and Crane, "The Genealogy of a Man of Feeling," 207, 229–30.

5. Sambrook, *Eighteenth Century*, 54; Voitle, *Shaftesbury*, 113. For the case that Shaftesbury derived much of his idea of moral sense from Locke, see Ernest Lee Tuveson, *The Imagination as a Means of Grace: Locke and the Aesthetics of Romanticism* (New York: Gordian Press, 1974 [1960]); see too Voitle, "Shaftesbury's Moral Sense," *Studies in Philosophy* 52 (1955): 17–38.

6. Anthony, Earl of Shaftesbury, *Characteristics of Men, Manners, Opinions, Times,* 2 vols. combined, ed. John M. Robertson (Indianapolis: Bobbs-Merrill, 1964 [1900]), 1:260, 270; 2:137.

7. Shaftesbury, *Characteristics,* 2:129; Voitle, *Shaftesbury,* 322.

8. Voitle, *Shaftesbury,* 10–11. John Redwood suggests that Locke was himself influenced by Cambridge Platonism in *Reason, Ridicule, and Religion: The Age of Enlightenment in England, 1660–1750* (Cambridge, Mass.: Harvard University Press, 1976), 60.

9. Voitle, *Shaftesbury,* 15, 7.

10. Jay Fliegelman, *Prodigals and Pilgrims: The American Revolution against Patriarchal Authority, 1750–1800* (New York: Cambridge University Press, 1982), passim; Lawrence Stone, *The Family, Sex and Marriage in England, 1500–1800* (New York: Harper and Row, 1977), pts. 3 and 4; Edwin G. Burrows and Michael Wallace, "The American Revolution: The Ideology and Psychology of National Liberation," *Perspectives on American History* 6 (1972): 167–305.

11. John Locke to Edward Clarke, 1 September 1685, quoted in Voitle, *Shaftesbury,* 8–9; Locke's "Letters to Clarke on Education, 1684–91" are published in appendix 1, *The Educational Writings of John Locke,* ed. James Axtell (Cambridge: Cambridge University Press, 1968).

12. Voitle, *Shaftesbury,* 10–11; Locke to Edward Clarke, 8 February 1686, quoted in Voitle, *Shaftesbury,* 9.

13. Shaftesbury, *Characteristics,* 1:331.

14. Voitle, *Shaftesbury,* 60.

15. For illustrations of Shaftesbury's assumption of sensational psychology, see *Characteristics,* 2:76, 29, 34. Like most eighteenth-century writers, Shaftesbury also mixed in references to the old humoral model, for example, Shaftesbury, *Characteristics,* 1:39.

16. Shaftesbury, *Characteristics,* 1:189. G. S. Rousseau judges that Shaftesbury's *Characteristics,* Newton's *Opticks,* Locke's *Essay,* and Burke's *Sublime and Beautiful* were the "most influential books" of the century, and points out that they all shared the "paradigm" of the new nerve physiology. Rousseau, "Science," in Rogers, *The Eighteenth Century,* 193.

17. Voitle, *Shaftesbury,* 229, 65.

18. John K. Sheriff, *The Good-natured Man: The Evolution of a Moral Ideal, 1660–1800* (University: University of Alabama Press, 1982), 5; R. L. Brett, *The Third Earl of Shaftesbury: A Study in Eighteenth-Century Literary Theory* (London: Hutchinson's Universal Library, 1951), 28, 63.

19. This quotation in Voitle, *Shaftesbury,* 150, is from Shaftesbury's unpublished "Exercises," at the Public Record Office.

20. Voitle, *Shaftesbury,* 229–30, 98, 53, 5–6, 302.

21. Voitle calls Shaftesbury a "Commonwealthman" throughout, see for example 26 and 73; see Caroline Robbins, *The Eighteenth-Century Commonwealthman: Studies in the Transmission, Development and Circumstance of English Liberal Thought from the Restoration of Charles II until the War with the Thirteen Colonies* (Cambridge, Mass.: Harvard University Press), 1959), 128–132.

22. Voitle, *Shaftesbury,* 390.

23. Ibid., 120; Shaftesbury to Michael Ainsworth, 3 June 1709, quoted in ibid., 230. For illustrations of Shaftesbury's implicit and explicit criticisms of Locke, in addition to his central notion of a moral sense, see *Characteristics* 1:193–6; 2:63. For illustrations of his criticism of Hobbes, see *Characteristics,* 1:61, 72; and 2:83. See too Grean's "Introduction" to this Bobbs-Merrill edition of *Characteristics,* xxix–xx; and Sambrook, *Eighteenth Century,* 53–5.

24. Grean, "Introduction," vii.

25. Voitle, *Shaftesbury,* 112–3, 111; Redwood, *Reason and Religion,* 182–4; Grean, "Introduction," xxxi; Stuart Andrews, *Methodism and Religion* (London: Longman, 1970), 4. Both Richardson and Fielding attacked Shaftesbury as an atheist fostering libertinism; Samuel Richardson, *Clarissa: or, The History of a Young Lady,* 4 vols. (London: J. M. Dent, 1932 [1748]), 2:59; Henry Fielding, *The History of Tom Jones, a Foundling* (New York: New American Library, 1963 [1749]), 180, 626.

26. Sheriff, *Good-Natured Man,* 7.

27. Sambrook, *Eighteenth Century,* 203; Shaftesbury, *Characteristics,* 1:261, 270; Brett, *Shaftesbury,* 171.

28. Shaftesbury, *Characteristics,* 2:125, 123.

29. One passage from *Characteristics* (2:123) anticipated manifold sentimental representations of "romantic" nature (Shaftesbury uses the word in this context), from some of Turner's paintings to the closely related scenic descriptions in Ann Radcliffe's *The Mysteries of Udolpho.*

30. Shaftesbury, *Characteristics,* 2:112, 97, 126; 1:279.

31. Ibid., 1:250; see Brett, *Shaftesbury,* 74.

32. Sambrook, *Eighteenth Century,* 54; Shaftesbury, *Characteristics,* 2:129, 98; Voitle, *Shaftesbury,* 321.

33. Shaftesbury, *Characteristics,* 1:5–39; Grean, "Introduction," xx–xxi; Voitle, *Shaftesbury,* 325.

34. Shaftesbury, *Characteristics,* 2:130, 143.

35. Ibid., 2:34, 32, 29, 257. See Ian Watt, *The Rise of the Novel: Studies in Defoe, Richardson, and Fielding* (Berkeley: University of California Press, 1967 [1957]), 16.

36. Shaftesbury, *Characteristics,* 2:249; Voitle, *Shaftesbury,* 352, 391, 159, 353. Shaftesbury's plate is reproduced in Paulson, *Breaking and Remaking,* plate 7.

37. Voitle, *Shaftesbury,* 350.

38. Ibid., 205ff, 177–81, 165, 391, 339.

39. Neil McKendrick, "The Commercialization of Fashion," in McKendrick, et al. *Birth of a Consumer Society,* 34–98; 37–8, 70, 71.

40. Boulton quoted in McKendrick, "Commercialization of Fashion," 77; Paul Langford, *A Polite and Commercial People: England, 1727–1783* (Oxford: Clarendon Press, 1989), 69; the second quotation of Boulton is in Peter Borsay, *The English Urban Renaissance: Culture and Society in The Provincial Town, 1660–1770* (Oxford: Clarendon Press, 1989), 258.

41. Voitle, *Shaftesbury,* 135–6, 152, 278, 151, 286, 404, 112, 353.

42. Ibid., 161, 283–9, 161, 344, 345.

43. Ibid., 132, 163, 114, 119; Shaftesbury, *Characteristics,* 2:314.

44. Quoted in Voitle, *Shaftesbury,* 53.

45. Louis C. Jones, *The Clubs of the Georgian Rakes* (New York: Columbia University Press, 1942), 39–40, 84, 96–106; Peter Burke, *Popular Culture in Early Modern Europe* (New York: Harper and Row, 1978), 270. See too Richard M. Berrong, *Rabelais and Bakhtin: Popular Culture in Gargantua and Pantagruel* (Lincoln: University of Nebraska Press, 1987), 63–4.

46. Quoted in Voitle, *Shaftesbury,* 78.

47. Shaftesbury, *Characteristics,* 2:12, 24, 148; 1:48.

48. Ibid., 1:203, 2:8, 10, 95; see, too, the quotation in Voitle, *Shaftesbury,* 255–6.

49. Shaftesbury, *Characteristics,* 1:313.

50. Ibid., 2:115–116.

51. Ibid., 1:313; 2:32, 144; Borsay, *Urban Renaissance,* 260.

52. McKeon, *Origins of the Novel,* 183; Shaftesbury, *Characteristics,* 2:9, 7, 8, 5–6.

53. Shaftesbury, *Characteristics,* 2:204, 169n.2; 2:147.

54. Shaftesbury wrote in 1701, "Our Adversaries have after 12 years mistake, learnt their right Game; they act the Commonwealthsmen & herd with us." Voitle, *Shaftesbury,* 207, 210. See too M. M. Goldsmith, *Private Vices, Public Benefits: Bernard Mandeville's Social and Political Thought* (Cambridge: Cambridge University Press, 1984), 14, 27, 84.

55. Quoted in McKeon, *Origins of the Novel,* 170.

56. Shaftesbury, *Characteristics,* 1:175–6, and see 1:331.

57. Quoted in Voitle, *Shaftesbury,* 331.

58. Shaftesbury, *Characteristics,* 2:314; 1:170, 173, 172.

59. Ibid., 1:176, 175, 176, 180, 181.

60. No. 446 (1 August 1712), *The Spectator,* 8 vols. (London: T. Hamilton, 1808 [1711–2]), 6:205–7. Steele was "the great promoter and popularizer of sentimental moral comedy," and Addison's *Cato* (1713) was "possibly the most admired of all eighteenth-century English tragedies." Sambrook, *The Eighteenth Century,* 172. Cato combined the new sentimentality with the representation of public virtue advocated by country ideology and the reformation of manners. He was "a pattern for Britons to emulate." Hence the nom de plume of Trenchard and Gordon in *Cato's Letters.* Goldsmith, *Private Vices,* 20–1 and n.37.

61. George Berkeley, "An Essay towards Preventing the Ruin of Great Britain," *The Works of George Berkeley, Bishop of Cloyne,* 8 vols., ed. A. A. Luce and T. E. Jessup (London: Thomas Nelson, 1953), 6:69–85.

62. Shaftesbury, *Characteristics,* 2:6; the characterization of Christ quoted in Voitle, *Shaftesbury,* 358.

63. Shaftesbury, *Characteristics,* 2:179; Keith Thomas, "Women and the Civil War Sects," *Past and Present,* no. 13 (1958): 42–62; Clarendon quoted in McKeon, *Origins of the Novel,* 187.

64. Shaftesbury, *Characteristics,* 2:314–6; 1:176–7; David Roberts, *The Ladies: Female Patronage of Restoration Drama, 1660–1700* (New York: Oxford University Press, 1989); Voitle, *Shaftesbury,* 262, 404.

65. Shaftesbury, *Characteristics,* 1:45; 2:10.

66. Ibid., 2:11, 12. At the same place, he expressed his admiration for "doughty knighthood" when "the fair" were merely "witnesses to . . . feats of arms."

67. Shaftesbury, *Characteristics*, 2:220, 174, 1:224.

68. Ibid., 2:257; Brett, *Shaftesbury*, 131.

69. Tuveson, *Imagination*, 52; Sambrook, *Eighteenth Century*, 54. See Crane, "Genealogy," 207; Voitle, *Shaftesbury*, 133, 130, 144; Brett, *Shaftesbury*, 28.

70. Bernard Mandeville, *The Fable of the Bees: or, Private Vices, Publick Benefits*, ed. F. B. Kaye (Oxford: Clarendon Press, 1924), 2:380–5; see too Richard I. Cook, *Bernard Mandeville* (New York: Twayne, 1974), ch. 1.

71. Mandeville, *Fable of the Bees*, 1:168; Schama, *Embarrassment of Riches*, 371, 338.

72. Schama, *Embarrassment of Riches*, 371, 335–7. For Mandeville's bibliography, see *Fable of the Bees*, 2:386–400; Cook, *Mandeville*, 165–6; Hector Monro, *The Ambivalence of Bernard Mandeville* (Oxford: Clarendon Press, 1975), 270–2; Goldsmith, *Private Vices*, 165–7.

73. Mandeville, *Fable of the Bees*, 1:11–12, 93. Historian Peter Clark has explained how, increasingly at the time Mandeville was writing, "justices relied on brewers to discipline ale-house keepers" who refused to be "tied" to a brewery. *The English Ale-house: A Social History 1200–1830* (London: Longman, 1983), 184. Schama describes Dutch "sheriffs, constables, and bailiffs"—public officials—"giving themselves up to shameless debauchery and drunkenness." *Embarrassment of Riches*, 202, and see too 195.

74. Mandeville, *Fable of the Bees*, 166; Norman O. Brown, *Life against Death: The Psychoanalytical Meaning of History* (Middletown, Conn.: Wesleyan University Press, 1985 [1959]), ch. 13.

75. Mandeville, *Fable of the Bees*, 1:166, 135, 124, 6–7.

76. Ibid., 1:95, 151; 2:179; compare McKeon, *Origins of the Novel*, 203.

77. Quoted in Cook, *Mandeville*, 124, which calls Mandeville a "Cultural Evolutionist." This historical view is apparent throughout *The Fable of the Bees*, and Goldsmith lays it out very clearly in ch. 3 of his *Private Vices*.

78. Mandeville, *Fable of the Bees*, 2:128; Cook, *Mandeville*, 142; see too Goldsmith, *Private Vices*, 68, 71, 73.

79. Mandeville, *Fable of the Bees*, 1:103, 104–5, 245.

80. Ibid., 117, 118. Mandeville may be referring to the putative effects of masturbation on young lads; a popular Dutch sex manual, published when Mandeville was seventeen, had "warned that four or five ejaculations per night was the maximum for health." Schama, *Embarrassment of Riches*, 424; see too Mandeville, *A Modest Defence of Public Stews: or, An Essay upon Whoring, as It Is Now Practis'd in These Kingdoms*, publication no. 162 (Los Angeles: Augustan Reprint Society 1973 [1724]), 30–1. Goldsmith challenges the ascription of this work to Mandeville in his *Private Vices*, 149, 150n.47, although see too 90. Cook, Monro, and Schama accept it.

81. Mandeville, *Fable of the Bees*, 1:119, 120–1; he discussed the same change in *The Virgin Unmask'd: or, Female Dialogues betwix't an Elderly Maiden Lady and Her Niece in Several Diverting Discourses on Love, Marriage, Memoirs, and Morals, etc., of the Times* (London: G. Strahan, 1724), 128–32.

82. Mandeville, *Fable of the Bees,* 1:86, 130, 148, 103.

83. Ibid., 1:130, II: 259.

84. Ibid., 1:25, 148, 247–8; Goldsmith, *Private Vices,* 140, 136.

85. Mandeville, *Fable of the Bees,* 1:381–6, xxvi; Cook, *Mandeville,* ch. 8; Mandeville, *Public Stews,* 11; For Heidegger see Terry Castle, *Masquerade and Civilization: The Carnivalesque in Eighteenth-Century English Culture and Fiction* (Stanford: Stanford University Press, 1986), 10. Redwood agrees with Mandeville that one motive for clerics joining the puritanical fray was preferment. *Reason,* 219.

86. Mandeville, *Public Stews,* 60; Mandeville's 1723 case against charity schools, "An Essay on Charity, and Charity Schools," is published in Kaye's edition of *Fable of the Bees,* 1:253–322. For Mandeville's view of dueling see *Fable of the Bees,* 1:82–99; see too Monro, *Ambivalence of Mandeville,* 8–10; and Goldsmith, *Public Benefits,* 36–7.

87. Mandeville, *Fable of the Bees,* 1:8, 161–2; this is Rochester's description of the typical parson:

> Who from his Pulpit vents more peevish Lyes,
> More bitter railings, scandals, Calumnies,
> Than at a Gossipping are thrown about,
> When the good *Wives* get drunk, and then fall out.
> None of that sensual Tribe whose Tallents lye,
> In Avarice, *Pride, Sloth,* and *Gluttony,*
> Who hunt good Livings, but abhor good Lives,
> Whose Lust exalted to that height arrives,
> They act *Adultery* with their own *Wives,*
> And e're a score of Years compleated be,
> Can from the Lofty *Pulpit* proudly see,
> Half a large *Parish,* their own *Progeny.*
> ("Satyr," *The Poems of John Wilmot, Earl of Rochester,* ed. Keith Walker [Oxford: Basil Blackwell, 1984], 97)

McKeon provides a persuasive interpretation of Swift's identical view, *Origins of the Novel,* 218.

88. Mandeville, *Public Stews,* iv–ix, x, 15.

89. Mandeville, *Fable of the Bees,* 2:51; Voitle, *Shaftesbury,* 5, 15, 225–72; Benjamin Franklin, *Autobiography and Other Writings* (Boston: Houghton Mifflin, 1958 [1793]), 39; Sambrook, *Eighteenth Century,* 56; Mandeville, *Fable of the Bees,* 1:105–6. Mandeville's symbolic recipe for a punchbowl reflected the culinary possibilities of domestic and imperial trade. It may be compared to the Dutch "hutsepot" to which Schama gives the same significance, *Embarrassment of Riches,* 176.

90. Mandeville, *Fable of the Bees,* 2:43–53; Kaye summarizes their differences in *Fable of the Bees,* 1:lxxiii–xxv.

91. Ibid., 1:234n; 2:46.

92. The "caged" phrase is Kaye's, ibid., cxiii n.1; see too 1:cii–iii, lxv–vi.

93. Mandeville, *Fable of the Bees,* 2:180–1, 56.

94. Ibid., 2:222, 55. See Goldsmith, "Regulating Anew the Moral and Po-

litical Sentiments of Mankind: Bernard Mandeville and the Scottish Enlightenment," *Journal of the History of Ideas* 49, no. 4 (1988): 597.

95. Mandeville, *Fable of the Bees,* 1:43, 72–3; 148 (and see Kaye's note). Goldsmith observes that "Mandeville's whole argument presses toward a recognition of the diversity of human pleasures and desires and consequent diversity of satisfying ways of life." *Private Vices,* 140.

96. Mandeville, *Fable of the Bees,* 1:165, 2:53, 59–60, 51–2.

97. Goldsmith, *Private Vices,* 122, 127, 158–9, 141.

98. Ibid., 133–5, 158, 142–44. In *Tom Jones,* Fielding describes a society in which "many different codes of honour . . . exist concurrently." He "does not find relativism alarming, because he feels to understand codes other than your own is likely to make your judgements better." William Empson, *Using Biography* (Cambridge, Mass.: Harvard University Press, 1984), 141, 142.

99. Mandeville, *Public Stews,* ix, iii, 25.

100. Mandeville, *Virgin Unmask'd,* 3.

101. Mandeville, *Public Stews,* 30, 31, 6, 7.

102. Mandeville, *Fable of the Bees,* 11:259; 44 and 49.

103. Schama, *Embarrassment of Riches,* 407, 410–2, 418–20; Mandeville, *Fable of the Bees,* 2:168, 172, 122, 124, 69, 71; Mandeville may well have been criticizing Locke in this regard: in *Some Thoughts Concerning Education,* Locke had written, "too much shamefacedness better becomes a girl than too much confidence." *The Educational Writings of John Locke,* 315.

104. Mandeville, *Fable of the Bees,* 2:65.

105. Ibid., 2:124; see too 71–2.

106. Ibid., 1:75; see too *Public Stews,* 11; and *Virgin Unmask'd,* passim.

107. Mandeville, *Fable of the Bees,* 1:142, 143; see too 1:73–6, 204–5; *Public Stews,* 41; *Virgin Unmask'd,* 2, 19–20, 31.

108. Mandeville, *Fable of the Bees,* 1:143–4.

109. Mandeville, *Public Stews,* 40–1.

110. Thomas Laqueur, "Orgasm, Generation, and the Politics of Reproductive Biology," *Representations* 14 (Spring 1986): 4, 12–4, and 2; Schama, *Embarrassment of Riches,* 424; Mandeville, *Fable of the Bees,* 1:143–4.

111. Goldsmith, *Private Vices,* 157, 156.

112. Mandeville, *The Female Tatler* 88 (27 January 1710), quoted in Goldsmith, *Private Vices,* 156.

113. Mandeville, *Virgin Unmask'd,* 115–6.

114. Schama, *Embarrassment of Riches,* pp. 403–7 (Shaw quoted 404). Franklin recorded the successful, independent management of a printing business by a widow in Charleston, South Carolina, during the 1730s, which he explained by her "being born and bred in Holland . . . where the knowledge of accounts makes a part of the female education." *Autobiography,* 90; Bathsua Pell Makin, *An Essay to Revive the Antient Education of Gentlewomen* (1673), in *First Feminists: British Women Writers, 1578–1799,* ed. Moira Ferguson (Bloomington: Indiana University Press, 1985), 137; Drake's *Essay* is also in *First Feminists,* 206–7. There is some question about the authorship of this, compounded by the existence of another "J. Drake," Judith's brother, also a

doctor. For the actual roles of women in business in London at the time Mandeville was writing, see Peter Earle, *The Making of the English Middle Class: Business, Society and Family Life in London, 1660–1730* (London: Methuen, 1989), ch. 6.

115. Goldsmith, *Private Vices,* 155; for this criticism of Astell see below, 196–7.

116. Mandeville, *Virgin Unmask'd,* 23–4, 27–8, 18.

117. Ibid., 27, 30, 28–9.

118. Philip Young, *Three Bags Full: Essays in American Fiction* (New York: Harcourt Brace Jovanovich, 1972), 212 n.

119. Mandeville, *Virgin Unmask'd,* 120, 150ff.

120. Ibid., 102–6, 169.

121. Ibid., 67, 79–80, 78, 95.

122. Richardson, *Clarissa,* 3:145. The converted Belford attacked Mandeville's view, *Clarissa,* 4:9. Mandeville wrote that rakes made the best husbands because their experience of other women made them more tolerant of imperfections in their wives (*Defence of Stews,* 37); however, Mandeville also expressed disapproval of "abandon'd Rakehells." Cook, *Mandeville,* 108.

123. Mandeville, *Fable of the Bees,* 2:286. In *The Virgin Unmask'd* he refers to the same phenomenon as "dumb language," 186: it was because tears were involuntary that Mandeville said it is not unmanly to weep. *Fable of the Bees,* 159–60.

124. David Hume, *Essays, Moral, Political, and Literary,* 2 vols., ed. T. H. Green and T. H. Grose (London: Longmans, Green, 1875), 1:301; Adam Smith, *The Theory of Moral Sentiments,* ed. A. L. MacFie and D. D. Raphael (Indianapolis: Liberty Classics, 1979), 9, 209.

125. Borsay, *Urban Renaissance,* 104; V. G. Kiernan, *The Duel in European History: Honour and the Reign of Aristocracy* (Oxford: Oxford University Press, 1988), 177; quotations in Christopher Lawrence, "The Nervous System and Society in the Scottish Enlightenment," in *Natural Order: Historical Studies of Scientific Culture,* ed., Barry Barnes and Steven Shapin (Beverly Hills and London: Sage, 1979), 29–30; Lawrence makes the case for a relationship between the Scottish Enlightenment and its physical setting; a relationship between English manners and architecture is implicit throughout Borsay, *Urban Renaissance* (see for example 256).

126. Robertson quoted in Burke, *Popular Culture,* 279; Hume, "Of the Delicacy of Taste and Passion," *Essays* 1:93; Sambrook, *The Eighteenth Century,* 269; Lawrence, "Nervous System," passim.

127. Hume, *A Treatise of Human Nature,* ed. Ernest Mossner (New York: Penguin, 1985 [1739–40]), 13; T. H. Green and T. H. Grose, "History of the Editions" in their edition of Hume, *Essays,* 1:33–43; Hume, "My Own Life," in *Essays,* 1:1–8; see too "Of the Study of History," in *Essays,* 2:390.

128. Hume, "Refinement," 300, 305. For a fuller treatment of the relations between Mandeville, Hume, and Smith, one extending to Hutcheson, too, see Goldsmith, "Mandeville and the Scottish Enlightenment."

129. Hume, "Refinement," 299–300, 302–3, 306.

130. Ibid., 299, 301.

131. Ibid., 301–3; Enfield, *History of Liverpool* (1773), quoted in Borsay, *Urban Renaissance*, 266, 267–9; William Enfield, *The Speaker: or, Miscellaneous Pieces Selected from the Best English Writers*, etc. (Gainesborough: Henry Morley, 1774); John Mullan, *Sentiment and Sociability: The Language of Feeling in the Eighteenth Century* (Oxford: Clarendon Press, 1988).

132. Hume, "The Stoic," *Essays*, 1:207: "Of the Delicacy of Taste and Passion," *Essays*, 1:92; "The Stoic," 1:208–9.

133. Hume, "Refinement," 304.

134. David Hume, *The History of England: From the Invasion of Julius Caesar to the Revolution in 1688*, 6 vols. (Indianapolis: Liberty Classics, 1983 [1778]), 4:352–3; Wollstonecraft, *The Female Reader: or, Miscellaneous Pieces in Prose and Verse; Selected from the Best Writers . . .* (Delmar, N.Y.: Scholars Facsimiles and Reprints, 1984 [1788]), 389; Wollstonecraft quoted another passage illustrating Hume's sympathetic view of women in *Vindication of the Rights of Woman* (New York: Penguin, 1975 [1792]), 145.

135. Smith, *Theory*, 308–14. See Goldsmith, "Mandeville and the Scottish Enlightenment," 587, 596–601.

136. Smith, *The Wealth of Nations* (New York: Penguin, 1970 [1776]), 447, 133. Compare Hume, *Treatise of Human Nature*, 361.

137. Smith, *Theory*, 9, 201, and see too 63.

138. Ibid., 313; Smith, *Wealth of Nations*, 447–9, 161, 181.

139. Smith, *Wealth of Nations*, 170–1; Smith assumed that a woman's labor was in and for a male-headed family.

140. Smith, *Theory*, 8–9, 18, 20–5.

141. Smith, *Wealth of Nations*, 182, 181; Smith, *Theory*, 39, 152.

142. Smith, *Theory*, 13, 17, 2, 200–211, 255–6. For the differences between Mandeville's vision of historical evolution and Smith's see Goldsmith, *Private Vices*, 164.

143. Raphael and MacFie, "Introduction" to Smith's *Theory*, 3–10; Smith, *Theory*, 152; Adam Smith to William Strahan, 26 August, 1776, in Hume, *Essays*, 1:13.

144. Smith, *Theory*, 30–31, 205–6, 28.

145. Quoted in Laqueur, "The Politics of Reproductive Biology," 22.

146. Fordyce quoted in Alice Browne, *The Eighteenth Century Feminist Mind* (Brighton, Sussex: Harvester Press, 1987), 28; Smith, *Theory*, 209.

147. Smith, *Theory*, 25, and passim; see Raphael and MacFie, "Introduction," 7, 16–17.

148. Smith, *Theory*, 40.

149. Smith, *Wealth of Nations*, 181: the liberal Smith here echoes the conservative Swift.

150. Samuel Richardson, *A Collection of the Moral and Instructive Sentiments, Maxims, Cautions, and Reflexions, Contained in the Histories of "Pamela," "Clarissa," and "Sir Charles Grandison"* (Delmar, N.Y.: Scholars Facsimiles and Reprints, 1980 [1755]), 204–5.

151. This is part of the well-known October 1748 letter of Fielding to Richardson published in Edward L. McAdam, Jr., in "A New Letter from Fielding," *Yale Review* 38 (1948): 300–310.

152. Fielding, *Tom Jones* 413.

153. Fielding, *Joseph Andrews and Shamela* (Boston: Houghton Mifflin, 1961 [1742 and 1741]), 145, 163, 13; Fielding, *Tom Jones,* 89, 555, 830.

154. Richardson, *Clarissa,* 1:205.

155. Charlotte Lennox, *The Female Quixote: or, The Adventures of Arabella* (London: Pandora, 1986 [1752]), 314, 315; see too Browne, *Feminist Mind,* 47. Women novelists' concern with manliness is discussed below.

156. Jane Spencer, *The Rise of the Woman Novelist: From Aphra Behn to Jane Austen* (Oxford: Basil Blackwell, 1986), 185; Sheriff, *Good-natured Man,* 30–36, 46, 73–91; Mullan, *Sentiment and Sociability,* 127; Fliegelman, *Prodigals and Pilgrims,* 254; Clive T. Probyn, *English Fiction of the Eighteenth Century, 1700–1789* (London and New York: Longman, 1987), 157, 162. See too Langford, *Polite and Commercial People,* 481.

157. Sir Walter Scott, "Memoir of Henry MacKenzie," *Works of Henry MacKenzie,* 8 vols. (Edinburgh: Archibald Constable, William Creech, and Manners and Miller, 1808), 1:8–9; Probyn, *English Fiction,* 231. In his "Memoir," Scott notes that MacKenzie "shot game of every description" (8–9). That a huntsman presents Harley's manuscript in *The Man of Feeling* to have been used as wadding for shooting may well have reflected MacKenzie's chariness of Harley's kind of manhood. *The Man of Feeling* (New York: Oxford University Press, 1970 [1771]), 5.

158. Scott, "MacKenzie," 6–7.

159. Ibid., 12.

160. MacKenzie, *Mirror,* no. 42 (19 June 1779), and no. 72 (15 January 1780), in *Miscellaneous Works* (New York: Harper and Brother, 1836), 479, 498–9.

161. MacKenzie, *Mirror,* no. 72, and no. 101 (25 April 1780), in *Miscellaneous Works,* 499–500, 501.

162. Scott, "MacKenzie," 13; Sheriff, *Good-natured Man,* 81–91, esp. 82; Brian Vickers, "Introduction," in MacKenzie, *The Man of Feeling,* vii; Sheriff, *Good-Natured Man,* p. 89; Probyn, *English Fiction,* 161.

163. Scott, "MacKenzie," 12; Scott wrote of MacKenzie in his journal: we "would suppose a retired, modest, somewhat affected man, with a white handkerchief and a sigh ready for every sentiment. No such thing, H. M. is as alert as a contracting tailor's needle in every sort of business, a politician and a sportsman—shoots and fishes in a sort even to this day [MacKenzie was eighty] and is the life of the company in anecdote and fun." Quoted by Vickers, "Introduction" to MacKenzie, *Man of Feeling,* viii n.2.

164. MacKenzie, *Lounger,* no. 100 (30 December 1786), in *Miscellaneous Works,* 170–4.

165. Ibid., 170–1; Smith, *Theory,* 312. Hume had made the same argument of the value of the cultivation of feeling to men of business. "Delicacy of Taste," 93–4.

166. MacKenzie, *Lounger,* no. 100, pp. 172–3.

167. Ibid., 174.

168. Ibid., no. 20 (18 June 1785), in *Collected Works,* 5:176–87; Hannah More, "Sensibility, a Poem," in *Sacred Dramas, Chiefly Intended for Young Persons*

(Philadelphia: Thomas Dobson, 1787 [1784]), 187. Compare Scott's diary entry quoted in n. 163, above.

169. MacKenzie, *Lounger,* no. 20, pp. 177, 179, 182.

170. MacKenzie, *Lounger,* no. 20, pp. 181, 182–3.

171. Ibid., 177–8; Fielding, *Tom Jones,* 409, 183.

172. MacKenzie, *Lounger,* no. 20, pp. 179–80, 186–7.

173. MacKenzie, "The Effects of Religion on Minds of Sensibility," *Mirror,* no. 42, p. 479; *Lounger,* no. 20, p. 178, 479.

174. John Brewer, *Party Ideology and Popular Politics at the Accession of George III* (Cambridge: Cambridge University Press, 1976), 41–2; Goldsmith, *Private Vices,* 19, 24; Barker-Benfield, "Mary Wollstonecraft: Eighteenth-Century Commonwealthwoman," *Journal of the History of Ideas* 50, no. 1 (1989): 98–100.

175. Gibbon, *The Decline and Fall of the Roman Empire,* 3 vols. (New York: Modern Library, n.d. [1776]), 1:9, 15; Gibbon, *Memoirs of My Life* (New York: Penguin, 1984 [1796]).

176. Adapting Clausewitz, McKeon writes that "literature . . . is politics by other means," *Origins of the Novel,* 173.

177. Robbins, *Eighteenth-Century Commonwealthman,* 156, 166; Probyn, *English Fiction,* 222, 150, 155, 154; see too Reeve, *Plans of Education: With Remarks on the Systems of Other Writers* (New York: Garland Publishing, 1974 [1792]), 67, and passim.

178. John Brand, *Observations on Popular Antiquities including the whole of Mr. Bourne's Antiquitates Vulgares* (1777), 21, quoted in J. M. Golby and A. W. Purdue, *The Civilisation of the Crowd: Popular Culture in England, 1750–1900* (New York: Schocken Books, 1984), 50–1; Langford, *Polite and Commercial People,* 479.

179. Robbins, *Eighteenth-Century Commonwealthman,* 373–4; Robert Alan Cooper, "Thomas Day (1748–89)" *Biographical Dictionary of Modern British Radicals,* vol. 1, *1770–1830,* ed. Joseph O. Baylen and Norbert J. Grossman (Sussex: Harvester Press; New Jersey: Humanities Press, 1979), 116–8.

180. Thomas Day, *The History of Sandford and Merton* (Philadelphia: n.p., n.d.), 48–57. Cooper, "Day," 117. For a remarkable illustration of Day's middle-class values see his rewriting of the history of Pizarro's conquest of the Incas, *Sandford and Merton,* 81–2.

181. Cooper, "Day," 116; Day, *Sandford and Merton,* 403, is one of many illustrations of the point.

182. Day, *Sandford and Merton,* 351.

183. Ibid., 147, 209–10, 211, 508, 466; Griffith quoted in Patricia Meyer Spacks "Ev'ry Woman Is at Heart a Rake," *Eighteenth-Century Studies* 8 (1974): 27–46, esp. 43.

184. Day, *Sandford and Merton,* 208, 210, 211.

185. Ibid., 533–4, 489, 422, 364.

186. Ibid., 11–2, 137, 479, 133.

187. Ibid., 241, 283, 426, 483, 523, 348, 533.

188. Ibid., 531, 451, 524, 217, 281, 253, 394. Clara Reeve's 1792 *Plan of*

Education, perhaps influenced by Day's recently published *Sandford and Merton,* made the same historical case against luxury, warning against "those pleasures which emasculate the mind and enervate the body," fearing that like the youth of the ancient Persians or Romans "our young men are grown effeminate" and, typically, "our daughters ignorant, affected, and dissipated." It was a recognizable historical morphology: in "a nation which has ascended to the highest degree of cultivation; when the language and manners, arts and sciences, are in the greatest perfection—refinement . . . becomes fastidious, wanton, effeminate." Reeve, *Plan of Education,* 33, 34–35, 58, 28.

189. Day, *Sandford and Merton,* 285, 206–7.

190. Burke, *Popular Culture,* 14, and ch. 1, passim.

191. Godwin draft letter dated 19 September 1797, quoted in Gary Kelly, *The English Jacobin Novel, 1780–1805* (Oxford: Clarendon Press, 1976), 226; Wollstonecraft to Godwin, 1 July 1796 in *Collected Letters of Mary Wollstonecraft,* ed. Ralph M. Wardle (Ithaca: Cornell University Press, 1979), 331; Don Locke, *A Fantasy of Reason: The Life and Thought of William Godwin* (London: Routledge and Kegan Paul, 1980), 139–42; Barker-Benfield, "Biography as Autobiography: William Godwin's Revelations about Himself in his *Memoirs of the Author of the Vindication of the Rights of Woman* (1798)," Conference on Autobiography and Biography, Stanford University, 11 April 1986.

192. Gerard Barker, *Grandison's Heirs: The Paragon's Progress in the Late Eighteenth-Century English Novel* (Newark: University of Delaware, 1985); Probyn, *English Fiction,* 168–9; Sheriff, *Good-natured Man,* 76; Peter L. Thorsley, Jr., *The Byronic Hero: Types and Prototypes* (Minneapolis: University of Minnesota press, 1962). This direction has been detected in Godwin's fiction, too, by B. Sprague Allen, "William Godwin as a Sentimentalist," *Publication of the Modern Language Association* 23, no. 1, n.s. (1924): 1–29, esp. 11; and Kelly, *The English Jacobin Novel,* 238. The dramatic individualism of Wordsworth emerged out of his sense of being "a man possessed of more than usual organic sensibility"; his poetry was "the spontaneous overflow of powerful feelings" as he described it in his manifesto for romantic poetry, the 1800 "Preface" to *Lyrical Ballads: The Poetical Works of Wordsworth,* ed. Paul D. Sheets (Boston: Houghton Mifflin, 1982), 791. See too Todd's remarks on Wordsworth's early "Sonnet, on seeing Miss Helen Maria Williams weep at a Tale of Distress," *Sensibility,* 62–3. For an intriguing argument connecting romanticism and consumerism, see Colin Campbell, *The Romantic Ethic and the Spirit of Modern Consumerism* (Oxford and New York: Basil Blackwell, 1987), pt. 2.

193. Day, *Sandford and Merton,* 348.

194. Ibid., 71–2; Eardley-Wilmot quoted in Philip Mason, *The English Gentleman: The Rise and Fall of an Ideal* (New York: William Morrow, 1982), 83.

Chapter 4. Women and Eighteenth-Century Consumerism

1. Peter Burke, *Popular Culture in Early Modern Europe* (New York: Harper Torchbooks, 1978), 49; Judith Bennett, *Women in the Medieval English Countryside: Gender and Household in Brigstock before the Plague* (New York: Oxford University Press, 1987), 37, and see 177. Peter Laslett, *The World We Have Lost,*

Further Explored (New York: Charles Scribner's, 1984), 73–44; J. M. Golby and A. W. Purdue, *The Civilisation of the Crowd: Popular Culture in England, 1750–1900* (New York: Schocken, 1985), 138–9. Duchess of Newcastle quoted in Hilda Smith, *Reason's Disciples: Seventeenth-Century English Feminists* (Urbana: University of Illinois Press, 1982), 82.

2. Roy Porter, *English Society in the Eighteenth Century* (Harmondsworth, Middx.: Penguin, 1982), 160, 101, 38, 42, 47; Bennett, *Women in the English Countryside,* 47, 7, 129, 133–41; Laslett points out how fundamental marriage was to the English social structure in *World We Have Lost,* 101; Paul Langford, *A Polite and Commercial People: England, 1727–83* (Oxford: Clarendon Press, 1989), 110; Barbara A. Hanawalt, "Peasant Women's Contribution to the Home Economy in Late Medieval England," in *Women and Work in Preindustrial Europe,* ed. Hanawalt (Bloomington: Indiana University Press, 1986), 17. For the necessary dismantling of the fantasy of a "golden age" of greater sexual equality see Mary Beth Norton, *Liberty's Daughters: The Revolutionary Experience of American Women 1759–1800* (Boston: Little Brown, 1980); Olwen Hufton, "Women in History: Early Modern Europe," *Past and Present* 101 (November 1983), 125–57; Bennett, *Women in the Medieval English Countryside,* 4–8; and Patricia West, "The Search for the *Bon Vieux Temps:* The Historiography of Women's Status in Pre-industrial Families" (unpublished paper, State University of New York, Binghamton, 1989). See too Laslett, *World We Have Lost,* 4; and Hanawalt, "Introduction," *Women and Work in Late Medieval Europe,* xii-xviii. The Reformation gave a new charge to this ancient myth; see R. H. Tawney, *Religion and the Rise of Capitalism* (West Drayton, Middx.: Pelican Books, 1948), 95. For the recharging of the myth under the impact of the industrial revolution see Neil McKendrick, "Home Demand and Economic Growth: A New View of the Role of Women and Children in the Industrial Revolution," *Historical Perspectives: Studies in English Thought and Society,* ed. McKendrick (London: Europa Press, 1974), 163–4. Addressing the period 1580–1680, Keith Wrightson warns that "we must avoid the painting of too black a picture of marital relations." He says that "conventionalized misogyny" and legal disabilities were offset by "positive elements," of complementarity and mutuality. Keith Wrightson, *English Society, 1580–1680* (London: Hutchinson, 1982), 90–1. For brief summaries of women's legal position in the late seventeenth and eighteenth centuries see Peter Earle, *The Making of the English Middle Class: Business, Society and Family Life in London, 1660–1730* (London: Methuen, 1989), 158–60, 198–200; Katherine M. Rogers, *Feminism in Eighteenth-Century England* (Urbana: University of Illinois Press, 1982), 7–14; and Alice Browne, *The Eighteenth Century Feminist Mind* (Brighton, Sussex: Harvester Press, 1987), 15–7 and 130–6; Browne describes favorable if minor changes in this position later in the century.

3. Carole Shammas, "The Domestic Environment in Early Modern England and America," *Journal of Social History* 14, no. 1 (1990): 6. The two quotations are, respectively, in Bennett, *Women in the Medieval English Countryside,* 118, and Lorna Weatherill, *Consumer Behavior and Material Culture in Britain 1660–1760* (London: Routledge, 1988), 137.

4. Bennett, *Women in the Medieval English Countryside,* 116–118; Hanawalt,

"Peasant Women's Contribution," 11, and passim; see too Shammas's quotation of Fitzherbert's *Book of Husbandry* (1534), "Domestic Environment," 5. In some places, women worked as agricultural laborers all year, Laslett, *World We Have Lost,* 126.

5. Bennett, *Women in the Medieval English Countryside,* 116–7, 198.

6. Carole Shammas, *The Pre-industrial Consumer in England and America* (Oxford: Clarendon Press, 1990), 40, 291, and passim.

7. Porter, *Eighteenth Century,* 99; John Rule, *The Labouring Classes in Early Industrial England 1750–1850* (London and New York: Longman, 1986), 13–14; Shammas, "Domestic Environment," 8, 7, 10, 17.

8. Weatherill, *Consumer Behaviour,* 146–9; R. N. K. Rees and Charles Fenby, "Meals and Mealtimes," *Englishmen at Rest and Play: Some Phases of English Leisure 1558–1714,* ed. Reginald Lennard (Oxford: Clarendon Press, 1931), 221; Shammas, "Domestic Environment," 17, 5; Mary Wollstonecraft, *Vindication of the Rights of Woman* (New York: Penguin, 1975 [1792]), 159. See too Earle, *English Middle Class,* 272–81. Elizabeth David points out that "until the late seventeenth century "recorded recipes" were predominantly those of royal households of the nobility, . . . the princes of the Church and . . . prosperous merchants." *Spices, Salts, and Aromatics in the English Kitchen* (New York: Penguin, 1970), 8.

9. Bennett, *Women in the Medieval English Countryside,* 117; Hanawalt, "Peasant Women's Contribution," 9–11; Harrison quoted in Shammas, *Pre-industrial Consumer,* 157, 158; Neil McKendrick, "The Consumer Revolution of Eighteenth-Century England," in *The Birth of a Consumer Society: The Commercialization of Eighteenth-Century England,* by McKendrick, John Brewer, and J. H. Plumb (Bloomington: Indiana University Press, 1982), 27; Shammas, "Domestic Environment," 6–8.

10. Shammas, "Domestic Environment," 7, 8, 6; see too Shammas, *Pre-industrial Consumer,* 88, 77, 161, 168.

11. Shammas, *Pre-industrial Consumer,* 186, 159; Earle, *English Middle Class,* 292; Shammas, "Domestic Environment, 8, 7, 10, 17. See too Shammas, *Pre-industrial Consumer,* 96, 100. For a nice picture of mid-eighteenth century knives and forks, see plate 4 in Weatherill, *Consumer Behaviour,* 36.

12. Shammas, *Pre-industrial Consumer,* 183, 185; Weatherill, *Consumer Behaviour,* 159–60; McKendrick, "Consumer Revolution," 26.

13. French traveler quoted in *The Early Hanoverian Age 1714–1760: Commentaries of an Era,* ed. A. F. Scott (London: Croom Helm, 1980), 230; Earle, *English Middle Class,* 298. For some further discussion of cleaning, see Shammas, "Domestic Economy," 17; and Weatherill, *Consumer Behaviour,* p. 151.

14. Peter Borsay, *The English Urban Renaissance: Culture and Society in The Provincial Town 1660–1770* (Oxford: Clarendon Press, 1989), 224–70, 8; Earle, *English Middle Class,* 77–8, 210, 298. Smollett was proud to be able to report quite late in the century that in Edinburgh "the water is brought in leaden pipes from a mountain in the neighbourhood, to a cistern in on the Castle-Hill, from whence it is distributed to public conduits in different parts

of the city. From these it is carried in barrels, on the backs of male and female porters, up two, three, four, five, six, seven, and eight pair of stairs, for the use of the particular families." Tobias Smollett, *The Expedition of Humphry Clinker* (New York: New American Library, 1960 [1771]), 219. That using water remained an enormous burden for many working-class women is suggested in Jane Rendall, *The Origins of Modern Feminism: Women in Britain, France, and the United States, 1780–1860* (Houndsmill, Basingstoke, Hampshire: MacMillan, 1985), 191–3.

15. McKendrick, "Josiah Wedgewood and the Commercialization of the Potteries," in *Birth of a Consumer Society,* by McKendrick et al., 142; McKendrick, "Home Demand," 202.

16. Shammas, *Pre-industrial Consumer,* 107; Weatherill, *Consumer Behaviour,* plate 13 on 158, and plate 3 on 35. See, too, plate 16 in Earle, *English Middle Class,* 178.

17. "Unfortunate shrine" quoted in Shammas, "Domestic Environment," 14; Alice Browne, *The Eighteenth Century Feminist Mind* (Brighton, Sussex: Harvester, 1987), 47.

18. Shammas, "Domestic Environment," 14–16; Peter Clark, *The English Alehouse: A Social History 1200–1830* (London: Longman, 1983), 297; Weatherill, *Consumer Behaviour,* 157.

19. Shammas, "Domestic Environment," pp. 13, 10, 18; Weatherill, *Consumer Behaviour,* 152–9. Here the author aligns her account of these changes with Elias's "civilizing process," but, echoing Mandeville's criticism of Shaftesbury's condemnation of coarse public manners, Weatherill also reminds us that the earlier mode of eating food may be regarded as simply a different set of manners (155).

20. Shammas, "Domestic Environment," 17; Eden quoted in Shammas, *Pre-industrial Consumer,* 188.

21. Shammas, *Pre-industrial Consumer,* 172, 201; Wollstonecraft, *Rights of Woman,* 266, 132, 319n.3.

22. Porter, *Eighteenth Century,* 41; see too Laslett, *World We Have Lost,* 124–6.

23. Lawrence Stone, "The New Eighteenth Century," *New York Review of Books* 31 no. 5 (29 March 1984), 42–8; see E. A. Wrigley, "Marriage, Fertility and Population Growth in Eighteenth-Century England," in *Marriage and Society,* ed. R. B. Outhwaite (London: Europa, 1981), 137–85; Harold Perkin, *The Origins of Modern English Society 1780–1880* (London: Routledge and Kegan Paul, 1972), 102–5.

24. Laslett, *World We Have Lost,* 139; "the strongest link between the current price of food and demographic behaviour was with marriages," 140.

25. Shammas, *Pre-industrial Consumer,* 157, 186.

26. Shammas, "Domestic Environment," 17, 18; compare Donald Meyer, *Sex and Power: The Rise of Women in America, Russia, Sweden, and Italy* (Middletown, Conn.: Wesleyan University Press, 1987), 430; Wrightson makes the argument about the change in marriage, modifying Lawrence Stone's well-known case in *The Family, Sex and Marriage in England, 1500–1800* (New York:

Harper and Row, 1977) by suggesting seventeenth-century marriage could be placed on the continuum between the roles of the patriarchal and companionate forms. *English Society,* 90–105.

27. Shammas, "Domestic Environment," 17, 6. More time in cooking, cleaning, and childcare is a constellation historians have detected in the shift to a popular consumer economy in industrializing America. See Meyer, *The Positive Thinkers: Religion as Pop Psychology from Mary Baker Eddy to Oral Roberts* (New York: Pantheon, 1980 [1965]), 48–51; Nancy Cott, *The Bonds of Womanhood: "Woman's Sphere" in New England, 1780–1835* (New Haven: Yale University Press, 1977), chs. 1 and 2; Ruth Schwartz Cowan, *More Work for Mother: The Ironies of Household Technology from the Open Hearth to the Microwave* (New York: Basic Books, 1983).

28. Wrightson, *English Society,* 118; compare Perkin, *Origins of Modern English Society,* 156–7.

29. Compare Carole Klein, *Mothers and Sons* (Boston: G. K. Hall, 1985), 83.

30. Bennett, *Women of the Medieval English Countryside,* 47.

31. Ian Watt, *The Rise of the Novel: Studies in Defoe, Richardson and Fielding* (Berkeley and Los Angeles: University of California Press, 1967 [1957]), 188; Wollstonecraft, *Rights of Woman* 149; Shammas, "Domestic Environment," 7; and *Pre-industrial Consumer,* 161; Earle, *English Middle Class,* 209–12; Rhys Isaac, *The Transformation of Virginia 1740–1790* (Chapel Hill: University of North Carolina Press, 1982), 307.

32. Watt, *Rise of the Novel,* 188, 189.

33. J. Paul Hunter, *Before Novels: The Cultural Contexts of Eighteenth-Century Fiction* (New York: Norton, 1990), 272; William Stafford, *Socialism, Radicalism, and Nostalgia: Social Criticism in Britain, 1775–1830* (Cambridge: Cambridge University Press, 1987), 29; Richardson, *Clarissa,* 1:156–7.

34. Quoted in Fliegelman, *Prodigals and Pilgrims,* 29; Spencer, *Woman Novelist,* 23; 1766 letter quoted in Norton, *Liberty's Daughters,* 133.

35. Watt, *Rise of the Novel,* 43–7; J. H. Plumb, "The Commercialization of Leisure in Eighteenth-Century England," in *The Birth of a Consumer Society: The Commercialization of Eighteenth-Century England,* by Neil McKendrick, John Brewer, and Plumb (Bloomington: Indiana University Press, 1982), 265–85; 269–70; Golby and Purdue, *The Civilisation of the Crowd,* 33; Stone, *The Family, Sex, and Marriage,* 206. The most recent reassessment of English literacy rates in the seventeenth and eighteenth centuries is Hunter, *Before Novels,* ch. 3.

36. Burke, *Popular Culture,* 251; Golby and Purdue, *Civilization,* 32; J. F. C. Harrison, *The Common People of Great Britain: A History from the Norman Conquest to the Present* (Bloomington: Indiana University Press, 1985), 165, 163, 164; Hunter, *Before Novels,* 72–3; Smith, *Reason's Disciples,* 25–6; see too Jean E. Hunter, "The 18th-Century Englishwoman, According to the Gentleman's Magazine," in *Women in the Eighteenth Century and Other Essays,* ed. Paul Fritz and Richard Morton (Toronto and Sarasota: S. S. Hakkert, 1976), 74; and Patricia Crawford, "Women's Published Writings 1600–1700," in *Women in English Society 1500–1800,* ed. Mary Prior (London: Methuen, 1985), 216. For a sensitive account of the achievement of literacy within popular culture during the later sixteenth and seventeenth centuries, insisting on "the transfor-

mation of the cultural horizons of a significant minority among the common people," see Wrightson, *English Society,* 196–9.

37. Clive Probyn, *English Fiction of the Eighteenth Century 1700–1789* (London and New York: Longman, 1987), 24n.5; Ruth Perry, *The Celebrated Mary Astell: An Early English Feminist* (Chicago: University of Chicago Press, 1986), 83; Stone, *Family,* 353, 206; Harrison, *Common People,* 286; Hunter, *Before Novels,* 72, 73. The late figures hide very significant fluctuations, the effects of the toll taken by the industrial revolution.

38. Dr. Johnson quoted in J. M. S. Tompkins, *The Popular Novel in England, 1770–1800* (Westport, Conn.: Greenwood Press, 1976 [1961]), 119.

39. Smith, *Reason's Disciples,* 26, 23, 21, and passim; see too Browne, *Feminist Mind,* ch. 5 and p. 103.

40. P. J. Miller, "Women's Education, 'Self-Improvement,' and Social Mobility—a Late Eighteenth-Century Debate," *British Journal of Education Studies* 20 (1978): 306; Roy Porter, *English Society,* 180–1; Plumb, "The New World of Children in Eighteenth-Century England," in *Birth of a Consumer Society,* by McKendrick et al., 292; Barbara Schnorrenberg with Jean E. Hunter, "The Eighteenth-Century Englishwoman," in *The Women of England: From Anglo-Saxon Times to the Present,* ed. Barbara Kanner (Hamden, Conn.: Archon Books, 1979), 186; see too Tompkins, *Popular Novel,* 2; and Browne, *Feminist Mind,* 31; Maurice Quinlan, *Victorian Prelude: A History of English Manners 1700–1830* (Hamden, Conn.: Archon books, 1965 [1941]), 63.

41. Bernard Mandeville, *The Virgin Unmasked: or, Female Dialogues, . . .* (London: G. Strahan 1724), 38.

42. Janet Spencer, *The Rise of the Woman Novelist: From Aphra Behn to Jane Austen* (Oxford: Basil Blackwell, 1986), 6; Plumb, "New World of Children," 300; Porter, *English Society,* 180–1; Miller, "Women's Education," 313, 306; G. J. Barker-Benfield, "Mary Wollstonecraft: Eighteenth-Century Commonwealthwoman," *Journal of the History of Ideas* 50, no. 1 (1989): 100.

43. For an introduction to various aspects of the commercialization of publishing and the development of a popular readership among both sexes, see Watt, *Rise of the Novel,* ch. 2; Tompkins, *Popular Novel,* ch. 1; Pat Rogers, "Introduction: The Writer and Society," in *The Context of English Literature: The Eighteenth Century,* ed. Rogers (London: Methuen, 1978), 1–80; Terry Lovell, *Consuming Fiction* (New York: Verso, 1987), 49–53, and passim; Porter, *English Society,* 248; Peter Borsay, *The English Urban Renaissance: Culture and Society in the Provincial Town, 1660–1770* (Oxford: Clarendon Press, 1989), 127–32; Langford, *Polite and Commercial People,* 90–9.

44. Shammas, "Domestic Environment," 8; Weatherill, *Consumer Behaviour,* 83, 29, 173–85; Perry, *Mary Astell,* appendix B.

45. Joseph Addison, Richard Steele, et al., *The Spectator,* 8 vols. (London: T. Hamilton and R. Ogle, 1808), 1:151; Richardson's correspondent quoted in Probyn, *English Fiction,* 1; James Boswell, *Life of Johnson* (London and Oxford: Oxford University Press, 1953 [1787]), 979.

46. Watt, *Rise of the Novel,* 51–2, 55–6; Rogers, "Writer and Society," 51; Browne, *Feminist Mind,* 25; Plumb, "Commercialization of Leisure," 268–269.

47. Hunter, *Before Novels,* 68; Watt, *Rise of the Novel,* 42, 47; Stafford, *Socialism, Radicalism, and Nostalgia,* 28; Probyn, *English Fiction,* 11.

48. Watt, *Rise of the Novel,* 47; Hannah Gasse, *The Art of Cookery Made Plain and Easy* (1747), quoted by Weatherill, *Consumer Behaviour,* 150.

49. Chudleigh quoted in *First Feminists: British Women Writers, 1578–1799,* ed. Moira Ferguson (Bloomington: Indiana University Press; and Old Westbury, New York: The Feminist Press, 1985), 217; Spencer, *Woman Novelist,* 186; Smith, *Reason's Disciples,* 26; Miller, "Women's Education," 306; Hunter, *Before Novels,* 74.

50. Watt, *Rise of the Novel,* 56; Rogers, "Writer and Society," 16; Probyn, *English Fiction,* 179n.3; quotation in Spencer, *Woman Novelist,* 4; Probyn, *English Fiction,* 7; see Watt, *Rise of the Novel,* 56, 43. McKeon also embraces the law of the marketplace, in his own phrasing, "the dialectical relation of production and consumption as a constitutive force in the origins of the English novel." *Origins of the English Novel 1600–1740* (Baltimore: Johns Hopkins University Press, 1987), 52; it is fundamental, too, to Hunter's *Before Novels,* see xix, and passim.

51. Jocelyn Harris, *Samuel Richardson* (New York: Cambridge University Press, 1987), 39; Terry Eagleton, *The Rape of Clarissa: Writing, Sexuality and Class Struggle in Samuel Richardson* (Minneapolis: University of Minnesota Press, 1982), 6; Jerry C. Beasley, *Novels of the 1740s* (Athens: University of Georgia Press, 1982), 134.

52. Spencer, *Woman Novelist,* 89; Watt, *Rise of the Novel,* 55; and see McKeon, *Origins of the Novel,* 357.

53. Katharine Rogers, "Richardson's Empathy with Women," in *The Authority of Experience: Essays in Feminist Criticism,* ed. A. Diamond and L. R. Edwards (Amherst: University of Massachusetts, 1977), 118–37. There is now a fine and growing volume of books on this subject, beginning with Christopher Hill, "Clarissa Harlowe and Her Times," *Essays in Criticism* 5, no. 4 (October 1955), 315–40; and the relevant chapters (5, 6, and 7) in Watt, *Rise of the Novel;* and continuing through R. F. Brissenden, *Virtue in Distress: Studies in the Novel of Sentiment from Richardson to Sade* (New York: Harper and Row, 1974); Margaret Ann Doody, *A Natural Passion: A Study of the Novels of Samuel Richardson* (Oxford: Oxford University Press, 1974); William Warner, *Reading Clarissa: The Struggle over Interpretation* (New Haven: Yale University Press, 1979); Eagleton, *Rape of Clarissa;* Rachel Brownstein, *Becoming a Heroine: Reading about Women in Novels* (New York: Penguin, 1984); Rita Goldberg, *Sex and Enlightenment: Women in Richardson and Diderot* (Cambridge: Cambridge University Press, 1984); particularly valuable for its conciseness, balance, and originality is Jocelyn Harris, *Samuel Richardson.*

54. Quoted in McKeon, *Origins of the Novel,* 382.

55. Probyn, *English Fiction,* 12; Brissenden, *Virtue in Distress,* 160; Hunter, *Before Novels,* 22.

56. Probyn, *English Fiction,* 12.

57. Lackington quoted ibid., 9–10; Beasley, "Politics and Moral Idealism: The Achievements of Some Early Women Novelists," in *Fetter'd or Free? British Women Novelists, 1760–1815* (Columbus: Ohio University Press, 1985): 220;

Schnorrenberg and Hunter, "Eighteenth-Century Englishwoman," 197; Rogers, "Writer and Society," 26; Tompkins, *Popular Novel,* 122, 119; Porter, *English Society,* 257–8; Browne, *Feminist Mind,* 13.

58. Probyn, *English Fiction,* 2; Spencer, *Woman Novelist,* 4; Rogers, *Feminism in Eighteenth-Century England,* 22.

59. Tompkins, *Popular Novel,* 121; Smollett, *Humphry Clinker,* 133.

60. Nancy Armstrong writes that women "suddenly began writing and were recognized as women writers [was] a central event in the history of the novel," *Desire and Domestic Fiction: A Political History of the Novel* (New York: Oxford University Press, 1987), 7; Spencer refers to the "feminization of literature," *Women Novelist,* xi; and Probyn refers to "the alleged feminization of the novel," *English Fiction,* 20.

61. Tompkins, *Popular Novel,* 119; Crawford, "Women's Writings," 215; *The Spectator,* no. 92 (15 June 1711), 2:49, 47; McKeon, *Origins of the Novel,* 51. See too Samuel Croxall's preface to his 1720 collection of "histories and romances," quoted in Watt, *Rise of the Novel,* 49.

62. Fielding, *Tom Jones,* 409; see too Watt, *Rise of the Novel,* 51; Kames quoted in John Vladimir Price, "Religion and Ideas," in Rogers, ed., *The Eighteenth Century,* 140.

63. Anna Laetitia Aikin [Barbauld], "On Romances, an Imitation," in *Miscellaneous Pieces in Prose,* by J. and A. L. Aikin (London: J. Johnson, 1773), 42, 44, 40–1; Rogers, "Writer and Society," 17, 18; Rousseau, "Science," 150, 156; Watt, *Rise of the Novel,* 48.

64. Spencer, *Woman Novelist,* 7, 34n.17; Charles Scruggs, "Phillis Wheatley and the Poetical Legacy of Eighteenth-Century England," *Studies in Eighteenth-Century Culture,* vol. 10, ed. Harry C. Payne (Madison: University of Wisconsin Press, 1981), 279–95.

65. Coventry quoted in Jerry C. Beasley, *Novels of the 1740s* (Athens: University of Georgia Press, 1982), 2; Richardson, *Clarissa: or, The History of a Young Lady,* 4 vols. (London: John Dent, 1932), 4:495; reviewer of *Della Stanhope* quoted in Spencer, *Woman Novelist,* 89, 79. See too Armstrong, *Domestic Fiction,* 7, 30.

66. Compare Watt, *Rise of the Novel;* Probyn, *English Fiction,* 12–15; and Browne, *Feminist Mind,* 8.

67. Margaret Kirkham, *Jane Austen, Feminism and Fiction* (New York: Methuen, 1986), 33. While valuably refining Watt's forty-year-old explanation for the rise of the novel, McKeon's *Origins of the Novel* shears off virtually any consideration of women. Fortunately, Hunter's *Before Novels* restores it. The case for naming Burney "Frances" is made by Margaret Anne Doody, *Frances Burney: The Life in the Works* (Cambridge: Cambridge University Press, 1989).

68. Burney, *Evelina: or, The History of a Young Lady's Entrance into the World* (Oxford and New York: Oxford University Press, 1982 [1778]), 3–5; Diary entries quoted in Edward A. Bloom and Lillian D. Bloom, "Introduction," Burney, *Evelina,* vii–viii. Discussing *Pamela,* Armstrong writes that "the progressive empowerment of individual merit leads in the end to the radical case of women," *Domestic Fiction,* 380.

69. Mary Hays, *Memoirs of Emma Courtney* (London: Pandora Press, 1987 [1796]), 119. Hays here is heavily influenced by William Godwin.

70. Jane Austen, *Northanger Abbey* (New York: Penguin, 1985 [1818]), 57–8.

71. Austen, *Northanger Abbey,* 58.

72. Christopher Hill, *Reformation to Industrial Revolution* (Harmondsworth, Middx.: Penguin, 1969), 171; Fielding, *Tom Jones,* 35–6; Richardson, *The History of Sir Charles Grandison,* in 3 vols. (London: Oxford University Press, 1974 [1753–4]), 1:331; McKendrick, "Commercialization of Fashion," 95, 46; Porter, *Eighteenth Century,* 241; David, *The English Kitchen,* 8; Shammas, *Pre-industrial Consumer,* 216; Armstrong, *Domestic Fiction,* 70, 71.

73. Earle, *English Middle Class,* 285; no. 42 (12 March 1710/11), 1:44, Wollstonecraft, *Rights of Woman,* 170; Samuel Richardson *The History of Sir Charles Grandison,* 3 parts (London: Oxford University Press, 1972 [1753]), 1:331.

74. McKendrick, "Home Demand," 202; quotation from McKendrick, "The Commercialization of Fashion," 95; Mandeville, *Fable of the Bees,* 1:138. Wollstonecraft discusses why women were more addicted to clothing than men, *Rights of Woman,* 170.

75. Mandeville, *Fable of the Bees,* 1:128.

76. Elizabeth Wilson suggests that the mass production of industrial capitalism "made possible the use of fashion as a means of self-expression for the majority," reminding us at the same place that the price for this democratization of fashion has been "the world-wide exploitation of largely female labor." *Adorned in Dreams: Fashion and Modernity* (Berkeley and Los Angeles: University of California, 1987), 12.

77. Mandeville, *Fable of the Bees,* 1:226.

78. Mandeville, *Fable of the Bees,* 1:225–6; Laslett, *World We Have Lost,* 73.

79. Defoe quoted in Langford, *Polite and Commercial People,* 101; Borsay, *Urban Renaissance,* 151–62. Writing of London, 1660–1730, Earle suggests that women had "considerable freedom to move alone about the city and to go to public places where they were likely to meet men." *English Middle Class,* 193.

80. Langford, *Polite and Commercial People,* 109; see too Earle, *English Middle Class,* 193.

81. Langford, *Polite and Commercial People,* 109, 101.

82. Shammas describes the difficulty of this issue, *Pre-industrial Consumer,* 180, 188, 210, 266, 298. As Bennett reminds us, many contingencies—of necessity and the particularities of each marriage—"fit poorly with the expectation of male authority and female dependence." *Women of the Medieval English Countryside,* 9. See too Wrightson, *English Society,* 92–104.

83. Wollstonecraft, *Rights of Woman,* 159; Mandeville, *Fable of the Bees,* 1:226–228.

84. Mandeville, *Fable of the Bees,* 1:228; Fielding, *Tom Jones,* 745.

85. Golby and Purdue, *Civilization of the Crowd,* 141; Peter Clark, *The English Alehouse: A Social History 1200–1830* (London: Longman, 1983), 148, 156; Louise A. Tilly and Joan W. Scott, *Women, Work and Family* (New York: Holt,

Rinehart and Winston, 1978), 136–40; Shammas, "Domestic Environment," 19–20; Meyer, *Sex and Power,* 271.

86. *A Trip through the Town* quoted in McKendrick, "Commercialization of Fashion," 60; Earle, *English Middle Class,* 220; Thomas Taylor, *A Vindication of the Rights of Brutes,* (Gainesville, Fla.: Scholars Facsimiles and Reprints, 1966 [1792]), vi–vii, Mandeville, *Fable of the Bees,* 1:129; see too McKendrick, "Commercialization of Fashion," 55.

87. Collett's painting is reproduced as plate 8 in Weatherill, *Consumer Behaviour,* 140; *The World* quoted in McKendrick, "Commercialization of Fashion," 54; Wollstonecraft, *Rights of Woman,* 252, 260, and see 170.

88. McKendrick, "Consumer Revolution," 25, 14; McKendrick, "Commercialization of Fashion," 55, 95, 96, 116, and passim; Porter, *Eighteenth Century,* 87, 240; Browne, *Feminist Mind,* 35; see too Harold Perkin, *The Origins of Modern English Society, 1780–1880* (London and Henley: Routledge and Kegan Paul, 1969), 91–4. Advancing the significance of Latitudinarian psychology's evolving into sensibility and "autonomous hedonism," Colin Campbell has challenged this emphasis on social emulation in *The Romantic Ethic and the Spirit of Modern Consumerism* (Oxford and New York: Basil Blackwell, 1987), 17–24. Weatherill, too, expresses doubts about its adequacy as an explanation, *Consumer Behaviour,* 20, 81, 194–6. It is not incompatible with other motives. Sugar, tobacco, and caffeine indicate that one of them was addiction.

89. Jean J. Hecht, *The Domestic Servant Class in Eighteenth-Century England* (London: Routledge and Kegan Paul, 1956), 200–228; McKendrick, "Consumer Revolution," 21–2; see too Golby and Purdue, *Civilisation of the Crowd,* 49; Rendall, *Modern Feminism,* 180n.; Borsay, *Urban Renaissance,* 312–3.

90. McKendrick, "Commercialization of Fashion," 59–60, 49, 60; Golby and Purdue, *Civilisation of the Crowd,* 140; Hecht, *Domestic Servant Class,* 200; Nottingham quotation in Porter, *English Society,* 237; Shammas, *Pre-industrial Consumer,* 137.

91. Langford, *Polite and Commercial People,* 118; Borsay, *Urban Renaissance,* 293; Perry, *Astell,* 263–4.

92. For example, Fielding, *The Life of Jonathan Wild, the Great* (New York: New American Library, 1960 [1743]), 87; Henry MacKenzie, *The Man of Feeling* (London: Oxford; New York: Oxford University Press, 1970 [1771]), 108–9.

93. Richardson, *Clarissa,* 4:423; Fielding, *Tom Jones,* 229–300, esp. 244; Smollett, *Humphry Clinker,* 58, and see 211; Montagu quoted in Borsay, *Urban Renaissance,* 228; Langford, *Polite and Commercial People,* 101.

94. Smollett, *Humphry Clinker,* 52; McKendrick, "Commercialization of Potteries," 141–2, and see "Commercialization of Fashion," 71; Porter, *Eighteenth Century,* 206; McKendrick, "Commercialization of Fashion," 46; Sophia quoted in Jerome Nadelhaft, "The Englishwoman's Sexual Civil War: Feminist Attitudes towards Men, Women, and Marriage, 1650–1740," *Journal of the History of Ideas* 43 (October 1982), 570; Wollstonecraft, *Rights of Woman,* 176.

95. "A Letter from Artemiza in the Towne to Chloe in the Countrey," *The Poems of John Wilmot, Earl of Rochester,* ed. Keith Walker (Oxford: Basil Blackwell, 1984), 85.

96. Rachel Pengelly's account book quoted in Weatherill, *Consumer Behaviour,* 127; Porter, *Eighteenth Century,* 241, 209; McKendrick, "Commercialization of Fashion," 95; for a careful discussion of the influence of towns on consumption see Weatherill, *Consumer Behaviour,* 89, and ch. 4, passim.

97. *Connoisseur* quoted in Porter, *Eighteenth Century,* 241; Fielding, *Tom Jones,* 147.

98. Byng quoted in Porter, *Eighteenth Century,* p. 243. For Stubbs, see McKendrick's discussion in "Commercialization of Fashion," 61–2, which persuasively dismisses John Barrell's reading of this picture in his *The Dark Side of the Landscape: The Rural Poor in English Painting, 1730–1840* (Camridge: Cambridge University Press, 1980), 25, 31. Barrell also finds the country women in Gainsborough's "Cottage with Children Playing" "surrisingly well turned out" (70). Nonetheless, Barrell's larger interpretation of the representation of peasants in eighteenth-century painting is sugestive.

99. Perkins, *Origins of Modern English Society,* 94; Porter, *Eighteenth Century,* 85–6; Golby and Purdue, *Civilisation of the Crowd,* 31; for illustrations of the presence of harpsichords, pianos, novels, and other signs of culture in aspiring households see Miller, "Women's Education," 309, 310; see too George Eliot's 1856 reference to this presence in the households of "tenant-farmers and small proprietors" of "half a century ago" in "The Natural History of German Life," *Westminster Review* (July 1856), in *Selected Essays, Poems and Other Writings,* ed. A. S. Byatt and Nicholas Warren (New York: Penguin, 1990), 113.

100. Terry Castle, *Masquerade and Civilization: The Carnivalesque in Eighteenth-Century English Culture and Fiction* (Stanford: Stanford University Press, 1986), 2, 9–10.

101. Ibid., 27; Richardson, *Clarissa,* 1:501; see too 4:544; Castle herself shows that regular, weekly masquerades were embedded in the new commercial and literate apparatus of London. *Masquerade,* 2, 9–10, 3.

102. Castle, *Masquerade,* 100, 27, 11, 85.

103. Ibid., 41–2, 48; Natalie Zemon Davis, "Women on Top," *Society and Culture in Early Modern France* (Stanford: Stanford University Press, 1975), 136–7.

104. Castle, *Masquerade,* 34; Elizabeth Robins Pennell, *Mary Wollstonecraft* (Boulton: Roberts Brothers, 1884), 108.

105. Critics quoted in Castle, *Masquerade,* 46, 39.

106. Ibid., 44, 45, 51, 53, 41.

107. Ibid., 63, 96. This may have been a mockery, a double-masquerade, as it were. Smollett in *Humphry Clinker* describes an all-male club of "cawdies" in Edinburgh—errand boys and pimps—giving a dinner and a ball, to which they invited young noblemen, gentlemen, and "celebrated ladies of pleasures," where the cawdies ran the proceedings. At the end the toastmaster declared, "Now we're your honours cawdies again" (228–30). This does seem

to be a modernized version of the reversals in Feast of Fools / Lords of Misrule tradition.

108. Castle, *Masquerade,* 92–4.

109. Ibid., 77.

110. John Trenchard and Thomas Gordon, *Cato's Letters,* no. 17 (18 February 1720), in David L. Jacobson, *The English Libertarian Heritage: From the Writings of John Trenchard and Thomas Gordon* (Indianapolis: Bobbs-Merrill, 1965), 55; Castle, *Masquerade,* 2; Fielding and Foster quoted in McKendrick, "Consumer Revolution," 24–5, 11. Simon Schama paints a similar picture of "cultural fusion" in Paris in the last decades of the ancien regime, under the impress of fashion and consumption. *Citizens: A Chronicle of the French Revolution* (New York: Knopf, 1989), 133–7.

111. Smollett, *Humphry Clinker,* 96.

112. Wilson, *Adorned in Dreams,* 9–10; McKeon, *Origins of the Novel,* 374.

113. Castle, *Masquerade,* 77, 104. Following in the footsteps of Mikhail Bakhtin, Castle asserts that the waning of the masquerade in the 1780s and 1790s was an expression of the general victimization of the carnivalesque by industrial capitalism and its production of class consciousness. The masquerade succumbed to the "rationalist ideology" of individualism, finished off by the efforts of moral reformers, who helped impose an "ideology of respectability." *Masquerade,* 101. For an historian's very severe criticism of Bakhtin's representation of history (in his *Rabelais and His World*), see Richard M. Berrong, *Rabelais and Bakhtin: Popular Culture in Gargantua and Pantagruel* (Lincoln: University of Nebraska Press, 1986). Berrong's account of Bakhtin's use of social history as a mask wherewith to criticize Stalinist representations of the folk is drawn from Katerina Clark and Michael Holquist, *Mikhail Bakhtin* (Cambridge: Harvard University Press, 1984). See Berrong, *Rabelais and Bakhtin,* 105–9.

114. Maria Edgeworth, *Belinda* (London, Boston, and Henley: Pandora, 1986 [1801]), 51, 36, 27, 150, 151, 91.

115. Richardson, *Sir Charles Grandison,* 1:168; Fielding, *Tom Jones,* 605ff; Elizabeth Inchbald, *A Simple Story* (London and New York: Pandora, 1987 [1791]), 139; Edgeworth, *Belinda,* 16–17, 55, 33, 50, 107.

116. Austen, *Northanger Abbey,* 58.

117. Fielding, *Tom Jones,* 298; Charlotte Lennox, *The Female Quixote or The Adventures of Arabella* (London: Pandora, 1986 [1752]), 373, 165; Inchbald, *Simple Story,* 13; Fiennes quoted in Borsay, *Urban Renaissance,* 170.

118. Smollett, *Humphry Clinker,* 48–9, 50, 57–8, 99–7, 100–102; Borsay also calls the Bath of this period a "consumer's paradise." *Urban Renaissance,* 35.

119. Burney, *Evelina,* 24, 37, 178.

120. Ibid., 57, 37, 38–9, 36–7.

121. Ibid., 36, 11, 243, 24–6, 27.

122. Ibid., 179, 392–3.

123. Borsay, *Urban Renaissance,* 243–8; Langford, *Polite and Commercial People,* 113–6; Earle, *English Middle Class,* 185–98, esp. 186–7. See too Stone, *Family, Sex and Marriage,* 274–81, 316–7.

124. Edgeworth, *Belinda,* 27–8; McKendrick, "George Packwood and the Commercialization of Shaving: The Art of Eighteenth-Century Advertizing or 'The Way to Get Money and Be Happy,'" in McKendrick et al., *Birth of Consumer Society,* 147; see too Edgeworth, *Belinda,* 298.

125. Smith, *Reason's Disciples,* 3; Anne Finch, Countess of Winchilsea, *Selected Poems,* ed. Katherine Rogers (New York: Frederick Ungar, 1979), 5; Chudleigh quoted in Smith, *Reason's Disciples,* 64, 134. A fine and late representation of the transcience of a woman's beauty is Rowlandson's colored drawing *Gilding the Lily* (c. 1800–10), first exhibited in 1984. It is reproduced in John Hayes, *The Art of Thomas Rowlandson* (Alexandria, Va.: Art Services International, 1990), plate 76.

126. Maureen Mulvihill, "Makin[s], Bathsua," in Janet Todd, *A Dictionary of British and American Writers 1660–1800* (London: Methuen, 1987), 207–9; Bathsua Pell Makin, "An Essay to Revive the Antient Education of Gentlewomen," extracted in Ferguson, *First Feminists,* 129, 138, 137. Hunter points out that the concern for women's education "permeated all segments of society well before Locke," and "Locke was in fact uttering mostly commonplaces of educational theory." *Before Novels,* 270. The determinative assumption was environmental psychology, which also preceded Locke, as I pointed out in Ch. 1.

127. Makin, "Revive Education," 134, 135, 130, 137, 139, 138, 136.

128. Ibid., 139, 140, 141, 130, 139.

129. Ibid., 140, 138, 141, 140, 141.

130. Perry, *Astell,* 14; Smith, *Reason's Disciples,* 117. The frequency of my citations of it expresses my indebtedness to Perry's fine biography of Astell.

131. Perry, *Astell,* 54, 61, 148, 210, chap. 8 passim.

132. Ibid., 73, 221–8; Perry, "Mary Astell and the Feminist Critique of Possessive Individualism," *Eighteenth-Century Studies* 23, no. 4 (Summer 1990): 444–57.

133. Astell, "A Serious Proposal to the Ladies," in Ferguson, *First Feminists,* 182; Rogers, *Feminism,* 80.

134. Quoted in Smith, *Reason's Disciples,* 125; Astell, "Serious Proposal," 195; Astell also accepted Newton's argument for the existence of God, Perry, *Astell,* 11–2.

135. Norris quoted in Perry, *Astell,* 138; Perry, *Astell,* 50, 51.

136. Perry, *Astell,* 91, 19; *The Tatler* quoted in Perry, *Astell,* 229. (The writer of a "Ladies Supplement" to *A Gentleman Instructed* [1753] declared that "ill education" was the "fatal Source of their Misery, the true Origin of all their Failings. Young Ladies are brought up as if God created 'em meerly for a Seraglio, and that their only Business was to charm a brutish *Sultan:* One would think they had no Souls, there is such a care taken for their Bodies," quoted in Hunter, *Before Novels,* 269). Here is the origin of "passionlessness," the feminist rationale for sexual puritanism detected later in the century by Nancy F. Cott, "Passionlessness: An Interpretation of Victorian Sexual Ideology, 1790–1850," in *A Heritage of Her Own,* ed. Cott and Elizabeth H. Pleck (New York: Simon and Schuster, 1979), 162–82. See too Perry, *Astell,* 160.

137. Perry, *Astell,* 142, 160. See Rogers, *Eighteenth-Century Feminism,* 71–80.

138. Astell, "Serious Proposal," 186; Perry, *Astell,* 146, 144.

139. Perry, *Astell,* 48–9, 137, 82.

140. Ibid., 124, 127, 123, 24, 88, 323.

141. Ibid., 168–9, 60, 21.

142. Mandeville, *Virgin Unmask'd,* 107–11, 113, 20–2, 115. See Richard I. Cook, *Bernard Mandeville* (New York: Twayne Publishers, 1974), 59.

143. Astell quoted in Smith, *Reason's Disciples,* 75; esp. 73; Dudley North, *Discourses upon Trade* quoted in McKendrick, "Consumer Revolution," 15.

144. Perry, *Astell,* 66–9, 63; Smith, *Reason's Disciples,* 24; Perry, *Astell,* 64, 246.

145. Perry, *Astell,* 296, 287–8, 315, 288; Browne, *Feminist Mind,* 34. Compare Simon Schama, *The Embarrassment of Riches: An Interpretation of Dutch Culture in the Golden Age* (Berkeley: University of California Press, 1988), 310.

146. Perry, *Astell,* 305–8, 245–7.

147. Earle, *English Middle Class,* 173–4; Langford, *Polite and Commercial People,* 572–4.

148. Borsay, *Urban Renaissance,* 249. Schama supplies evidence for women's appetite to play in lotteries in the seventeenth-century Dutch capitalist culture. *Embarrassment of Riches,* 307–10.

149. Borsay, *Urban Renaissance,* 250 (here, as well as for the quotations by Steele and "Mrs. C's Complaint for the Loss of the Ace of Hearts" in a 1741 number of the *Bath Miscellany,* I am very much in Professor Borsay's debt); Fanny Burney, *Camilla: or, A Picture of Youth* (Oxford: Oxford University Press, 1983 [1796]), 687.

150. McKeon writes of Haywood's *Philidore and Placentia* (1727) that it shows "insight into the analogous pathologies of exchange value and sexual libertinage." *Origins of the Novel,* 262.

151. Richardson, *Clarissa,* 4:537–41; for the eighteenth-century association between warmth and a woman's sexual arousal see Thomas Laqueur, "Orgasm, Generation and the Politics of Reproductive Biology," *Representations,* no. 14 (Spring 1986): 10–11, 13.

152. Richardson, *Sir Charles Grandison,* 1:191; Shammas, *Pre-industrial Consumer,* 225; Richardson, *Clarissa,* 4:553.

153. Fielding, *Tom Jones,* 29; and see 429; Fielding, *Jonathan Wild,* 70; Lennox, *Female Quixote,* 295, 313; Smollett, *Humphry Clinker,* 43–7, 66.

154. Smollett, *Humphry Clinker,* 66, 320; see too 101–2; Inchbald, *A Simple Story,* 36; Thomas Day, *History of Sandford and Merton* (Philadelphia: n.p., n.d. [1783–9]), 33, 330, and see 331, 211, 327; Clara Reeve, *Plans of Education: With Remarks on the Systems of Other Writers* (New York: Garland Publishing, 1974 [1792]), 70, 47.

155. Smollett, *Humphry Clinker,* 95; see too Fielding, *Jonathan Wild,* 111; Fielding, *Tom Jones,* 390; MacKenzie, *Man of Feeling,* passim; and Day, *Sandford and Merton,* 241. See James Sambrook, *The Eighteenth Century: The Intellectual and Cultural Context of English Literature, 1700–1789* (London: Longman, 1986), 78–79; Janet Todd, *Sensibility: An Introduction* (London: Methuen, 1986), 14.

156. Schama, *Embarrassment of Riches,* 447, 433. See Mary Douglas, *Purity and Danger: An Analysis of the Concepts of Pollution and Taboo* (London: Routledge and Kegan Paul, 1966).

157. Richardson, *Clarissa,* 4:501; Fielding, *Tom Jones,* 624, 631–2.

158. Mrs. Barbauld to John Aikin, 19 January 1778, Barbauld, *Works,* 2:19; Wollstonecraft, *Original Stories from Real Life: With Conversations Calculated to Regulate the Affections and Form the Mind to Truth and Goodness* (n.p.: Folcroft Library, n.d. [1788]), 21); Wollstonecraft, *Rights of Woman,* 169.

159. Wollstonecraft, *Rights of Woman,* 151, 310, 315, 170, 306, 315, 81, 145, 147–8, 81, 260, 158, 152, 179, 156n.

160. Langford, *Polite and Commercial People,* 601–3, 607, 606, and plates 11(a), 11(b); Patricia Meyer Spacks, "Ev'ry Woman Is at Heart a Rake," *Eighteenth-Century Studies* 8 (1974): 43; More quoted by Langford, *Polite and Commercial People,* 607. Describing the reaction to fashionable, self-assertive women in seventeenth-century Holland, Schama points out that "the battle of the trousers" "echoed ancient refrains in Renaissance and Reformation antifeminism" and appeared "in almost all northern European popular literature in the sixteenth as well as the seventeenth century." The "partition of worlds was of such paramount importance within Dutch culture *and* gender roles so often threatened with a blurring ambiguity that it may have cut particularly deep notches on the collective psyche of Dutch men." *Embarrassment of Riches,* 447–8.

161. John Brewer, "Commercialization and Politics," in *Birth of Consumer Society,* by McKendrick et al., 200.

162. Sambrook, *Eighteenth Century,* 168; *The Universal Spectator* quoted in James T. Boulton's introduction to Burke's *A Philosophical Enquiry into the Origin of our Ideas of the Sublime and Beautiful* (Notre Dame: University of Notre Dame Press, 1958 [1757]), xxvii.

163. *Universal Spectator* quoted in McKendrick, "Commercialization of Fashion," 53–5; Shammas, *Pre-industrial Consumer,* 219–20.

164. Richardson quoted in McKeon, *Origins of the Novel,* 414; David Hume, "Of the Standard of Taste," in *Essays, Moral, Political, and Literary,* ed. T. H. Green and T. H. Grose, 2 vols. (London: Longmans, Green, 1875) 1:273, 274; Ronald Paulson, *Breaking and Remaking: Aesthetic Practice in England, 1700–1820* (New Brunswick: Rutgers University Press, 1989), 168–92.

165. Suggestive in this regard are Carole Fabricant, "Binding and Dressing Nature's Loose Tresses: The Ideology of Augustan Landscape Design," in *Studies in Eighteenth-Century Culture,* vol. 8, ed. Roseanne Runte (Madison: University of Wisconsin Press, 1979); and Doody, "Deserts, Ruins and Troubled Waters: Female Dreams in Fiction and the Development of the Gothic Novel," *Genre* 10, no. 4 (Winter 1977): 529–72.

166. Wollstonecraft, *Original Stories,* 29; Anne Radcliffe, *The Mysteries of Udolpho* (Oxford: Oxford University Press, 1980 [1794]), 40, 98, 139, 166.

167. Radcliffe, *Udolpho,* 49 (see too Radcliffe, *The Romance of the Forest* [London: W. Nicholson, n.d. (1791)],5); Wollstonecraft, *Original Stories,* 22, 23; Radcliffe, *Udolpho,* 190.

168. Bennet quoted in Porter, *Eighteenth Century,* 325; Schama, *Embarrassment of Riches,* 82; Wollstonecraft, *Rights of Woman,* 221, 162, 112, 153.

169. For *The Compleat Housewife,* see Armstrong, *Domestic Fiction,* 82; Richardson, *Clarissa,* 4:417, 420, 424–5.

170. Smollett, *Humphry Clinker,* 25, 66–7.

171. Inchbald, *Simple Story,* 213; Radcliffe, *Udolpho,* 119, 94–5, 97.

172. Hays, *Emma Courtney,* 157; Austen, *Mansfield Park* (New York: New American Library, 1979 [1814]), 120–1. Recognizing the point, Armstrong quotes exactly the same kind of passage from Gaskell's *Mary Barton* (1848), *Domestic Fiction,* 87.

173. McKendrick, "Commercialization of Fashion," 47 and n.41.

174. MacKenzie, *Man of Feeling,* 8; Edgeworth, *Belinda,* 387; *Saturday Review* and *Spectator* quoted under "Cambric" in the OED.

175. McKendrick, "Commercialization of Fashion," 76; McKendrick, "Josiah Wedgewood and the Commercialization of the Potteries," in *Birth of a Consumer Society,* by McKendrick et al., 100–145; Langford, *Polite and Commercial People,* 661.

176. McKendrick, "Commercialization of Fashion," 76.

177. Ibid., 76; Wedgewood quoted in Langford, *Polite and Commercial People,* 666.

178. Boulton quoted in Borsay, *Urban Renaissance,* 258; E. P. Thompson, "Time, Work-Discipline, and Industrial Capitalism," in *Essays in Social History,* ed. M. W. Flinn and T. C. Smout (Oxford: Clarendon Press, 1974), 57; Langford, *Polite and Commercial People,* 482–5; Gerald Cragg, *The Church and the Age of Reason, 1648–1789* (New York: Penguin, 1983), 129–34; F. K. Prochaska, *Women and Philanthropy in 19th Century England* (Oxford: Oxford University Press, 1980), passim. Reforming "the design of everyday consumer items" "embodied the ideal of social reform" in late nineteenth- and early twentieth-century France. Rosalind H. Williams, *Dream Worlds: Mass Consumption in Late Nineteenth-Century France* (Berkeley: University of California, 1982), 13, ch. 5. Of course, the renewal and spread of this hope at this time, accompanying the spread of manufacturing and mass marketing, was an international phenomenon, stretching from Vienna, through London, to New York.

179. Langford, *Polite and Commercial People,* 668, 659, 670–1.

180. Aileen Dawson, *Masterpieces of Wedgewood in the British Museum* (Bloomington: Indiana University Press, 1984), plate 13. Dickens referred to the familiarity of the figure and its motto which, he said, was "so often represented in tracts and cheap prints," *Martin Chuzzlewit* (New York: New American Library, 1965 [1843–4]), 308; Jean Fagan Yellin, *Women and Sisters: The Antislavery Feminists in American Culture* (New Haven: Yale University Press, 1988), 7, 10, 13, 5, 14, 15.

181. A good illustration in women's fiction is Evelina's response to Macartney, before she realizes he is in fact her blood brother. Burney, *Evelina,* 214.

182. Brewer, "Commercialization and Politics," 237, 241, 258, 239.

183. Yellin describes the sexual distinctions between the figures. *Women and Sisters,* 8–10.

184. Brewer, "Commercialization and Politics," 256.

Chapter 5. A Culture of Reform

1. Jane Spencer, *The Rise of the Woman Novelist: From Aphra Behn to Jane Austen* (Oxford: Basil Blackwell, 1986), 32.

2. A. R. Humphreys, "'The Friend of Mankind' (1700–1760)—An Aspect of Eighteenth-Century Sensibility," *Review of English Studies* 24 (1948): 203–18; R. F. Brissenden, *Virtue in Distress: Studies in the Novel of Sentiment from Richardson to Sade* (New York: Harper and Row, 1974), 29–30; Richard O. Allen, "If You Have Tears: Sentimentalism as Soft Romanticism," *Genre* 8 (1975): 125; Norman Fiering, "Irresistible Compassion: An Aspect of Eighteenth-Century Sympathy and Humanitarianism," *Journal of the History of Ideas* 37 (1976): 195–218; Christopher Lawrence, "The Nervous System and Society in the Scottish Enlightenment," in *Natural Order: Historical Studies of Scientific Culture,* ed. Barry Barnes and Steven Shapin (Beverly Hills and London: Sage, 1979), 27–33; John K. Sheriff, *The Good-natured Man: The Evolution of a Moral Ideal, 1660–1800* (University: University of Alabama Press, 1982), 16–17; Jay Fliegelman, *Prodigals and Pilgrims: The American Revolution against Patriarchal Authority, 1750–1800* (Cambridge and New York: Cambridge University Press, 1982), 25–6; Charlotte Lennox, *The Female Quixote: or, The Adventures of Arabella* (London: Pandora, 1986 [1752]), 421; Anne Radcliffe, *The Mysteries of Udolpho* (Oxford: Oxford University Press, 1980 [1794]), 29, 229, 195, 308.

3. Samuel Richardson, *The History of Sir Charles Grandison,* 3 vols. (London: Oxford University Press, 1972 [1753–4]), 1:277; Mary Hays, *Memoirs of Emma Courtney* (London: Pandora, 1987 [1796]), 120, 82.

4. Maria Edgeworth, *Belinda* (London: Pandora, 1986 [1801]), 197; Henry Fielding, *The History of Tom Jones, a Foundling* (New York: New American Library, 1963 [1749]), 652, 851; Spencer, *Rise of Woman Novelist,* 21; Henry MacKenzie, *The Man of Feeling* (London: Oxford University Press, 1970 [1771]), 70; Radcliffe, *Udolpho,* 672; Edgeworth, *Belinda,* 196–7.

5. Richardson quoted in *The Letters of Doctor George Cheyne to Samuel Richardson* (1733–43), ed. Charles F. Mullett, University of Missouri Studies 18, no. 1 (Columbia: University of Missouri Press, 1943), 81–2n.76; Richardson, *Clarissa: or, The History of a Young Lady* (London: J. M. Dent, 1932 [1748]), 4:60; MacKenzie, *The Man of the World* (London: Routledge, n.d. [1773]), 300.

6. Edgeworth, *Belinda,* 215, and see 84; Beth Kowaleski-Wallace, "Home Economics: Domestic Ideology in Maria Edgeworth's *Belinda*" (unpublished paper), 21, 18. Kowaleski-Wallace quotes a male expert of 1803 who uses terms typical of the criticism of the willfully consuming "woman of the world" to condemn women's not breast-feeding: "Women, enervated by luxury, allured by a false taste for mistaken pleasure, and encouraged by shameless example, are eager to spend the time thus gained from the discharge of duty in dissipation or indolence."

7. Fielding, *The Life of Jonathan Wild, the Great* (New York: New American Library, 1961 [1743]), 142–50; Fielding, *Tom Jones,* 610–2; Elizabeth Inchbald, *A Simple Story* (London: Pandora, 198 [1791]), 233–4; Wollstonecraft,

Original Stories from Real Life: With Conversations, Calculated to Regulate the Affections, and Form the Mind to Truth and Goodness (n.p.: Folcroft Library Editions, n.d. [1788]), 29; illustrations of scenes of reconciliation are Inchbald, *Simple Story*, ch. 11; Fielding, *Tom Jones*, 389; and Tobias Smollett, *The Expedition of Humphry Clinker* (New York: New American Library, 1960 [1771]), 174.

8. Edgeworth, *Belinda*, 197; Jerry C. Beasley, *Novels of the 1740s* (Athens: University of Georgia Press, 1982), 75; see too G. A. Starr, "'Only A Boy': Notes on Sentimental Novels," *Genre* 10 (1977): 501–27; Richardson, *Clarissa*, 3:505; Adam Smith, *The Theory of Moral Sentiments*, ed. D. D. Raphael and A. L. MacFie (Indianapolis: Liberty Classics, 1979 [1759]), 40; Fanny Burney, *Evelina: or, The History of a Young Lady's Entrance into the World* (Oxford: Oxford University Press, 1968 [1778]), 164.

9. Radcliffe, *Udolpho*, 444ff. Compare J. M. S. Tompkins, *The Popular Novel in England, 1770–1800* (Westport, Conn.: Greenwood Press, 1963), 148; Allen, "Tears," 128, 139; Janet M. Todd, *Sensibility: An Introduction* (London: Methuen, 1986), 85; John Mullan, *Sentiment and Sociability: The Language of Feeling in the Eighteenth Century* (Oxford: Clarendon Press, 1988), 213.

10. Todd, *Sensibility*, 97; Richardson, *Clarissa*, 4:9; Combe quoted in Paul Langford, *A Polite and Commercial People: England 1727–1783* (Oxford: Clarendon Press, 1989), 465; MacKenzie, *Man of Feeling*, 75, 61, 62, 87–98, 31.

11. Compare Donald Meyer, *Sex and Power: The Rise of Women in America, Russia, Sweden, and Italy* (Middletown, Conn.: Wesleyan University Press, 1987), 274.

12. Fielding, *Tom Jones*, 561.

13. Richardson, *Clarissa*, 3:64; Burney, *Evelina*, 259, 267; Gamini Salgado, "Introduction," in *Three Restoration Comedies* (Baltimore: Penguin, 1968), 21, 30. Patricia Meyer Spacks makes the same point in connection with Burney's *Cecilia* (1782) and *Camilla* (1796), "Ev'ry Woman Is at Heart a Rake," *Eighteenth-Century Studies* 8 (1974), 29, 30, and 31.

14. Mary Wollstonecraft to Gilbert Imlay, 23 September [1794], *The Collected Letters of Mary Wollstonecraft*, ed. Ralph M. Wardle (Ithaca: Cornell University Press, 1979), 264.

15. Richardson, *Sir Charles Grandison*, 1:96; Burney, *Evelina*, 131; Radcliffe, *Udolpho*, 155; Hays, *Emma Courtney*, 130; Fielding, *Joseph Andrews* and *Shamela* (Boston: Houghton Mifflin, 1961), 154, 155; Richardson, *Pamela: or, Virtue Rewarded* (New York: Norton, 1950 [1740]), 483, 252, 253; Lennox, *Female Quixote*, 101; Edgeworth, *Belinda*, 193, 174; Hays, *Emma Courtney*, 99, 47.

16. Lennox, *Female Quixote*, 5, 7; MacKenzie, *Man of the World*, 155–6; Radcliffe, *Udolpho*, 2, 11, 12, 465.

17. Todd, *Sensibility*, 95; *The Works of Anna Laetitia [Aikin] Barbauld*, 2 vols. (London: Longman Hurst, Rees, Orme, Brown, and Green, 1825), 1:168–72; Inchbald, *Simple Story*, 191; Radcliffe, *Udolpho*, 591, 113; William Godwin, *Memoirs of Mary Wollstonecraft*, ed. and retitled by W. Clark Durant (New York: Haskell House, 1927 [1798]), 14.

18. Wollstonecraft, *Letters Written during a Short Residence in Sweden, Norway, and Denmark* (Lincoln and London: University of Nebraska, 1976 [1796]), 59;

Philipe Ariès is the authority here, in *The Hour of Our Death,* trans. Helen Weaver (New York: Vintage, 1982), ch. 8, and passim. See, too, David Stannard, ed., *Death in America* (Philadelphia: University of Pennsylvania Press, 1975), 25–26, and Jean Starobinski, "Burying the Dead," *New York Review of Books* 32, nos. 21, 22 (16 January 1986),20.

19. Clive Probyn, *English Fiction of the Eighteenth Century, 1700–1789* (London and New York: Longman, 1987), 156; Brissenden, *Virtue in Distress,* 79–86, and ch. 3; Langford, *Polite and Commercial People,* 485, 492ff; Tompkins, *Popular Novel in England,* 142; Moira Ferguson and Janet Todd, *Mary Wollstonecraft* (Boston: Twayne, 1984), 60; see too Mona Scheuerman, *Social Protest in the Eighteenth-Century English Novel* (Columbus: Ohio State University Press, 1985).

20. Winthrop Jordan, *White over Black: American Attitudes toward the Negro, 1550–1812* (Baltimore: Penguin 1969), 368–72; Alice Browne, *The Eighteenth Century Feminist Mind* (Brighton, Sussex: Harvester, 1987), 129–30; Langford's summary of the dawning British opposition to racism and slavery is in his chapter entitled, "The Birth of Sensibility," *Polite and Commercial People,* 516–8; Wollstonecraft, *Vindication of the Rights of Woman* (New York: Penguin, 1975 [1792]), 257, and see 117 and 121. Wollstonecraft's work, suffused with "Commonwealth" thought, and the constant references in the writings of women throughout the eighteenth century, makes it crystal clear that their representation of themselves as "slaves" to men was derived from classical thought. Thence women carried it to their opposition to race slavery in the modern world.

21. John Howard, *The State of the Prisons* (London: J. M. Dent, 1929 [1777]); D. L. Howard, *John Howard: Prison Reformer* (New York: Archer House, 1963). Compare Jean Fagan Yellin, *Women and Sisters: The Antislavery Feminists in American Culture* (New Haven: Yale University Press, 1989), 18.

22. Jordan, *White over Black,* 370–1; Claudia L. Johnson, review of Janet Todd, *Sensibility: An Introduction* (1986), *Eighteenth-Century Studies* 21, no. 1 (Fall 1988): 112. It may have been the case that "to focus attention on simple folk and to idealize them at least prepares the way and provides materials for more adequate social criticism," but "the link between the cult of feeling and genuine social concern is not a necessary or universal one." William Stafford, *Socialism, Radicalism, and Nostalgia: Social Criticism in Britain, 1775–1830* (Cambridge: Cambridge University Press, 1987), 46, 43.

23. For a recent discussion of the motives of humanitarian men see the three articles by David Brion Davis, John Ashworth, and Thomas L. Haskell in a special issue of the *American Historical Review* 92, no. 4 (October 1987), 797–879.

24. Aphra Behn, *Oronooko: or, The Royal Slave* (New York: W. W. Norton, 1973 [1688]), 57; Brissenden, *Virtue in Distress,* 32; Burney, *Evelina,* 13, 53, 122–3, 216–7, and see 225; Inchbald, *Simple Story,* 257; Radcliffe, *Udolpho,* 267; Wollstonecraft, *Rights of Woman,* 159, 191, 295, and see 157. "Benevolence" was also a quality long trumpeted by the culture of sensibility as a facet of its opposition to Hobbesian selfishness and hard-heartedness. Ernest Lee Tuveson, *The Imagination as a Means of Grace: Locke and the Aesthetics of Roman-*

ticism (New York: Gordian Press, 1974 [1960]), 162. For the origins of the term "benevolence" see Fliegelman, *Prodigals and Pilgrims,* 101; and for the distinction between "benevolence" and "sympathy" see Mullan, *Sentiment and Sociability,* 29n.33; see too Todd, *Sensibility,* 91.

25. Richardson, *Pamela,* 183; Brissenden, *Virtue in Distress,* 20; Radcliffe, *Udolpho,* 194, 46; Wollstonecraft, *Rights of Woman,* 219–20; see too Hays *Emma Courtney,* 120, 82.

26. For example Michael McKeon, *The Origins of the English Novel 1600–1740* (Baltimore: Johns Hopkins University Press, 1987), 256, 287.

27. Richardson, *Clarissa,* 4:152; Wollstonecraft, *Rights of Woman,* 80.

28. Madame de Cambon, *Young Grandison: A Series of Letters from Young Persons to their Friends, Trans. from the Dutch, with Alterations and Improvements* [the latter, not the translation, by Wollstonecraft], 2 vols (London: J. Johnson, 1790); Stafford, *Socialism,* 44; Pat Rogers, "The Writer and Society," ch. 1 of *The Context of English Literature: The Eighteenth Century,* ed. Rogers (London: Methuen, 1978), 28; see too John Barrell, *The Dark Side of the Landscape: The Rural Poor in English Painting, 1730–1840* (Cambridge: Cambridge University Press, 1980), 76; Raymond Williams, *The Country and the City* (New York: Oxford University Press, 1973), 93; Tompkins, *Popular Novel,* 104.

29. Brooke quoted in Walter Francis Wright, *Sensibility in English Prose Fiction, 1760–1814: A Reinterpretation* (n.p.: Folcroft Press, 1970 [1937]), 41; Radcliffe, *Udolpho,* 28; see, too 3–4, 43, 40, 420. For scenes of tasteful simplicity, etc., see 500, 212, 472, 167–8. Describing Holman Hunt's 1852 painting, "The Hireling Shepherd," George Eliot said its peasants "were not much more real than the idyllic swains and damsels of our chimney ornaments." This still prevalent convention had been inherited from eighteenth-century literature.

> The notion that peasants are joyous, that the typical moment to represent a man in a smock coat is when he is cracking a joke and showing a row of sound teeth, that cottage matrons are usually buxom, and village children necessarily rosy and merry, are prejudices difficult to dislodge from the artistic mind, which looks for its subjects into literature instead of life. The painter is still under the influence of idyllic literature, which has always expressed the imagination of the cultivated and town-bred, rather than the truth of rustic life. ("The Natural History of German Life," *Westminster Review* [July 1856], in George Eliot, *Selected Essays, Poems and Other Writings,* ed. A. S. Byatt and Nicholas Warren [New York: Penguin, 1990], 108–9)

30. A scene from *Belinda* illustrates with these typical assumptions: from her guest room Belinda exclaims, "hark, there's the sound of music!" Lady Anne's maid, with ties to the local village, has told her mistress of a village wedding. Inevitably, the bride is "pretty," and cultists are able to bestow property on the bridal pair, in this case "a pretty little farm." "They looked out of the window, and they saw a troop of villagers, gaily dressed, going to the wedding, Lady Anne, who was always eager to promote innocent festivity, sent immediately to have a tent pitched in the park." Edgeworth, *Belinda,* 235.

31. See Brissenden, *Virtue in Distress,* 81; Todd, *Sensibility,* 31; Starr, "'Only a Boy,'" 513, 514.

32. Ian Watt, *The Rise of the Novel: Studies in Defoe, Richardson, and Fielding* (Berkeley: University of California Press, 1967 [1957]), passim; McKeon, *Origins of the Novel,* 19, 164–9, and passim; Langford, *Polite and Commercial People,* 460.

33. George Cheyne, *The English Malady,* . . . (Delmar, N.Y.: Scholars Facsimiles and Reprints, 1976 [1733]), iii; David Hume, "Of the Middle Station in Life," in *Essays, Moral, Political, and Literary,* ed. T. H. Green and T. H. Grose, 2 vols. (London: Longmans Green, 1875), 2:375–80; Wollstonecraft, *Rights of Woman,* 81; here Wollstonecraft may have been influenced by either Smith or by Joseph Priestley, with whose works she was also very familiar, Priestley being a close ally of Richard Price, one of Wollstonecraft's early mentors. But many held this view at the time. Roy Porter, *English Society in the Eighteenth Century* (Harmondsworth, Middx.: Penguin, 1982), 99.

34. Jeremy Taylor is quoted in Rita Goldberg, *Sex and Enlightenment: Women in Richardson and Diderot* (Cambridge: Cambridge University Press, 1984), 36; Sabbatarians quoted in W. P. Baker, "The Observance of Sunday," *Englishmen at Rest and Play: Some Phases of English Leisure 1558–1714,* ed. Reginald Lennard (Oxford: Clarendon Press, 1931), 79–144; Richardson, *Pamela,* 276, 387, 494–6; Richardson, *Clarissa,* 2:308, 395; 4:407, 408–9; see too Fielding, *Tom Jones,* 613–4.

35. Richardson, *Clarissa,* 4:425–6, 178; Richardson, *Pamela,* 494; Richardson, *Sir Charles Grandison,* 1:96; D. L. Howard, *Howard,* 27.

36. Wollstonecraft to Eliza W. Bishop, 5 November [1786], *Collected Letters,* 124; Wollstonecraft, *Original Stories,* 59–60; Hays, *Emma Courtney,* 154; Radcliffe, *Udolpho,* 583.

37. Hannah More, *Strictures on the Modern System of Female Education: With a View of the Principles and Conduct Prevalent among Women of Rank and Fortune,* vols. 7 and 8 of *The Works of Hannah More* (London: T. Caddell and W. Davies, 1818 [1799]), 8:32. Compare Nancy Armstrong, *Desire and Domestic Fiction: A Political History of the Novel* (New York: Oxford University Press, 1987), 93.

38. Laurence Sterne, *A Sentimental Journey through France and Italy* (Harmondsworth, Middx.: Penguin, 1967 [1768]), 142–4; Henry Mackenzie, *The Man of Feeling* and *The Man of the World* (London: Routledge, n.d. [1773]), 352–5; Wollstonecraft, *Original Stories,* 36–37; Thomas Day, *History of Sandford and Merton* (Philadelphia: n.p., n.d. [1783–9]), 296–7; Clara Reeve, *Plans of Education: With Remarks on the Systems of Other Writers* (New York: Garland, 1974 [1792]), 89; Radcliffe, *Udolpho,* 67–8, 616.

39. The title of ch. 4 of McKeon's *Origins of the Novel* is "The Destabilization of Social Categories"—to the categories he discusses must be added those of gender; Barrell, *Dark Side of the Landscape,* 16, 18, 20–1, 22, 59, 78–9, 85. See too Brissenden, *Virtue in Distress,* 238–9; Todd, *Sensibility,* 13, 83; Peter Burke, *Popular Culture in Early Modern Europe* (New York: Harper Torchbooks, 1978), 9–11, 18–19, 280–1.

40. Radcliffe, *Udolpho,* 207, 167–8; Edgeworth, *Belinda,* 223–5.

41. Keith Thomas, *Man and the Natural World: A History of the Modern Sensibility* (New York: Pantheon, 1983), 174–180, 181.

42. Thomas, *Natural World,* 154, 99, 183–4, 107; Wollstonecraft, *Rights of Woman,* 292, 284.

43. Thomas, *Natural World,* 191; MacKenzie, *The Man of Feeling* (Oxford: Oxford University Press, 1970 [1771]), 88; MacKenzie, *Man of the World,* 355; Radcliffe, *Udolpho,* 539.

44. Thomas, *Natural World,* 246, 251, 186.

45. J. H. Plumb, "The Acceptance of Modernity," in *The Birth of a Consumer Society: The Commercialization of Eighteenth-Century England,* by Neil McKendrick, John Brewer, and Plumb (Bloomington: Indiana University Press, 1982), 316–36; Simon Schama, *The Embarrassment of Riches: An Interpretation of Dutch Culture in the Golden Age* (Berkeley: University of California Press, 1988), 350–66.

46. Wollstonecraft, *Rights of Woman,* 120; for Cobbe in this regard see Richard D. French, *Antivivisection and Medical Science in Victorian Society* (Princeton: Princeton University Press, 1975), passim.

47. Cavendish quoted in Thomas, *Natural World,* 173, 170.

48. Thomas, *Natural World,* 128.

49. Cavendish quoted in Thomas, *Natural World,* 222, 128; Cavendish, "Philosophical and Physical Opinions," in *First Feminists: British Women Writers, 1578–1799,* ed. Moira Ferguson (Bloomington: Indiana University Press; and Old Westbury, New York: Feminist Press, 1985), 85.

50. Thomas, *Natural World,* 34, 125, 151, 147; Richardson, *Clarissa,* 2:328, 245–6, and see 2:23; Wollstonecraft, *Rights of Woman,* 292, 146. The belief that ill-treating animals had a brutalizing effect on men was ancient. Thomas, *Natural World,* 150.

51. Richardson, *Sir Charles Grandison,* 1:64; Richardson, *Pamela,* 134; MacKenzie, *Man of the World,* 189, 266; Fielding, *Tom Jones,* 88.

52. Richardson, *Sir Charles Grandison,* 1:64; Richardson, *Clarissa,* 1:350, 2:30, 55, and 160; Griffith quoted in Tompkins, *Popular Novel,* 160.

53. Radcliffe, *Udolpho,* 477, 16–7; Barbauld, *Works,* 1:39–46; Radcliffe, *Udolpho,* 16–7, 119; Burney, *Evelina,* 177, 175; Langford, *Polite and Commercial People,* 504.

54. See Ch. 2, n. 271.

55. Plumb, "New World of Children," 304, 302; Mitzi Myers, "Impeccable Governesses, Rational Dames, and Moral Mothers: Mary Wollstonecraft and the Female Tradition in Georgian Children's Books," in *Children's Literature* 14 ed. Francelia Butler, Margaret Higonnet, and Barbara Rosen (New Haven: Yale University Press, 1986): 31–59.

56. (London: Longman, 1798), review, *The Scientific Magazine and Freemason's Repository* 10 (June 1798), 404.

57. Trimmer, *History of the Robins* (New York: Garland Publishing, 1977 [1786]); Barbara Brandon Schnorrenberg, "Trimmer, Sarah [Kirby] 1741–1810," in *A Dictionary of British and American Women Writers, 1660–1800,* ed. Todd (London: Methuen, 1987), 306–7; Trimmer, *The Oeconomy of Charity: or, An Address to Ladies; Adapted to the Present State of Charitable Institutions in*

England, 2 vols. (London: J. Johnson and F. and C. Rivington, 1801 [1787]); Mary Wollstonecraft to Everina Wollstonecraft, 15 November 1787, *Collected Letters,* 166; Wollstonecraft, *Original Stories,* 45, and see 9.

58. Quoted in C. Beasley, *Novels of the 1740s,* 165; Burney, *Evelina,* 3–4. The same argument might be made of efforts to reform the treatment of children; Langford compares the appeal of animals to that of children, noting "their helplessness, their utter dependence on parental benevolence and enlightenment." *Polite and Commercial People,* 503.

59. Brissenden, *Virtue in Distress,* 121–2; see too Margaret Kirkham, *Jane Austen, Feminism and Fiction* (New York: Methuen, 1986), 13–4; Mary Poovey, *The Proper Lady and the Woman Writer: Ideology as Style in the Works of Mary Wollstonecraft, Mary Shelley, and Jane Austen* (Chicago: University of Chicago Press, 1984), 15.

60. Tompkins, *Popular Novel,* 147. Fliegelman, *Prodigals and Pilgrims,* passim. For this theme in the archetypal *Clarissa* see Probyn, *English Fiction,* 183–4.

61. Fielding, *Tom Jones,* 745; Fliegelman, *Prodigals and Pilgrims,* 36; Tompkins, *Popular Novel,* 84; Wollstonecraft, *Rights of Woman,* chs. 10 and 11. Suggesting that the father-daughter relationship "seems to have provided for many women the model of emotional satisfaction and safety." Spacks writes that this therefore expressed the wish "to retain the advantages of childhood," in effect contributing to female infantilization. "Ev'ry Woman Is at Heart a Rake," 45.

62. Lennox, *The Female Quixote,* 152; Richardson, *Pamela,* 349–53; the phrase "dark leep" is the eighteenth-century Massachusetts letter writer, Pamela Sedgewick's, quoted in Norton, *Liberty's Daughters,* 42; Edgeworth, *Belinda,* 122; Elizabeth Carter quoted in Katharine M. Rogers, *Feminism in Eighteenth-Century England* (Urbana: University of Chicago Press, 1982), 146; Hays, *Letters and Essays, Moral and Miscellaneous* (New York: Garland, 1974 [1793]), 30. Female "conduct books" made the same declaration of female mind; Armstrong, *Desire and Domestic Fiction,* ch. 2.

63. Watt, *Rise of the Novel,* 226; Richardson, *Clarissa,* 2:370 (and see 142, 147), 15, 400; 3:74; 2:403; Harris, *Richardson,* 99.

64. Richardson, *Clarissa,* 3:236; 2:16, 55–6, 273; 4:14–5; 3:149, 125.

65. Richardson, *Clarissa,* 2:41; 1:406; 2:488; Richardson, *Sir Charles Grandison,* 1:158; Burney, *Evelina,* 347; Smollett, *Humphry Clinker,* 312; Richardson, *Clarissa,* 2:147, 182.

66 Richardson, *Clarissa,* 2:396, 3:122.

67. Ibid., 3:181–3; 2:187–8.

68. Ibid., 2:39, 192–3. Only much later could women be able to declare "that the way to deal with Don Juan was not to attack sex." Meyer, *Sex and Power,* 188.

69. For example, Burney, *Evelina,* 110, 80, 343; Radcliffe, *Udolpho,* 144, 196, 198, 199, 200, 201, 210.

70. Mark Philp, *Godwin's Political Justice* (London: Duckworth, 1986), 177.

71. Burney, *Evelina,* 13, 195, 196, 197, 200, 201, Compare Louis C. Jones, *The Clubs of Georgian Rakes* (New York: Columbia University Press, 1942), 13.

72. Burney, *Evelina,* 231, 233–4. The detail of Gainsborough's "The Mall in St. James's Park" (1783), used to illustrate the cover of the World's Classics editions of *Evelina,* is well chosen, showing as it does a man lurking behind the trees framing several fashionably dressed young ladies walking there.

73. Burney, *Evelina,* 273, 275, 276.

74. Ibid., 141. For an account of this "frolick," see 147–50.

75. Ibid., 150, 151, 152; Radcliffe, *Udolpho,* 319.

76. Fielding, *Tom Jones,* 100, 255, 360, 259, 284. For castration in popular male leisure culture in Virginia, see Rhys Isaac, *The Transformation of Virginia, 1740–1790* (Chapel Hill: University of North Carolina Press, 1982), 95.

77. Fielding, *Tom Jones,* 284, 285; another male of the same type as Squire Western in *Tom Jones* was the brother of the Man of the Hill. The Man of the Hill, on the other hand, was a man of feeling, "compassionate," of "true learning and almost universal knowledge" who despised "the contemptible art" of sportsmen and was unacquainted with their "phrases." Fielding, *Tom Jones,* 397.

78. Smollett, *Humphy Clinker,* 319, 168–9; Oliver Goldsmith, *She Stoops to Conquer* (New York: Appleton-Century-Crofts, 1951 [1773]); see, for example, scene I and scene II, but the contrast pervades the play.

79. The phrase "that common race of country squires" is printed in the Norton edition of *The Man of Feeling* (1958), 39; the Oxford edition I have quoted elsewhere prints the second, corrected edition, substituting the phrase "that athletic order," 57; Sindall description in MacKenzie, *Man of the World,* 185–7.

80. Burney, *Evelina,* 287, 279, 290, 295; Burke, *Popular Culture,* 184.

81. Burney, *Evelina,* 295, 311–3.

82. Ibid., 288; Wollstonecraft, *Rights of Woman,* 187; Edgeworth, *Belinda,* 86.

83. Wollstonecraft, *Mary* and *The Wrongs of Woman* (Oxford and New York: Oxford University Press, 1980 [1788 and 1798]), 1; Day, *Sandford and Merton,* 18; Inchbald, *A Simple Story,* 214, 215, 216, 249.

84. William Godwin, *Caleb Williams* (London: Oxford University Press, 1970 [1794]), 86, 5, 10, 127, 9, 16, 17, 21.

85. Jane Austen, *Northanger Abbey* (New York: Penguin, 1985 [1818]), 66–67, 83, 85, 102.

86. Ibid., 47, 48, 49, 50.

87. Edgeworth, *Belinda,* 133, 135. The dissenting Edgeworth also shows the related type, "a buck parson," whose common practice was "to leap from his horse at the church door on a holiday, after following a pack of hounds, huddle on his surplice, and gabble over the service with the indecent mockery of religion." *Belinda,* 289.

88. Edgeworth, *Belinda,* 76, 77–8, 83, 80, 8, 79.

89. For Voltaire, "Le Mondain," and Mandeville, see Rosalind H. Williams, *Dream Worlds: Mass Consumption in Nineteenth-Century France* (Berkeley: University of California Press, 1982), 39–40; Fielding, *Tom Jones,* 205. Compare McKeon, *Origins of the Novel,* 202, 208.

90. Fielding, *Jonathan Wild,* 63, 34, 83, 121, 172, 66, 65. Compare William

Empson, "Tom Jones," in *Using Biography* (Cambridge, Mass.: Harvard University Press, 1984), 137, 143.

91. Fielding, *Jonathan Wild,* 73, 79, 216; Richardson, *Clarissa,* 3:32–40. The "modernity" of the man of the world is illustrated by Lovelace, who capitalized on his mastery of that world's attractions to women by using the masquerade to begin his successful seduction of Sally Martin. Lovelace embodied squire, rake, and man of the world. It may be true that, in certain respects, Lovelace was "an old-style libertine or Restoration relic," an aristocrat of the traditional landed class, a Filmerian in his politics, who resisted the "embourgeoisement" represented by Clarissa. Watt, *Rise of the Novel,* 227; Terry Eagleton, *The Rape of Clarissa: Writing, Sexuality and Class Struggle in Samuel Richardson* (Oxford: Blackwell, 1982), 90; Jocelyn Harris, *Samuel Richardson* (Cambridge: Cambridge University Press, 1987), 63. Lovelace expressed his contempt for "the dignity of trade in this mercantile nation." Richardson, *Clarissa,* 4:129. At the same time, however, Lovelace's city know-how, his consumer psychology, his pursuit of material pleasures, and his ability to manipulate and dissemble made him the embodiment of "the man of the world" according to the culture's own terms. If he was a "tyrannical Filmer," he "poses as a liberal Locke." Harris, *Richardson,* 63, and see 83 and 170. Richardson identified Lovelace's belief system explicitly with Mandeville's materialism and the advocacy of the pursuit of private vices. Lovelace knew he would have made "an admirable lawyer." He was, his friend Belford told him, a man "born for intrigue, full of invention, intrepid, remorseless, able to watch for any opportunity, not hurried as most men are by gusts of violent passion." *Clarissa,* 4:230–1; 2:159. William Warner's *Reading Clarissa: The Struggle of Interpretation* (New Haven: Yale University Press, 1979), interprets Lovelace as "a modern man, playing parts" (ch. 2, passim). Mr. B embodied the same combination, as McKeon observes in *Origins of the Novel,* 366.

92. MacKenzie, *Man of the World,* 200, 219–20, 221, 193; MacKenzie, *Man of Feeling,* 25; see too Smollett, *Humphry Clinker,* 306.

93. Radcliffe, *Udolpho,* 296, 243, 122, 362. John Graham makes the same observation of Charlotte Smith's *Desmond* (1792), noting that the contrast between the moral sign of one's face revealing one's emotions and the inexpressive face concealing a villainous heart was one made in many novels of the time. John Graham, "Lavater's Physiognomy in England," *Journal of the History of Ideas* 22 (1961): 568.

94. Radcliffe, *Udolpho,* 195–6, 267, 182, 395, 358, 182; Wollstonecraft, *Rights of Woman,* 143n.5, and see 144.

95. *The Fair Moralist* quoted in Beasley, *Novels of the 1740s,* 420; Burney, *Evelina,* 256.

96. Tompkins, *Popular Novel,* 131; Gerard A. Barker, *Grandison's Heirs in the Late Eighteenth-Century English Novel* (Newark: University of Delaware Press, 1985), 9.

97. Tompkins, *Popular Novel,* 130; Sheriff, *Good-natured Man,* 70.

98. Richardson quoted in Kirkham, *Feminism and Fiction,* 27.

99. Harris, *Richardson,* 125.

100. Ibid., 140.

101. See for example Richardson, *Clarissa,* 2:15; Fielding, *Tom Jones,* 551; Richardson, *Sir Charles Grandison,* 1:182. Howard contradicted the prereform traditions of working an animal to death or killing it once it was useless by insisting that his "horse must have his range when he is past his labour." D. L. Howard, *Howard,* 143.

102. Radcliffe, *Udolpho,* 8; Thomas Day, *History of Sandford and Merton* (Philadelphia: n.p., n.d. [1783–9]), 12; Burney, *Evelina,* 80; Fielding, *Tom Jones,* 161.

103. Burney, *Evelina,* 283, and see 96; Richardson, *Sir Charles Grandison,* 1:181.

104. Fordyce quoted in Alice Browne, *The Eighteenth Century Feminist Mind* (Brighton, Sussex: Harvester, 1987), 28–29.

105. MacKenzie, *Man of the World,* 237; Burney, *Evelina,* 125, 109; Mary Hays, *Emma Courtney,* 128; Barbauld, "Thoughts on Devotional Taste, and on Sects and Establishments," in *Works,* 2:234; Richardson, *Clarissa,* 2:236.

106. Fielding, *Tom Jones,* 138; Burney, *Evelina,* 330, 276.

107. Fielding, *Tom Jones,* 265; Radcliffe, *Udolpho,* 106; Richardson, *Clarissa,* 1:139; Burney, *Evelina,* 241, 34.

108. Margaret Ann Doody, "Deserts, Ruins, and Troubled Waters: Female Dreams in Fiction and the Development of the Gothic Novel," *Genre* 10, no. 4 (Winter 1977): 529; Edgeworth quoted in Browne, *Feminist Mind,* 29.

109. Beasley, *Novels of the 1740s,* 143.

110. Richardson, *Pamela, Or Virtue Rewarded* (New York: W. W. Norton, 1958 [1740]), 482, 382–3, 522, 449, 379, 371, 373, 371, 521.

111. Richardson quoted in Eagleton, *Rape of Clarissa,* 89; Tompkins, *Popular Novel,* 155.

112. Richardson, *Clarissa,* 4:389, "Preface," xv; 4:389. Lady Charlotte says it was "the envious, the censorious" who "malign" women by charging them with "the love of rakes and libertines." Richardson, *Sir Charles Grandison,* 1:291; see Harris, *Richardson,* for Richardson's conversion from *Pamela's* conclusion.

113. Richardson, *Clarissa,* 1:200; see too 3:335, 4:337. Even after Lovelace rapes her and she therefore refuses to marry him, Clarissa hopes for his reform; dying, she says, "Poor man . . . I once could have loved him . . . Would he have permitted me to have been a humble instrument to have made him good, I think I could have made him happy. But tell him not this if he be *really* penitent—it may too much affect him! . . . But pray tell him that if I could know that my death might be a means to reclaim and save him, it would be an inexpressible satisfaction to me!" (3:336, 4:306).

114. Harris, *Richardson,* 3:170; Richardson, *Clarissa,* 4:437, 444–5.

115. Fielding, *Jonathan Wild,* 35, 23; Smollett, *Humphry Clinker,* 175; Burney, *Evelina,* 274; Terry Castle, *Masquerade and Civilization: The Carnivalesque in Eighteenth-Century English Culture and Fiction* (Stanford: Stanford University Press, 1986), 64. Someone dressed as the devil mocked Wollstonecraft's party

at the masquerade Pennell claims she attended. Fuseli was provoked to tell him/her to "Go to Hell!" Elizabeth Robins Pennell, *Mary Wollstonecraft* (Boston: Roberts Brothers, 1884), 108.

116. Richardson, *Clarissa,* 3:219, 170; 2:461. Belford points out that Lovelace's "remorses" are "transient," 4:389. See Watt, *Rise of the Novel,* 236–7; Brissenden, *Virtue in Distress,* 185; Mullan, *Sentiment and Sociability,* 69ff.

117. Radcliffe, *Udolpho,* 366; see too Inchbald, *Simple Story,* 284.

118. Richardson, *Clarissa,* 2:477, 1:147.

119. Ibid., 2:155. See too MacKenzie, *Man of the World,* 184; Godwin, *Caleb Williams,* 16.

120. Richardson, *Clarissa,* 4:248; 2:159; 4:16, 248.

121. Ibid., 4:552, 147, 347.

122. Ibid., 4:389, 448–9, 8, 448.

123. Ibid., 4:389, 549, and see 447.

124. Fielding, *Tom Jones,* 118.

125. Ibid., 830–1, 833–4. In Empson's judgment, whether or not Tom Jones is a "libertine" is "a decisive question" in Sophia's mind. And by the end of the novel, Tom has become "a Gospel Christian." "Tom Jones," 146, 144.

126. MacKenzie, *Man of the World,* 421–2; see too Smollett, *Humphry Clinker,* 258.

127. Burney, *Evelina,* 176–7, 15, 338–40.

128. Ibid., 372, 383–7, 351.

129. Inchbald, *Simple Story,* 3, 17, 22, 11–2.

130. Ibid., 29, 100, 129, 148, 116.

131. Ibid., 171–2, 199.

132. Ibid., 236, 283.

133. Radcliffe, *Udolpho,* 292–5, 509, 515, 516; Hays, *Emma Courtney,* 110, 180.

134. Edgeworth, *Belinda,* 5–6, 113, 33–4, 113, 267, 256, 257, 258, 259, 294.

135. See "Introduction," n.10.

136. Donald Meyer, *The Positive Thinkers: Religion as Pop Psychology from Mary Baker Eddy to Oral Roberts* (New York: Pantheon, 1980), 67. The culture of sensibility was a transatlantic phenomenon. This has been assumed by, for example, Nancy Cott, in *The Bonds of Womanhood: "Woman's Sphere" in New England, 1780–1855* (New Haven: Yale University Press, 1977), ch. 5, as her sources demonstrate.

137. William Haller, *The Elect Nation: The Meaning and Relevance of Foxe's Book of Martyrs* (New York: Harper and Row, 1963), 52; Fliegelman, *Prodigals and Pilgrims,* 26; see too Todd, *Sensibility,* 4, 136; Mullan, *Sentiment,* 223–4; Todd, *Sensibility,* 136.

138. Steele quoted in McKeon, *Origins of the Novel,* 50; Johnson, *The Rambler,* no. 4 (31 March 1750), in *Selected Essays from the Rambler, Adventurer and Idler,* ed. W. J. Bate (New Haven: Yale University Press, 1968), 12; Kames quoted in Fleigelman, *Prodigals,* 214–5 Burke attributed the same power to words in *A Philosophical Enquiry into our Ideas of the Sublime and the Beautiful,*

ed. James T. Boulton (Notre Dame: University of Notre Dame Press, 1958 [1757]), 166, 175–6. See too Hugh Blair, *Critical Dissertation on the Poems of Ossian* (1763), quoted in Sambrook, *Eighteenth Century,* 125.

139. Fielding, *Tom Jones,* 243.

140. Beasley, *Novels of the 1740s,* chs. 1 and 5; "A.B.," "Letter," in *Man: A Paper for Ennobling the Species,* no. 43 (22 October 1755), 5; Inchbald, *Simple Story,* 246; MacKenzie, *Man of the World,* 307.

141. Richardson quoted in McKeon, *Origins of the Novel,* 414; Fielding, *Tom Jones,* 709, 554; Griffin quoted in Brissenden, *Virtue in Distress,* 160; Robert Darnton, "Readers Respond to Rousseau: The Fabrication of Romantic Sensitivity," *The Great Cat Massacre and Other Episodes in French Cultural History* (New York: Basic Books, 1984), 248, 249, 251–2. On the first page of his *Confessions,* Rousseau addresses God in a prayer-like declaration about the forthcoming revelations: "I have bared my secret soul, as Thou thyself hast seen it, Eternal Being!" He calls each of his readers to "reveal his heart at the foot of Thy throne with equal sincerity." As a young man, his "preference was for the ministry, for [he] fancied [himself] as a preacher." *The Confessions,* trans. J. M. Cohen (New York: Penguin, 1954 [1781]).

142. Fielding, *Tom Jones,* bk. 6, ch. 6; see too bk. 6, ch. 11, "A Short Chapter; But Which Contains Sufficient Matter to Affect the Good-natured Reader." Inchbald, *Simple Story,* 169; Lennox, *Female Quixote,* 54, 367.

143. Beasley, *Novels of the 1740s,* 145; Edward L. McAdams, Jr., "A New Letter from Fielding," *Yale Review* 38 (1948): 300–310. The characterizations "masculine" and "feminine" are Martin C. Battestin's; see his introduction to Fielding, *Joseph Andrews* and *Shamela* (Boston: Houghton-Mifflin, 1961), v.

144. Burney quoted in Mullan, *Sentiment and Sociability,* 141; Lady Louisa Stuart quoted in Brian Vickers introduction to *The Man of Feeling,* viii; Godwin, *Memoirs,* 84; see Darnton, "Readers Respond to Rousseau," 240–3, 248.

145. *The Anti-Jacobin Review,* passim; Browne, *Feminist Mind,* 69. Burke declared on behalf of Englishmen: "We are not the converts of Rousseau." *Reflections on the Revolution in France* (New York: Penguin, 1968 [1790]), 181.

146. Quoted by Probyn, *English Fiction,* 169.

147. Fielding, *Jonathan Wild,* 22; MacKenzie, *Man of Feeling,* 52; Browne, *Feminist Mind,* 66; Hays, *Emma Courtney,* 25, 59, 60–1, 120; Darnton, "Readers Respond to Rousseau," 235–41; Radcliffe, *Udolpho,* 175, 248.

148. Donnellan quoted in Watt, *Rise of the Novel,* 184; Richardson quoted in McKeon, *Origins of the Novel,* 416; Todd, *Sensibility,* 108–9; Mullan, *Sentiment,* 173; MacKenzie, *Man of the World,* 149; see too Harris, *Richardson,* 39.

149. Vivian de Sola Pinto, *Enthusiast in Wit: A Portrait of John Wilmot Earl of Rochester, 1647–1680* (London: Routledge and Kegan Paul, 1982), 19; Schama, *Citizens,* 157–8 (the owner of Ermenonville sometimes filled the estate "with rustics, trained to look jolly, disporting themselves in innocent pastimes and musical games"); Barbauld, "Devotional Taste," 244; Langford, *Polite and Commercial People,* 69; Godwin, *Essay on Sepulchres: or, A Proposal for Erecting Some Memorial of the Illustrious Dead in All Ages in the Spot Where Their*

Remains Have Been Interred (London: W. Miller, 1809). That this was a widespread impulse in Europe is illustrated by Ugo Foscolo's famous *Dei Sepolari* (1807) and placed in context by Starobinski, "Burying the Dead."

150. Sterne, *A Sentimental Journey through France and Italy* (New York: Penguin, 1907 [1768]), 141 (Brissenden quotes an apostrophe to Rousseau in a work indebted to Sterne—Francois Vernes, *Le voyageur sentimental, ou ma promenade à Yverdan* [1786], *Virtue in Distress,* 7); MacKenzie, "The Effects of Religion on Minds of Sensibility," *The Mirror,* nos 42, 43, and 44 (19–26 June 1779), *Works,* 479–89; MacKenzie, "Effects of Sentiment and Sentimentality on Happiness: From a 'Guardian,'" *The Mirror,* no. 101 (25 April 1780), *Works,* 504; Barbauld, "Devotional Taste," 243–4.

151. MacKenzie, *The Lounger,* no. 20 (18 June 1785), *Collected Works,* 8 vols. (Edinburgh: Constable, Creech, Manners and Miller; London: Cadell and Davies), 5:176–83.

152. Don Locke, *A Fantasy of Reason: The Life and Thought of William Godwin* (London: Routledge and Kegan Paul, 1980), plate X; Butler, *War of Ideas,* 107, 88 (and see Todd, *Sensibility,* ch. 4) (the Gillray cartoon is in the collection of prints at the Lewis Walpole Library, Farmington, Conn.); William Hazlitt, "Methodists," *Selected Writings,* ed. Ronald Blythe (New York: Penguin, 1970), 413–5, 413; Coleridge quoted in Sydney G. Dimond, *The Psychology of the Methodist Revival: An Empirical and Descriptive Study* (London: Oxford University Press, 1970), 117.

153. Langford has observed that sentiment "had a special appeal to middle-class England at a time of economic growth and rising standards of living," and he associates it with "gentility." *Polite and Commercial People,* 464. There still exist groups of readers with cultic values resembling those described. Dena Kleiman headed an article about them: "Societies Answer Yearnings of the Literary Soul," *New York Times* (3 April 1986), sec. c, 21. She wrote that they provided foci whereby "members can identify with their literary idols . . . secret friends, the type of confidantes who understand them in ways no one else could." The Ibsen Society of America publishes its "Credo" "dedicated" to maintaining "the living legacy" of Ibsen's "body of plays" and "the paradigm of his life," as a "generative force" in the American drama. Perhaps the expression of twentieth-century popular culture which can better suggest the power of the earlier consumer cult is that of popular music. Playable privately or in emotional congregations, it too generates its idols and devotees, and it is part of a larger culture in which gender ideals and sexual practices are in flux. See too Patrick Pacheco, "Fan Clubs—from Engelbert to Mr. Ed," Arts and Leisure Section, *New York Times* (4 November 1990), 1, 20–1.

154. Sheriff, *Good-natured Man,* 72; Haywood quoted in Beasley, *Novels of the 1740s,* 177. She is deliberately echoing Richardson's *Pamela,* 530.

155. Probyn, *English Fiction,* 17; Sambrook, *Eighteenth Century,* 278; Probyn, *English Fiction,* 23, 22.

156. Richardson, *Clarissa,* 4:389–90; Hays, *Emma Courtney,* 3–5; Darnton, "Readers Respond to Rousseau," 248; Wollstonecraft to Godwin, 1 July 1796, *Collected Letters,* (New York: Cornell University Press, 1979), 331.

157. Gregory quoted in Probyn, *English Fiction,* 169; Harris, *Richardson,* 51;

Radcliffe, *Udolpho,* 184; Rosaline, "The Birth of Sensibility: An Imitation," *London Magazine* 45 (1776), 194–5; Hays, *Emma Courtney,* 172.

158. Charles Scruggs, "Phillis Wheatley and the Poetical Legacy of Eighteenth Century England," *Studies in Eighteenth-Century Culture,* vol. 10, ed. Harry C. Payne (Madison: University of Wisconsin Press, 1981), 290; Anna Seward's *Elegy on Captain Cook* quoted by Langford, who wryly contrasts it with Cook's own expression of motive, "to go as far as man could possibly go," *Polite and Commercial People,* 515. Hannah More, "Sensibility, a Poem" (alternatively subtitled "A Poetical Epistle to the Hon. Mrs. Boscawen), in *Sacred Dramas, Chiefly Intended for Young Persons* (Philadelphia: Thomas Dobson, 1787 [1784]), 177–94; 180–1, 183, 186, 187, 179.

159. More "Sensibility," 180, 186, 180, 185, 187.

160. Todd, "Williams, Helen Maria (1761–1827)," in *A Dictionary of British and American Writers, 1660–1800,* ed. Todd (London: Methuen, 1987), 323–6; Helen Maria Williams, "To Sensibility," in *Poems,* 2 vols. (London: Thomas Cadell), 1–28. The phrase "life-long creed" is Deborah Kennedy's in "Storm of Sorrow: The Poetry of Helen Maria Williams" (paper delivered at the Annual Meeting of the Canadian Society for Eighteenth-Century Studies, Montreal, October 1989). The judgments, "fashionable" and "popular," are Todd's.

161. Wollstonecraft, *Rights of Woman,* 143–4. At this point Wollstonecraft touches the keenest difference between herself and Barbauld, their views of female sensibility, but it should be noted that their careers and views overlapped, too. They were both friends of their publisher, the dissenter Joseph Johnson, and they both were public supporters of the repeal of the Corporation and Test Acts at the same, crucial time, Wollstonecraft in her *A Vindication of the Rights of Man* (1790), and Barbauld in her "An Address to the Opposers of the Repeal of the Corporation and Test Acts" (1793) in *Works,* 2:353–78. Wollstonecraft quoted Barbauld's "Thoughts on Devotional Taste" in the preface to her 1789 anthology, *The Female Reader . . . Selected for the Best Writers . . . from the Improvement of Young Women,* published by Johnson and wished by him to be modeled in a similar work for young men published by another dissenter, William Enfield, a friend of Barbauld and her family (Wollstonecraft to Johnson [July 1788]), *Collected Letters,* 179). Wollstonecraft said Barbauld's essay did "honour to a female pen" and she included Barbauld's poem "Address to the Deity." Yet, despite endorsing Barbauld's views, Wollstonecraft also declared in *The Female Reader*'s "Preface" that we (women) must be free "to run the race ourselves, and by our own exertions acquire virtue," a view fundamental to the *Rights of Woman,* published three years later.

162. Barbauld, "The Rights of Woman," in *Works,* 1:185–7. The editor of her works, her niece, Lucy Aikin, arranged Barbauld's writings chronologically, and "The Rights of Woman," while undated, immediately followed a poem dated December 1792. I am grateful to Professor William McCarthy of Iowa State University for clarification of this point, which is supported by the evidence of the poem and Wollstonecraft's *Rights of Woman.* Professor McCarthy is preparing a complete scholarly edition of Barbauld's works.

163. Barbauld, "Rights of Woman," 185.

164. Margaret Maison, "'Thine, Only Thine!' Women Hymn Writers in Britain, 1760–1835," in *Religion in the Lives of English Women*, ed. Malmgreen, 12, 29, 12, 14, 15, 23, 26, 29, and 21.

165. Wesley quoted in Maurice Quinlan, *Victorian Prelude: A History of English Manners, 1700–1835* (Hamden, Conn.: Archon, 1961), 31; *Monthly Review* 18 (April 1773), 268, quoted in Brissenden, *Virtue in Distress*, 257. Scholars noting this resemblance include Alfred Kuhn in his "Introduction" to *Three Sentimental Novels* . . . (New York: Holt, Rinehart, Winston, 1970), ix; and Todd, *Sensibility*, 22–3.

166. Compare Isaac, *Transformation of Virginia*, 264.

167. Neil McKendrick, "The Consumer Revolution of the Eighteenth Century," in *The Birth of a Consumer Society: The Commercialization of Eighteenth-Century England*, by McKendrick, John Brewer, and J. H. Plumb (Bloomington: Indiana University Press, 1982), 16; Richard I. Cook, *Bernard Mandeville* (New York: Twayne, 1974), 133.

168. Gerald Cragg, *The Church and the Age of Reason, 1648–1789* (New York: Penguin, 1982), 153; Alan D. Gilbert, *Religion and Society in Industrial England: Church, Chapel, and Social Change, 1740–1914* (London: Longman, 1976), 83; Horton Davies, *Worship and Theology in England: From Watts and Wesley to Maurice, 1690–1850* (Princeton, Princeton University Press 1961), 159.

169. Quoted in Stuart Andrews, *Methodism and Society* (London: Longman, 1970), 45, and Dimond, *Methodist Revival*, 215; Isaac, *Transformation of Virginia*, 165.

170. David Hempton, *Methodism and Politics in British Society, 1750–1850* (Stanford: Stanford University Press, 1984), 14; see too Isaac, *Transformation of Virginia*, 172–3.

171. Wesley remarked that "persons pretended to see or feel what they did not" in responding to his sermons. Andrews, *Methodism*, 42.

172. Michael J. Crawford, "Origins of the Eighteenth-Century English Revival: England and New England Compared," *Journal of British Studies* (October 1987): 395.

173. Gilbert, *Religion and Society*, 56; MacArthur, *Economic Ethics*, 90; Cragg, *Church and the Age of Reason*, 149; Hempton, *Methodism and Politics*, 43.

174. Quoted in Stafford, *Socialism*, 87.

175. Wesley quoted in Cragg, *Church in the Age of Reason*, 147; Andrews, *Methodism*, 26, 34, 52, 36; Gilbert, *Religion and Society*, 56; John Vladimir Price, "Religion and Ideas," ch. 3 of *The Context of English Literature: The Eighteenth Century*, ed. Pat Rogers (London: Methuen, 1978), 138; Cragg, *Church and the Age of Reason*, 149; Kathleen Walker MacArthur, *The Economic Ethics of John Wesley* (New York: Abingdon Press, 1936), 92.

176. Cragg, *Church and the Age of Reason*, 147.

177. John Walsh, "Methodism and the Mob in the Eighteenth Century," *Studies in Church History: Popular Belief and Practice*, ed. G. J. Cuming and Derek Baker (Cambridge: Cambridge University Press, 1972), 218. See too Gilbert, *Religion and Society*, 73.

178. Wesley's *Journal* quoted in Andrews, *Methodism*, 105; see too Price, "Religion and Ideas," 138.

179. Quoted in Hempton, *Methodism and Politics,* 29.

180. Gilbert, *Religion and Society,* 52; W. R. Ward, "The Religion of the People and the Problem of Control, 1790–1830," *Popular Belief and Practice,* 253.

181. Thomas, "Women and the Civil War Sects," *Past and Present,* no. 13 (1958): 42–62; Christopher Hill, *The World Turned Upside Down: Radical Ideas during the English Revolution* (New York: Viking Press, 1972), ch. 15; Phyllis Mack, "Women as Prophets during the English Civil War," *Feminist Studies* 8 (1982):19–26. The life of Jane War Lead or Leade (1624–1704) illustrates the continuity of this tradition; see Katherine Rogers, *Feminism in Eighteenth-Century England* (Urbana: University of Illinois Press, 1982), 269.

182. Robert Glen, "Methodist Women Mocked in Eighteenth-Century England," Annual Meeting of the American Society for Eighteenth-Century Studies, Cincinnati, Ohio, April 1987; D. Colin Dews, "Ann Carr and the Female Revivalists of Leeds," ch. 4 of Malmgreen, *Religion in the Lives of Women,* 68–9, 84; Langford, *Polite and Commercial People,* 275; McKeon, *Origins of the Novel,* 76; Meyer, *Positive Thinkers,* 429.

183. Glen, "Methodist Women Mocked," 1; Dews, "Ann Carr," 70–71; for these and others see Earl Kent Brown, *Women of Mr. Wesley's Methodism* (New York: Edwin Mellen, 1983).

184. Dews, "Ann Carr," 79; Malmgreen, "Introduction," 9; Williams quoted in Dews, "Ann Carr," 82; Hempton, *Methodism and Politics,* 86–9; Ward, "Religion of the People," 238.

185. Hempton, *Methodism and Politics,* 14; Walsh, "Methodism and the Mob," 221; Isaac, *Transformation of Virginia,* 170; Andrews, *Methodism,* 105; Hempton, *Methodism and Politics,* 13; Paul Johnson, *A Shopkeepers' Millennium: Society and Revivals in Rochester, New York, 1815–1837* (New York: Hill and Wang, 1978), 108; Mary Ryan, *Cradle of the Middle Class: The Family in Oneida County, New York, 1790–1865* (New York: Cambridge University Press, 1981), ch. 2; Ian C. Bradley, *The Call to Seriousness: The Evangelical Impact on the Victorians* (New York: Macmillan, 1976), 46ff.; Leonore Davidoff and Catherine Hall, *Family Fortunes: Men and Women of the English Middle Class, 1780–1850* (London: Hutchinson, 1987), 123–6; Hempton, *Methodism and Politics,* 14; Currie et al., *Church and Churchgoers,* 46. And Sunday School children could rope parents into evangelism, too. Gilbert, *Religion and Society,* 57.

186. J. M. Golby and A. W. Purdue, *The Civilisation of Crowd: Popular Culture in England, 1750–1900* (New York: Schocken, 1985), 140–1, 178–9; Louise A. Tilly and Joan W. Scott, *Women, Work and Family* (New York: Holt, Rinehart and Winston, 1978), 138–41. Anglican seating arrangements separating women from men could have contributed to the changes in self-conception encouraged by the sermons. Thomas, *Religion and the Decline of Magic* (New York: Scribners, 1971), 152.

187. John Redwood, *Reason, Ridicule, and Religion: The Age of Enlightenment in England 1660–1750* (Cambridge, Mass.: Harvard University Press, 1976), 19; Malmgreen, "Introduction," 1–2.

188. Scholars who have used the phrase the "feminization of religion" include Malmgreen, "Introduction," 2; and Spencer, *Rise of the Woman Novelist,* xi. Rita Goldberg addresses the issue in her analysis of *Clarissa* in *Sex and*

Enlightenment, ch. 1. Her "Afterword" acknowledges her debt on the score of "feminization" to Ann Douglas, *The Feminization of American Culture* (New York: 1977), to which must be added Barbara Welter, "The Feminization of American Religion: 1800–1860," ch. 6 of her *Dimity Convictions: The American Woman in the Nineteenth Century* (Athens: Ohio University Press, 1976), the chapter first published in 1973. See too Cott, *The Bonds of Womanhood,* 132. Richard Shiels entitled a piece "The Feminization of American Congregationalism, 1730–1835," *American Quarterly* 33 (1981): 46–62. Spencer also uses the phrases "feminization of culture" as well as "feminization of literature" in *Rise of the Woman Novelist,* xi; Todd, *Sensibility* refers to the "feminization of culture," 43; and Eagleton, in *The Rape of Clarissa,* refers to a "deep-seated feminization of values throughout the eighteenth century," 13–14. Armstrong heads one section of her chapter on "The Rise of the Domestic Woman," "The Power of Feminization," *Desire and Domestic Fiction,* 88.

189. Brown, *Women of Mr. Wesley's Methodism,* xi; Hempton recognizes both that "the role of women is virtually unrecorded and that "there were probably more women than men in eighteenth-century Methodism," *Methodism and Politics,* 13; Malmgreen, *Religion in the Lives of Women,* 2, 9–10n.5. A few statistics pointing in the same direction for 1739–43 are in Dimond, *Methodist Revival;* of his 234 cases, 69 recorded gender; 44 were female, 25 male, (128); Gilbert, *Religion and Society,* 67. Unfortunately the compendious Robert Currie, Alan Gilbert, and Lee Horsley, *Church and Churchgoers: Patterns of Church Growth in the British Isles since 1700* (Oxford: Clarendon Press, 1977) ignores women almost entirely—it mentions them on 72.

190. Hempton, *Methodism and Politics,* 14; Clive Field, "The Social Structure of English Methodism: Eighteenth-Twentieth Centuries," *British Journal of Sociology* 28, no. 2 (1977): 202.

191. Langford, *Polite and Commercial People,* 275.

192. Walpole quoted in Andrews, *Methodism,* 112; Glen, "Methodist Women Mocked," passim; Dews, "Ann Carr," 69, 79; Wollstonecraft, *Rights of Woman,* 225.

193. In *Tom Jones,* Fielding showed an upper-class, fashionable woman-about-town being converted and thereby revolutionized in manners and morals (617). Smollett insisted on Methodism's particular attractiveness to women of all ranks: housemaids, a housekeeper, townswomen, country-gentry, and an aristocrat. He shows, too, Tabitha Bramble leaning on her housemaids to become Methodists like her. He suggests a relationship between the immersion of Lydia Melford in sentimental fiction and her attraction to Methodist "enthusiasm" and depicts the conversion to Methodism of a gaoler's wife and "silly old women." *Humphry Clinker,* 144, 156–60, 141, 151, 143, and see 14. When she was sick and vulnerable, Edgeworth's aristocratic and fashionable Londoner, Lady Delacour, found herself susceptible to "the early impressions made on her mind in her childhood, by a methodistical mother." Edgeworth, *Belinda,* 246–7, and ch. 22.

194. Hempton, *Methodism and Politics,* 129; Currie et al., *Church and Churchgoers,* 71; Malmgreen, "Introduction," 7. Ward, "The Religion of the People,"

and Michael Hennell, "Evangelicalism and Worldliness, 1770–1870," *Popular Belief and Practice,* 229–36, both point to the reestablishment of gender orthodoxy; see too Davidoff and Hall, *Family Fortunes,* 106, 119; One Methodist male said of a Methodist woman preacher in 1810, "I believe she will prove to be a witch." Quoted in Ward, "The Religion of the People," 241. The acceptance of women preachers by Methodist males had always varied greatly from locality to locality. As Wesleyanism purged women preachers, Wesleyan women moved into the leadership of Primitive Methodism and successfully resisted the attempts of male preachers to control their preaching. There were other well-known female leaders of popular religions who continued the Protestant preaching tradition into the nineteenth century, notably, Mary Evans, Mrs. Buchan, and Joanna Southcott. J. F. C. Harrison, *The Second Coming: Popular Millenarianism, 1780–1850* (New Brunswick, N.J.: Rutgers University Press, 1979), 29, 31–3, ch. 5; Dews, "Ann Carr," 72, 71, 76, 71, 80–1, 84.

195. Andrews, *Methodism,* 76; Hempton, *Methodism and Politics,* 13; V. K. Kiernan, "Evangelicalism and the French Revolution," *Past and Present,* no. 1 (1952–3), 45–46; Andrews, *Methodism,* 71; F. K. Prohaska, *Women and Philanthropy in Nineteenth-Century England* (Oxford: Clarendon Press, 1980), 26, 73–9.

196. She was at the time the unmarried Anna Laetitia Aikin. She had received a very similar education to the male students whom Warrington Academy prepared for the dissenting ministry, because her father and her brother (her future husband was also a pupil) were, respectively, a teacher and a pupil there, although she received that education privately, at home. Barbauld became a kind of self-appointed theologian of the cult of sensibility—her "Thoughts on Devotional Taste" was complemented by her other writings, notably her "An Inquiry into Those Kinds of Distress Which Excite Agreeable Sensations," in *Works,* 2:214–1, as well as the poem, "The Rights of Woman," discussed above. Brian Vickers calls Barbauld the "theorist" of "the cult of distress" in his introduction to *The Man of Feeling,* x.

197. Barbauld, "Devotional Taste," 232–46, 235.

198. Ibid., 232, 233.

199. Ibid., 240, 232, 245–6, 235, 234, 242, 253, 242.

200. Ibid., 237, 240–1, 238, 232–3, 240.

201. Ibid., 239, 232, 234, 246.

202. Armstrong reaches comparable conclusions from a very different direction. *Desire and Domestic Fiction,* 23–4, 89, 100.

203. Plumb, "New World of Childhood," 303; Peter Earle, *The Making of the English Middle Class: Business, Society and Family Life in London, 1660–1730* (London: Methuen, 1989), 237.

204. Meyer, *Sex and Power,* 271; again, compare Armstrong, *Desire and Domestic Fiction,* 3, 125.

205. Carole Shammas, "The Domestic Environment in Early Modern England and America," *Journal of Social History* 11, no. 1 (1980): 3–24; 4, 18–19.

206. Judith M. Bennett, *Women in the Medieval English Countryside: Gender and Household in Brigstock before the Plague* (New York: Oxford University Press

1987), 45; Cheyne, *Letters to Richardson*, 81–2n.76; Richardson, *Clarissa*, 1:2, 11, 357; 4:442–3; Anon, *The Rake: or, The Libertine's Religion* (London: R. Taylor, 1693); Anthony, Earl of Shaftesbury, *Characteristics of Men, Manners, Opinions, Times*, 2 vols. (Indianapolis: Bobbs-Merrill, 1964 [1711]), 1:321–3; Bernard Mandeville, *The Fable of the Bees: or, Private Vices, Publick Benefits*, 2 vols. (Oxford: Clarendon Press, 1924), 1:144, 76, 250.

207. Hays, *Emma Courtney*, 6, 8–10; Wollstonecraft, *Mary*, 4; Edgeworth, *Belinda*, 33–4; Inchbald, *A Simple Story*, 4, 36, 83–4, 17.

208. Norton, *Liberty's Daughters*, 95; *Female Government* quoted in Langford, *Polite and Commercial People*, 606; Day, *Sandford and Merton*, 19, 311–3, 329, 331–2, 342 (it is Tommy's father who initiates his son's restoration to manhood, 20–1); Jane Rendall, *The Origins of Modern Feminism: Women in Britain, France, and the United States, 1780–1860* (Houndsworth, Hants: MacMillan, 1985), ch. 2.

209. Wollstonecraft, *Rights of Woman*, 274–5, 161, 298.

210. Ibid., 319, 156, 108–9, 298, 132, 319n.3, and see 102–3.

211. Ibid., 80, 265 (and see 254, 313); See too Browne, *Feminist Mind*, 5.

212. Wollstonecraft, *Rights of Woman*, 86.

213. Ibid., 86–7; M. M. Goldsmith, *Private Vices, Public Benefits: Bernard Mandeville's Social and Political Thought* (Cambridge: Cambridge University Press, 1988), ch. 1; Barker-Benfield, "Mary Wollstonecraft: Eighteenth-Century Commonwealthwoman," *Journal of the History of Ideas* 50 (1989): 95–115; Wollstonecraft, *Rights of Woman*, 251. Schama suggests that the cult of sensibility played an important part in the "construction" of a French citizen. *Citizens*, 145–62.

214. Wollstonecraft, *A Vindication of the Rights of Men in a Letter to the Right Honourable Edmund Burke . . .* (Gainesville, Fl.: Scholars' Facsimiles and Reprints, 1960 [1790]), 136–7; Wollstonecraft, *Rights of Woman*, 156.

215. Wollstonecraft, *Rights of Woman*, 291, 292, 80. She also criticized women who paraded their "sensibility" for maltreated animals while keeping their own coachmen and horses waiting outside in terrible weather for hours (292).

216. Wollstonecraft, *Rights of Woman*, 299, 293.

217. Ibid., 254–5, 266.

218. Ibid., 254.

219. Ibid., 254.

220. Ibid., 254, 255. Lorna Weatherill observes that washing and cleaning were "low-status" household activities, in *Consumer Behaviour and Material Culture in Britain 1660–1760* (London: Routledge, 1988), 149. Cf. Earl, *English Middle Class*, 222–3.

221. Godwin, *Memoirs*, 62.

222. Wollstonecraft, *Rights of Woman*, 255; Wollstonecraft, *Original Stories*, 22, 23.

223. Wollstonecraft, *Rights of Woman*, 255.

224. Ibid., 142.

225. Ibid., 142; Meyer, *Sex and Power*, 271.

Chapter 6. Women and Individualism: Inner and Outer Struggles over Sensibility

1. Norbert Elias, *Power and Civility: The Civilizing Process,* vol. 2, trans. Edmund Jephcott (New York: Pantheon, 1982 [1939]), 78–82; Elias, *The Court Society,* trans. Edmund Jephcott (New York: (New York: Pantheon, 1983), 243–4; Elias notes exceptional ladies, reared to warriorhood, becoming "viragos," "taking part in all the pleasures and dangers of the knights around" them, *Power and Civility,* 78–9.

2. Baldesar Castiglione, *The Book of the Courtier,* trans. George Bull (Hamondsworth, Middx.: Penguin, 1976), 13, 11. The festive and carnivalesque inversions of the sexual order in early modern Europe, whereby women were "on top" for a moment, probably expressed the same wish, although such reversals also can be seen merely to have "clarified" the unchallenged structure. Natalie Zemon Davis, "Women on Top," in *Society and Culture in Early Modern France* (Stanford: Stanford University Press, 1975), 124–51. One might refer, too, to the influence of salons in seventeenth-century France, the "extension of the institutionalized court which, since the early sixteenth century, had accorded royal women positions of leadership in matters of taste and pleasure." Carolyn C. Lougee, *Le paradis des femmes: Women, Salons, and Social Stratification in Seventeenth-Century France* (Princeton: Princeton University Press, 1976), 5. Established by the "wives and mistresses" of nobles and the higher reaches of the bourgeoisie, the salon was extremely important to the "civilizing process." Rosalind M. Williams, *Dream Worlds: Mass Consumption in Late Nineteenth-Century France* (Berkeley: University of California Press, 1982), 36.

3. Castiglione, *Courtier,* 255, 210–2, 214–6.

4. Ibid., 211–2, 213.

5. Michael McKeon, *The Origins of the English Novel, 1600–1740* (Baltimore: Johns Hopkins University Press, 1987), 158, 156 (compare J. Paul Hunter, *Before Novels: The Cultural Contexts of Eighteenth-Century Novels* (New York: Norton, 1990), 271–2; Samuel Richardson, *Clarissa: or, The History of a Young Lady,* 4 vols. (London: J. M. Dent, 1932 [1748]), 2:392; Dr. Armstrong quoted in Paul Langford, *A Polite and Commercial People: England, 1727–1783* (Oxford: Clarendon Press, 1987), 120. Rogers's novel quoted in J. M. S. Tompkins, *The Popular Novel in England, 1770–1800* (Westport, Conn.: Greenwood Press, 1976 [1961]), 124–5.

6. Mary Poovey, *The Proper Lady and the Woman Writer: Ideology as Style in the Works of Mary Wollstonecraft, Mary Shelley, and Jane Austen* (Chicago: University of Chicago, 1984), 20; Hunter, *Before Novels,* 264 (Hunter suggests *The Ladies Calling* and *The Gentlemans Calling* were by Richard Allestree); Nancy Armstrong, *Desire and Domestic Fiction: A Political History of the Novel* (Oxford: Oxford University Press, 1987), 61.

7. *Ladies Calling* quoted in Poovey, *Proper Lady,* 20; Armstrong, *Desire and Domestic Fiction,* 67; *The Spectator,* no. 217 (8 November 1711), in *The Spectator,* by Joseph Addison, Richard Steele, et al. 8 vols. (London: T. Hamilton and

R. Ogle, 1808), 3:201–2; for "delicatesse" see Elias, *The History of Manners: The Civilizing Process,* vol. 1 (New York: Pantheon, 1978), 115–6, where he describes the relationship between "eating and speech." See too Arthur M. Wilson, "Sensibility in France in the Eighteenth Century," *French Quarterly* 13 (1931):35–46.

8. Fordyce quoted in Alice Browne, *The Eighteenth Century Feminist Mind* (Brighton, Sussex: Harvester, 1987), 34; Lady Mary Wortley Montagu quoted in McKeon, *Origins of the Novel,* 41; the Northern expression quoted in Roy Porter, *English Society in the Eighteenth Century* (Harmondsworth, Middx.: Penguin, 1982), 24; Adam Smith, *The Theory of Moral Sentiments* (Indianapolis: Liberty Press, 1979 [1759]), 308; Tobias Smollett, *The Expedition of Humphry Clinker* (New York: New American Library, 1960 [1771]), 46.

9. Mrs. Thrale quoted in Browne, *Feminist Mind,* 155; the *Gentleman's Magazine* quoted in Maurice Quinlan, *Victorian Prelude: A History of English Manners, 1700–1830* (Hamden, Conn.: Archon Books, 1965 [1941]), 66–7; Mary Anne Radcliffe quoted in Browne, *Feminist Mind,* 133.

10. Wollstonecraft, *Vindication of the Rights of Woman* (New York: Penguin, 1975 [1792]), 229n, 234n, 235, and 235n. See too her introduction to her translation of Christian Gotthilf von Salzmann, *Elements of Morality* (London: Joseph Johnson, 1790).

11. Wollstonecraft, *Rights of Woman,* 231, 230n, 229, 231, 139, 109, 121, and see 120 and 139.

12. Ibid., 160, 247, 228, 234, 235; Wollstonecraft, *Original Stories from Real Life* (n.p.: Folcroft Library, 1972 [1788]), 32 (and see Patricia Meyer Spacks, "Ev'ry Woman Is at Heart a Rake," *Eighteenth-Century Studies* 8 [1974]: 39; review of *Vindication of the Rights of Woman . . . Critical Review* in 2 parts, N.S. 4 (1792):389–98; N.S. 5 (1792), 137, 139.

13. Henry Fielding, *The History of Tom Jones, a Foundling* (New York: New American Library, 1963 [1749]), 230; Maria Edgeworth, *Belinda* (London: Pandora, 1986 [1801]), 39; John Gregory, *A Father's Legacy to His Daughters* (London: W. Strahan and T. Cadell, 1774), 83; Richardson, *Pamela: or, Virtue Rewarded* (New York: W. W. Norton, 1950 [1740]), 74, 302–3; Fielding, *Joseph Andrews* and *Shamela* (Boston: Houghton Mifflin, 1961), 70–2; Fielding, *Tom Jones,* 148–52; see K. D. M. Snell, *Annals of the Labouring Poor: Social Change and Agrarian England* (Cambridge: Cambridge University Press, 1985), ch. 1; Roy Porter, *English Society in the Eighteenth Century* (Harmondsworth, Middx.: Penguin, 1982), 46.

14. Brooke quoted in Walter Frances Wright, *Sensibility in English Prose Fiction, 1760–1814: A Reinterpretation* (n.p.: Folcroft Press, 1970 [1937]), 40; Carole Shammas, *The Pre-industrial Consumer in England and America* (Oxford: Clarendon Press, 1990), 137–45.

15. Neil McKendrick, "The Commercialization of Fashion," in *The Birth of a Consumer Society: The Commercialization of Eighteenth-Century England,* by McKendrick, John Brewer, and J. H. Plumb, (Bloomington: Indiana University Press, 1982), 34–98; 59, 82. McKendrick, "George Packwood and the Commercialization of Shaving: The Art of Eighteenth-Century Advertizing or 'The Way to Get Money and Be Happy,' in *Birth of a Consumer Society,* by

McKendrick et al., 185, 184. Packwood, the manufacturer of razor strops and a paste to accompany them and a pioneer of advertising techniques, suggested that ladies spread his reputation "in gratitude for the comfort they enjoy by their lovers and husband's beards being so closely shorn." McKendrick, "Packwood," 162. "Personal appearance was central to the pursuit of status. A well-shaped body provided a useful foundation, particularly in the case of a woman, but of far greater importance were the garments and accessories adorning it." Peter Borsay, *The English Urban Renaissance: Culture and Society in the Provincial Town, 1660–1770* (Oxford: Clarendon Press, 1989), 237.

16. Cynthia Griffin Wolff, *Samuel Richardson and the Eighteenth-Century Puritan Character* (Hamden, Conn.: Archon Books, 1972), 4–54; Rita Goldberg, "Clarissa and the Puritan Conduct Books," ch. 1 of *Sex and Enlightenment: Women in Richardson and Diderot* (Cambridge: Cambridge University Press, 1984), 24–65; Richardson, *Clarissa,* 1:504; Clara Reeve repeated and endorsed John Gregory's words in her *The Progress of Romance* (1785), both quoted in Clive Probyn, *English Fiction of the Eighteenth Century 1700–1789* (London and New York: Longman, 1987), 169, 181n.26.

17. Ian Watt, *The Rise of the Novel: Studies in Defoe, Richardson, and Fielding* (Harmondsworth, Middx.: Penguin, 1958); Terry Eagleton, *The Rape of Clarissa: Writing, Sexuality and Class Struggle in Samuel Richardson* (Minneapolis: University of Minnesota Press, 1982), 3, 7–10; Colin Campbell, *The Romantic Ethic and the Spirit of Modern Consumerism* (New York: Basil Blackwell, 1987), 26; Armstrong, *Desire and Domestic Fiction,* 61, 67.

18. Richardson, *Clarissa,* 1:23; Fielding, *Tom Jones,* 672, 240.

19. Aphra Behn, *Oronooko: or, The Royal Slave* (New York: Norton, 1973 [1688]), 18.

20. Spacks, "Ev'ry Woman Is at Heart a Rake," 32; Jane Spencer, *The Rise of the Woman Novelist: From Aphra Behn to Jane Austen* (Oxford: Basil Blackwell, 1986), ch. 3; Wright, *Sensibility,* 59–60.

21. Fielding, *Tom Jones,* 255, 680, 250; Fielding was in fact the kind of character that we have seen Anne Donellan imagined, physically and verbally abusive, his cursing "as well-known as his dirtiness and his love of eating and drinking to excess," Fielding was an extravagant gambler and spendthrift. When Samuel Foote described Fielding as "a dirty Fellow . . . a Quid of Tobacco in his Jaws that run up and down . . . begging Money," Fielding pronounced the sentence that Foote "be pissed upon . . . with the utmost Scorn and Contempt." Margaret Anne Doody, "Henry Fielding's Improbable Life," *Manchester Guardian Weekly* (23 September 1990), 20.

22. Samuel Richardson to Hester Chapone, in *Selected Letters of Samuel Richardson,* ed. John Carroll (Oxford: Oxford University Press, 1964), 173n.68.

23. Armstrong, *Desire and Domestic Fiction,* 62–3.

24. Tompkins, *Popular Novel,* 51; Brissenden, *Virtue in Distress,* 77–81.

25. Brissenden, *Virtue in Distress,* 241–2n.62.

26. "One tear shed in private / Over the unfortunate is worth it all." Wollstonecraft, *The Female Reader: or, Miscellaneous Pieces in Prose and Verse's Selected from the Best Writers, and Disposed under Proper Heads; for the Improvement of*

Young Women (New York: Scholars' Facsimiles and Reprints, 1980 [1789]), 300–301; Rev. William Enfield's *The Speaker: or, Miscellaneous Pieces, Selected from the Best English Writers, . . .* (Gainsborough: Henry Mozley [1774]) (see Wollstonecraft to Joseph Johnson, July 1788, in *Collected Letters of Mary Wollstonecraft,* ed. Ralph M. Wardle [Ithaca, N.Y.: Cornell University Press, 1979] 179); Mullan, *Sentiment and Sociability,* 156.

27. Brissenden, *Virtue in Distress,* 113; Mullan, *Sentiment and Sociability,* 155. One reviewer defended *A Sentimental Journey* against charges of "sensuality," in order to preserve Sterne's authority for the cultivation of sensibility.

> What delicacy of feeling, what tenderness of sentiment, yet what simplicity of expression here! Is it *possible* that a man of *gross ideas* could ever *write* in a strain so pure, so refined from the dross of sensuality! (Quoted in Mullan, *Sentiment and Sociability,* 200)

Of course, such rhetoric was open to opposite interpretations.

28. Robert D. Mayo, *Novel in Magazines, 1740–1815* (Evanston, Ill.: Northwestern University Press, 1962), 336–42.

29. Quoted in Quinlan, *Victorian Prelude,* 62.

30. Ibid., 66. See too Ruth Perry, *Women, Letters and the Novel* (New York: AMS Press, 1980), 151; and Browne, *Feminist Mind,* 28–9.

31. Henry Austen, "Biographical Notice of the Author," in Jane Austen, *Northanger Abbey* (New York: Penguin, 1985 [1818]), 33; Austen, *Northanger Abbey,* 58–9. For a brilliant recreation of Austen's historical context, see Warren Roberts, *Jane Austen and the French Revolution* (New York: St. Martin's Press, 1981); see too Armstrong, *Desire and Domestic Fiction,* 138f.

32. Johnson quoted by Janet Todd, in *Sensibility: An Introduction* (London and New York: Methuen, 1986), 33.

33. Todd, *Sensibility,* ch. 3; see too Sheriff, *Good-natured Man,* 19–20.

34. Todd, *Sensibility,* 37; Langford, *Polite and Commercial People,* 466; Ian Donaldson, "Cato in Tears: Stoical Guises of the Man of Feeling," in *Studies in the Eighteenth Century,* ed. R. F. Brissenden. (Toronto: University of Toronto Press, 1973), 389. According to Donaldson, Addison attempted "to transform Cato into an eighteenth-century Man of Feeling" (382).

35. Langford, *Polite and Commercial People,* 308; Todd, *Sensibility,* 34; Gibbon, *Memoirs of My Life* (New York: Penguin, 1984 [1788–93]), 148; Mullan, *Sentiment and Sociability,* 174; Todd, *Sensibility,* 36.

36. Todd, *Sensibility,* 47; Borsay, *Urban Renaissance,* 259–60; J. M. Golby and A. W. Purdue, *The Civilisation of the Crowd: Popular Culture in England, 1750–1900* (New York: Schocken, 1985), 39, 67–8; Fanny Burney, *Evelina: or, The History of a Young Lady's Entrance into the World* (Oxford: Oxford University Press, 1982 [1778]), 78.

37. Richardson, *Clarissa,* 4:198.

38. C. J. Rawson, "Some Remarks on Eighteenth-Century 'Delicacy,' with a Note on Hugh Kelly's '*False Delicacy*' (1768)," *Journal of English and Germanic Philosophy* 61, no. 1 (January 1962), 3 and 4; *Prompter* quoted in Erik Erämetsä, *A Study of the World Sentimental and of other Linguistic Characteristics of Eighteenth Century Sentimentalism in England* (Helsinki: Helsingin Liikekirjapaino Oy, 1951), 61; Griffith quoted in Rawson, "Delicacy," 1; Langford, *Polite*

and Commercial People, 109 (and see Spencer, *Woman Novelist,* 123–24; and Mullan, *Sentimental and Sociability,* 80); Richardson, *Clarissa,* 1:426 (see too 2:260).

39. Henry MacKenzie, *The Man of Feeling* (New York: Oxford University Press, 1970 [1771]), 73; Burney, *Evelina,* 336; see too Edgeworth, *Belinda,* 69.

40. Ann Radcliffe, *The Mysteries of Udolpho* (Oxford: Oxford University Press, 1980 [1794]), 5; Brooke quoted in Rawson, "Delicacy," 136.

41. Elizabeth Inchbald, *A Simple Story* (London: Pandora, 1987 [1791]), 294; *The Hermit of Snowden* and Lady Mary Wortley Montagu quoted in Spacks, "Ev'ry Woman Is at Heart a Rake," 42, 37. The "mainly homosexual" phrase is in the same article, 34n.15.

42. Spacks, "Ev'ry Woman Is at Heart a Rake," 37; Frances Burney, *Camilla: or, A Picture of Youth* (Oxford: Oxford University Press, 1983 [1796]), 680; Knox quoted in Langford, *Polite and Commercial People,* 478.

43. Charlotte Lennox, *The Female Quixote: or, The Adventures of Arabella* (London: Pandora, 1986 [1752]), 203, 103; Spacks, "Ev'ry Woman Is at Heart a Rake," 34; Elizabeth Inchbald, *Simple Story,* 161; Radcliffe, *Udolpho,* 127, 270; Richardson, *The History of Sir Charles Grandison,* 3 vols. (London: Oxford University Press, 1972 [1753–4]), 1:21.

44. For further illustration, see *Modern Novel Writing* (1796) and *Azemia* (1797) by Elizabeth Hervey, significantly published under the name of her stepbrother, William Beckford, (Gainesville: Scholars Facsimiles and Reprints, 1970). Probyn, *English Fiction,* 221.

45. Clara Reeve, *Plans for Education: With Remarks on the Systems of Other Writers* (New York: Garland Publishing, 1974 [1792]), 122, 124; Wollstonecraft, *Rights of Woman,* 116; it "must be very improper that a young lady should dream of a gentleman before the gentleman is known to have dreamt of her." Austen, *Northanger Abbey, 51;* Mary Hays, *Memoirs of Emma Courtney* (London: Pandora Press, 1987 [1796]), 33; Maria Edgeworth, *Belinda* (London: Pandora Press, 1986 [1801]), 233.

46. Wollstonecraft, *Rights of Woman,* 240, 153, 147, 154.

47. Ibid., 81 (this is a persistent theme); Barker-Benfield, "Mary Wollstonecraft: Eighteenth-Century Commonwealthwoman," *Journal of the History of Ideas* 50, no. 1 (1989): 95–115. See too Cora Kaplan, "Wild Nights: Pleasure/Sexuality/Feminism," in *The Ideology of Conduct: Essays on Literature and the History of Sexuality,* ed. Nancy Armstrong and Leonard Tennenhouse (New York: Methuen, 1987), 170. Of course, Marx and Engels would reflect eighteenth-century thought in declaring in 1848 that there was an opposition between "sentimentalism" and "egotistical calculation," associating the former with "heavenly ecstasies of religious fervor" and subsuming it under "patriarchal" feudalism. *The Communist Manifesto* (Harmondsworth, Middx.: Penguin, 1967 [1848; trans. 1888]), 82. One can interpret Wollstonecraft's analysis in McKeon's terms: she applied "progressive ideology" to women in whom male aristocratic honor had been "relocated." "The progressive critique of aristocratic ideology" had demystified "prescribed honor" for men "as an imaginary value explaining virtue as a quality that is not prescribed by status but demonstrated by achievement." McKeon, *Origins of the Novel,* 212.

48. Wollstonecraft, *Rights of Woman,* 215; Griffith quoted in Spacks, "Ev'ry Woman Is at Heart a Rake," 43; Barker-Benfield, "Wollstonecraft: Eighteenth-Century Commonwealthwoman," 106.

49. Richard O. Allen, "If You Have Tears: Sentimentalism as Soft Romanticism," *Genre* 8 (1975): 128, 138–9; Spacks, "Ev'ry Woman Is at Heart a Rake," 46; Ernest Lee Tuveson, *The Imagination as a Means of Grace: Locke and the Aesthetics of Romanticism* (New York: Gordian Press, 1974 [1960]), 88, and see 136; Todd, *Sensibility,* 6; Donald Meyer, *Sex and Power: The Rise of Women in America, Russia, Sweden, and Italy* (Middletown, Conn.: Wesleyan University Press, 1987), 617; Mullan, *Sentiment and Sociability,* 236–7; Lennox, *Female Quixote,* 47.

50. Allen, "Tears," 134, and passim; B. J. Tysdahl, *William Godwin as Novelist* (London: Athlone Press, 1981), 114.

51. Borsay, *Urban Renaissance,* 250; Probyn, *English Fiction,* 22; compare Watt, *Rise of the Novel,* 18, 21, and passim; Goldberg, *Sex and Enlightenment,* 207; Poovey, *The Proper Lady,* 27–9; Armstrong, *Desire and Domestic Fiction,* 8; Peter Laslett, *The World We Have Lost: England before the Industrial Age,* 3d ed. (New York: Scribner's, 1984), 19.

52. Burney, *Evelina,* 17.

53. Spacks, "Ev'ry Woman Is at Heart a Rake," 33, 38, 40, 42–3; Patricia Crawford, "Women's Published Writings 1600–1700," in *Women in English Society, 1500–1800,* ed. Mary Prior (London: Methuen, 1985), 216–7; Jane Spencer, *The Rise of the Woman Novelist: From Aphra Behn to Jane Austen* (Oxford: Basil Blackwell, 1986), 32, 75–8, and passim.

54. *The Spectator,* no. 10 (12 March 1710–1), 1:44–5.

55. *The Spectator,* no. 10, 1:43; *The Spectator,* no. 294 (6 February 1711–2), 4:175; Crawford, "Women's writings," 223–4, 213.

56. Jerry C. Beasley, "Politics and Moral Idealism: The Achievement of Some Early Woman Novelists," in *Fetter'd or Free? British Women Novelists, 1760–1815,* ed. Mary Anne Schofield and Cecilia Macheski (Columbus: Ohio University Press, 1985), 216–36; Borsay, *Urban Renaissance,* 280.

57. Peter Earle, *The Making of the English Middle Class: Business Society and Family Life in London, 1660–1730* (London: Methuen, 1989), 263–4 and 268. *The Spectator,* no. 81 (2 June 1711), 2:1, 4; no. 125 (24 July 1711), 2:178.

58. *The Spectator,* no. 242 (7 December 1711), 3:301.

59. Katherine M. Rogers, "The Feminism of Daniel Defoe," in *Women in Eighteenth-Century England and Other Essays,* ed. Paul Fritz and Richard Morton (Toronto: Hakkert, 1976), 22; *The Spectator,* no. 274, 4:93; no. 231, 3:257; no. 10, 1:45.

60. Borsay, *Urban Renaissance,* 280; Langford, *Polite and Commercial People,* 110 (here Langford concedes that women exercised at least some political rights); Simon Schama, *The Embarrassment of Riches: An Interpretation of Dutch Culture in the Golden Age* (Berkeley: University of California, 1987), 454–5; Suzanne Lebsock, *The Free Women of Petersburg: Status and Culture in a Southern Town, 1764–1860* (New York: W. W. Norton, 1984), ch. 3.

61. Earle, *English Middle Class,* 166–74; Karl Von Den Steinen, "The Discovery of Women in Eighteenth-Century English Political Life," in *The Women of England from Anglo-Saxon Times: Interpretive Bibliographical Essays,* ed. Bar-

bara Kanner (Hamden, Conn.: Archon Books, 1979), 229–57; Barker-Benfield, "Wollstonecraft: Eighteenth-Century Commonwealthwoman," 113; Richardson, *Pamela: or, Virtue Rewarded* (New York: Norton, 1950 [1740]), 428–9. Women are recorded to have voted much earlier in R. H. Hilton, "Women in the Village," in *The English Peasantry in the Late Middle Ages* (Oxford: Oxford University Press, 1975), 105–6, although Judith Bennett suggests this was "a very peculiar election," *Women in the Medieval English Countryside: Gender and Household in Brigstock before the Plague* (New York: Oxford University Press, 1987), 5. Bennett also describes elite women "politicking," 187. For the nineteenth century, see Patricia Hollis, *Ladies Elect: Women in English Local Government, 1865–1914* (Oxford: Oxford University Press, 1987).

62. *The Spectator,* 37 (12 April 1711), 1:150–4; Richardson, *Clarissa,* 4:220; Johnson quoted in Probyn, *English Fiction,* 20.

63. Compare Margaret Kirkham, *Jane Austen, Feminism and Fiction* (New York: Methuen, 1983), 13, Spencer, *Woman Novelist,* 115–6; Lennox, *Female Quixote,* 71, 128; Inchbald, *Simple Story,* 235; Austen, *Northanger Abbey,* ch. 14; Edgeworth, *Belinda,* 60.

64. Henry Austen, "Biographical Notice of the Author," 29–33.

65. Barbauld quoted in Lucy Aikin, "Memoir" in *The Works of Anna Laetitia Barbauld,* 2 vols. (London: Longman, Hurst, Rees, Orme, Brown, and Green, 1825), 1:xviii-xiv; Hume, *Essays, Moral, Political and Literary,* 2 vols., ed. T. H. Grose and T. H. Green (London: Longman, Green, 1875), 1:388–92. *The Ladies Library* quoted in Hunter, *Before Novels,* 395n.38. Langford makes the same point, *Polite and Commercial People,* 98.

66. Austen, *Northanger Abbey,* 123, 122.

67. Peter Burke, *Popular Culture in Early Modern Europe* (New York: Harper Torchbooks, 1978), 256; Todd, *Sensibility,* 134; see too Hunter, *Before Novels,* 79; Fordyce quoted in Spencer, *Rise of the Woman Novelist,* 186; Anna Laetitia Aikin [Barbauld], "On Romances, an Imitation," in J. and A. L. Aikin, *Miscellaneous Pieces in Prose* (London: J. Johnson, 1773), 44, 45; Burney, *Camilla,* 680.

68. Colin Campbell, *The Romantic Ethic and the Spirit of Modern Consumerism* (Oxford: Basil Blackwell, 1987), 72; Fielding, *Tom Jones,* 372; Edgeworth, *Belinda,* 424–5.

69. Richardson, *Clarissa,* 2:288; see too 1:472, 38, 431, and 4:524; Hays, *Emma Courtney,* 139, 140.

70. Barker-Benfield, "Mary Wollstonecraft's Depression and Diagnosis: The Relation between Sensibility and Women's Susceptibility to Nervous Disorders," *Psychohistory Review* 13, no. 4 (Spring 1985): 15–31; Wollstonecraft to George Blood, 4 February [1786], *Collected Letters,* 102; Wollstonecraft to Everina Wollstonecraft, 22 March 1788, *Collected Letters,* 173; Wollstonecraft, *Mary* and *The Wrongs of Woman,* ed. James Kinsley and Gary Kelly (Oxford: Oxford University Press, 1980 [1788 and 1798]), 82; Radcliffe, *Udolpho,* 249.

71. Fielding, *Tom Jones,* 141; Radcliffe, *Udolpho,* 163; review of *Man of Feeling* quoted in Mullan, *Sentiment and Sociability,* 123; Radcliffe, *Udolpho,* 383; 1776 writer quoted in Tompkins, *Popular Novel,* 146.

72. Richardson, *Pamela,* 15, 239–51, 258; Richardson, *Clarissa,* 4:356, 348, 351.

73. Lennox, *Female Quixote,* 59, 29, 53, 40, 44, 307, 52; Probyn, *English Fiction,* 10; see too Spencer, *Woman Novelist,* 187–92.

74. Mary Wollstonecraft, "Advertisement," *Mary,* xxxi.

75. Beasley, *Novels of the 1740s,* 29; Probyn, *English Fiction,* 15; Edith Birkhead, "Sentiment and Sensibility in the Eighteenth-Century Novel," in *Essays and Studies by Members of the English Association* 11, collected by Oliver Elton (London: Wm. Dawson and Sons, 1966 [1925]), 98–9; McKeon, *Origins of the Novel,* 57, 273; Marianne Shapiro, *The Poetics of Ariosto* (Detroit: Wayne State University Press, 1988), passim.

76. McKeon, *Origins of the Novel,* 54; see too Ronald Paulson, *Satire and the Novel in Eighteenth-Century England* (New Haven: Yale University Press, 1967).

77. Spencer, *Rise of the Woman Novelist,* 181; Bakhtin quoted in McKeon, *Origins of the Novel,* 12; see too Beasley, *Novels of the 1740s* (Athens: University of Georgia Press, 1982), 23, 35; and McKeon, *Origins of the Novel,* 267–8.

78. Richardson, *Pamela,* 242–3, 229; see n.46 above; for further discussion of this passage and romance/antiromance in Richardson's work, see Armstrong, *Desire and Domestic Fiction,* 119; McKeon *Origins of the Novel,* 2, 259–60; Jocelyn Harris, "Introduction," Richardson, *The History of Sir Charles Grandison,* ed. Jocelyn Harris, 3 vols. (London: Oxford University Press, 1972 [1753–4]), xvi.

79. Lennox, *Female Quixote,* 23, 16, 360; Kemble to Inchbald quoted in Gary Kelly, *The English Jacobin Novel, 1780–1815* (Oxford: Clarendon Press, 1976), 66; Wollstonecraft, *Mary,* 2.

80. Spencer, *Woman Novelist,* 186 (see too Tompkins, *Popular Novel,* 211; and McKeon, *Origins of the Novel,* 3); Burney, *Evelina,* "Preface," 8.

81. Spencer, *Woman Novelist,* 18.

82. Compare Gary Kelly, *English Fiction of the Romantic Period, 1789–1830* (London: Longman, 1989), 48–9.

83. Radcliffe, *Udolpho,* 468, 469, 5.

84. Spencer, *Woman Novelist,* 181.

85. Burke, *Popular Culture,* 157 (see too McKeon, *Origins of the Novel,* 54); Congreve's *Incognita* (1692) quoted in Probyn, *English Fiction,* 2; Spencer, *Woman Novelists,* 184; Beasley, *Novel of the 1740s,* 25. Burke refers to "the gradual diffusion of the romances of chivalry" as literature "descended the social scale." "Like the French nobility, the English gentry abandoned the romance of chivalry to the lower classes," those "of the weakest judgment and reason, such as women, children and ignorant and superstitious persons." But he reminds us that the minds of such people were "not blank paper, but stocked with ideas and images." Hence "descending" ideas were modified, adapted to the needs of a new audience. *Popular Culture,* 59, 270.

86. Samuel Johnson, *The Rambler,* no. 4 (31 March 1750) in *Essays from the Rambler, Adventurer, and Idler,* ed. W. J. Bate (New Haven and London: Yale University Press, 1968), 12, 14, 13; compare Kirkham, *Jane Austen,* 13–15, 18; Burney, *Evelina,* "Preface."

87. Richardson, *Clarissa,* 1:149; compare Beasley, *Novels of the 1740s,* 37–8.

88. Wollstonecraft, *Wrongs of Woman,* 79. McKeon's remarks on the relationship between "ideology" and "reality" are relevant. *Origins of the Novel,* 223.

89. Jane Austen to Cassandra Austen, 7 January 1807, *Jane Austen's Letters to her Sister Cassandra and Others,* collected and ed. R. W. Chapman (London: Oxford University Press, 1952), 173 (see too Probyn, *English Fiction,* 19).

90. Austen, *Northanger Abbey,* 199, 202; Browne, *Feminist Mind,* 16; Austen, *Northanger Abbey,* 223.

91. Austen, *Northanger Abbey,* 211, 162, 182, 107, 179, 163, 171. Harold Perkin's concise account of a county's revolving around "the big house" is nicely illustrated by Northanger Abbey. *The Origins of Modern English Society 1780–1880* (London: Routledge and Kegan Paul, 1972), 42.

92. Austen, *Northanger Abbey,* 231, 230, 224, 225.

93. *Spectator,* no. 278 (18 January 1711–12), 4:108–9.

94. Harris, *Richardson,* 54–5; Richardson, *Clarissa,* 1:156, 287, 161–2, 158, and see 183.

95. Mary Beth Norton, *Liberty's Daughters: The Revolutionary Experience of American Women, 1750–1800* (Boston: Little-Brown, 1980), 44; Wollstonecraft, *The Wrongs of Woman,* 73–4; Wollstonecraft to Imlay, 19 February 1795, 17 August 1794, 30 December 1794, *Collected Letters,* 280, 258, 272, and passim.

96. Richardson, *Sir Charles Grandison,* 1:48–9; Burney, *Evelina,* 360–2; Mary Hays, *Memoirs of Emma Courtney,* 115.

97. Fielding, *Tom Jones,* 71.

98. Richardson, *Pamela,* 525. Clarissa's native "dignity" made her acceptable to Lovelace's more aristocratic family, *Clarissa,* 3:395, another illustration of the redefinition of honor. A "man ennobles the woman he takes, be she *who* she will . . . but a woman, though ever so nobly born, debases herself by a mean marriage . . . when a duke marries a private person, is he still not her *head,* by virtue of being her husband? But when a lady descends to marry a groom, is not the groom her *head,* being her husband?" Richardson, *Pamela,* 447. The problem Pamela's class subversion caused some of the novels' readers is described in Richard Gooding, "*Pamela, Shamela,* and the 'Horizon of Expectations' in 1741" (paper delivered at the Annual Meeting of the Canadian Society for Eighteenth-Century Studies, October 1989, Montréal). See Spencer, *Woman Novelist,* 186; McKeon, *Origins of the Novel,* 364–6. McKeon also links the subversiveness of Pamela's literacy to the apprehensions over a "trade in counterfeit references" written by servants. *Origins of the Novel,* 369–70.

99. Quoted in Spencer, *Woman Novelist,* 6.

100. Borsay, *Urban Renaissance,* 138; Quinlan, *Victorian Prelude,* 63; P. J. Miller, "Women's Education, 'Self-Improvement,' and Social Mobility: A Late Eighteenth-Century Debate," *British Journal of Educational Studies* 20 (1972): 307.

101. Reeve, *Plans of Education,* 111, 62; Thomas Day, *History of Sandford and Merton* (Philadelphia: n.p., n.d. [1783–9]), 533–4, 551. That in American "settlements" reformers of education were making precisely the same con-

trast as Day, is demonstrated in Linda K. Kerber, *Women of the Republic: Intellect and Ideology in Revolutionary America* (Chapel Hill, N.C.: University of North Carolina Press, 1980), 203–4. Day also blamed English "public" schools for making boys effete, and teaching them envy, vice, and folly, *Sandford and Merton,* 314.

102. Inchbald, *A Simple Story,* 294, 4.

103. Reeve, *Plans of Education,* 68, 113; Miller, "Womens' Education," 311–2; Browne, *Feminist Mind,* 42–3; Howlett quoted in Langford, *Polite and Commercial People,* 113; for the romanticized view of female health in the past see Neil McKendrick, "Home Demand and Economic Growth: A New View of the Role of Women and Children in the Industrial Age," in *Historical Perspectives: Studies in English Thought and Society* (London: Europa, 1974), 161, 163, 165. Several of McKendrick's sources illustrate the integral relationship between the view of women presented in literature and the view presented in Parliamentary Blue Books.

104. Sara Delamont and Lorna Duffin, *The Nineteenth-Century Woman: Her Cultural and Physical World* (London: Croom Helm; and New York: Barnes and Noble, 1978), ch. 5; see too Frances Power Cobbe, "Life in an English Boarding School" and Frances Mary Buss's testimony before the Schools Inquiry Commission 1867–8, both published in *Victorian Women: A Documentary Account of Women's Lives in Nineteenth-Century England, France and the United States,* ed. Erna Olafson Hellerstein, Leslie Parker Hume, and Karen M. Offen (Stanford: Stanford University Press, 1981), 72–80.

105. Tobias Smollett, *The Expedition of Humphry Clinker* (New York: New American Library, 1960 [1771]), 18, 22; Edgeworth, *Belinda,* 371; Browne, *Feminist Mind,* 43; see too Wright, *Sensibility,* 91; and Langford, *Polite and Commercial People,* 477–8.

106. Compare Crawford, "Women's Writings," 219; Sandra M. Gilbert and Susan M. Gubar, *The Madwoman in the Attic: The Woman Writer and the Nineteenth Century Literary Imagination* (New Haven: Yale University Press, 1979), 45–92.

107. For example, Lennox, *Female Quixote,* 193; Smollett, *Humphry Clinker,* 310; Burney, *Evelina,* 249, 257–8; Radcliffe, *Udolpho,* 127; Clara Reeve's *Plans of Education* required that her pupils could not send or receive letters without their being inspected. Reeve, *Plans of Education,* 150.

108. Lawrence Stone, *The Family, Sex, and Marriage in England, 1500–1800* (New York: Harper and Row, 1977), 35–7; Richardson, *Clarissa,* 2:280; Spencer, *Woman Novelist,* 186; Langford, *Polite and Commercial People,* 478.

109. Bernard Mandeville, *The Virgin Unmask'd: or, Female Dialogues betwixt an Elderly Maiden Lady and her Niece* (London: G. Strahan, 1724 [1709]), 20, 22; Richard I. Cook, *Bernard Mandeville* (New York:Twayne Publishers, 1974), 54.

110. Todd, *Sensibility,* 134; Browne, *Feminist Mind,* 37; Armstrong, *Desire and Domestic Fiction,* 106; see too Langford, *Polite and Commercial People,* 109.

111. Colman quoted in Browne, *Feminist Mind,* 36; Henry MacKenzie, *The Man of Feeling* (New York: Oxford University Press, 1972 [1771]), 55, 57; Spencer, *Woman Novelist,* 186; Probyn, *English Fiction,* 20.

112. Thomas Laqueur, "Orgasm, Generation, and the Politics of Reproductive Biology," *Representations* 14 (Spring 1986): 10–11. For copious illustration of the persistence through the nineteenth century see Anon., *My Secret Life* (New York: Grove Press, 1966), passim.

113. Donald Meyer, *Sex and Power: The Rise of Women in America, Russia, Sweden, and Italy* (Middletown, Conn.: Wesleyan University Press, 1987), 437; Spacks, "Ev'ry Woman Is at Heart a Rake," 38. Compare Richardson's observation on writing about sex: "To be sure there is no Writing on these Subjects to please such a Gentleman as that in the Tatler; who cou'd find Sex in a *laced Shoe,* when there was none in the foot to wear it." Richardson to George Cheyne, 4 August 1741, in *The Letters of Doctor George Cheyne to Samuel Richardson* (1733–1743), ed. Charles F. Mullett, University of Missouri Studies 18, no. 1 (Columbia: University of Missouri, 1943), 68.

114. Stone, *Family,* 488–9; Bennett, *Women in the Medieval English Countryside,* 102–3.

115. Wollstonecraft, *Mary,* 1–2. For suggestive discussions of the symbolism of hair see Orlando Patterson, *Slavery and Social Death: A Comparative Study* (Cambridge, Mass.: Harvard University Press, 1982), 60; and Anne Hollander, *Seeing through Clothes* (New York: Avon, 1980), 72–3.

116. Wollstonecraft, *Mary,* 2–3.

117. Ibid., 3; Wollstonecraft, *Rights of Woman,* 168. Wollstonecraft to Eliza W. Bishop, 27 June 1787, *Collected Letters,* 155. Compare Spacks, "Ev'ry Woman Is at Heart a Rake," 39.

118. Wollstonecraft, *Mary,* p. 4.

119. For example Nancy F. Cott, "Passionlessness: An Interpretation of Victorian Sexual Ideology," in *A Heritage of Her Own,* ed. Cott and Elizabeth Pleck (New York: Simon and Schuster, 1979), 162–87; Laqueur, "Orgasm," 24, 39n.45; Langford points out that the well-established view that women were sexually more voracious than men came under attack earlier in the century. *Polite and Commercial People,* 115–6.

120. René Spitz, "Authority and Masturbation," *Psychoanalytic Quarterly* 21 (1952): 490–577; E. H. Hare, "Masturbatory Insanity: The History of an Idea," *Journal of Mental Science* 108, no. 452 (January 1962): 1–21; Robert H. MacDonald, "The Frightful Consequences of Onanism: Notes on the History of a Delusion," *Journal of the History of Ideas* 28, no. 3 (1967): 423–4; R. P. Neuman, "Masturbation, Madness, and the Modern Concepts of Childhood and Adolescence," *Journal of Social History* 8 (1975): 2–5; Alex Comfort, "The Rise and Fall of Self-Abuse," ch. 3 of *The Anxiety Makers: Some Curious Preoccupations of the Medical Profession* (New York: Dell Publishing, 1970); see too Wayland Young, *Eros Denied: Sex in Western Society* (New York: Grove Press, 1964), ch. 20. Masturbation phobia also overlapped with the "formidable increase in illegitimacy" in England as well as all over Continental Europe. Peter Laslett, *Family Life and Illicit Love in Earlier Generations: Essays in Historical Sociology* (Cambridge: Cambridge University Press, 1977), 107. Laslett is "wary" of explaining this phenomenon by "attitudinal changes," but McKeon is less so. *Origins of the Novel,* 158–9.

121. There was a connection made in France, too, between the cult of sen-

sibility and masturbation, focused ultimately on the representations of Marie Antoinette. Schama, *Citizens: A Chronicle of the French Revolution* (New York: Knopf, 1989), 225.

122. Spacks, "Ev'ry Woman Is at Heart a Rake," 37; Richardson to Cheyne, 4 August 1741, in Cheyne, *Letters to Richardson,* 67–8.

123. Quinlan, *Victorian Prelude,* 66–7; Reeve quoted by Spencer, *Woman Novelist,* 76; Spacks, "Ev'ry Woman Is at Heart a Rake," 28; see Spencer, *Woman Novelist,* 60–1; Browne, *Feminist Mind,* 28; Keith Thomas, "The Double Standard," *Journal of the History of Ideas* 20, no. 2 (April 1959): 215; Roy Porter, "Mixed Feelings: The Enlightenment and Sexuality in Eighteenth-Century Britain," in *Sexuality in Eighteenth-Century Britain,* ed. Paul Gabriel Boucé (Manchester, N.J.: Barnes and Noble, 1982), 18–9; Christopher Lawrence, "The Nervous System and Society in the Scottish Enlightenment," in *Natural Order: Historical Studies of Scientific Culture,* ed. Barry Barnes and Steven Shapin (Beverly Hills and London: Sage, 1979), 30.

124. Spencer, *Rise of the Woman Novelist,* 98; Reeve, *Plans of Education,* 62.

125. Behn quoted in McKeon, *Origins of the Novel,* 27.

126. Inchbald, *Simple Story,* 171; Wollstonecraft, *Rights of Woman,* 222.

127. Brissenden, *Virtue in Distress,* 271–2.

128. Castiglione, *Courtier,* 258; Mandeville, *Virgin Unmask'd,* 182–91; J. G. A. Pocock, *Virtue, Commerce, and History: Essays on Political Thought and History, Chiefly in the Eighteenth Century* (New York: Cambridge University Press, 1985), 49. Compare Langford, *Polite and Commercial People,* 115–6.

129. Fielding, *The Life of Mr. Jonathan Wild, the Great* (New York: New American Library, 1982 [1743]), 70; Richardson, *Clarissa,* 1:502, 3:125; Richardson, *Sir Charles Grandison,* 1:24; Fielding, *Tom Jones,* 493, 499, 500.

130. Lennox, *Female Quixote,* 83, 133, 144–5; Richardson, *Clarissa,* 2:191; Cheyne, *Letters to Richardson,* 121.

131. Fielding, *Tom Jones,* 30, 445; MacKenzie, *Man of Feeling,* 57–8; MacKenzie, *The Man of Feeling* and *The Man of the World* (London: Routledge, n.d. [1773]), 189; Burney, *Evelina,* 41–2, 48.

132. Jane Austen, *Sense and Sensibility* (New York: New American Library, 1961 [1811]), 19, 18, 17, and see 39.

133. Ibid., 36, 37, 40, 41, 78, 41, 151.

134. Ibid., 257–8, 67, 277, 256–7.

135. Ibid., 147; Edgeworth, *Belinda,* 218–9.

136. Richardson, *Clarissa,* 2:472, 4:23, and see 1:160; Lady Bradshaigh quoted in Mullan, *Sentimental and Sociability,* 105–6.

137. Richardson, *Clarissa,* 1:502, 2:33, 1:353; 4:24, and see too 4:560–61; see Harris, *Richardson,* 108–9.

138. Fielding, *Jonathan Wild,* 51; MacKenzie, *Man of the World,* 176–7; Fielding, *Tom Jones,* 679; Inchbald, *Simple Story,* 104–5, 171.

139. Francis Greville's "Prayer for Indifference," quoted in Todd, *Sensibility,* 61; see Betty Rizzo, "Greville, Francis (1726[?]-89)" in *A Dictionary of British and American Women Writers 1660–1800,* ed. Todd (London: Methuen, 1987), 139–40; Hannah More, "Sensibility, a Poem," in *Sacred Dramas, Chiefly In-*

tended for Young Persons, . . . (Philadelphia: Thomas Dobson, 1787 [1784]), 184–5; Wollstonecraft to Imlay, 27 September and 4 October 1795, *Collected Letters,* 313, 317; Dr. Johnson quoted in Brian Vickers, "Introduction" to MacKenzie, *Man of Feeling,* xxxiii; Rawson, "Delicacy," 8; see too Spacks, "Ev'ry Woman Is at Heart a Rake," 31–2.

140. Barbauld, *Works,* 2:219, 228–9, 215, 225, and 223–4.

141. Austen, *Sense and Sensibility,* 69; Mayo, *Novels in Magazines,* 371.

142. Austen, *Sense and Sensibility,* 52, 86, 138, 133, 69, 132.

143. Richardson, *Clarissa,* 2:55, 1:270; Wollstonecraft, *Rights of Woman,* 223, 215; compare Brissenden, *Virtue in Distress,* 171.

144. Lady Mary Wortley Montagu and Burney quoted in Spacks, "Ev'ry Woman Is at Heart a Rake," 34, 28. Part of the "worldly" knowledge of rakes was their wider knowledge of women and sexuality, including the attractions of rakery's manhood to women. Mrs. Howe tells Hickman that "you *good* young gentlemen know nothing at all of our sex." *Clarissa,* 1:336. Scholars who suggest rakes represented the attractions of "the world to women" include Richard O. Allen in "If You Have Tears," 139 and Harris in *Richardson,* 72.

145. Fielding, *Tom Jones,* 428, 415; see too Brissenden's introduction to the Penguin edition of *Joseph Andrews* (1977).

146. Richardson, *Sir Charles Grandison,* 1:181; Burney, *Evelina,* 288, 262.

147. Richardson, *Clarissa,* 4:354; Burney, *Evelina,* 283; Inchbald, *Simple Story,* 57.

148. Brissenden, *Virtue in Distress,* 209; Todd, *Sensibility,* 100, and see 116 and 69; Mullan, *Sentiment and Sociability,* 89; see G. A. Starr, "'Only a Boy': Notes on Sentimental Novels," *Genre* 10 (Winter 1977), 501–27; Harris, *Richardson,* 140, 34; and Eagleton, *Rape of Clarissa,* 99. Like Todd, Mullan follows Eagleton here: taking male writers for his subject, Mullan describes them as finding it increasingly difficult to distinguish between the figures of the "virtuous hero, . . . virtuous heroine," or "isolated hysteric," *Sentiment and Sociability,* 16. It has also been suggested that the males of the culture were "invested with female signifiers" (for example Yorick's calling himself "weak as a woman," in addition to the widespread use of the term "effeminate") because their refusal of "the world" brings them to the condition of women. Todd, *Sensibility,* 101; see too Spencer, *Rise of the Women Novelist,* 185. Browne, *Feminist Mind,* 110; and Kerber, *Women of the Republic,* 31.

149. Compare Brissenden, *Virtue in Distress,* 154.

150. Burney, *Evelina,* 261.

151. Edmund Burke, *A Philosophical Enquiry in the Origin of Ideas of the Sublime and the Beautiful* (Notre Dame: University of Notre Dame Press, 1958 [1757]), 111; Radcliffe, *Udolpho,* 528; 486; Inchbald, *Simple Story,* 286, 20. In *Mary,* Wollstonecraft's first novel, the hero—a man of feeling—is already deprived of "any threatening sexuality" by his chronic illness, before dying without "physical consummation" with the eponymous heroine of sensibility; Moira Ferguson and Janet Todd, *Mary Wollstonecraft* (Boston: Twayne Publishers, 1984), 35.

152. Richardson, *Clarissa,* 3:390; MacKenzie, *Man of the World,* 407; Marquis de Sade, "Eugenie de Franval," in *Crimes of Love,* trans. Lowell Blair (New York: Bantam Books, 1964), 4–74.

153. Wright, *Sensibility in English Prose Fiction,* 89; Radcliffe, *Udolpho,* 31, 34, 168, 159, 155.

154. Radcliffe, *Udolpho,* 23, 157, 172, 192, 173, 302, 316, and see 580; Wollstonecraft, *Rights of Woman,* p. 225.

155. Burney, *Evelina,* 406; Wollstonecraft, *Rights of Woman,* 199, 203, 114. There was "not direct evidence of felt female sexuality," despite the hints teased out in Spacks, "Ev'ry Woman Is at Heart a Rake."

156. Compare Meyer, *Sex and Power,* 270–2, 429–35, 627, and passim.

157. Quoted in Rogers, "Feminism of Defoe," 22; Richardson, *Pamela,* 221, 443; Richardson, *Clarissa,* 2:512, 118, 465; 3:116; 1:112; 2:15, 14. Lovelace's successor-rake in *Sir Charles Grandison,* also raping away his prey, tells her, "sweet and ever adorable creature . . . your very terror is beautiful. I can *enjoy* your terror, madam." *Sir Charles Grandison,* 1:152.

158. Fielding, *Jonathan Wild,* 110: Fielding, *Tom Jones,* 291, 671, 185, 291; MacKenzie, *Man of Feeling,* 53; MacKenzie, *Man of the World,* 255. Compare Richardson, *Sir Charles Grandison,* 1:332.

159. Sterne, *A Sentimental Journey through France and Italy* (Baltimore: Penguin, 1967 [1768]), 66; Richardson, *Clarissa,* 2:512; 1780 writer quoted in Tompkins, *Popular Novel,* 98; Wollstonecraft, *Rights of Woman,* 112. Compare Kirkham, *Feminism and Fiction,* 43.

160. Wollstonecraft, *Rights of Woman,* 191; James Fordyce, *Sermons to Young Women,* 2 vols. (London: A Millar and T. Cadell, . . . , 1766), 2:225; see Spencer, *Rise of the Woman Novelist,* 16–18; and Browne, *Feminist Mind,* 28–9.

161. Wollstonecraft, *Rights of Woman,* 192; Thrale's diary quoted in Spacks, "Ev'ry Woman Is at Heart a Rake," 32; Wollstonecraft, *Rights of Woman,* 192–3.

162. Wollstonecraft, *Rights of Woman,* 224; Wollstonecraft, *Thoughts on the Education of Daughters: With Reflections on Female Conduct, or the More Important Duties of Life* (London: J. Johnson, 1787), 8; Wollstonecraft, *Rights of Woman,* 154, 83, 223, 224, 225.

163. Wollstonecraft, *Rights of Woman,* 81, 126–7n.2; Emily W. Sunstein, *A Different Face: The Life of Mary Wollstonecraft* (Boston: Little Brown, 1975), 173.

164. Wollstonecraft, *Rights of Woman,* 123; Wollstonecraft, *Wrongs of Woman,* 147; Jardine quoted by Browne, *Feminist Mind,* 116.

165. Wollstonecraft, *Rights of Woman,* 123, 249. This was Wollstonecraft's extension to women of Commonwealthmen's concern over the effeminacy of men; see Barker-Benfield, "Wollstonecraft: Eighteenth-Century Commonwealthwoman."

166. Wollstonecraft, *Wrongs of Woman,* 146; Wollstonecraft, *A Vindication of the Rights of Men, in a Letter of the Rights Honourable Edmund Burke . . .* (Gainesville, Fla.: Scholars Facsimiles and Reprints, 1960 [1790]), 114.

167. Austen, *Northanger Abbey,* 125; Edgeworth, *Letters for Literary Ladies* (New York: Garland Publishing Company, 1974 [1795]), 45; Robert Alan Cooper, "Day, Thomas (1748–89)," *Biographical Dictionary of Modern British*

Radicals, vol. 1, 1770–1830, ed. Joseph O. Baylen and Norbert J. Gossman (Sussex: Harvester; and Atlantic Highlands, N.J.: Humanities Press, 1979), 116–8; Edgeworth, *Belinda,* ch. 26.

168. Wollstonecraft, *Rights of Man,* 114; Spencer, *Rise of the Woman Novelist,* 115; de Sade quoted in Brissenden, *Virtue in Distress,* 81; Wollstonecraft, *Rights of Woman,* 173–91. Her response to Rousseau's ideas, which at first had bowled her over, remained ambivalent throughout her life, as her gift of *Heloïse* to Godwin illustrates. See Kelly, "Godwin, Wollstonecraft, and Rousseau," *Women and Literature* 3 (Autumn, 1975): 21–6.

169. Inchbald, *Simple Story,* 89. With irony, Inchbald writes that "there are no tortures a lover would not suffer, rather than cease to love." *Simple Story,* 84.

170. Brissenden, *Virtue in Distress,* 273, 94.

171. Ibid., 273. Wollstonecraft, *Rights of Woman,* 173–91. In France, Rousseau provoked Laclos's *Les liaisons dangeureuses* (1782), and then de Sade's *La nouvelle Justine, ou les malheurs de la vertu* (1792). Both suggested that the sentimental male ideal—"social, sympathetic, generous, benevolent, and good natured"—denied "the sexual element in his nature" as well as "his inherent violence, aggression, selfishness, and cruelty." Brissenden, *Virtue in Distress,* 294, 286. Compare: Fuseli's art "argued that human behavior of all kinds has to do with sex and power and that any utopian vision that does not take repressed impulses and desires into account is deluded and cramped." Michael Brenson, "Henry Fuseli's Drawings of Life's Lusts and Compulsions," Art Review, *New York Times* (4 January 1991), c. 20. Wollstonecraft was deeply attracted to Fuseli, and her own language asking him to return her letters suggests the same element of self-destructiveness running through her correspondence with Imlay. She writes she would "fain tear from my heart its treacherous sympathies . . . wounding my bosom." Wollstonecraft to Fuseli, c. 1795, *Collected Letters,* 324. Sunstein suggests that "Fuseli's sadistic side fascinated Mary Wollstonecraft." *A Different Face,* 184.

172. At some level, Inchbald, capable of masquerading as a man, seems to have played with this long familiar dyad in her 1791 novel, reversing roles in having Miss Milner attempt to humiliate the sensitive Dorriforth and make him "the veriest slave of love." *Simple Story,* 119. Perhaps this is further evidence of the attractions of rakery in the hearts of women. Miss Milner is severely punished and realism replaced by the pious harmonies of properly educated sensibility. Of course, Inchbald was also alluding to the old feminist point to which Wollstonecraft referred in quoting Dryden against Rousseau, who, she said, degraded woman by "making her the slave of love.

—Cursed vassalage
First idolized till love's hot fire be o'er,
Then slave to those who courted us before.
Wollstonecraft, *Rights of Woman,* 190.

173. Roberts, *Jane Austen and the French Revolution,* 128–9. As far as sexuality was concerned, Austen expressed "sheer wish, the wish that sex could be welcomed without disturbing social order, the wish for sex without price." Meyer, *Sex and Power,* 627.

174. Brissenden, *Virtue in Distress,* 284; Wollstonecraft, *Rights of Woman,* 215.

Chapter 7. Wollstonecraft and the Crisis of Sensibility in the 1790s

1. Wollstonecraft, *Vindication of the Rights of Woman* (New York: Penguin, 1975 [1792], 80.

2. Herbert Jennings Rose and Charles Martin Robertson, "Amazons," *The Oxford Classical Dictionary,* ed. N. G. L. Hammond and H. H. Scullard (Oxford: Clarendon Press, 1970), 50. See Abby Wettan Kleinbaum, *The War Against the Amazons* (New York: McGraw Hill, 1983).

3. Clive Probyn, *English Fiction of the Eighteenth Century, 1700–1789* (London and New York: Longman, 1987), 158. Maureen Duffy, *The Passionate Shepherdess: Aphra Behn 1640–89* (New York: Avon Books, 1977), 188, 30; that the Amazon had been a convention of seventeenth-century romance is illustrated by Michael McKeon, *The Origins of the English Novel, 1600–1740* (Baltimore: John Hopkins University Press, 1987), 95, derived in part from the "viragos" of feudal record. Norbert Elias, *Power and Civility,* vol. 2 of *The History of Manners,* trans. Edmund Jephcott (New York: Pantheon, 1982), 78–9. That the convention appeared in French romance may be illustrated by reference to Mademoiselle l'Heritier's "reworkings of an old French tale in *The French Amazon* (1718), described in Natalie Zemon Davis, "Women on Top," in *Society and Culture in Early Modern France* (Stanford: Stanford University Press, 1975), 133. Images of "the vicious virago" appeared in seventeenth-century Dutch culture, conflated with the boundary-crossing women of the world, scorning the "division of spheres." Simon Schama, *The Embarrassment of Riches: An Interpretation of Dutch Culture in the Golden Age* (Berkeley: University of California Press, 1988), 400–401.

4. "The Introduction," in *Selected Poems of Anne Finch, Countess of Winchilsea,* ed. Katharine M. Rogers (New York: Frederick Ungar, 1979), 5–7. Characterization of Astell, Manley, and Elstob quoted in Ruth Perry, *The Celebrated Mary Astell: An Early English Feminist* (Chicago: University of Chicago Press, 1986), 229; Elstob's life and work are described by Perry in her introduction to George Ballard, *Memoirs of Several Ladies of Great Britain, . . .* (Detroit: Wayne State University Press, 1985), 21–5. Other kinds of unorthodox female behavior, aside from women's learning, writing, publishing, and their political demonstrations, were called "Amazonian." There were cases of eighteenth-century women who, dressed in men's uniforms, served as soldiers (this has been a feature of many centuries, many societies). One of them was Christina Davis, who petitioned Queen Anne for a pension. Perceiving she was pregnant, Anne paid for the costs of her lying-in, and in 1717 Davis became the only female pensioner at the Chelsea Royal Hospital for veterans. Perry, *Astell,* 297. Her life became a pseudoliterary one when her "autobiography" was published as *The Life and Adventures of Mrs. Christian Davies, the British Amazon, Commonly Called Mother Ross.* Jerry C. Beasley, *Novels of the 1740s* (Athens: University of Georgia Press, 1982), 68–9.

5. Henry Fielding, *The History of Tom Jones, a Foundling* (New York: Signet, 1979 [1749]), 229–30.

6. Ibid., 232, 727, 130, 132. Fielding combined this kind of femininity with his subscription to the reform of male manners, described in Ch. 5.

7. Fielding, *Tom Jones,* 145, 439, 149, 147, 72; bk 6, ch. 2, passim.

8. Johnson quoted in Probyn, *English Fiction,* 12; Margery Kirkham, *Jane Austen, Feminism and Fiction* (New York: Methuen, 1986), 18, 16; Kathyrn Shevelow, "Lennox, Charlotte," in *A Dictionary of British and American Writers, 1660–1800,* ed. Janet Todd (London: Methuen, 1987), 196–8; James Boswell, *Life of Johnson* (London: Oxford University Press, 1970 [1791]), 14; Shevelow, "Lennox," 197; see too Phillipe Séjourné, *The Mystery of Charlotte Lennox: First Novelist of Colonial America (1727[?]-1804)* (Aix-En-Provence: Publications des Annales de la Faculté des Lettres, 1967), 20–2.

9. Shevelow, "Lennox," 198; Charlotte Lennox, *The Female Quixote: or, The Adventures of Arabella* (London: Pandora, 1986 [1752]), 413, 415, 408.

10. Lennox, *The Female Quixote,* 139, 305, 80.

11. Ibid., 80; Davis, "Women on Top," 133, 145; Steele quoted in Peter Borsay, *The English Urban Renaissance: Culture and Society in the Provincial Town, 1660–1770* (Oxford: Clarendon Press, 1989), 262; Stubbs's paintings include *The Countess of Coningsby in the Livery of the Charlton Hunt* (c. 1760); *John and Sophia Musters Riding at Colwick Hall* (1777); and *Laetitia, Lady Lade* (1793); Paul Langford, *A Polite and Commercial People: England, 1727–1783* (Oxford: Clarendon Press, 1989), 602–3.

12. Fanny Burney, *Evelina: or, The History of a Young Lady's Entrance into the World* (Oxford and New York: Oxford University Press, 1982 [1778]), 268; Betty Rizzo, "Greville, Frances [1726[?]-1789)," in Todd, *Dictionary,* 139–40.

13. Burney, *Evelina,* 268–9.

14. Ibid., 357–8, 361, 362.

15. Burney's diary and letters quoted by Edward and Lillian Bloom, "Introduction," Burney, *Evelina,* vii-viii.

16. *Lady's Monthly Museum* quoted in Lawrence Stone, *The Family, Sex and Marriage in England, 1500–1800* (New York: Harper and Row, 1977), 283.

17. Edward Royle and James Walvin, *English Radicals and Reformers, 1760–1848* (Brighton, Sussex: Harvester, 1982), 41–43; Wollstonecraft, *An Historical and Moral View of the Origin and Progress of the French Revolution and the Effect It Has Produced on Europe* (London: Joseph Johnson, 1794), 218, v, and passim; R. F. Brissenden, *Virtue in Distress: Studies in the Novel of Sentiment from Richardson to Sade* (New York: Harper and Row, 1974), 57–8 (Schama has recently developed the theme of a relationship between the cult of sensibility and the Revolution in *Citizens: A Chronicle of the French Revolution* [New York: Knopf, 1989], 152); Walvin, "The Impact of Slavery on British Radical Politics: 1787–1838," *Annals of New York Academy of Sciences* 292 (Summer 1977): 346; Royle and Walvin, *English Radicals,* 60; Marilyn Butler, *Jane Austen and the War of Ideas* (Oxford: Clarendon Press, 1975); Gary Kelly, *The English Jacobin Novel, 1780–1805* (Oxford: Clarendon Press, 1976); Warren Roberts, *Jane Austen and the French Revolution* (New York: St. Martin's Press, 1979); see too Kelly, *English Fiction of the Romantic Period, 1789–90* (London: Longman, 1989), ch. 2.

18. Barker-Benfield, "Mary Wollstonecraft: Eighteenth-Century Common-

wealthwoman," *Journal of the History of Ideas* 50 (1989): 95–115; James Kinsley and Gary Kelly, "Introduction" to Wollstonecraft, *Mary* and *The Wrongs of Woman* (Oxford: Oxford University Press, 1980 [1788 and 1798]), ix; Brissenden, *Virtue in Distress,* 62–3, 64; Kelly, *Romantic Period,* 59–69; Butler, *War of Ideas,* 90, 111n.3, and ch. 4, passim.

19. Charlotte Smith quoted in Walter Francis Wright, *Sensibility in English Prose Fiction, 1760–1814: A Reinterpretation* (n.p.: Folcroft Press, 1970 [1937]), 76–7 (Godwin read Smith's *Desmond* in 1793 [Kelly, *Jacobin Novel,* p. 191]); Sir Walter Scott, "Memoir of Henry Mackenzie," *Works of Henry MacKenzie,* 8 vols. (Edinburgh: Constable, Creech, Manners, and Miller; London: Cadell and Davies, 1808), 1:1–16, 6–7; E. P. Thompson, *The Making of the English Working Class* (New York: Vintage, 1963), 126–8.

20. Albert J. Kuhn, "Introduction," *Three Sentimental Novels: Sterne, A Sentimental Journey; MacKenzie, The Man of Feeling; Day, The History of Sandford and Merton* (New York: Holt, Rinehart, Winston, 1970), xx; Janet Todd, *Sensibility: An Introduction* (London: Methuen, 1986) 144; *British Critic* quoted in Ian Watt, "On Sense and Sensibility," in *Jane Austen: A Collection of Critical Essays,* ed. Ian Watt (Englewood Cliffs, N.J.: Prentice Hall, 1963), 43–4; Butler, *War of Ideas,* 54–55, 183; Wollstonecraft, *Rights of Woman,* 135–39 and 156–58.

21. Jane Austen, *Sense and Sensibility* (New York: New American Library, 1961 [1811]), 8.

22. For the relationship between Austen's ideas and those of Wollstonecraft see Roberts, *Jane Austen,* 156–7.

23. Wollstonecraft, *Rights of Woman,* 258.

24. Barker-Benfield, "Mary Wollstonecraft's Depression and Diagnosis: The Relation between Sensibility and Women's Susceptibility to Nervous Disorders," *Psychohistory Review* 13, no. 4 (Spring 1985): 15–31; see too the introduction by Kinsley and Kelly to Wollstonecraft's *Mary* and *The Wrongs of Woman* cited in n.8 above, which is a brilliant if brief piece on Wollstonecraft's thought.

25. Wollstonecraft, *Rights of Woman,* 192, 82, 309.

26. Wollstonecraft, *Letters Written during a Short Residence in Sweden, Norway, and Denmark* (Lincoln and London: University of Nebraska Press, 1976 [1796]), "Advertisement," 58. Here is another good illustration of "sentimental jargon":

> Let me catch pleasure on the wing—I may be melancholy tomorrow. Now all my nerves keep tune to the melody of nature. Ah! Let me be happy whilst I can. The tear starts when I think of it. I must fly from thought, and find refuge from sorrow in strong imagination—the only solace for a feeling heart. Phantom of bliss . . . wipe clear from my remembrance the disappointments, which render the sympathy painful, which experience rather increases than damps; by giving the indulgence of feeling the sanction of reason. (*Letters from Sweden,* 100)

27. Per Nystrom, *Mary Wollstonecraft's Scandinavian Journey* (Gothenburg: Acts of the Royal Society of Arts and Sciences of Gothenburg, Humaniora, no. 17, 1980). This is conveniently summarized by Richard Holmes in his

introduction to Wollstonecraft, *A Short Residence in Sweden, Norway and Denmark* and William Godwin, *Memoirs of the Author of the Rights of Woman* (New York: Penguin, 1987), 21–5.

28. Wollstonecraft, review of *Edward and Harriet, or the Happy Recovery: A Sentimental Novel by a Lady, Analytical Review* 1 (1788): 207–8; William Godwin, *Memoirs of Mary Wollstonecraft,* ed. and retitled W. Clark Durant (New York: Haskell House, 1927 [1798]), 84; Wollstonecraft, *Rights of Woman,* 157, 146.

29. Wollstonecraft to Gilbert Imlay, 17 June 1795 and 4 October 1795, *The Collected Letters of Mary Wollstonecraft,* ed. Ralph M. Wardle (Ithaca: Cornell University Press, 1979), 296, 316.

30. Wollstonecraft, *Rights of Woman,* 179; it could be argued that Wollstonecraft came to terms with her lifelong conflict in her late thirties. The best evidence for this is a letter Wollstonecraft wrote to Godwin, 4 September 1796, *Collected Letters,* 244–5; it requires careful analysis. For further remarks on the meanings for men and women of the conflict between reason and sensibility, see Patricia Meyer Spacks, "Ev'ry Woman Is at Heart a Rake," *Eighteenth-Century Studies* 8 (1974): 41–4.

31. *The General Magazine* 6 (1792): 187–91; *Analytical Review* 12 (March 1792): 241–9; *Monthly Review* 8 (May-August 1792): 198–209; *Literary Magazine and British Review* 8 (1792), 133–9; *New Annual Register: or, General Repository of History, Politics and Literature* (1792), 298; see R. M. Janes, "On the Reception of Mary Wollstonecraft's *A Vindication of the Rights of Woman,*" *Journal of the History of Ideas* 39 (1978): 293–302; Nicholas McGuinn, "George Eliot and Mary Wollstonecraft," in *The Nineteenth-Century Woman: Her Cultural and Physical World,* ed. Sara Delamont and Lorna Duffin (New York: Barnes and Noble, 1978), 188–205. For some privately expressed, positive views of the *Rights of Woman,* see Emily W. Sunstein, *A Different Face: The Life of Mary Wollstonecraft* (Boston: Little Brown, 1975), 215.

32. *Literary Magazine,* 138; *Monthly Review,* 106.

33. *Critical Review,* N.S. 4 (1792), 389–98; N.S. 5 (1792) 132–41; 5:133, 137–8, 139.

34. Wollstonecraft, *Letters from Sweden,* 67, 169, 64, 116, 14; *British Critic* 7 (1796), 607–8.

35. Todd, "Hays, Mary (1760–1843)," in Todd, *Dictionary,* 156–7. (The object of Hays's affection was William Frend). Mary Hays, *Memoirs of Emma Courtney* (London: Pandora, 1987 [1796]), "Preface," 6–7, 83, 134, 120.

36. Hays's novel would give " a more striking and affecting lesson that abstract philosophy can ever afford," *Emma Courtney,* 5. Godwin's *Caleb Williams* had illustrated his *Political Justice;* and Wollstonecraft's *The Wrongs of Woman* would illustrate her *Vindication of the Rights of Woman.*

37. Hays, *Emma Courtney,* 89, 90.

38. Ibid., xix, xxviii, 5, 120, 130–1, 126.

39. Ibid., 134, 82, 126.

40. Ibid., 120, 89, 103. In asserting here that the freedom of mutual affection "transcended mere custom," Hays's heroine was making the same argu-

ment that MacKenzie's libertine, Sir Thomas Sindall, made to Harriet Annesley in attempting to seduce her. MacKenzie, *Man of the World,* 197, 268.

41. Hays, *Emma Courtney,* 90, 103, 120; Wollstonecraft, *Rights of Woman,* 220; for Victorian separate spheres see *Victorian Women: A Documentary Account of Women's Lives in Nineteenth-Century England, France, and the United States,* ed. Erna Olafson Hellerstein, Leslie Parker Hume, and Karen M. Offen (Stanford: Stanford University Press, 1981), 118–33, and passim; see too Jane Rendall, *The Origins of Modern Feminism: Women in Britain, France, and the United States, 1780–1860* (Houndsworth, Hampshire: MacMillan, 1985), and Leonore Davidoff and Catherine Hall, *Family Fortunes: Men and Women of the English Middle Class, 1780–1830* (London: Hutchinson, 1987).

42. Hays, *Emma Courtney,* 125, 134, 44, 131, 125.

43. Butler, *Jane Austen and the War of Ideas,* 117; Hays, *Emma Courtney,* 120, 103, 60; *Critical Review* quoted in Spencer, *Woman Novelist,* 136.

44. Royle and Walvin, *English Radicals,* 71; Godwin's pamphlet was *Cursory Strictures on the Charges Delivered by Lord Chief Justice Eyre to the Grand Jury* (1794); see Don Locke, *A Fantasy of Reason: The Life and Thought of William Godwin* (London, Boston and Henley: Routledge and Kegan Paul, 1980), 83–4.

45. Royle and Walvin, *English Radicals,* 79, 81; Wollstonecraft, *Letters from Sweden,* 157; in their introduction to *The Wrongs of Woman,* Hinsley and Kelly write of Wollstonecraft's Jacobin trial scene that the judge rejects Maria's "French principles" because "the trial is only a symbol for the Government's legal suppression of English Jacobinism after the Treason Trials of 1794" (xix).

46. Royle and Walvin, *English Radicals,* 80–81, 89; Butler, *War of Ideas,* 105, 106.

47. Godwin, *Memoirs,* 40–41; Ralph M. Wardle, *Mary Wollstonecraft: A Critical Biography* (Lawrence: University of Kansas Press, 1951), 318–9; Claire Tomalin, *The Life and Death of Mary Wollstonecraft* (New York: Harcourt, Brace, Jovanovich, 1974), 237; McGuinn, "Eliot and Wollstonecraft," 191; review of *Memoirs . . . , European Magazine and London Review* 33 (April 1798); 247; see too review of *Memoirs . . . , British Critic* 12 (September 1798), 230.

48. Richard Polwhele, *The Unsex'd Females: A Poem;* and Mary Ann Radcliffe, *The Female Advocate: or, An Attempt to Recover the Rights of Women from Male Usurpation,* ed. Gina Luria (New York: Garland, 1974 [1798]), 28.

49. This is evident in, for example, Wollstonecraft to Amelia Alderson, 11 April 1797, *Collected Letters,* 389–90.

50. Peter H. Marshall, *William Godwin* (New Haven: Yale University Press, 1984), 126; Locke, *Fantasy of Reason,* 89; review of Godwin's *Memoirs, The Scientific Magazine and Freemasons Repository* 10 (June 1798): 404; Godwin, *Memoirs,* 5; *Anti-Jacobin Review,* 1:94; see too *European Magazine,* 33:246.

51. Barker-Benfield, "Biography as Autobiography: William Godwin's Revelations about Himself in his *Memoirs of the Author of the Vindication of the Rights of Woman* (1798)" (paper delivered at the Conference on Autobiography and Biography: Gender, Text and Context, Stanford University, April 11, 1986).

52. Patricia Jewell McAlexander, "The Creation of the American Eve: The Cultural Dialogue on the Nature of the Role of Women in Late Eighteenth-Century America," *Early American Literature* 9 (1975): 262.

53. Godwin, *Memoirs,* 53–4, 130, 73. The points in this paragraph are laid out by Barker-Benfield, "Biography as Autobiography." Clear illustrations of Godwin's conflict over the issue of male sensibility and effeminacy (to be read alongside his conclusion to his revised edition of the *Memoirs*) are his *St. Leon: A Tale of the Sixteenth Century,* 4 vols. (New York: Garland Publishing Co., 1974 [1799]); and his *Fleetwood: or, The New Man of Feeling* (New York: Garland, 1979 [1805]). *Caleb Williams,* discussed in Ch. 3, points to the same conflict, and it can be detected in Godwin's earliest novels.

54. Godwin, *Memoirs,* 106, 101–2, 61; Godwin, *Caleb Williams* (London: Oxford University Press, 1970 [1794]), 103.

55. Brissenden, *Virtue in Distress,* 243, 258–60; Godwin, *Memoirs,* 19, 73. Langford describes a widespread apprehension from the 1770s that suicide was on the increase as a result of "the cult of feeling," apprehensions that reached a climax after 1779, when *Werther* was translated into English, *Polite and Commercial People,* 479.

56. Godwin, *Memoirs,* 6, 73, 80.

57. Butler, *War of Ideas,* 106; review of *Memoirs . . . , Anti-Jacobin Review and Magazine* 1 (1798): 98.

58. [Dr. Bisset], review of *The False Friend: A Domestic Story,* by Mary Robinson, in *Anti-Jacobin Review* (May 1799): 40; Godwin, *Memoirs,* 73, 181–2; *British Critic,* 12:232, 231.

59. *European Magazine,* 33:243; *Anti-Jacobin Review,* 1:100.

60. Wollstonecraft, *Vindication,* 162, 232; Thomas James Matthias, *The Shade of Alexander Pope on the Banks of the Thames: A Satirical Poem with Notes* (Philadelphia: A. Dickins, 1800 [London, 1798]), 1, 37.

61. Review of *Posthumous Works of the Author of a Vindication of the Rights of Woman,* in *British Critic, a New Review* 12 (1798): 235; *Anti-Jacobin Review,* 1:96.

62. *Monthly Review* (September–December 1798), 324; *Analytical Review* 27 (January–June 1798): 235–40; "Memoirs of Mrs. Godwin: Author of *A Vindication of the Rights of Women* [sic]."

63. *Monthly Visitor* 3 (February 1798): 108–24, 326–42, the actual review of the *Memoirs* and the *Posthumous Works,* by the same writer, is in the following issue of the *Monthly Visitor* 3 (March 1798):311–8.

64. *Monthly Visitor,* 3:112–3.

65. Ibid., 3:115–24. Reprinted in nineteenth and early twentieth centuries as romantic literature, these letters finally found scholarly treatment in Wardle's edition of Wollstonecraft's *Collected Letters.*

66. *Monthly Visitor,* 3:315, 313.

67. L. M., "Reflections on the Character of Mary Wollstonecraft Godwin," *Monthly Magazine and American Review* 1, no. 1 (1799), 330, 331, 332, 333, 334.

68. Polwhele, *Unsex'd Females,* 16.

69. Ibid., 17, 16, 11, 10; Wollstonecraft, *Rights of Woman,* 162.

70. Polwhele, *Unsex'd Females,* 14–15, 23; compare Austen's characterization of Elinor in *Sense and Sensibility,* 110.

71. *Anti-Jacobin Review,* 1:94; Polwhele, *Unsex'd Females,* 21; *European Magazine,* 33:251.

72. Godwin, *Memoirs,* 56, 55. Kelly, *Jacobin Novel,* 294, argues that both Jacobins and Anti-Jacobins expressed the values of a single "expanding and increasingly powerful professional middle class." This view was criticized by Raymond Williams, "The Fiction of Reform: Gary Kelly's *The English Jacobin Novel,*" *Times Literary Supplement* (25 March 1977), 330–1.

73. Polwhele, *Unsex'd Females,* 23, 13, 22, 6–7. Langford points out that the "stormy sexual politics" of the 1770s, a long-brewing reaction to feminism, had been expressed in the "controversy concerning female fashions." *Polite and Commercial People,* 603.

74. Polwhele, *Unsex'd Females,* 6, 15–20. In addition to her early sympathy for the Revolution, Barbauld had supported the repeal of the Test and Corporation Acts. See Ch. 6, n. 161.

75. Wollstonecraft, *Rights of Woman,* 229, 234n; Rev. Christian Gotthilf Salzman, *Elements of Morality, for the Use of Children . . . ,* trans. [Wollstonecraft], 3 vols. (London: J. Johnson, 1791) 1:xiv-xv; *British Critic,* 12:233.

76. Polwhele, *Unsex'd Females,* 29.

77. Ibid., 31–5; Anne Radcliffe, *The Mysteries of Udolpho* (Oxford: Oxford University Press, 1987 [1794]), 464.

78. Janet M. Todd, "The Polwhelean Tradition and Richard Cobb," *Studies in Burke and his Time* 16 (1975): 271–7; Matthias, *Shade of Pope,* 37–8.

79. Perry, "Introduction," in Ballard, *Memoirs of Several Ladies,* 28, 15, 35, 25, 37.

80. Hays, *Letters and Essays, Moral and Miscellaneous,* 108–11; Hays, *Emma Courtney,* 134, 52, 103; Edgeworth quoted by Francies Jeffrey, review of *Leonora, Edinburgh Review* 8 (1806): 206–13. For Jacobinism's appeal to women, see Kelly, *Jacobin Novel,* 112. J. Paul Hunter suggests that because women were members of the "underclasses" they saw change as "an inevitable and . . . a personal opportunity to join the future," and they opposed "the Augustan desire to preserve traditional values." This was one reason for their support of the novel from its beginnings. *Before Novels: The Cultural Contexts of Eighteenth-Century English Fiction* (New York: W. W. Norton, 1990), 97–8.

81. Review of *Posthumous Works, British Critic,* 12:234; *European Magazine* 33:251; Editorial, "To Correspondents," *Monthly Magazine* (November 1796): 792.

82. Jane West quoted in Tomalin, *Wollstonecraft,* 241.

83. Cecil S. Emden, "The Composition of Northanger Abbey," *Review of English Studies* 19, no. 75 (1968): 279–83; Cassandra Austen's letter quoted in Anne Henry Ehrenpreis, "Introduction" to Jane Austen, *Northanger Abbey* (New York: Penguin, 1985 [1816]), 9. For a scrupulous account of "how the political turbulence unleashed by the French Revolution entered Austen's life," see Roberts, *Jane Austen,* ch. 4.

84. Austen, *Northanger Abbey,* 58. Polwhele wrote, "The united merits of *Evelina, Cecilia* and *Camilla,* must place Mrs. D'Arblay, above all the Novel-

writers that have existed, since the first invention of this delightful species of composition." *Unsex'd Females,* 34. His phrasing and condescending judgment should be compared to Austen's irony: "It is only *Cecilia,* or *Camilla,* or *Belinda;* or, in short, only some work in which the greatest powers of the human mind are displayed," etc. (58).

85. Austen, *Northanger Abbey,* 58; Polwhele, *Unsex'd Females,* 15; Wollstonecraft, *Mary,* "Advertisement." See too Cora Kaplan, "Wild Nights: Pleasure/Sexuality/Feminism," in *The Ideology of Conduct: Essays on Literature and the History of Sexuality,* ed. Nancy Armstrong and Leonard Tennenhouse (London: Methuen, 1987), 174–5.

86. Roberts, *Jane Austen,* 207; Austen, *Persuasion* (New York: New American Library, 1980 [1818]), 223. Here, as elsewhere, I am extremely grateful to Professor Roberts, who reminded me of this quotation and discussed it with me.

87. Roberts, *Jane Austen,* 205, 200; Polwhele, *Unsex'd Females,* 35–36.

88. Margarette Smith, "More, Hannah (1745–1833)," in Todd, *Dictionary,* 224–7, esp. 27.

89. Hannah More, *Strictures on the Modern System of Female Education: With a View of the Principles and Conduct Prevalent among Women of Rank and Fortune,* vols. 7 and 8 of *Works of Hannah More* (London: T. Caddell and W. Davies, 1818 [1799]), 8:27, 29, 30.

90. More, *Strictures,* 8:30–1.

91. Ibid., 3:31, 7:210; Compare to 7:32.

92. Wollstonecraft, *Rights of Woman,* 80: More, *Strictures,* 8:33–5. See the discussion of evangelical "Doctrines on Femininity" in Leonore Davidoff and Catherine Hall, *Family Fortunes: Men and Women of the English Middle Class, 1780–1830* (London: Hutchinson, 1987), 114–8.

93. More, *Strictures,* 8:35–6; Wollstonecraft, *Rights of Woman,* 141n, 154; Harris suggests that the fact that the eighteenth century's image of Christ lacked traditional masculinity meant that he served "as a model for many a heroine or hero." Jocelyn Harris, *Samuel Richardson* (Cambridge: Cambridge University Press, 1987), 140.

94. Maria Edgeworth, *Belinda* (London: Pandora, 1986 [1801]), 3, 4, 5, 20–1; Michael Hennell, "Evangelicalism and Worldliness, 1770–1870," *Popular Belief and Practice,* ed. G. J. Cuming and Derek Baker (Cambridge: Cambridge University Press, 1972), 229–36.

95. Edgeworth, *Belinda* 20–1, 26, 151.

96. Ibid., 23–4, 26.

97. Ibid., 29–30, 33, 34, 31, 34.

98. Ibid., 34; Burney, *Evelina,* 362; Edgeworth, *Belinda,* 37–9, 200. In his 1728 poem, "The Masquerade," Fielding blamed its subject for creating an "Amazonian race" of women and warning, "when men women turn—why then / May not women be chang'd to men?" Quoted in Terry Castle, *Masquerade and Civilization: The Carnivalesque in Eighteenth-Century English Culture and Fiction* (Stanford: Stanford University Press, 1986), 47.

99. Edgeworth, *Belinda,* 46, 38, 34, 35.

100. Ibid., 38, 284; Matthias, *Shade of Pope,* 37.

101. Edgeworth, *Belinda,* 283, 280, 209, 208.
102. Ibid., 206–7.
103. Ibid., 350.
104. Ibid., 269: quoting Godwin, *Memoirs,* 38, 230.
105. Edgeworth, *Belinda,* 207; Godwin, *Memoirs,* 54–5.
106. Edgeworth, *Belinda,* 283, 282, 41, 31–3, 38–9.
107. Godwin, *Memoirs,* 105–6.
108. Edgeworth, *Belinda,* 42–3.
109. Wollstonecraft, *Rights of Woman,* 80.
110. Compare Roberts's observations on *Belinda,* in *Jane Austen,* 184.
111. Edgeworth, *Belinda,* 54; Roberts, *Jane Austen,* ch. 4 passim.
112. Edgeworth, *Belinda,* 47, 175, 55, 51, 107, 147, 104, 91.
113. Ibid., 107, 245, 294, 267. For an interpretation of *Belinda*'s domestic ideology see Beth Koweski-Wallace, "Home Economics: Domestic Ideology in Maria Edgeworth's *Belinda*" (unpublished paper).
114. Quotations from *Leonora* in Francis Jeffrey, "*Leonora* by Miss Edgeworth," *Edinburgh Review* 8 (1806): 206–13.
115. Compare Thomas Laqueur, "Orgasm, Generation, and the Politics of Reproductive Biology," *Representations* 14 (Spring 1986): 2.
116. Butler, "Edgeworth, Maria (1768–1849)," in Todd, *Dictionary,* 111.
117. Jeffrey, "*Leonora* by Miss Edgeworth," 207.
118. Ibid., 207; More, *Strictures on Education,* 7:218–9; J. F. C. Harrison, *The Common People of Great Britain: A History from the Norman Conquest to the Present* (Bloomington: University of Indiana Press, 1985), 286–9; Hendell, "Evangelicalism and Worldliness," 233; George Eliot, "Silly Novels by Lady Novelists," *Westminster Review* (October 1856), in Eliot, *Selected Essays, Poems and Other Writings,* ed. A. S. Byatt and Nicholas Warren (New York: Penguin, 1990), 140, 141. Complementarily, Eliot wrote to a woman friend in 1870: "We women are always in danger of living too entirely in the affections; and though our affections are perhaps the best gift we have, we ought also to have our share of the more independent life." Quoted in Eliot, "Introduction," *Essays,* xiv. She found "the helplessness of sweet women" "piteous," and she was contemptuous of "sentimentality." Eliot, "The Natural History of German Life," *Essays,* 109. Eliot had praised Wollstonecraft's *Rights of Woman* the previous year, distinguishing it from the by then "vague prejudice in some quarters . . . as in some way or other a reprehensible book," when in fact it is "eminently serious, severely moral." "Margaret Fuller and Mary Wollstonecraft," *Essays,* 333.
119. More, *Strictures on Education,* 7:219.
120. Henry Thompson, *The Life of Hannah More: With Notices of Her Sisters* (London: T. Cadell; and Edinburgh: W. Blackwood, 1838), 1, and ch. 1, passim. This book's final chapter explains to its readers how they are to be instructed by More's example. Nancy Cott also claims that More's *Strictures of Female Education* was "a weighty English progenitor of the American canon of domesticity." *The Bonds of Womanhood: "Woman's Sphere" in New England, 1780–1835* (New Haven: Yale University Press, 1977), 99.

121. F. K. Prochaska, *Women and Philanthropy in Nineteenth-Century England* (Oxford: Oxford University Press, 1980); M. Jeanne Peterson, *Family, Love, and Work in the Lives of Victorian Gentlewomen* (Bloomington: Indiana University Press, 1989). If eighteenth-century women (except some aristocratic ones) came more quickly and unambivalently to the campaign against dueling than men, associating it with other male habits, "especially drunkenness and libertinism," the antidueling associations of 1810 and 1843 were among the host of reformation-of-manners societies set up and largely wo-manned by the strong-minded paragons who combined the purged virtues of sensibility with evangelized self-assertion in public life. V. K. Kiernan, *The Duel in European History: Honor and the Reign of the Aristocracy* (Oxford: Oxford University Press, 1988), 183–4, 216.

122. Thompson, Dedication, *Life of More;* that this combination carried on is suggested by Sara Delamont, "The Contradictions in Ladies' Education," in *The Nineteenth-Century Woman,* ch. 5, p. 139, and illustrated in Nancy Armstrong, *Desire and Domestic Fiction: A Political History of the Novel* (Oxford: Oxford University Press, 1987), 77, and passim. The point is implicit in the middle-class origins and arguments of British suffragists; see Susan Kingsley Kent, *Sex and Suffrage in Britain, 1860–1914* (Princeton: Princeton University Press, 1987), 16, and passim.

Index

Note: Italicized numbers indicate page numbers of figures.